TimeOut

New York

timeout.com/newyork

Published by Time Out Guides Ltd, a wholly owned subsidiary of Time Out Group Ltd.
Time Out and the Time Out logo are trademarks of Time Out Group Ltd.

© Time Out Group Ltd 2006
Previous editions 1990, 1992, 1994, 1996, 1997, 1998, 1999, 2000, 2001, 2002, 2003, 2004.

10 9 8 7 6 5 4 3 2 1

This edition first published in Great Britain in 2005 by Ebury Publishing
Ebury Publishing is a division of The Random House Group Ltd,
20 Vauxhall Bridge Road, London SW1V 2SA

Random House Australia Pty Limited 20 Alfred Street, Milsons Point, Sydney, New South Wales 2061, Australia
Random House New Zealand Limited 18 Poland Road, Glenfield, Auckland 10, New Zealand
Random House South Africa (Pty) Limited Isle of Houghton, Corner Boundary
Road & Carse O'Gowrie, Houghton 2198, South Africa

Random House UK Limited Reg. No. 954009

Distributed in USA by Publishers Group West
1700 Fourth Street, Berkeley, California 94710

Distributed in Canada by Penguin Canada Ltd
10 Alcorn Avenue, Toronto, Ontario, Canada M4V 3B2

For further distribution details, see www.timeout.com

ISBN
To 31 December 2006: 1-904978-92-4
From 1 January 2007: 9781904978923

A CIP catalogue record for this book is available from the British Library

Colour reprographics by Icon, Crowne House, 56-58 Southwark Street, London SE1 1UN

Printed and bound in Germany by Appl

Papers used by Ebury Publishing are natural, recyclable products made from wood grown in sustainable forests

Contents

Time Out Guides Limited
Universal House
251 Tottenham Court Road
London W1T 7AB
Tel + 44 (0)20 7813 3000
Fax + 44 (0)20 7813 6001
Email guides@timeout.com
www.timeout.com

Editorial

Editor Keith Mulvihill
Consultant Editor Elizabeth Barr for *Time Out New York*
Deputy Editor Ruth Jarvis
Fact checkers/researchers Doug Troland, Lisa Troland
Copy editing Edoardo Albert, Peterjon Cresswell, Sally Davies, Lily Dunn, Eleila Ferro, Will Fulford-Jones, Tom Lamont, Lisa Ritchie, Ros Sales
Proofreader Sylvia Tombesi-Walton
Indexer Anna Norman
Mapping Patrick Welch, with Sid Amin, Zara Burdett and Gabriel Bailey

Editorial/Managing Director Peter Fiennes
Series Editor Ruth Jarvis
Deputy Series Editor Lesley McCave
Business Manager Gareth Garner
Guides Co-ordinator Holly Pick
Accountant Kemi Olufuwa

Design

Art Director Scott Moore
Art Editor Tracey Ridgewell
Senior Designer Josephine Spencer
Digital Imaging Dan Conway
Ad Make-up Jenni Prichard

Picture Desk

Picture Editor Jael Marschner
Deputy Picture Editor Tracey Kerrigan
Picture Researcher Helen McFarland

Advertising

Sales Director Mark Phillips
International Sales Manager Ross Canadé
International Sales Executive Simon Davies
Advertising Sales (New York) Siobhan Shea Rossi
Advertising Assistant Lucy Butler

Marketing

Marketing Director Mandy Martinez
Marketing & Publicity Manager, US Rosella Albanese

Production

Production Director Mark Lamond
Production Controller Marie Howell

Time Out Group

Chairman Tony Elliott
Managing Director Mike Hardwick
Group Financial Director Richard Waterlow
Group Commercial Director Lesley Gill
Group General Manager Nichola Coulthard
Group Circulation Director Jim Heinemann
Group Art Director John Oakey
Online Managing Director David Pepper
Group Production Director Steve Proctor
Group IT Director Simon Chappell

Contributors

History Kathleen Squires (*What lies beneath* Alan Mozes). **Architecture** Pablito Nash (*Thoroughly modernist melee, On the right track* EJ Mundell). **Wiseguys in New York** Jerry Capeci. **New York Today** Billie Cohen. **Where to Stay** Heather Tierney **Tour New York** Keith Mulvihill. **Downtown** Carole Braden (*Freeman's Alley* Carole Braden; *A Downtown reborn* EJ Mundell). **Midtown,** **Uptown** Mark Sinclair, Keith Mulvihill (*Heaven in hell* EJ Mundell; *Rock on* Keith Mulvihill; *Saturday in the city* Eric Mendelsohn; *Garden of delights* Keith Mulvihill; *How the nest was won* Keith Mulvihill). **Brooklyn** Jules Verdone (*Battle of Bed-Stuy* Justin Rocket Silverman). **Queens** Karen Tina Harrison. **The Bronx, Staten Island** Kathleen Squires (*VIP, RIP* Karen Tina Harrison). **Museums** Clare Lambe. **Restaurants** Heather Tierney (*History in the round* Charlotte Kaiser). **Shops & Services** Kelly McMasters (*On the record* Michael Silverberg). **Festivals & Events** Ethan LaCroix. **Art Galleries** Emily Weiner. **Books & Poetry** Michael Miller. **Cabaret &Comedy** Adam Feldman (cabaret), Jane Borden (comedy). **Children** Barbara Aria (*Here's to the babies who brunch* Katie Quirk). **Clubs** Bruce Tantum. **Film & TV** Joshua Rothkopf. **Gay & Lesbian** Beth Greenfield. **Music** Mike Wolf, K Leander Williams, Jay Ruttenberg (popular); Steve Smith (classical). **Sports & Fitness** Keith Mulvihill. **Theatre & Dance** David Cote (theatre), Amy Norton (dance) (*Times Square south* Alan Mozes). **Trips Out of Town** Adapted from *Time Out New York* magazine.

Maps JS Graphics (john@jsgraphics.co.uk).

Photography Alys Tomlinson, except: page 31 Santiago Calatrava SA/© Albert Vecerka/Esto; page 32 Images courtesy the City of New York, © 2004; pages 35, 127 PA/Empics; pages 100, 212 Talia Simhi; page 106 Bettmann/Corbis; page 107 Allison Sparks; page 124 John Cassidy; page 132 Cinzia Reale Costello; page 134 Lincoln Karim; page 145 courtesy of A'Lelia Bundles/Walker Family Collection; page 153 courtesy of the Library of Congress; pages 156, 206 Sarina Finkelstein; page 161 Tara Di Giovanni; page 163 Steinway & Sons; page 164 courtesy of the Los Angeles Dodgers; pages 181, 182, 196 Patrik Rytikangas; page 191 Alexa Vachon; pages 202, 203 Astrid Stawiarz; page 205 Philip Friedman; page 218 Seth Kushner; page 226 Jeff Harris; page 244 Dave Sanders; page 261 Getty Images; page 264 Wellington Lee; page 297 Susan Pittard; page 303 courtesy of Cattyshack; page 315 Jasper Coolidge; page 321 Christina Jensen; page 331 Marty Sohl/Metropolitan Opera; page 332 Chris Lee; page 334 Duomo/Corbis; page 341 Eric McNatt; page 357 Bill Jacobson; page 358 NJ Commerce, Economic Growth & Tourism Commission; page 362 Mick Hales; page 363 Masayuki Nagare. The following images were provided by the featured establishments/artist: pages 47, 57, 67, 68, 69, 72, 123, 189, 266.

The Editor would like to thank Joe Angio, Elizabeth Barr, Annie Bell, Carole Braden, Maile Carpenter, Nestor Cervantes, Erin Clements, Melisa Coburn, Sarina Finkelstein, Brian Fiske, Chad Frade, Louise Gore, Howard Halle, Stacy Hillegas, Killian Jordan, Gia Kourlas, Eric Medelsohn, Amy Plitt, Stephanie Rosenbaum, Andrea Scott, Mark Sinclair, Cyndi Stivers, Heather Tierney, Alison Tocci, Reed Tucker and all contributors to previous editions of the *Time Out New York Guide*, whose work forms the basis for parts of this book.

Introduction

People come to New York for a million different reasons: to get famous, to be a face in the crowd, to escape, to put down roots, to get loaded, to step out in style, to blow money, to chase dreams. And, remarkably, there are always new wonders, new dreams and more money.

Even now, the fifth anniversary of the terrorist attacks of September 11th – the city's darkest days in living memory – her magnetic pull continues to draw millions of new admirers. Like no other major American city, Manhattan is a sparkling array of art and architecture, culture and cranks, history and novelty – all crammed into the priciest real estate known to man. Newcomers and residents alike gaze on this place as they would a natural wonder, like the Grand Canyon or Niagara Falls. And yet there is nothing natural about it. Even Central Park, the city's largest green space, was carefully crafted by master landscapers over 150 years ago.

How can it be that on such a small strip of land, only 13 miles long and three miles at its widest, so many superlatives have been racked up? New York, at one time or another, has been home to the world's tallest buildings, the longest bridges, the busiest ports, the crabbiest cabbies, the super-ist super heroes – not to mention the most beloved and honoured police and fire departments in the nation. Like the world's largest, most complex ant farm, NYC is a crazy kaleidoscope of life on display 24 hours a day, seven days a week, 52 non-stop, exciting, exhausting, fulfilling weeks a year.

There's a big misconception that New York is simply too big to get to know in a single visit – and it's true that even the city's long-time residents find themselves continually discovering the city anew. But even if your stay only lasts a few days the trick is not to speed things up but, rather, to slow them down. Linger over brunch in the West Village and stroll the charming cobbled streets; spend an afternoon sipping martinis at the Carlyle as if it were a weekly ritual; take a midnight walk under the dazzling lights of Times Square – if you act as if you own this city it won't fail to leave you with a storehouse of rich memories.

The point of this book is to help you seize those special moments and make them your own. Take heart in the fact that its written by a crew of New York diehards eager to share their personal delight in seeking out hidden gems, unseen pleasures and places and the monuments and minutiae of a city waiting to make you her newest admirer.

ABOUT THE TIME OUT CITY GUIDES

The *Time Out New York Guide* is one of an expanding series of travel books produced by the people behind the successful listings magazines in London, New York and Chicago. Our guides, now numbering around 50, are written and updated by resident experts who strive to provide you with the most up-to-date information you'll need to explore the city, whether you're a first-time visitor or a local.

Many of the staff of *Time Out New York* magazine worked on this, the 14th edition, of the Time Out New York Guide. TONY has been 'the obsessive guide to impulsive entertainment' for all city dwellers (and visitors) for over ten years. Many chapters have been written from scratch; all have been thoroughly revised and offer new feature boxes.

THE LOWDOWN ON THE LISTINGS

Above all, we've tried to make this book as useful as possible. Websites, telephone numbers, transport information, opening times, admission prices and credit-card details are included in our listings. And we've given details on facilities, services and events, all checked and correct at press time. However, owners and managers can change their policies with little notice. Before you go out of your way, we strongly advise you to call and check opening times, dates of exhibitions and other particulars. While every effort has been made to ensure the accuracy of the information in this guide, the publishers cannot accept responsibility for any errors it may contain.

PRICES AND PAYMENT

Our listings give the major credit cards – American Express (AmEx), Diners Club (DC), Discover (Disc), MasterCard (MC) and Visa (V) – taken by each venue. Many will also accept traveller's checks issued by a major financial institution (such as American Express).

The prices we've supplied should be treated as guidelines, not gospel. Fluctuating exchange rates and inflation can cause prices to change

rapidly, especially in shops and restaurants. If costs vary wildly from those we've quoted, then ask whether there's a good reason – and please email us to let us know. We aim to give the best and most up-to-date advice, so we always want to know if you've been badly treated or overcharged.

THE LAY OF THE LAND

Many of our listings are divided up into area sections. Those areas are consistent with the demarcations we describe in our Sightseeing chapters, and are marked on our maps on pages 402 to 412. The maps now also pinpoint specific locations of hotels (**❶**), restaurants and cafés (**❶**) and bars (**❶**).

We've also included cross streets with every address, so you can more easily find your way around.

TELEPHONE NUMBERS

All telephone numbers printed in this guide are written as dialed within the United States. Note that you must always dial 1 and an area code, even if the number you're calling is in the same area code as the one you're calling from. Manhattan area codes are 212 and 646; those in Brooklyn, Queens, the Bronx and Staten Island are 718 and 347; generally (but not always), 917 is reserved for cell phones and pagers.

Numbers preceded by 800, 877 and 888 can be called free of charge from within the US, and some of them can be dialled (though not usually for free) from the UK.

To dial numbers given in this book from abroad, use your country's exit code (00 in the UK) then the number as printed. The '1' acts as the US's country code.

For more details on telephone use, *see p380.*

ESSENTIAL INFORMATION

For any practical information you might need for visiting the city – including visa and customs information, disabled access, emergency telephone numbers, a list of useful websites and the ins and outs of the local transport network, see the Directory (*p366-386*) at the back of this guide.

LET US KNOW WHAT YOU THINK

We hope you enjoy the *Time Out New York Guide*, and we'd like to know what you think of it. We welcome tips for places that you believe we should include in future editions and appreciate your feedback on our choices. Please e-mail us at guides@timeout.com.

There is an online version of this book, along with guides to over 45 other international cities, at **www.timeout.com**.

In Context

Features

Peter Stuyvesant.
See p13.

History

How New York became its inimitable self.

The greatest city in the world wasn't built with courtesy, all right? Call it attitude or chutzpah; cojones or street smarts: a pioneering amalgamation of inconsiderate characters has made this city what it is. A brief look back at New York's history shows just how its residents earned such a reputation, and explains why having what many would consider a rude 'tude has gotten them everywhere.

TRIBES AND TOURISTS

Members of the indigenous Lenape tribe were the original native New Yorkers. They lived among the meadows, forests and farms of the land they called Lenapehoking pretty much undisturbed by outsiders for thousands of years, until 1524, when their idyll was interrupted by tourists from the Old World. The first European sightseer to cast his eyes upon this land was Giovanni da Verrazano, an Italian explorer commissioned by the French to find a shortcut to the Orient. Instead, he found Staten Island. Recognizing that he was on the wrong track, Verrazano pulled up anchor nearly as

quickly as he had dropped it, never setting foot on land. Eighty-five years later, Englishman Henry Hudson was more favourably disposed. Commissioned by the Dutch, with the same goal of finding a shortcut to the Far East, Hudson sailed into Manhattan's natural deep-water harbour in September 1609, and was entranced by what lay before him. He lingered long enough to explore the entire length of the river that now bears his name, but it wasn't his fate to grow old in the place he admired and described in his logs as a 'rich and pleasant land': on a return trip in 1611, Hudson's crew mutinied and cast him adrift. Still, his tales of the lush, river-crossed countryside had captured the Dutch imagination, and in 1624 the Dutch West India Company sent 110 settlers to establish a trading post here. They planted themselves at the southern tip of the island called Mannahata and christened the colony New Amsterdam. In bloody battles against the local Lenape, they did their best to drive the natives away from the little company town. But the Lenape were immovable.

In 1626, a man named Peter Minuit, New Amsterdam's first governor, thought he had solved the Lenape problem by pulling off the city's very first real-estate rip-off. The tribe had no concept of private land ownership, so Minuit made them an offer they couldn't refuse: he 'bought' the island of Manhattan – all 14,000 acres of it – from the Lenape for 60 guilders' worth of goods. Legend famously values the purchase price at $24, but modern historians set the amount closer to $500. (These days, that wouldn't cover a month's rent for a closet-size studio apartment.) It was a slick trick, and a precedent for countless ungracious business transactions that would occur over the centuries.

The Dutch quickly made the port of New Amsterdam a centre for fur trading. The population didn't grow as fast as the business, however, and the Dutch West India Company had a hard time finding recruits to move to an unknown island an ocean away. The company instead gathered servants, orphans and slaves, and other, more unsavoury, outcasts such as thieves, drunkards and prostitutes. The population grew to 400 within ten years, but given that one in every four structures was a tavern, drunkenness, crime and squalor prevailed. If the colony was to thrive, it needed a strong leader. Enter Dutch West India Company director Peter Stuyvesant.

THE FIRST TOUGH-GUY MAYOR
A one-legged, puritanical bully with a quick temper, Stuyvesant was less than popular: rudeness was a way of life for Peg-leg Pete, as he was known. But he was the colony's first effective governor. He made peace with the Lenape, formed the first policing force (consisting of nine men) and cracked down on debauchery by shutting taverns and outlawing drinking on Sunday. He established the first school, post office, hospital, prison and poorhouse. Within a decade, the population quadrupled, and the settlement became an important trading port.

Lined with canals and windmills, and dotted with gabled farmhouses, New Amsterdam began to resemble its namesake city. Newcomers arrived to work in the fur and slave trades, or to farm. Soon, a dozen and a half languages could be heard in the streets – a fact that made the bigoted Stuyvesant nervous. In 1654, he attempted to quash immigration by turning away Sephardic Jews who were fleeing the Spanish Inquisition. But, surprisingly for the time, the corporate honchos at the Dutch West India Company reprimanded him for his intolerance and overturned his decision, leading to the establishment of the earliest Jewish community in the New World. That was the

first time the inflexible Stuyvesant was made to bend his ways. The second time would put an end to the 40-year Dutch rule for good.

REVOLUTIONARY CITY
In late August 1664, English warships sailed into the harbour, set on taking over the now prosperous colony. To avoid bloodshed and destruction, Stuyvesant quickly surrendered. Soon after, New Amsterdam was renamed New York (after the Duke of York, brother of King Charles II), and Stuyvesant quietly retired to his farm. Unlike Stuyvesant, the English battled with the Lenape; by 1695, those members of the tribe who weren't killed off were sent packing upstate, and New York's European population shot up to 3,000. Over the next 35 years, Dutch-style farmhouses and windmills gave way to stately townhouses and monuments to English royals. By 1740, the slave trade had made New York the third-busiest port in the British Empire. The city, now home to more than 11,000 residents, continued to be prosperous for a quarter-century more. But resentment was beginning to build in the colony, fuelled by the ever-heavier burden of British taxation.

> **'Fearing the brewing revolution, New York's citizenry fled in droves in 1775, causing the population to plummet from 25,000 to just 5,000.'**

One very angry young man was Alexander Hamilton, the illegitimate son of a Scottish nobleman. Hamilton arrived in New York from the West Indies in 1772. A fierce intellectual, he enrolled in King's College (which is now Columbia University) and became politically active – writing anti-British pamphlets, organising an artillery company and serving as a lieutenant colonel in General George Washington's army. In these and other ways, Hamilton played a key role in a movement that would change the city – and the country – forever.

Fearing the brewing revolution, New York's citizenry fled in droves in 1775, causing the population to plummet from 25,000 to just 5,000. The following year, 100 British warships sailed into this virtual ghost town, carrying an intimidating army of 32,000 – nearly four times the size of Washington's militia. Despite the British presence, Washington organised a reading of the Declaration of Independence, and patriots tore the statue of King George III from its pedestal. Revolution was inevitable.

Local legend

Before there was a Greenwich Village or even a George Washington, there was an **English Elm** standing in this spot. Three hundred or so years later, it's still here, towering over the north-west corner of Washington Square Park, one of the oldest and, with a diameter of 61in, largest-known trees in the city. As a 17th-century sapling, it rested in what was then a forest north of the city. In the early 1800s, the tree stood in a field used for duelling and for burying victims of the frequent cholera and yellow-fever breakouts. Because the field also hosted public hangings until 1819, the tree earned its name, the Hangman's Elm, and the persistent urban myth arose that criminals once hung from the tree itself. When the city bought the land in 1827, the elm survived landscaping and exhumation of the burial ground, and bore witness to a stately neighbourhood cropping up around the new park. Today, it's mostly the squirrels that pay attention to the elm, though it proudly bears a sign designating it as one of New York's Great Trees.

The battle for New York officially began on 26 August 1776, and Washington's army sustained heavy losses. Nearly a quarter of his men were slaughtered in a two-day period. As Washington retreated, a fire – thought to have been lit by patriots – destroyed 493 buildings, including Trinity Church, the tallest structure on the island. The British found a scorched city, and a populace living in tents.

The city continued to suffer for seven long years. Eventually, of course, Washington's luck turned. As the British left, he and his troops marched triumphantly down Broadway to reclaim the city as part of the newly established United States of America. A week and a half later, on 4 December 1783, the general bade farewell to his dispersing troops at Fraunces Tavern, which still stands on Pearl Street.

Alexander Hamilton, for his part, got busy in the rebuilding effort, laying the groundwork for New York institutions that remain vital to this day. He started by establishing the city's first bank, the Bank of New York, in 1784. When Washington was inaugurated as the nation's first president in 1789, at Federal Hall on Wall Street, he brought Hamilton on board as the first secretary of the treasury. Thanks to Hamilton's business savvy, trade in stocks and bonds flourished, leading to the establishment

in 1792 of what would eventually be known as the New York Stock Exchange. In 1801, Hamilton founded the *Evening Post* newspaper, still in circulation today as the *New York Post*. By 1804, he had helped make New York a world-leading financial centre. The same year that his dream was realised, however, Hamilton was killed by political rival Aaron Burr in a duel in Weehawken, New Jersey.

BOOMTOWN

New York continued to grow and prosper for the next three decades. Maritime commerce soared, and Robert Fulton's innovative steamboat made its maiden voyage on the Hudson River in 1807. Eleven years later, a group of merchants introduced regularly scheduled shipping (a novel concept at the time) between New York and Liverpool on the Black Ball Line. Reflecting the city's status as America's shipping centre, the urban landscape was ringed with sprawling piers, towering masts and billowing sails. A boom in the maritime trades lured hundreds of European labourers, and the city – still entirely crammed below Houston Street – grew more and more congested. Where Dutch farms and English estates once stood, taller, more efficient structures took hold, and Manhattan real estate became the most expensive in the world.

The first man to conquer the city's congestion problem was Mayor DeWitt Clinton, a brilliant politician and a protégé of Alexander Hamilton. Clinton's dream was to organise the entire island of Manhattan in such a way that it could cope with the eventual population creep northwards. In 1807, he created a commission to map out the foreseeable sprawl. It presented its work four years later, and the destiny of this new city was made manifest: it would be a regular grid of crossing thoroughfares, 12 avenues wide and 155 streets long.

Then Clinton literally overstepped his boundaries. In 1811, he presented a plan to build a 363-mile canal linking the Hudson River with Lake Erie. Many thought it impossible: at the time, the longest canal in the world ran a mere 27 miles. But he pressed on and, with a silver tongue to rival a certain modern-day Clinton, raised a staggering $6 million for the project.

Work on the Erie Canal, begun in 1817, was completed in 1825 – three years ahead of schedule. It shortened the journey between New York City and Buffalo from three weeks to one, and cut the shipping cost per ton from about $100 to $4. Goods, people and money poured into New York, fostering a merchant elite that moved northwards to escape the urban crush. Estates multiplied above Houston Street even as 3,000 new buildings were erected below it – each grander and more imposing than its modest colonial forerunners. Once slavery was officially abolished in New York in 1827, free blacks became an essential part of the workforce. In 1831, the first public transportation system began operation, pulling passengers in horse-drawn omnibuses to the city's far reaches.

BUMMERTOWN

As the population grew (swelling to 170,000 by 1830), so did New York City's problems. Tensions bubbled between immigrant newcomers and those who could trace their American lineage back a generation or two. Crime rose and lurid tales filled the 'penny press', the city's proto-tabloids. While wealthy New Yorkers were moving as far 'uptown' as Greenwich Village, the infamous Five Points neighbourhood – the city's first slum – festered in the area now occupied by City Hall, the courthouses and Chinatown. Built on a fetid drained pond, Five Points became the ramshackle home of poor immigrants and blacks. Brutal gangs with colourful names like the Forty Thieves, Plug Uglies and Dead Rabbits often met in bloody clashes in the streets, but what finally sent a mass of 100,000 people scurrying from downtown was an outbreak of cholera in 1832. In just six weeks, 3,513 New Yorkers died.

In 1837, a financial panic left hundreds of Wall Street businesses crumbling. Commerce stagnated at the docks, the real-estate market collapsed, and all but three city banks closed down. Fifty thousand New Yorkers lost their jobs, while 200,000 teetered on the edge of poverty. In 1849, a xenophobic mob of 8,000 protesting the performance of an English actor at the Astor Place Opera House was met by a militia that opened fire, killing 22 people. But the Draft Riots of 1863, known as 'the bloodiest riots in American history', were much worse. After a law was passed exempting men from the draft for a $300 fee, the (mostly Irish) poor rose up, forming a 15,000-strong mob that rampaged through the city. They trashed police stations, draft boards, newspaper offices, expensive shops and wealthy homes before the chaos took a racial turn. Fuelled by anger about the Civil War (for which they blamed blacks), and fearful that freed slaves would take away jobs, the rioters set fire to the Colored Orphan Asylum and vandalised black homes. Blacks were beaten in the streets, and some were lynched. A federal force of 6,000 men was sent to subdue the violence. After four days and at least 105 deaths, peace was finally restored.

PROGRESSIVE CITY

Amid the chaos of the mid-19th century, the pace of progress continued unabated. Compared with the major Southern cities, New York

Political **Alexander Hamilton**. *See p13.*

What lies beneath

National Historic Landmark designation aside, a passer-by might be forgiven for not immediately appreciating the enormous significance of an unassuming quarter-acre rectangle situated in the heart of Lower Manhattan. But it's what lies beneath it that's important: the 17th- and 18th-century remains of an estimated 20,000 African slaves and freed slaves, who were stacked in layers, buried 16 to 25ft under street level and spread across a five to seven acre stretch of what is now prime downtown real-estate just north of City Hall. No colonial-era tombstones or markers speak of the lives and deaths of those interred. But the sheer scope of the burial ground nonetheless offers a poignant testimony to a surprising fact: in its 18th-century infancy, New York City held the dubious distinction of being home to more enslaved Africans than any other English settlement save one (that being Charleston, South Carolina, which can claim sad bragging rights to top-dog status).

The slave trade first reached the Dutch colony of New Amsterdam in about 1625. After the British assumed control in 1665, the colony's African population was given permission to bury their dead in areas outside the town perimeters. Around the year 1795 – by which point roughly a staggering 40 per cent of New York households owned at least one slave – the graveyard was closed down, surveyed, sub-divided, and sold in lots. Construction landfill preserved the remains for nearly 200 years – it became

a case of out of sight and mind – below a cityscape of 19th- and 20th-century office buildings and busy streets.

A 1991 excavation for the construction of a 34-storey office tower led to the rediscovery of the graveyard, the unearthing of 1.5 million burial artefacts and the disinterment of 419 remains. A community uproar led to the nixing of building plans, the re-interment of remains, and heated discussions regarding the building of a permanent memorial. Finally, in 2005 a government-led panel selected a stone memorial drafted by architect Rodney Leon – a 36-year-old African-American New Yorker. The two-storey-tall curved monument draws heavily on African architecture and contains a spiral path leading to an ancestral chamber. 'I wanted it to reflect the diversity of Africans who were buried there, and to address the sacredness of the place,' says Leon. 'It's a big responsibility, and you just hope you're doing the right thing.'

However, New York City councilman Charles Barron – who is part of the grass-roots Committee of the Descendants of the Afrikan Ancestral Burial Ground – believes very strongly that Leon and the powers that be are not doing the right thing. 'We don't want a bunch of stuff on top of our ancestors,' says Barron. 'They're disrespecting and desecrating a graveyard. There's supposed to be a museum and we want that to happen, but we want the site open, with some eternal flames, and history marked outside the site so that people will

emerged nearly unscathed from the Civil War. The population ballooned to 2 million, and new technologies revolutionised daily life. The elevated railway, for example, helped extend the population into what is now the Upper East and Upper West Sides, while other trains connected the city with upstate New York, New England and the Midwest. By 1871, train traffic had grown so much that rail tycoon Cornelius Vanderbilt built the original Grand Central Depot, which could accommodate a then-considerable 15,000 passengers at a time. (It was replaced in 1913 by the current Grand Central Terminal.)

One ambitious project was inspired by the harsh winter of 1867. The East River froze over, halting water traffic between Brooklyn and Manhattan for weeks. Brooklyn, by then, had become the nation's third most populous city,

and its politicians, businessmen and community leaders realised that the boroughs had to be linked. Thus, the New York Bridge Company was incorporated. Its goal was to build the world's longest bridge, spanning the East River between downtown Manhattan and southwestern Brooklyn. Over 16 years (four times longer than projected), 14,000 miles of steel cable were stretched across the 1,595ft span, while the towers rose a staggering 276ft above the river. Disasters, worker deaths and corruption dogged the project, but the Brooklyn Bridge opened with triumphant fanfare on 24 May 1883. It remains one of the city's most beloved symbols.

CORRUPT CITY

As New York recovered from the turmoil of the mid 1800s, one extremely indecorous man – William M 'Boss' Tweed – was pulling the

never forget that New York was indeed a slave state. There are going to be demonstrations. We're going to fight.'

'I disagree,' counters Howard Dodson, director of the Schomburg Center for Research in Black Culture, in Harlem. 'We have the better part of 200 years of history in which nothing was placed on the site to mark it as a sacred place. As a consequence we have courthouses and office buildings. To leave it bare is to invite a repeat of that history.'

Thankfully, this time around, people are listening and attention is finally being paid.

African Burial Ground

Duane Street, between Broadway & Centre Street, behind 290 Broadway (www.africanburialground.com). Subway: N, Q R, W to Canal Street; J, M, Z to Chambers Street; 4, 5, 6 to Brooklyn Bridge-City Hall. **Open** 9am-4pm Mon-Fri. **Admission** free.

strings. Using his ample charm, the six-foot tall, 300-pound bookkeeper, chairmaker and volunteer firefighter became one of the city's most powerful politicians. He had been an alderman and district leader; he served in the US House of Representatives and as a state senator; and he was a chairman of the Democratic General Committee and leader of Tammany Hall, a political organisation formed by craftsmen to keep the wealthy class's political clout in check. But even though Tweed opened orphanages, poorhouses and hospitals, his good deeds were overshadowed by his and his cohorts' gross embezzlement of city funds.

By 1870, members of the 'Tweed Ring' had established a new city charter, granting themselves control of the City Treasury. Using fake leases and wildly inflated bills for city supplies and services, Tweed and his cronies

may ultimately have pocketed as much as $200 million, and caused the city's debt to triple. The work of cartoonist Thomas Nast, who lampooned Tweed in the pages of *Harper's Weekly*, helped to bring the Boss's transgressions to light. Tweed was eventually sued by the city for $6 million, and charged with forgery and larceny. In 1875, while being held in debtor's prison pending bail, he escaped. He was caught in Spain a year later and died in the slammer in 1878. But before his fall from power, Tweed's insatiable greed hurt many: as he was emptying the city's coffers, poverty spread. Then the bond market collapsed, the stock market took a nosedive, factories closed, and railroads went bankrupt. By 1874, New York estimated its homeless population at 90,000 souls. That winter, *Harper's Weekly* reported, 900 New Yorkers starved to death.

Further reading

Herbert Asbury The Gangs of New York: An Informal History of the Underworld
A racy journalistic portrait of the city at the turn of the 20th century.

Robert A Caro The Power Broker
A biography of Robert Moses, New York's mid-20th-century master builder, and his checkered legacy.

Federal Writers' Project The WPA Guide to New York City
A wonderful snapshot of the 1930s by writers who were employed under FDR's New Deal.

Sanna Feirstein Naming New York
How Manhattan places got their names.

Mitchell Fink and Lois Mathias Never Forget: An Oral History of September 11, 2001
A collection of first-person accounts.

Alice Rose George (ed) Here Is New York
A collection of nearly 900 powerful amateur photos that document the aftermath of September 11, 2001.

Clifton Hood 722 Miles: The Building of the Subways and How They Transformed New York
The title adequately describes the content.

Kenneth T Jackson (ed) The Encyclopedia of New York City
An ambitious and useful reference guide.

David Levering Lewis When Harlem Was in Vogue
A study of the Harlem Renaissance.

Shaun O'Connell Remarkable, Unspeakable New York
The history of New York as literary inspiration.

Mitchell Pacelle Empire
The story of the fight to build the Empire State Building.

Jacob A Riis How the Other Half Lives
A pioneering photojournalistic record of squalid tenement life.

Marie Salerno and Arthur Gelb The New York Pop-up Book
An interactive historical account of NYC.

Luc Sante Low Life
Opium dens and brothels in New York from the 1840s to the 1920s.

Mike Wallace and Edwin G Burrows Gotham: A History of New York City to 1898
The first volume in a planned mammoth history of NYC.

THE TWO HALVES

In September 1882, a new era dawned brightly when Thomas Alva Edison lit up half a square mile of lower Manhattan with 3,000 electric lamps. One of the newly illuminated offices belonged to a man known for brushing people aside when he strode down the sidewalks: financier JP Morgan, who was essential in bringing New York's – and America's – economy back to life. By bailing out a number of failing railroads, then merging and restructuring them, Morgan jump-started commerce in New York once again. Goods, jobs and businesses returned to the city, and soon aggressive businessmen with names like Rockefeller, Carnegie and Frick wanted a piece of the action (none of them, by the way, was noted for his courtesy, either). They made New York the HQ of Standard Oil and US Steel, corporations that would go on to shape America's economic future and New York's reputation as the country's centre of capitalism.

A shining symbol for less fortunate immigrants also made New York its home around that time: to commemorate America's freedom 100 years after the Declaration of Independence, and to celebrate an international friendship, the French gave the Statue of Liberty to the United States. Sculptor Frédéric-Auguste Bartholdi had created the 151ft-tall amazon using funds donated by French citizens, but their generosity could not cover the expense of building her base. Although the project was initially met with apathy by the US government, Hungarian immigrant and publisher Joseph Pulitzer used his *World* newspaper to encourage Americans to pay for a pedestal. When she was finally unveiled in 1886, Lady Liberty measured 305ft high – taller than the towers of the Brooklyn Bridge.

> ### 'With little land left to develop in lower Manhattan, the city began a vertical race, building 66 skyscrapers by 1902.'

Between 1892 and 1954, the statue welcomed more than 12 million immigrants into the harbour. Ellis Island, which was an immigration-processing centre, opened in 1892, expecting to accommodate 500,000 people annually; it processed twice that number in its first year. In the 34-building complex, crowds of would-be Americans were herded through examinations, inspections and interrogations. Fewer than two per cent were sent home, and others moved on, but 4 million stayed, turning New York into what British playwright Israel Zangwill called 'the great melting pot where all the races of Europe are melting and reforming'.

Many of these new immigrants crowded into dark, squalid tenements on the Lower East Side, while millionaires like the Vanderbilts were building huge French-style mansions along Fifth Avenue. Jacob A Riis, a Danish immigrant and police reporter for the *New York Tribune*, made it his business to expose this dichotomy, however impolite it may have seemed to the wealthy. Employing the relatively new technology of photography to accompany his written observations, Riis's 1890 book, *How the Other Half Lives,* revealed, in graphic terms, the bitter conditions of the slums. The intrepid reporter scoured filthy alleys and overcrowded, unheated tenements, many of which lacked the barest minimum of light, ventilation and sanitation. Largely as a result of Riis's work, the state passed the Tenement House Act of 1901, which called for drastic housing reforms.

EXPANDING CITY

By the close of the 19th century, 40 fragmented governments had formed in and around Manhattan, creating political confusion on many different levels. On 1 January 1898, the boroughs of Manhattan, Brooklyn, Queens, Staten Island and the Bronx consolidated to form New York City, America's largest city.

More and more companies started to move their headquarters to this new metropolis, increasing the demand for office space. With little land left to develop in lower Manhattan, New York embraced the steel revolution and grew skywards. Thus began an all-out race to build the tallest building in the world. By 1902, New York boasted 66 skyscrapers, including the 20-storey Fuller Building (which is now known as the Flatiron Building) at Fifth Avenue and 23rd Street, and the 25-storey New York Times Tower in Longacre (now Times) Square. Within four years, these two buildings would be completely dwarfed by the 47-storey Singer Building on lower Broadway, which enjoyed the status of tallest building in the world – but for only 18 months. The 700ft Metropolitan Life Tower on Madison Square claimed the title from the Singer Building in 1909, but the 792ft Woolworth Building on Broadway and Park Place topped it in 1913 – and amazingly held the distinction for nearly two decades.

If that wasn't enough to demonstrate New Yorkers' unending ambition, the city burrowed below the streets at the same time, starting work on its underground transit system in 1900. The $35-million project took nearly four and a half years to complete. Less than a decade after opening, it was the most heavily travelled subway system in the world, carrying almost a billion passengers on its trains every year.

Ellis Island. *See p18.*

CITY OF MOVEMENT

By 1909, 30,000 factories were operating in the city, churning out everything from heavy machinery to artificial flowers. Brutal conditions worsened the situation for workers, who toiled long hours for meager pay. Young immigrant seamstresses worked 60-plus hours for just $5 a week. Mistrusted and abused, factory workers faced impossible quotas, had their pay docked for minor mistakes, and were often locked in the factories during working hours. In the end, it would take a tragedy for real changes to be made.

On 25 March 1911, a fire broke out at the Triangle Shirtwaist Company. Though it was a Saturday, some 500 workers – most of them teenage girls – were toiling in the Greenwich Village factory. Flames spread rapidly through the fabric-filled building. But as the girls rushed to escape, they found many of the exits locked. Roughly 350 made it out on to the adjoining rooftops before the inferno closed off all exits, but 146 young women perished. Many jumped to their deaths from windows on the eighth, ninth and tenth floors. Even in the face of such tragedy, justice was not served: the two factory owners, tried for manslaughter, were acquitted. But the disaster did spur labour and union organisations, which pushed for – and won – sweeping reforms for factory workers.

Another sort of rights movement was taking hold during this time as well. Between 1910 and 1913, New York City was the site of the largest women's-suffrage rallies in the United States. Harriet Stanton Blatch (who was the daughter of famed suffragette Elizabeth Cady Stanton and founder of the Equality League of Self Supporting Women) and Carrie Chapman Catt (the organiser of the New York City Women's Suffrage party) arranged attention-getting demonstrations intended to pressure the state into authorising a referendum on a woman's right to vote. The measure's defeat in 1915 only steeled the suffragettes' resolve. Finally, with the support of Tammany Hall, the law passed in 1919, challenging the male stranglehold on voting throughout the country. (With New York leading the nation, the 19th Amendment was ratified in 1920.)

In 1919, as New York welcomed troops home from World War I with a parade along Fifth Avenue, the city also celebrated its emergence on the global stage. It had supplanted London as the investment capital of the world, and it was the centre of publishing, thanks to two men: Pulitzer and Hearst. The *New York Times* had become the country's most respected newspaper; Broadway was the focal point of American theatre; and Greenwich Village, once the home of an elite gentry, had become a world-class bohemia, where flamboyant artists, writers and political revolutionaries gathered in galleries and coffeehouses. John Reed, reporter on the Russian revolution and author of *Ten Days That Shook the World*, lived here, as did Edna St Vincent Millay, famous for her poetry and her public, unfettered love life.

The more personal side of the women's movement also found a home in New York City. A nurse and midwife who grew up in a family of 11 children, Margaret Sanger was a fierce advocate of birth control and family planning. She opened the first ever birth-control clinic in Brooklyn on 16 October 1916. Finding this unseemly, the police closed the clinic soon after and imprisoned Sanger for 30 days. She pressed on and, in 1921, formed the American Birth Control League – the forerunner of Planned Parenthood – which researched birth control and provided gynecological services.

Forward-thinking women like Sanger set the tone for the Jazz Age, a time when women, now a voting political force, were moving beyond the moral conventions of the 19th century. The country ushered in the Jazz Age in 1919 by ratifying the 18th Amendment, which outlawed the distribution and sale of alcoholic beverages. Prohibition turned the city into the epicentre of bootlegging, speakeasies and organised crime. By the early 1920s, New York boasted 32,000 illegal watering holes – twice the number of legal bars before Prohibition.

Brooklyn Bridge.
See p16.

In 1925, New Yorkers elected the magnetic James J Walker as mayor. A charming ex-songwriter (as well as a speakeasy patron and skirt-chaser who would later leave his wife for a dancer), Walker matched his city's flashy style, hunger for publicity and consequences-be-damned attitude. Fame flowed in the city's veins: home-run hero Babe Ruth drew a million fans each season to the New York Yankees' games, and sharp-tongued Walter Winchell filled his newspaper columns with celebrity titbits and scandals. Alexander Woollcott, Dorothy Parker, Robert Benchley and other writers met daily to trade witticisms around a table at the Algonquin Hotel; the result, in 1925, was *The New Yorker*.

The Harlem Renaissance blossomed at the same time. Writers such as Langston Hughes, Zora Neale Hurston and James Weldon Johnson transformed the African-American experience into lyrical literary works, and white society flocked to the Cotton Club to see genre-defining musicians like Bessie Smith, Cab Calloway, Louis Armstrong and Duke Ellington. (Blacks were not welcome here unless they were performing.) Downtown, Broadway houses were packed out, thanks to brilliant composers and lyricists like George and Ira Gershwin, Irving Berlin, Cole Porter, Lorenz Hart, Richard Rodgers and Oscar Hammerstein II. Towards the end of the '20s, New York-born Al Jolson wowed audiences in the wonderful *The Jazz Singer*, the first ever talking picture.

THE FALL AND RISE

The dizzying excitement ended on Tuesday, 29 October 1929, when the stock market completely crashed and widespread hard times set in. Corruption eroded Mayor Walker's hold on the city: despite a tenure that saw the opening of the Holland Tunnel, the completion of the George Washington Bridge and the construction of the Chrysler and Empire State Buildings, Walker's lustre faded in the growing shadow of graft accusations. He resigned in 1932, as New York, caught in the depths of the Great Depression, had a staggering 1 million inhabitants who were out of work.

In 1934, an unstoppable force named Fiorello La Guardia took office as mayor, rolling up his sleeves to crack down on mobsters, gambling, smut and government corruption. La Guardia was the son of an Italian father and a Jewish mother. He was a tough-talking politician known for nearly coming to blows with other city officials, and he described himself as 'inconsiderate, arbitrary, authoritative, difficult, complicated, intolerant and somewhat theatrical'. La Guardia's act played well: he ushered New York into an era of unparalleled

It happened here

Booze clues During the 13 years of national buzz-kill known as Prohibition, New York City was the tap through which the nation's bootlegged liquor endlessly flowed, and mob bosses like Al Capone were the barkeeps. Locals, too, had to have their hooch, so speakeasies flourished, and people imbibed more than ever. The most famous place to wet your whistle, Jack and Charlie's 21, took its name from its address, 21 West 52nd Street; it still lives on today as the somewhat more respectable '21' Club (*see p124*).

prosperity over the course of his three terms. During World War II, the city's ports and factories proved essential to the war effort. New Yorkers' sense of unity was never more visible than on 14 August 1945, when 2 million people spontaneously gathered in Times Square to celebrate the end of the war. The 'Little Flower', as La Guardia was known, streamlined city government, paid down the debt and updated the transportation, hospital, reservoir and sewer systems. Additional highways made the city more accessible, and North Beach (now La Guardia) Airport became the city's first commercial landing field.

Helping La Guardia to modernise the city was Robert Moses, a hard-nosed visionary who would do much to shape – and in some cases, destroy – New York's landscape. Moses spent

It happened here

Pleasure and pain Before ultra-trendy eaterie Vento moved into 28 Ninth Avenue, the triangular-shaped building had a long, varied history, with two relative constants: uniforms and pain. During the Civil War, the building served as a hospital, where the Union Army's wounded were separated from their gangrenous limbs. However, excruciation became recreation in the 1980s, when the legendary gay S&M club the Manhole moved in. Today, the only agony to be found is the sprained ankles that are suffered by fashionistas negotiating the cobblestones in their Jimmy Choo stilettos.

44 years stepping on toes to build expressways, parks, beaches, public housing, bridges and tunnels, creating such landmarks as Shea Stadium, the Lincoln Center, the United Nations complex and the Verrazano-Narrows Bridge.

THE MODERN CITY

Despite La Guardia's belt-tightening and Moses' renovations, New York began to fall apart financially. When WWII ended, 800,000 industrial jobs disappeared from the city. Factories in need of space moved to the suburbs, along with nearly 5 million residents. But more crowding occurred as rural African-Americans and Puerto Ricans flocked to the metropolis in the '50s and '60s, only to meet with ruthless discrimination and a dearth of jobs. Robert Moses' Slum Clearance Committee reduced many neighbourhoods to rubble, forcing out residents in order to build huge, isolating housing projects that became magnets for crime. In 1963, the city also lost Pennsylvania Station – McKim, Mead & White's architectural masterpiece. Over the protests of picketers, the Pennsylvania Railroad Company demolished the site to make way for a modern station and Madison Square Garden. It was a giant wake-up call to New Yorkers: architectural changes were hurtling out of control.

But Moses and his wrecking ball couldn't knock over one steadfast West Village woman. An architectural writer and urban-planning critic named Jane Jacobs organised local residents when the city unveiled its plan to clear a 14-block tract of her neighbourhood to make space for yet more public housing. Her obstinacy was applauded by many, including an influential councilman named Ed Koch (who would become mayor in 1978). The group fought the plan and won, causing Mayor Robert F Wagner to back down. As a result of Jacobs's efforts in the wake of Pennsylvania Station's demolition, the Landmarks Preservation Commission – the first such group in the US – was established in 1965.

At the dawning of the age of Aquarius, the city harboured its share of innovative creators. Allen Ginsberg, Jack Kerouac and their fellow Beats gathered in Village coffeehouses to create a new voice for poetry. A folk-music scene brewed in tiny clubs around Bleecker Street, showcasing musicians such as Bob Dylan. A former advertising illustrator from Pittsburgh named Andy Warhol began turning the images of mass consumerism into deadpan, ironic art statements. Gay men and women, long a hidden part of the city's history, came out into the streets in 1969's Stonewall riots, sparked when patrons at the Stonewall Inn on Christopher Street resisted a police raid – giving birth to the modern gay-rights movement.

By the early 1970s, deficits had forced heavy cutbacks in city services. The streets were dirty, subway cars and buildings were scrawled with graffiti, crime skyrocketed and the city's debt deepened to $6 billion. Despite the downturn, construction commenced on the World Trade Center; when completed, in 1973, its twin 110-storey towers were the world's tallest buildings. Even as the Trade Center rose, the city became so desperately overdrawn that Mayor Abraham Beame appealed to the federal government for financial assistance in 1975. Yet President Gerald Ford refused to bail out the city, and New Yorkers faced his decision, summed up by the immortal *Daily News* headline: 'Ford to city: drop dead'.

The President's callousness certainly didn't help matters during this time. Around the mid '70s, Times Square steadily degenerated into a sleazy morass of sex shops and porn palaces, drug use escalated and subway ridership hit an all-time low. To make situations worse, in 1977, serial killer Son of Sam terrorised the city, and a blackout one hot August night that same year led to widespread looting and arson. The angst of the time fuelled the angry punk culture that rose up around downtown clubs like CBGB, where the Ramones and other bands played fast and loud. At the same time, celebrities, designers and models converged on midtown to disco their nights away at Studio 54.

The Wall Street boom of the '80s and some adept fiscal petitioning by then-mayor Ed Koch brought money flooding back into New York. Gentrification glamourised neighbourhoods like Soho, Tribeca and the East Village. But deeper ills persisted. In 1988, a demonstration against the city's efforts to impose a curfew and displace the homeless in Tompkins Square Park erupted into a violent clash with the police. Crack use was epidemic in the ghettos, homelessness was rising and AIDS became a

new scourge. By 1989, citizens were restless for change. They turned to David N Dinkins, electing him the city's first African-American mayor. A distinguished, soft-spoken man, Dinkins held office for only a single term – one marked by a record murder rate, flaring racial tensions in Washington Heights, Crown Heights and Flatbush, and the explosion of a terrorist bomb in the World Trade Center that killed six, injured 1,000 and foreshadowed the catastrophic attacks of 2001.

Deeming the polite Dinkins ineffective, New Yorkers voted in former federal prosecutor Rudolph Giuliani. Like his predecessors Peter Stuyvesant and Fiorello La Guardia, Giuliani was an abrasive leader who used bully tactics to get things done. His 'quality of life campaign' cracked down on everything from drug dealing and pornography to unsolicited windshield-washing. Even as multiple cases of severe police brutality grabbed the headlines, crime plummeted, tourism soared and New York became cleaner and safer than it had been in decades. Times Square was transformed into a family-friendly tourist destination, and the dot-com explosion brought a generation of young wannabe millionaires to the Flatiron District's Silicon Alley. Giuliani's second term as mayor would close, however, on a devastating tragedy.

On 11 September 2001 terrorists flew two hijacked passenger jets into the Twin Towers of the World Trade Center, collapsing the entire complex and killing nearly 2,800 people. But the

The **Cotton Club** helped power the Harlem Renaissance of the 1920s. *See p21.*

Ground Zero. *See p23.*

attack triggered a citywide sense of unity, and New Yorkers did what they could to help their fellow citizens, from feeding emergency crews around the clock to cheering on workers en route to Ground Zero.

> ### 'New Yorkers continue to uphold their hard-edged reputation.'

Two months later, billionaire Michael Bloomberg was elected mayor and took on the daunting task of repairing not only the city's skyline but also its battered economy and shattered psyche. He proved adept at steering the city back on the road to health as the stock market revived, downtown businesses reemerged and plans for rebuilding the Trade Center were drawn. True to form, however, New Yorkers debated the future of the site for more than a year until architect Daniel Libeskind was awarded the redevelopment job in 2003. His plan, called 'Memory Foundations', aims to reconcile rebuilding and remembrance, with parks, plazas, a cultural centre, a performing arts centre, a memorial and a sleek new office tower. Nevertheless, conflict continues to plague every step of the project.

The summer of 2003 saw a blackout that shut down the city (and much of the eastern seaboard). New Yorkers were sweaty but calm,

and again proved that they possessed surprisingly strong reserves of civility as the city's cafés set up candlelit tables and bodegas handed out free ice-cream.

And yet, despite Bloomberg's many efforts to make New York a more considerate and civil place – imposing a citywide smoking ban in bars and restaurants and a strict noise ordinance that would even silence the jingling of ice-cream vans – New Yorkers continue to uphold their hard-edged reputation. The 2004 Republican National Convention brought out hundreds of thousands of peace marchers who had no trouble expressing how they really felt about the war in Iraq. Still, the oft-cranky citizenry swooned for Christo and Jeanne-Claude's *The Gates* – the 7,503 billowing orange-fabric-and-metal gates that lined 23 miles of paths in Central Park for two weeks in February 2005. But just as quickly, it was back to business as usual: local bellyaching helped kill a plan to build a 75,000-seat stadium on Manhattan's West Side, squashing Bloomberg and Co's dream to bring the 2012 Olympic Games to the Big Apple.

But let's face it, if any of these rude, abrasive or inconsiderate people had their attitudes adjusted, New Yorkers wouldn't be where they are today: thriving in a city that is widely looked upon as the capital of the world. And no doubt they would offer a big, disrespectful Bronx cheer to those who disagree.

Key NYC events

1524 Giovanni da Verrazano sails into New York Harbour.
1624 First Dutch settlers establish New Amsterdam at the foot of Manhattan Island.
1626 Peter Minuit purchases Manhattan for goods worth 60 guilders.
1639 The Broncks settle north of Manhattan.
1646 Village of Breuckelen founded.
1664 Dutch rule ends; New Amsterdam renamed New York.
1754 King's College (now Columbia University) founded.
1776 Battle for New York begins; fire ravages the city.
1783 George Washington's troops march triumphantly down Broadway.
1784 Alexander Hamilton founds the Bank of New York.
1785 New York becomes the nation's capital.
1789 President Washington inaugurated at Federal Hall on Wall Street.
1792 New York Stock Exchange founded.
1804 New York becomes the country's most populous city, with 80,000 inhabitants; New York Historical Society founded.
1811 Mayor DeWitt Clinton's grid plan for Manhattan introduced.
1825 New York Gas Light Company completes installation of first gas lamps on Broadway; Erie Canal completed.
1827 Slavery officially abolished in New York.
1833 The *New York Sun*'s lurid tales give birth to tabloid journalism.
1851 The *New York Daily Times* (now the *New York Times*) published.
1858 Work on Central Park begins; Macy's opens.
1870 Metropolitan Museum of Art founded.
1883 Brooklyn Bridge opens.
1886 Statue of Liberty unveiled.
1890 Jacob A Riis publishes *How the Other Half Lives*.
1891 Carnegie Hall opens with a concert conducted by Tchaikovsky.
1892 Ellis Island opens.
1895 Oscar Hammerstein's Olympia Theater opens, creating Broadway theatre.
1898 The city consolidates the five boroughs.
1902 The Fuller (Flatiron) Building becomes the world's first skyscraper.
1903 The New York Highlanders (later the New York Yankees) play their first game.
1904 New York's first subway line opens; Longacre Square becomes Times Square.

1908 First ball dropped to celebrate the new year in Times Square.
1911 The Triangle Shirtwaist Fire claims nearly 150 lives, spurring unionisation.
1923 Yankee Stadium opens.
1924 First Macy's Christmas Parade held; now the Thanksgiving Day Parade.
1929 The stock market crashes; Museum of Modern Art opens.
1931 George Washington Bridge completed; the Empire State Building opens; the Whitney Museum opens.
1934 Fiorello La Guardia takes office; Tavern on the Green opens.
1939 New York hosts a World's Fair.
1946 The New York Knickerbockers play their first game.
1950 United Nations complex completed.
1953 Robert Moses spearheads building of the Cross Bronx Expressway; 40,000 homes demolished in the process.
1957 The New York Giants baseball team moves to San Francisco; Brooklyn Dodgers move to Los Angeles.
1962 New York Mets debut at the Polo Grounds; Philharmonic Hall (later Avery Fisher Hall), the first building in Lincoln Center, opens; first Shakespeare in the Park performance.
1964 Verrazano-Narrows Bridge completed; World's Fair held in Flushing Meadows–Corona Park in Queens.
1970 First New York City Marathon held.
1973 World Trade Center completed.
1975 On the verge of bankruptcy, the city is snubbed by the federal government; *Saturday Night Live* debuts.
1977 Serial killer David 'Son of Sam' Berkowitz arrested; Studio 54 opens; 4,000 arrested during citywide blackout.
1989 David N Dinkins elected the city's first black mayor.
1993 A terrorist bomb explodes in the World Trade Center, killing six and injuring 1,000.
1997 Murder rate lowest in 30 years.
2001 Hijackers fly two jets into the Twin Towers, killing nearly 2,800 and demolishing the World Trade Center.
2004 The Statue of Liberty reopens for the first time since 9/11; the Republican National Convention brings out hundreds of thousands of protesters.
2005 Christo and Jeanne-Claude decorate Central Park with art installation *The Gates*; New York loses its bid for the 2012 Olympics.

Astor Palace. *See p34.*

Architecture

From humble beginnings to the almighty tower.

Under New York's gleaming exoskeleton of steel and glass lies the heart of a 17th-century Dutch city. It began at the Battery and New York Harbor, one of the greatest naturally formed deep-water ports in the world. The former Alexander Hamilton Custom House, now the **National Museum of the American Indian** (*see p89*), was built by Cass Gilbert in 1907 and is a symbol of the harbour's significance in Manhattan's growth. Before 1913, the city's chief source of revenue was customs duties. Gilbert's domed marble edifice is suitably monumental – its carved figures of the Four Continents are by Daniel Chester French, the sculptor of the Lincoln Memorial in Washington, DC.

The Dutch influence is still traceable in the downtown web of narrow, winding lanes, reminiscent of the streets in medieval European cities. Because the Cartesian grid that rules the city was laid out by the Commissioners' Plan in 1811, only a few samples of actual Dutch architecture remain, mostly off the beaten path. One of these is the 1785 **Dyckman Farmhouse Museum** (4881 Broadway, at 204th Street, www.dyckmanfarmhouse.org) in Inwood, Manhattan's northernmost neighbourhood. Its gambrel roof and decorative brickwork reflect the architectural fashion of the late 18th century. The oldest house still standing in the five boroughs is the **Pieter Claesen Wyckoff House Museum** (5816 Clarendon Road, at Ralph Avenue, Flatbush, Brooklyn, www.wyckoffassociation.org). Erected around 1652, it's a typical Dutch farmhouse with shingled walls and deep eaves. The **Lefferts**

In Context

Homestead (Prospect Park, Flatbush Avenue, Prospect Heights, Brooklyn), built between 1777 and 1783, combines a gambrel roof with column-supported porches, a hybrid style popular during the Federal period.

In Manhattan, the only building extant from pre-Revolutionary times is the stately columned and quoined St Paul's Chapel (see p94), completed in 1766 (a spire was added in 1796). George Washington, a parishioner here, was officially received in the chapel after his 1789 presidential inauguration. The Enlightenment ideals upon which this nation was founded influenced the church's democratic, non-hierarchical layout. Trinity Church (see p94) of 1846, one of the first and finest Gothic Revival churches in the country, was designed by Richard Upjohn. It's difficult to imagine now that Trinity's crocketed, finialed 281-foot-tall spire held sway for decades as the tallest structure in Manhattan.

Hold-outs remain from each epoch of the city's architectural history. An outstanding example of Greek Revival from the first half of the 19th century is the 1842 Federal Hall National Memorial (see p94), the mighty marble colonnade which was built to mark the site where George Washington took his oath of office. A larger-than-life statue of Washington by the sculptor John Quincy Adams Ward stands in front. The city's most celebrated blocks of Greek Revival townhouses, built in the 1830s, are known simply as the Row (1-13 Washington Square North, between Fifth Avenue & Washington Square West); they're exemplars of the more genteel metropolis of Henry James and Edith Wharton.

'Once engineers perfected steel, the sky was the limit.'

Greek Revival gave way to Renaissance-inspired Beaux Arts architecture, which reflected the imperial ambitions of a wealthy young nation during the Gilded Age of the late 19th century. Like Emperor Augustus, who boasted that he had found Rome a city of brick and left it a city of marble, the firm of McKim, Mead & White built noble civic monuments and palazzi for the rich. The best-known buildings of the classicist Charles Follen McKim include the main campus of Columbia University (see p143), which was begun in the 1890s, and the austere 1906 Morgan Library (see p117). His partner, socialite and bon vivant Stanford White (scandalously murdered by his mistress's husband in 1906), designed more festive spaces, such as the Metropolitan Club (1 E 60th Street, at Fifth Avenue) and

the extraordinarily luxe Villard Houses of 1882, now incorporated into the New York Palace hotel (see p62).

Another Beaux Arts treasure from the city's grand metropolitan era is Carrère & Hastings's sumptuous white-marble New York Public Library of 1911 (see p122), built on a former Revolutionary War battleground; the site later hosted an Egyptian Revival water reservoir and, presently, the greensward of Bryant Park. The 1913 travertine-lined Grand Central Terminal (see p127) remains the elegant foyer of the city, thanks to preservationists (most prominently, Jacqueline Kennedy Onassis; see p127 Local legend) who saved it from the wrecking ball.

MOVIN' ON UP

Cast-iron architecture peaked in the latter half of the 19th century, coinciding roughly with the Civil War era. Iron and steel components freed architects from the bulk, weight and cost of stone construction and allowed them to build higher. Cast-iron columns, cheap to mass-produce, could support a tremendous amount of weight. The façades of many Soho buildings, with their intricate details of Italianate columns, were manufactured on assembly lines and could be ordered in pieces from catalogues.

This led to an aesthetic of uniform building façades, which had a direct impact on the steel skyscrapers of the following generation. To enjoy one of the most telling vistas of skyscraper history, gaze northwards from the 1859 Cooper Union (see p104), the oldest existing steel-beam-framed building in America.

The most visible effect of the move towards cast-iron construction was the way it opened up solid stone façades to expanses of glass. In fact, window-shopping came into vogue in the 1860s. Mrs Lincoln bought the White House china at the Haughwout Store (488-492 Broadway, at Broome Street). The 1857 building's Palladian-style façade recalls Renaissance Venice, but its regular, open fenestration was also a portent of the future. (Look carefully: the cast-iron elevator sign is a relic of the world's first working safety passenger elevator, designed by Elisha Graves Otis in 1852.)

Once engineers perfected steel, which is stronger and lighter than iron, and created the interlocking steel-cage construction that distributed the weight of a building over its entire frame, the sky was the limit. New York is fortunate to have one building by the great skyscraper innovator Louis Sullivan, the 1898 Bayard-Condict Building (65-69 Bleecker Street, between Broadway & Lafayette Street). Though only 13 storeys tall, Sullivan's building, covered with richly decorative terracotta, was one of the earliest to apply a purely vertical design rather than imitate horizontal styles of the past. Sullivan wrote that a skyscraper 'must be tall, every inch of it all.… From bottom to top, it is a unit without a single dissenting line'.

Chicago architect Daniel H Burnham's 1902 **Flatiron Building** (*see p113*) is another standout; its modern design – breathtaking even today – combined with traditional masonry decoration, was made possible only by steel-cage construction.

The new century saw a frenzy of skyward manufacture, resulting in buildings of record-breaking height; the now modest-looking 30-storey, 391-foot-tall **Park Row Building** (15 Park Row, between Ann & Beekman Streets) was, when it was built in 1899, the tallest building in the world. That record was shattered by the 612-foot Singer Building in 1908 (demolished in the 1960s); the 700-foot **Metropolitan Life Tower** (1 Madison Avenue, at 24th Street) of 1909, modelled after the Campanile in Venice's Piazza San Marco; and Cass Gilbert's Gothic masterpiece, the 792-foot **Woolworth Building** (*see p97*). The Woolworth reigned in solitary splendour until William van Alen's metal-spired homage to the Automobile Age, the 1930 **Chrysler Building** (*see p128*), soared to 1,046 feet.

> **'The Empire State Building remains the quintessential skyscraper, one of the most recognisable in the world.'**

In a highly publicised race, the Chrysler was outstripped 13 months later, in 1931, by Shreve, Lamb & Harmon's 1,250-foot-tall **Empire State Building** (*see p122*), which has since lost its title to other giants: the 1,450-foot Sears Tower in Chicago (1974); the 1,483-foot Petronas Towers in Kuala Lumpur, Malaysia (1996); and the current record holder, the 1,671-foot Taipei 101 in Taiwan (2004). But the Empire State remains the quintessential skyscraper, one of the most recognisable buildings in the world, with its broad base, narrow shaft and distinctive needled crown. (The giant ape that scaled the side might have something to do with it too.)

The Empire State's setbacks, retroactively labelled art deco (such buildings were then simply called 'modern'), were actually a response to the zoning code of 1916, which required a building's upper storeys to be tapered in order not to block sunlight and air circulation to the streets. The code engendered some of the city's most fanciful designs, such

as the ziggurat-crowned **Paramount Building** (1501 Broadway, between 43rd & 44th Streets) of 1926, and the romantically slender spire of the former **Cities Service Building** (70 Pine Street, at Pearl Street), illuminated from within like a rare gem.

BRAVE NEW WORLD

The post-World War II period saw the rise of the International Style, pioneered by such giants as Le Corbusier and Ludwig Mies van der Rohe. The style's most visible symbol was the all-glass façade, like that found on the sleek slab of the **United Nations Headquarters** (*see p128*). The International Style relied on a new set of aesthetics: minimal decoration, clear expression of construction, an honest use of materials and a near-Platonic harmony of proportions. **Lever House** (390 Park Avenue, between 53rd & 54th Streets), designed by Gordon Bunshaft of Skidmore, Owings & Merrill, was the city's first all-steel-and-glass structure when it was built in 1952 (it recently received an award-winning brush-up). It's almost impossible to imagine the radical vision this glass construction represented on the all-masonry corridor of Park Avenue, because nearly every building since has followed suit. Mies van der Rohe's celebrated bronze-skinned **Seagram Building** (375 Park Avenue, between 52nd & 53rd Streets), which reigns in imperious isolation on its own plaza, is the epitome of the architect's cryptic dicta 'Less is more' and 'God is in the details'. The Seagram's detailing is exquisite – the custom-made bolts securing the miniature bronze piers that run the length of the façade must be polished by hand annually to keep them from oxidizing and turning green. It can truly be called the Rolls-Royce of skyscrapers.

High modernism began to show cracks in its façade during the mid 1960s. By then, New York had built too many such structures in midtown and below, and besides, the public had never fully warmed to the undecorated style (though for those with a little insight, the best glass boxes are fully rewarding aesthetic experiences). And the International Style's sheer arrogance in trying to supplant the traditional city structure didn't endear the movement to anyone, either. The **MetLife Building** (200 Park Avenue, at 45th Street), originally the Pan Am Building of 1963, was the prime culprit, not so much because of its design by Walter Gropius of the Bauhaus, but because of its presumptuous location, straddling Park Avenue and looming over Grand Central. There was even a plan at the time to raze Grand Central and build a twin Pan Am in its place. The International Style had obviously

Thoroughly modernist mêlée

The only New Yorker without an opinion on beleaguered 2 Columbus Circle may be Columbus himself, who stares at the marble modernist monolith 24/7 from his perch across the plaza.

'This building is like a beacon coming down Broadway – it glows,' enthuses retiree Ann Bragg, who, on a hot summer afternoon, linked arms with fellow '2CC' supporters in a kind of preservationist daisy chain around the base of the ten-storey tower. Bragg was part of a last-ditch community effort to convince the city's Landmarks Preservation Commission to grant the building landmark status. That might save the nearly windowless 1964 edifice, now slated for redesign by its new owner, the Museum of Arts & Design. The building's cool, perforated white marble curves were financed by grocery-store magnate Huntington Hartford in the early '60s to house his personal art collection. His choice as architect: disaffected modernist Edward Durell Stone, who also helped design the original Museum of Modern Art (MOMA). The building's critics call its interior 'dark and claustrophobic', while MOMA's present-day chief curator of architecture, Terence Riley, has dismissed 2CC as being 'of no consequence whatsoever'.

Derelict since the mid 1990s, the building's new owners have hired architect Brad Cloepfil to remove its marble façade – once famously derided by über-critic Ada Louise Huxtable as 'a die-cut Venetian palazzo on lollipops' – and reclothe it, instead, in a minimalist sheath of incised terracotta.

That's when the big guns came out.

With oversized behemoths like the Time Warner Center and Trump International Hotel & Tower now dominating the plaza, 2CC 'is the only thing that holds Columbus Circle together', said *Bonfire of the Vanities* author Tom Wolfe, who's already contributed two op-ed pieces to the *New York Times* supporting the preservation of the building as is. Wolfe described Stone's incorporation of surface detailing and luxe interiors as an American bourgeois reimagining of modernism. 'In fact, the modern movement never caught up with it,' he said. In contrast, Cloepfil's new façade is 'a Band-Aid box with the Band-Aid stuck on the outside', Wolfe said. Cloepfil, on the other hand, has dismissed the novelist as a 'populist' engaged in a 'lifelong crusade against modern architecture'.

In the meantime, major preservationist groups such as the Preservation League of New York State, the National Trust for Historic Preservation and the World Monuments Fund have placed 2CC on their 'must-save' lists, with design bigwigs such as Yale dean of architecture Robert Stern and *Times* critic Herbert Muschamp rallying to the cause.

Still, the Landmarks Preservation Commission continues to deny the building either landmark status – it became eligible in 1994 – or a public hearing on the issue.

'What more is it going to take?' asked Kate Wood, executive director of preservationist group Landmark West! as she rallied the troops outside the building. Design historian Michael Henry Adams, wearing a snappy boater and oversized jewellery, called 2CC's impending makeover 'a shameful event', while seven-year-old Owen O'Hara (who was chaperoned by mom Elizabeth) deemed the building as being 'pretty cool'.

Gazing down, Columbus held his tongue.

reached its end when Philip Johnson, who was instrumental in defining the movement with his book *The International Style* (co-written with Henry-Russell Hitchcock), began disparaging the aesthetic as 'glass-boxitis'.

POSTMODERNISM AND BEYOND

Plainly, new blood was needed. A glimmer on the horizon was Boston architect Hugh Stubbins's silvery, triangle-topped **Citicorp Center** (Lexington Avenue, between 53rd & 54th Streets), which utilised daring contemporary engineering (the building cantilevers almost magically on high stilts above street level), while harking back to the decorative tops of yesteryear. The sly old master Philip Johnson turned the tables on everyone with the heretical Chippendale crown on his **Sony Building**, originally the AT&T Building (350 Madison Avenue, between 55th & 56th Streets), a bold throwback to decoration for its own sake.

Postmodernism provided a theoretical basis for a new wave of buildings that mixed past and present, often taking cues from the environs. Some notable examples include Helmut Jahn's 425 Lexington Avenue (between 43rd and 44th Streets) of 1988; David Childs's diamond-tipped **Worldwide Plaza** (825 Eighth Avenue, between 49th & 50th Streets) of 1989; and the honky-tonk agglomeration of Skidmore, Owings & Merrill's **Bertelsmann Building** (1540 Broadway, between 45th & 46th Streets) of 1990. But even postmodernism became old hat. Too many architects relied on fussy fenestration and Milquetoast commentary on other styles instead of creating vital new building façades.

The electronic spectacle of Times Square provides one possible direction. Upon seeing the myriad electric lights of Times Square in 1922, the British wit GK Chesterton remarked: 'What a glorious garden of wonder this would be, to anyone who was lucky enough to be unable to read.' This particular crossroads of the world continues to be at the cybernetic cutting edge: the 120-foot-tall, quarter-acre-in-area NASDAQ sign; the real-time stock tickers and jumbo TV screens everywhere; the news zipper on the original *New York Times* Tower (1 Times Square, between Broadway & Seventh Avenue). The public's appetite for new images seems so insatiable that a building's fixed profile no longer suffices here – only an ever-shifting electronic skin will do. The iconoclastic critic Robert Venturi, who taught us how to learn from Las Vegas, calls this trend 'iconography and electronics upon a generic architecture'.

Early 21st-century architecture is moving beyond applied symbolism to radical new forms facilitated by computer-based design methods. A stellar example is Kohn Pedersen Fox's stainless-steel-and-glass 'vertical campus', the **Baruch College Academic Complex** (55 Lexington Avenue, between 24th & 25th Streets). The resulting phantasmic designs that curve and dart in sculptural space are so beyond the timid window-dressing of postmodernism that they deserve a new label.

Known for designs that owe as much to conceptual art as to architecture, the firm of Diller & Scofidio is working on an eye-popping addition to staid Chelsea, the **Eyebeam** art and technology centre, to be completed in 2007. The curvilinear walls of the planned museum are suggestive of film looping through a projector.

Since the late 19th century, New York City has been the world's prime outdoor skyscraper museum. It may be founded on a very deliberate grid, but its growth has been organic. In the next decade, Manhattan may come to look like a sculpture garden, as computer-aided designs bridge the gap between what is possible and what can be imagined.

> **'The splashy Westin Hotel is a crisp-edged glass tower sheathed in purple, aqua and tangerine reflective glass.'**

NEW YORK NOW

New York continues to be the pre-eminent skyscraper city in the world, although perhaps on a more modest scale (with regard to height) after the tragedy of 9/11. Less than 60 storeys tall appears to be the preferred limit these days, making any new buildings commensurate with most of the towers in midtown. Still, a roster of world-renowned architects befitting a global capital has been added to the mix.

The steel is in the ground, and Italian architect Renzo Piano's translucent glass-skinned 52-storey tower for the *New York Times* is on schedule for completion in 2007 across from the Port Authority of New York bus terminal. Midtown West is looking decidedly more colourful with the addition of the splashy **Westin Hotel** (270 W 43rd Street, between Seventh & Eighth Avenues), a crisp-edged glass tower sheathed in purple, aqua and tangerine reflective glass by the Miami-based firm Arquitectonica. Another stunning addition to the skyline is Lord Norman Foster's 46-storey, 597-foot-high faceted tower for the **Hearst Building** (959 Eighth Avenue, between W 56th & W 57th Streets), which includes the

Santiago Calatrava's breathtaking vision of the future: **80 South Street**. *See p34.*

On the right track

In the early 1980s the last train to use the elevated High Line dropped off its final load, a wagon of frozen turkeys. Not only was it the end of the line, it was the end of an era. Then, for more than two decades this 22-block-long, three-storey-high ribbon of rail on Manhattan's far west side between Gansevoort Street in the Meatpacking District and 34th Street in midtown was abandoned – an urban afterthought made lush by nature.

In 2000 photos taken by renowned lensman Joel Sternfeld helped awaken New Yorkers to the High Line's hidden beauty, which during the 1980s and '90s faced constant threat from the wrecking ball. Sternfeld's photos revealed something remarkable: a miles-long artery of serene, verdant pasture coursing through the city's overstressed heart.

'What attracted me to saving the High Line was exactly that strangeness – this steel structure with wild flowers growing on top of it, in the middle of the city,' said Robert Hammond, 36, who in 1999 founded the Friends of the High Line along with Joshua David, 42. The two Chelsea residents started pitching a simple idea to anyone who would listen: save the High Line and turn it into an elevated, urban oasis.

Now, seven years later, the project has garnered the support of all major city politicians plus cultural heavyweights like Diane von Furstenberg and actor Edward Norton, all the while raising more than $60 million in public

funding. In 2005 the line's owner, CSX Transportation, officially released the High Line from the national rail grid, freeing it for development as a public trail. Note to visitors: for now, the High Line's mystery remains off-limits and trespassers will be prosecuted. But the winning design team – landscapers Field Operations plus architects Diller, Scofidio & Renfro – has already drawn up preliminary plans for a restored High Line, with groundbreaking slated for late 2005 (for design details, go to www.thehighline.org). The first segment – from Gansevoort Street in the Meatpacking District to 15th Street in Chelsea – is expected to open to the public in late 2007 or early 2008. The proposed design 'opens the High Line to the public but still refers back to the magic we found it in, in its wild state,' David enthused. Instead of setting strict borders between walkways and vegetation, planking tapers off raggedly, allowing wild flowers and grass to blur borders in the same way they soften the line's rusting rails. In one imaginative 'wetlands' segment, a shoulder-high, glassed-in pond will flank those walking by. But David and Hammond say the design stresses the High Line's 1930s-era industrial identity too. 'It really celebrates that steel structure,' Hammond said.

Once-neglected neighbourhoods touched by the High Line are undergoing rapid change, and the new park has already become a magnet for projects such as the new DIA contemporary art museum (planned for the Line's southern terminus), André Balazs's Standard Hotel at 13th Street, and a Frank Gehry-designed building slated for 19th Street. Even though the High Line's surface is currently off-limits, David and Hammond urge visitors to the city to walk under and alongside it, using the Line as a kind of 'overhead thread' linking the Meatpacking District, Chelsea and Hudson Yards.

They hope the High Line will inspire too. 'We were just a small community group against pretty big odds when we started this,' David said, looking back. 'We really hope that when visitors come and look at it they'll understand that they can do this in their cities too.'

original art deco-style base built in 1928 by Joseph Urban. With its unusual angled contours made of glass triangles trimmed in steel, the Hearst Building is one of the city's first fully 'green', or eco-friendly, office buildings.

Midtown features some small-scale surprises. French architect Christian de Portzamparc's eccentrically angled translucent and coloured-glass **LVMH Tower** (19 E 57th Street, between Fifth & Madison Avenues) stands like a postmodernist mini glacier among more sober storefronts on this famous shopping strip, and glows from within at night. Austria native Raimund Abraham's **Austrian Cultural Forum** (11 E 52nd Street, between Fifth & Madison Avenues) presents a starkly chiselled façade that glowers like a primitive mask, breaking free of the perpendicular street front.

There are other signs that New York is not afraid to build big. A new set of Twin Towers, the **Time Warner Center** (10 Columbus Circle, at Broadway) designed by David Childs, arose seemingly from the ashes of the World Trade Center. With its eye-catching mix of high-end stores, the Jazz at Lincoln Center performance space and an enormous Whole Foods gourmet food court, the upscale shopping mall has made a destination of what was once a near-dead neighbourhood.

Other tall towers include Costas Kondylis's 72-storey **Trump World Tower** (845 First Avenue, between E 47th & E 48th Streets) a slick, 863-foot black glass slab that was briefly the tallest residential building in the world. Skyscraper buffs will be interested in comparing it with the stately 41-storey Beaux Arts **Ritz Tower** (109 E 57th Street, at Park Avenue), once the world's tallest residence when it was built in 1925. Nearby is Cesar Pelli's 868-foot-tall **Bloomberg Tower** (731 Lexington Avenue, between 58th & 59th Streets), with a torqued conical open space.

Imposing, sentinel-like skyscrapers mark the southern entry to the electric carnival that is Times Square: the **Condé Nast Building** (4 Times Square, at 42nd Street) and the **Reuters Building** (3 Times Square, at 42nd Street), both by Fox & Fowle, complement Kohn Person Fox's postmodern **5 Times Square** (Seventh Avenue, at 42nd Street) and the recent addition of David Childs's **Times Square Tower** (7 Times Square, between Broadway & Seventh Avenue). The crossroads of the world is quickly becoming wall-to-wall skyscrapers, with the addition of Fox & Fowle's sharp-edged, wedge-shaped, 35-storey glass tower at **11 Times Square** (42nd Street, between Seventh & Eighth Avenues).

Plans for New York's most significant commemorative site were literally left hanging in the air when it was belatedly discovered that the Freedom Tower at the World Trade Center violated certain security measures set for US embassies around the world. It was found at the eleventh hour that Daniel Libeskind and David Childs's design for the 1,776-foot spire was only 25 feet from a major roadway, making it vulnerable to attack from a truck bomb, an almost unbelievable oversight considering the towers were subject to a truck bombing in 1993, before the devastating attack by two 727s flown by terrorists on 11 September 2001. The setback came after delays because of lengthy in-fighting between the original master architect of the site, Libeskind, and the developer Larry A Silverstein, who brought in his own architect, Childs, who has ultimate control over the Freedom Tower. In a comedy of errors, Donald Trump stepped into the arena last spring, offering his version of the Twin Towers, two Saltine boxes that lacked the detailing of the original towers by the Japanese architect Minoru Yamasaki. The first part of the complex to rise again was David Childs's 52-storey, 750-foot-tall **7 World Trade Center**, built on a 10-storey pedestal that looks like a block of stainless steel from which the 45-foot-tall lobby was scooped.

'On the drafting board is David Childs's spectacular clamshell-shaped glass and steel addition to Penn Station.'

The new World Trade Center site will feature a museum that will house the International Freedom Center and the Drawing Center, designed by the Norwegian firm Snøhetta. It will be a wood and glass sheathed structure that evokes the reflecting pools of the memorial plaza called Reflecting Absence, a meditative grotto 30 feet below street level, with two pools that will occupy the footprints of the original towers. The building floats on large pillars above a ground-level plaza, with a mirrored light well in the centre. The museum will feature multimedia presentations on the World Trade Center and the theme of freedom. A Freedom Walk circulates around the perimeter of the building.

Yoshio Taniguchi's airy, minimalist makeover of the venerable **Museum of Modern Art** (*see p125*) is at the vanguard of ambitious cultural plans throughout the city, including an extraordinary eight-storey, glass-walled boomerang-shaped building to house

the Brooklyn Public Library's Visual & Performing Arts Library (*see p154*).

Architects in New York are not only housing the arts, but also their well-heeled patrons. Gwathmey Siegel's curved, free-standing 21-storey residential tower **Astor Place** (445 Lafayette Street, at the corner of Astor Place), sheathed in reflective green glass, with condos that sell for more than $12 million, stands like an expensive perfume bottle among the old brick buildings of the Lower East Side. Richard Meier has added a third sleek glass tower (165 Charles Street, between West & Washington Streets) to his other postmodernist residences overlooking the Hudson on the Lower West Side. More straightforward, though no less elegant than the other two, the transparent, 16-storey condominium features lofts with the narrowest of mullions between floor levels. The ultimate work of art is one that you live in. The Spanish architect Santiago Calatrava is looking to build an abstract sculpture of 12 four-storey cube-shaped, glass-walled townhouses cantilevered breathtakingly from an 835-foot-tall mast at 80 South Street overlooking the East River.

Transportation is a major theme in the coming decade in the city. The revitalisation of downtown in the wake of 9/11 continues with Frederic Schwartz Architects' shiny new $201 million, 200,000-square-foot update of the Staten Island Ferry terminal in Lower Manhattan. The prow-shaped, green-glass-and-stainless-steel encased structure frames panoramic views of the Brooklyn Bridge and the Lady in the Harbor under a broad sloping ceiling. The space provides a foretaste of Santiago Calatrava's much-anticipated World Trade Center PATH Station, which will feature a suspended ribbed-steel, wing-shaped canopy over a public space that promises to be larger than Grand Central Station. The station will alight like a dove of peace at the base of the World Trade complex. Another transportation annexe on the drafting board is David Childs's spectacular clamshell-shaped glass-and-steel addition to Penn Station to be built mid block behind the imposing Corinthian colonnade of McKim, Mead & White's landmarked **General Post Office** of 1913 (421 Eighth Avenue, between 31st & 33rd Streets). The transparent multi-level station recalls the awe-inspiring experience of arrival by train in the original majestic Penn Station.

The best place to keep tabs on upcoming architectural developments in the city, like Enrique Norten's exciting plans for a double slab skyscraper in Harlem and a condominium at One York Street in Tribeca, is the **AIA Center for Architecture** (*see p107*).

Bailed: **Stephen Caracappa** (centre).

Wise Guys of New York

Did NYC cops work for the mob? This and other tales of the mafia in New York City. By Jerry Capeci.

Founded in 1820, the New York Eye and Ear Infirmary is recognised across the country as a leader in the field. It proudly boasts of being the oldest speciality hospital in the western hemisphere. If you visit its flag-draped nerve centre at 310 East 14th Street (at the corner of Second Avenue) in downtown Manhattan, or browse brochures detailing its mission or its history, you won't read a word about its role in the city's latest Mafia scandal, which just happens to be also the biggest scandal in the history of the New York Police Department. Here, *Time Out* lays it out for you.

On 8 November 1990, recently retired NYPD detective Louis Eppolito reportedly swaggered into the hospital carrying a copy of that day's *New York Daily News* opened to a story about the latest mob hit during a particularly bloody five-year stretch. 'Cohort of Gotti slain in

Brooklyn!' screamed the headline above an account of the death of Gambino family mobster Edward Lino, who was shot as he drove his Mercedes-Benz on a service road of the Belt Parkway near Sheepshead Bay. When Eppolito reached the room where Burton Kaplan, a mob-connected businessman-drug dealer, was convalescing after eye surgery, he walked in and tossed the paper on Kaplan's chest with a flourish, and allegedly said with a grin: 'It's done. We did it.'

Eppolito's purpose, it is claimed, was to tell Kaplan that after six months of trying, they had finally carried out their assignment from the Lucchese crime family and killed Lino, a top gun in the rival Gambino family, then headed by the swashbuckling Dapper Don, John Gotti. This version of the story, of course, is based on what investigators say happened after a lengthy probe that led to a murder and racketeering indictment against Eppolito and his long-time partner, Stephen Caracappa, in March 2005. The two retired NYPD detectives were soon nicknamed the 'Mob Cops' in the local tabloids and sensational allegations swirled around them for months. Both men have vehemently denied all charges.

'Gangsters have long been associated with myriad well-known endeavours.'

RESIDENT EVIL

If you live, work or spend any time in New York, it's a virtual certainty that you have brushed up against the American Mafia in one way or another, whether you're aware if it or not. For more than 75 years, the mob has had a firm hand in the financial fabric of the city. Through its infiltration of labour unions and investments in many affiliated legitimate businesses, gangsters have long been associated with myriad well-known endeavours. They're *On The Waterfront,* not only in the movie classic starring Marlon Brando, but on the docks in Brooklyn, Staten Island and Manhattan. Ditto the Fulton Fish Market and the Garment District.

Through decades of union domination, the mob has held sway in the trucking, construction, private sanitation, and hotel and restaurant industries. Names like Lucky Luciano, Meyer Lansky, Vito Genovese, Dutch Schultz, Joe Bonanno and Al Capone (yes, *that* Al Capone; he was a big-time gangster in Brooklyn before he took over the Chicago mob) are synonymous with organised crime in the Big Apple. In addition to the Lucchese and Gambino families, New York is home to the Genovese, Colombo and Bonanno clans, the notorious Five Families, as well as the Newark-based DeCavalcante family – the so-called *real* Sopranos – whose leaders live, play and die here, occasionally in stunning, memorable ways.

WHACK JOBS

In the city that supposedly never sleeps, wise guys sure have an uncanny way of putting guys to bed – permanently. Joe Colombo, a pseudo civil-rights leader, got it at a rally of the Italian American Civil Rights League at Columbus Circle in front of 50,000 witnesses on 28 June 1971. Crazy Joe Gallo, a pretender to Colombo's crown, got his the following year at Umberto's Clam House, which has since relocated from 129 to 178 Mulberry Street, while celebrating his 43rd birthday. Right outside Sparks Steak House (210 East 46th Street, near

the corner of Third Avenue) – is where Mafia boss Paul Castellano and his key aide were whacked in truly spectacular fashion. They were blown away during the height of the 1986 Christmas shopping season by four gunmen dressed alike in trench coats and dark, Russian-style fur hats. Gotti, who orchestrated the bloody show and watched it evolve from a car parked diagonally across Third Avenue, rode the double slaying to the top of the Gambino crime family. Killing a boss without authorisation has been outlawed since 1931 when the Mafia Commission established rules against it. But as the saying goes, rules are made to be broken.

'Many former top wise guys are no longer around, either away in prison or dead...'

The slaying irked some rival leaders, most notably the bosses of the Lucchese and Genovese crime families, for entirely selfish reasons. They didn't relish the notion that ambitious mobsters in their families might think they could get away with killing them. They tried to kill Gotti with a remote-controlled bomb as he got into his car on 86th Street, near the corner of Bay 8th Street in the Bensonhurst section of Brooklyn. They failed, killing his underboss instead.

MOB COPS?

This all brings us back to the alleged Mob Cops. Eppolito and Caracappa's indictment charges them with taking part in eight mob slayings between 1986 and 1991, including the aforementioned Edward Lino. The lead architect in that slaying, Lucchese underboss Anthony 'Gaspipe' Casso, told authorities that he marked Lino for death because he feared that if the Luccheses and Genoveses ever succeeded in killing Gotti, Lino would retaliate. Casso asked 'the cops' to kill Lino, he said, because he believed – quite correctly, it turned out – that the veteran gangster would be less likely to smell out an assassin wearing a badge.

At press time the ex-detectives were slated for trial in early 2006 in the same federal courthouse (225 Cadman Plaza East) in downtown Brooklyn that was the scene of Gotti's stunning acquittal of murder and racketeering charges in 1987, and his conviction five years later for Castellano's murder. During their trial – the prosecution estimates it will last three months – you might catch them at lunch at the Park Plaza Restaurant (220 Cadman Plaza West), a huge one-storey red-brick Greek diner across the street from the courthouse and a small park. Eppolito is the beefy, gregarious one, Caracappa is slight and reserved. The Park

It happened here: Wise guy wheres

Sparks steakhouse
210 46th Street (1-212 687 4855).
Mob boss Paul Castellano was killed outside here in 1985 in a hit arranged by John Gotti.

Skyline Hotel
725 Tenth Avenue (1-212 586 3400).
Although not a mob-run establishment, word on the street is that wise guys like to meet here.

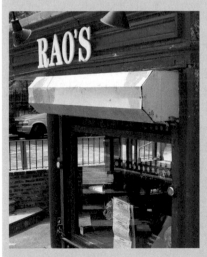

Rao's restaurant
455 114th Street (1-212 722 6709).
Once frequented by some major wise guys, this tiny place is now a movie-star hangout.

Umberto's Clam House
178 Mulberry Street (1-212 431 7545).
Its previous location was where Crazy Joe Gallo was shot dead.

Plaza is where Gotti and his crew ate during his first encounter with the feds, before his bail was revoked. It's also the place the lawyers, and Gotti supporters like his brother Peter, often met for lunch during the Dapper Don's second trial. Look for the big round 'Gotti table' in the back if you're part of a large group.

BEEN THERE, DONE THAT

New York mobsters and their rackets have certainly been battered and bruised by the law during the last 25 years. Many former top wise guys are no longer around, either away in prison or dead, some from natural causes, others by two in the back of the head. If you were to visit Gotti's former Manhattan headquarters, the Ravenite Social Club (247 Mulberry Street) in Little Italy, you won't find the big card table where the Dapper Don held court and plotted mob hits under a framed picture of himself. You'll find beautiful, slender people browsing for fashionable accessories at Amy Chan's trendy women's boutique. As you walk out of the front door, turn your head left and focus your eyes on the big picture window on the left side of the sixth floor of the brick building two blocks north on East Houston Street. That's where the FBI

> ### 'There are still plenty of hotspots in Little Italy with bona fide ties to the mob.'

placed the video cameras that caught Gotti & Co in countless comings and goings that absorbed jurors at his trial and numerous others in Brooklyn Federal Court.

The Ravenite is gone, but there are still plenty of hotspots in Little Italy and around town, that have bona fide ties to the mob. Da Nico (164 Mulberry Street), a favourite Italian eaterie of former mayor Rudolph Giuliani and other

bigwigs, was linked to the mob at Massino's trial when its owner, Perry Criscitelli, was identified as a Bonanno mobster. An Italian restaurant frequented by wise guys from Brooklyn and Staten Island is in Bay Ridge, Brooklyn, not far from the Verrazano Bridge that connects the two boroughs. This is not to say that the owners of the popular place, Areo's (8424 Third Avenue), are mob-connected – only that wise guys like to eat there. To name just a few who have dined there, according to official court records, we offer: Michael 'Mikey Scars' DiLeonardo, a turncoat Gambino capo; Alphonse Persico, the son of the jailed Colombo boss; and Anthony 'Sonny' Ciccone, a capo who ran the Brooklyn and Staten Island docks for John Gotti.

If you ever get to Corona, Queens, there's the Parkside Restaurant (107-01 Corona Avenue), where former US Senator Alfonse D'Amato and scads of other politicians and just plain folk have dined for years. Anthony 'Tough Tony' Federici, a Genovese capo who owns the building and manages the restaurant, goes the extra mile to keep the riff-raff out. A few years ago, he grabbed his shotgun, ran to the roof and fired away at pigeon hawks that had swooped down on the prized racing pigeons he keeps cooped on the roof. 'The hawks were murdering the defenceless pigeons. They were flying away with them in their mouths, blood gushing from the hawks' mouths, for months,' explained Federici's lawyer, Mathew Mari. His client, he said, has sworn off any repeat performances, noting, however, that he doubts whether the need would ever arise again. 'For some unexplained reason,' deadpanned Mari, 'the hawks have stopped coming.'

● Mafia expert Jerry Capeci writes a weekly 'Gang Land' column for the *New York Sun* that also appears online at www.ganglandnews.com. His latest book, *The Complete Idiot's Guide to the Mafia*, was published in 2005.

New York Today

A resident's view of the capital of the world.

New York City isn't exactly a place that no one's ever heard of. It's not like you told your friends, 'I'm going to New York on holiday', and they looked at you and said, 'Huh?' No, the unofficial capital of the USA is not a mystery to visitors. Its renowned restaurants, distinguished museums and rich variety of theatre, opera and sports events are not something hidden or obscure. In marketing terms, the brand recognition of this city is right up there with, say, Nike or Coca-Cola. People know what this city is, and they know what it's all about. Nevertheless, this past year Mayor Michael Bloomberg kick-started an effort to rebrand Gotham, to buff up its image and present a newly scrubbed and shined face to the world. In February 2005 the city applied to trademark the phrase 'The World's Second Home' as its new tagline. Of course, a volley of op-ed pieces ensued, wondering why such a first-rate town should settle for being 'second', but that's not really the point. The point is that this application is one of several efforts to trademark phrases, logos and images in order to (a) raise the iconic profile of New York City and (b) make money on products and clothing that bear those images, which by the way is also a typically New Yorkish profit-making

scheme. From the day he took office, Mayor Bloomberg, a media-empire billionaire in his own right, has run the city as if it were a business, and this step certainly follows that model. (He is, unfortunately, a little late to the game: Citibank already owns a variation of the phrase 'the city that sleeps' and the New York Pizzeria and Delicatessen – in Florida! – owns NYPD.)

Still, Bloomberg's not the only one who's grabbed on to this marketing concept: the NYC Taxi and Limousine Commission (ironically referred to as TLC) is selling T-shirts with its newly redesigned medallion, which refers to both the metal ornament stapled to the hood of licensed vehicles and the actual licence given to drivers to operate a taxi.

Even the city's official tourism board, NYC & Co, hopped on the better-marketing bandwagon, commissioning a new theme song. 'New York: For the Time of Your Life' – written by Broadway composer Frank Wildhorn (*Jekyll & Hyde*, *The Scarlet Pimpernel*) – is an old-timey-sounding tune with somewhat corny lyrics that could have been taken right out of a 1960s musical: 'It's the Yankees and Knicks, the Rockettes doin' kicks/You can sail Sheepshead Bay, see a show on Broadway.'

What was wrong with Sinatra's 'New York, New York', you might ask? 'One doesn't replace another,' says Lisa Mortman, a spokesperson for NYC & Co. 'This is a city that has a lot of great music in it and a lot of different sounds that work together in a unique harmony.'

But if there's one sound that brings everyone in this city together, it's the sound of money.

CASH COW

Whether they're fully loaded or flat broke, New Yorkers are obsessed with money. Wonder why? How about the fact that a recent *Forbes* poll of US cities determined that in order to live well in this town (that is, two cars, private school for the kids, a holiday home), you'd have to pull in an annual wage of almost half a million dollars after taxes, compared to $370,000 in Los Angeles. Forbes calculated that NYC is the second-most expensive place to live in this country (after Seattle, Washington). Still, a large part of the population in NYC is rich enough to afford this state of affairs – and for better and for worse, these are the people who have been increasingly affecting things.

Not in every way, but in enough ways that regular people not only know what Manolo Blahniks are, but they want to spend what little money they have to buy a pair. Fashion has always been integral to the New York look and feel, but in the wake of the trendsetting television series *Sex and the City* (which has returned to TV – on the WB network and TBS cable channel), everyone wants to be *fabulous*. That's what the real brand identity of New York City is these days.

If we can't all be rich, well, then we'll value what the rich value and make the pursuit of money and luxury lifestyles the mantra of our rebounding city (all while still riding the subway every day, just like Bloomberg). Hey, why reach for the brass ring, when you can go for the gold?

OLYMPIAN EFFORT

One of the early pushes that Mayor Bloomberg made in the name of revitalising NYC was a bid to be the site of the 2012 summer Olympics. Despite the protests, articles and blogs of an ambivalent public, the proponents made it to the final selection round, but not without stirring up controversy. The efficacy of NYC as an Olympic site hinged on the construction of a new stadium, and although the five boroughs already have several, none was deemed good enough for the Olympics. The proposed West Side Stadium (which was to be occupied and partly funded by major-league football team the New York Jets) became the dividing argument of 2004-5, pleasing many fans who thought the

city deserved a world-class stadium and the Olympics, and angering many opponents who thought the money could be better spent on things like schools and affordable housing. The city ended up losing the bid for the Olympics to London and the fate of the West Side Stadium was sealed: with no grand Olympic need to keep it going, the unpopular project may just keel over and die.

The idea of spending ridiculous amounts of money on a sports arena when so many city residents are struggling to afford housing is a good illustration of New York's current mood, and it is buoyed by the rise of a new class: the super-rich. In 2004, a full 38 of the *Forbes* 400 (which lists the richest Americans) lived in New York City. Those few dozen aren't the only people making bank, and they're certainly not the only ones willing to spend it. A large portion of New Yorkers pay half their salaries just to have a flat here.

At a new breed of very high-end restaurants you can fork out up to a thousand bucks for a meal. People are even willing to spend handfuls of money to keep their dogs well dressed (*see p256* **Creature comforts**).

Clearly, this is not New York's time of sanity. In this super-rich time, transforming two historic hotels (the Plaza and the Gramercy) into luxury condos that trade on high-profile brand names is the kind of move that has come to be expected. And the monied class isn't the only one that's building, growing and generally movin' on up. All over the city, new homes are being constructed faster than spin-offs of *The Apprentice*. New apartment buildings are going up in neighbourhoods most people used to avoid – Long Island City, Bensonhurst, the South Bronx – and they're selling fast. The ensuing gentrification of historically poor or ethnic areas is, of course, as inevitable a consequence as it has always been, it just seems to be on fast forward lately (*see p156* **The battle for Bed-Stuy**).

THE PRICE OF SAFETY

One struggle that's brought most New Yorkers together is the struggle to maintain our safety. Although there has hardly been a perceptible rise in citywide anxiety, the 2005 bombings in London stirred some sleeping nerves. The biggest impact the attacks had over here was the beginning of random police searches of people's shopping bags and backpacks in the subway system. While some riders feel safer, because they believe that the searches act as a deterrent for terrorists, others contend that the 'random' searches are not random at all; that they are actually based on people's ethnic appearance. Soon after, the New York City

New Yorkers will bend over backwards to make a little extra cash.

Civil Liberties Union filed a suit against the city, claiming that the searches violate a constitutional prohibition against unlawful searches and that they do nothing to prevent terrorism. The issue of public safety at the expense of individual rights was one that was hotly debated after 9/11, and not just in New York. But in a city where people are so fiercely independent, these recent events have raised the concern anew.

MONEY ISN'T EVERYTHING

Despite all previous arguments to the contrary, NYC is not a town that's 'all about the Benjamins'. Sure, life here is easier if you're rich, but you don't need a lot of cash to enjoy the wealth of diversity it offers. New York is, at heart, a city for the masses. And most of those masses, as a smart lady once said, are poor, tired and huddled. Because of that underdog spirit, New York provides thousands of affordable diversions, from free summer

Shakespeare and rock concerts to pay-what-you-wish museum nights and always-free art galleries. There's a mother lode of delicious cheap eats here, and a mere $2 fare can take you to any of the city's international neighbourhoods. After all, Bloomberg is not wrong about New York being the world's second home – we want all visitors to feel that, no matter where they come from or how much they're willing to spend on shoes, they fit in here. That was the point from the moment the Statue of Liberty went up, and we certainly don't need any slogan or marketing ploy to remind people of that.

To understand the city, and to feel a part of it while you're here, you don't really need to know that the Indians supposedly sold the island of Manhattan to the Dutch for a few beads and some pocket lint. You do need to know about what's going on now, from a local's perspective. And how New Yorkers – never at a loss for an opinion – feel about it.

Where to Stay

Where to Stay   **44**

Features

Where to Stay

Style without the stretch.

So you're planning a trip to New York. You've heard the hotel horror stories: $500 a night buys you 50 square feet of space – and anything less than that will put you up in a room that smells like skid row and looks like something out of the *Rocky Horror Picture Show*. Much like real estate in this city, hotel room prices have been skyrocketing over the years with little noticeable effect on quality. Tourism has picked up since the post-9/11 slump, and city hotels have responded by hiking rates (in 2005, prices went up $10 to $50 per room). That said, a few hoteliers are starting to turn things around, opening accommodation at more affordable prices without sacrificing any of the style.

Celebrity hotelier André Balazs recently opened **Hotel QT** near Times Square, with rooms starting at just $125 a night. In a cheeky play on the budget backpackers' hostel, rooms are small and sparsely furnished with platform beds and floating bunks, but with luxuries like Egyptian cotton sheets, flat-panel TVs and a lobby pool with underwater music. At **Abingdon Guest House**, another budget-conscious hotel, $149 buys you a night in a room Ralph Lauren wouldn't mind crashing in, mere steps away from the still-happening Meatpacking District. Although considered small – even by New York standards – the ship cabin-esque rooms at Ian Schrager's **Hudson** start at $155 a night and come with white studded headboards and all-glass showers.

Hoteliers continue to carve out niches in various areas of the city. Chelsea offers stylish accommodation at budget prices; Soho is the land of designer chambers; and savvy uptown entrepreneurs are turning Harlem's beautiful brownstones into one-of-a-kind bed-and-breakfasts (*see p68* **Home Sweet Harlem**). New York has more small-chain and independent hotels than any other city in the country.

The best way to begin your hotel search is to choose the price range and neighbourhood that interest you. The prices quoted in our listings are not guaranteed, but they should give you a good indication of the hotel's average rack rates. And if you follow the tips below, you're likely to find slashed room prices, package deals and special promotions on offer. Make sure to include New York's 13.625 per cent room tax and a $2 to $6 per-night occupancy tax when planning your travel budget.

Weekend travellers should be warned that many smaller hotels adhere to a strict three-night-minimum booking policy.

HOTEL-RESERVATION AGENCIES

Pre-booking blocks of rooms allows reservation companies to offer reduced rates. Discounts cover most price ranges, including economy; some agencies claim savings of up to 65 per cent, though 20 per cent is more likely. If you simply want the best deal, mention the rate you're willing to pay, and see what's available. The following agencies are free of charge, though a few require payment for rooms at the time the reservation is made.

Hotel Reservations Network
Suite 400, 10440 North Central Expressway, Dallas, TX 75231 (1-214 369 1264/1-800 246 8357/ www.hotels.com).

Quikbook
3rd Floor, 381 Park Avenue South, New York, NY 10016 (1-212 779 7666/1-800 789 9887/ www.quikbook.com).

The best Hotels

... for theatre buffs on a budget
The **Americana Inn** (*see p65*), the **Big Apple Hostel** (*see p70*), **the Broadway Inn** (*see p65*).

... for celebrity sightings
The **Mercer**, the **Hotel Gansevoort** (for both, *see p54*) and the **Four Seasons** (*see p62*).

... for rooms with a view
The **Bentley Hotel** (*see p71*), the **Hotel on Rivington** (*see p46*) and the **Maritime Hotel** (*see p47*).

... for style on a shoestring
The **Hotel QT**, the **Hudson** (for both, *see p66*) and the **Chelsea Hotel** (*see p51*).

... for cosy comfort
The **Inn on 23rd** (*see p46*), the **Wyman House** (*see p72*) and the **Efuru Guest House** (*see p68*).

Maritime Hotel. *See p47*.

timeoutny.com

The Time Out New York website offers online reservations at more than 300 hotels. You can search for availability by arrival date or hotel name. (Full disclosure: TONY receives a commission from sales made through our partner hotel-reservation sites.)

APARTMENT RENTALS AND B&BS

Thousands of B&B rooms are available in New York, but in the absence of a central organisation, some are hard to find. Many B&Bs are unhosted, and breakfast is usually continental (if it's served at all), but the ambience is likely to be more personal than that of a hotel. A sales tax of 8.625 per cent is added on hosted rooms – though not on unhosted apartments – if you stay more than seven days. For a longer visit, it can be cheaper and more convenient to rent a place of your own; several of the agencies listed below specialise in short-term rentals of furnished apartments. One caveat: last-minute changes can be costly. For gay-friendly B&Bs, *see p304* – straight guests are welcome too.

CitySonnet

Village Station, PO Box 347, New York, NY 10014 (1-212 614 3034/www.citysonnet.com). **Rates** *B&B room $80-$165; hosted artist's loft $80-$125; unhosted artist's loft $165-$375; private apartment $135-$375.* **Credit** AmEx, Disc, MC, V.

This amiable artist-run agency specialises in downtown locations but has properties all over Manhattan. B&B rooms and short-term apartment rentals are priced according to room size, number of guests, and whether the bathroom is private or shared.

New York Habitat

Suite 306, 307 Seventh Avenue, between 27th & 28th Streets (1-212 255 8018/www.nyhabitat. com). **Rates** *unhosted studio $85-$165; unhosted 1-bedroom apartment $135-$225; unhosted 2-bedroom apartment $200-$375.* **Credit** AmEx, DC, Disc, MC, V.

A variety of services is offered, from hosted B&Bs to short-term furnished-apartment rentals, which can be charged by the day, week or month.

STANDARD HOTEL SERVICES

In the categories Expensive and Moderate, every hotel has the following services (unless otherwise stated): alarm clock, business centre, cable TV, concierge, conference facility, currency exchange, dry-cleaning, fax (in its business centre or in the rooms), hairdryer, in-room safe, laundry, minibar, modem line, parking, radio, one or more restaurants, one or more bars, room service and voicemail. Additional services are

> ❶ Green numbers given in this chapter correspond to the location of each hotel as marked on the street maps. *See pp402-412.*

noted at the end of each listing. All hotels have air-conditioning unless otherwise noted.

Most hotels in all categories have access for the disabled, non-smoking rooms (and smoking rooms, at least on request) and an iron with ironing board in the room or on request. Call to confirm. 'Breakfast included' may mean either muesli and milk or a more generous continental spread. While many hotels claim 'multilingual' staff, that term may be used loosely.

Downtown (below 23rd Street)

Expensive ($200-$350)

Hotel on Rivington

107 Rivington Street, between Essex & Ludlow Streets (1-212 475 2600/www.hotelonrivington.com). Subway: F to Delancey Street; J, M, Z to Delancey-Essex Streets. **Rates** from $265 single/double; call or visit website for more rates. **Rooms** 110. **Credit** AmEx, Disc, MC, V. **Map** p403 G29 ❶

Hotel on Rivington has a high cool factor for a place that's not even fully complete yet (at press time a lobby-level gift shop stocked with high-design accessories, two invitation-only lounges, and a bar-restaurant piloted by Wallsé chef Kurt Gutenbrunner were in the works). Floor-to-ceiling windows are a theme throughout the hotel: the second-floor lobby overlooks the storefronts of Rivington Street, and every India Mahdavi-designed room has an unobstructed city view. In the future, guests are promised 24-hour room service, but for now, mini-fridges hold single-serving cans of Sofia (as in Coppola) champagne, and wood-panelled drawers hide binoculars and an 'intimacy kit' stocked with surprises from nearby Toys in Babeland if you're feeling frisky. **Photo** *p47.*
Hotel services *Complimentary breakfast. Fitness centre. Gift shop. Spa. Valet.* **Room services** *CD player. DVD library. Flat-panel TV. High-speed wireless internet. Room service (24hrs).*

Inn on 23rd Street

131 W 23rd Street, between Sixth & Seventh Avenues (1-212 463 0330/www.innon23rd.com). Subway: A, C, E to 14th Street; L to Eighth Avenue. **Rates** $209-$279 queen/king; $329-$359 suite. **Rooms** 14. **Credit** AmEx, MC, V. **Map** p404 D26 ❷

This real-deal B&B in the heart of Chelsea gives you a warm and fuzzy feeling from the moment you enter – the sun-drenched library is brimming with comfy couches and chairs. Owners and innkeepers Annette and Barry Fisherman renovated a 19th-century townhouse into a homey inn with 14 themed rooms (all accessible by elevator and each with its own private bathroom). Rooms are exceptionally plush: pillow-topped mattresses, double-pane windows and white-noise machines will ensure a decent night's sleep. An expanded continental breakfast is served daily in the lobby or breakfast room. **Photo** *p50.*

Hotel services *Complimentary continental breakfast. high-speed wireless internet.* **Room services** *Complimentary high-speed internet. Complimentary local and national long distance phone calls.*

Inn at Irving Place

56 Irving Place, between 17th & 18th Streets (1-212 533 4600/1-800 685 1447/www.innatirving.com). Subway: L, N, Q, R, W, 4, 5, 6 to 14th Street-Union Square. **Rates** $325-$495 standard/deluxe; $475-$495 junior suite. **Rooms** 12. **Credit** AmEx, DC, Disc, MC, V. **Map** p403 F27 ❸

Inn at Irving Place may be one of Manhattan's smallest hotels, but it is also one of its most endearing. Housed in a pair of brownstones near Gramercy Park, it's dotted with fresh flowers and antique furnishings. While some rooms are petite, each is decorated with turn-of-the-20th century elegance. Leave the little ones at home (children under 12 are not permitted). At Lady Mendl's (1-212 533 4466, reservations required), the inn's pretty tearoom, damask love seats and a lavish tea and dessert menu create the perfect spot for brushing up on your manners. Edith Wharton would feel right at home.
Hotel services *Complimentary breakfast. Ticket desk.* **Room services** *CD player. Digital cable. High-speed internet. Room service (24hrs). VCR.*

Maritime Hotel

363 W 16th Street, between Eighth & Ninth Avenues (1-212 242 4300/www.themaritimehotel.com). Subway: A, C, E to 14th Street; L to Eighth Avenue. **Rates** $285-$325 single/double; $650-$1,350 suite. **Rooms** 125. **Credit** AmEx, DC, Disc, MC, V. **Map** p403 C27 ❹

What are porthole windows doing on a hotel in Chelsea? Well, it's not *all* for show – the building is the former headquarters of the Maritime Union. In 2002, architects at cool Eric Goode and Sean MacPherson took this nautical theme and spun it into the high-gloss Maritime Hotel, blending the look of a luxury yacht with a chic 1960s airport lounge. The lobby is a bit dank and dark, but the rooms are much more eye-catching. Modelled after ship cabins, each has one large porthole window and lots of glossy teak panelling. For more space, book one of the two penthouses, which have their own private terrace with an outdoor shower. The hotel offers four food and drink spaces: Matsuri, a gorgeous Japanese restaurant; La Bottega (*see p197*), an Italian trattoria with a lantern-festooned patio; Cabana, an airy rooftop bar; and Hiro, a basement lounge that draws a buzzing crowd. **Photo** *p45 & p53.*
Hotel services *Complimentary pass to New York Sports Club. Discount parking and valet service. DVD library. Fitness centre. Pet-friendly.* **Room services** *CD player. Complimentary in-room movies. DVD player. Flat-panel TV. High-speed wireless internet. Room service (24hrs). Two-line telephone.*

SoHo Grand Hotel

310 West Broadway, between Canal & Grand Streets (1-212 965 3000/1-800 965 3000/www.sohogrand.com). Subway: A, C, E, 1 to Canal Street. **Rates** $259-$499 single/double; $1,699-$3,500 suite. **Rooms** 366. **Credit** AmEx, DC, Disc, MC, V. **Map** p403 E30 ❺

Regarded by many as Soho's living room, the Grand makes good use of industrial materials like poured concrete, cast iron and bottle glass. Built in 1996,

View New York's city skyline from your bed at the **Hotel on Rivington**. *See p46.*

Soho's first high-end hotel features Bill Sofield-designed rooms, which include two spacious penthouse lofts, use a restrained palette of greys and beiges, and sport photos from local galleries. Sip cocktails in the Grand Bar and Lounge, or dine on haute macaroni and cheese in the Gallery.
Hotel services *Beauty salon. Fitness centre. Mobile phone rental. Pet-friendly. Ticket desk. Valet. Video library.* **Room services** *CD player. High-speed internet. Plasma TV. VCR.*
Other locations: Tribeca Grand Hotel, 2 Sixth Avenue, between Walker & White Streets (1-877 519 6600).

Wall Street District Hotel

15 Gold Street, at Platt Street (1-212 232 7700/ www.wallstreetdistricthotel.com). Subway: A, C to Broadway-Nassau Street; J, M, Z, 2, 3, 4, 5 to Fulton Street. **Rates** *$199-$399 single/double; $299-$599 suite.* **Rooms** 138. **Credit** AmEx, DC, Disc, MC, V. **Map** p402 F32 ❻
This small, tech-savvy hotel might be the best value for business travellers, nicely fusing comfort with amenities like automated check-in kiosks. For just $50 more, you can upgrade to a deluxe room with higher-tech amenities (PCs with free internet, white-noise machines); things to help prepare you for the big meeting (shoe shiner, trouser press, complimentary breakfast); and a few low-tech mood lifters (gummy bears!). The hotel's restaurant and bar, San Marino Ristorante, serves casual Italian cuisine.
Hotel services *Business centre. CD, periodical and video-game library. Fitness centre. Mobile phone rental. Pet-friendly.* **Room services** *CD player. Complimentary newspaper. Laptop-computer rental. Room service (24hrs). VCR on request. Web TV.*

W New York-Union Square

201 Park Avenue South, at 17th Street (1-212 253 9119/www.whotels.com). Subway: L, N, Q, R, W, 4, 5, 6 to 14th Street-Union Square. **Rates** *$249-$549 single/double; $599-$1,800 suite.* **Rooms** 270. **Credit** AmEx, DC, Disc, MC, V. **Map** p403 E27 ❼
For review, *see p65* W New York-Times Square.

Moderate ($100-$200)

Abingdon Guest House

13 Eighth Avenue, between Jane & W 12th Streets (1-212 243 5384/www.abingdonguesthouse.com). Subway: A, C, E to 14th Street; L to Eighth Avenue. **Rates** *$149-$199 single/double; $229-$239 suite.* **Rooms** 9. **Credit** AmEx, DC, Disc, MC, V. **Map** p403 D28 ❽
This charm-saturated B&B (without the breakfast) is a good option if you want to be near the Meatpacking District but can't afford the Gansevoort. Named after nearby Abingdon Square, the nine-room townhouse offers European ambience for a reasonable price. Each room is painted a different colour and has plush fabrics, four-poster beds and private bath. The popular Brewbar Coffee doubles as a check-in desk and café, and you can sip your latte in the trellised garden (if you're lucky enough to get the garden room).

It happened here

If these walls could talk... and talk and talk, you'd need a few weeks to absorb the legendary history behind the lavish Queen Anne façade of the **Chelsea Hotel**, located at 222 W 23rd Street. The infamous bohemian hangout got it's start as a co-op in 1884 and was later converted to a hotel in 1905. While Titanic survivors crashed a few nights here in 1912, its the mother lode of writerly types, artists and musicians that has given the place a mountain of notoriety. Among the famous residents are Mark Twain, Eugene O'Neil, Arthur Miller and Allen Ginsberg. Thomas Wolfe wrote *You Can't Go Home Again* while living in Room 831. Poet Dylan Thomas downed his last 18 straight whiskies in Room 206. William S Burroughs, under the influence, penned *Naked Lunch* here. Andy Warhol's film *Chelsea Girls* was shot on location at the hotel. Both Bob Dylan and Joni Mitchell wrote songs about Chelea and, last but not least, the Sex Pistols' Sid Vicious lived up to his surname and stabbed his girlfriend, Nancy Spungen, to death in Room 100. *See also p51.*

Inn on 23rd Street. *See p46.*

Hotel services *Coffeebar.* Room services *Complimentary local calls. Direct-dial phone numbers. High-speed wireless internet. VCR in some rooms.*

Chelsea Hotel

222 W 23rd Street, between Seventh & Eighth Avenues (1-212 243 3700/www.hotelchelsea.com). Subway: C, E, 1 to 23rd Street. Rates $125-$150 single/double with shared bath; $185-$275 single/double with private bath; $225 double studio; $325-$785 suite. Rooms 400. Credit AmEx, DC, Disc, MC, V. Map p404 D26 ❾

Built in 1884, the Chelsea has a long (and infamous) past: Nancy Spungen was murdered in Room 100 by her boyfriend, Sex Pistol Sid Vicious. This funky hotel has seen an endless parade of noteworthy guests: in 1912, Titanic survivors stayed here; other former residents include Mark Twain, Dee Dee Ramone, Thomas Wolfe and Madonna. Rooms are generally large with high ceilings, but certain amenities, like flat-panel TVs, washer-dryers and marble fireplaces, vary. The lobby doubles as an art gallery, and the basement cocktail lounge, Serena (1-212 255 4646), draws a downtown crowd with nightly DJs. Hotel services *Beauty salon. Fitness centre. Pet-friendly. Valet.* Room services *Fireplace, flat-panel TV, and kitchenette or refrigerator in some rooms. High-speed wireless internet. Washer-dryer in some rooms.*

Cosmopolitan

95 West Broadway, at Chambers Street (1-212 566 1900/1-888 895 9400/www.cosmohotel.com). Subway: A, C, 1, 2, 3 to Chambers Street. Rates $119-$169 single/double. Rooms 120. Credit AmEx, DC, MC, V. Map p402 E31 ❿

Despite the name, you won't find any trendy pink cocktails at this well-maintained hotel (or even a bar to drink them in). That's because the Cosmopolitan is geared towards budget travellers with little need for luxury. Open continuously since the 1850s, it remains a tourist favourite for its Tribeca address and affordable rates. Mini-lofts – multilevel rooms with sleeping lofts – start at $119. Hotel services *Discount parking.* Room services *Smoking permitted in all rooms.*

Pioneer of SoHotel

341 Broome Street, between Elizabeth Street & Bowery (1-212 226 1482/www.sohotel-ny.com). 6 to Spring Street Subway; J, M, Z to Bowery. Rates $90-$105 standard/double; $129-$139 suite. Rooms 105. Credit AmEx, DC, Disc, MC, V. Map p403 F30 ⓫

At press time, this European-style hotel was getting a complete renovation, but will remain open for business throughout the construction. The Pioneer is a bit of a pioneer itself – it's the only hotel in Nolita, which is a rapidly developing area known for its boutiques and cafés. Rooms are small and basic, but have decorative paintings and hardwood floors; most have private baths. Larger rooms have charming stucco walls and vaulted ceilings. Morning complimentary coffee is served in the lobby. Hotel services *Complimentary coffee.*

St Mark's Hotel

2 St Mark's Place, at Third Avenue (1-212 674 0100/www.stmarkshotel.qpg.com). Subway: 6 to Astor Place. Rates $110-$140 single/double. Rooms 67. No credit cards. Map p403 F28 ⓬

Positioned among all the tattoo parlours and piercing shops of St Mark's Place, this small hotel is unexpectedly bright, clean and understated (and the staff were surprisingly tattoo-less when we visited). The basic rooms have double beds with their own private baths. St Marks's biggest asset is its location – it's perfectly situated for immersing yourself in the East Village's historic punk-rock culture and new-found restaurant scene. Note that the hotel is in a pre-war walk-up building (no elevators). Room services *Satellite TV.*

Wall Street Inn

9 South William Street, at Broad Street (1-212 747 1500/www.thewallstreetinn.com). Subway: 2, 3 to Wall Street; 4, 5 to Bowling Green. Rates $189-$399 single/double. Call for corporate and weekend rates. Rooms 46. Credit AmEx, DC, Disc, MC, V. Map p402 E33 ⓭

The area surrounding this boutique hotel in the financial district has seen a reincarnation in recent years, sprouting new pâtisseries, bars and restaurants along its cobblestone streets. The Wall Street Inn started a trend in 1998 by transforming the 1830s Lehman Brothers Bank building into tastefully appointed accommodation with marble baths. To lure travellers beyond financiers, the hotel offers hefty discounts on weekends. There's no restaurant or room service, but breakfast is included. Hotel services *Complimentary breakfast. Fitness centre. Mobile phone rental. Video library.* Room services *Complimentary newspaper. High-speed wireless internet. Refrigerator. Two-line phone. VCR.*

Washington Square Hotel

103 Waverly Place, between MacDougal Street & Sixth Avenue (1-212 777 9515/1-800 222 0418/www.washingtonsquarehotel.com). Subway: A, B, C, D, E, F, V to W 4th Street. Rates $141-$194 single/double; $204-$210 quad. Rooms 165. Credit AmEx, MC, V. Map p403 E28 ⓮

This quintessential Greenwich Village hotel has a rock 'n' roll past: Bob Dylan and Joan Baez both lived here back when they sang for change in nearby Washington Square Park. Today, the century-old hotel remains popular with travellers aiming to soak up Village life. This past year, the deluxe rooms were expanded into larger chambers decked out with art deco furnishings and leather headboards. Other recent renovations include a refurbished lobby and the addition of a cosy bar-lounge that serves afternoon tea and light fare. Rates include a complimentary continental breakfast – or you can splurge on the Sunday jazz brunch at North Square (1-212 254 1200), the hotel's restaurant. Hotel services *Complimentary breakfast. Fitness centre. High-speed wireless internet. Massage service.* Room services *Complimentary newspaper. High-speed internet in some rooms.*

Budget (less than $100)

Chelsea Lodge

318 W 20th Street, between Eighth & Ninth Avenues (1-212 243 4499/www.chelsealodge.com). Subway: C, E to 23rd Street. **Rates** $95-$110 single/double with shared bath; $135-$150 deluxe with private bath; $195-$225 suite with private bath (each additional person $15; maximum 4 people). **Rooms** 26. **Credit** AmEx, DC, Disc, MC, V. **Map** p403 D27 ⑮

If Martha Stewart decorated a log cabin, it would look not unlike this 22-room inn, housed in a landmark brownstone. All rooms (including four suites down the block at 334 West 20th Street) have new beds, televisions, showers and air-conditioners. Although most are fairly small, the rooms are so aggressively charming that reservations fill up quickly. (Psst! There's no sign outside, so be sure to write down the address.) **Photo** *p57.*
Room services *High-speed wireless internet. Kitchenette and VCR in suites.*

Chelsea Star Hotel

300 W 30th Street, at Eighth Avenue (1-212 244 7827/1-877 827 6969/www.starhotelny.com). Subway: A, C, E to 34th Street-Penn Station. **Rates** $30 per person dorms; $69-$105 single/double/triple/quad with shared bath; $129-$149 double with private bath; $159-$179 suite. **Rooms** 30. **Credit** AmEx, MC, V. **Map** p403 D25 ⑯

Tired of sleeping in a boring beige box? Check in to this whimsical place, where your quarters might be decked out in Japanese paper screens (the Madame Butterfly). The 16 themed rooms are on the small side though less pricey, and lavatories are shared. A recent renovation more than doubled the hotel's size; there are now 18 superior rooms and deluxe suites with custom mahogany furnishings, flat-panel TVs and private baths. Ultracheap, shared hostel-style dorm rooms are also available.
Hotel services *Bicycle and in-line-skate rental. Internet kiosk. Laundry. Safe-deposit boxes.* **Room services** *DVD and flat-panel TV in some rooms.*

East Village Bed & Coffee

110 Avenue C, between 7th & 8th Streets (1-212 533 4175/www.bedandcoffee.com). Subway: F, V to Lower East Side-Second Avenue; L to First Avenue. **Rates** $80-$100 single; $90-$130 double quad. **Rooms** 9. **Credit** AmEx, MC, V. **Map** p403 G28 ⑰

Popular with European travellers, this unassuming East Village B&B (breakfast meaning coffee) is a great place in which to immerse yourself in downtown culture without dropping the cash. The nine guest rooms come with eclectic furnishings and quirky themes, such as the Black and White Room and 110 Downing Street. Shared areas include three separate loft-like living rooms, bathrooms and fully equipped kitchens. In nice weather, sip your complimentary java in the private garden.
Hotel services *Digital cable. Fax. Free bicycle rental and local phone service. Garden. High-speed wireless internet. Kitchen. Stereo. VCR. Video library.*

Maritime Hotel. *See p47.*

Downtown deluxe

Sleeping over in any one of these luxurious hot spots is simply divine. Hanging out with the fabulous in any one of these lobbies, in-house bars or restaurants is pretty cool too.

Hotel Gansevoort

18 Ninth Avenue, at 13th Street (1-212 206 6700/1-877 726 7386/www.hotel gansevoort.com). Subway: A, C, E to 14th Street; L to Eighth Avenue. **Rates** *$395-$475 single/double; $725-$675 suite; from $5,000 duplex penthouse.* **Rooms** *187.* **Credit** *AmEx, DC, Disc, MC, V.* **Map** *p403 C28* ⬤

It's hard to miss this commanding hotel – a soaring 14-floor contemporary structure that stands out against the cobblestone streets and warehouse-store fronts of the Meatpacking District. Opened in early 2004 and blueprinted by Stephen B Jacobs, this full-service luxury hotel gets strong marks for style. The hotel's entrance is framed by four 18ft light boxes, which change colour throughout the evening, and the world's tallest revolving door. Inside the rooms, colour gets less play, but the quarters are spacious and come with original photography from local artists and Molton Brown bath products. The private roof garden features a glassed-in heated pool with underwater music and 360-degree views of the city. Jeffrey Chodorow's glossy Japanese eaterie Ono has a covered terrace, private dining huts and a robatayaki bar – all behind a red velvet rope. At press time, the G Spa was due to open in autumn 2005. **Hotel services** *Pet-friendly. Spa.* **Room services** *CD player. Complimentary*

newspapers and magazines. Cordless phone. DVD player on request. High-speed wireless internet. LCD or plasma TV. Room service (24hrs).

Mercer

147 Mercer Street, at Prince Street (1-212 966 6060/1-888 918 6060/www.mercer hotel.com). Subway: N, R, W to Prince Street. **Rates** *$410-$620 single/double; $1,100-$2,300 suite.* **Rooms** *75.* **Credit** *AmEx, DC, Disc, MC, V.* **Map** *p403 E29* ⬤

Although now over seven years old, Soho's first luxury boutique hotel still has small touches that keep it a notch above nearby competitors, which is perhaps why Marc Jacobs takes up residence here when he returns to New York. The lobby, appointed with oversized white couches and chairs and shelves lined with colourful books, acts as a bar, library and lounge – open exclusively to hotel guests. Rooms are large by New York standards and feature furniture by Christian Liagre, oversize washrooms with tubs for two and Face Stockholm products.

Other locations: Second Home on Second Avenue, 221 Second Avenue, between 13th and 14th Streets (1-212 677 3161/www.secondhome.citysearch.com).

Hotel 17

225 E 17th Street, between Second & Third Avenues (1-212 475 2845/www.hotel17ny.com). Subway: L to Third Avenue; N, Q, R, W, 4, 5, 6 to 14th Street-Union Square. **Rates** *$60-$120 single/double; $75-$150 triple.* **Rooms** *120.* **Credit** *MC, V.* **Map** *p403 F27* ⬤

Equivalent to a good dive bar, Hotel 17 is part of the grungy cachet that draws you in. Except for a recent sprucing up of the lobby, the place remains a little rough and funky. The hotel has been used for numerous films (Woody Allen shot scenes from

The restaurant, Mercer Kitchen (1-212 966 5454), serves Jean-Georges Vongerichten's stylish version of casual American cuisine. **Hotel services** *Book and magazine library. CD/DVD library. Complimentary pass to nearby gym. Mobile phone and laptop-computer rental. Pet-friendly. Ticket desk. Valet.* **Room services** *Cassette and CD players. Complimentary newspaper. DVD player and VCR on request. Fireplace in some rooms. Plasma TV. PlayStation.*

60 Thompson

60 Thompson Street, between Broome & Spring Streets (1-212 431 0400/1-877 431 0400/www.60thompson.com). Subway: C, E to Spring Street. **Rates** *$370-$450 single/double; $520-$655 suite; $3,500 penthouse suite.* **Rooms** 98. **Credit** AmEx, DC, Disc, MC, V. **Map** p403 E30 ③

Don't be surprised if you have to walk through a fashion shoot when you enter this stylish hotel – it's a favoured location for fashionistas. A60, which is the exclusive guests-only rooftop bar, offers commanding city views and is particularly magazine-spread-worthy. Designed by Thomas O'Brien of Aero Studios, 60 Thompson has been luring fashionable jet-setters since it opened five years ago. The modern rooms are dotted with pampering details like pure down duvets and pillows, and a 'shag bag' filled with fun items to get you in the mood. The highly acclaimed restaurant Kittichai (*see p187*) serves creative Thai cuisine beside a pool filled with floating orchids. In warmer months, make sure to request a table on the sidewalk terrace. **Photo p54.** **Hotel services** *CD/DVD library. Fitness centre. Laptop computer on request. Mobile phone rental. Valet.* **Room services** *CD/DVD player. Complimentary newspaper. High-speed internet. Microwave oven on request. Plasma TV.*

Manhattan Murder Mystery here), as well as magazine shoots. Labyrinthine corridors lead to tiny high-ceilinged rooms filled with discarded dressers and mismatched 1950s wallpaper. Expect to share the hallway bathroom with other guests. The affiliated Hotel 31 (*see p70*) has even less ambience, but it suffices as a Gramercy budget hotel.
Room services *VCR in some rooms.*

Larchmont Hotel

27 W 11th Street, between Fifth & Sixth Avenues (1-212 989 9333/www.larchmonthotel.com). Subway: F, V to 14th Street; L to Sixth Avenue. **Rates** $75-$89 single; $99-$109 double; $109-$119 queen. **Rooms** 60. **Credit** AmEx, DC, Disc, MC, V. **Map** p403 E28 ⑲

Housed in a 1910 Beaux Arts building, the attractive, affordable Larchmont Hotel may be the best value in the heart of Greenwich Village. The decor (wicker furniture, floral bedspreads) recalls the set of *The Golden Girls*, but with prices this reasonable, you can accept low marks for style. All baths are shared, but your room comes equipped with a washbasin, a robe and a pair of slippers.
Hotel services *Complimentary breakfast. Kitchenette on some floors.* **Room services** *Digital TV.*

Off-Soho Suites Hotel

11 Rivington Street, between Bowery & Chrystie Street (1-212 979 9808/1-800 633 7646/www.offsoho.com). Subway: B, D to Grand Street; F, V to Lower East Side-Second Avenue; J, M, Z to Bowery. **Rates** $79-$109 2-person suite with shared bath; $139-$209 4-person suite with private bath. **Rooms** 38. **Credit** AmEx, MC, V. **Map** p403 F30 ⑳

These no-frill suites became a great deal more popular after the reclusive-hipster destination restaurant Freemans (see p184) opened at the end of the alley across the street. The suites are good value for the thriving Lower East Side (a couple of blocks from – not in – Soho). Rooms are bland but clean and spacious, and they have fully equipped kitchens.
Hotel services *Café. Fitness room. High-speed wireless internet. Pet-friendly.* **Room services** *Digital TV. Kitchen.*

Union Square Inn

209 E 14th Street, between Second & Third Avenues (1-212 614 0500/www.nyinns.com). Subway: L to Third Avenue; N, Q, R, W, 4, 5, 6 to 14th Street-Union Square. **Rates** $89-$149 single/double. **Rooms** 45. **Credit** AmEx, MC, V. **Map** p403 F27 ㉑ For review, see p70 Murray Hill Inn.

Hostels

Bowery's Whitehouse Hotel of New York

340 Bowery, between 2nd & 3rd Streets (1-212 477 5623/www.whitehousehotelofny.com). Subway: B, D, F, V to Broadway-Lafayette Street; 6 to Bleecker Street. **Rates** $34-$57 single/double; $71-$81 triple. **Rooms** 220. **Credit** AmEx, Disc, MC, V. **Map** p403 F29 ㉒

Even though the Bowery progressively looks more sleek than seedy, with pricey restaurants and flashy clubs popping up in recent years, the unapologetically second-rate Whitehouse Hotel remains steadfastly basic. Built in 1919 as housing for railroad workers, the renovated hotel offers semi-private cubicles (ceilings are an open latticework, so be warned that snorers or sleep talkers may interrupt

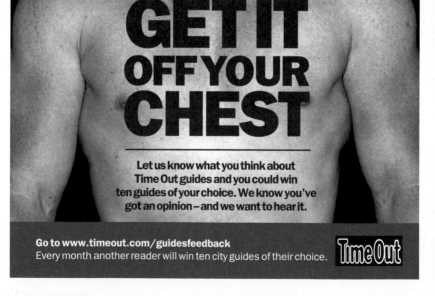

your slumber) at unbelievably low rates. Towels and linens are provided. A microwave and large-screen TV are available in the lounge at all times.
Hostel services Concierge. DVD library. DVD player, internet and TV in lobby. Fax. Luggage storage. Safe-deposit boxes. Self-service laundry. TV in some rooms.

Midtown

Expensive ($200-$350)

Blakely New York

136 W 55th Street, between Sixth & Seventh Avenues (1-212 245 1800/www.blakelynewyork.com). Subway: F, N, Q, R, W to 57th Street. **Rates** $275-$320 single/double; $315-$360 suite. **Rooms** 120. **Credit** AmEx, DC, Disc, MC, V. **Map** p405 D22 ㉓
Trimmed in oak and appointed with cherry-wood furniture and paintings of fox hunts, the Blakely recalls more an old English manor than a midtown hotel in New York City. In 2004, the designers of superhip hotels the Maritime and the Mercer transformed the former dated Gorham Hotel into a more traditional accommodation, favouring comfort over style. Handsome marble bathrooms – some of which are equipped with deep jacuzzi tubs – are stocked with Frette robes and toiletries from British line Penhaligon's. Abboccato, an upscale eatery from the owners of Molyvos, offers modern Italian cuisine in a room that Frank Sinatra would have loved.
Hotel services Mobile spa. **Room services** CD/DVD player. Complimentary newspapers. Flat-panel TV. High-speed wireless internet. Kitchenette. Video library.

Bryant Park Hotel

40 W 40th Street, between Fifth & Sixth Avenues (1-212 642 2200/www.bryantparkhotel.com). Subway: B, D, F, V to 42nd Street-Bryant Park; 7 to Fifth Avenue. **Rates** $265-$395 single/double; $395-$615 suite. **Rooms** 128. **Credit** AmEx, DC, MC, V. **Map** p404 E24. ㉔
This midtown hotel has seen a lot more action ever since Koi, the East Coast branch of the splashy Los Angeles restaurant, opened on site in spring 2005. Ian Schrager's partner Philip Pilevsky converted the 1924 American Radiator Building into his first New York property, and it seems as though the hotel has all the right accessories to lure a trend-setting crowd: there's a gorgeous 70-seat screening room with red velour chairs and built-in desks, and, thanks to the hotel's close proximity to Bryant Park, a well-heeled clientele checks in each year during Fashion Week. But oddly, the rooms are stark, and – aside from the LCD TVs – they look as if they were furnished from the IKEA catalogue. But you can always head downstairs for a cocktail in the vaulted Cellar Bar.
Hotel services Beauty salon. Fitness centre. Screening room. Spa. Valet. **Room services** CD player. Digital movies on demand. High-speed internet. Room service (24hrs). VCR.

Dream Hotel

210 W 55th Street, between Broadway & Seventh Avenue (1-212 247 2000/1-866 437 3266/www. dreamny.com). Subway: N, Q, R, W to 57th Street. **Rates** $275-$575 single/double; $509-$5,000 suite. **Rooms** 216. **Credit** AmEx, Disc, MC, V. **Map** p405 D22 ㉕
In 2004, hotelier Vikram Chatwal, who brought us the Time Hotel, enlisted boldfaced names to turn the old Majestic Hotel into a luxury lodge with a trippy slumberland theme. David Rockwell dressed up the restaurant, an outpost of Serafina; Deepak Chopra conceived the ayurvedic spa. The lobby sums up the resulting aesthetic – walls are cloaked in Paul Smith-style stripes, a crystal boat dangles from the ceiling, and an enormous gold statue of Catherine the Great stands guard. But the rooms are more streamlined, with white walls, satin headboards and an ethereal blue backlight that glows under the bed. Luxurious touches include feather-duvet-topped beds, plasma TV with movies on demand and an iPod – loaded with ambient music – with Bose speakers. Ava, the rooftop bar, has panoramic views of the city.
Hotel services Fitness centre. Flat-panel TV. Pet-friendly. Spa. **Room services** CD/DVD player on request. High-speed internet. iPod. Movies on demand.

Dylan

52 E 41st Street, between Madison & Park Avenues (1-212 338 0500/1-800 553 9526/www.dylanhotel. com). Subway: 42nd Street S, 4, 5, 6, 7 to 42nd Street-Grand Central. **Rates** $329-$549 single/ double; $495-$1,200 suite. **Rooms** 107. **Credit** AmEx, DC, Disc, MC, V. **Map** p404 E24 ㉖

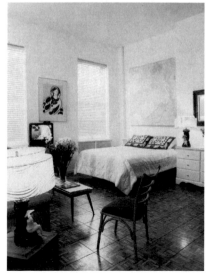

Charming **Chelsea Lodge**. *See p53.*

If you're a closet science geek, you'll love this breathtaking boutique hotel, fashioned out of the once-crumbling 1903 landmark Chemist Club building. The lobby has a grand marble staircase, fluted columns and beautifully ornate mouldings. Most rooms are flooded with natural light and have 11ft ceilings. Bathrooms sport bowl sinks, and beakers stand in for water glasses. The stunning Gothic Alchemy Suite, modelled after a medieval alchemist's lab, has leaded floor-to-ceiling windows and a spacious outdoor terrace. At press time, the hotel Bar & Grill was set to open in the autumn of 2005.
Hotel services *Fitness centre. Ticket desk. Valet.* **Room services** *CD player and VCR on request. Complimentary newspaper. High-speed wireless internet.*

Flatotel

135 W 52nd Street, between Sixth & Seventh Avenues (1-212 887 9400/www.flatotel.com). Subway: N, R, W to 49th Street; 1 to 50th Street. **Rates** $329-$489 single/double; $629-$3,800 suite. **Rooms** 288. **Credit** AmEx, DC, MC, V. **Map** p404 D23 ㉗
Upon entrance, the Flatotel seems ultra-hip: techno beats pump through the granite lobby, where dimly lit nooks and cowhide couches are filled with cocktailers. But that's where the sleek stops as rooms are more basic, although still modern and spacious. A slew of reality-TV shows, including *America's Next Top Model*, has been filmed in the penthouse suites. The in-house restaurant, Moda (1-212 887 9880), serves Italian-inspired fare; in temperate weather, catch a breeze with your cocktail in the restaurant's alfresco atrium. For private imbibing, call the Martini butler, who will mix the drink right in your room.
Hotel services *Fitness centre. Gift shop. Mobile phone rental. Spa. Valet.* **Room services** *CD player. High-speed internet. Microwave. Mini-fridge. Room service (24hrs). VCR.*

Hotel Chandler

12 E 31st Street, between Fifth & Madison Avenues (1-212 889 6363/www.hotelchandler.com). Subway: 6 to 33rd Street. **Rates** $255-$355 single/double; $495-$650 suite. **Rooms** 120. **Credit** AmEx, DC, Disc, MC, V. **Map** p404 E25 ㉘
Rooms at this delightful hotel are style-conscious, with black-and-white photographs of New York streetscapes on the walls, checkered carpeting, and Frette robes and Aveda products in the bathroom. The in-house 12:31 bar offers cocktails and light nibbles. And turndown service means a chocolate on your pillow and a next-day weather forecast.
Hotel services *DVD library. Fitness centre. Valet.* **Room services** *CD/DVD player. High-speed internet. Nintendo/WebTV (free).*

Hotel Elysée

60 E 54th Street, between Madison & Park Avenues (1-212 753 1066/www.elyseehotel.com). Subway: E, V to Lexington Avenue-53rd Street; 6 to 51st Street. **Rates** $285-$395 single/double; $525 suite. **Rooms** 101. **Credit** AmEx, DC, Disc, MC, V. **Map** p405 E22 ㉙

The Hotel Elysée is a well-preserved piece of New York's Jazz Age: quarters are appointed with a touch of romance (period fabrics, antique furniture), and some rooms have coloured-glass conservatories and terraces. Elysée is popular with publishers and literary types, who convene over complimentary wine and cheese in the evening. Downstairs is the Steakhouse at Monkey Bar (1-212 838 2600), where a well-coiffed clientele dines on fine cuts. For sister hotels, see Casablanca Hotel (*p65*), the Library Hotel (*p59*) and the ultra modern Hotel Gansevoort (*p54*).
Hotel services *Complimentary breakfast and pass to nearby gym. Valet. Video library.* **Room services** *CD player in suites. High-speed wireless internet. VCR.*

Hotel Roger Williams

131 Madison Avenue, at 31st Street (1-212 448 7000/1-888 448 7788/www.rogerwilliamshotel.com). Subway: 6 to 33rd Street. **Rates** $255-$340 single/double; $325-$450 suite. **Rooms** 191. **Credit** AmEx, DC, Disc, MC, V. **Map** p404 E25 ㉚
In 2004, an $8 million renovation brought in a vibrant colour palette of greens and bright tangerine to this small, stylish hotel. The soaring lobby has floor-to-ceiling windows, plenty of textured wood and a live jazz band (Wed-Fri). Room amenities, such as bottled water, Aveda bath products and a modern office area, make you feel at home – if you're lucky enough to live like this. Each room on the penthouse level has access to a shared wraparound terrace. Lounge at the Roger, the hotel's new restaurant and bar, serves light fare and cocktails as well as room service, and the recently opened Veranda 411 is a fourth-floor garden open for private events.

Hotel services *Complimentary newspapers and magazines. Fitness centre. Mobile phone rental. Valet.* Room services *High-speed wireless internet. Plasma TV.*

Iroquois

49 W 44th Street, between Fifth & Sixth Avenues (1-212 840 3080/1-800 332 7220/www.iroquoisny. com). Subway: B, D, F, V to 42nd Street-Bryant Park; 7 to Fifth Avenue. Rates *$219-$425 single/double; $475-$685 suite.* Rooms 114. Credit AmEx, DC, Disc, MC, V. Map p404 E24 ③①

The Iroquois is what you might find if you were to walk into a posh doorman apartment building on the Upper East Side. It boasts a polished-stone lobby, a mahogany-panelled library and spacious and elegant rooms – all the result of a massive renovation that morphed a modest inn into a full-service luxury hotel. Nine suites include additional treats like decorative fireplaces, jacuzzis and Frette bathrobes. The James Dean Suite (No.803), which is decorated with photographs of the rebel without a cause, commemorates the actor, who lived here in the 1950s. There's also a fitness centre, a sauna and a library with computer access. Haute French fare is served in the hotel's restaurant, Triomphe (1-212 453 4233).

Hotel services *Fitness centre. Mobile phone rental. Sauna. Ticket desk. Video library.* Room services *CD player. Flat-screen TVs. Room service (24hrs). VCR. Wireless internet.*

Kitano

66 Park Avenue, at 38th Street (1-212 885 7000/1-800 548 2666/www.kitano.com). Subway: 42nd Street S, 4, 5, 6, 7 to 42nd Street-Grand Central. Rates *$250-$480 single/double; $400-$715 junior suite; $715-$2,100 suite.* Rooms 149. Credit AmEx, DC, Disc, MC, V. Map p404 E24 ③②

The first and only Japanese-owned and operated hotel in New York City is also the only hotel to offer heated commodes. Rooms feature silk-covered walls, smooth stone floors, Shiseido bath products and complimentary green tea. A one-of-a-kind tatami suite boasts painted shoji screens and a separate tea-ceremony room. Dine with chopsticks at the hotel's two casual Japanese restaurants, Hakubai (1-212 885 7111) and Garden Café (1-212 885 7123).

Hotel services *Bar/lounge with jazz Wed-Sat. Complimentary pass to nearby gym. Gift shop. Laundry drop-off. Ticket desk. Valet.* Room services *CD player in some rooms. High-speed internet.*

Library Hotel

299 Madison Avenue, at 41st Street (1-212 983 4500/www.libraryhotel.com). Subway: 42nd Street S, 4, 5, 6, 7 to 42nd St-Grand Central; 7 to Fifth Avenue. Rates *$335-$395 single/double; $435 suite.* Rooms 60. Credit AmEx, DC, MC, V. Map p404 E24 ③③

More than 6,000 books were handpicked from indie-fave bookstore the Strand to match the themes of the rooms they adorn at this literary-themed boutique hotel. Even before you enter, you'll see quotes from famous authors inscribed in the sidewalk. Lodgings are organised according to the Dewey decimal system and furnished by theme (Botany, Fairy Tales). For instance, the Love Room is strewn with rose petals; Casanova's autobiography sits on a bedside table in the Erotica Room. Rates include breakfast, evening wine and cheese gatherings in the second-

Where to Stay

Hotel QT. *See p66.*

Selective about where you sleep?

So are we.

TabletHotels.com
Unique Hotels for Global Nomads

floor Reading Room, and access to the mahogany-lined writer's den (which has a lovely tiny terrace and a glowing fireplace). The casual seafood destination, Branzini, is conveniently located in the lobby. Hotel Giraffe, which is a sister hotel, embodies modern European style 15 blocks south.
Hotel services *Complimentary breakfast, pass to nearby gym, and wine and cheese every evening. Mobile phone rental. Ticket desk. Valet. Video library.* **Room services** *CD player. High-speed internet. VCR.*
Other locations Hotel Giraffe, 365 Park Avenue South, at 26th Street (1-212 685 7700/1-877 296 0009/www.hotelgiraffe.com).

Metropolitan Hotel

569 Lexington Avenue, at 51st Street (1-212 752 7000/1-800 836 6471/www.metropolitannyc.com). Subway: E, V to Lexington Avenue-53rd Street; 6 to 51st Street. **Rates** $189-$500 single/double; $379-$700 suite. **Rooms** 722. **Credit** AmEx, DC, Disc, MC, V. **Map** p404 F23 ③④
The Metropolian has reinvented itself more times than Madonna: it was unveiled in 1961, and known as the Summit, with an art deco look, later transformed into a more toned-down Loews Hotel in the '80s, and in 2000 architect Morris Lapidus – designer of many 1950s-era hotels – returned the building to its original look. Its most recent reincarnation emerged in 2004, when hospitality-industry giant Doubletree acquired the place and a $35 million renovation added some badly needed style. Rooms are now freshly outfitted with fluffy down comforters, flat-panel TVs and original artwork. The Met Grill offers casual American cuisine, and a lobby lounge draws guests and local imbibers. In keeping with Doubletree tradition, everyone receives a warm chocolate-chip cookie at check-in.
Hotel services *Barbershop. Fitness centre (24hrs).* **Room services** *Cordless phone. High-speed internet. LCD TV.*

Michelangelo

152 W 51st Street, between Sixth & Seventh Avenues (1-212 765 1900/1-800 237 0990/www.michelangelohotel.com). Subway: N, R, W to 49th Street; 1 to 50th Street. **Rates** $255-$495 single/double; $595-$1,735 suite. **Rooms** 178. **Credit** AmEx, DC, Disc, MC, V. **Map** p404 D23 ③⑤
Appointed with Italian luxuries like peach marble, Venetian fabrics and oil paintings, this Renaissance-inspired hotel is the only US location of a 21-branch Italian chain. The sizeable rooms are accoutred in styles ranging from French country to art deco, and each contains two TVs and a large soaking tub. Complimentary breakfast includes Italian coffee and pastries. Fully equipped apartments are available for extended stays ($4,000 to $12,000 per month).
Hotel services *Complimentary breakfast every day and limousine service to Wall Street (Mon-Fri). Fitness centre (24hrs). Mobile phone rental. Valet.* **Room services** *CD player. Complimentary newspaper and shoe shine. DVD player, laptop computer and VCR on request. High-speed internet.*

Park South Hotel

122 E 28th Street, between Park Avenue South & Lexington Avenue (1-212 448 0888/1-800 315 4642/www.parksouthhotel.com). Subway: 6 to 28th Street. **Rates** $209-$270 single/double; $330-$350 suite. **Rooms** 141. **Credit** AmEx, DC, Disc, MC, V. **Map** p404 E26 ③⑥
Everything about this quaint boutique hotel says 'I love New York'. The mezzanine library is crammed with books on historic Gotham, and the walls are covered with images from the New York Historical Society. Rooms are appointed in warm amber and brown tones, and some have dazzling views of the Chrysler Building. Bathrooms are stocked with essential oil products and thick terry-cloth bathrobes. The hotel's bar-restaurant, Black Duck (1-212 204 5240), serves live jazz with brunch.
Hotel services *Complimentary breakfast and newspaper. Fitness centre. Video library.* **Room services** *DVD player. High-speed internet.*

Roger Smith

501 Lexington Avenue, between 47th & 48th Streets (1-212 755 1400/1-800 445 0277/www.rogersmith. com). Subway: E, V to Lexington Avenue-53rd Street; 6 to 51st Street. **Rates** $265-$295 single/double; $330-$450 junior suite; $275-$400 suite. **Rooms** 130. **Credit** AmEx, DC, Disc, MC, V. **Map** p404 F23 ③⑦
The spacious chambers at this arty spot make it a good option for families. Each room is decorated with unique furnishings and colourful wallpaper. Lily's restaurant serves breakfast for now (a full service is expected by the time this guide is published) in a bright space with playful murals. The Roger Smith Gallery hosts rotating exhibitions, and a few interesting pieces by artist James Knowles (whose family owns the hotel) adorn the lobby.
Hotel services *Valet. Video library.* **Room services** *CD player. Coffeemaker. Complimentary local phone calls. High-speed wireless internet. Refrigerator. VCR.*

Time

224 W 49th Street, between Broadway & Eighth Avenue (1-212 320 2900/1-877 846 3692/www.the timeny.com). Subway: C, E, 1 to 50th Street; N, R, W to 49th Street. **Rates** $199-$429 single/double; $329-$529 suite; $2,500-$6,000 penthouse suite. **Rooms** 193. **Credit** AmEx, DC, Disc, MC, V. **Map** p404 D23 ③⑧
Have you ever wondered what it's like to feel, taste and smell colour? Adam Tihany designed this boutique hotel with the idea of stimulating the senses through a single primary colour (guest rooms are furnished entirely in either red, yellow or blue). Expect to find matching duvets, jelly beans and reading materials, as well as a chromatically inspired scent. At press time, Océo, the hotel's creative American restaurant, was closed but expected to reopen as a restaurant by another name.
Hotel services *Fitness centre. Mobile phone rental. Personal shopping. Ticket desk.* **Room services** *CD player and VCR on request. High-speed internet.*

Classic New York

In a New York state of mind? Check out these venerable NYC icons.

Algonquin

59 W 44th Street, between Fifth & Sixth Avenues (1-212 840 6800/1-800 555 8000/ www.thealgonquin.net). Subway: B, D, F, V to 42nd Street-Bryant Park; 7 to Fifth Avenue. **Rates** *$200-$299 single/double; $299-$549 suite.* **Rooms** *174.* **Credit** *AmEx, DC, Disc, MC, V.* **Map** *p404 E24* ⑰

This landmark hotel with a strong literary past (greats like Alexander Woollcott and Dorothy Parker gathered at the famous Round Table in the Rose Room to gossip) is beautifully appointed with upholstered chairs, old lamps and large paintings of important figures of the Jazz Age. In 2004 the entire hotel underwent renovations, which spiffed up the small quarters with new bedspreads and mahogany furniture, and many rooms now have flat-panel TVs. But there's still a sense of old New York: hallways are covered with *New Yorker*-cartoon wallpaper to commemorate Harold Ross, who secured funding for the magazine over long meetings at the Round Table. Quarters are on the small side and the decor is a bit dated, but the feel is still classic New York. Catch readings by local authors on some Mondays; cabaret performers take over in the Oak Room (*see pXXx*) Tuesday through to Saturday.
Hotel services *Fitness centre (24hrs). Ticket desk.* **Room services** *CD player and VCR in suites. Complimentary magazines and newspapers. High-speed wireless internet. Refrigerator in suites or on request.*

Four Seasons Hotel

57 E 57th Street, between Madison & Park Avenues (1-212 758 5700/1-800 332 3442/www.fourseasons.com). Subway: N, R, W to Lexington Avenue-59th Street; 4, 5, 6 to 59th Street. **Rates** *$455-$895 single/double; $1,550-$11,000 suite.* **Rooms** *368.* **Credit** *AmEx, DC, Disc, MC, V.* **Map** *p405 E22* ⑱

New York's quintessential luxury hotel hasn't slipped a notch from its heyday. Everybody who's anybody – from music-industry executives to political figures – continues to drop in for a dose of top-notch New York service. Renowned architect IM Pei's sharp geometric design (in neutral cream and honey tones) is sleek and modern, and rooms are among the largest in the city (the three-

bedroom Royal Suite measures 2,000sq ft). From the higher floors, the views of the city are superb. In 2004, the spa was renovated and now features high-tech 'spa-ology', and in 2005 the presidential suites were renovated and reopened. The hotel is known for catering to a guest's every need; your 4am hot-fudge sundae is only a room-service call away.
Hotel services *Fitness centre. Gift shop. Spa.* **Room services** *CD/DVD library. Flat-panel TV. High-speed internet. VCR in suites.*

New York Palace Hotel

455 Madison Avenue, between 50th & 51st Streets (1-212 888 7000/1-800 697 2522/www.newyorkpalace.com). Subway: E, V to Fifth Avenue-53rd Street. **Rates** *$315-$745 single/double; $900-$12,000 suite.* **Rooms** *896.* **Credit** *AmEx, DC, Disc, MC, V.* **Map** *p404 E23* ⑲

Stepping inside the palace is like stepping inside a fairy tale, complete with red carpet, twinkling lights and fancy tea parties. So it's hard to believe that the hotel was once owned by real-estate tycoon (and former jailbird) Leona Helmsley. Designed by McKim, Mead & White, the cluster of mansions now holds nearly 900 rooms ornamented in art deco or neo-classic style. Triplex suites have a top-tier terrace, solarium and private rooftop garden. The famous restaurant Le Cirque 2000 is now closed, but you can still sip a Manhattan in the extravagant Louis XVI-style Villard Bar and Lounge. And the Istana Restaurant, which will satisfy all New American and exotic cocktail needs, is also located in this hotel.
Hotel services *Complimentary limousine service to Wall Street and shoe shine. Fitness centre. Video library.* **Room services** *Complimentary breakfast, dessert and newspaper in suites. Dual-line phone. Room service (24hrs).*

Pierre

2 E 61st Street, at Fifth Avenue (1-212 838 8000/1-800 743 7734/www.fourseasons. com/pierre). Subway: N, R, W to Fifth Avenue-59th Street. **Rates** *$425-$950 single; $475-$995 double; $625-$3,800 suite.* **Rooms** *201.* **Credit** *AmEx, DC, Disc, MC, V.* **Map** *p405 E22* ㉚

A landmark of New York glamour, the Pierre marked its 75th birthday in 2005. A black-and-white checkered sidewalk leads up to the

gleaming gold lobby. Front rooms overlook Central Park, and you'll find wares from fancy neighbouring stores on display in the lobby. In addition to a dry cleaning service, the hotel offers hand-laundering for precious garments. There are three restaurants, including the opulent Café Pierre.
Hotel services *Beauty salon. Fitness centre. Free shuttle to Theater District. Mobile phone rental. Ticket desk. Valet.* **Room services** *CD player. Exercise equipment. High-speed wireless internet. PlayStation and VCR on request.*

Waldorf-Astoria

301 Park Avenue, at 50th Street (1-212 355 3000/1-800 924 3673/www.waldorf.com). Subway: E, V to Lexington Avenue-53rd Street; 6 to 51st Street. **Rates** *$275-$450 single; $300-$450 double; $400-$900 suite.* **Rooms** 1,425. **Credit** AmEx, DC, Disc, MC, V. **Map** p404 E23 ③①
First built in 1893, the Waldorf-Astoria was the city's largest hotel (and the birthplace of the Waldorf salad), but it was demolished to make way for the Empire State Building. The current art deco Waldorf opened in 1931 and now has protected status as a historic landmark. In addition to the grandeur, guests will be impressed by the $2 million renovation that has turned 24 rooms into 12 reconfigured 'Astor Suites'. The Waldorf still caters to the high and mighty (guests have included Princess Grace, Sophia Loren and a long list of US presidents). Double-check your attire before entering the hotel

– you won't be terribly welcome if you're wearing a baseball cap, T-shirt or even fashionably ripped jeans. **Photo** *above.*
Hotel services *Beauty salon. Complimentary newspaper. Copier/printer. Fitness centre. High-speed internet. Kitchenette in some suites. Mobile phone rental. Spa. Valet. Wireless internet in lobby.* **Room services** *Complimentary newspaper. Copier/printer. High-speed internet. Kitchenette in some suites.*

Warwick New York Hotel

65 W 54th Street, at Sixth Avenue (1-212 247 2700/1-800 223 4099/ www.warwickhotels.com). Subway: E, V to Fifth Avenue-53rd Street; F to 57th Street. **Rates** *$189-$475 single/double; $405-$3,500 suite.* **Rooms** 426. **Credit** AmEx, DC, MC, V. **Map** p405 E22 ③②
You'd never know it from its dated façade, but the grand Warwick was frequented by Elvis and the Beatles during their tours, and the top-floor suite with wrap-around balcony was once the home of Cary Grant. Built by William Randolph Hearst in 1927, the Warwick is listed by the National Trust for Historic Preservation. Rooms are exceptionally large by midtown standards, and have feminine touches like floral curtains and bedspreads. The Murals on 54 eatery has been refurbished to reveal a scenerie of light filled murals.
Hotel services *Fitness centre. Business centre. Mobile phone rental. Valet.* **Room services** *High-speed wireless internet. VCR on request.*

W New York-Times Square

*1567 Broadway, at 47th Street (1-212 930 7400/
1-877 976 8357/www.whotels.com). Subway: N, R,
W to 49th Street; 1 to 50th Street.* **Rates** $259-$339
single/double; $499-$2,500 suite. **Rooms** 509. **Credit**
AmEx, DC, Disc, MC, V. **Map** p404 D23 ③
'Whatever, whenever' is the motto of this luxury
boutique chain, and the hotel's concierge is always
at the ready to fill your bathtub with champagne,
chocolate or whatever else your heart desires. NYC's
fifth and flashiest W location has a street-level
vestibule with a waterfall (reception is on the seventh floor). To your right, the Living Room is a massive sprawl of white leather seating. Every private
room features a floating-glass desk and a sleek bathroom stocked with Bliss spa products, but it's the
bed-to-ceiling headboard mirror and sexy room-service menu that get the mind racing. Steve Hanson's
Blue Fin (1-212 918 1400) serves stellar sushi and
cocktails. The second hotel bar, Living Room Bar, is
on the seventh floor. **Photo** *p67.*
Hotel services *Fitness centre. Gift shop. Mobile
phone rental. Pet-friendly. Screening room. Spa.
Valet.* **Room services** *CD/DVD player. High-speed
wireless internet. VCR.*
Other locations: W New York, 541 Lexington
Avenue, at 49th Street (1-212 755 1200); W New
York-The Court, 130 E 39th Street, between Park
Avenue South & Lexington Avenue (1-212 685
1100); W New York-The Tuscany, 120 E 39th Street,
between Park Avenue South & Lexington Avenue
(1-212 686 1600); W New York-Union Square, 201
Park Avenue South, at 17th Street (*see p49*).

Moderate ($100-$200)

Americana Inn

*69 W 38th Street, at Sixth Avenue (1-212
840 6700/www.newyorkhotel.com). Subway:
B, D, F, N, Q, R, V, W to 34th Street-Herald
Square; B, D, F, V to 42nd Street.* **Rates**
$95-$105 standard/double. **Rooms** 53. **Credit**
AmEx, MC, V. **Map** p404 E24 ④
This budget hotel, situated close to Times Square,
has a speakeasy feel: the signage is very discreet,
and you'll have to ring the doorbell to enter through
the second-floor lobby. What the Americana might
lack in ambience (with its linoleum floors and fluo-
rescent lighting), it makes up for in location (a rhine-
stone's throw from the major Broadway shows) and
reasonable prices (rooms start at just under $100).
And although all bathrooms are shared, rooms come
with a mini-sink and large walk-in closets.
Hotel services *Ticket desk. Modem. Shared
kitchenette.*

Broadway Inn

*264 W 46th Street, at Eighth Avenue (1-212 997
9200/1-800 826 6300/www.broadwayinn.com).
Subway: A, C, E to 42nd Street-Port Authority.*
Rates $99-$199 single/double; $199-$399 suite.
Rooms 41. **Credit** AmEx, DC, Disc, MC, V.
Map p404 D23 ④

Theatre junkies should take note: this endearing little hotel can arrange a 35 to 40% discount on theatre tickets; it also offers several Broadway
dinner-and-show combinations. The warm lobby
has exposed-brick walls, ceiling fans and shelves
that are loaded with bedtime reading material. The
fairly priced basic guest rooms and suites get lots of
natural light. On the downside, there are no elevators, and the hotel is strict about its three-night-minimum policy on weekends and holidays.
Hotel services *Complimentary breakfast.* **Room
services** *High-speed wireless internet. Kitchenette
in suites.*

Casablanca Hotel

*147 W 43rd Street, between Sixth Avenue &
Broadway (1-212 869 1212/1-800 922 7225/www.
casablancahotel.com). Subway: B, D, F, V to 42nd
Street-Bryant Park; N, Q, R, W, 42nd Street S, 1, 2,
3, 9, 7 to 42nd Street-Times Square.* **Rates** $225-
$365 single/double; $295-$395 suite. **Rooms** 48.
Credit AmEx, DC, MC, V. **Map** p404 D24 ④
Run by the same people who own the Library Hotel
(*see p59*), this 48-room boutique hotel has a cheerful
Moroccan theme. The lobby is an oasis in the middle of Times Square: walls are adorned with blue
and gold Mediterranean tiles, and giant bamboo
shoots stand in tall vases. The theme is diluted in
the basic rooms, but wicker furniture, wooden shut-
ters and new carpets and sofas warm up the space.
Rick's Café serves free wine and cheese to guests
Monday through Saturday. Breakfast is complimentary, as is your copy of *Casablanca*.
Hotel services *Complimentary breakfast and pass
to nearby gym. Cybercafé. Mobile phone rental. Spa.
Valet. Video library.* **Room services** *CD player.
High-speed wireless internet. VCR.*

414 Hotel

*414 W 46th Street, between Ninth & Tenth Avenues
(1-212 399 0006/www.414hotel.com). Subway: A, C,
E to 42nd Street-Port Authority.* **Rates** $99-$329
single/double. **Rooms** 22. **Credit** AmEx, MC, V.
Map p404 C23 ④
This small hotel's shockingly affordable rates and
reclusive location (tucked away on the Theater
District's Restaurant Row) make it feel like a secret
you've been lucky to stumble upon. Immaculate
rooms are tastefully appointed with suede headboards, vases full of colourful roses and framed
black-and-white photos of the city. There's a glowing fireplace and computer available to guests in the
lobby and a leafy courtyard outside.
Hotel services *Complimentary breakfast. High-
speed wireless internet.* **Room services** *Refrigerator
in some rooms.*

Hotel Edison

*228 W 47th Street, at Broadway (1-212 840 5000/
1-800 637 7070/www.edisonhotelnyc.com). Subway:
N, R, W to 49th Street; 1 to 50th Street.* **Rates** $150
single; $170 double (each additional person $20,
maximum 5 people); $170-$295 suite. **Rooms** 1,000.
Credit AmEx, DC, Disc, MC, V. **Map** p404 D23 ④

Theatre lovers flock to this newly renovated art deco hotel for its affordable rates and convenient location. Rooms are of a standard size but are decidedly spruced up. Café Edison (1-212 840 5000), a classic diner just off the lobby, is a long-time favourite of Broadway actors and their fans – Neil Simon was so smitten that he put it in one of his plays.

Hotel services *Fitness centre. Gift shop. Ticket desk. Valet.* **Room services** *High-speed wireless internet.*

Hotel 41

206 W 41st Street, between Seventh & Eighth Avenues (1-212 703 8600/www.hotel41.com). Subway: N, Q, R, W, 42nd Street S, 1, 2, 3, 7. 9 to 42nd Street-Times Square. **Rates** $289-$309 single/double; $369-$589 suite. **Rooms** 47. **Credit** AmEx, Disc, MC, V. **Map** p404 D24 ⑮

Although its looks are cool, this tiny boutique hotel feels comfy-warm: reading lamps extend from dark-wood headboards, and triple-paned windows effectively filter out the cacophony from the streets below. The penthouse suite has a large private terrace with potted trees and views of Times Square. Bar 41 serves breakfast, lunch and dinner.

Hotel services *CD/DVD library. Complimentary breakfast. Espresso bar. Pet-friendly. Valet.* **Room services** *CD/DVD player. High-speed internet.*

Hotel Metro

45 W 35th Street, between Fifth & Sixth Avenues (1-212 947 2500/1-800 356 3870/www.hotelmetro nyc.com). Subway: B, D, F, N, Q, R, V, W to 34th Street-Herald Square. **Rates** $195-$325 single/double; $275-$450 suite. **Rooms** 179. **Credit** AmEx, DC, MC, V. **Map** p404 E25 ⑯

It's not posh, but the Metro has good service and a retro vibe. Black-and-white portraits of Hollywood legends adorn the lobby, and the tiny rooms are clean. Take in views of the Empire State Building from the rooftop bar of Metro Grill (1-212 947 2500).

Hotel services *Beauty salon. Complimentary breakfast. Fitness centre. Library. Ticket desk. Valet.* **Room services** *High-speed wireless internet. Refrigerator.*

Hotel Pennsylvania

401 Seventh Avenue, between 32nd & 33rd Streets (1-212 736 5000/1-800 223 8585/www.hotelpenn. com). Subway: A, C, E, 1, 2, 3 to 34th Street-Penn Station. **Rates** $129-$200 single/double; $350-$1,000 suite. **Rooms** 1,700. **Credit** AmEx, DC, Disc, MC, V. **Map** p404 D25 ⑰

One of the city's largest hotels. Its reasonable rates and convenient location (directly opposite Madison Square Garden and Penn Station) make it popular for tourists. Rooms are basic but pleasant. The hotel's Café Rouge Ballroom once hosted such greats as Duke Ellington and the Glenn Miller Orchestra.

Hotel services *Gift shop. Pet-friendly. Ticket desk. Valet.* **Room services** *Internet.*

Hotel QT

125 West 45th Street, between Sixth & Seventh Avenues (1-212 354 2323/www.hotelqt.com). Subway: N, Q, R, W, 42nd Street S, 1, 2, 3, 7, 9 to 42nd Street-Times Square. **Rates** $125-$285 single/double; $250-$375 suite. **Rooms** 140. **Credit** AmEx, Disc, MC, V. **Map** p404 D23 ⑱

Celebrity hotelier André Balazs has mastered almost every type of property, from hip LA hotels (the Standard) to art deco resorts (the Raleigh) in Miami to luxury condominiums in Manhattan. This year he's taking a stab at a youth hostel: well, one with Egyptian cotton sheets, flat-screen TVs and a lobby pool with underwater music. Yep, rooms start at just $125 – a shockingly low price for a midtown hotel. This brand new stylish hotel for the budget-minded traveller is the last thing you'd expect to find in the middle of Times Square. That and the trippy corridors, which get smaller as you get to your room. Which is also likely to be narrow, but with fittings well adapted to the space. **Photo** *p59.*

Hotel services *Complimentary breakfast. Fitness centre. Magazine library. Pool.* **Room services** *Flat-screen TVs. Two-line speakerphones.*

Hotel Thirty Thirty

30 E 30th Street, between Madison Avenue & Park Avenue South (1-212 689 1900/1-800 497 6028/ www.thirtythirty-nyc.com). Subway: 6 to 28th Street. **Rates** $110-$215 single/double; $160-$305 suite. **Rooms** 250. **Credit** AmEx, DC, Disc, MC, V. **Map** p404 E25 ⑲

Before it became a tony hotel, Thirty Thirty was a residence for single women, and 60 tenants still live here. Ambient music sets the tone in the spare, fashionable, block-long lobby. Rooms are small but sleek and complemented by clean lines and textured fabrics. Executive-floor rooms are slightly larger, with nifty workspaces and slate bathrooms. The hotel's restaurant, Zanna, serves Mediterranean fare.

Hotel services *Complimentary pass to nearby gym. Florist. Ticket desk.* **Room services** *CD player. Internet.*

Hudson

356 W 58th Street, between Eighth & Ninth Avenues (1-212 554 6000/www.hudsonhotel.com). Subway: A, B, C, D, 1 to 59th Street-Columbus Circle. **Rates** $155-$295 single/double; $330-$5,000 suite. **Rooms** 803. **Credit** AmEx, DC, Disc, MC, V. **Map** p405 C22 ㊿

Sure, the rooms get points for looks, but just try turning around, or even finding a place to put down your suitcase. Outside of its teeny bedrooms, though, the Hudson has lots to offer. A lush courtyard is shaded with enormous potted trees, and a rooftop terrace overlooks the Hudson River, and a glass-ceilinged lobby with imported English ivy is crawling with beautiful people. The Hudson Cafeteria and the three on-site bars lure the fabulous. This is the third New York palace in Ian Schrager's hip-hotel kingdom, which includes Morgans and the Royalton.

Hotel services *Fitness centre. Mobile phone rental. Rooftop terrace.* **Room services** *CD player. Internet.* **Other locations**: Morgans, 237 Madison Avenue, between 37th & 38th Streets (1-212 686 0300/1-800 334 3408); Royalton, 44 W 44th Street, between Fifth & Sixth Avenues (1-212 869 4400/1-800635 9013).

Lose yourself in modern pleasure at the luxurious **W New York** chain. *See p65.*

Marcel

201 E 24th Street, at Third Avenue (1-212 696 3800/www.nychotels.com). Subway: 6 to 23rd Street. **Rates** $185-$250 single/double. **Rooms** 97. **Credit** AmEx, DC, Disc, MC, V. **Map** p404 F26 ⑤
Frequented by fashion-industry types, because of its easy access to the Flatiron and Garment Districts, the Marcel features compact rooms with nice touch-es like modern wood furniture and multicoloured, padded headboards. An added bonus is the complimentary espresso bar in the lobby that's always open. You'll find the same chic perks and low prices at four sister hotels: Ameritania Hotel, Amsterdam Court, the Moderne and the Bentley Hotel (*see p71*). **Hotel services** *Espresso bar. Ticket desk.* **Room services** *CD player. PlayStation. VCR on request.*

Home Sweet Harlem

Just a quick subway ride from the crowds and tiresome hotel chains of central Manhattan lies a neighbourhood rich in history, abounding in brownstones and brimming with energy. It's Harlem, and it's back in full swing. The latest – and best – way to get an authentic taste of uptown life is to stay at a freshly renovated bed and breakfast. For far less than the price of a beige-on-beige midtown room, you can tap into the heart of residential life in a vibrant urban neighbourhood.

There's a lot going on uptown these days. New residents and dedicated long-time inhabitants are restoring this once-blighted 'hood to its historic grandeur. Harlem Week – originally the first week in August – has now extended informally to fill the entire month with free outdoor concerts, street fairs, walking tours, a film festival and the largest African-American book fair in the country, drawing over 40,000 people. The Studio Museum in Harlem (see p145) anchors a burgeoning art scene; the famed Apollo Theater (see p314) jumps with performances by musical artists as diverse as Al Green and Morrissey; while black church services and gospel brunches draw visitors by the busload. You can bulk up on soul food at famous diners nearby, like Amy Ruth's or Pan Pan (500 Malcolm X Blvd [Lenox Avenue], at 135th Street), where Alicia Keys shot her You Don't Know My Name video.

Harlem may not have a hotel, but a handful of enterprising locals have turned their historic brownstones into bed and breakfasts, with a personal service and, in some cases, superluxe amenities, all within walking distance of Harlem's best-known landmarks. Three of the B&Bs listed below are in central Harlem, near 125th Street; the fourth, the Harlem Landmark Guest House, is further north, on Sugar Hill (at 145th Street), Harlem's historic Gold Coast. Harlem Landmark is also the only one to serve a breakfast included in the room rate. Both 102Brownstone and Efuru Guest House refer guests to Settepani (1-917 492 4806), the café-pâtisserie across the street (102 provides a coupon for a free continental breakfast there), while the Harlem Flophouse offers a home-cooked breakfast for an extra charge. All four request deposits ranging from 20 to 50 per cent and suggest booking at least a month in advance. (Word to the wise: many deposits are non-refundable after a certain time, so cancellations may cost you.)

Efuru Guest House

106 W 120th Street, at Malcolm X Blvd (Lenox Avenue) (1-212 961 9855/www.efuru-nyc.com). Subway: 2, 3 to 116th Street. **Rates** $95-$125 double with shared or private bath. **Rooms** 3. **Credit** MC, V. **Map** p407 D14 ❽❻

Efuru, a Nigerian word meaning 'daughter of heaven', is the brainchild of owner Lydia Smith, who bought the once-abandoned property through a lottery system in the late '90s and then endured a five-year renovation process. The result is a homey inn where guests can enjoy total privacy – each garden-level room has an entrance and patio – or mingle in a communal living room decorated with cosy antique couches and a working fireplace.

The three suites, painted in serene hues of green and blue, are basic but clean and comfy. All have queen beds and refrigerators, most have private baths and some have a kitchenette. The parlour floor is sometimes rented for parties or art exhibitions.

B&B services *Garden. High-speed internet. Kitchenette in some rooms. TV in rooms.*
Nearby attractions Apollo Theater. Bayou restaurant. Lenox Lounge jazz club. 125th Street shopping. Studio Museum in Harlem.

Harlem Flophouse

242 W 123rd Street, between Adam Clayton Powell Jr Boulevard (Seventh Avenue) & Frederick Douglass Boulevard (Eighth Avenue) (1-212 662 0678/www.harlemflophouse. com). Subway: A, B, C, D to 125th Street. **Rates** *$100 single with shared bath; $125 double with shared bath.* **Rooms** *4.* **Credit** *MC, V.* **Map** *p407 D14* ⑰

The dark-wood interior, moody lighting and lilting jazz make the Flophouse feel like a 1930s speakeasy. Owner René Calvo, a globe-trotting thespian and former graphic designer, has created a sleepy hideaway filled with artefacts from his travels. The airy suites have restored tin ceilings, glamorous chandeliers and working sinks in antique cabinets. For $15 a person ($25 per couple), you can eat a home-cooked breakfast in the communal dining room or garden. Want to stay in your pjs? A staff member will bring your meal to your room. **Photo** below.

B&B services *Garden. High-speed wireless internet. Laundry service. Private sink and dressing areas.*

Nearby attractions Apollo Theater. Harlem USAMall. Kitchenette Uptown restaurant. Studio Museum in Harlem.

Harlem Landmark Guest House

437 W 147th Street, at Convent Avenue (1-212 694 8800). Subway: A, B, C, D to 145th Street. **Rates** *$125-$175 double.* **Rooms** *12.* **Credit** *AmEx, MC, V.* **Map** *p408 C10* ⑧⑧

In 2002, when the Duncan-White family purchased this 1893 Romanesque-revival house, relatives from far and wide started visiting. The Duncan-Whites had so many guests, they decided to convert their single-family home and adjacent building into a 12-room guesthouse (which has recently doubled in size). Tall stamped-tin ceilings, mosaic-tiled fireplaces, elegantly carved banisters and original wood floors are redolent of the past. Each room is named after an icon of African-American music: the Ella Fitzgerald Egyptian suite features a private jacuzzi set below a skylight; the Nat 'King' Cole honeymoon suite is decked out with an antique four-poster bed.

B&B services *Continental breakfast. In-room massage. Jacuzzi. Private on-site Pilates instruction (by appointment). Spray-on tanning.*

Nearby attractions Hamilton Grange (287 Convent Avenue, at 142nd Street, 1-212 666 1640). Londel's Supper Club. Strivers' Row.

102Brownstone

102 W 118th Street at Malcolm X Blvd (Lenox Avenue) (1-212 662 4223/www.102 brownstone.com). Subway: 2, 3 to 116th Street. **Rates** *$200 suite; $250 studio apartment.* **Rooms** *6.* **Credit** *AmEx, MC, V.* **Map** *p407 D14* ⑳

Located near Marcus Garvey Park on tree-lined street, 102 features five substantial suites, all newly renovated and individually themed by lively proprietor Lizette Lanoue, who owns and lives in the 1892 Greek Revival row house with her husband. Individual rooms include the Zen Suite, which combines Japanese accents and antique Chinese furniture. The Luna Studio has deep burgundy walls, velvet curtains and leopard-print rugs. The showpiece of 102 is the Café Au Lait, a two-bedroom apartment, with full kitchen.

B&B services *DVD player. High-speed internet. Jacuzzi. Kitchenette in some rooms.*

Nearby attractions Studio Museum. Amy Ruth's restaurant. Harlemade boutique. Marcus Garvey Park. Native restaurant. St Martin's Episcopal Church (230 Malcolm X Blvd [Lenox Avenue], at 122nd Street).

Other locations: Ameritania Hotel, 230 W 54th Street, at Broadway (1-888 664 6835); Amsterdam Court, 226 W 50th Street, between Broadway & Eighth Avenue (1-888 664 6835); Moderne, 243 W 55th Street, between Broadway & Eighth Avenue (1-888 664 6835).

Roosevelt Hotel

45 E 45th Street, at Madison Avenue (1-212 661 9600/1-888 833 3969/www.theroosevelthotel.com). Subway: 42nd Street S, 4, 5, 6, 7 to 42nd Street-Grand Central. **Rates** *$159-$419 single/double; $350-$750 suite.* **Rooms** *1,013.* **Credit** *AmEx, DC, Disc, MC, V.* **Map** p404 E23 ⓒ2️⃣*
Several films have been shot here, including *Wall Street*, *The French Connection* and, more recently, *Maid in Manhattan*. Built in 1924, the enormous hotel was once a haven for celebs and socialites, and a certain nostalgic grandeur lives on in the lobby, which is decked with fluted columns and acres of marble. Teddy's Table serves light bites, and the Madison Club Lounge (1-212 885 6192) dispenses cocktails in a gentleman's club-like setting.
Hotel services *Ballroom. Fitness centre. Gift shop. Ticket desk. Valet.* **Room services** *High-speed wireless internet. PlayStation. Room service (24hrs).*

Budget (less than $100)

Carlton Arms Hotel

160 E 25th Street, at Third Avenue (1-212 679 0680/www.carltonarms.com). Subway: 6 to 23rd Street. **Rates** *$70-$80 single; $85-$99 double; $110-$120 triple.* **Rooms** *54.* **Credit** *MC, V.* **Map** p404 F26 ⓒ3️⃣*
The Carlton Arms Art Project started in the late 1970s, when a small group of creative types brought new paint and fresh ideas to a run-down shelter. Today, the site is home to a bohemian hotel with themed spaces (check out the English-cottage room). Discounts are offered for students, overseas guests and patrons on weekly stays. Most guests share baths; tack on an extra $15 for a private lavatory. Rooms are usually booked early, so reserve in advance.
Hotel services *Safe. Telephone in lobby.*

Gershwin Hotel

7 E 27th Street, between Fifth & Madison Avenues (1-212 545 8000/www.gershwinhotel.com). Subway: N, R, W, 6 to 28th Street. **Rates** *$33-$53 per person in 4- to 8-bed dorm; $99-$200 for 1-3 people in private room; $179-$289 suite.* **Rooms** *58 beds in dorms; 133 private.* **Credit** *AmEx, MC, V.* **Map** p404 E26 ⓒ4️⃣*
Works by Lichtenstein line the hallways, and an original Warhol soup-can painting hangs in the lobby of this funky Pop Art-themed budget hotel. Rates are extremely reasonable for a location just off Fifth Avenue. All rooms received a facelift in 2005, which brought in new chairs and upholstery. If you can afford a suite, book the Lindfors (named after the building's designer), which has screen-printed walls and a sitting room. Just off the lobby, but unaffiliated, is Gallery at the Gershwin, a bar and lounge with glowing countertops and mod Lucite orbs.
Hotel services *Internet kiosk. Transportation desk.*

Hotel 31

120 E 31st Street, between Park Avenue South & Lexington Avenue (1-212 685 3060/www.hotel31.com). Subway: 6 to 33rd Street. **Rates** *$85-$120 single/double; $125-$140 triple.* **Rooms** *60.* **Credit** *MC, V.* **Map** p404 E25 ⓒ5️⃣*
For review, *see p54* Hotel 17.

Murray Hill Inn

143 E 30th Street, between Lexington & Third Avenues (1-212 683 6900/1-888 996 6376/www.nyinns.com). Subway: 6 to 28th Street. **Rates** *$79-$95 double with shared bath; $95-$149 single/double with private bath.* **Rooms** *50.* **Credit** *AmEx, MC, V.* **Map** p404 F25 ⓒ6️⃣*
A recent renovation added hardwood floors and new bathrooms – most of which are private – to this affordable inn. Discounted weekly and monthly rates are available. Book well in advance, or try the sister locations: Amsterdam Inn, Central Park Hostel and Union Square Inn (*see p73* and *p55*).
Hotel services *Complimentary breakfast. High-speed wireless internet. Flat-panel TVs.*

Pickwick Arms

230 E 51st Street, between Second & Third Avenues (1-212 355 0300/1-800 742 5945/www.pickwickarms.com). Subway: E, V to Lexington Avenue-53rd Street; 6 to 51st Street. **Rates** *$79-$119 single; $139-$145 double.* **Rooms** *370.* **Credit** *AmEx, DC, MC, V.* **Map** p404 F23 ⓒ7️⃣*
Rooms at this no-frills hotel are clean and bright, and many have baths. (Some share an adjoining facility; otherwise, the lavatories are down the hall.) There are two on-site restaurants and a rooftop garden.
Hotel services *Internet in lobby.*

Hostels

Big Apple Hostel

119 W 45th Street, between Sixth & Seventh Avenues (1-212 302 2603/www.bigapplehostel.com). Subway: B, D, F, V to 42nd Street; N, Q, R, S, W, 1, 2, 3, 7 to Times Square-42nd Street. **Rates** *$35 dorm; $92 private room.* **Rooms** *112 dorm beds; 11 private.* **Credit** *AmEx, DC, Disc, MC, V.* **Map** p404 D23 ⓒ8️⃣*
Increasingly popular with backpackers, this basic hostel is lacking in frills, but the rooms are spotless and as cheap as they come. The Big Apple puts you just steps from the Theater District and the bright lights of Times Square. Beware if you're travelling in August: dorm rooms are without air-conditioning. Take refuge in the breezy back patio, equipped with a grill for summer barbecues. Linens are provided, but remember to pack a towel.
Hostel services *Air-conditioning in private rooms.*

Chelsea Center

313 W 29th Street, between Eighth & Ninth Avenues (1-212 643 0214/www.chelseacenterhostel.com). Subway: A, C, E to 34th Street-Penn Station; 1 to 28th Street. **Rates** *$33 per person in dorm.* **Beds** *20.* **No credit cards.** **Map** p404 D25 ⓒ9️⃣*

Re-live your student days in a small, women-only hostel with shared rooms and a communal kitchen and living area. Bathrooms are clean, and a patio garden is out back. Rooms are non-smoking and lack air-con, but the fee includes breakfast.
Hostel services *Garden. Internet. Kitchen. TV.*

Above 59th Street

Expensive ($200 to $350)

Melrose Hotel

140 E 63rd Street, between Lexington & Third Avenues (1-212 838 5700/www.melrosehotel.com). Subway: F to Lexington Avenue-63rd Street; N, R, W to Lexington Avenue-59th Street; 4, 5, 6 to 59th Street. **Rates** $219-$319 single/double; $349-$1,200 suite. **Credit** AmEx, DC, Disc, MC, V. **Map** p405 F21 ⑥⓪
From 1927 to 1981, this was the Barbizon Hotel, an exclusive women-only hotel and host to the likes of Grace Kelly and Liza Minnelli. In 2002, it reopened as the Melrose, spiffed up with cherry-wood furniture, gilded mirrors and the original marble floor restored. Tower suites boast landscaped balconies with Corinthian pillars and views of the city lights. The Library Bar offers cocktails and a full menu.
Hotel services *CD/video library. Fitness centre. Spa. Ticket desk. Valet.* **Room services** *CD player. High-speed internet. PlayStation. VCR.*

On the Ave Hotel

2178 Broadway, at 77th Street (1-212 362 1100/1-800 509 7598/www.ontheave-nyc.com). Subway: 1 to 79th Street. **Rates** $225-$365 single/double; $275-$395 suite; $425-$795 penthouse. **Rooms** 266. **Credit** AmEx, DC, Disc, MC, V. **Map** p405 C19 ⑥①
Stylish additions here include industrial-style bathroom sinks and penthouse suites with fantastic balcony views of Central Park. (All guests have access to a balcony on the 16th floor.) On the Ave's Citylife Hotel Group sibling is Hotel Thirty Thirty (*see p66*).
Hotel services *Video library.* **Room services** *CD player. Complimentary newspaper. High-speed internet. Plasma TV. VCR.*

Moderate ($100 to $200)

Bentley Hotel

500 E 62nd Street, at York Avenue (1-212 644 6000/1-888 664 6835/www.nychotels.com). Subway: F to Lexington-63rd Street; 4, 5, 6 to 59th Street. **Rates** $150-$250 single/double; $200-$275 suite. **Rooms** 200. **Credit** AmEx, DC, Disc, MC, V. **Map** p405 G22 ⑥②
It's hard to notice anything in the Bentley's sleek rooms other than the sweeping vistas from the floor-to-ceiling windows. Converted from an office building in 1998, this slender 21-storey hotel is an ideal getaway for weary execs, thanks to solid sound-proofing and blackout shades. Sip cappuccinos in the mahogany-panelled library or take in even more views from the glittering rooftop restaurant.

Hotel services *Complimentary pass to nearby gym.* **Room services** *CD player. Complimentary newspaper. High-speed wireless internet.*
Other locations: Ameritania Hotel, 230 W 54th Street, at Broadway (1-888 664 6835); Amsterdam Court, 226 W 50th Street, between Broadway & Eighth Avenue (1-888 664 6835); Marcel (*see p67*); Moderne, 243 W 55th Street, between Broadway & Eighth Avenue (1-888 664 6835).

Country Inn the City

270 W 77th Street, between Broadway & West End Avenue (1-212 580 4183/1-800 572 4969/www. countryinnthecity.com). Subway: 1 to 79th Street. **Rates** $150-$210 single/double. **Rooms** 4. **No credit cards. Map** p405 C19 ⑥③
The name of this charming bed and breakfast on the West Side is actually quite telling: you can escape to the country without leaving the city. Four-poster beds, flagons of brandy, and moose heads in the hallways make this intimate inn a special retreat.
Room services *Complimentary local phone calls. Kitchenette.*

Hotel Beacon

2130 Broadway, between 74th and 75th Streets (1-212 787 1100/1-800 572 4969/www.beaconhotel. com). Subway: 1, 2, 3 to 72nd Street. **Rates** $180-$235 single/double; $250-$500 suite. **Rooms** 245. **Credit** AmEx, DC, Disc, MC, V. **Map** p405 C20 ⑥④
The Hotel Beacon offers very good value in a desirable residential neighbourhood that's only a short walk from Central and Riverside Parks. Rooms are clean and spacious and include marble baths. For only $5, guests can purchase a pass to the nearby Synergy gym. But make sure you quell your post-workout hunger at the classic diner Viand Café.
Hotel services *Babysitting. internet.* **Room services** *Kitchenette.*

Hotel Belleclaire

250 W 77th Street, at Broadway (1-212 362 7700/ www.hotelbelleclaire.com). Subway: 1 to 79th Street. **Rates** $100-$119 single with shared bath; $189-$219 single/double with private bath; $289-$229 suite. **Rooms** 200. **Credit** AmEx, DC, Disc, MC, V. **Map** p405 C19 ⑥⑤
Housed in a landmark building near Lincoln Center and Central Park, the sleek Belleclaire is a steal for savvy budget travellers. Rooms feature goose-down comforters, sleek padded headboards and mod lighting fixtures. Every room comes with a refrigerator – perfect for chilling your protein shake while you're hitting the new state-of-the-art fitness centre.
Hotel services *Fitness centre. Gift shop. Massage service. Mobile phone rental.* **Room services** *CD player. Direct-dial phone numbers. Internet. Nintendo.*

Lucerne

201 W 79th Street, at Amsterdam Avenue (1-212 875 1000/1-800 492 8122/www.thelucernehotel. com). Subway: 1 to 79th Street. **Rates** $180-$280 single/double; $220-$400 suite. **Rooms** 187. **Credit** AmEx, DC, Disc, MC, V. **Map** p405 C19 ⑥⑥

Chain gang

Many of the familiar global chains have locations in New York, and although they don't offer oodles of cachet, they do have reasonable rates and reliable amenities.

The scruffy-trendy Lower East Side may be the last place you'd expect to find a HoJo's, but the Howard Johnson's Express Inn (135 E Houston Street, between First & Second Avenues, 1-212 358 8844, www.hojo.com) is clean and affordable and provides a complimentary breakfast. High-end rooms have two double beds and a jacuzzi.

It's hard to miss the assertive 45-storey tower of the Westin New York at Times Square (270 W 43rd Street, at Eighth Avenue, 1-888 627 7149, www.westinny.com; pictured). The lobby boasts a soaring seven-storey atrium, while rooms have flat-panel televisions and, above the 15th floor, amazing views of Times Square.

Farther north, in Hell's Kitchen, the Holiday Inn Midtown (440 W 57th Street, between Ninth and Tenth Avenues, 1-800 465 4329, www.hi57.com) offers a heated outdoor pool, a fitness centre and two restaurants.

If it's romance you're after, hop over the East River to downtown Brooklyn's New York Marriott at the Brooklyn Bridge (333 Adams Street, between Tillary and Willoughby Streets, Brooklyn Heights, 1-718 246 7000, www.brooklynmarriott.com; pictured), where for an extra $99, your room can be showered with white rose petals, dotted with scented candles and furnished with bubble-bath supplies. A bottle of Aria Estate champagne completes the package.

The elaborate pre-war façade and ornate columns of this historic hotel may fool you into thinking the rooms are equally stunning. They are, however, far from fabulous. Instead, seek style in the hotel's breezy ground-floor French bistro, Nice Matin (1-212 873 6423), or on the rooftop patio, which offers views of Central Park and the Hudson River.
Hotel services *Fitness centre.* **Room services** *High-speed internet. Plasma TV.*

Wyman House

36 Riverside Drive, at 76th Street (1-212 799 8281/ www.wymanhouse.com). Subway: 1, 2, 3 to 72nd Street. **Rates** $175-$250 single/double. **Rooms** 6. **No credit cards. Map** p404 B20 ⑰
Since 1986, Pamela and Ron Wyman have hosted many happy travellers at their home (the building of which dates back to 1888). Each of the six apartment-style suites available has a unique shabby-chic

decor. The Conservatory is the largest suite and boasts sunny yellow walls and a Moroccan-themed bathroom. Note that all rooms are reached by stairs, the minimum booking is for three nights, and children under 12 are not allowed in the hotel.
Hotel services *Complimentary breakfast first day of stay. Complimentary local phone calls.* **Room services** *High-speed wireless internet. Kitchenette. VCR.*

Budget ($100 or less)

Amsterdam Inn

340 Amsterdam Avenue, at 76th Street (1-212 579 7500/www.amsterdaminn.com). Subway: 1 to 79th Street. **Rates** $69-$89 single/double with shared bath; $79-$149 with private bath. **Rooms** 30. **Credit** AmEx, MC, V. **Map** p405 C19 ⑱
For review, *see p70* Murray Hill Inn.

Hostels

Central Park Hostel

19 W 103rd Street, at Central Park West (1-212 678 0491/www.centralparkhostel.com). Subway: B, C to 103rd Street. **Rates** $26-$35 for a bed in shared room; $99-$129 private room with shared bath. **Beds** 250. **Credit** MC, V. **Map** p406 D16 ⑥⑨

Housed in a recently renovated brownstone, this tidy hostel offers dorm-style rooms that sleep four, six or eight people; private chambers with two beds are also available. All baths are shared.
Hostel services *Lockers. Travel desk.*

Hostelling International New York

891 Amsterdam Avenue, at 103rd Street (1-212 932 2300/www.hinewyork.org). Subway: 1 to 103rd Street. **Rates** $29-$40 dorm rooms; $120 family rooms; $135 private room with bath. **Beds** 624. **Credit** AmEx, DC, MC, V. **Map** p406 C16 ⑦⓪

This budget lodging is actually the city's only real hostel (ie a non-profit accommodation that belongs to the International Youth Hostel Federation), but it's also one of the most architecturally stunning. The gabled, Gothic-inspired brick-and-stone building spans the length of an entire city block. The immaculate rooms are spare but air-conditioned. There is a shared kitchen and a large backyard.
Hostel services *Café. Conference facility. Courtyard. Fax. Games room. Gift shop. Internet kiosk. Library. Lockers. Self-service laundry. Shuttles. Travel desk. TV lounge.* **Room services** *Air-conditioning.*

International House

500 Riverside Drive, at Tiemann Place (1-212 316 8436/www.ihouse-nyc.org). Subway: 1 to 125th Street. **Rates** $120-$130 single; $135-$145 double/suite. **Rooms** 11. **Credit** MC, V. **Map** p407 B13 ⑦①

Primarily a dormitory for foreign graduate students, this housing facility is a good reliable bet for short-term summer travellers (when all the students have checked out). Located on a peaceful block overlooking Grant's Tomb and the small but well-tended Sakura Park, this hostel has simple rooms with private bathrooms and refrigerators.
Hostel services *Bar. Cafeteria. Self-service laundry.* **Room services** *Air-conditioning. Cable TV.*

Jazz on the Park Hostel

36 W 106th Street, between Central Park West & Manhattan Avenue (1-212 932 1600/www.jazz hostel.com). Subway: B, C to 103rd Street. **Rates** $25-$38, 4- to 12-bed dorm; $50-$85 2-bed dorm (maximum 2 people); $110 private room with bath. **Beds** 310. **Credit** MC, V. **Map** p406 D16 ⑦②

Jazz on the Park might be the trendiest hostel in the city – the lounge is outfitted like a space-age techno club and sports a piano and pool table. But some visitors have been known to complain about the customer service, so make sure to double-check your room type and check-in date before you arrive. In summer, the back patio hosts a weekly barbecue. Linens and a continental breakfast are complimentary, while lockers come at a surcharge.

Hostel services *Air-conditioning. Café. Complimentary breakfast. Fax. Internet. Private lockers. Self-service laundry. TV room.*
Other locations: Jazz on the Town Hostel, 307 E 14th Street, between First & Second Avenues (1-212 228 2780).

Brooklyn

Akwaaba Mansion

347 MacDonough Street, between Lewis & Stuyvesant Avenues, Bedford-Stuyvesant (1-718 455 5958/www.akwaaba.com). Subway: A, C to Utica Avenue. **Rates** $150 single/double weekdays; $165 single/double weekends (each additional person $30, maximum 4 people). **Rooms** 4. **Credit** MC, V. **Map** p410 W10 ⑦③

Akwaaba means 'welcome,' in Ghanaian, a fitting name for this gorgeous restored 1860s mansion with a wide screened-in porch and flower gardens. The individually themed rooms are decorated with African artefacts and textiles. A hearty Southern-style breakfast and complimentary afternoon tea are served in the dining room or on the porch.

Awesome Bed & Breakfast

136 Lawrence Street, between Fulton & Willoughby Streets, Fort Greene, Brooklyn (1-718 858 4859/ www.awesome-bed-and-breakfast.com). Subway: A, C, F to Jay Street-Borough Hall; M, R to Lawrence Street; 2, 3 to Hoyt Street. **Rates** $72-$150 single/double; $150-$200 triple/quad. **Rooms** 7. **Credit** AmEx, MC, V. **Map** p410 T10 ⑦④

'Awesome' isn't normally a word used to describe a bed and breakfast, but this bi-level guesthouse is an exception. The themed rooms could be a setting for MTV's *The Real World*, with details like giant daisies and purple drapes. The equally snazzy bathrooms are communal, and a complimentary breakfast is delivered to your door promptly at 8am. Plans to double the capacity are in the works.

Bed & Breakfast on the Park

113 Prospect Park West, between 6th & 7th Streets, Park Slope, Brooklyn (1-718 499 6115/www.bbnyc. com). Subway: F to Seventh Avenue. **Rates** $155-$225 single/double; $250-$325 suite. **Rooms** 7. **Credit** AmEx, MC, V (cheques preferred). **Map** p410 T12 ⑦⑤

Staying at this 1895 parkside brownstone is like taking up residence on the set of *The Age of Innocence*. The parlour floor is crammed with antique furniture, and guest rooms are outfitted with love seats and canopy beds swathed in French linens.

Union Street Bed & Breakfast

405 Union Street, between Hoyt & Smith Streets, Carroll Gardens (1-718 852 8406). Subway: F, G to Carroll Street. **Rates** $100 single; $165 double. **Rooms** 7. **Credit** AmEx, MC, V. **Map** p410 S10 ⑦⑥

This quasi-Victorian-style inn is housed in an 1898 brownstone with a pleasant back garden. Room prices decrease with each additional night's stay. Great restaurants are just steps away on Smith Street, Brooklyn's restaurant row.

Sightseeing

Features

'Imagine' memorial mosaic. *See p132.*

Introduction

How to get the most out of the city that never sleeps.

The variety and scope of places to visit in New York City can be dizzying to a newcomer. Since whole days can be spent wondering through the Metropolitan Museum of Art, Soho or the Bronx Zoo, you'll need to draw up a plan. Start by listing your must-see places and then be sure to consult the guide for hours of operation (also *see p80* **Timing is everything**). Whether your weakness is window-shopping, art, jazz, food or architecture, the options we list here are sure to keep you busy. Iconic New York – the Empire State Building, the Brooklyn Bridge, Ellis Island – almost never fail to satisfy even the most jaded souls. Just be sure to save a chunk of time to roam around without a schedule; some of the best attractions this city has to offer are the hidden surprises it has waiting for you to discover.

THE LIE OF THE LAND
New York City is made up of five boroughs: Brooklyn, the Bronx, Manhattan, Queens and Staten Island. What the island of Manhattan lacks in landmass (it's the smallest of the bunch), it more than makes up for in cultural and commercial power. Manhattan is bordered by New Jersey, just over the Hudson River, to the west; Brooklyn and Queens are due east, on the other side of the East River; the Bronx is just to the north, above the Harlem River, and Staten Island is south, at the mouth of New York harbour. Within each borough, areas of varying size are broken down into neighbourhoods like Midtown, Chinatown and the Upper East Side (*see p78* **New York at a glance**), all marked on the maps at the back of this book.

STREET SMARTS
Setting out into our teeming metropolis, we guarantee that you are going to feel overwhelmed if not downright lost. Take heart: even New Yorkers get turned around and frequently can't remember which way is which. Your best bet is to take a few moments to study our maps on pages 402 to 412 before hitting the streets and to have a look at the **Getting Around** section (*see p368*) in the directory located in the back of this book.

VISITING MUSEUMS
Visiting several venues in a single day can be exhausting. Similarly, it's self-defeating to attempt to hit all the major collections during

one visit to an institution as large as the Met or the American Museum of Natural History. So plan, pace yourself, and don't forget to eat: a host of excellent museum cafés and restaurants afford convenient breaks. Delicious spots for refuelling include Sarabeth's at the **Whitney Museum of American Art** (*see p185*); the elegant Café Sabarsky at the **Neue Galerie** (*see p135*); the **Jewish Museum**'s Café Weissman (*see p136*); and a more formal option, the Modern, at the **Museum of Modern Art** (MoMA; *see p124*). It may be tempting to save museums for a rainy day, but remember that most sites offer cool, air-conditioned relief on sticky summer days and cosy warmth come winter.

If the weather is too gorgeous to stay indoors, bear in mind that gardens are the hidden gems of several New York museums. The Brooklyn Museum abuts the **Brooklyn Botanic Garden** (*see p154*) where enticements include a Japanese garden complete with pavilion, wooden bridges and a Shinto shrine. The **Cloisters** (*see p149*), in northern Manhattan's Fort Tryon Park, was John D Rockefeller's gift to New York. The reconstructed monastery houses the Met's stellar collection of medieval art. In summer, bring a picnic and relax on lush grounds that provide spectacular views of the Hudson River and the rocky cliffs of New Jersey's Palisades.

Brace yourself for local admission prices; they can be steep (tickets to the recently renovated MoMA cost $20 per adult). This is because most of the city's museums are privately funded and receive little or no government support. Even so, a majority of them, including MoMA, the Whitney and the Guggenheim, either waive admission fees or make them voluntary at least one evening a week. Most museums also offer discounts to students and senior citizens with valid IDs. And although the Met suggests a $12 donation for adults, you can pay what you wish whenever you visit.

Nothing is more exciting than discovering the secrets of a new museum on your own, but many institutions offer tours that are both entertaining and educational. For example, the audio tour at the **Ellis Island Immigration Museum** (*see p87*) and the (mandatory) guided tours at the **Lower East Side Tenement Museum** (*see p103*) and the **Museum of**

Sightseeing

New York at a glance

Broadway & Times Square (p118)
Night-time under the world's most famous array of twinkling lights is positively thrilling.

Chelsea (p110)
The city's gayest neighbourhood is also home to hundreds of art galleries west of Tenth Avenue, between 19th and 26th Streets.

Chinatown (p101)
You'll feel like you are in another country walking among the Asian restaurants and groceries here. Canal Street offers myriad designer knock-offs.

East Village (p104)
Tompkins Square Park (just off Avenue A) is the heart of this young, edgy 'hood. No specific tourist destinations to mention (save CBGB, the infamous punk-rock club). Fun to wander.

Fifth Avenue (p122)
The well-heeled still shop here (Tiffany's, Bergdorf Goodman), but mall stores are nudging in. Landmarks a-plenty: the Empire State Building, Rockefeller Center, St Patrick's Cathedral.

Greenwich Village (p106)
Leafy streets and bohemian Washington Square Park, where folks embrace a slower pace. Literary associations abound.

Harlem (p144)
Broad, sunny boulevards with stunning examples of late 19th- and early 20th-century architecture. And soul food galore.

Lower East Side (p102)
See how waves of immigrants lived at the Lower East Side Tenement Museum. Today, young hipsters have recently opened up all kinds of indie-boutiques and hot new bars but the delis and pickle shops remain.

Midtown East (p127)
Lots of office buildings and bustling streets, but it's the United Nations and Grand Central Terminal that beckon.

Soho (p97)
The city's former art district is now a must-see stop for trendy shoppers. Tons of cafés and restaurants to cool your heels.

Tribeca (p97)
Actor Robert De Niro put this area on the map when he debuted the Tribeca Film Festival here in 2002. Chic bars and restaurants nestled between enormous cast-iron warehouses (now expensive residential lofts) are worth a look.

Upper East Side (p134)
Super-rich and important, chock-full of embassies and billionaires. Dozens of museums, including the Metropolitan Museum of Art and the Guggenheim, up the culture quotient.

Upper West Side (p139)
Lovely turn-of-the-century architecture and lush green havens on either side (Central Park to the east, Riverside Park to the west).

Wall Street (p93)
The oldest area of the city and the epicentre of capitalism. Offers a glimpse of traders (between trades) and a chance to stroll narrow streets darkened by tall skyscrapers. Home of the New York Stock Exchange and Trinity Church, where the signatories of the Declaration of Independence are buried.

West Village & Meatpacking District (p109)
Quiet, cobblestoned streets offer plenty of opportunity to peer into picturesque 19th-century brownstones. Comes alive after sundown, when throngs flock to the trendy restaurants and bars along Ninth Avenue.

Beyond Manhattan
Particularly worth the trip over to Brooklyn are **Williamsburg** (see *p155*), with dozens of über-hip cafés, bars and shops; the promenade in **Brooklyn Heights** (*p160*) and its breathtaking views of lower Manhattan; and the Brooklyn Bridge; and Coney Island's delightful **Astroland Amusement Park** (*p159*).

Jewish Heritage (*see p93*) offer fascinating insights into NYC's immigrant roots.

Most New York museums are closed on major US holidays (*see p383* **Holidays**). Nevertheless, some institutions are open on certain Monday holidays, such as Columbus Day and Presidents' Day. A few places, like **Dia:Beacon** and the **Queens Museum of Art**, change their hours seasonally; it's wise to call before setting out.

Security has been tightened at most museums. Guards at all public institutions will ask you to open your bag or backpack for inspection; umbrellas and large bags must be checked (free of charge) at a cloakroom.

Most museums are accessible to people with disabilities, and furnish free wheelchairs.

PACKAGE DEALS

If you're planning to take in multiple museums – and you're likely to add a Circle Line tour or a visit to the Empire State Building (where you can bypass the first queue) – consider buying a nine-day **CityPass** for $53 ($41 6-17s, free under-6s). Similarly, the **New York Pass** covers admission to over 40 of the city's top attractions and cultural institutions, and provides discounts on shopping, eating and other activities. The card is $49 for the day ($39 2-12s) and $139 for the week ($99 2-12s). You can compare benefits and purchase at www.citypass.com and www.newyorkpass.com.

Timing is everything

Whether you're just visiting or you've lived here for years, figuring out the best time to go somewhere – the Empire State Building, a museum or a theatre box office – is tricky. With that in mind, we've approached our local experts for the inside scoop on getting into some of NYC's most popular happenings.

American Museum of Natural History

See p141 for listing.
Security guard Carmine Torrisi suggests, 'Start at 10 o'clock on any day and you'll be fine. Weekdays after 2pm are good also'. Whatever you do, stay away on the day after Thanksgiving – when 20,000 visitors descend on the place to pick over the bones.

Chelsea galleries

See p269 for listing.
Go on a Tuesday morning, which is the art world's equivalent of Monday morning. Chelsea is guaranteed to be a ghost town, and proprietors will be positively thrilled to see you.

Empire State Building

See p122 for listing.
The staff here advises lining up for the first viewing at 8.30am. (As if!) Other off-peak times include lunch and dinner hours Mondays through Wednesdays, and most times on cold winter days – with the exception of just before and just after Christmas. To avoid waiting in an endless line in the dreaded ESB basement, buy your tickets online and print them out from your computer.

Metropolitan Museum of Art

See p135 for listing.
Rule No.1: never go on a Sunday; crowds get so thick that the museum prohibits strollers. Staffers advise you to opt instead for weekdays – either early mornings or from 3pm to 4pm, to avoid endless busloads of schoolkids. Summer afternoons are ideal, but be aware that the museum café draws a lunchtime crowd.

The Nutcracker

See p264 for listing.
In-the-know parents advise those with kids to take advantage of the 6pm performances Tuesdays through Thursdays, rather than the matinées. To up your chances of getting in, attend during the first two weeks of December or after Christmas. (The show runs from 26 November to 2 January.)

Rockefeller Center Ice Rink

See p339 for listing.
'Morning is the quietest part of every day,' says Justin, who rents out skates at the rink. Also try weekdays between 2pm and 4pm – after lunch and before school is dismissed – or any afternoon when it's lightly raining, snowing or bitterly cold.

TKTS

See p382 for listing.
David LeShay, spokesperson for TKTS, suggests forgoing the Times Square booth and heading to the one at the South Street Seaport. Though a line forms at 11am when TKTS first opens, by noon the wait is down to about five minutes. If Times Square is more convenient for you, go after 6pm; shows often release more tickets late in the day.

Union Square Greenmarket

See p115 for listing.
Go on Monday, Wednesday or Friday. Lunchtime, predictably, is the busiest at the Greenmarket, as is that last frantic hour before the 6pm closing. Vendors say you'll have no trouble if you stick to mornings and early afternoons (2pm to 4pm). Or you could just enjoy the bustle at busy times.

Tour New York

Round round get around.

The possibilities for taking in the majestic sights of New York are seemingly endless. Whether you prefer traditional (the ubiquitous red double-decker bus) or offbeat (a pilgrimage to the East Village haunts frequented by your punk-rock heroes), there's a tour badge with your name on it. For additional inspiration, refer to the Around Town section of *Time Out New York* magazine, where you'll find a weekly listing of urban outings to suit all tastes.

By bicycle

For more city biking, *see p337* **Active sports**.

Bike the Big Apple

1-201 837 1133/www.bikethebigapple.com. **Tours** Call or visit website for schedule. **Tickets** $49-$69 (includes bicycle and helmet rental). **Credit** AmEx, DC, Disc, MC, V.

Licensed guides take cyclists through both historic and newly hip neighbourhoods. Half- and full-day rides are family-friendly and gently paced, and they can be customised to your interests and riding level. Check the website for seasonal events and deals.

Central Park Bike Tours

Bite of the Apple Tours (1-212 541 8759/www. centralparkbiketour.com). **Tours** *Apr-Oct* 10am, 1pm, 4pm daily. *Nov-Mar* by reservation only. **Tickets** $35; $20 under-15s (includes bicycle rental). **Credit** AmEx, Disc, MC, V.

Bite of the Apple focuses on Central Park. The main tour visits the John Lennon memorial at Strawberry Fields, Belvedere Castle and the Shakespeare Garden. Film buffs will enjoy the Central Park Movie Scenes Bike Tour (10am, 1pm, 4pm Sat, Sun), passing locations for *When Harry Met Sally...* and *Wall Street*. Most tours run a leisurely two hours; hard-core cyclists might consider the three-hour Manhattan Island Bicycle Tour ($45, by appointment only). Spanish-language tours are available.

By boat

Adirondack

Chelsea Piers, Pier 62, 22nd Street, at the Hudson River (1-646 336 5270/www.sail-nyc.com). Subway: C, E to 23rd Street. **Tours** *May-15 Oct* 1pm, 3.30pm, 6pm, 8.30pm Mon-Sat; 10.30am Sun. **Tickets** $35 for day sails; $45 for evening and Sunday-brunch sails. **Credit** AmEx, MC, V.

Built in 1994, the *Adirondack* is a beautiful three-masted replica of a classic 19th-century schooner. Sip your complimentary glass of wine (or beer) as the ship sails from Chelsea Piers to Battery Park, past Ellis Island, to the Statue of Liberty, and around to Governors Island and the Brooklyn Bridge.

Circle Line Cruises

Pier 83, 42nd Street, at the Hudson River (1-212 563 3200/www.circleline.com). Subway: A, C, E to 42nd Street-Port Authority. **Tours** Call or visit website for schedule. **Tickets** $28; $23 seniors; $15 children. **Credit** AmEx, DC, Disc, MC, V.

Circle Line's famed three-hour, guided circumnavigation of Manhattan is a great way to see the sights. Themed tours include a New Year's Eve cruise, a DJ dance party or a fall foliage ride to Bear Mountain in the Hudson Valley. From April to October, there's a fun 30-minute speedboat ride on *The Beast*. **Other locations**: South Street Seaport, Pier 16, by Burling Slip & Fulton Street (1-212 630 8888).

Walk his way

Justin Ferate has been giving tours for more than 20 years, and he knows his stuff – after all, he's the guy the Department of Consumer Affairs tapped to write the licensing test required for all city tour guides.

In addition to toting around that bounty of knowledge, he also brings a lot of character to his tours, marked by his dandyish elocution, bow tie and old-timey tales. His hokey jokes and tricks to get folks physically involved are often, he admits, 'pure shtick' – like when he plucks a participant from the group and the pair runs around Grand Central Terminal's main concourse to illustrate how the width of the floor tiles exactly matches the stride of a rushing commuter – but they make for a fun tour.

Starting from the familiar, Ferate veers off into what he calls 'the weirdness', while pointing out architectural and design details and quirky social history. He is the sort of guide who can linger over a statue for 15 minutes, so don't expect to hit all of the usual sites – just enjoy the trip. *1-212 223 2777/www.justins newyork.com.* **Tours** Free Grand Central tours are offered every Friday at 12.30pm. See website for additional tours.

The ultimate traveling companion.

MetroCard can take you to all the famous places in the entire city. And, with an Unlimited Ride Card, you can hop on and off New York City Transit subways and local buses as many times as you like, all day long. It's the fastest, least expensive way to see it all.

You can choose from several Unlimited Ride MetroCards, including our 1-Day Fun Pass and our 7-Day Unlimited Ride MetroCard.

You can buy MetroCard at many hotels, the New York Convention & Visitors Bureau (810 7th Avenue at 53rd Street), and the New York Transit Museum in Brooklyn Heights and the Museum's Gallery & Store at Grand Central Terminal. You can also buy it at subway station vending machines with your debit or credit card, or cash.

For more information, call 800-METROCARD (800-638-7622); in NYC, call 212-METROCARD.

www.mta.info

George E. Pataki
Governor, State of New York

Peter S. Kalikow
Chairman, MTA

NY Waterway
Pier 78, 38th Street, at the Hudson River (1-800 533 3779/www.nywaterway.com). Subway: A, C, E to 42nd Street-Port Authority. **Tours** Call or see web for schedule. **Tickets** 2-hr Manhattan cruise $26; $21 seniors; $13 children. **Credit** AmEx, Disc, MC, V.
The scenic two-hour ride makes a complete circuit around Manhattan's landmarks. A 60-minute tour focuses on the skyline of lower Manhattan.
Other locations: World Financial Center Pier, Pier 11, Wall Street.

Pioneer
South Street Seaport Museum, 207 Front Street, between Beekman & Fulton Streets (1-212 748 8786/www.southstreetseaportmuseum.org). Subway: A, C to Broadway-Nassau Street; J, M, Z, 2, 3, 4, 5 to Fulton Street. **Tours** Call for schedule. **Tickets** $30; $15 under-12s. **Credit** AmEx, MC, V.
Built in 1885, the 102ft *Pioneer* is the only iron-hulled merchant sailing ship still in existence. Sails billow as you cruise the East River and New York Harbor. Educational children's programmes also on offer.

Shearwater Sailing
North Cove, Hudson River, between Liberty & Vesey Streets (1-212 619 0885/1-800-544 1224/www.shearwatersailing.com). Subway: R/W to City Hall; 2, 3, 4, 5, A, C to Fulton Street/Broadway-Nassau Street. **Tours** 15 Apr-15-Oct five times daily. Call for schedule. **Tickets** $45; $25 children. **Credit** AmEx, DC, Disc, MC, V.
Set sail on the *Shearwater*, an 82ft luxury yacht built in 1929. The champagne brunch or full-moon sail are lovely ways to take in the skyline.

Staten Island Ferry
Battery Park, South Street, at Whitehall Street (1-718 727 2508/www.siferry.com). Subway: 1 to South Ferry; 4, 5 to Bowling Green. **Open** 24hrs daily. **Tickets** free.
During this commuter barge's 25-minute crossing, you get superb panoramas of lower Manhattan and the Statue of Liberty. Boats leave South Ferry at Battery Park. Call or see the website for schedules.

By bus

D3 Busline
1-212 533 1664/1-866 336 4837/www.d3busline.com. **Tours** 8pm-2am Fri, Sat. **Tickets** $60. **Credit** AmEx, MC, V.
A night out on the leather-seated 'trans-lounge limo bus' includes an open bar and a DJ, plus VIP entry into select Manhattan hotspots. The Brooklyn tour takes in area bars and nightclubs. The fee includes everything but drinks at the venues. Groups only.

Gray Line
777 Eighth Avenue, between 47th & 48th Streets (1-212 445 0848/1-800 669 0051 ext 3/www.graylinenewyork.com). Subway: A, C, E to 42nd Street-Port Authority. **Tours** Call or see web for schedule. **Tickets** $37-$81. **Credit** AmEx, Disc, MC, V.

This is your grandma's classic red double-decker (the line runs other buses too), but with something to interest everyone. Gray Line offers more than 20 bus tours, from a basic two-hour ride (with more than 40 hop-on, hop-off stops) to the guided Manhattan Comprehensive, which lasts eight and a half hours and includes lunch, admission to the United Nations tour and a boat ride to Ellis Island and the Statue of Liberty.

By helicopter, carriage or rickshaw

Liberty Helicopter Tours
Downtown Manhattan Heliport, Pier 6, East River, between Broad Street & Old Slip (1-212 967 6464/1-800 542 9933/www.libertyhelicopters.com). Subway: R, W to Whitehall Street; 1 to South Ferry. **Tours** *Jan, Feb* 9am-7pm daily. *Mar-Dec* 9am-9pm daily. **Tickets** $63-$169. **Credit** AmEx, MC, V.
There won't be any daredevil swooping and diving – Liberty's helicopters provide a fairly smooth flight – but the views are excitement enough. Even a five-minute ride (durations vary) is long enough to give you a thrilling look at the Empire State Building and Central Park.
Other locations: VIP Heliport, Twelfth Avenue, at 30th Street.

Manhattan Carriage Company
200 Central Park South, at Seventh Avenue (1-212 664 1149/www.ajnfineart.com/mcc.html). Subway: N, Q, R, W to 57th Street. **Tours** 10am-2am Mon-Fri; 8am-2am Sat, Sun. **Tickets** $40 per 20-minute ride (extended rides by reservation only). Hours and prices vary during holidays. **Credit** AmEx, MC, V (reserved tours only).
The beauty of Central Park seems even more romantic from the seat of a horse-drawn carriage. Choose your coach from those lined up on the streets along the southern end of the park, or book in advance.

Manhattan Rickshaw Company
1-212 604 4729/www.manhattanrickshaw.com. **Tours** noon-midnight Tue-Sun by appointment. **Tickets** $10-$50, depending on duration and number of passengers. **No credit cards**.
Manhattan Rickshaw's pedicabs operate in Greenwich Village, Soho, Times Square and the Theater District. If you see one that's available, hail the driver. (Determine your fare before you jump in.) For a pre-arranged pick-up, make reservations 24 hours in advance. **Photos** *p85* and *p86*.

On foot

Adventure on a Shoestring
1-212 265 2663. **Tours** Sat, Sun. Call for schedule and reservations. **Tickets** $5. **No credit cards**.
The motto of this organisation, which celebrates its 43rd anniversary this year, is 'Exploring the world within our reach… within our means', and founder

Taxi talk

In 2006, 13,087 taxicabs will blaze New York City streets, with many racking up as many as 70,000 miles on their odometers. While the vast majority (11,637 at last count) of the city's taxis are the Ford Crown Victoria model, the fleet also boasts just over a thousand mini-vans, about two dozen Ford Explorer sports utility vehicles – and one London cab tossed in for good measure. Still, in coming years, the taxicab as we know it may get a make-over.

Last year, city officials, taxi commission honchos and designers launched a campaign to redesign the taxicab – and we're not talking about just adding more legroom. Some of the ideas that have been bandied about include sunroofs, front passenger seats that face the backseat, and even the possibility of hailing a cab with a mobile phone. However, that flashy shade of yellow is staying put.

Howard Goldberg is dedicated to revealing the 'real' New York. The walks take you from one charming neighbourhood to another, and topics can include Millionaire's Row and Haunted Greenwich Village. Special celebrity theme tours, including tributes to Jackie O, Katharine Hepburn and Marilyn Monroe, are also available.

Big Onion Walking Tours

1-212 439 1090/www.bigonion.com. **Tours** *Sept-May* 1-3pm Fri-Sun and major holidays. *Jun-Aug* 1-3pm Wed-Sun. **Tickets** $12; $10 seniors and students. **No credit cards**.

New York was known as the Big Onion before it became the Big Apple. The tour guides will explain why, and they should know – all guides hold advanced degrees in history (or a related field), resulting in astoundingly informative tours of the city's historic districts and ethnic neighbourhoods. Check the website for meeting locations. Private tours are also available.

Bronx Tours

1-646-685 7725/www.bronxtours.net. **Tours** Call for schedule and to make reservations. **Tickets** $40. **Credit** AmEx, Disc, MC, V.

On these van tours, Bronx native Maurice Valentine shows that there's more to his borough than Yankee Stadium and the Bronx Zoo. Hip-hop music provides a funky aural backdrop as passengers are guided through unsung neighbourhoods like Fordham, Hunts Point and Mott Haven.

Greenwich Village Literary Pub Crawl

New Ensemble Theatre Company (1-212 613 5796/ www.geocities.com/newensemble). Tour meets at the White Horse Tavern, 567 Hudson Street, at 11th Street. Subway: 1 to Christopher Street-Sheridan Square. **Tours** 2pm Sat (reservations requested). **Tickets** $15; $12 seniors and students (drinks not included). **No credit cards**.

Local actors from the New Ensemble Theatre Company take you to the past haunts of famous writers. Watering stops include Chumley's (a former speakeasy) and Cedar Tavern, where Jack Kerouac and a generation of abstract expressionist painters, including Jackson Pollock, drank with their peers.

Harlem Heritage Tours

1-212 280 7888/www.harlemheritage.com. **Tours** Call or visit website for schedule and meeting locations. **Tickets** $20-$100 (reservations required). **Credit** AmEx, MC, V.

Now operating more than 15 bus and walking tours, Harlem Heritage shows visitors the soul of Harlem. Harlem Song, Harlem Nights takes you to landmarks such as the Apollo Theater. The Renaissance

Manhattan Rickshaw Company. *See p83.*

Follow that pedicab! – the **Manhattan Rickshaw Company**. *See p83*.

tour walks you through Prohibition-era speakeasies, nightclubs and one-time residences of artists, writers and musicians.

Municipal Art Society Tours

1-212 935 3960/recorded information 1-212 439 1049/www.mas.org. **Tours** Call or visit website for schedule and meeting locations. **Tickets** $12-$15 (reservations may be required for some tours). **No credit cards**.

The society organises bus and walking tours in New York and even New Jersey. Many, like Art Deco Midtown, have an architectural bent. There's also a free guided walk through Grand Central Terminal on Wednesdays at 12.30pm (suggested donation $10). Private tours are available by appointment.

NYCDiscovery Walking Tours

1-212 465 3331/nycdiscovery@hotmail.com. **Tours** Sat, Sun. Call for schedule and meeting locations. **Tickets** $12; food tours $17-$18 (food included). **No credit cards**.

These walking tours cover six different themes: American history (American Revolution to Civil War), biography (George Washington to John Lennon), culture (art to baseball), neighbourhood (Brooklyn Bridge area to Central Park), indoor winter (like the Secrets of Grand Central) and tasting-and-tavern (food and drink landmarks; drinks not included). The company has 80 year-round selections; private tours are available by appointment.

Radical Walking Tours of New York

1-718 492 0069/www.radicalwalkingtours.com. **Tours** Call or visit website for schedule and meeting locations. **Tickets** $10 (no reservations required). **No credit cards**.

Historian and author Bruce Kayton guides these walks through Greenwich Village, the Lower East Side and other bastions of the counterculture.

Rock 'n' Roll Walking Tour

Rock Junket NYC (1-212 696 6578/www.rock junket.com). **Tours** Mon-Fri by appointment; 1pm Sat. **Tickets** $20. **No credit cards**.

Rocker guides and liggers supreme Bobby Pinn and Ginger Ail lead this East Village walk to legendary rock, punk and glam sites (from famous album-cover locations to where the Ramones called home) from the 1960s to the present day.

Soundwalk

1-212 674 7407/www.soundwalk.com. **Tours** CDs and MP3s are available for purchase on website and in various stores. **Tickets** vary.

These inventive self-guided audio tours provide insight into life in Chinatown, Times Square, Little Italy, Dumbo and other 'nabes'. The cinematic soundtracks layer the voices of narrators, selected for their connection to the 'hood, with various sound clips and street noises. Celebrated writer Paul Auster recently narrated the Ground Zero Sonic Memorial Soundwalk.

Downtown

Lower Manhattan becomes a little more uptown with each passing year.

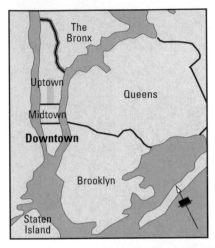

The southern tip of Manhattan has experienced a demographic sea change. For most of its life it has been populated by a down-to-earth crowd, from newly settled immigrants who packed their families into Lower East Side tenements to Greenwich Village beatniks who needed little more to live than coffee, cigs and jam sessions. Nowadays, Downtown is home to some of the priciest real estate on earth, as formerly grungy neighbourhoods like the Meatpacking District and the East Village become ritzified, and the value of a loft in Soho or Tribeca continues to skyrocket. But despite its streets of gold and such fancy-pants developments as the designer-boutique explosion on the west end of Bleecker Street, the area still has a great big heart. Downtowners adore their meandering streets, their historical touchstones, their newly revitalised waterfront, their underground fashion and music scenes, even their minuscule apartments – so much so, they've been known to avoid going north of 14th Street. A day or two of exploring is all it takes to see why.

Battery Park

Manhattan doesn't generally feel island-like – until you reach the southern tip. Down here, Atlantic Ocean breezes remind you how millions of people once travelled to New York: on

overcrowded, creaking sailing ships. Trace their journey past the golden torch of the **Statue of Liberty**, through the immigration and quarantine centres of **Ellis Island** (for both, *see p91*) and, finally, to the statue-dotted **Battery Park promenade**. If it's summertime, this strip – the closest thing this largely green area has to a main drag – will pull you back to the present as you behold a harbour filled with sailboats and jet-skiers, and sidewalks crowded with hurried urbanites who've just ferried to work from their Staten Island homes.

The promenade is a bench-lined location for quiet contemplation, but also a stage for applause- (and money-) hungry performers, who entertain crowds waiting to hop on the boats to the Statue of Liberty and Ellis Island. The park itself plays host to a variety of events, including the River to River Festival (www.rivertoriver nyc.com), a celebration of downtown culture featuring free outdoor goings-on from music and movies to comedy and kids' programmes on summer evenings. **Castle Clinton**, in the park, is an intimate, open-air setting for concerts. Built in 1812 to defend against attacks by the British, the castle, really a former fort, has been a theatre and an aquarium; it now also serves as a visitors' centre and ticket booth for Statue of Liberty and Ellis Island tours.

As you join the throngs making their way to Lady Liberty, you'll head south-eastwards along the shore, from which several ferry terminals jut into the harbour. The **Whitehall Ferry Terminal** is the boarding place for the famous **Staten Island Ferry** (*see p83*). First constructed in 1907, it has been completely rebuilt in recent years, after being damaged by fire in 1991. The new terminal opened in early 2005; it's the place to catch one of the city's three new ferry boats: the *Guy V Molinari*, named after the former Staten Island borough president; the *Sen John J Marchi*, honouring the veteran Republican legislator; and the *Spirit of America*, which commemorates the teamwork of Staten Islanders on 9/11. The 25-minute ride to the Staten Island shore is one of the few things in NYC that is free; quite a bargain, considering it offers an unparalleled view of the downtown Manhattan skyline and, of course, a closer look at the iconic statue. In the years before the Brooklyn Bridge was built, the Battery Maritime Building (11 South Street,

THE WORLD'S YOUR OYSTER

There's no freedom from the crowds on the ferry to the **Statue of Liberty**. *See p91.*

between Broad & Whitehall Streets) served as a terminal for ferry services between Manhattan and Brooklyn. Get a better view, cocktail in hand, from the terrace of the Rise Bar, on the 14th floor of the luxe Ritz-Carlton New York hotel (2 West Street, 1-917 790 2626).

Once you're refreshed, head north of Battery Park to the triangle of **Bowling Green**, the city's oldest park and the recipient of an expensive makeover completed in 2004. This grass triangle is also the front lawn of the 1907 Beaux Arts Alexander Hamilton Custom House, now home to the **National Museum of the American Indian** (*see p91*). On its north side, sculptor Arturo DiModica's muscular bronze bull represents the potent capitalism of the Financial District, while to the east sits the

Skyscraper Museum (*see p90* **High times**), where you can learn about the high-rise buildings that have made the city's skyline iconic, and explore the World Trade Center Dossier, an exhibit about the fallen towers and what will replace them.

Other see-worthy historical sites are close by: the rectory of the **Shrine of St Elizabeth Ann Seton**, a 1790 Federal building dedicated to the first American-born saint; and **New York Unearthed**, a tiny offshoot of the South Street Seaport Museum, whose collection documents 6,000 years of New York's archaeological past. The **Fraunces Tavern Museum** is a restoration of the alehouse where George Washington celebrated his victory over the British. After a bite, you can examine the

High times

Good things come in small packages, but the last place you'd expect to learn that lesson is at the **Skyscraper Museum**. Still, after six years of mounting exhibitions in various Lower Manhattan spaces, the once peripatetic institution has settled into a small but exhilarating new home on the ground floor of the 38-storey Ritz-Carlton tower in Battery Park City. In just 5,000 square feet – very modest by institutional standards – the space manages to evoke the scale and aspirations of the Skyscraper Museum's subject matter.

To achieve this, architects Skidmore, Owings & Merrill panelled the ceilings and floors in reflective stainless steel. 'The ceilings are actually only about 12 feet at their highest,' says Carol Willis, the museum's founder and director, 'but the material creates a much greater sense of space.' Strolling through the place is both thrilling and unnerving. 'An electrician described it best,' Willis says. 'It reminded him of being up in a building under construction. The architects loved hearing that, because it was exactly what they were after.' A ramp running along the glassed-in front of the building rises from the main entrance to a pair of second-floor galleries, which are dominated by tall rolling vitrines that seem to go on forever, thanks to the mirror-like ceilings.

Besides creating the illusion of walking the steel high above Manhattan, the new space allows the museum to operate like any other. 'Our function is to collect, preserve and interpret history,' Willis says. But collecting was difficult during the institution's itinerant years. Now acquisitions of photographs, architectural renderings, blueprints and assorted ephemera occur more frequently. A group of artefacts relating to the Woolworth Building, for example, includes not only period photos and drawings, but also an item straight out of the old five-and-dime: a cardboard packet of sewing needles adorned with an image of Cass Gilbert's architectural masterpiece.

Education is the word that Willis, an architectural historian, uses most often to describe the museum's main function. Two photo murals, for instance, depict the tip of Manhattan. The first, from 1955, shows a scene basically unchanged from the 1920s; the next picture, taken in 1975, looks completely different, thanks in large part to the addition of the World Trade Center. The murals are textbook illustrations of the degree to which construction in New York depends on the boom-and-bust cycles of real estate, Willis explains, adding that the museum itself was the beneficiary of a market lull that prodded the building's owners, Millennium Partners, to donate vacant space.

The whole enterprise is clearly a personal passion for Willis, and she evinces the single-minded intensity of someone who had a dream and saw it through. In her office, she pulls out an album of 500 photographs of the Empire State Building under construction, compiled by the original contractors. The pictures aren't terribly beautiful, but they illustrate the techniques that enabled the edifice to rise skywards at a breathtaking pace – in little more than a year, from start to finish. Willis's eyes light up as she peruses the images. 'Everyone knows the Lewis Hines photos,' she says, referring to the iconic images of ironworkers labouring on what was then the tallest building in the world, 'but these show you how it got done.' At the Skyscraper Museum, that story is just as important as the Empire State Building itself.

Skyscraper Museum

39 Battery Place, between Little West Street & 1st Place (1-212 968 1961/www. skyscraper.org). Subway: 4, 5 to Bowling Green. **Open** *noon-6pm Wed-Sun.* **Admission** *$5; $2.50 seniors and students.* **Credit** *MC, V.* **Map** *p402 E34.*

Revolution-era relics displayed in the tavern's period rooms. For all, *see p91*. The **New York Vietnam Veterans Memorial** (55 Water Street, between Coenties Slip & Hanover Square, www.nyvietnamveteransmemorial.org) stands one block to the east. Erected in 1985 and refreshed with a newly designed plaza a few years ago, it features the Walk of Honor – a pathway inscribed with the names of the 1,741 New Yorkers who lost their lives fighting in that South-east Asian conflict and a touching memorial etched with excerpts from letters, diary entries and poems written during the war.

Nearby, the **Stone Street Historic District** is built around one of Manhattan's oldest roads. The once-derelict bit of Stone Street between Coenties Alley and Hanover Square is charming; office workers and visitors now frequent its shops, restaurants and bars, including popular watering hole Ulysses (95 Pearl Street, at Stone Street, 1-212 482 0400) and Financier Patisserie (62 Stone Street, between Hanover Square & Mill Lane, 1-212 344 5600).

Fraunces Tavern Museum

54 Pearl Street, at Broad Street (1-212 425 1778/ www.frauncestavernmuseum.org). Subway: J, M, Z to Broad Street; 4, 5 to Bowling Green. **Open** noon-5pm Tue-Fri; 10am-5pm Sat. **Admission** $4; $3 seniors and 6-18s; free under-6s . **No credit cards**. **Map** p402 E33.
This 18th-century tavern was George Washington's watering hole and the site of his famous farewell to the troops at the Revolution's close. During the mid to late 1780s, the building housed the fledgling nation's departments of war, foreign affairs and treasury. In 1904, Fraunces became a repository for artefacts collected by the Sons of the Revolution in the State of New York. Ongoing exhibits include George Washington: Down the Stream of Life, which examines America's first president. The tavern and restaurant (1-212 968 1776) serve hearty fare at lunch and dinner, Monday through Saturday.

National Museum of the American Indian

George Gustav Heye Center, Alexander Hamilton Custom House, 1 Bowling Green, between State & Whitehall Streets (1-212 514 3700/www.nmai. si.edu). Subway: R, W to Whitehall Street; 1 to South Ferry; 4, 5 to Bowling Green. **Open** 10am-5pm Mon-Wed, Fri-Sun; 10am-8pm Thur. **Admission** free. **Map** p402 E33.
This branch of the Smithsonian Institution displays its collection around the grand rotunda of the 1907 Custom House, at the bottom of Broadway (which, many moons ago, began as an Indian trail). The life and culture of Native Americans is presented in rotating exhibitions – from intricately woven fibre Pomo baskets to beaded buckskin shirts – along with contemporary artwork. On show through November 2006 is Born of Clay: Ceramics from the National

Museum of the American Indian, a collection of more than 300 examples of pottery from the Andes, Meso-America and eastern and southwestern America dating from 3000 BC up to the late 20th century.

New York Unearthed

17 State Street, between Pearl & Whitehall Streets, behind the Shrine of St Elizabeth Ann Seton (1-212 748 8628). Subway: R, W to Whitehall Street. **Open** by appointment only Mon-Fri. **Admission** free. **Map** p402 E34.
At the city's only museum dedicated to urban archeology, visitors can watch resident archeologists catalogue some of the millions of artefacts excavated from various sites in and around the city. A fun stop for sidewalk-weary kids and their bushed parents.

Shrine of St Elizabeth Ann Seton

7 State Street, between Pearl & Whitehall Streets (1-212 269 6865/www.setonshrine-ny.org). Subway: R, W to Whitehall Street. **Open** 6.30am-5pm Mon-Fri; by appointment only Sat; before and after 11am Mass Sun. **Admission** free. **Map** p402 E34.

Statue of Liberty & Ellis Island Immigration Museum

Statue of Liberty (1-212 363 3200/www.nps.gov/stli). Travel: R, W to Whitehall Street; 1 to South Ferry; 4, 5 to Bowling Green; then take the Statue of Liberty ferry (1-212 269 5755), departing every 25 minutes from gangway 4 or 5 in southernmost Battery Park. **Open** Ferry runs 8.30am-3.30pm daily. Purchase tickets at Castle Clinton in Battery Park. **Admission** $10; $8 seniors; $4 4-12s; free under-4s. **Credit** AmEx, MC, V.
Frédéric-Auguste Bartholdi's *Liberty Enlightening the World*, a gift from the people of France, was unveiled in 1886. After security concerns placed the statue off-limits for nearly three years, its pedestal finally reopened for guided tours in summer 2004 (you still can't climb up to the crown, and backpacks and luggage are not permitted on the island). Still, there's ample room to absorb the 1883 Emma Lazarus poem that includes the renowned lines 'Give me your tired, your poor/Your huddled masses yearning to breathe free'. On the way back to Manhattan, the ferry will stop at the popular Immigration Museum, on Ellis Island, through which more than 12 million entered the country between 1892 and 1954. The exhibitions are a moving tribute to the people from so many different countries who made the journey to America, dreaming of a better life. The $6 audio tour, narrated by Tom Brokaw, is informative and inspiring. **Photo** *p89*.

Battery Park City & Ground Zero

The streets around **Ground Zero**, the former site of the **World Trade Center**, have been drawing crowds since the terrorist attacks of 2001. People come in droves to pay their respects to the nearly 2,800 people who lost

Sightseeing

Recharge in **Battery Park City**'s green spaces...

their lives on September 11 that year, and the area is surrounded by a high fence on which pictures of the devastation are hung; signs posted along the barrier say 'Please help us to maintain this site as a very special place' and ask tourists not to buy souvenirs or give any money to people soliciting donations. The mood here has turned at least a little bit optimistic now that reconstruction is under way – but rebuilding has already proved arduous (*see p95* **A Downtown reborn**). The good news: construction on the 9/11 memorial is set to begin in 2006; along with a transport centre, a museum and a performing-arts complex, it is slated for completion in 2009. The 1,776-foot Freedom Tower, planned as the world's tallest building but stalled by security issues in 2005, will eventually rise as well.

Immediately to the west of Ground Zero, the city-within-a-city **World Financial Center** (*see p93*) is fully recovered from its 9/11 injuries, and is a pretty place for a walk-through. Completed in 1988, architect Cesar Pelli's four glass-and-granite, postmodern office towers – each crowned with a different geometric form – surround an upscale retail area and a series of eaterie-lined plazas ringing a marina where private yachts and water taxis to New Jersey are docked. The glass-roofed

Winter Garden is a popular venue for concerts. To the east of Ground Zero, shopaholics can amuse themselves at the enormous discount-designer-duds vault Century 21 (22 Cortlandt Street, between Broadway & Church Street, 1-212 227 9092).

Just west of the World Financial Center lies **Battery Park City**, devised by Nelson A Rockefeller (the governor of New York from 1959 to 1973) as a site of apartment housing and schools in an area that is otherwise all business. Home to roughly 9,000 people, the self-contained neighbourhood includes restaurants, cafés, shops and a marina amid 92 glorious riverside acres. Sweeping views of the Hudson River and close proximity to the downtown financial scene have also made this an ideal spot for office space. Still, the most impressive aspects of BPC are its esplanade, a paradise for bikers, skaters and joggers, and strolling park (officially called Nelson A Rockefeller Park), which run along the Hudson River north of the Financial Center and connect to Battery Park at the south. Close by the marina is the 1997 **Police Memorial** (Liberty Street, at South End Avenue), a granite pool and fountain that symbolically trace the lifespan of a police officer through the use of moving water, with names of the fallen etched in the wall. The

...or stroll around its marina.

Irish Hunger Memorial (Vesey Street, at North End Avenue) is here too, paying tribute to those who suffered during the Irish Famine.

One of the larger chunks of green along this stretch is Rockefeller Park's sprawling North Lawn. This spot, located adjacent to the well-respected Stuyvesant High School, becomes a veritable beach in summer, where sunbathers, kite fliers and soccer players vie for turf. Basketball and handball courts, concrete tables inlaid with chess and backgammon boards, and playgrounds with swings are some of the built-in recreation options. Continue north and you'll find a jogging and bike trail and, on piers 25 and 26, all kinds of activities, from kayaking and fishing to a trapeze-swinging school.

Situated between Battery Park City and Battery Park are the inventively designed South Cove, the new **Teardrop Park**, a two-acre space designed to evoke the Hudson River Valley, and Robert F Wagner Jr Park, where the grass is as soft as a golf green and an observation deck offers fabulous views of the harbour and the Verrazano-Narrows Bridge. New York City's Holocaust-remembrance archive, the **Museum of Jewish Heritage** (see below) is tucked in amid the green spots, and the entire park area is dotted with sculptures, including Tom Otterness's

whimsical *The Real World* – which, by the way, has nothing to do with MTV's long-running reality show of the same name, although both debuted the same year: 1992.

Battery Park City Authority
1-212 417 2000/www.batteryparkcity.org.
The neighbourhood's official website lists events and has a great map of the area.

Museum of Jewish Heritage
Robert F Wagner Jr Park, 36 Battery Place at First Place (1-646 437 4200/www.mjhnyc.org). Subway: 1, 9 to South Ferry; 4, 5 to Bowling Green. **Open** 10am-5.45pm Mon-Tue, Thur, Sun; 10am-8pm Wed; 10am-3pm Fri, eve of Jewish holidays (until 5pm in the summer). **Admission** $10; $7 seniors; $5 students; free under-12s; free 4-8pm Wed. **Credit** AmEx, MC, V. **Map** p402 E34.
Opened in 1997 and expanded in 2003, this museum offers one of the most moving cultural experiences in the city. Detailing the horrific attacks on (and inherent joys of) Jewish life during the past century, the collection consists of 24 documentary films, 2,000 photographs and 800 cultural artefacts, many donated by Holocaust survivors and their families. The Memorial Garden features English artist Andy Goldsworthy's permanent installation *Garden of Stones*: 18 fire-hollowed boulders, each planted with a dwarf oak sapling.

World Financial Center & Winter Garden
From Albany to Vesey Streets, between the Hudson River & West Street (1-212 945 2600/www. worldfinancialcenter.com). Subway: A, C to Broadway-Nassau Street; E to World Trade Center; J, M, Z, 2, 3, 4, 5 to Fulton Street. **Map** p402 D32.
Go online to download a calendar of free events ranging from folk concerts to silent-film festivals.

Wall Street

Since the city's earliest days as a fur-trading post, wheeling and dealing has been New York's main activity, and commerce the backbone of its prosperity. The southern tip of Manhattan is generally known as the **Financial District** because, in the days before telecommunications, banking institutions established their headquarters here to be near the city's active port. While this nib is bisected vertically by the ever-bustling Broadway, it's that east-west thoroughfare **Wall Street** (or merely 'the Street' in trader lingo) that is synonymous with the world's greatest den of capitalism.

Wall Street, which took its name from a defensive wooden wall built by the Dutch in 1653 to mark what was then the northern limit of New Amsterdam, is big on legend but is less than a mile long – it's truncated by Broadway on its western end, and therefore only spans about half the width of the island. Here at

Sightseeing

Broadway rises the Gothic Revival spire of **Trinity Church** (*see below*) – proof, perhaps, that God and capitalism are not mutually exclusive. This Episcopalian house of worship was the island's tallest structure when it was completed in 1846 (the original burned down in 1776; a second was demolished in 1839). A set of gates north of the church on Broadway allow access to the adjacent cemetery, where cracked and faded tombstones mark the final resting places of dozens of past city dwellers, including signatories of the Declaration of Independence and the Constitution. The church is also home to the **Trinity Church Museum**, which displays an assortment of historic diaries, photographs, sermons and burial records.

St Paul's Chapel (*see below*), a satellite of Trinity Church, is an oasis of peace in the midst of frantic business activity. The chapel is the city's only extant pre-Revolutionary building (it dates from 1766) and one of the finest Georgian structures in the country. Miraculously, both landmark churches survived the World Trade Center attack; although mortar fell from their façades, the steeples remained intact.

A block east of Trinity Church, the **Federal Hall National Memorial** (closed for renovations until autumn 2006) is an august Greek Revival building in its own right, and – in a previous incarnation – the site of George Washington's inauguration in 1789.

It was along this stretch that corporate America made its first audacious architectural statements, and a continued walk eastwards offers much evidence of what money can buy. Notable structures include **40 Wall Street** (between Nassau & William Streets), which went head-to-head with the Chrysler Building in 1929 battling for the title of 'world's tallest building' (the Empire State Building trounced them both a year later), and the former **Merchants' Exchange** at 55 Wall Street (between Hanover & William Streets), with its stacked rows of Ionic and Corinthian columns, giant doors and a remarkable 12,000-square-foot ballroom inside. Back around the corner is another example: the **Equitable Building** (120 Broadway, between Cedar & Pine Streets), whose greedy use of vertical space helped to instigate the zoning laws now governing skyscrapers (stand across the street from the building to get the optimal view).

The nerve centre of the US economy is the **New York Stock Exchange** (11 Wall Street, between Broad and New Streets). For security reasons, the Exchange is no longer open to the public, but the street outside offers an endless pageant of brokers, traders and their minions. For a lesson on Wall Street's influence through the years, check out the **Museum of**

American Financial History (*see below*), on the ground floor of what was once John D Rockefeller's Standard Oil Building.

The **Federal Reserve Bank** (*see below*), a block north on Liberty Street, is an imposing structure built in the Florentine style. It holds the nation's largest store of gold – just over 9,000 tons – in a vault five storeys below street level, an exhibit about which is open to the public (advance reservations required). Fans of *NYPD Blue, Law & Order*, or any of the seemingly endless stream of New York Police Department themed TV shows will want to take a quick detour to the **New York City Police Museum**, located two blocks south of Wall Street, between Water and South Streets.

Federal Reserve Bank

33 Liberty Street, between Nassau & William Streets (1-212 720 6130/www.newyorkfed.org). Subway: 2, 3, 4, 5 to Wall Street. **Open** 9.30-11.30am, 1.30-2.30pm Mon-Fri. **Tours** every hour on the half hour. Tours must be arranged at least one week in advance; tickets are sent by mail. **Admission** free. **Map** p402 E33.

Museum of American Financial History

28 Broadway, between Beaver Street & Exchange Place (1-212 908 4110/www.financialhistory.org). Subway: 1 to Rector Street. **Open** 10am-4pm Tue-Sat. **Admission** $2. **Credit** AmEx, MC, V. **Map** p402 E33.

The permanent collection, which traces the development of Wall Street and America's financial markets, includes ticker tape from the morning of the big crash of 29 October 1929, an 1867 stock ticker and the earliest known photograph of Wall Street.

New York City Police Museum

100 Old Slip, between South & Water Streets (1-212 480 3100/www.nycpolicemuseum.org). Subway: 2, 3 to Wall Street; 4, 5 to Bowling Green. **Open** 10am-5pm Tue-Sat (10am-5pm Sun in summer). **Admission** suggested donation $5; $3 seniors; $2 6-18s; free under-6s. **No credit cards**. **Map** p402 F32.

The New York Police Department's tribute to itself features exhibits on its history and the tools and transportation of the trade. You can also pick up officially licensed NYPD paraphernalia.

St Paul's Chapel

209 Broadway, between Fulton & Vesey Streets (1-212 233 4164/www.saintpaulschapel.org). Subway: A, C to Broadway-Nassau Street; J, M, Z, 2, 3, 4, 5 to Fulton Street. **Open** 10am-6pm Mon-Sat; 9am-4pm Sun. **Map** p402 E32.

Trinity Church Museum

Broadway, at Wall Street (1-212 602 0872/www.trinitywallstreet.org). Subway: R, W to Rector Street; 2, 3, 4, 5 to Wall Street. **Open** 9-11.45am, 1-3.45pm Mon-Fri; 10am-3.45pm Sat; 1-3.45pm Sun. Closed during concerts. **Admission** free. **Map** p402 E33.

A Downtown reborn

Living in the shadow of Ground Zero

Artist Maria Leather has lived on Maiden Lane, 500 yards from the World Trade Center site, since 1999. In those days permanent residents were few and far between, so the neighbourhood's streets were more or less deserted after brokers rang Wall Street's closing bell.

Then came September 11, which Leather calls 'the most frightening thing I've ever had to deal with'. For months afterwards, a film of ash and dust lay thick on the blocks around her home.

'The weirdest thing about the months after the terrorist attacks is that it felt like it did back in 1975 when I was a kid here – there weren't any people around at all,' says Vincent Barile, a manager at Bubby's (120 Hudson Street, at North Moore Street), a hip neighbourhood café and hangout that was way ahead of the curve when it opened in 1990. Barile grew up in Tribeca and recalls

people getting excited when limousines started pulling up to the Tribeca Grill after it opened in the early 1990s, heralding the start of a promising new era for the out-of-the-way neighbourhood.

Leather, Barile and many others wondered if the attacks would be the death knell for their home. Not a chance – in fact, Lower Manhattan is experiencing a boom not previously seen since the city began here 400 years ago. Residents say it's a testament to the spirit of New Yorkers that attacks meant to destroy their neighbourhood may be leading to its rebirth.

Thanks to the tax-free Liberty Bonds programme created by Congress post 9/11, this part of the city is now the fastest-growing residential neighbourhood in New York, according to Stefan Pryor, president of the Lower Manhattan Development Corporation (LMDC).

Of course, Ground Zero remains the sombre centrepiece of all this urban renewal. The site itself is better managed now than in the past, with vendors hawking cheesy WTC paperweights and graphic photobooks now banished to the periphery. Most New Yorkers wince at this kind of profiteering, and a new LMDC-sponsored Tribute Center is due to open on the Liberty Street side of the site by spring 2006. Mementoes will be on sale, 'with all proceeds going to worthy causes', says Pryor.

For the best all-weather views of Ground Zero, head to the glassed-in second-floor observation area in the Winter Garden, part of the World Financial Center to the west of the site (open 10am-7pm Mon-Fri; 11am-5pm Sat; noon-5pm Sun).

The LMDC has also set up a special installation on the Winter Garden's ground floor that uses videos and 3-D models to give visitors a sense of the planned development, which includes the Freedom Tower, a 9/11 memorial, a museum and a performing-arts complex.

'Today, life has regrown much stronger than it was even before September 11,' says Barile. 'There are more people coming down here than ever before, and I think it means a lot to everyone who worked so hard to keep the area alive.'

South Street Seaport

New York's importance as a port has diminished, but its initial fortune rolled in on the swells that crash around its deep-water harbour. The city was perfectly situated for trade with Europe; after 1825, goods from the Western Territories arrived via the Erie Canal and the Hudson River. Of course, because by 1892 New York had become the point of entry for many millions of immigrants, its character was shaped by more than commodities – it grew from the waves of humanity that arrived at its docks. The South Street Seaport is the best place to appreciate this seafaring heritage.

If you enter the Seaport area from Water Street, the first thing you'll notice is the whitewashed *Titanic* **Memorial Lighthouse**, originally erected on top of the Seaman's Church Institute (Coenties Slip and South Street) in 1913, the year after the great ship sank. The monument was moved to its current location in 1976. Check out the fine views of the **Brooklyn Bridge** that this corner of the neighbourhood offers.

The Seaport, which was redeveloped in the mid 1980s, is lined with reclaimed and renovated buildings that have been converted to shops, restaurants, bars and a museum. It's not an area that New Yorkers often visit, despite its rich history. The Seaport's public spaces, including blocks of both Fulton and Front Streets where cars are barred, are a favourite of street performers. At 11 Fulton Street, the **Fulton Market** (open daily), with its gourmet food stalls and seafood restaurants, is a great place for people-watching and oyster-slurping. Familiar national-chain stores such as J Crew and Abercrombie & Fitch line the surrounding thoroughfares. The shopping area of **Pier 17**, though little more than a picturesque mall by day and an after-work watering hole by night, is worth a quick walk-through. (Outdoor concerts in summertime actually do attract locals, and may justify a sit-down even for a determined sightseer.) Antique vessels are docked at neighbouring piers. The **South Street Seaport Museum** (*see below*), which details New York's maritime history, is located within the restored 19th-century buildings of Schermerhorn Row (2-18 Fulton Street, 91-92 South Street and 189-195 Front Street); these structures were constructed on an extension built of landfill in 1812.

South Street Seaport Museum

Visitors' Center, 12 Fulton Street, at South Street (1-212 748 8600/www.southstseaport.org). Subway: A, C to Broadway-Nassau Street; J, M, Z, 2, 3, 4, 5 to Fulton Street. **Open** *Apr-Oct* 10am-6pm Tue-Sun. *Nov-Mar* 10am-6pm Fri-Sun. **Admission** $8; $6 students; $4 5-12s; free under-5s. **Credit** AmEx, MC, V. **Map** p402 F32.
Occupying 11 blocks along the East River, the museum is an amalgam of galleries, historic ships, 19th-century buildings and a visitors' centre. Wander around the rebuilt streets and pop in to see an exhibition on marine life and history before climbing aboard the four-masted 1911 *Peking*. The seaport is generally thick with tourists, but it's still a lively place to spend an afternoon, especially for families with children, who are likely to enjoy the atmosphere and intriguing seafaring memorabilia. In spring 2006, the museum launches World Port New York an ambitious exhibition highlighting the economic and social importance of New York's bustling seaport to the city, country and world beyond.

Civic Center & City Hall

The business of running New York takes place in the many grand buildings of the **Civic Center**, an area that formed the budding city's northern boundary in the 1700s. **City Hall Park**, at the south end of which you'll find a granite 'time wheel' tracking the park's history, was treated to an extensive renovation just before the millenium arrived, and the pretty landscaping and abundant benches make it a popular weekday lunching spot for local office

New York Stock Exchange. *See p94.*

workers. Like the steps of City Hall, the park has been the site of press conferences and political protests for years. (Under former mayor Rudy Giuliani, the steps were closed to such activities unless they were approved by Hizzoner's office. A federal district judge declared the ban unconstitutional in April 2000, after a celebration of the Yankees' World Series victory took place, but an event commemorating World AIDS Day was snuffed.) **City Hall**, at the northern end of the park, houses the mayor's office and the legislative chambers of the City Council, and is therefore usually buzzing with preparations for VIP comings and goings. When City Hall was completed in 1812, its architects were so confident the city would grow no farther north that they didn't bother to put any marble on its northern side. The building, a beautiful blend of Federalist form and French Renaissance detail, is closed to the public (except for scheduled group tours). Facing City Hall, the much larger, golden-statue-topped **Municipal Building** contains other civic offices, including the marriage bureau; note the nervous, blushing brides- and grooms-to-be awaiting their ceremonies, particularly in the early morning.

Park Row, east of City Hall Park, is now lined with cafés, electronics shops and the campus of **Pace University**. It once held the offices of 19 daily papers and was known as Newspaper Row (these days, scoop-driven crime reporters from the major newspapers share one cramped office, affectionately known as 'the Shack', which is located nearby at 1 Police Plaza). This strip was also the site of Phineas T Barnum's sensationalist American Museum, which burned down in 1865.

Facing the park from the west is Cass Gilbert's famous **Woolworth Building** (233 Broadway, between Barclay Street & Park Place), a vertically elongated Gothic cathedral-style office building considered by many to be the Mozart of skyscrapers (and, alternatively, nicknamed the Cathedral of Commerce). Be sure to look skywards, both as you face the striking façade and as you stand in the stunning lobby.

The houses of crime and punishment are also located in the Civic Center, near Foley Square, which was once a pond and later the site of the city's most notorious 19th-century slum, Five Points. These days, you'll find the State Supreme Court in the **New York County Courthouse** (60 Centre Street, at Pearl Street), a hexagonal Roman Revival building; the beautiful rotunda is decorated with the mural *Law Through the Ages*. The **United States Courthouse** (40 Centre Street, between Duane & Pearl Streets) is a Corinthian temple crowned with a golden pyramid. Next to City Hall, on Chambers Street,

is the 1872 Old New York County Courthouse, more popularly known as the **Tweed Courthouse**, a symbol of the runaway corruption of mid-19th-century municipal government. Boss Tweed, leader of the political machine Tammany Hall, famously pocketed $10 million of the building's huge $14 million construction budget. What he didn't steal bought a beautiful edifice; the Italianate detailing is exquisite. The **Criminal Courts Building and Bernard Kerik Detention Complex** (100 Centre Street, between Leonard & White Streets), still known as 'the Tombs' despite its official renaming in 2001, is the district's most intimidating pile. The hall's architecture – great granite slabs and looming towers guarding the entrance – is downright Kafkaesque.

All of these courts are open to the public weekdays from 9am to 5pm. Your best bets for legal drama: the Criminal Courts. If you can't slip into a trial, you can at least observe legal eagles and their clients. Or, for a grim twist on dinner theatre, observe the pleas here at the Arraignment Court (the action lasts till 1am).

A major archaeological discovery, the **African Burial Ground** (Duane Street, between Broadway & Centre Street) is a small remnant of a five-and-a-half-acre cemetery where between 10,000 and 20,000 African men, women and children were buried long ago. The cemetery, which closed in 1794, was unearthed during construction of a federal office building in 1991 and designated a National Historic Landmark (*see p16* **What lies beneath**).

City Hall

City Hall Park, from Vesey to Chambers Streets, between Broadway & Park Row (1-212 788 3000/ www.nyc.gov). Subway: J, M, Z to Chambers Street; 2, 3 to Park Place; 4, 5, 6 to Brooklyn Bridge-City Hall. **Map** p402 E32.
For group tours only; call two weeks in advance.

Tribeca & Soho

Tribeca (the Triangle Below Canal Street) is a textbook example of the gentrification process in lower Manhattan. Much of the neighbourhood throbs with energy, but a few pockets appear abandoned – the cobblestones crumbling and dirty, the cast-iron buildings chipped and unpainted. Don't let your eyes fool you; derelict areas like these are transformed with deluxe makeovers, seemingly overnight.

The rich and famous weren't really here first, but visible gentrification has led some to think of them as pioneers: many big-name celebs (Robert De Niro and Christy Turlington among them) and established, successful artists such as Richard Serra live in the area. There's a host of haute restaurants here, including Chanterelle

Built to last

Tribeca's high concentration of distinctive late-19th-century structures makes the neighbourhood an architecture buff's dream. About three quarters of these buildings occupy a designated historical district, which protects not just the edifices but also the stone-paved streets and metal awnings left over from the days when the Washington Market's wholesale food vendors dominated Tribeca's west side. Thanks to the activism of preservationists in the '80s, these sites will be around for years to come. Here are a few favourites.

6 Harrison Street

Between Greenwich & Hudson Streets.
The red-brick and granite Mercantile Exchange was built between 1872 and 1884 to regulate the trade of butter and cheese and, in the late 1980s, was made into an office building. An ornate cupolaed clock tower caps its five storeys. The American Institute of Architects declares it a 'hearty pile and a must-see work'.

135 Hudson Street

At Beach Street.
Once a Pony Express office, this 1886 masonry warehouse was one of the earliest commercial buildings to be converted into artists' studios. Its street-level arches are supported by massive cylindrical brick columns.

451 Washington Street

Between Desbrosses & Watts Streets.
Completed in 1871, the original Fleming Smith warehouse is a golden-hued, late-Victorian stunner, with steep gables, dormer windows and contrasting brick trim. Copper cornice detailing gilds the lily even further. The bistro Capsouto Frères has occupied the first floor since 1980.

85 Leonard Street

Between Broadway & Church Street.
The marvel of cast-iron technology changed the face of Soho and Tribeca in the mid-19th century. Slender, mass-produced columns allowed for much larger windows, brightening dim interiors. Cast iron's premier architect, James Bogardus, had his own warehouse here. Note to those in line at the Knitting Factory next door: this building is the only one in the city known for certain to be the work of Bogardus.

(2 Harrison, at Hudson Street, 1-212 966 6960) and Nobu (*see p201*); the long-running Odeon (145 West Broadway, at Duane Street, 1-212 233 0507), immortalised by Jay McInerney in his 1984 novel *Bright Lights, Big City,* is still a beautiful-people hotspot.

Many of the buildings in Tribeca are large, hulking former warehouses; those near the river, in particular, are rapidly being converted into modern condos, but fine small-scale cast-iron architecture still stands along White Street and the parallel thoroughfares (*see p98* **Built to last**). You'll find galleries, salons, furniture stores, spas and other businesses here that cater to the neighbourhood's stylish residents. Architecture star Frank Gehry designed the multimillion-dollar interior for the Tribeca Issey Miyake boutique (119 Hudson Street, at North Moore Street, 1-212 226 0100).

Tribeca is also the unofficial headquarters of New York's film industry. De Niro's **Tribeca Film Center** (375 Greenwich Street, at Franklin Street) houses screening rooms and production offices in the old Martinson Coffee Building; his restaurant, Tribeca Grill, is on the ground floor. A few blocks away, his recently acquired **Tribeca Cinemas** (54 Varick Street, at Laight Street, 1-212 941 2000) hosts film premières and parties when it is not acting as a venue for the **Tribeca Film Festival** (*see p260*), which grows bigger each year. In 2005, during its two-week run, organisers held 700 movie screenings, to which they sold a whopping 135,000 tickets.

Soho, New York's glamorous downtown shopping destination, was once an industrial zone known as Hell's Hundred Acres. In the 1960s, the neighbourhood was earmarked for destruction, but its signature cast-iron warehouses were saved by the many artists who inhabited them. (Urban-planning theorist Chester A Rapkin coined the name Soho, for South of Houston Street, in a 1962 study of the neighbourhood.) The **King** and **Queen of Greene Street** (respectively, 72-76 Greene Street, between Broome & Spring Streets, and 28-30 Greene Street, between Canal & Grand Streets) are prime examples of the area's beloved architecture landmarks. Not surprisingly, as loft living became fashionable and buildings were renovated for residential use, landlords sniffed the potential for profits, and Soho morphed into a playground for the young, the beautiful and the rich. While it can still be a pleasure to stroll around the cobblestoned streets on weekdays, large chain stores have moved in among the boutiques and bistros, bringing with them a shopping-mall-at-Christmas-time crush every Saturday and Sunday. The commercialism and crowds have caused a number of hip shops to head to other neighbourhoods, and most of the galleries that made Soho an art mecca in the 1970s and '80s have decamped to cheaper (and now trendier) neighbourhoods like West Chelsea and Brooklyn's Dumbo. Surprisingly, some garment-factory sweatshops remain in Soho, especially near Canal Street, though the same elegant buildings may also house design studios, magazine publishers and record labels.

Upscale hotels like the Mercer, 60 Thompson (for both, *see p54* **Downtown deluxe**) and SoHo Grand (*see p47*) keep the fashionable coming to the area; high-end clothing stores include Prada and Agnès b, and swanky home furnishings rule at Euro-cool design stores such as Moss and Cappelletti. And the goods aren't all that's worldly in these parts. West Broadway, Soho's main thoroughfare, is a magnet for out-of-towners. At weekends, you're as likely to hear French, German and Italian as you are to catch a blast of Brooklynese.

The **New Museum of Contemporary Art** (*see p113*) has left the neighbourhood (it's inhabiting a temporary space in Chelsea until its new home on the Bowery is ready). A remaining museum in Soho that is worth a tour is the **New York City Fire Museum** (*see below*), a former fire station housing a collection of antique engines dating from the 1700s.

Just west of West Broadway, tenement- and townhouse-lined streets contain remnants of the Italian community that once dominated the area. Elderly men and women walk along Sullivan Street to the St Anthony of Padua Roman Catholic Church (No.155, at W Houston Street), which was dedicated in 1888. You'll find old-school neighbourhood flavour in businesses such as Joe's Dairy (No.156, between Houston & Prince Streets, 1-212 677 8780), Pino's Prime Meat Market (No.149, between Houston & Prince Streets, 1-212 475 8134) and, on Prince Street, the Vesuvio Bakery (160 Prince Street, between Thompson Street & West Broadway, 1-212 925 8248), whose old-fashioned façade has appeared in dozens of commercials.

New York City Fire Museum

278 Spring Street, between Hudson & Varick Streets (1-212 691 1303/www.nycfiremuseum.org). Subway: C, E to Spring Street; 1 to Houston Street. **Open** 10am-5pm Tue-Sat; 10am-4pm Sun. **Admission** suggested donation $5; $2 seniors and students; $1 under-12s. **Credit** AmEx, DC, Disc, MC, V. **Map** p403 D30.

An active firehouse from 1904 to 1959, this museum is filled with gadgetry and pageantry, from late 18th-century hand-pumped fire engines to present-day equipment. The museum also houses a permanent exhibit commemorating firefighters' heroism after the attack on the World Trade Center. **Photo** *p102.*

Little Italy & Nolita

Little Italy, which once ran from Canal to Houston Streets between Lafayette Street and the Bowery, hardly resembles the insular

You'll find shops and ships at **South Street Seaport**. *See p96.*

Alley cat

Meet the man who saved a whole street from extinction.

If you've managed to find clandestinely cool restaurant **Freeman's** (*see p184*) – located at the end of Freeman Alley, on the north side of Rivington Street between Chrystie Street and the Bowery – you have one man to thank: artist and alley resident Jimmy Wright. That 'Freeman Alley' sign you were so glad to spot from down the block? He owns it.

When Wright bought his building in 1980, the street's name was unofficial. 'It supposedly no longer existed,' says Sanna Feirstein, who wrote the 2001 book *Naming New York*. The corridor is visible on maps dating back to at least 1853, but in 1914 the city demapped it, removing street signs and all traces of it from tax rolls. It took him more than two decades, but Wright resurrected the address. For five years now, it's been 1 Freeman Alley.

Wright describes the area in the old days as an open-air heroin market. His first priority was to clean it up, so he started a block association, and made contacts at Community Board 3 and the Fifth Police Precinct. His hazy address, however, slowed down everything – including gettin a gas line. Mail carriers consistently misdelivered his bills, and violations committed in other buildings haunted him. Over the years, Wright filed a mass of paperwork, finally earning approvals from the Manhattan borough president's office and NYC's Department of Transportation. Wright paid $350 for the sign, which was installed by the DOT in 2001. Freeman Alley was official.

Little is known about the origins of Freeman Alley. Some historians, including Feirstein, think it was named after Uzal Freeman, a surveyor who lived in the neighbourhood in the early 19th century. Others, like Joyce Mendelsohn, author of 2001's *The Lower East Side Remembered and Revisited*, think that the cul-de-sac was once open at both ends, and named after an African burial ground. 'Freeman Alley,' Mendelsohn says, 'is believed to have been a road to that graveyard.' The lot, then on the city's outskirts, was laid with graves relocated from a City Hall area cemetery closed in 1794. (In 1853, the interred were again moved, to Harlem and the Bronx.)

These days, Wright is a sort of mayor of the micro-neighbourhood, proudly supporting both the restaurant and Silo, an art gallery on the first floor of his three-storey building. Some folks would perhaps prefer a traffic-free street, but to him, the sounds of heels clicking and glasses tinkling are sweet.

community famously portrayed in Martin Scorsese's *Mean Streets*. Italian families have fled Mott Street and gone to the suburbs, Chinatown has crept north, and rising rents have forced mom-and-pop businesses to surrender to the stylish boutiques of Nolita – North of Little Italy (a misnomer, since it technically lies within Little Italy). Another telling change in the 'hood: **St Patrick's Old**

Cathedral (260-264 Mulberry Street, between Houston & Prince Streets) now holds services in English and Spanish, not Italian. Completed in 1809 and restored after a fire in 1868, this was New York's premier Catholic church until it was demoted, upon consecration of the Fifth Avenue cathedral of the same name. But ethnic pride remains. Italian-Americans flood in from the outer boroughs to show their love for the old neighbourhood during the **Feast of San Gennaro** (*see p265*) every September. Tourist-oriented Italian cafés and restaurants line Mulberry Street between Canal and Houston Streets, but nearby pockets of the past still linger. Elderly locals (and in-the-know young ones) buy olive oil and fresh pasta from venerable shops such as DiPalo's Fine Foods (200 Grand Street, at Mott Street, 1-212 226 1033) and sandwiches packed with salami and cheeses at the Italian Food Center (186 Grand Street, at Mulberry Street, 1-212 925 2954).

Of course, Little Italy is the site of several notorious Mafia landmarks. The brick-fronted store occupied by accessories boutique Amy Chan (247 Mulberry Street, between Prince & Spring Streets) was once the Ravenite Social Club – Mafia kingpin John Gotti's HQ from the mid 1980s until his arrest (and imprisonment) in 1990. Mobster Joey Gallo was shot to death in 1972 while celebrating a birthday at Umberto's Clam House, which has since moved around the corner to 178 Mulberry Street, at Broome Street (1-212 431 7545). The restaurants in the area are mostly undistinguished grill-and-pasta houses, but two reliable choices are Il Cortile (125 Mulberry Street, between Canal & Hester Streets, 1-212 226 6060) and La Mela (167 Mulberry Street, between Broome & Grand Streets, 1-212 431 9493). Drop in for dessert and espresso at Caffè Roma (385 Broome Street, at Mulberry Street, 1-212 226 8413), which opened in 1891.

Chi-chi restaurants and boutiques have taken over **Nolita**. Elizabeth, Mott and Mulberry Streets, between Houston and Spring Streets in particular, are now the source of everything from perfectly cut jeans to hand-blown glass. The young, the insouciant and the vaguely European still congregate outside forever-hip eateries like Bread (20 Spring Street, between Elizabeth & Mott Streets, 1-212 334 1015) and Café Habana (17 Prince Street, at Elizabeth Street, 1-212 625 2001). Even before the Nolita boom, the grand Police Headquarters Building (240 Centre Street, between Broome & Grand Streets) had been converted into pricey apartments.

Chinatown

Take a walk in the area south of Broome Street and west of Broadway, and you'll feel as though you've entered a completely different continent. You won't hear much English spoken along the crowded streets of **Chinatown**, lined by fish-, fruit- and vegetable-stocked stands. Manhattan's Chinatown is the largest Chinese community outside Asia. Even though some residents eventually decamp to one of the four other Chinatowns in the city (two each in Queens and Brooklyn), a steady flow of new

arrivals keeps this hub full-to-bursting, with thousands of legal and illegal residents packed into the area surrounding East Canal Street. Many work and live here and rarely leave the neighbourhood. Chinatown's busy streets get even wilder during the **Chinese New Year** festivities, in February (*see p266*), and around the Fourth of July, when the area is the city's best source of (illegal) fireworks.

Food is everywhere. The markets on Canal Street sell some of the best, most affordable seafood and fresh produce in the city – you'll see buckets of live eels and crabs, neat stacks of greens and piles of hairy rambutans (cousins of the lychee). Street vendors sell satisfying snacks such as pork buns and sweet egg pancakes by the bagful. Mott Street, between Kenmare and Worth Streets, is lined with restaurants representing the cuisine of virtually every province of mainland China and Hong Kong; the Bowery, East Broadway and Division Street are just as diverse. Adding to the mix are myriad Indonesian, Malaysian, Thai and Vietnamese eateries and stores.

Canal Street, a bargain hunter's paradise, is infamous as a source of (illegal) knockoff designer handbags, perfumes and other goods. The area's many gift shops are stocked with fun, inexpensive Chinese products, from good-luck charms to pop-culture paraphernalia.

One site of historical interest is Wing Fat Shopping, a strange little subterranean mall with its entrance at Chatham Square (No.8, to the right of the OTB parlour), rumored to have been a stop on the Underground Railroad 25 years before the Chinese began populating this area in the 1880s.

A statue of the philosopher marks **Confucius Plaza**, at the corner of the Bowery and Division Street. In Columbus Park, at Bayard and Mulberry Streets, elderly men and women gather around card tables to play mah-jong and dominoes (you can hear the clacking tiles from across the street), while younger folks practise martial arts. The **Museum of Chinese in the Americas** hosts exhibitions and events that explore the Chinese immigrant experience in the western hemisphere. In the **Eastern States Buddhist Temple of America**, you'll be dazzled by the glitter of hundreds of Buddhas and the aroma of wafting incense. Donate $1 and you'll receive a fortune slip. For both, *see p102*.

For a different perspective on the area's culture, visit the noisy, dingy Chinatown Fair (at the southern end of Mott Street), an amusement arcade where some of the East Coast's best Street Fighter players congregate. Older kids hit Chinatown to eat and drink: Joe's Shanghai (9 Pell Street, between Bowery &

New York City Fire Museum. *See p99.*

Mott Street, 1-212 233 8888) is famous for its soup dumplings, boiled pillows of dough filled with pork and broth; and Happy Ending (302 Broome Street, between Eldridge & Forsyth Streets, 1-212 334 9676), a popular nightspot for downtown denizens of every ethnic group, occupies a former massage parlour (the name of the bar is a nod to its sexually charged roots).

Eastern States Buddhist Temple of America

64 Mott Street, between Bayard & Canal Streets (1-212 966 6229). Subway: J, M, N, Q, R, W, Z, 6 to Canal Street. **Open** *9am-6pm daily.* **Map** *p403 F29.*

Museum of Chinese in the Americas

Second Floor, 70 Mulberry Street, at Bayard Street (1-212 619 4785/www.moca-nyc.org). Subway: J, M, N, Q, R, W, Z, 6 to Canal Street. **Open** *noon-6pm Tue-Thur, Sat, Sun; noon-7pm Fri.* **Admission**

suggested donation $3; $1 seniors and students; free under-12s. Free Friday. **No credit cards.** **Map** p402 F31.

In the heart of downtown Manhattan's Chinatown, a century-old former schoolhouse holds a two-room museum focused on Chinese-American history and the Chinese immigrant experience. Call for details about walking tours of the neighbourhood.

Lower East Side

The **Lower East Side** was shaped by New York's immigrants, millions upon millions of whom poured into the city from the late 19th century onwards. The resulting patchwork of dense communities is great for dining and exploration – though today, the Lower East Side is less and less dominated by Asian and Latino families, and more and more ruled by chic boutiques, restaurants and the stylish types who frequent them. Early inhabitants of this area were mostly Eastern European Jews, and mass tenement housing was built to accommodate the 19th-century influx of immigrants, which included many German, Hungarian, Irish and Polish families. The unsanitary, airless and overcrowded living conditions suffered by these people were documented near the end of that century by photographer and writer Jacob A Riis in *How the Other Half Lives*; the book's publication fuelled reformers, who prompted the introduction of building codes. To better understand how these immigrants lived, tour the **Lower East Side Tenement Museum** (*see below*).

Between 1870 and 1920, hundreds of synagogues and religious schools were established. Yiddish newspapers and associations for social reform and cultural studies flourished, as did vaudeville and classic Yiddish theatre. (The Marx Brothers, Jimmy Durante, Eddie Cantor, and George and Ira Gershwin were just a few of the entertainers who once lived in the district.) Currently, only about 10 per cent of the LES population is Jewish; the **Eldridge Street Synagogue** often has a hard time rounding up the ten adult males required to conduct a service. Still, the synagogue has not missed a Sabbath or holiday service in more than 115 years. **First Shearith Israel Graveyard** (on the southern edge of Chinatown) is the burial ground of the country's first Jewish community. It has gravestones that date from 1683, including those of Spanish and Portuguese Jews who fled the Inquisition.

Puerto Ricans and Dominicans began to move to the Lower East Side after World War II. Colourful awnings still mark the area's bodegas, and many restaurants serve Caribbean standards.

In the 1980s, a new breed of immigrant began moving in: young artists and musicians attracted by low rents. Bars, boutiques and music venues sprang up on and around Ludlow Street, creating an annexe to the East Village. This scene is still thriving, though rents have risen like mercury in August. For live music, check who's playing at Arlene's Grocery, the Bowery Ballroom (for both, *see p314*) and Tonic (*p321*). The sign at Pianos (*see p320*), a popular bi-level bar, is a remnant from the piano store that occupied its address for decades. A local art scene has also taken root; Rivington Arms and Participant Inc (*see p268*) are storefront galleries showcasing young artists.

The Lower East Side's reputation as a haven for political radicals lives on at ABC No Rio (*see p278* **Our unorganicized reading**), which was established in 1980 after squatters took over an abandoned ground-floor space; it now houses a gallery and performance space. Meanwhile, luxe apartment complexes have moved in. Hotel on Rivington (*see p46*), one of the new crop of high-rise buildings in this low-rise 'hood, is difficult to miss.

Despite the trendy shops that have cropped up along the block, Orchard Street below Stanton Street remains the heart of the **Orchard Street Bargain District**, a row of stores selling utilitarian goods. This is the place for cheap hats, luggage, sportswear and T-shirts. In the 1930s, Mayor Fiorello La Guardia forced pushcart vendors off the streets and into large indoor marketplaces. Although many of these bazaars are now a thing of the past, **Essex Street Markets** (120 Essex Street, between Delancey & Rivington Streets) is still going strong and is packed with purveyor of all sorts of things Latino, Jewish and Chinese, from plantains to kosher wine and soy dumplings.

Some other vestiges of the neighbourhood's Jewish roots remain. Katz's Delicatessen (205 E Houston Street, 1-212 254 2246) sells some of the best pastrami in New York (FYI, Meg Ryan's famous 'orgasm' scene in *When Harry Met Sally…* was filmed here). People come from all over for the crunchy dills at Guss' Pickles (*see p241*), another Lower East Side favourite and film star (it's in *Crossing Delancey*).

The Lower East Side is a carb-craver's paradise. Pay tribute to the neighbourhood's Eastern European origins with a freshly baked bialy from Kossar's Bialystoker Kuchen Bakery (367 Grand Street, between Essex & Norfolk Streets, 1-212 473 4810). If you're in need of a sweeter hunk of dough, head a few doors over to the Doughnut Plant (379 Grand Street, between Essex & Norfolk Streets, 1-212 505 3700), for high-quality organic doughnuts.

Eldridge Street Synagogue

12 Eldridge Street, between Canal & Division Streets (1-212 219 0888/www.eldridgestreet.org). Subway: F to East Broadway. **Tours** 11am-4pm Tue, Wed, Thur, Sun and by appointment. Guided tours on the hour between 11am and 3pm. **Admission** $5; $3 seniors and students; $1 self-guided tours. **Map** p402 F31.

First Shearith Israel Graveyard

55-57 St James Place, between James & Oliver Streets. Subway: J, M, Z to Bowery. **Map** p402 F31.

Lower East Side Tenement Museum

90 Orchard Street, at Broome Street (1-212 431 0233/www.tenement.org). Subway: F to Delancey Street; J, M, Z to Delancey-Essex Streets. **Open** *Visitors' center* 11am-5.30pm Mon; 11am-6pm Tue-Fri; 10.45am-5.30pm Sat, Sun. **Admission** $12; $10 seniors and students. **Credit** AmEx, MC, V. **Map** p403 G30.

Housed in an 1863 tenement building along with a gallery, shop and video room, this fascinating museum is accessible only by guided tour. The tours, which regularly sell out (definitely book ahead), explain the daily life of typical tenement-dwelling immigrant families. (See the website for 360-degree views of the museum's interior.) From April to December, the museum also leads walking tours of the Lower East Side.

East Village

Scruffier than its genteel western counterpart, the **East Village** has a long history as a countercultural hotbed. Originally considered part of the Lower East Side, the neighbourhood boomed in the 1960s, when writers, artists and musicians moved in, transforming it into the hub for the period's social revolution.

Clubs and coffeehouses thrived, including the Fillmore East, on Second Avenue, between 6th & 7th Streets (the theatre has been demolished), and the Dom (23 St Marks Place, between Second & Third Avenues), where the Velvet Underground often headlined (the building is now a condo). In the '70s, the neighbourhood took a dive as drugs and crime prevailed – but that didn't stop the influx of artists and punk rockers. In the early '80s, East Village galleries were among the first to display the work of groundbreaking artists Jean-Michel Basquiat and Keith Haring. The nabe's past as an alt-scene nexus of arts and politics gets a nod with **Howl!** (*see p264*) – a late-summer festival organised by the Federation of East Village Artists. Poetry, music and film events celebrate the community's vibrant heritage.

The area east of Broadway between Houston and 14th Streets is less edgy today, but remnants of its spirited past endure. A generally amiable population of ravers, punks, yuppies, hippies, homeboys, vagrants and trustafarians (those wannabe bohos funded by family money) has crowded into the neighbourhood's tenements, alongside a few elderly holdouts from previous waves of immigration. Check out the indie record shops, bargain restaurants, grungy bars, punky clubs and funky, cheap clothing stores.

For a historical and cultural tour of the neighbourhood, start on the corner of 10th Street and Second Avenue. Here, on the eastern end of historic Stuyvesant Street (one of only a few streets in this area that break the grid), sits the East Village's unofficial cultural centre: **St Mark's Church in-the-Bowery** (*see p354* **Danspace project**). St Mark's was built in 1799 on the site of Peter Stuyvesant's farm, and the old guy himself, one of New York's first governors, is buried in the adjacent cemetery.

The Episcopal church holds regular services, and also hosts arts groups, such as the experimental theatre troupe Ontological at St Mark's (1-212 533 4650).

St Marks Place (8th Street, between Lafayette Street & Avenue A) is the East Village's main drag. In 1917, the Bolshevik Leon Trotsky ran a printing press at 77 St Marks Place (between First & Second Avenues), and poet WH Auden lived at the address from 1953 to 1972. Lined with stores, bars and street vendors, St Marks stays packed until the wee hours with crowds browsing for bargain T-shirts, records and books. Since tattooing became legal again in New York City in 1997 (it had been banned in 1961), a number of parlours have opened up, including the famous Fun City (94 St Marks Place, between First Avenue & Avenue A, 1-212 353 8282), whose awning advertises cappuccino and tattoos.

Astor Place, with its 1970s balanced-cube sculpture – which made news in 2005, when its spinning base got stuck – is always swarming with young skateboarders and other modern-day street urchins. It is also the site of Peter Cooper's Cooper Union; home to schools of art, architecture and engineering, it bears the distinction of being the only full-scholarship (as in free) private college in the United States. During the 19th century, Astor Place marked the boundary between the slums to the east and some of the city's most fashionable homes. **Colonnade Row** (428-434 Lafayette Street, between Astor Place & E 4th Street) faces the distinguished Astor Public Library building, which theatre legend Joseph Papp rescued from demolition in the 1960s. Today, the old library is the **Public Theater** (*see p349*) – a haven for first-run American plays, the headquarters of the Shakespeare in Central Park festival (*see p262*) and the trendy Joe's Pub (*see p317*).

Below Astor Place, Third Avenue (one block east of Lafayette Street) becomes the **Bowery**. The street, for ages the city's famous flophouse strip and the home of missionary organisations catering to the down-and-out, has in recent years been sanitised and invaded by swanky restaurants and clubs. Hallowed CBGB (*see p315*), the birthplace of American punk, is still here though, and continues to pack in guitar bands and nostalgia seekers. Many other bars and clubs successfully apply the cheap-beer-and-loud-music formula, including Continental (*see p315*) and the Mercury Lounge (*see p319*).

East 7th Street is a Ukrainian stronghold; the focal point is the Byzantine **St George's Ukrainian Catholic Church** at No.30. Across the street, there's often a long line of beefy fraternity types waiting to enter McSorley's Old Ale House (*see p216*), which

Chinatown. *See p101.*

Sightseeing

touts itself as the city's oldest pub in a single location (1854); it still serves just one kind of beer – its own brew, available in light and dark formulas. For those who would rather shop than sip, the eclectic boutiques of young designers and vintage-clothing dealers dot 7th, 8th and 9th Streets.

Curry Row, on 6th Street, between First & Second Avenues, is one of several Little Indias in New York. Roughly two dozen Indian restaurants sit side by side (contrary to a oft-told joke, they do not share a single kitchen), and they remain popular with diners on an extremely tight budget. The line of shiny Harleys on 3rd Street, between First & Second Avenues, tells you that the New York chapter of the **Hell's Angels** is based here.

Alphabet City, occupying Avenues A through D, stretches towards the East River. The once largely working-class Latino population has been overtaken by professionals willing to pay higher rents. Avenue C is known as Loisaida Avenue, an approximation of 'Lower East Side' when pronounced with a Spanish accent. The neighbourhood's long romance with the drug trade is mostly a thing of the past.

For those who appreciate funky charm, Alphabet City has its attractions. Two churches on 4th Street are built in the Spanish-colonial style: San Isidro y San Leandro (345 E 4th Street, between Avenues C & D) and Iglesia Pentecostal Camino Damasco (289 E 4th Street, between Avenues B & C). The Nuyorican Poets Cafe (*see p278*), a more than 30-year-old clubhouse for espresso-drinking beatniks, is famous for its poetry slams, in which performers do lyric battle before a score-keeping audience.

Tompkins Square Park (from 7th to 10th Streets, between Avenues A & B), which honours Daniel D Tompkins, governor of New York from 1807 to 1817 and vice president during the Monroe administration, has a past as a site for demonstrations and rioting. The last major uprising was about 15 years ago, when the city evicted squatters from the park and renovated it to suit the area's increasingly affluent residents; in the summer of 2004, a permit request for a 20,000-person protest camp during the Republican National Convention was denied. The square also plays host to the city's on-again, off-again drag celebration, Wigstock. This is the community park of the East Village, and a place where Latino bongo beaters, longhairs with acoustic guitars, punky squatters, mangy dogs, yuppie stroller-pushers and the homeless all mingle.

North of Tompkins Square, around First Avenue and 11th Street, are remnants of earlier communities: discount fabric dealers, Italian cheese shops, Polish butchers and two great

Local legend

In 1917 **Edna St Vincent Millay**, already a gifted poet, moved to Greenwich Village, where she immediately took to the bohemian lifestyle; here women were allowed to smoke in public, dress casually and go out at night unaccompanied. Embracing unconventionality, Millay freely took both male and female lovers. In 1921 she wrote *Recuerdo*, a romantic poem about being up all night and riding the Staten Island Ferry: 'We were very tired, we were very merry – /We had gone back and fourth all night on the ferry.' In 1923 she was the first woman to be awarded the Pulitzer Prize for poetry. That same year she moved into 75½ Bedford Street, one of the narrowest homes in the city, measuring a mere nine feet wide. A talented actress, St Vincent Millay also helped found the Cherry Lane Theater around the corner on Commerce Street – an experimental-theatre landmark.

Italian coffee-and-cannoli houses: De Robertis (176 First Avenue, between 10th & 11th Streets, 1-212 674 7137) and Veniero's Pasticceria and Caffè (342 E 11th Street, at First Avenue, 1-212 674 7264).

Greenwich Village

Stretching from Houston Street to 14th Street, between Broadway and Sixth Avenue, **Greenwich Village**'s leafy streets have inspired bohemians for almost a century. It's a place for idle wandering, for candlelit dining in out-of-the-way restaurants, and for hopping between bars and cabaret venues. The Village gets mobbed in mild weather and has lost some of its quaintness, but much of what has always attracted painters and poets to New York still exists. Sip a fresh roast in honour of the Beats – Jack Kerouac, Allen Ginsberg and their buddies – as you sit in their former haunts. Kerouac's favourite was Le Figaro Café (184 Bleecker Street, at MacDougal Street, 1-212 677 1100). The Cedar Tavern (82 University Place, between 11th & 12th Streets, 1-212 929 9089), which was originally at the corner of 8th Street, is where the leading figures of abstract expressionism's boys' club discussed how best to apply paint: Franz Kline, Jackson Pollock, Larry Rivers and Willem de Kooning drank under this banner in the 1950s.

The hippies who tuned out in **Washington Square Park**, once a potter's field, are still there in spirit, and often in person: the park hums with musicians and street artists (though the once ubiquitous pot dealers have disappeared thanks to hidden surveillance cameras). In warmer months, this is one of the best people-watching spots in the city. Chess hustlers and students from New York University join in, along with today's new generation of idlers: hip-hop kids who drive down to West 4th Street in their booming Jeeps, and Generation-Y skateboarders who clatter around the fountain and near the base of the Washington Arch. A modest-size replica of Paris's Arc de Triomphe, the arch was built in 1895 to honour George Washington, and was recently unveiled after a seemingly endless refurbishment. A $16-million redesign of the park began in late 2005.

The Village has been fashionable since the 1830s, when the wealthy built handsome townhouses around Washington Square. A few of these properties are still privately owned and occupied; many others have become part of the ever-expanding **New York University** campus. NYU also owns the Washington Mews, a row of charming 19th-century buildings that were once stables; they line a tiny cobblestoned alley just north of the park between Fifth Avenue and University Place. Several literary figures, including Henry James, Herman Melville and Mark Twain, lived on or near the square. In 1871, the local creative community founded the **Salmagundi Club** (see p109), America's oldest artists' club, which is now situated north of Washington Square on Fifth Avenue. The landmark building hosts exhibitions, lectures and art auctions.

Greenwich Village continues to change with the times, for better and for worse. Eighth Street is currently a long procession of piercing parlours, punky boutiques and shoe stores; in the 1960s, it was the closest New York got to San Francisco's Haight Street. (Jimi Hendrix's Electric Lady Studios is still at 52 W 8th Street, between Fifth & Sixth Avenues.)

Once the dingy but colourful stomping ground of Beat poets and folk and jazz musicians, the well-trafficked strip of Bleecker Street between La Guardia Place and Sixth Avenue is now simply an overcrowded stretch of poster shops, cheap restaurants and music venues for the college crowd. Bob Dylan lived at and owned 94 MacDougal Street (on a row of historic brownstones near Bleecker Street) through much of the 1960s, performing in Washington Square Park and at clubs such as Cafe Wha? on MacDougal Street, between Bleecker & West 3rd Streets. The famed Village Gate jazz club once stood at the corner of Bleecker and Thompson Streets; it's been carved up into a CVS pharmacy and a small theatre, though the Gate's sign is still in evidence. The new **AIA Center for Architecture** (see p108), a comprehensive resource for building and planning in New York, is just up the street, on La Guardia Place.

In the triangle formed by Sixth Avenue, Greenwich Avenue and 10th Street, you'll see the Gothic-style Jefferson Market Library (a branch of the New York Public Library); the

Lower East Side. See p102.

Sightseeing

Village life on and around **Bleecker Street**. *See p107.*

lovely flower-filled garden facing Greenwich Avenue once held the art deco Women's House of Detention (Mae West did a little time there in 1926, on obscenity charges stemming from her Broadway show *Sex*), torn down in 1974. On Sixth Avenue at West 4th Street, stop by 'the Cage', outdoor basketball courts where outstanding schoolyard players showcase their shake-and-bake moves.

AIA Center for Architecture

536 La Guardia Place, between Bleecker &
W 3rd Streets (1-212 683 0023/www.aiany.org).
Subway: A, B, C, D, E, F, V to W 4th Street.
Open 9am-8pm Mon-Fri; 11am-5pm Sat.
Admission free. **Map** p403 E29.
After five years of planning, the Center for Architecture opened to acclaim in autumn 2003. Founded in 1867, the organisation languished for years on the sixth floor of a Lexington Avenue

edifice, far out of sight (and mind) of all but the most devoted architecture aficionados. In 1997, recognising its isolation and perceived insularity, the American Institute of Architects (AIA) began searching Soho and the Village for new digs, finally opting for a vacant storefront in an early 20th-century industrial building. After a design competition, Andrew Berman Architect was chosen to transform the space into a fitting home for architectural debate.

The sweeping, light-filled design is a physical manifestation of AIA's goal of promoting transparency in its access and programming. Berman cut away large slabs of flooring at the street and basement levels, converting underground spaces into bright, museum-quality galleries. He also installed a glass-enclosed library and conference room – open to the public – on the first floor, and a children's gallery and workshop on the mezzanine level. The building is New York's first public space to use an energy-efficient geothermal system. Fifty-five-degree water, from two 1,260ft wells, is piped through the building to help heat and cool it.

Salmagundi Club

47 Fifth Avenue, at 12th Street (1-212 255 7740/ www.salmagundi.org). Subway: L, N, Q, R, W, 4, 5, 6 to 14th Street-Union Square. **Open** *1-5pm daily for exhibitions only; phone for details.* **Admission** *free.* **Map** *p402 E28.*

West Village & Meatpacking District

While the **West Village** now harbours a wide range of celebrities (Sarah Jessica Parker and hubby Matthew Broderick live here, as does former NYC mayor Ed Koch, and the trio of Richard Meier towers at the end of Perry and Charles Streets houses A-listers galore), it has managed to retain a low key, everyone-knows-one-another feel.

The area west of Sixth Avenue to the Hudson River, from 14th Street to Houston Street, still possesses the features that moulded the Village's character. Only in this neighbourhood could West 10th Street cross West 4th Street, and Waverly Place cross…Waverly Place. (The West Village's layout follows not the regular grid pattern but the original horse paths that settlers used to navigate it.) Locals and tourists fill the bistros along Seventh Avenue and Hudson Street (aka Eighth Avenue), the neighbourhood's main drags, and patronise the increasingly high-rent shops, including three Marc Jacobs boutiques, three Ralph Lauren outposts and a new James Perse shop, which line this newly hot end of Bleecker Street.

The north-west corner of this area is known as the **Meatpacking District**. Beginning in

the 1930s, it was primarily a wholesale meat market; until the 1990s, it was also a choice haunt for prostitutes, many of them transsexual. In recent years, however, the atmospheric cobblestoned streets of this landmark district have seen the arrival of a new type of tenant: the once lonely Florent (69 Gansevoort Street, between Greenwich & Washington Streets, 1-212 989 5779), a 24-hour French diner that opened in 1985, is now part of a chic scene that includes swinging watering holes and the restaurants Pastis (9 Ninth Avenue, at Little W 12th Street, 1-212 929 4844) and 5 Ninth (5 Ninth Avenue, at Little W 12th Street, 1-212 929 9460), among many others. The recent opening of the boutique Hotel Gansevoort (*see p54* **Downtown deluxe**) has made this region an official tourist destination. The district also lures the fashion faithful with hot destinations such as Jeffrey New York, Alexander McQueen, Catherine Malandrino, Stella McCartney and rockin' Le Dernier Cri. As rents rose, many of the meatpacking plants were forced out to make space for the trendy (on hot summer days, however, you can still smell the meat dealers that remain).

The neighbourhood's bohemians may have dwindled – they surely could not afford the current rents in this astronomically priced area – but several historic nightlife spots soldier on to the south: the White Horse Tavern (567 Hudson Street, at 11th Street, 1-212 989 3956) is supposedly where poet Dylan Thomas went on the last drinking binge before his death, in 1953. Earlier in the century, John Steinbeck and John Dos Passos passed time at Chumley's (*see p217*), a still-unmarked Prohibition-era speakeasy at 86 Bedford Street. Writer Edna St Vincent Millay lived at 75½ Bedford Street (*see p106* **Local legend**), built in 1873; subsequent inhabitants of this building include Cary Grant and John Barrymore. Only nine feet wide, it's one of the narrowest residential buildings in the entire city. On and just off Seventh Avenue South are jazz and cabaret clubs, including Village Vanguard (*see p325*).

The West Village is also renowned as a gay neighbourhood, though the scene is more happening in Chelsea, to the north (*see p110*). The Stonewall (*see p307*), on Christopher Street, is next to the original Stonewall Inn, the site of the 1969 rebellion that marked the birth of the modern gay-liberation movement. Same-sex couples stroll along Christopher Street (from Sheridan Square to the Hudson River), and plenty of shops, bars and restaurants are out and proud. The Hudson riverfront features grass-covered piers, food vendors, picnic tables and volleyball courts – ideal for warm-weather dawdling by folks of any sexual persuasion.

Sightseeing

Midtown

The heart of Manhattan pulses with excitement 24/7.

Sightseeing

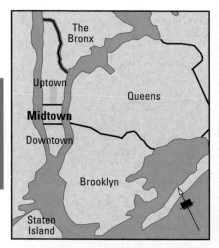

Jostling shoulder to shoulder with the masses in Midtown, it's hard to believe that Manhattan was once a sleepy wooded island, traded for a handful of beads and some pocket lint way back when. Every day, Midtown (occupying the slice of the island between 14th Street and 59th Street) earns its reputation as one of the most hectic, breathtaking urban landscapes on earth. During the day, people elbow their way along the sidewalks as yellow cabs and bicycle messengers dart every which way and streetlights restrain walls of impatient traffic. The frenetic action continues above and below ground: each skyscraper is a monument to the buzz of commercial activity, while hordes of commuters ride an around-the-clock network of underground trains and subways. The city's most famous landmarks – the **Empire State Building**, the **Chrysler Building**, **Rockefeller Center**, **Times Square** and **Grand Central Terminal** – are found here. High- and low-brow fashion is conceived around Seventh Avenue, publicised on Madison and sold along Fifth. But there's more to Midtown than glistening towers and high-octane commerce. Cultural heavyweights such as the **Museum of Modern Art**, **Broadway** and the **Theater District**, **Carnegie Hall** and the **New York Public Library** draw their own crowds. Midtown

is also where you'll find the folksy **Union Square Greenmarket** and the quaint tree-lined streets of **Chelsea**, **Tudor City** and **Gramercy Park**. Everywhere you look, you'll see shopping galore, from street peddlers pushing designer knockoffs to soigné boutiques and world-class department stores. It may sound like a corny line from a Broadway musical, but Midtown's got it all.

Chelsea

Not so long ago, Chelsea was a mostly working-class and industrial neighbourhood. Now it's the epicentre of the city's gay life, but residents of all types inhabit the blocks between 14th and 29th Streets west of Fifth Avenue. There's a generous assortment of bars and restaurants, most of which are clustered along Eighth Avenue, the main hub of activity. Pioneers such as **Dia:Chelsea** (*see p112*) led the art crowd northwards from Soho, and the whole western edge of Chelsea is now the city's hottest gallery zone. The far-west warehouse district, a nesting ground for fashionable lounges and nightclubs, is also seeing more residential use. The most exciting thing to happen to Chelsea of late are the plans to turn a defunct elevated train, known as the High Line, into a 1.5 mile long promenade (*see p32* **On the right track**).

Don't miss the weekend flea markets tucked between buildings in parking lots on 25th Street, between Sixth Avenue and Broadway, or the rummage-worthy **Garage** (*see p48*). Ornate wrought-iron balconies distinguish the **Chelsea Hotel** (*see p51*), which has been a magnet for international bohemians since the 1950s. In the '60s and '70s, Andy Warhol's superstars (the Chelsea Girls) made the place infamous; punk rock conferred its notoriety in the '80s, when Nancy Spungen was stabbed to death by boyfriend Sid Vicious in Room 100. Stop by for a peek at the lobby artwork and the grunge-glamorous guests, and linger over a drink in the luxe basement lounge, Serena. Occupying the long stretch of 23rd Street between Ninth and Tenth Avenues, London Terrace is a distinctive 1920s Tudor-style apartment complex that's home to some famous names, including Debbie Harry, Chelsea Clinton and Teri Hatcher (of *Desperate Housewives*).

Chrysler Building. *See p128.*

Chelsea has its fair share of cultural offerings. The **Joyce Theater** (*see 352*) is a brilliantly renovated Art Deco cinema that presents better-known contemporary dance troupes. The **Dance Theater Workshop** (*see p354*) performs at the Bessie Schönberg Theater (219 W 19th Street, between Seventh & Eighth Avenues, 1-212 691 6500), and towards the river on 19th Street sits the **Kitchen** (*see p354*), a pioneering experimental-arts centre. If sex is on your mind, head to Fifth Avenue and check out the **Museum of Sex** (*see p112*).

Cushman Row (406-418 W 20th Street, between Ninth & Tenth Avenues), in the Chelsea Historic District, is an example of how the area looked when it was developed in the mid 1800s (although its grandeur was later affected by the intrusion of noisy elevated railways). Just north is the block-long **General Theological Seminary of the Episcopal Church** (*see p112*), whose gardens offer a pleasant respite for reflection. The seminary's land was part of the estate known as Chelsea, owned by the poet Clement Clarke Moore (best known for "Twas the night before Christmas').

The former Nabisco plant on Ninth Avenue – where the first Oreo cookie was made, in 1912 – has been renovated and is now home to the **Chelsea Market** (75 Ninth Avenue, between 15th & 16th Streets, www.chelseamarket.com). The former factory site is a conglomeration of 18 structures built between the 1890s and the 1930s. The ground-floor food arcade offers artisanal bread, lobster, wine, hand-decorated cookies and imported Italian foods, among other treats. Upper floors house several media companies, including the Oxygen Network and the Food Network studios, where shows such as *Emeril Live* and *Molto Mario* are taped.

Chelsea's art galleries, occupying former warehouses in the 20s west of Tenth Avenue, draw an international audience, especially at weekends. Many of the major galleries that were priced out of Soho (retail shops replaced them) found new homes here; bars and restaurants on the prowl for cheaper space followed suit. Evolving much like Soho did, this area has become just as expensive. In 2006, the **New Museum of Contemporary Art** (*see p113*) will call the nabe home while new digs are being built.

Union Square: spinmeisters lure the crowds away from...

On Seventh Avenue at 27th Street is the **Fashion Institute of Technology** (www.fitnyc.edu), a state college for those who aspire to vie with renowned alumni Jhane Barnes and Calvin Klein in making their mark on fashion. Fashionistas won't want to miss the school's museum (*see below*) a block away, which mounts stellar free exhibitions.

You can watch the sunset from one of the spectacular Hudson River piers, which were once terminals for the world's grand ocean liners. Many other city piers remain in a state of ruin, but the four between 17th and 23rd Streets have been transformed into the mega sports centre and TV- and film-studio complex **Chelsea Piers**. When you're down by the river, the **Starrett-Lehigh Building** (601 W 26th Street, at Eleventh Avenue) comes into view. The stunning 1929 structure was left to fall into disrepair until the dot-com boom of the late '90s, when media companies, photographers and fashion designers snatched up the loft-like spaces.

Dia:Chelsea

548 W 22nd Street, between Tenth & Eleventh Avenues (1-212 989 5566/www. diachelsea.org). **Closed** until late 2007. **Map** p404 C26.
The Chelsea branch of this New York stalwart, usually given to single-artist projects, is undergoing renovation and will reopen sometime in late 2007. For Dia:Beacon, Dia Art Foundation's magnificent new outpost in the Hudson Valley, *see p356*.

General Theological Seminary of the Episcopal Church

175 Ninth Avenue, between 20th & 21st Streets (1-212 243 5150/www.gts.edu). Subway: C, E to 23rd Street. **Open** *Gardens* noon-3pm Mon-Thur; 11am-3pm Fri, weather permitting. **Admission** free. **Map** p403 C27.

Museum at FIT

Seventh Avenue, at 27th Street (1-212 217 5800/www.fitnyc.edu). Subway: 1 to 28th Street. **Open** noon-8pm Tue-Fri; 10am-5pm Sat. **Admission** free. **Map** p404 D26.
The Fashion Institute of Technology houses one of the world's most important collections of clothing and textiles, curated by the influential fashion historian Valerie Steele. Incorporating everything from extravagant costumes to sturdy denim work clothes, the exhibitions touch on the role fashion has played in society since the beginning of the 20th century.

Museum of Sex

233 Fifth Avenue, at 27th Street (1-212 689 6337/ www.museumofsex.org). Subway: N, R, W, 6 to 28th Street. **Open** 11am-6.30pm Mon-Fri, Sun; 11am-8pm Sat. **Admission** $14.50; $13.50 students. Under-18s not admitted. **Credit** AmEx, MC, V. **Map** p404 E26.
Despite the subject matter, don't expect too much titillation at this museum, which opened in 2002 to mixed reviews. Instead, you'll find presentations of historical documents and items – many of which were too risqué to be made public in their own time – that explore prostitution, burlesque, birth control, obscenity and fetishism. In 2002, the museum acquired an extensive collection of pornography

... **Union Square Greenmarket**. *See p114.*

from a retired Library of Congress curator (apparently, he applied his professional skills to recreational pursuits as well). Thus, the Ralph Whittington Collection features thousands of items, including 8mm films, videos, blow-up dolls and other erotic paraphernalia.

New Museum of Contemporary Art

Temporary location 556 W 22nd Street, at Eleventh Avenue (1-212 219 1222/www.new museum.org). Subway: C, E to 23rd Street.
Open noon-6pm Tue, Wed, Fri, Sat; noon-8pm Thur. **Admission** $6; $3 seniors and students; free under-18s. Half-price 6-8pm Thur.
Credit AmEx, Disc, MC, V. **Map** p404 C26.
While its new digs on the Bowery are under construction (the opening is slated for 2007), the New Museum will occupy 7,000sq ft of ground-floor space in the Chelsea Art Museum. Its retrospectives of mid-career artists – South Africa's William Kentridge, Los Angeles' Paul McCarthy, New York's Carroll Dunham – attract serious crowds, though group shows can be less successful.

Flatiron District & Union Square

The Flatiron District, which extends from 14th to 29th Streets between Fifth and Park Avenues, gives Downtown a run for its money in terms of cachet – and cool. This chic enclave is full of retail stores that are often less expensive but just as stylish as those below 14th Street. The area is compact enough that tourists can hit all the sights on foot and then relax with a cocktail at a local watering hole.

Two public commons lie within the district: Madison and Union Squares. **Madison Square** (from 23rd to 26th Streets, between Fifth & Madison Avenues) was the site of PT Barnum's Hippodrome and the original Madison Square Garden – the scene of the scandalous murder of its architect, Stanford White (recounted in EL Doctorow's novel *Ragtime*, also adapted as a film). After years of neglect, the statue-filled Madison Square Park finally got a facelift in 2001. For ages, the vicinity bordering the park's east side was notable only for the presence of the monolithic New York Life Insurance Company building (51 Madison Avenue, between 25th & 26th Streets) and the Appellate Division Courthouse (35 E 25th Street, at Madison Avenue). Now, numerous swank dining options have injected some café-society liveliness, including Tom Colicchio's glorious side-by-side-by-side trifecta 'wichcraft, Craft, Craftbar (*see p198*).

During warmer months, stop by Danny Meyer's Shake Shack (south side of Madison Square Park, near 23rd Street at Madison Avenue, 1-212 889 6600), a hot-dog, hamburger and ice-cream stand where you can dine alfresco, surrounded by lush foliage.

Just south of Madison Square is a famously triangular Renaissance palazzo, the **Flatiron Building** (175 Fifth Avenue, between 22nd & 23rd Streets). The 22-storey edifice is clad in white terracotta: its light colour was revealed again by cleaning and restoration in the early 1990s. The surrounding neighbourhood was christened in honour of the structure, which was the world's first steel-frame skyscraper.

In the 19th century, the neighbourhood went by the moniker of Ladies' Mile, thanks to the ritzy department stores that lined Broadway and Sixth Avenue to the west. These huge retail palaces attracted the carriage trade, wealthy women who bought the latest imported fashions and household goods. By 1914, most of the department stores had moved north, leaving their proud cast-iron buildings behind. Today, the area is peppered with bookshops and photo studios and labs (it was known as New York's photo district well into the 1990s), and supermodels. The area has also reclaimed its fashionable history and is once again a prime shopping destination. Broadway between 14th and 23rd Streets is a tasteful home-furnishings strip; be sure to take a spin through the eclectic, expensive six-storey home-design store **ABC Carpet & Home** (*see p249*). Fifth Avenue below 23rd Street is a clothing mecca: many upscale shops, including the exclusive Paul Smith, showcase the latest designs. In the mid

Sightseeing

1990s, big internet companies began colonising the lofts on Fifth Avenue and Broadway, and the district was dubbed Silicon Alley, a name that stuck even after the boom flattened out.

Union Square (from 14th to 17th Streets, between Union Square East & Union Square West) is named after neither the Union of the Civil War nor the lively labour rallies that once took place here, but simply for the union of Broadway and Bowery Lane (now Fourth Avenue). From the 1920s until the early 1960s, Union Square had a reputation as the favourite location for rabble-rousing political oratory, from AFL-CIO rallies to anti-Vietnam War protests. Following September 11, 2001, the park became a focal point for the city's outpouring of grief. Today, it's probably best known as the home of the **Union Square**

Walk this way: Saturday in the city

Start: Empire State Building
Finish: Merchant's House Museum
Length: about 1.5 miles
Time: 2 to 3 hours, depending on how long you linger.
Note: this walk is best on Saturdays, when the flea markets and the farmers' market are in full swing.

In old New York it would have been referred to as a constitutional – a stroll taken for health, mental stimulation and culture. This walk includes all three: a tour of some of the city's vintage treasures and a chance to reverse the clock and see how folks lived last century.

The journey back in time begins on the south-west corner of Fifth Avenue and East 34th Street in the shadow of Manhattan's 102-storey, 75-year-old, gleaming silver ambassador: the **Empire State Building**. Built during the Depression drawing design inspiration from a common pencil, this art deco masterpiece represents the ultimate marriage of Manhattan sophistication with technical dominance – not to mention serving as the notorious rendezvous for a certain female beauty with a rather large ape (no, not Meg Ryan and Tom Hanks).

Saunter west on 34th Street and it'll only take you a city block to arrive at **Herald Square**, home for over 100 years to another icon of Manhattan's urban streetscape, **Macy's** department store (*see p225*). From first-day sales totalling a mere $11.06, this dry goods shop blossomed into the titanic mega-retailer it is today.

Turn south down Sixth Avenue and stroll past the handbag, T-shirt and hat wholesalers. When you reach 25th Street you'll be in the heart of Manhattan's antiquarian soul – the flea market and collectibles district. Turn right (west) along 25th Street (peek in one of the many collectable co-operative shops along the way) until you get to the indoor Garage Flea

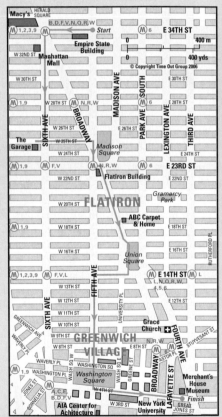

markets, located on bi-level floors of a gigantic parking garage to your left. Here you can spend hours hunting among junk and jewels, trash and treasure, posh and porn. When you're done browsing, head back east on 25th Street. If the weather is decent, don't

Greenmarket (*see p116*), an excellent farmers' market fast becoming a New York institution. The buildings flanking the square are used for a variety of commercial purposes. They include the W New York-Union Square hotel, the giant Zeckendorf Towers residential complex (1 Irving Place, between 14th & 15th Streets), a Virgin Megastore and a Barnes & Noble bookstore. Facing south, look up (and slightly east) and marvel at what three million bucks can buy: the ugly sculpture-wall before you, called *Metronome,* was installed in 1999 (and remains one of the largest private commissions of public art in the city's history). What the hell is it? We thought you'd never ask: 'The entire work symbolises the intangibility of time,' according to its makers (artists Kristin Jones and Andrew Ginzel). Reading from left

miss the outdoor flea market nestled in a weekday parking lot on 25th Street between Sixth Avenue and Broadway.

One block's walk further west will get you to Broadway, where you'll be staring into the shady copse of **Madison Square Park**. A public space in the city since 1686, this park (later named after President James Madison) is in the centre of Manhattan's vibrant Flatiron District. It once housed the Statue of Liberty's arm while funds were secured for the rest of her. Enjoy canine antics at the dog run and then head out the south-west exit to get a close look at the district's namesake – the Flatiron Building – named for its resemblance to a... oh, you'll figure it out.

Make your way south down Broadway. A tony trove of shops housed in 19th-century, mansard-roofed buildings awaits you, notable among them the crown jewel of housewares: **ABC Carpet & Home** (*see p249*).

If you're really a glutton for period authenticity, shop for food the way they did in Manhattan's early days at the Greenmarket farmers' market, a few more blocks south in **Union Square Park**. A showcase of produce from over 200 farmers, this is the spot to load up on flowers, fruits, veggies, handicrafts, even wines and handmade pretzels, from the tri-state area.

Exit the park's south side at University Place, then head west on 14th Street. When you get to Fifth Avenue, turn left and walk south until you get to an indisputable gem of Manhattan history, the unofficial capitol of Greenwich Village: **Washington Square Park** (pictured). Through its famed arch you'll find the epicentre of the city's bohemian life, as well as history up the wazoo: the park served as a potter's field for yellow-fever victims, public gallows (the hanging tree still stands), a beatnik meeting place in the 1950s and, more recently, a skateboarders' paradise.

At the southern end of the park you'll find yourself on 4th Street. Stroll east and make a social call at No.29 East 4th Street, the **Merchant's House Museum** (1-212 777 1089, merchantshouse.com), the city's only preserved family home from the 19th century. Built in 1832, the house is a virtual portal into domestic life of the time and the perfect way to wrap up a day of nostalgia, time travel and treasure hunting in a city that once sold for $24 in beads and blankets.

to right, the digital readout on the installation's main panel displays an artist's impression of the current time.

If you worked up an appetite contemplating the time of day, several decent restaurants are in close proximity, most notably the elegant (and famously expensive) Union Square Café (21 E 16th Street, between Fifth Avenue & Union Square West, 1-212 243 4020). In summer, the outdoor Luna Park bar (Union Square Park, 17th Street, between Broadway & Park Avenue South, 1-212 475 8464) beckons the cocktail crowd, while skateboarders commandeer the Greenmarket space during the evenings. Just off the square to the east is the **Vineyard Theatre** (*see p349*), an Off Broadway venue featuring the works of such well-respected playwrights as Craig Lucas and Paula Vogel. Tony-Award winning musical *Avenue Q* got its start here.

Union Square Greenmarket

From 16th to 17th Streets, between Union Square East & Union Square West (1-212 788 7476). Subway: L, N, Q, R, W, 4, 5, 6 to 14th Street-Union Square. **Open** 8am-6pm Mon, Wed, Fri, Sat. **Map** p403 E27.
Shop elbow-to-elbow with top chefs for all manner of regionally grown culinary pleasures. **Photo** *p113*.

Heaven in hell

Overwhelmed by the elbow-to-elbow crowds and the same theme restaurants (and Starbucks!) you can get at home? It's a shame so many visitors to Times Square miss out on a neighbourhood gem just two blocks west of Broadway.

Infamously known as **Hell's Kitchen**, the neighbourhood retains the laid-back Latin ambience that was made famous in *West Side Story*, but the triple-X grittiness and gangs that swamped the area in the 1970s and '80s are gone.

How did the area get that name in the first place? The appellation appears to have worked its way into the city vocabulary in the late 1850s. Some say it was borrowed from a notorious slum in London; others claim it was derived from a conversation between two cops witnessing a riot on 39th Street between Tenth and Eleventh Avenues – a stretch known back then as Battle Row. 'This place is Hell itself,' one cop supposedly remarked. 'Hell's a mild climate,' allegedly replied the other cop, '*This* is Hell's kitchen'.

Today, the strip of Ninth Avenue between 42nd and 52nd Streets is especially inviting with its hip boutiques and a virtual United Nations of cheap, delicious cuisine. The **Westway Diner** (614 Ninth Avenue, between 43rd & 44th Streets) is where Jerry Seinfeld and Larry David dreamed up their famous sitcom about nothing. Just up the street is the grandmama of area eateries: **Poseidon Bakery** (629 Ninth Avenue, at 44th Street), where proprietor Lili Fable and son Paul are the third and fourth generation respectively to run the place since it opened in the 1920s. At **Rice 'n' Beans** (744 Ninth Avenue, at 50th Street), owner Maria Lemos serves up cheap, delicious Brazilian specialities. For lighter fare, join the actor-dancer-singer wannabes lolling on thrift-shop sofas at local caffeine hangout the **Coffee Pot** (350 W 49th Street). Then there's **Amy's Bread** (672 Ninth Avenue, between 46th and 47th Streets), a neighbourhood fave loaded with some of the most mouthwatering baked goods in the city. In the middle of all this lies a little known escape, **Clinton Community Garden** (pictured), a tiny landscaped retreat tucked into 48th Street (between Ninth & Tenth Avenues). Lovingly tended by neighbourhood volunteers, the gated (but public) garden is open to any visitor who shows up (with a smile) and simply asks to be let in: a little piece of heaven in Hell's Kitchen.

Gramercy Park & Murray Hill

You need a key to enter **Gramercy Park**, a tranquil, gated green square at the bottom of Lexington Avenue (between 20th and 21st Streets). Who gets a key? Only the lucky people who live in the beautiful townhouses and apartment buildings that ring the park. Anyone, however, can enjoy the charms of the surrounding district. Gramercy Park was developed in the 1830s to resemble a London square. The Players (16 Gramercy Park South, between Park Avenue South & Irving Place), a private club and residence, is housed in an 1845 brownstone formerly owned by actor Edwin Booth; the 19th-century superstar was the brother of Abraham Lincoln's assassin, John Wilkes Booth. Edwin had the interior revamped as a club for theatre professionals. Next door (No.15) is the Gothic-Revival Samuel Tilden House, which now houses the **National Arts Club**, whose members often donate their work in lieu of annual dues. The busts of famous writers (Shakespeare, Dante, etc) that grace the façade were chosen to reflect Tilden's library, which, along with his vast fortune helped create the New York Public Library.

Irving Place, a strip leading south from the park to 14th Street, is named after author Washington Irving. Near the corner of 15th Street, **Irving Plaza** (*see p317*), a medium-size live-music venue that has been around since the early 1990s (when the Dave Matthews Band played here as an opening act), hosts everyone from old-timers like Van Morrison to newer acts like the Ted Leo/Pharmacists. At the corner of Park Avenue South and 17th Street stands the final headquarters of the once-omnipotent Tammany Hall political machine. Built in 1929, the building now houses the New York Film Academy and a theater.

A few blocks away, the **Theodore Roosevelt Birthplace**, a national historic site, holds a small museum. The president's actual birthplace was demolished in 1916, but it has since been fully reconstructed, complete with period furniture and a trophy room. The low, fortress-like 69th Regiment Armory (68 Lexington Avenue, between 25th & 26th Streets), now used by the New York National Guard, hosted the sensational 1913 Armory Show, which introduced Americans to Cubism, Fauvism and Dadaism. The tradition continues at the annual **Armory Show** (*see p260*).

The largely residential area bordered by 23rd and 30th Streets, Park Avenue and the East River is known as **Kips Bay**, named after Jacobus Henderson Kip, whose farm covered the area in the 17th century. Third Avenue is the neighbourhood's main thoroughfare, and a locus of ethnic eateries representing a variety of eastern cuisines, including Afghan, Tibetan and Turkish, along with nightspots such as the **Rodeo Bar & Grill** (*see p325*), a Texas-style roadhouse that offers food and live roots music. Lexington Avenue between 27th and 30th Streets has been dubbed Curry Hill because of its many Indian restaurants and grocery stores.

Murray Hill spans 30th to 40th Streets between Third and Fifth Avenues. Townhouses of the rich and powerful were once clustered around Madison and Park Avenues. While it's still a fashionable neighbourhood, only a few streets retain the elegance that made Murray Hill so distinctive. Sniffen Court (150-158 E 36th Street, between Lexington & Third Avenues) is an unspoiled row of 1864 carriage houses located within earshot of the Queens Midtown Tunnel's ceaseless traffic. One of the area's most impressive attractions, the **Morgan Library** (*see below*), also on 36th Street, is closed for renovation until spring 2006. The charming exhibition space occupies two buildings (one of which was J Pierpont Morgan's personal library) and holds books, manuscripts, prints, and silver and copper collections accumulated by the famously acquisitive banker. If contemporary European culture interests you more, visit nearby **Scandinavia House: the Nordic Center in America** (*see p118*).

Morgan Library

29 E 36th Street, between Madison & Park Avenues (1-212 685 0008/www.morganlibrary.org). Subway: 6 to 34th Street. **Closed** until spring 2006. **Map** p404 E25.

After undergoing a dramatic expansion in which Pritzker Prize-winning architect Renzo Piano fused the Morgan's three landmark buildings and built yet more galleries underground, the library is set to open its doors in spring 2006. Serving as both museum and research library, the impressive, light-filled space (glass walls in the main pavilion allow visitors to see more of the 1906 Charles McKim building and a naturally lit reading room tops the Madison Avenue structure) is home to an awe-inspiring collection of rare books, illuminated manuscripts, drawings and prints. Among the treats in store will be etchings and drawings by Rembrandt, Michelangelo and Leonardo da Vinci, Mary Shelley's own copy of *Frankenstein* marked with notes and revisions, a 1488 first edition of the Hebrew *Bible*, and one of the first printed copies of the Declaration of Independence.

National Arts Club

15 Gramercy Park South, between Park Avenue South & Irving Place (1-212 475 3424/www.national artsclub.org). Subway: 6 to 23rd Street. **Open** For exhibitions only. Call or visit website for current exhibition information. **Map** p404 E27.

Scandinavia House: The Nordic Center in America

*58 Park Avenue, between 37th & 38th Streets
(1-212 879 9779/www.scandinaviahouse.org).
Subway: 42nd Street S, 4, 5, 6, 7 to 42nd
Street-Grand Central.* **Open** noon-6pm Tue-Sat.
Admission suggested donation $3; $2 seniors and
students. **Credit** AmEx, MC, V. **Map** p404 E24.
You'll find all things Nordic, from Ikea designs to
the latest Finnish film, at this modern centre, the
leading cultural link between the US and the five
Nordic countries (Denmark, Finland, Iceland,
Norway and Sweden). As well as exhibitions, it
stages films, concerts, lectures, symposia and readings, plus kid-friendly programming. The AQ Café
is a bustling lunch spot with a menu by NYC's most
famous Swedish chef, Marcus Samuelsson.

Theodore Roosevelt Birthplace

*28 E 20th Street, between Broadway & Park
Avenue South (1-212 260 1616/www.nps.gov/thrb).
Subway: 6 to 23rd Street.* **Open** 9am-5pm Tue-Sat.
Tours 10am-4pm Tue-Sat; tours depart on the hour.
Admission $3; free under-18s. **No credit cards**.
Map p403 E27.

Herald Square & Garment District

The heart of America's multibillion-dollar
clothing industry is New York's **Garment
District** (roughly from 34th to 40th Streets,
between Broadway and Eighth Avenue),
where platoons of designers – and thousands
of workers – create the clothes we'll be wearing
next season. The main drag, Seventh Avenue,
has a fitting (although rarely used) moniker,
Fashion Avenue. Although most garment-
manufacturing has left Manhattan, the area is
still gridlocked by delivery trucks and workers
pushing racks of clothes up and down the
streets. Trimming, button and fabric shops
line the sidewalks, especially on 38th and 39th
Streets. At the north-east corner of 39th Street
and Seventh Avenue, you'll spy a gigantic
needle and button sculpture, signalling that
you are in the fashion centre. **The Fashion
Center Information Kiosk** alongside the
sculpture provides spools of information to both
professional and budding designers, buyers and
manufactures. A once-thriving fur market is in
retreat, now occupying only 28th to 30th Streets
between Seventh and Eighth Avenues.

Beginning on 34th Street at Broadway
and stretching all the way to Seventh Avenue,
Macy's (*see p225*) is still the biggest – and
busiest – department store in the world. Across
the street at the junction of Broadway and
Sixth Avenue is **Herald Square**, named after
a long-gone newspaper, surrounded by a retail
wonderland. The area's lower section is known

as **Greeley Square**, after Horace Greeley,
owner of the *Herald*'s rival, the *Tribune* (which
employed Karl Marx as a columnist); the
previously grungy square now offers bistro
chairs and rest areas for weary pedestrians.
To the east, the many restaurants and shops of
Koreatown line 32nd Street between Broadway
and Madison Avenue.

The giant circular building on Seventh
Avenue between 31st and 33rd Streets is the
sports and entertainment arena **Madison
Square Garden** (*see p313*). It occupies the
site of the old Pennsylvania Station, a McKim,
Mead & White architectural masterpiece that
was razed in the 1960s – an act so soulless,
it spurred the creation of the Landmarks
Preservation Commission. The railroad
terminal, now known as **Penn Station**, lies
beneath the Garden and serves approximately
600,000 people daily, more than any other
station in the country. Fortunately, the aesthetic
tide has turned. The city has approved a $788
million restoration-and-development project to
move Penn Station across the street, into the
General Post Office (formally known as the
James A Farley Post Office Building; 421
Eighth Avenue, between 31st & 33rd Streets,
1-800 275 8777), another McKim, Mead & White
design. The project will connect the post office's
two buildings with a soaring glass-and-nickel-
trussed ticketing hall and concourse. When the
new Penn Station is finally realised (no earlier
than 2007), Amtrak services will roll in (along
with rail links to Newark, La Guardia and JFK
airports), while the current Penn Station will
remain a hub for New Jersey Transit and the
Long Island Rail Road.

Broadway & Times Square

Around 42nd Street and Broadway, an area
sometimes called 'the crossroads of the world',
the night is illuminated not by the moon and the
stars but by acres of glaring neon and sweeping
arc lamps. Even native New Yorkers are
electrified by this larger-than-life light show
of corporate logos. No area better represents
the city's glitter than **Times Square**, where
zoning laws actually require businesses to
include a certain level of illuminated signage
on their facades.

Originally called Longacre Square, Times
Square was renamed after the *New York Times*
moved to the site in the early 1900s, and it
announced its arrival with a spectacular New
Year's Eve fireworks display. At the present
1 Times Square building (formerly the Times
Tower), the *Times* erected the world's first
ticker sign, and the circling messages – the
stockmarket crash of 1929, JFK's assassination,

the 2001 World Trade Center attack – have been known to stop the midtown masses in their tracks. The Gray Lady is now located on 43rd Street between Seventh and Eighth Avenues but will move soon to a new $84 million tower on Eighth Avenue between 40th and 41st Streets. However, the sign remains at the original locale and marks the spot where New Year's Eve is traditionally celebrated.

Times Square is really just the elongated intersection of Broadway and Seventh Avenue, but it's also the heart of the **Theater District**. More than 40 stages showcasing extravagant dramatic productions are situated on the streets that cross Broadway. Times Square's once-famous sex trade is now relegated to short stretches of Seventh and Eighth Avenues (just North and South of 42nd Street).

The Theater District's transformation began in 1984, when the city condemned many properties along 42nd Street ('the Deuce') between Seventh and Eighth Avenues. A few years later, the city changed its zoning laws, making it harder for adult-entertainment establishments to operate. The results include places like Show World (669 Eighth Avenue, between 42nd & 43rd Streets), formerly a noted sleaze palace that now gets by with X-rated video sessions instead of live 'dance' shows.

The streets west of Eighth Avenue are filled with eateries catering to theatregoers, especially along **Restaurant Row** (46th Street, between Eighth & Ninth Avenues). This stretch is also popular after the theatres let out, when the street's bars host stand-up comedy and campy drag cabaret.

The area's office buildings are filled with entertainment companies: recording studios, record labels, theatrical agencies and screening rooms. The Brill Building (1619 Broadway, at 49th Street) has long been the headquarters of music publishers and producers, and such luminaries as Jerry Lieber, Mike Stoller, Phil Spector and Carole King wrote and auditioned their hits here. Visiting rock royalty and aspiring musicians drool over the selection of new and vintage guitars (and other instruments) for sale along **Music Row** (48th Street, between Sixth & Seventh Avenues). Eager teens congregate under the windows at MTV's home base (1515 Broadway, at 45th Street), hoping for a wave from a guest celebrity like Beyoncé from the second-floor studio above. The glittering glass case that serves as headquarters to magazine-publishing giant Condé Nast (Broadway, at 43rd Street) gleams at 4 Times Square – home to *Vogue*, *GQ*, and *The New Yorker* among many other titles. The NASDAQ electronic stock market is housed in the same building, and its

Intrepid Sea-Air-Space Museum. *See p121.*

MarketSite Tower, a cylindrical eight-storey video screen, dominates Times Square.

Glitzy attractions strive to outdo one another in ensnaring the endless throngs of tourists. **Madame Tussaud's New York**, a Gothamised version of the London-based wax-museum chain, showcases local legends such as Woody Allen and Jennifer Lopez. On Broadway, the noisy **ESPN Zone** (1472 Broadway, at 42nd Street, 1-212 921 3776) offers hundreds of video games and enormous TVs showing all manner of sporting events, and the 110,000-square-foot **Toys 'R' Us** flagship store boasts a 60-foot-tall indoor Ferris wheel.

Make a brief detour uptown on Seventh Avenue for a glimpse of the great classical-music landmark **Carnegie Hall** (*see p322*), on 57th Street, two blocks south of Central Park. Nearby is the famous Carnegie Deli (854 Seventh Avenue, at 55th Street, 1-212 757 2245), maestro of the Reuben sandwich. **ABC Television Studios**, at 7 Times Square, draw dozens of early morning risers hoping to catch a glimpse of the *Good Morning America* crew.

West of Times Square, in the vicinity of the Port Authority Bus Terminal (on Eighth Avenue) and the Lincoln Tunnel's traffic-knotted entrance, is an area historically known as **Hell's Kitchen**, where a gang- and crime-ridden Irish community scraped by during the 19th century. Italians, Greeks, Puerto Ricans, Dominicans and other ethnic groups followed. The neighbourhood maintained its tough reputation into the 1970s, when, in an effort to invite gentrification, local activists renamed it Clinton, after one-time mayor (and governor) DeWitt Clinton. Crime has indeed abated, and in-the-know theatregoers fill the ethnic eateries along Ninth Avenue, which cost less and serve more interesting food than the traditional pre-theatre spots. (*See p116* **Heaven in Hell**.)

The extreme West Side remains somewhat desolate, but in the past year a burgeoning theatre scene has taken root (*see p353*). Since plans for a new stadium in the neighbourhood were quashed last year, hopes for expanding the unlovely Jacob K Javits Convention Center (Eleventh Avenue, between 34th & 39th Streets) have stalled. Still, the massive black glass structure draws huge crowds to its various trade shows. Maritime enthusiasts will appreciate the area along the Hudson River between 46th and 52nd Streets. The **Intrepid** (*see below*), a retired naval aircraft carrier, houses a sea, air and space museum (and a Concorde jet), and big crowds flock to the river when cruise ships, especially the world's largest ocean liner, the *Queen Mary 2*, dock at the terminal near 50th Street. During Fleet Week (*see p261*), the West Side fills with white-uniformed sailors on shore leave. The Circle Line terminal is on 42nd Street at Pier 83.

Intrepid Sea-Air-Space Museum

USS Intrepid, *Pier 86, 46th Street, at the Hudson River (1-212 245 0072/www.intrepidmuseum.org). Travel: A, C, E to 42nd Street-Port Authority, then M42 bus to Twelfth Avenue.* **Open** *Apr-Sept* 10am-5pm Mon-Fri; 10am-6pm Sat, Sun. *Oct-Mar* 10am-5pm Tue-Sun. *Last admission* 1hr before closing. **Admission** $16.50; $12.50 seniors and students; $11.50 6-17s; $4.50 2-5s; free under-2s, veterans, servicepeople on active duty. **Credit** AmEx, MC, V. **Map** p404 B23.

Climb inside a model of a wooden Revolutionary-era submarine, try out a supersonic-flight simula-tor, and explore dozens of military helicopters, fighter planes and more aboard this retired aircraft carrier. A barge next to the *Intrepid* displays a British Airways Concorde and holds exhibitions on the history of supersonic flight. Additional arte-facts in the collection include a Cobra attack heli-copter and a Tomcat fighter jet. During Fleet Week (*see p261*) in summer, the *Intrepid* hosts contests and other fun events. **Photo** *p120*.

Madame Tussaud's New York

234 W 42nd Street, between Seventh & Eighth Avenues (1-800 246 8872/www.nyc wax.com). Subway: A, C, E to 42nd Street-Port Authority; N, Q, R, W, 42nd Street S, 1, 2, 3, 7 to 42nd Street-Times Square. **Open** 10am-8pm daily. **Admission** $29; $26 seniors; $23 4-12s; free under-3s. **Credit** AmEx, MC, V. **Map** p404 D24.

If you're a fan of frozen, life-sized celebs, every few months they roll out a new posse of waxed victims.

Times Square Visitors' Center

1560 Broadway, between 46th & 47th Streets, entrance on Seventh Avenue (1-212 869 1890/www.timessquarebid.org). Subway: N, R, W to 49th Street; 1 to 50th Street. **Open** 8am-8pm daily. **Map** p404 D23.

The light stuff

Originally illuminated with one large searchlight in 1932 to herald Franklin D Roosevelt's presidential election, the Empire State Building now requires nearly 1,400 lights for its iconic nightly display. White light remains the basic ESB staple, though coloured lights were introduced in 1976, during the bicentennial, to bathe the tower in patriotic red, white and blue. The pizza-sized coloured gels take a full four hours to fit and are used in dozens of colour combinations to celebrate holidays (red and green at Christmas) and charity causes (pink for breast-cancer awareness). Lights come on at sundown and turn off, Cinderella-like, at the stroke of midnight each night except New Year's Eve, New Year's Day, St Patrick's Day, Christmas Eve and Christmas Day. On these nights the edifice becomes the world's largest night-light, shining on until 3am.

Fifth Avenue

Synonymous with the chic and moneyed, Fifth Avenue caters to the elite; it's also the main route for the city's many ethnic (and inclusive) parades: National Puerto Rican Day, St Patrick's Day, Gay and Lesbian Pride, and many more. Even without a parade, the street hums with activity as the sidewalks fill with all types, from gawking tourists to smartly dressed society matrons.

The **Empire State Building** (*see p124*), located smack-dab in the centre of midtown, is visible from most parts of the city and beyond (at night, it's lit in showy colours to celebrate a holiday or special event in progress; *see p121* **The light stuff**). Craning your neck at the corner of 34th Street to see storey after storey extend into the sky gives a breathtaking perspective of the gargantuan structure. The building's 86th-floor observation deck offers brilliant views in every direction; go at sunset to glimpse the longest urban shadow you'll ever see, cast from Manhattan all the way across the river to Queens. For a weekday break from sightseeing, catch a few winks in a cosy MetroNaps pod (1-212 239 3344), located in the famous skyscraper. This new company welcomes midtown executives and others looking to recharge with a quick snooze.

Impassive stone lions, dubbed Patience and Fortitude by Mayor Fiorello La Guardia, guard the steps of the humanities and science collection of the **New York Public Library** (*see p126*), a beautiful Beaux Arts building at 41st Street. (A lovely library gift shop is just across Fifth Avenue.) The Rose Main Reading Room, on the library's top floor, is a hushed sanctuary of 23-foot-long tables and matching oak chairs, where bibliophiles can read, write and do research. Situated behind the library is **Bryant Park**, a well-cultivated green space that hosts a dizzying schedule of free entertainment during the summer (*see p261*), when it also attracts outdoor internet users with its free wireless access. The luxury **Bryant Park Hotel** (*see p57*) occupies the former American Radiator Building on 40th Street. Designed by architect Raymond Hood in the mid 1920s and recently renovated, the structure is faced with near-black brick and trimmed in gold leaf. Alexander Woollcott, Dorothy Parker and friends held court and traded barbs at the **Algonquin** (*see p62*); the lobby is still a great place to meet for a drink.

Veer off Fifth Avenue into the 19 buildings of **Rockefeller Center** (*see p126*) and you'll see why this interlacing of public and private space is so lavishly praised. After plans for an expansion of the Metropolitan Opera on the site

American Folk Art Museum. *See p123.*

fell through in 1929, John D Rockefeller Jr, who had leased the land on behalf of the Met, set about creating a complex to house radio and television corporations. Designed by Raymond Hood and many other prominent architects, the 'city within a city' grew over the course of more than 40 years, with each new building conforming to the original master plan and art deco design. Last autumn (2005), the legendary observation deck atop 30 Rockefeller Plaza, reopened after 20 years (*see p123* **Rock on**).

As you stroll through the Channel Gardens from Fifth Avenue, the stately **General Electric Building** gradually appears above you. The sunken plaza in the complex is the winter home of an oft-packed ice-skating rink (*see p339*); a giant Christmas tree looms above it each holiday season. The plaza is the most visible entrance to the restaurants and shops in the underground passages that link the buildings. It is also home to the famous art auction house **Christie's** (*see p124*)

The centre is filled with murals, sculptures, mosaics and other artwork. Perhaps the most famous pieces are the rink-side *Prometheus* sculpture, by Paul Manship, and José María Sert's murals in the GE Building. But wander around, and you'll be treated to many more

Rock on

In 1933, John D Rockefeller Jr witnessed the completion of the monumental 30 Rockefeller Center, aka the RCA Building (now referred to as the General Electric Building) – the crown jewel in one of the country's most significant (and copied) urban design projects. Back in the day, the top floor, 70 storeys up, was done up like the upper decks of a 1930s ocean liner, replete with deck chairs and air vents resembling smoke stacks.

One of the most impressive elements of the art deco tower – its stunning observation decks, with unparalleled 360-degree views of Manhattan – was declared off-limits in 1986, when another RCA landmark, the glamorous Rainbow Room on the 65th floor, underwent a renovation and expansion, cutting off access to the roof. Twenty years later, the observatory, which occupies the 67th to 70th floors, opened with great fanfare in the autumn of 2005. 'Every inch of the place that

we could restore to its original glamour, we did,' says Peter Dillon of Rockefeller Center. (Those details include the cast-aluminium fleur de lis panels and tiled mosaics).

While the view alone is worth the price of admission, the folks at 30 Rock have also designed an exciting three-storey atrium lobby housing a modern gallery space that explores the storied history of Rockefeller Center. Even the elevator gets in on the act, with a fun video projection on its glass-panelled ceiling of bygone decades.

Top of the Rock

30 Rockefeller Plaza, just off W 50th Street, between Fifth & Sixth Avenues (1-212 698 2000/tickets 1-877 692 7625/www.topoftherocknyc.com). Subway: B, D, F, V to 47-50th Streets-Rockefeller Center. **Open** 8.30am-midnight daily. **Admission** $14; $12 seniors; $9 6-11s. **Credit** AmEx, MC, V. **Map** p404 E23.

masterworks. On weekday mornings, a crowd of (mainly) tourists gathers at the **NBC** television network's glass-walled, ground-level studio (where the *Today* show is shot), at the south-west corner of Rockefeller Plaza and 49th Street (*see p126*). When the show's free concert series in the plaza hosts big-name guests like Norah Jones, Sting and Queen Latifah, the throng swells mightily.

Radio City Music Hall, on Sixth Avenue, at 50th Street, was the world's largest cinema

when it was built, in 1932. This art deco jewel (the backstage tour is one of the best in town) was treated to a $70 million restoration in 1999; it's now used for music concerts and for traditional Christmas and Easter shows featuring the renowned Rockettes.

Facing Rockefeller Center is the beautiful **St Patrick's Cathedral** (*see p127*), the largest Catholic cathedral in the United States. A few blocks north, a cluster of museums – the **American Folk Art Museum** (*see p124*), the

Museum of Arts & Design (*see below*) and the **Museum of Television & Radio** (*see p125*) – is anchored by the recently renovated **Museum of Modern Art** (*see p125*). Swing Street, or 52nd Street, between Fifth and Sixth Avenues, is a row of 1920s speakeasies; the only venue still open from that period is the '21' Club (21 W 52nd Street, between Fifth & Madison Avenues, 1-212 582 7200; *see p21* **It happened here**). The bar buzzes at night; upstairs, the restaurant is a popular power-lunch spot.

The blocks off Fifth Avenue between Rockefeller Center and Central Park South showcase expensive retail palaces bearing names that were famous long before the concept of branding was developed. Along the stretch between Saks Fifth Avenue (49th to 50th Streets; *see p226*) and Bergdorf Goodman (at 58th Street; *see p225*), the rents are the highest in the world; tenants include Cartier, Versace, Tiffany & Co, and Gucci. Fifth Avenue is crowned by Grand Army Plaza at 59th Street. A gilded statue of General William Tecumseh Sherman presides over this public space; to the west stands the elegant Plaza Hotel (which is closed while being transformed into condos); to the north, the luxe Pierre hotel. From here, you can access Central Park (*see p129*), where the city din gives way to relative serenity.

American Folk Art Museum

45 W 53rd Street, between Fifth & Sixth Avenues (1-212 265 1040/www.folkartmuseum.org). Subway: E, V to Fifth Avenue-53rd Street. **Open** 10.30am-5.30pm Tue-Thur, Sat, Sun; 10.30am-7.30pm Fri. **Admission** $9; $7 seniors and students; free under-12s. Free to all 5.30-7.30pm Fri. **Credit** AmEx, Disc, MC, V. **Map** p404 E22.

Celebrating traditional craft-based work is the American Folk Art Museum (formerly the Museum of American Folk Art). Designed by architects Billie Tsien and Tod Williams, the architecturally stunning eight-floor building is four times larger than the original Lincoln Center location (now a branch of the museum) and includes a café. The range of decorative, practical and ceremonial folk art encompasses pottery, trade signs, delicately stitched log-cabin quilts and wind-up toys.

Other locations: 2 Lincoln Square, Columbus Avenue, between 65th & 66th Streets (1-212 595 9533).

Christie's

20 Rockefeller Plaza, 49th Street, between Fifth & Sixth Avenues (1-212 636 2000/www.christies.com). Subway: B, D, F, V to 47-50th Streets-Rockefeller Center. **Open** 9.30am-5.30pm Mon-Fri. **Admission** free. **Map** p404 E23.

Dating from 1766, Christie's joins Sotheby's as one of New York's premier auction houses. Architecturally, the building alone is worth a visit, particularly for its cavernous three-floor lobby featuring a specially commissioned mural by artist Sol LeWitt. Most auctions are open to the public, with viewing hours scheduled in the days leading up to the sale. Hours vary with each exhibition, so call or visit the website for details.

Empire State Building

350 Fifth Avenue, between 33rd & 34th Streets (1-212 736 3100/www.esbnyc.com). Subway: B, D, F, N, Q, R, V, W to 34th Street-Herald Square. **Open** 9.30am-midnight daily (closed during extreme weather). Last elevator up 11.15pm. **Admission** $12; $11 seniors and 12-17s; $7 6-11s; free under-5s. **No credit cards. Map** p404 E25.

To say they don't build 'em like they used to is an understatement. The Empire State Building was financed as a speculative venture by General Motors executive John J Raskob; builders broke the ground in 1930. It sprang up in 14 months with amazing speed, completed more than a month ahead of schedule and $5 million under budget. The 1,250ft tower snatched the title of world's tallest building from under the nose of the months-old, 1,046ft Chrysler Building, conveniently showing up Raskob's Detroit rival Walter P Chrysler.

Museum of Arts & Design

40 W 53rd Street, between Fifth & Sixth Avenues (1-212 956 3535/www.americancraftmuseum.org). Subway: E, V to Fifth Avenue-53rd Street. **Open**

It happened here

Leave it to **Marilyn Monroe** to make even a subway grate sexy. It was here, on the northwest corner of Lexington Avenue at 52nd Street, that the blond bombshell filmed the famous dress-blowing scene from 1955's *The Seven Year Itch*. The pose Marilyn struck – mischievous, smiling as she girlishly forces the front of her white dress down with both hands – became iconic. The grate, however, lives on unrecognised.

Museum of Modern Art.

Museum of Television & Radio.

10am-6pm Mon-Wed, Fri-Sun; 10am-8pm Thur. **Admission** $9; $6 seniors and students; free under-12s. Voluntary donation 6-8pm Thur. **Credit** AmEx, Disc, MC, V. **Map** p404 E23.
Formerly the American Crafts Museum, this is the country's leading museum for contemporary crafts in clay, cloth, glass, metal and wood. It changed its name to emphasise the correspondences among art, design and craft. The museum plans to move to a new home in the former Huntington Hartford building at Columbus Circle in late 2007, but for now, visitors can come here to peruse the jewellery, ceramics and other objects displayed on four floors.

Museum of Modern Art (MoMA)

11 W 53rd Street, between Fifth & Sixth Avenues (1-212 708 9400/www.moma.org). Subway: E, V to Fifth Avenue-53rd Street. **Open** 10.30am-5.30pm Mon, Wed, Thur, Sat, Sun; 10.30am-8pm Fri. **Admission** (includes admission to film programmes) $20; $16 over-65s; $12 full-time students; free under-16s (must be accompanied by an adult). Free to all 4-8pm Fri. **Credit** AmEx, MC, V. **Map** p404 E23.
The Museum of Modern Art contains the world's finest and most comprehensive holdings of 20th-century art and, thanks to a sweeping redesign by architect Yoshio Taniguchi completed in 2004, it is now able to show off much more of its immense permanent collection in serene, high-ceilinged galleries that almost outshine the art on display. Inside, the soaring five-storey atrium is the central artery from which six curatorial departments – Architecture and Design, Drawings, Painting and Sculpture, Photography, Prints and Illustrated Books, and Film and Media – display works that include the best of Matisse, Picasso, van Gogh, Giacometti, Lawrence, Pollock, Rothko and Warhol, among many others.

Outside, Philip Johnson's sculpture garden has been restored to its original, larger plan from 1953, and its powerful minimalist sculptures and sheer matt-black-granite-and-glass wall are overlooked by the sleek high-end restaurant and bar the Modern, which is run by Midas-touch restaurateur Danny Meyer. The museum's eclectic exhibition of design objects is a must-see, with examples of art nouveau, the Bauhaus and the Vienna Secession lining up alongside a vintage 1946 Ferrari and architectural drawings and models from the likes of Rem Koolhaas and Mies van der Rohe.
In summer 2006 MoMA stages the first major US museum show dedicated to the avant-garde Dada movement. Max Ernst, Marcel Duchamp, Man Ray and Hans Richter are among nearly 50 artists represented in a multimedia display of 400 works including sound and film recordings, paintings, sculpture and photography (18 June-11 Sept). Following this, Plane Image: A Brice Marden Retrospective traces the development of one of America's most important abstract artists from early monochromatic panels to the shimmering wreaths of colour in later works (22 Oct-Jan) and Comic Abstraction looks at the growth of comic strips and cartoons as a medium to address social and political issues (29 Oct-Jan). **Photo** *above.*

Museum of Television & Radio

25 W 52nd Street, between Fifth & Sixth Avenues (1-212 621 6800/www.mtr.org). Subway: B, D, F, V to 47-50th Streets-Rockefeller Center; E, V to Fifth Avenue-53rd Street. **Open** noon-6pm Tue-Sun; noon-8pm Thur. **Admission** $10; $8 seniors and students; $5 under-14s. **No credit cards. Map** p404 E23.
This nirvana for boob-tube addicts and pop-culture junkies contains an archive of more than 100,000

Full of grace: the US's largest Catholic church, **St Patrick's Cathedral**.

radio and TV programmes. Head to the fourth-floor library to search the computerised system for your favourite *Star Trek* or *I Love Lucy* episodes, then walk down one flight to take a seat at your assigned console. (The radio listening room operates the same way.) Screenings of modern cartoons, public seminars and special presentations are offered. Recent programmes were devoted to television superheroes, American political ads, and the history of gay and lesbian characters on TV. **Photo** *above*.

NBC

30 Rockefeller Plaza, 49th Street, between Fifth & Sixth Avenues (1-212 664 3700/www.nbc. com). Subway: B, D, F, V to 47-50th Streets-Rockefeller Center. **Admission** $17.95; $15.50 seniors, students and 6-16s; under-6s not admitted. **Tours** 8.30am-5.30pm Mon-Sat; 9.30am-4.30pm Sun. Tours depart every 15 minutes. **Credit** AmEx, MC, V. **Map** p404 E23.

Peer through the *Today* show's studio window with a horde of fellow onlookers, or pay admission (at the NBC Experience Store, www.shopnbc.com) for a guided tour of the studios. The tours are led by pages, many of whom – Ted Koppel, Kate Jackson, Michael Eisner, Marcy Carsey, and others – have gone on to bigger and better things in showbiz. (For information on NBC tapings, *see p300*.)

New York Public Library

455 Fifth Avenue, at 42nd Street (1-212 930 0830/www.nypl.org). Subway: B, D, F, V to 42nd Street-Bryant Park; 7 to Fifth Avenue. **Open** 11am-7.30pm Tue, Wed; 10am-6pm Thur-Sat. **Admission** free. **Map** p404 E24.

When people mention 'the New York Public Library,' most are referring to this imposing Beaux Arts building. (In fact it houses only NYPL's humanities and social sciences collection; for other locations, *see p375*.) Two massive stone lions, dubbed Patience and Fortitude by former mayor Fiorello La Guardia, flank the main portal. Free guided tours (at 11am and 2pm) stop at the beautifully renovated Rose Main Reading Room and the Bill Blass Public Catalog Room, which offers free Internet access. Lectures, author readings and special exhibitions are definitely worth checking out.

Radio City Music Hall

See p320 for listing. **Tours** 11am-3pm daily. **Admission** $17; $14 seniors; $10 under-12s. **Credit** AmEx, MC, V. **Map** p404 E23.

Rockefeller Center

From 48th to 51st Streets, between Fifth & Sixth Avenues (1-212 632 3975/tickets 1-212 664 7174/www.rockefellercenter.com). Subway: B, D, F, V to 47-50th Streets-Rockefeller Center. **Admission** $18; $16 seniors and 6-16s; no under-6s. **Tours** 10am-5pm Mon-Sat; 10am-4pm Sun. Tours depart on the hour. **Credit** AmEx, MC, V. **Map** p404 E23.

Exploring the centre is free. For guided tours in and around the historic buildings, however, advance tickets are necessary and available by phone, online or at the NBC Experience Store. For information about newly opened Top of the Rock, the observation deck at 30 Rockefeller Center, *see p123* **Rock on**.

St Patrick's Cathedral
Fifth Avenue, between 50th & 51st Streets (1-212 753 2261). Subway: B, D, F to 47-50th Streets-Rockefeller Center; E, V to Fifth Avenue-53rd Street. **Open** 6.30am-8.45pm daily. **Admission** free. **Tours** Call for tour dates and times. **Map** p404 E23.
St Patrick's adds gothic grace to Fifth Avenue. The diocese of New York bought the land for an orphanage in 1810, but then in 1858, it switched gears and began construction on what would become the country's largest Catholic church. Today, the white marble spires are dwarfed by Rockefeller Center but, inside, visitors are treated to a still-stunning array of vaulted ceilings, stained-glass windows from Charres and altars by Tiffany & Co.

Midtown East

The area east of Fifth Avenue may seem less appealing to visitors than Times Square or Rockefeller Center. Although the neighbourhood is home to some of the city's most recognisable landmarks – the United Nations, Grand Central Terminal and the Chrysler Building – the grid of busy streets is lined with large, imposing buildings, and the bustling sidewalks are all business. The area is a little thin on plazas and street-level attractions, but it compensates with a dizzying array of world-class architecture.
  Grand Central Terminal, a 1913 Beaux Arts train station, is the city's most spectacular point of arrival, even though it isn't a national gateway (unlike Penn Station, Grand Central is used only for commuter trains). The station stands at the junction of 42nd Street and Park Avenue, the latter rising on a viaduct that curves around the terminal. The station played an important role in the nation's historic preservation movement, after a series of legal battles that culminated in the 1978 Supreme Court decision affirmed NYC's landmark laws (*see p127* **Local legend**). Since its 1998 renovation, the terminal itself has become a destination, with classy restaurants and bars, such as the Campbell Apartment cocktail lounge (off the West Balcony, 1-212 953 0409), the expert and attitudinous Grand Central Oyster Bar & Restaurant (Lower Concourse, 1-212 490 6650) and star chef Charlie Palmer's Métrazur (East Balcony, 1-212 687 4600). The Lower Concourse food court spans the globe with its fairly priced lunch options. One notable oddity: the constellations on the Main Concourse ceiling are drawn in reverse, as if seen from outer space.
  Rising like a phoenix behind Grand Central, the **MetLife Building**, formerly the Pan Am Building, was once the world's largest office tower. Now its most celebrated tenants are the peregrine falcons that nest on the roof and feed on pigeons snatched mid-air. On Park Avenue is the famed **Waldorf-Astoria** (*see p63*), formerly located on Fifth Avenue but rebuilt here in 1931 after the original was demolished to make way for the Empire State Building. Other must-see buildings in the area include **Lever House** (390 Park Avenue, between 53rd & 54th Streets), the **Seagram Building** (375 Park Avenue, between 52nd & 53rd Streets), **Citicorp Center** (from 53rd Street to 54th Street, between Lexington & Third Avenues) and the stunning art deco skyscraper that anchor the corner of Lexington Avenue and 51st Street, formerly the **General Electric Building** (and before that, the RCA Victor Building). A Chippendale crown tops Philip

Local legend

It took more than ten years of unflagging – and very public – effort for the notoriously private **Jacqueline Kennedy Onassis** to save Grand Central Terminal, America's most famous train station. After the glorious (original) Pennsylvania Station was demolished in 1964, developers unveiled plans for an office tower over the crumbling Grand Central. But Jackie O would have none of it. She drafted civic leaders, architects and celebrities for her Committee to Save Grand Central, which in 1978 finally won a Supreme Court decision affirming landmark status for the beloved Beaux Arts building.

Ideas above its station: the exquisite, inspirational hall of **Grand Central Terminal**.

Johnson's postmodern icon, the **Sony Building** (550 Madison Avenue, between 55th & 56th Streets), formerly the AT&T Building. Inside, the Sony Wonder Technology Lab (*see p286*) delivers a hands-on thrill zone of science in action.

Along the river to the east lies **Tudor City**, a pioneering 1925 residential development and a high-rise version of England's Hampton Court. The neighbourhood is dominated by the **United Nations Headquarters** (*see below*) and its famous glass-walled Secretariat building. Although you don't need a passport, you will be leaving US soil when you enter the UN complex – it's an international zone, and the vast buffet at the Delegates Dining Room (fourth floor, 1-212 963 7626) puts cultural diversity on the table. The grounds and the Peace Garden along the East River are off-limits for security reasons. Unless you pay for a guided tour, the only accessible attractions are the exhibitions in the lobby and the bookstore and gift shop on the lower level. But right across First Avenue is **Dag Hammarskjöld Plaza** (47th Street, between First & Second Avenues), named for the former UN secretary general. Here, you can stroll through a lovely garden honouring Katharine Hepburn (who used to live nearby in Turtle Bay Gardens, a stretch of townhouses on 48th and 49th Streets, between Second and Third Avenues). Nearby is the **Japan Society** (*see p128*).

East 42nd Street holds still more architectural distinction, including the Romanesque-revival hall of the former **Bowery Savings Bank** (No.110) and the art deco details of the **Chanin Building** (No.122). Completed in 1930, the gleaming **Chrysler Building** (at Lexington Avenue) pays homage to the automobile.

Architect William Van Alen outfitted the main tower with colossal radiator-cap eagle 'cargoyles' and a brickwork relief sculpture of racing cars complete with chrome hubcaps. A needle-sharp stainless-steel spire was added to the blueprint so the finished product would be taller than 40 Wall Street, which was under construction at the same time. The Daily News Building (No.220), another art deco gem designed by Raymond Hood, was immortalised in the *Superman* films; although the namesake tabloid no longer has offices here, the lobby still houses the paper's giant globe.

Grand Central Terminal

From 42nd to 44th Streets, between Vanderbilt & Lexington Avenues. Subway: 42nd Street S, 4, 5, 6, 7 to 42nd Street-Grand Central. **Tours** Call 1-212 697 1245 for information. **Map** p404 E24. **Photo** *above.*

Japan Society

333 E 47th Street, at First Avenue (1-212 832 1155/ www.japansociety.org). Subway: E, V to Lexington Avenue-53rd Street; 6 to 51st Street. **Open** 11am-6pm Tue-Thur; 11am-9pm Fri; 11am-5pm Sat, Sun. **Admission** $12; $10 seniors & students; free under-16s. **Credit** AmEx, Disc, MC, V. **Map** p404 F23.
In a serene space complete with waterfall and bamboo garden, the Japan Society presents performing arts, lectures, exchange programmes and special events. The gallery will be closed for refurbishment throughout summer and will reopen in autumn 2006.

United Nations Headquarters

UN Plaza, First Avenue, between 42nd & 48th Streets (1-212 963 7710/tours 1-212 963 8687/www.un.org). Subway: 42nd Street S, 4, 5, 6, 7 to 42nd Street-Grand Central. **Admission** $10.50; $8 seniors; $7 students; $6 5-14s; under-5s not admitted. **Tours** *Mar-Dec* 9.30am-4.45pm Mon-Fri; 10am-4.30pm Sat, Sun. *Jan, Feb* 9.30am-4.45pm Mon-Fri. **Credit** AmEx, MC, V. **Map** p404 G24.

Uptown

Central Park's beauty, Fifth Avenue's culture and Harlem's urban style make a lasting impression.

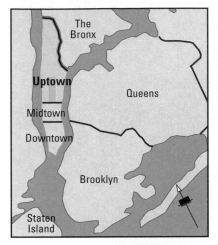

Sightseeing

As you get above 57th Street in Manhattan you'll notice that the crowds thin out and the frenetic pace slows down considerably: welcome to Uptown. While it's definitely calmer up here, there are still plenty of attractions to get your heart racing. For starters, there's Central Park, the city's gigantic emerald playground in spring and summer and magical oasis of quiet solitude in autumn and winter. The cultural offerings found uptown are stellar: Lincoln Center, the Metropolitan Museum of Art, the Guggenheim and the Studio Museum in Harlem, to name just a few. The city's wealthiest residents are huddled together in spectacular mansions on the Upper East Side – we guarantee a walk up Fifth Avenue will leave you breathless. The very northern tip of Manhattan not only provides glorious views of the Hudson River, but take a look back: the medieval castle of the Cloisters sits majestically in Fort Tryon Park (where this chapter's walk is based; see p140).

Central Park

Two and a half miles long and half a mile wide, this patch of the great outdoors was the first man-made public park in the US. In 1853, the newly formed Central Park Commission chose landscape designer Frederick Law Olmsted and architect Calvert Vaux to turn this vast tract of rocky swampland into a rambling oasis of greenery. The commission, inspired by the great parks of London and Paris, imagined a place that would provide city dwellers respite from the crowded streets. A noble thought, but one that required the eviction of 1,600 mostly poor or immigrant inhabitants, including residents of Seneca Village, the city's oldest African-American settlement. But clear the area the city did, and the rest is history.

The park recently celebrated its 150th anniversary, and it has never looked better, thanks to the Central Park Conservancy, a private non-profit civic group formed in 1980 that has been instrumental in restoration and maintenance. A horse-drawn carriage is still the sightseeing vehicle of choice for many tourists (and even a few romantic locals, though they'd never admit it); plan on paying $34 for a

'Imagine' memorial mosaic. See p132.

Central Park.

Central Park, season by season

Even without Christo's recent *Gates* project in 2005 – a spectacular art installation of 7,500 archways hung with sheets of saffron-hued fabric – a stroll through Manhattan's grandest park is worth a visit in any season. In summer, thousands of visitors flood the famous green spot to take advantage of a slew of mostly free operas, concerts and plays, but the park is a boon to locals and tourists throughout the year. Here are a few of our favourite activities, ranging from alfresco tango lessons in June to cosy carriage rides in December. For a list of day-by-day happenings, visit the Central Park Conservancy at www.centralparknyc.org.

Spring

Chick watch From green herons to snowy egrets and red-tailed hawks, more than 70 species of birds reside in the park, and hundreds more drop in during the spring and fall migrations. The densely wooded Ramble is a birders' paradise, as is the north end of the park above 103rd Street. To see what's been spotted lately, scan the birders' journal on display in the Loeb Boathouse.

Board silly At the Chess and Checkers House, just west of the Dairy at 65th Street, get your butt kicked by an old guy at one of 24 outdoor playing tables. Chess and checker sets can be borrowed from the Dairy with ID.

Flower power Celebrate the return of spring with a stroll through the Conservatory Garden at the northeast end of the park. In March and April, flower beds are filled with daffodils, crocuses and tulips, and magnolia, quince and crab apple trees are in bloom.

Summer

Get reel The fishing is strictly catch-and-release, but the Charles A Dana Discovery Center provides free rods and bait to help you land largemouth black bass, catfish and bluegills in the Harlem Meer. Tuesdays through Sundays, mid-April to mid-October.

Be ballsy Informal pickup games happen all over the park during the summer. *Basketball*: the most popular games are at the Great Lawn playground, Saturdays 9am till dusk, and Sundays 1pm till dusk. *Ultimate Frisbee*: from Memorial Day to Labor Day, join the Central Park Nomads at the 'Dustbowl,' at 97th Street on the east side of the park (6pm-dusk Tue, Thur; 3-6pm Sat). *Soccer*: an international crowd convenes next to

SummerStage, south of 72nd Street near Fifth Avenue, on Wednesdays at 6pm and Saturdays from 11am to 1pm.

Take two From June to September, tango aficionados dance at the south end of the Mall near the Shakespeare Statue (6 to 9pm every Saturday). Live music is provided twice monthly, and there's a free lesson at 7pm.

Fall

Cheer-a-thon Applaud the sweaty throngs as they cross the finish line of the world-famous New York City Marathon in early November. Runners enter the Park at Engineers' Gate (Fifth Avenue, at 90th Street), head south to exit the park at 59th Street and then re-enter it at Columbus Circle to end their five-borough trek near Tavern on the Green. Participants begin the course at 10am; front-runners finish between noon and 1pm. By mid afternoon, the south end of the park is mobbed with limping, water-guzzling marathoners wrapped in the day's most coveted accessory – the Mylar sheets handed out at the finish line. For more information, go to www.nyrrc.org.

Splash of colour Watch the brilliant changing leaves of maple and oak trees reflected in the water as you row a rental boat around Central Park Lake, or go the romantic route and ride in an authentic Venetian gondola.

On a string Catch the puppets in action at the Swedish Cottage Marionette Theater (*see p289*). This newly refurbished 1876 building is the headquarters of the Citywide Puppets in the Parks programme as well as the home base for one of the country's few remaining marionette companies. Productions based on classic fairytales run throughout the year.

Winter

Slip and slide Beat the crowd at Wollman Rink by hitting the ice just as the rink opens at 10am. Or come down for a moonlit after-dinner spin before closing time. *See p339*.

Snuggle up Get cosy in a horse-drawn carriage and enjoy the park in winter as you clip-clop under snow-dusted trees. Then warm up with a hot toddy at the lovely Park Hyatt Stanhope Hotel at 995 Fifth Avenue.

Downhill racer Cedar Hill (east side between 76th & 79th Streets) and Pilgrim Hill (just past the Conservatory Water) have been snow-day sledding destinations for generations of city youngsters. Feel like a kid again as you watch them zoom by.

20-minute tour. (You can usually hail a carriage on Central Park South, where they line up between Fifth Avenue and Columbus Circle.)

The park is dotted with landmarks. **Strawberry Fields**, near the West 72nd Street entrance, memorialises John Lennon, who lived in the nearby Dakota Building (pictured p143). Also called the International Garden of Peace, this sanctuary features a mosaic of the word 'imagine', donated by the Italian city of Naples. More than 160 species of flowers and plants from all over the world bloom here (including strawberries, of course). The statue of Balto, a heroic Siberian husky (East Drive, at 67th Street), is a favourite sight for tots. Slightly older children appreciate the statue of Alice in Wonderland, just north of the **Conservatory Water** at the East 74th Street park entrance.

In winter, ice-skaters lace up at **Wollman Rink** (midpark, at 62nd Street; *see also p339*), where the skating comes with a picture-postcard view of the fancy hotels surrounding the park. A short stroll to about 64th Street brings you to the **Friedsam Memorial Carousel**, still a bargain at a dollar a ride. (For more park activities for children, *see p287*.)

Come summer, kites, frisbees and soccer balls fly every which way across **Sheep Meadow**, the designated quiet zone that begins at 66th Street. The sheep are gone (they grazed here until 1934), replaced by sunbathers improving their tans and scoping out the thonged throngs. The hungry (and affluent) can repair to the glitzy **Tavern on the Green** (Central Park West, at 67th Street, 1-212 873 3200), which sets up a grand outdoor café in the summer, complete with a 40ft bar made with trees from city parks. However, picnicking alfresco (or snacking on a hot dog from one of the park's food vendors) is the most popular option. East of Sheep Meadow, between 66th and 72nd Streets, is the **Mall**, where you'll find volleyball courts and plenty of in-line skaters. East of the Mall's **Naumburg Bandshell** is **Rumsey Playfield** – site of the annual Central Park SummerStage series (*see p262*), an eclectic roster of free and benefit concerts held from Memorial Day weekend to Labor Day weekend. One of the most popular meeting places in the park is the grand **Bethesda Fountain and Terrace**, near the midpoint of the 72nd Street Transverse Road. *Angel of the Waters*, the sculpture in the centre of the fountain, was created by Emma Stebbins, the first woman to be granted a major public-art commission in New York. North of it is the **Loeb Boathouse** (midpark, at 75th Street), where you can rent a rowing boat or gondola to take out on the lake, which is crossed by the elegant Bow Bridge.

The leafy reaches of Uptown.

It happened here

Does it go without saying that **Sheep Meadow** in Central Park got its name from a herd of sheep that grazed there until 1935? We thought not. Yet New York's history is, among other things, an agricultural one. Just 100 years ago the city counted more than 2,000 farms in the five boroughs, with an average acreage of 25. By 1930, only five per cent of those farms were still growing. The same year, Vincenzo Benedetto sold his farm at Broadway and 213th Street, marking the end of Manhattan farming – and perhaps the beginning of the fire-escape garden.

The bucolic park views enjoyed by diners at the nearby **Central Park Boathouse Restaurant** (midpark, at 75th Street, 1-212 517 2233) make it a lovely place for brunch or drinks, with an outdoor terrace and bar that's idyllic in summer. The thickly forested **Ramble**, between 73rd and 79th Streets, is a favourite spot for bird-watching, offering glimpses of more than 70 species.

Farther north is the popular **Belvedere Castle**, a recently restored Victorian building that sits atop the park's second-highest peak. It offers excellent views and also houses the **Henry Luce Nature Observatory** (*see below*). The open-air **Delacorte Theater** hosts Shakespeare in the Park (*see p349*), a summer tradition of free performances of plays by the Bard and others. The **Great Lawn** (midpark, between 79th and 85th Streets) is a sprawling stretch of grass that doubles as a rally point for political protests and a concert spot for just about any act that can rally a six-figure audience, as well as free shows by the Metropolitan Opera and the New York Philharmonic during the summer. (At other times, it's the favoured spot of seriously competitive soccer teams and much less cut-throat teams of Hacky Sackers and their dogs.) Several years ago, the Reservoir (midpark, between 85th and 96th Streets) was renamed in honour of the late Jacqueline Kennedy Onassis, who used to jog around it.

Central Park Zoo
830 Fifth Avenue, between 63rd & 66th Streets (1-212 439 6500/www.centralpark zoo.org). Subway: N, R, W to Fifth Avenue-59th Street. **Open** *Apr-Oct* 10am-5pm Mon-Fri; 10am-5.30pm Sat, Sun. *Nov-Mar* 10am-4.30pm daily. **Admission** $6; $1.25 seniors; $1 3-12s; free under-3s. **No credit cards.** **Map** p405 E21.

This is the only place in New York City where you can see a polar bear swimming underwater. The Tisch Children's Zoo was recently spiffed up, and the roving characters on the George Delacorte Musical Clock delight kids every half hour.

Charles A Dana Discovery Center
Park entrance on Malcolm X Boulevard (Lenox Avenue), at 110th Street (1-212 860 1370/www. centralparknyc.org). Subway: 2, 3 to 110th Street-Central Park North. **Open** 10am-5pm Tue-Sun. **Admission** free. **Map** p406 E15.
Stop by for weekend family workshops, cultural exhibits and outdoor performances on the plaza next to the Harlem Meer. From April to October, the centre lends out fishing rods and bait, and on selected Thursday mornings, park rangers lead bird-watching walks. Call ahead for the schedule.

Dairy
Park entrance on Fifth Avenue, at 65th Street (1-212 794 6564/www.centralparknyc.org). Subway: N, R, W to Fifth Avenue-59th Street. **Open** *Summer* 11am-5pm daily. *Winter* 10am-5pm daily. **Admission** free. **Map** p405 D21.
Built in 1872 to show city kids where milk comes from (cows, in this case), the Dairy is now the Central Park Conservancy's information centre, complete with interactive exhibits, videos explaining the park's history, and a gift shop.

Henry Luce Nature Observatory
Belvedere Castle, midpark, off the 79th Street Transverse Road (1-212 772 0210). Subway: B, C to 81st Street-Museum of Natural History. **Open** 10am-5pm Tue-Sun. **Admission** free. **Map** p405 D19.
During the spring and autumn hawk migrations, park rangers discuss the various birds of prey found in the park and help visitors spot raptors from the castle roof (*see also p134* **How the nest was won**). You can also borrow a naturalist kit that includes binoculars, maps and bird-identification guides.

How the nest was won

Carving out your own little place to call home on the island of Manhattan is rough for anyone – rich or poor it takes real chutzpah. So when a nobody from the country alights on one of the city's most exclusive residences on swank Fifth Avenue – home to the likes of Mary Tyler Moore, CNN's Paula Zahn and a clutch of super-rich Wall Street big shots – people definitely take notice. In this town, nerve like that is bound to ruffle a few feathers.

It all started back in 1993 when Pale Male – a red-tailed hawk – and his mate built a love nest on a slab of ornate moulding near the top of a chic 12-storey apartment building at 927 Fifth Avenue (at 74th Street), overlooking Central Park. However, the uptight human residents would have none of it and had the pile of twigs and branches removed. But soon after, they found themselves in hot water: they were admonished by the US Fish & Wildlife Service, which forbids such actions, and the hawks were allowed to rebuild. For 11 years, Pale Male and his various mates (the latest of several years is named Lola) have dazzled New Yorkers with their aerial acrobatics and cute chicks. In all his years here, Pale Male has sired 23 offspring and acquired a legion of devoted fans – a fervent crew of birdwatchers that faithfully congregate daily (with a slew of telescopes, binoculars and cameras) at the western edge of the model boat pond (aka Conservatory Water) in Central Park. Among them is Lincoln Karim, a 45-year-old Manhattanite who gladly spends his off-work hours letting passers by get a glimpse of the birds through his enormous telescope.

In December 2004, it was Karim who first noticed that the building residents were up to no good. Apparently they had done their regulatory homework and got the okay to remove the nest, based on a technicality – a nest with no eggs or chicks is deemed inactive. When the nest came down, Karim and a crowd of protesters released a firestorm of rage. Facing TV crews and reporters hunkered down to relay the battle, appearances by animal lover Mary Tyler Moore and the relentless chants of 'Bring back the nest!' the building's board of directors eventually gave in. Three weeks later, they installed a stainless steel cradle into the façade so that the birds might rebuild their nest. And rebuild they did as bird lovers around the city chirped with glee. Although Pale Male and Lola's efforts to hatch a new brood of chicks failed in spring 2005, there is a happy ending: their son, Junior, built his own love nest on the Trump Parc building on Central Park South. Last spring Junior made his mom and dad the proud grandparents of two hatchlings, which delighted New Yorkers all summer as they watched the youngsters grow up in the treetops of Central Park.

Upper East Side

Gorgeous pre-war apartments owned by blue-blooded socialites, soigné restaurants filled with the Botoxed ladies-who-lunch set… this is the picture most New Yorkers have of the Upper East Side, and you'll certainly see plenty of supporting evidence on Fifth, Madison and Park Avenues. There's a history to this reputation: encouraged by the opening of Central Park in the late 19th century, the city's more affluent residents began building mansions along Fifth Avenue. By the beginning of the 20th century, even the superwealthy had warmed to the idea of giving up their large homes for smaller quarters – provided they were near the park. As a result, flats and hotels began springing up. (A few years later, working-class folks settled around Second and Third Avenues, following construction of an elevated East Side train line.) Architecturally, the overall look of the neighbourhood, especially from Fifth to Park Avenues, is remarkably homogeneous. Along the expanse known as the Gold Coast – Fifth, Madison and Park Avenues from 61st to 81st Streets – you'll see the great old mansions, many of which are now foreign consulates. The structure at 820 Fifth Avenue (at 64th Street) was one of the earliest luxury-apartment buildings on the avenue. New York's ultimate gingerbread house is 45 East 66th Street (between Madison and Park Avenues). Stanford White designed 998 Fifth Avenue (at 81st Street) in the image of an Italian Renaissance palazzo. Some wonderful old carriage houses adorn 63rd and 64th Streets. Further east, at the intersection of Second Avenue and 60th Street, you'll spy a tram car that carries people off to Roosevelt Island, a submarine-shaped isle in the middle of the East River. Unless you have a thing for tram rides, take our word for it and feel free to skip a visit to the residential enclave created in 1975 and home to roughly 10,000 New Yorkers.

Philanthropic gestures made by the moneyed class over the past 130 years have helped to create a cluster of art collections, museums and cultural institutions. In fact, Fifth Avenue from 82nd to 104th Streets is known as Museum Mile because it is flanked by the **Metropolitan Museum of Art** (see p136); the Frank Lloyd Wright-designed **Solomon R Guggenheim Museum** (see p138); the **Cooper-Hewitt** (see below), which houses the National Design Museum in Andrew Carnegie's former mansion); the **Jewish Museum** (see p136); the **Museum of the City of New York** (see p138) and **El Museo del Barrio** (see below).

Madison Avenue from 57th to 86th Streets is New York's world-class ultra-luxe shopping strip. The snazzy department store **Barneys New York** (see p225) offers chic designer fashions and witty, sometimes audacious, window displays. For a post-spree pick-me-up, order a cup of divinely rich hot chocolate and a Paris-perfect pastry at **La Maison du Chocolat** (see p240). While bars and restaurants dominate most of the north–south avenues, hungry sightseers can pick up a snack (or picnic supplies) at the well-stocked **Grace's Market Place** (1237 Third Avenue, between 71st & 72nd Streets, 1-212 737 0600) or at the Italian gourmet-food shop **Agata & Valentina** (1505 First Avenue, at 79th Street, 1-212 452 0690). Savour your meal on a park bench along the East River promenade leading to **Carl Schurz Park** (see p139). The ritzy neighbourhood is also home to the **Asia Society & Museum** (see below), the **China Institute** (see below), the **Frick Collection** (see p136), the **Goethe-Institut New York/German Cultural Center** (see p136), the **Neue Galerie** (see p138) and the **Whitney Museum of American Art** (see p138).

Asia Society & Museum

725 Park Avenue, at 70th Street (1-212 288 6400/ www.asiasociety.org). Subway: 6 to 68th Street-Hunter College. **Open** 11am-6pm Tue-Thur, Sat,

Sun; 11am-9pm Fri. **Admission** $10; $7 seniors; $5 students; free under-16s. Free 6-9pm Fri. **No credit cards.** **Map** p405 E20.

The Asia Society sponsors study missions and conferences while promoting public programmes in the US and abroad. The headquarters' striking galleries host major exhibitions of art culled from dozens of countries and time periods – from ancient India and medieval Persia to contemporary Japan – and assembled from public and private collections, including the permanent Mr and Mrs John D Rockefeller III collection of Asian art. There's a spacious, atrium-like café with a pan-Asian menu and a beautifully stocked gift shop.

China Institute

125 E 65th Street, between Park & Lexington Avenues (1-212 744 8181/www.chinainstitute.org). Subway: F to Lexington Avenue-63rd Street; 6 to 68th Street-Hunter College. **Open** 9am-5pm Mon-Wed, Fri; 10am-8pm Thur; 10am-5pm Sat. **Admission** $5; $3 seniors, students; free under-12s. Free 6-8pm Tue, Thur. **Credit** AmEx, MC, V. **Map** p405 E21.

Consisting of just two small galleries, the China Institute is somewhat overshadowed by the nearby Asia Society. But its rotating exhibitions, including works by female Chinese artists and selections from the Beijing Palace Museum, are compelling. The institute offers lectures and courses on myriad subjects such as calligraphy, Confucius and cooking.

Cooper-Hewitt, National Design Museum

2 E 91st Street, at Fifth Avenue (1-212 849 8400/ www.cooperhewitt.org). Subway: 4, 5, 6 to 86th Street. **Open** 10am-5pm Tue-Thur; 10am-9pm Fri; 10am-6pm Sat; noon-6pm Sun. **Admission** $10; $7 seniors, students; free under-12s. **Credit** AmEx, Disc, MC, V. **Map** p406 E18.

The Smithsonian's National Design Museum was once the home of industrialist Andrew Carnegie (there is still a lovely lawn behind the building). Now it's the only museum in the US dedicated to domestic and industrial design, and it boasts a fascinating roster of temporary exhibitions. Starting 5 May 2006, check out a round-up of 500 years' worth of eating utensils titled Feeding Desire: The Tools of the Table, 1500-2005, on view until 29 October. From December 2006 through to July 2007, the museum stages the National Design Triennial 2006, which examines experimental projects and innovations in architecture, fashion, graphics and product design.

El Museo del Barrio

1230 Fifth Avenue, between 104th & 105th Streets (1-212 831 7272/www.elmuseo.org). Subway: 6 to 103rd Street. **Open** 11am-5pm Wed-Sun. **Admission** $6; $4 seniors, students; free under-12s when accompanied by an adult. Seniors free Thursday. **Credit** AmEx, MC, V. **Map** p406 E16.

Located in Spanish Harlem (aka El Barrio), El Museo del Barrio is dedicated to the work of Latino artists who reside in the US as well as Latin-American masters. The 8,000-piece collection ranges from pre-Columbian artefacts to contemporary installations. In 2006 (to 12 November) programmes include homages to printmaker Lorenzo Homar and poet Rev Pedro Pietri, and Héctor Méndez Caratini: the Eye of Memory, a collection of the artist's photography and videos reflecting the cultural heritage of emerging Caribbean nations.

Frick Collection

1 E 70th Street, between Fifth & Madison Avenues (1-212 288 0700/www.frick.org). Subway: 6 to 68th Street-Hunter College. **Open** 10am-6pm Tue-Sat; 1-6pm Sun. **Admission** $12; $8 seniors; $5 students, 10-18s (under-16s must be accompanied by an adult; under-10s not admitted). **Credit** AmEx, Disc, MC, V. **Map** p405 E20.

The opulent residence that houses this private collection of great masters (from the 14th through the 19th centuries) was originally built for industrialist Henry Clay Frick. The firm of Carrère & Hastings (which also did the New York Public Library) designed the 1914 structure in an 18th-century European style, with a beautiful interior court and reflecting pool. The permanent collection boasts world-class paintings, sculpture and furniture by the likes of Rembrandt, Vermeer, Renoir and French cabinet-maker Jean-Henri Riesener. In the autumn, two works from a series by Italian Renaissance master Cimabue will be reunited and displayed together for the first time in America.

Goethe-Institut New York/ German Cultural Center

1014 Fifth Avenue, at 82nd Street (1-212 439 8700/www.goethe.de/ins/us/ney). Subway: 4, 5, 6 to 86th Street. **Open** *Gallery* 10am-5pm Mon-Fri. *Library* noon-7pm Tue, Thur; noon-5pm Wed, Fri, Sat. **Admission** free. **Map** p405 E19.

Goethe-Institut New York is a branch of the international German cultural organisation founded in 1951. Housed in a landmark Fifth Avenue mansion across from the Metropolitan Museum of Art, the institute mounts shows featuring German-born contemporary artists and presents concerts, lectures and film screenings. German-language books, videos and periodicals are available in the library.

Jewish Museum

1109 Fifth Avenue, at 92nd Street (1-212 423 3200/www.thejewishmuseum.org). Subway: 4, 5 to 86th Street; 6 to 96th Street. **Open** 11am-5.45pm Mon-Wed, Sun; 11am-9pm Thur; 11am-3pm Fri. Closed on Jewish holidays. **Admission** $10; $7.50 seniors; free under-12s when accompanied by an adult. Voluntary donation 5-8pm Thur. **Credit** AmEx, MC, V. **Map** p405 E18.

The Jewish Museum, in the 1908 Warburg Mansion, contains a fascinating collection of more than 28,000 works of art, artefacts and media installations. A two-floor permanent exhibit, Culture and Continuity: The Jewish Journey examines Judaism's survival and the essence of Jewish identity. Temporary exhibitions in 2006 include Max Liebermann: From

Realism to Impressionism, in which most of the 45 modernist works on display have never before been shown in America (10 March-9 July). Eva Hesse, an exhibition focusing on large-scale drawings and sculpture from the influential minimalist artist's considerable body of work, runs from 12 May to 17 September. The Museum's Café Weissman serves contemporary kosher fare.

Metropolitan Museum of Art

1000 Fifth Avenue, at 82nd Street (1-212 535 7710/ www.metmuseum.org). Subway: 4, 5, 6 to 86th Street. **Open** 9.30am-5.30pm Tue-Thur, Sun; 9.30am-9pm Fri, Sat. No strollers Sun. **Admission** suggested donation $12; $7 seniors, students; free under-12s. **Credit** AmEx, DC, Disc, MC, V. **Map** p405 E19.

It could take days, even weeks, to cover the Met's two million square feet of gallery space, so it's best to be selective. Besides the enthralling temporary exhibitions, there are excellent collections of African, Oceanic and Islamic art, along with more than 3,000 European paintings from the Middle Ages up through the fin de siècle period, including major works by Titian, Brueghel, Rembrandt, Vermeer, Goya and Degas. Egyptology fans should head straight for the glass-walled atrium housing the Temple of Dendur. The Greek and Roman halls have received a graceful makeover, and the incomparable medieval armour collection – a huge favourite with adults and children – was recently enriched by gifts of European, North American, Japanese and Islamic armaments. The Met has also made significant additions to its modern-art galleries, including major works by American artist Eric Fischl and Chilean surrealist Roberto Matta. Contemporary sculptures are displayed each year in the Iris and B Gerald Cantor Roof Garden (May to late autmn, weather permitting).

Once you've sated your art cravings, we recommend seeking out a spot of relative privacy and calm. The Met is studded with them; you just have to know where to look. The Engelhard Court, which borders Central Park, has benches, a trickling fountain, trees, ivy and stunning examples of Tiffany stained glass. (If you'd like to grab a drink or a snack in less-than-hectic surroundings, try the American Wing Café.) The Astor Court, on the second floor, is a garden modelled on a Ming-dynasty scholar's courtyard. Wooden paths border a naturally lit, gravel-paved atrium. The nearby Asian galleries, full of superb bronzes, ceramics and rare wooden Buddhist images, seldom get heavy foot traffic. At the western end of the museum, rest on a bench in the Robert Lehman Wing, then commune with Botticelli's *Annunciation*.

A large, round desk in the Great Hall (staffed by volunteers who speak multiple languages) is the hub of the museum's excellent visitors' resources. The Met opens its doors on Monday holidays, including Martin Luther King Day, Presidents' Day, Memorial Day and the Monday between Christmas and New Year's Day.

Metropolitan Museum of Art.
See p136.

Exhibitions scheduled for 2006 include Robert Rauschenberg: Combines, a comprehensive look at the influential artist's multimedia assemblages (to 2 Apr); and American artist Kara Walker's cutpaper silhouettes (21 Mar-25 June). In Daughter of Re: Hatshepsut, the Met shows off its vast collection of Egyptian decorative arts, sculpture and architectural artefacts dating from the reign of Hatshepsut (21 Mar-9 July). **Photo** *p137*.

Museum of the City of New York

1220 Fifth Avenue, between 103rd & 104th Streets (1-212 534 1672/www.mcny.org). Subway: 6 to 103rd Street. **Open** 10am-5pm Tue-Sun. **Admission** suggested donation $7; $5 seniors, students, children; $15 families. **Credit** AmEx, MC, V. **Map** p405 E16.

Located at the northern end of Museum Mile, this institution contains a wealth of city history and includes paintings, sculptures, photographs, military and naval uniforms, theatre memorabilia, manuscripts, ship models and rare books. The extensive toy collection, full of New Yorkers' playthings dating from the colonial era to the present, is especially well loved. Toy trains, lead soldiers and battered teddy bears share shelf space with exquisite bisque dolls (decked out in extravagant Paris fashions) and lavishly appointed doll's houses. Don't miss the amazing Stettheimer Dollhouse, created during the 1920s by Carrie Stettheimer, whose artist friends re-created their masterpieces in miniature to hang on the walls. Look closely and you'll even spy a tiny version of Marcel Duchamp's famous *Nude Descending a Staircase. See also* p138 **Don't miss**.

Neue Galerie

1048 Fifth Avenue, at 86th Street (1-212 628 6200/www.neuegalerie.org). Subway: 4, 5, 6 to 86th Street. **Open** 11am-6pm Mon, Sat, Sun; 11am-9pm Fri. **Admission** $10; $7 seniors, students, 12-16s (must be accompanied by an adult); under-12s not admitted. **Credit** AmEx, MC, V. **Map** p405 E18.

Don't miss MCNY film

New York, New York, it's a hell of a town with a hell of a story. Since 1624, people on this little island have been fighting to live the American dream on a daily basis. Now, witness the evolution of our great metropolis for yourselves: *Timescapes*, a 25-minute multimedia film showing daily at the **Museum of the City of New York** (*see above*) uses specially made digital maps with historic images and film footage to piece together the rise of New York City over four centuries – bringing to life buildings and street corners you might otherwise breeze by.

This elegant museum is devoted entirely to late 19th- and early 20th-century German and Austrian fine and decorative arts. The creation of the late art dealer Serge Sabarsky and cosmetics mogul Ronald S Lauder, it has the largest concentration of works by Gustav Klimt and Egon Schiele outside Vienna. There's also a bookstore, a chic design shop and Café Sabarsky (*see* p207), serving updated Austrian cuisine and ravishing Viennese pastries.

Solomon R Guggenheim Museum

1071 Fifth Avenue, at 89th Street (1-212 423 3500/www.guggenheim.org). Subway: 4, 5, 6 to 86th Street. **Open** 10am-5.45pm Mon-Wed, Sat, Sun; 10am-8pm Fri. **Admission** $15; $10 seniors, students with a valid ID; free under-12s (must be accompanied by an adult). Half-price 5-8pm Fri. **Credit** AmEx, MC, V. **Map** p406 E18.

Even if your schedule doesn't allow time to view the collections, you must get a glimpse (if only from the outside) of this dramatic spiral building, designed by Frank Lloyd Wright. In addition to works by Manet, Kandinsky, Picasso, Chagall and Louise Bourgeois, the museum owns Peggy Guggenheim's haul of cubist, surrealist and abstract expressionist works, along with the Panza di Biumo Collection of American minimalist and conceptual art from the 1960s and '70s. In 1992, the addition of a ten-storey tower provided space for a sculpture gallery (with views of Central Park), an auditorium and a café.

Planned 2006 exhibitions include David Smith: A Centennial (3 Feb-14 May), a collection of drawings, sculptures and notebooks that highlight Smith's achievements in American abstraction; and The Wound of Time: Spanish Art from El Greco to Picasso (29 Sept-Jan 2007), an overview of Spanish art from the last five centuries.

Whitney Museum of American Art

945 Madison Avenue, at 75th Street (1-212 570 3676/1-800 944 8639/www.whitney.org). Subway: 6 to 77th Street. **Open** 11am-6pm Wed, Thur, Sat, Sun; 1-9pm Fri. **Admission** $12; $9.50 seniors, students; free under-12s. Voluntary donation 6-9pm Fri. **Credit** AmEx, MC, V. **Map** p405 E20.

Like the Guggenheim, the Whitney is set apart by its unique architecture: it's a Marcel Breuer-designed gray granite cube with an all-seeing upper-storey 'eye' window. When Gertrude Vanderbilt Whitney, a sculptor and art patron, opened the museum in 1931, she dedicated it to living American artists. Today, the Whitney holds about 15,000 pieces by nearly 2,000 artists, including Alexander Calder, Willem de Kooning, Edward Hopper (the museum holds his entire estate), Jasper Johns, Louise Nevelson, Georgia O'Keeffe and Claes Oldenburg.

Still, the museum's reputation rests mainly on its temporary shows, particularly the exhibition everyone loves to hate, the Whitney Biennial. Held in even-numbered years, the Biennial remains the most prestigious (and controversial) assessment of contemporary art in America. The Whitney's small midtown Altria branch, located in a corporate

that path that bisects the Heather Garden (the one just below the promenade). When you reach the end, head down the path along Billings Lawn and stop at the stone overlook. From here you can see the George Washington Bridge to your left. Across the Hudson River, you'll see the cliffs of the Palisades in New Jersey – towering up to 500 feet above the river; these rocky outcroppings were formed about 190 million years ago. Bear right as you walk along the path heading up past Pine Lawn towards Abbey's Lawn and then on to Cloisters Lawn. Notice the humungous Ginkgo Biloba tree in the centre of the lawn. As you cross over the street, stay on the path to the left that crosses in front of the Cloisters (see p148). The castle is built out of bits and pieces of five medieval monasteries and chapels from France and houses a glorious collection of medieval art. When you find yourself at the main entrance of the museum pop in for a look around, or continue the walk by crossing over the street and turn right on to the path. This walkway will soon curve east (to the left) and lead to a large stone gazebo and a fun dog run. If you stay to the left of the dog run and walk uphill, the path will go below an overpass and up a flight of stairs to the New Leaf Café where you can stop for a snack (and use the public restrooms). The path in front of the cafe will take you back to the main entrance of the park.

various ageing halls and construction of new buildings. Nearby you can also check out the **New York Public Library for the Performing Arts** (see p142).

The other, less formal, cultural venues on the Upper West Side include the **Makor/ Steinhardt Center** (35 W 67th Street, between Central Park West & Columbus Avenue, 1-212 601 1000, www.makor.org), where the public can attend lectures, films, readings and live music performances, often with a folky or Jewish flavour; **Symphony Space** (see p332), where the World Music Institute programmes music and dance performances and rated actors read short stories aloud as part of the Selected Shorts programme; and **El Taller Latino Americano** (2710 Broadway, at 104th Street, 1-212 665 9460, www.tallerlatino.org), which offers a full range of cultural events.

Around Sherman and Verdi Squares (from 70th to 73rd Streets, where Broadway and Amsterdam Avenue intersect) classic early 20th-century buildings stand cheek-by-jowl with newer, often mundane high-rises. The jewel is the 1904 **Ansonia Hotel** (2109 Broadway, between 73rd & 74th Streets). Over the years, Enrico Caruso, Babe Ruth and Igor Stravinsky have lived in this Beaux Arts masterpiece, which was also the site of the Continental Baths (the gay bathhouse and cabaret where Bette Midler got her start) and Plato's Retreat (a swinging '70s sex club). On Broadway, the crowded 72nd Street subway station, which opened in 1904, is notable for its Beaux Arts entrance. The **Beacon Theatre** (see p314), formerly Manhattan's only rococo-style 1920s movie palace, is now one of the city's premier mid-size concert venues, presenting an eclectic menu of music, African-American regional theatre and headliner comedy events.

Once Central Park was completed, magnificently tall residential buildings rose up along Central Park West to take advantage of the views. The first of these great buildings was the Dakota (at 72nd Street). The fortress-like 1884 luxury apartment building is known as the setting for *Rosemary's Baby* and the site of John Lennon's murder in 1980 (Yoko Ono still lives here). You might recognise 55 Central Park West (at 66th Street) from the movie *Ghostbusters*. Built in 1930, it was the first art deco building on the block. Heading north on Central Park West, you'll spy the massive twin-towered San Remo Apartments (at 74th Street), which also date from 1930. A few blocks north, the **New-York Historical Society** (see p142) is the city's oldest museum, built in 1804. Across the street, the glorious **American Museum of Natural History** (see p142) has been given an impressive facelift, making even the fossils look fresh again. Dinosaur skeletons, a permanent rainforest exhibit and an IMAX theatre (which shows Oscar-winning nature documentaries) lure adults and school groups. Perhaps most popular is the museum's newest wing, the amazing, glass-enclosed Rose Center for Earth and Space, which includes the retooled Hayden Planetarium.

The cluster of classic groceries and restaurants lining the avenues of the neighbourhood's northern end is where the Upper West Side shops, drinks and eats. To see West Siders in their natural habitat, get in line at the perpetually jammed smoked-fish counter at gourmet market **Zabar's** (see p241). **Café Lalo** (201 W 83rd Street, between Amsterdam

Avenue & Broadway, 1-212 496 6031) is famous for its lavish desserts; **H&H Bagels** (*see p208* **History in the round**) is the city's largest bagel purveyor; and the legendary (though scruffy) restaurant and deli **Barney Greengrass** ('the Sturgeon King', 541 Amsterdam Avenue, at 86th Street, 1-212 724 4707) has specialised in smoked fish and what may be the city's best chopped liver since 1908.

Designed by Central Park's Frederick Law Olmsted, **Riverside Park** is a sinuous stretch of riverbank that starts at 72nd Street and ends at 158th Street, between Riverside Drive and the Hudson River. The stretch of park below 72nd Street, called Riverside Park South, includes a pier and beautiful patches of grass with park benches, and is a particularly peaceful city retreat. You'll probably see yachts, along with several houseboats, berthed at the 79th Street Boat Basin; in the summertime, there's an open-air café in the adjacent park where New Yorkers unwind with a beer and watch the sun set over the Hudson River. Several sites provide havens for reflection. The Soldiers' and Sailors' Monument (89th Street, at Riverside Drive), built in 1902 by French sculptor Paul EM DuBoy, honours Union soldiers who died in the Civil War, and a 1908 memorial (100th Street, at Riverside Drive) pays tribute to fallen firemen. **General Grant National Memorial** (aka Grant's Tomb), the mausoleum of former president Ulysses S Grant, is also located in the park. Across the street stands the towering Gothic-style Riverside Church (Riverside Drive, at 120th Street, 1-212 870 6700, www.theriverside churchny.org), built in 1930. The tower contains the world's largest carillon: 74 bells, played every Sunday at 10.30am.

American Museum of Natural History/Rose Center for Earth & Space

Central Park West, at 79th Street (1-212 769 5100/www.amnh.org). Subway: B, C to 81st Street-Museum of Natural History. **Open** 10am-5.45pm daily. **Admission** $13 suggested donation; $10 seniors, students; $7.50 2-12s; free under-2s. **Credit** AmEx, MC, V. **Map** p405 C/D19.

The thrills begin when you cross the threshold of the Theodore Roosevelt Rotunda, where you're confronted with a towering barosaurus rearing up to protect its young from an attacking allosaurus. This impressive welcome to the world's largest museum of its kind acts as a reminder to visit the dinosaur halls, on the fourth floor. During a mid-1990s renovation, several specimens were remodelled to reflect updated scientific thinking. The T-Rex, for instance, was once believed to have walked upright, Godzilla-style; it now stalks prey with its head lowered and its tail parallel to the ground.

The rest of the museum is equally dramatic. The Hall of Biodiversity examines world ecosystems and environmental preservation, and a life-size model of a blue whale hangs from the cavernous ceiling of the Hall of Ocean Life. The impressive Hall of Meteorites was brushed up and reorganised in 2003. The space's focal point is Ahnighito, the largest iron meteor on display anywhere in the world, weighing in at 34 tons (more than 30,000 kilos). From October to May, the museum installs a tropical butterfly conservatory in the Hall of Oceanic Birds, where visitors can mingle with 500 live specimens.

The spectacular $210 million Rose Center for Earth and Space – dazzling at night – is a giant silvery globe where you can discover the universe via 3-D shows in the Hayden Planetarium and light shows in the Big Bang Theater. An IMAX theatre screens larger-than-life nature programmes, and you can always learn something new from the innovative temporary exhibitions, an easily accessible research library (with vast photo and print archives), several cool gift shops and friendly, helpful staff.

General Grant National Memorial

Riverside Drive, at 122nd Street (1-212 666 1640). Subway: 1, 9 to 125th Street. **Open** 9am-5pm daily. **Admission** free. **Map** p407 B14.

Who's buried in Grant's Tomb? Technically, no one – the crypts of Civil War hero and 18th president Ulysses S Grant and his wife, Julia, are in full aboveground view. Note: the memorial is closed on Thanksgiving, Christmas and New Year's Day.

New-York Historical Society

170 Central Park West, between 76th & 77th Streets (1-212 873 3400/www.nyhistory.org). Subway: B, C to 81st Street-Museum of Natural History. **Open** 10am-6pm Tue-Sun. **Admission** $10; $5 seniors, students; free under-12s when accompanied by an adult. **No credit cards**. **Map** p405 D20.

New York's oldest museum, founded in 1804, was one of America's first cultural and educational institutions. Highlights in the vast Henry Luce III Center for the Study of American Culture include George Washington's Valley Forge camp cot, a complete series of watercolours from Audubon's *The Birds of America* and the world's largest collection of Tiffany lamps. From March to September 2006, a group of artists consider the consequences of enslavement via painting, sculpture and performance in Legacies: Contemporary Artists Reflect on Slavery; in Group Dynamics: Family Portraits and Scenes of Everyday Life, diverse artworks – including painting, quilt-making and photography – are used to trace family culture in 19th-century America (31 Mar-6 Aug).

New York Public Library for the Performing Arts

40 Lincoln Center Plaza, at 65th Street (1-212 870 1630). Subway: 1 to 66th Street-Lincoln Center. **Open** noon-6pm Tue, Wed, Fri, Sat; noon-8pm Thur. **Admission** free. **Map** p405 C21.

One of the world's great performing-arts research centres, the New York Library for the Performing Arts houses a seemingly endless collection of films, letters, manuscripts, video – and half a million sound recordings. Visitors can browse through books, scores and recordings, or attend a concert or lecture.

Morningside Heights

Morningside Heights runs from 110th Street (also known west of Central Park as Cathedral Parkway) to 125th Street, between Morningside Park and the Hudson River. The Cathedral Church of St John the Divine and the campus of Columbia University exert considerable influence over the surrounding neighbourhood.

One of the oldest universities in the US, **Columbia** was chartered in 1754 as King's College (the name changed after the Revolutionary War). It moved to its present location in 1897. Thanks to the large student population of Columbia and its sister school, Barnard College, the area has an academic feel, with bookshops, inexpensive restaurants and coffeehouses lining Broadway between 110th and 116th Streets. **Mondel Chocolates** (2913 Broadway, at 114th Street, 1-212 864 2111) was the chocolatier of choice for the late Katharine Hepburn, whose standing monthly order is still tacked on the wall behind the counter, and **Tom's Restaurant** (2880 Broadway, at 112th Street, 1-212 864 6137) did duty for the exterior shots for the countless diner scenes on TV's *Seinfeld*.

If you wander into Columbia's campus entrance at 116th Street, you won't fail to miss the impressive Low Memorial Building: it's the only one modelled after Rome's Pantheon. The former library, completed in 1897, is now an admin building. The real attraction, however, is the student body sprawled out on its steps (or lawns out front) catching rays between classes.

The **Cathedral Church of St John the Divine** (*see below*) is the seat of the Episcopal Diocese of New York. Known affectionately by locals as St John the Unfinished, the enormous cathedral (already larger than Notre Dame in Paris) will undergo hammering and chiselling well into this century. Just behind is the green expanse of **Morningside Park** (from 110th to 123rd Streets, between Morningside Avenue & Morningside Drive) and across the street is the **Hungarian Pastry Shop** (1030 Amsterdam Avenue, between 110th & 111th Streets, 1-212 866 4230), a great place for coffee, dessert and mingling with cute Columbia co-eds.

Cathedral Church of St John the Divine

1047 Amsterdam Avenue, at 112th Street (1-212 316 7540/www.stjohndivine.org). Subway: B,

The **Dakota Building**. *See p132.*

C, 1 to 110th Street-Cathedral Parkway. **Open**
8am-6pm daily. **Fees** $5; $4 seniors, students.
Credit MC, V. **Map** p406 C15.

Construction on 'St John the Unfinished' began in
1892 in Romanesque style, was put on hold for a
Gothic Revival redesign in 1911, then ground to a
halt in 1941, when the US entered World War II. It
resumed in earnest in 1979, but a fire in 2001
destroyed the church's gift shop and damaged two
17th-century Italian tapestries, further delaying
completion. In addition to Sunday services, the
cathedral hosts concerts and tours. It bills itself as
a place for all people – and it means it. Annual events
include both winter and summer solstice celebrations; the Blessing of the Animals during the Feast
of St Francis, which draws pets and their people
from all over the city; and, would you believe it, the
Blessing of the Bikes, which kicks off the bicycle
season each spring.

Harlem

Harlem is not just a destination on Manhattan
island – it's the cultural capital of black
America. More than any other New York City
address, Harlem is a state of mind as well as a
geographical location. It is no longer the
neglected 'raisin in the sun', as it was described
in Langston Hughes's famous poem 'Harlem:
A Dream Deferred', and it's not the powder keg
of the 1960s that his words presaged, either.
The Harlem Renaissance of the 1920s and '30s –
the cultural explosion that gave us the likes
of Hughes, Zora Neale Hurston and Duke
Ellington – continues to live on in memory. But
these days, there's a new Harlem renaissance, in
large part due to private real-estate investment
and government support for local entrepreneurs
and business development.

Harlem began as a suburb for well-to-do
whites in the 19th century, after the West
Side railroad was built. Around 1900, plans
to extend the subway along Lenox Avenue
to 145th Street triggered a housing boom
that went bust just a few years later. White
landlords, previously unwilling to rent to blacks
were now desperate for tenants and slowly but
surely changed their renting habits. Still, blacks
reportedly paid up to $5 more per month than
whites to rent similar flats. It was a watershed
for the city's resident African-American
community, who, for the first time, finally had
an opportunity to live in well-built homes in a
stable community. By 1914, the black
population of Harlem rose above 50,000.

The area is blessed with stately brownstones
in varying stages of renovation, often right next
to blocks of towering public housing. Thanks to
a thriving black middle class, Harlem's cultural
and religious institutions are seeing renewed
interest and funding, and new commercial
enterprise abounds. Still, the neighbourhood's
history remains visible. Some of the fabled
locations of the original Harlem Renaissance
have been restored, and while many stages
in the celebrated jazz clubs, theatres and
ballrooms have been replaced by pulpits, the
buildings still stand.

West Harlem

West Harlem, between Fifth and St Nicholas
Avenues, is the Harlem of popular imagination,
and 125th Street ('the one-two-five') is its
lifeline. Start at the crossroads: the 274,000-
square-foot **Harlem USA Mall** (300 W
125th Street, between Adam Clayton Powell Jr
Boulevard [Seventh Avenue] & Frederick
Douglass Boulevard [Eighth Avenue],
www.harlem-usa.com). The mall features a
Magic Johnson multiplex movie theatre (1-212
665 6923) and the well-stocked Hue-Man
Bookstore (1-212 665 7400), specialising in
African-American titles, plus the usual retail
megastores. Across the street is the **Apollo
Theater** (*see p314*; pictured left), which still

Harlem's landmark **Apollo Theater**.

hosts live concerts, a syndicated television programme and the classic Amateur Night held every Wednesday. A few blocks west, other touches of old Harlem linger: **Showman's Bar** (375 W 125th Street, between St Nicholas & Morningside Avenues, 1-212 864 8941), a mecca for jazz lovers, and the reconstituted **Cotton Club** (656 W 125th Street, at Riverside Drive, 1-212 663 7980), which hosts gospel brunches and evening jazz and blues sessions.

To the east of the mall is the **Lenox Lounge** (*see p324*), still cooking with old-school jazz. A well-regarded fine-arts centre, the **Studio Museum in Harlem** (*see p147*) exhibits work by many local artists. The offices of former president Bill Clinton are at 55 W 125th Street (between Fifth Avenue & Malcolm X Boulevard [Lenox Avenue]). Harlem's rich history is preserved in the archives of the **Schomburg Center for Research in Black Culture** (*see below*). This branch of the New York Public Library contains more than five million documents, artefacts, films and prints relating to the cultures of peoples of African descent, with an emphasis on the African-American experience. The **Abyssinian Baptist Church** (*see below*), where Harlem's controversial 1960s congressman Adam Clayton Powell Jr once preached, is celebrated for its history, political activism and rousing gospel choir. It harbours a small museum dedicated to Powell, the first black member of New York's City Council.

Harlem has become a destination for stylish plus-size fashions. Check out the **Soul Brothers Boutique** (115 W 128th Street, between Malcolm X Boulevard [Lenox Avenue] & Adam Clayton Powell Jr Boulevard [Seventh Avenue], 1-212 749 9005), where you can find T-shirts that celebrate the neighbourhood,

black political figures and '70s blaxploitation films. (You may also want to visit Freedom Hall, an active radical-politics lecture facility and bookstore next door.)

That generously sized clothing will come in handy if you sample the smothered pork chops and collard greens with fatback at **Sylvia's** (328 Malcolm X Boulevard [Lenox Avenue], between 126th & 127th Streets, 1-212 996 0660), Harlem's tourist-packed soul-food specialist. **Bayou** (308 Malcolm X Boulevard [Lenox Avenue], between 125th & 126th Streets, 1-212 426 3800), the handsome Cajun eaterie down the street, is a more attractive alternative.

Walk off some of your meal with a stroll around **Marcus Garvey Park** (aka Mount Morris Park, 120th to 124th Streets, between Madison Avenue & Mount Morris Park West), where the brownstone revival is in full swing.

Abyssinian Baptist Church

132 W 138th Street, between Malcolm X Boulevard (Lenox Avenue) & Adam Clayton Powell Jr Boulevard (Seventh Avenue) (1-212 862 7474/www.abyssinian. org). Subway: 2, 3 to 135th Street. **Open** 9am-5pm Mon-Fri. **Admission** free. **Map** p407 E11.

Schomburg Center for Research in Black Culture

515 Malcolm X Boulevard (Lenox Avenue), at 135th Street (1-212 491 2200). Subway: 2, 3 to 135th Street. **Open** noon-8pm Tue, Wed; noon-6pm Thur, Fri; 10am-6pm Sat. **Admission** free. **Map** p407 D12.

An extraordinary trove of vintage literature and historical memorabilia relating to black culture and the African diaspora is housed in an institution founded in 1926 by its first curator, bibliophile Arturo Alfonso Schomburg. The centre also hosts jazz concerts, films, lectures and tours.

Sightseeing

Local legend

In 1916, **Madame CJ Walker**, the first African-American millionaire in the United States, bought a townhouse at 104 West 136th Street in Harlem. A master marketer and tireless promoter, Walker began her business empire with a homemade hair conditioner and later expanded the enterprise into an extensive line of hair-care and beauty products formulated for African-Americans. After her death in 1919, her daughter, A'Lelia, turned the house into a literary salon, which was frequented by the stars of the Harlem Renaissance. The Countee Cullen Regional Branch Library now stands on the site of the Walker home.

Harlem living.

Studio Museum in Harlem

144 W 125th Street, between Malcolm X Boulevard (Lenox Avenue) & Adam Clayton Powell Jr Boulevard (Seventh Avenue) (1-212 864 4500/www.studio museum.org). Subway: 2, 3 to 125th Street. **Open** noon-6pm Wed-Fri, Sun; 10am-6pm Sat. Guided tours by appointment. **Admission** suggested donation $7; $3 seniors, students; free under-12s. **No credit cards**. **Map** p407 D13.

When the Studio Museum opened in 1968, it was the first black fine-arts museum in the country, and it remains the place to go for historical insight into African-American art and that of the African diaspora. Under the leadership of director Lowery Stokes Sims (formerly of the Met) and chief curator Thelma Golden (formerly of the Whitney), this favourite has evolved into the city's most exciting showcase for contemporary African-American artists.

Mount Morris & Strivers' Row

Harlem's historic districts continue to gentrify. The **Mount Morris Historic District** (from 119th to 124th Streets, between Malcolm X Boulevard [Lenox Avenue] & Mount Morris Park West) contains charming brownstones and a collection of religious buildings in a variety of architectural styles. These days, new boutiques, restaurants and pavement cafés dot the walk down the double-wide **Malcolm X Boulevard** (Lenox Avenue). **Harlemade** (No.174 between 118th & 119th Streets, 1-212 987 2500, www.harlemade.com) sells tees with Afro- and Harlem-centric messages and images, along with postcards, books and other neighbourhood memorabilia.

Another area with a historic past is **Strivers' Row**, also known as the St Nicholas Historic District. Running from 138th to 139th Streets, between Adam Clayton Powell Jr Boulevard (Seventh Avenue) and Frederick Douglass Boulevard (Eighth Avenue), these blocks of majestic houses were developed in 1891 by David H King Jr and designed by three different architects, including Stanford White. In the 1920s, prominent members of the black community, the legendary Eubie Blake and WC Handy among them, lived in this area. Now, more upwardly mobile strivers are moving in, and so are stylish boutiques such as **Grandview** (2531 Frederick Douglass Boulevard [Eighth Avenue], between 135th & 136th Streets, 1-212 694 7324), which sells eclectic contemporary clothing and accessories, mostly by African-American designers.

Along the way, there's plenty of good eating: **Londel's Supper Club** (2620 Frederick Douglass Boulevard [Eighth Avenue], between 139th & 140th Streets, 1-212 234 0601), owned by former police officer Londel Davis, serves some of the best blackened catfish in town, and

Home Sweet Harlem Café (270 W 135th Street, at Frederick Douglass Boulevard [Eighth Avenue], 1-212 926 9616) is the place for smoothies, soy burgers and hearty soups.

The 'hood comes alive after dark, especially at the not-to-be-missed **St Nick's Pub** (773 St Nicholas Avenue, at 149th Street, 1-212 283 9728), where you can hear live jazz every night (except Tuesday) for a small cover charge.

Heading east on West 116th Street, you'll pass through a dizzying smörgåsbord of cultures. There's a West African flavour between Malcolm X and Adam Clayton Powell Jr Boulevards (Lenox and Seventh Avenues), especially at the Senegalese restaurant **Le Baobab** (No.120, 1-212 864 4700). On the north side of the street is one of the Reverend Al Sharpton's favourite restaurants, **Amy Ruth's** (No.113, 1-212 280 8779), where Southern-style ribs and fried or smothered chicken and waffles are de rigueur. Continue east, past the silver-domed **Masjid Malcolm Shabazz** (No.102, 1-212 662 2200), the mosque of Malcolm X's ministry, to the **Malcolm Shabazz Harlem Market** (No.52, 1-212 987 8131), an outdoor bazaar where vendors sell T-shirts, toiletries and (purportedly) African souvenirs. (Don't miss Harley the Buckle Man, maker of custom-made belt buckles for rap stars.)

East Harlem

East of Fifth Avenue is East Harlem, sometimes called Spanish Harlem but better known to its primarily Puerto Rican residents as El Barrio. North of 96th Street and east of Madison Avenue, El Barrio moves to a different beat. Its main east–west cross street, East 116th Street, shows signs of a recent influx of Mexican immigrants, but between Fifth and Park Avenues, the thoroughfare's main attraction is actually the unusually high concentration of botanicas, or shops that supply candles, charms, oils, potions, orisha-priestess readings and other elements of the Catholic-tinged Santeria religion. **Rendon Otto Chicas** (60 E 116th Street, at Madison Avenue, 1-212 289 0378) is particularly kid- and tourist-friendly. From 96th to 106th Streets, a little touch of East Village-style bohemia can be detected in such places as **Carlito's Café y Galería** (1701 Lexington Avenue, between 106th & 107th Streets, 1-212 348 7044), which presents music, art and poetry performances. Nearby is the **Graffiti Hall of Fame** (106th Street, between Madison & Park Avenues), a schoolyard that celebrates great old- and new-school 'writers'. Be sure to check out **El Museo del Barrio** (*see p135*), Spanish Harlem's community museum.

Sightseeing

Hamilton Heights

Hamilton Heights (named after Alexander Hamilton, who owned a farm and estate here in 1802) extends from 125th Street to the Trinity Cemetery at 155th Street, between Riverside Drive and St Nicholas Avenue. The former factory neighbourhood developed after the West Side elevated train was built in the early 20th century. Today, it's notable for the elegant turn-of-the-20th-century row houses in the Hamilton Heights Historic District, which extends from 140th to 145th Streets, between Amsterdam and Edgecomb Avenues – just beyond the Gothic Revival-style campus of the City College of New York (Convent Avenue, at 138th Street).

Washington Heights & Inwood

The area from West 155th Street to Dyckman (200th) Street is called Washington Heights; venture north of that and you're in Inwood, Manhattan's northernmost neighbourhood, where the Harlem and Hudson Rivers converge. A growing number of artists and young families are relocating to these parts, attracted by the art deco buildings, big parks, hilly streets and (comparatively) low rents.

The area's biggest claim to fame is the **Morris-Jumel Mansion** (*see p149*), a stunning Palladian-style mansion that served as a swanky headquarters for George Washington during the autumn of 1776.

Since the 1920s, waves of immigrants have settled in Washington Heights. In the post-World War II era, many German-Jewish refugees (including Henry Kissinger, Dr Ruth Westheimer and Max Frankel, a former executive editor of the *New York Times*) moved to the western edge of the neighbourhood. Broadway once housed a sizable Greek population – opera singer Maria Callas lived here in her youth. But in the last few decades, the southern and eastern parts of the area have become predominantly Spanish-speaking due to a large population of Dominican settlers. The **Hispanic Society of America** (*see p149*) has its headquarters here.

A trek along Fort Washington Avenue from about 173rd Street to Fort Tryon Park puts you in the heart of what is now being called **Hudson Heights** – the posh area of Washington Heights.

Start at the George Washington Bridge, the city's only bridge across the Hudson River. A pedestrian walkway (also a popular route for cyclists) allows for dazzling Manhattan views.

Under the bridge on the New York side is a diminutive lighthouse – those who know the children's book *The Little Red Lighthouse and the Great Gray Bridge,* by Hildegarde Swift, will recognise it immediately. When the 85-year-old landmark wasn't needed anymore (after the bridge was completed) fans of the book rallied against plans to put it up for auction. To see it up close, look for the footpath on the west side of the interchange on the Henry Hudson Parkway at about 170th Street. If you need to refuel, stop at Bleu Evolution (808 W 187th Street, between Fort Washington and Pinehurst Avenues, 1-212 928 6006) for a downtown-style vibe, or hold out for the lovely New Leaf Café (1 Margaret Corbin Drive, near Park Drive, 1-212 568 5323) within the Frederick Law Olmsted-designed **Fort Tryon Park** (*see p140* **Walk this way**).

At the northern edge of the park are the **Cloisters** (*see below*), a museum built in 1938 using segments of five medieval cloisters shipped from Europe by the Rockefeller clan. It currently houses the Metropolitan Museum of Art's permanent medieval-art collection, including the exquisite *Unicorn Tapestries*, woven circa AD 1500.

Inwood stretches from Dyckman Street up to 218th Street, the last residential block in Manhattan. Dyckman buzzes with street life and nightclubs from river to river, but, north of that, the island narrows considerably and the parks along the western shoreline culminate in the wilderness of **Inwood Hill Park**, another Frederick Law Olmsted legacy. Some believe that this is the location of the legendary 1626 transaction between Peter Minuit and the Native American Lenapes for the purchase of a strip of land called Manahatta – a plaque at the south-west corner of the ballpark near 214th Street marks the purported spot. The 196-acre refuge contains the island's last swathes of virgin forest and salt marsh. Today, with a bit of imagination, you can hike over the hilly terrain, scattered with massive glacier-deposited boulders (called erratics), and picture Manhattan as it was before development. In recent years, the city's Parks Department has used the densely wooded area as a fledging spot for newly hatched bald eagles.

Cloisters

Fort Tryon Park, Fort Washington Avenue, at Margaret Corbin Plaza (1-212 923 3700/ www.metmuseum.org). Subway: A to 190th Street, then take the M4 bus or follow Margaret Corbin Drive north, for about the length of five city blocks, to the museum. **Open** *Mar-Oct* 9.30am-5.15pm Tue-Sun. *Nov-Feb* 9.30am-4.45pm Tue-Sun. **Admission** suggested donation (includes admission to the Metropolitan

Museum of Art on the same day) \$15; \$10 seniors; \$7 students; free under-12s (must be accompanied by an adult). **Credit** AmEx, DC, Disc, MC, V. **Map** p409 B3.

Set in a lovely park overlooking the Hudson River, the Cloisters houses the Met's medieval art and architecture collections. A path winds through the peaceful grounds to a castle that seems to have survived from the Middle Ages. (It was built a mere 70 years ago, using pieces of five medieval French cloisters.) Be sure to check out the famous Unicorn Tapestries, the 12th-century Fuentidueña Chapel and the *Annunciation Triptych* by Robert Campin.

Hispanic Society of America

Audubon Terrace, Broadway, between 155th & 156th Streets (1-212 926 2234/www.hispanic society.org). Subway: 1 to 157th Street. **Open** 10am-4.30pm Tue-Sat; 1-4pm Sun. **Admission** free. **Map** p408 B9.

The Hispanic Society has the largest assemblage of Spanish art and manuscripts outside Spain. Look for two portraits by Goya and the lobby's bas-relief of Don Quixote. The collection is dominated by religious artefacts, including 16th-century tombs from the monastery of San Francisco in Cuéllar, Spain. Also on display are decorative-art objects and thousands of black-and-white photographs that document life in Spain and Latin America from the mid-19th century to the present. Note that the library is closed on Sundays.

Morris-Jumel Mansion

65 Jumel Terrace, between 160th & 162nd Streets (1-212 923 8008/www.morrisjumel.org). Subway: C to 163rd Street-Amsterdam Avenue. **Open** 10am-4pm Wed-Sun. **Admission** \$4; \$3 seniors, students; free under-12s. **No credit cards. Map** p408 C8.

Built in 1765, Manhattan's only surviving pre-Revolutionary manse was originally the heart of a 130-acre estate that stretched from river to river (on the grounds, a stone marker points south with the legend 'new york, 11 miles'). George Washington planned the battle of Harlem Heights here in 1776, after the British colonel Roger Morris moved out. The handsome 18th-century Palladian-style villa offers fantastic views. Its former driveway is now Sylvan Terrace, which boasts the largest continuous stretch (one block) of old wooden houses in Manhattan.

The **Cloisters**. *See p148.*

Sightseeing

Brooklyn

A step away from Manhattan hyperbole, but still very much NY.

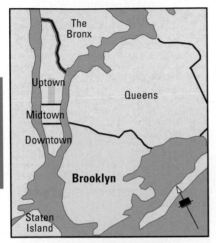

Most people who travel to New York for the first time never see anything beyond Manhattan (the trip from the airport aside) – but Brooklynites, and their admirers, know better. Almost one third of the city's population resides here, taking advantage of a vibrant array of social, cultural, dining, recreational and shopping destinations, as well as a pace that's typically a little less breakneck than you'll find in its more glorified neighbour.

Those with a taste for the archives will find no shortage of history to investigate: Europeans first settled here in the early 1600s, and **Brooklyn**, originally the Dutch settlement of Breuckelen, was a city from 1834 until 1898, when it became an official borough. Today, the area's diversity is still reflected in its spirited neighbourhoods. From the Russian families in Brighton Beach and the Polish residents of Greenpoint to the Italians in Bensonhurst, Chinese expats in Sunset Park and Caribbean immigrants in Bedford-Stuyvesant, almost 40 per cent of the people who call Brooklyn home were born outside the United States.

If that makes Brooklyn sound like a quaint old-world attraction, think again. Among the contemporary playgrounds for adults (not to mention kids) are the hipster enclaves of Williamsburg, the world-class Brooklyn Academy of Music and a wealth of lawn

lounging in Prospect Park and the Brooklyn Botanic Garden. And there are those those bridges, potent landmarks in these parts. Most famously, the Brooklyn Bridge, one of the greatest feats of engineering in the 19th century, not only linked two cities, it became an important symbol of progress. During the blackout of 14 August 2003, it was the Manhattan Bridge where borough president Marty Markowitz greeted hot, weary crowds through a bullhorn as they neared home: 'Everything's going to be all right now – you're back in Brooklyn!'

Sure, nothing is like Manhattan, but if you don't get a feel for Brooklyn, you can't really say that you know New York. Whether it's a bridge, a beach or premier music, dance and theatre you're after, it's easy to find it here. For more details on what the borough has to offer, contact **Brooklyn Information & Culture** (1-718 855 7882, www.brooklynx.org) or **Heart of Brooklyn: A Cultural Partnership** (1-718 638 7700, www.heartofbrooklyn.org). We've also put together a walk for you to take in some of the borough's most stunning sites; *see p158* **Walk this way**.

Brooklyn Heights & Dumbo

Brooklyn Heights has been the borough's toniest address since the end of World War II. The neighbourhood was born when entrepreneur Robert Fulton's first steam-powered ferry linked Manhattan to the quiet fishing village on the western edge of Long Island in 1814. The streets of Brooklyn Heights – particularly Cranberry, Hicks, Pierrepont and Willow – are lined with beautifully maintained Greek Revival and Italianate row houses dating from the 1820s. In 1965, 30 blocks of the area were designated Brooklyn's first historic district. Today, Henry and Montague Streets, the main drags, are packed with shops, restaurants and bars. The **Brooklyn Heights Promenade**, which offers spectacular vistas of Manhattan, is just a quick walk from the end of the magnificent **Brooklyn Bridge**. The vision of German-born civil engineer John Augustus Roebling (who did not live to see its completion), the bridge was the first to use steel cables. It connects downtown Brooklyn with Manhattan and provides glorious views of the

Statue of Liberty and New York Harbor. If you're more interested in underground goings-on, then a stop at the **New York Transit Museum**, housed in a former subway station, is a must. Visitors can learn a boatload about the complex engineering and construction feats that made the city's massive subway system.

More remnants of bygone Breuckelen abound at the **Brooklyn Historical Society** building, which, when completed in 1881, was the first in New York to use locally produced terracotta on its facade (it reopened in late 2003, following an extensive restoration). The grand **Borough Hall** (209 Joralemon Street, at Court Street, www.brooklyn-usa.org) stands as a monument to Brooklyn's past as an independent municipality. Completed in 1851, the Greek Revival edifice – later crowned with a Victorian cupola – was renovated in the late 1980s. The building is linked to the **New York State Supreme Court** (360 Adams Street, between Joralemon Street & Tech Place) by **Cadman Plaza** (from Prospect Street to Tech Place, between Cadman Plaza East & Cadman Plaza West). Nearby, at the junction of Court and Remsen Streets, farmers peddle produce on Tuesday, Thursday and Saturday mornings during most seasons.

If the Heights is too staid and stately for your taste, you might prefer the still-evolving waterside neighbourhood of **Dumbo** (Down Under the Manhattan Bridge Overpass), which also provides impressive sightlines

to Manhattan. A fine viewing perch is below the Brooklyn Bridge at the **Fulton Ferry Landing**, which juts out over the East River at Old Fulton and Water Streets, and is close to two newly refurbished parks – **Empire-Fulton Ferry State Park** and **Brooklyn Bridge Park** (riverside between the Manhattan and Brooklyn Bridges). Also at the water's edge is the posh and pricey River Café (1 Water Street, at Old Fulton Street, 1-718 522 5200); breathtaking views of the Manhattan skyline have made the adjacent pier a favourite photo site for Chinese wedding parties. You'll enjoy the view even more with a cone from the **Brooklyn Ice Cream Factory** (Fulton Ferry Landing, between Old Fulton & Water Streets, 1-718 246 3963). This area is also home to the **Fulton Ferry Historic District**, the only commercial district in the borough that is a designated historic district. Steam-powered ferry service between Brooklyn and Manhattan kicked off in 1814. As a result, the area bustled with activity and saw the construction of several Greek Revival, Italianate and cast-iron buildings. Most impressive is the Long Island Insurance Company (5-7 Front Street) and the Eagle Warehouse (now apartments) on Fulton Street.

Drawn by the cobblestone streets and loft spaces in red-brick warehouses, artists flocked to Dumbo in the 1970s and '80s, and then kept on coming. The arrival of several chic boutiques and home stores has some people saying that

One of Brooklyn's greatest assets: Manhattan views, as seen from the Brooklyn Bridge.

the area has lost its rough-hewn charm. Don't believe it. You can still get lost among the quiet side streets, and the **d.u.m.b.o.** arts centre (30 Washington Street, between Plymouth & Water Streets, 1-718 694 0831, www.dumboarts center.org) continues to promote the work of community artists through its gallery and sponsorship of the annual **d.u.m.b.o. art under the bridge** festival (*see p265*), held in mid October. **St Ann's Warehouse** (38 Water Street, between Dock & Main Streets, 1-718 254 8779) hosts offbeat concerts, readings and theatre productions that often feature high-profile artists.

Dumbo dining also boasts its share of attractions. Pizza lovers can sample a coal-fired pie at the venerable **Grimaldi's** (19 Old Fulton Street, between Front & Water Streets, 1-718 858 4300), which claims the title of America's first (and some say best) pizzeria. Linger over a latte and chit-chat with locals at the airy café and bar at the **Dumbo General Store** (111 Front Street, between Adams & Washington Streets, 1-718 855 5288), which also hawks art supplies. And don't miss the always-packed **Jacques Torres Chocolate** shop (*see p240*) or its fabulous hot chocolates.

Brooklyn Bridge
Subway: A, C to High Street; J, M, Z to Chambers Street; 4, 5, 6 to Brooklyn Bridge-City Hall.
The stunning views and awe-inspiring web of steel cables will take your breath away. As you walk, bike

or Rollerblade along its wide wood-planked promenade, look for plaques detailing the history of the bridge's construction.

Brooklyn Historical Society
128 Pierrepont Street, at Clinton Street, Brooklyn Heights (1-718 222 4111/www.brooklynhistory.org). Subway: A, C, F to Jay Street-Borough Hall; M, R to Court Street; 2, 3, 4, 5 to Borough Hall. **Open** noon-5pm Fri-Sun. **Admission** $6; $4 seniors, students and 12-18s; free under-12s. **Credit** AmEx, MC, V.
The permanent exhibit is sure to satisfy fans of Brooklyn. A major research library and photo archive are also housed here. Boat tours of the waterfront in summer are fun and fascinating.

New York Transit Museum
Corner of Boerum Place & Schermerhorn Street, Brooklyn Heights, Brooklyn (1-718 694 1600/www.mta.info/mta/museum). Subway: A, C, G to Hoyt-Schermerhorn. **Open** 10am-4pm Tue-Fri; noon-5pm Sat, Sun. **Admission** $5; $3 seniors and 3-17s; free under-3s. **No credit cards**.
Located underground in an authentic 1930s subway station, this museum allows visitors to climb aboard the museum's collection of vintage subway and el cars, explore a working signal tower and check out permanent exhibitions such as Moving the Millions: New York City's Subways from Its Origins to the Present. The museum also has a great gallery and gift shop in Grand Central Terminal.
Other locations: New York Transit Museum Gallery Annex & Store, Grand Central Terminal, adjacent to stationmaster's office, Main Concourse, 42nd Street, at Park Avenue (1-212 878 0106).

Beautiful **Brooklyn Heights**, Brooklyn's first preservation district. *See p150.*

Local legend

Lyman Beecher was a firebrand
Presbyterian minister whose controversial
abolitionist views led him from Boston
to Cincinnati to Brooklyn. Here he joined
his son, minister Henry Ward Beecher,
in preaching against the immorality of
slavery at the Plymouth Church, at 75
Hicks Street in Brooklyn Heights. Lyman's
daughter, Harriet Beecher Stowe, took up
the cause as well, publishing her classic
novel *Uncle Tom's Cabin* in 1852.

Boerum Hill, Carroll Gardens, Cobble Hill & Red Hook

One of Brooklyn's most striking examples of
rapid gentrification can be found on **Smith
Street**, which stretches from **Boerum Hill** to
Carroll Gardens and has come to be known
as the borough's **Restaurant Row**. This strip
was targeted for urban renewal in the 1990s
and given a facelift that included wrought-iron
streetlamps and new sidewalks. Both nabes
boast charming, walkable historic districts
lined with mid 19th-century Greek Revival
and Italianate homes and storefronts. Today,
affordable restaurants and cafés pack in the
diners. Hot eateries along trendy Smith Street
include classic bistro Bar Tabac (No.128, at
Dean Street, Boerum Hill, 1-718 923 0918);
French-Chinese Chance (No.223, at Butler

Street, Carroll Gardens, 1-718 242 1515) and
New American Chestnut (No.271, between
DeGraw & Sackett Streets, Carroll Gardens,
1-718 243 0049). Many of the area's shops are
run by artists and designers selling their own
wares; these stand shoulder to shoulder with a
swiftly shrinking number of Latino restaurants,
bodegas and social clubs that have (barely)
survived the transition. Playful, pretty women's
clothing is for sale at Frida's Closet (No.296,
between Sackett & Union Streets, Carroll
Gardens, 1-718 855 0311) and Flirt (No.252,
between DeGraw & Douglass Streets, 1-718
858 7931), where many of the pieces are made
by local designers.

Along nearby **Atlantic Avenue** are haute
home furnisher City Foundry (No.365, between
Bond & Hoyt Streets, Boerum Hill, 1-718 923
1786); Rico (No.384, between Bond & Hoyt
Streets, 1-718 797 2077), which sells art, lighting
and furnishings; and stylish women's clothier
Butter (No.389, between Bond & Hoyt Streets,
1-718 260 9033).

The mile-long stretch of Atlantic Avenue
between Henry and Nevins Streets, known by
locals as the **Fertile Crescent**, is crowded
with Middle Eastern restaurants and retail food
markets. The granddaddy of them all is Sahadi
Importing Company (No.187, between Clinton
& Court Streets, Cobble Hill, 1-718 624 4550), a
57-year-old neighbourhood institution that sells
olives, spices, cheeses, nuts and other gourmet
treats. Atlantic Avenue is also considered
the northern border of **Cobble Hill**, a quaint
neighbourhood with a small-town feel. Less
restaurant-heavy than nearby Smith Street,
shady **Court Street** is dotted with boutiques
and shops such as Book Court (No.163, between
Pacific and Dean Streets, 1-718 875 3677), which
carries Brooklyn guidebooks and histories; and
the charming Sweet Melissa (No.276, between
Butler & Douglass Streets, 1-718 855 3410)
which serves brunch, lunch and afternoon tea in
a pretty back garden. Farther south, you'll cross
into the still predominantly Italian-American
Carroll Gardens. Pick up a prosciutto loaf
from the Caputo Bakery (No.329, between
Sackett & Union Streets, Carroll Gardens, 1-718
875 6871) or an aged *soppressata* salami from
Esposito and Sons (No.357, between President
& Union Streets, 1-718 875 6863); then relax
in **Carroll Park** (from President to Carroll
Streets, between Court & Smith Streets) and
watch the old-timers play *bocce* (bowls). Take
a walk over the Brooklyn-Queens Expressway
to the industrial waterfront of Cobble Hill to
the corner building housing hip Mexican bistro
Alma (*see p210*), where the open-air rooftop
dining area has a great view of the East River
and lower Manhattan.

Sightseeing

Southwest of Cobble Hill and Carroll Gardens lies rough-and-tumble **Red Hook**, offering a mix of industrial-waterfront surrealism, local artist studios, and a fast-growing crop of bars and eateries. Getting to the 'hood is a challenge – from the F and G subway station at Smith-9th Street, it's either a long walk or a connecting B77 bus ride. But it's worth it for a glimpse of the tough, pre-gentrified life of old New York. Decaying piers are an appropriately moody backdrop for massive cranes, empty warehouses and trucks clattering over cobblestoned streets. To check out works by local artists, look for the hand-scrawled letters 'Gallery' on the doors of the Kentler International Drawing Space (353 Van Brunt Street, between Sullivan & Wolcott Streets, 1-718 875 2098). The Brooklyn Waterfront Artist Coalition (BWAC) hosts large group shows in the spring and autumn; visit the website (www.bwac.org) or call 1-718 596 2507 for a calendar. Warning: this slice of gritty Brooklyn of yore may not be around for long: in addition to the many restaurants and artists' lofts that have crept into the region, plans are afoot to turn one of the biggest waterfront warehouses into condos and to construct a massive Ikea store on a disused old pier. A pickup spot for the **New York Water Taxi** (1-212 742 1969, www.nywatertaxi.com) is sure to bring in a fresh crop of curious Manhattanites.

Park Slope & Prospect Heights

Welcome to Brooklyn's suburbs. **Park Slope** has a relaxed, upscale feel, owing to its charming Victorian brownstones, leafy streets and proximity to Prospect Park. Seventh Avenue is the main commercial drag here. Fifth Avenue is the hot strip for unique boutiques and good restaurants, including the highly thought of Venetian-accented Al di là (248 Fifth Avenue, at Carroll Street, 1-718 783 45665); the eclectic favourite Blue Ribbon Brooklyn (*see p185*); and the New American Stone Park Café (324 Fifth Avenue, at 3rd Street, 1-718 369 0082). Park Slope's lesbian community is very visible: at the **Lesbian Herstory Archives** (*see p303*), you can peruse books and memorabilia; at Ginger's Bar (*see p309*) you can peruse the readers. If you're more of the walking sort, you're in luck: along the western edge of Prospect Park, extending for a full 19 blocks, is a section of the **Park Slope Historic District**. Brownstones and several fine examples of Romanesque Revival and Queen Ann residences grace these streets.

Particularly charming are the brick edifices that line Carroll and Montgomery Streets.

Central Park may be bigger and more famous, but **Prospect Park** (main entrance on Flatbush Avenue, at Grand Army Plaza, Prospect Heights, 1-718 965 8999/www.prospect park.org) has a more rustic quality than its rectangular sibling to the west, and Brooklynites adore it. This masterpiece, also designed by Frederick Law Olmsted and Calvert Vaux, is a great spot for bird-watching, especially with a little guidance from the **Prospect Park Audubon Center at the Boathouse** (park entrance on Ocean Avenue, at Lincoln Road, Prospect Heights, 1-718 287 3400). Or pretend you've left the city altogether by boating or hiking amid the waterfalls, reflecting pools and wildlife habitats of the recently restored **Ravine District** (park entrances on Prospect Park West, at 3rd, 9th & 15th Streets, Park Slope). The rolling green park was created with equestrians in mind; you can saddle a horse at the nearby Kensington Stables (*see p339*) or hop on a bike and pedal alongside bladers and runners. Children enjoy riding the hand-carved horses at the park's antique Carousel (Flatbush Avenue, at Empire Boulevard) and playing with animals in the **Prospect Park Zoo** (park entrance on Flatbush Avenue, near Ocean Avenue, Prospect Heights, 1-718 399 7339).

The verdant expanse of **Green-Wood Cemetery** is about a 15-minute walk from Prospect Park. A century ago, this site vied with Niagara Falls as New York State's greatest tourist attraction. Filled with Victorian mausoleums, cherubs and gargoyles, Green-Wood is the resting place of some half-million New Yorkers, including Jean-Michel Basquiat, Leonard Bernstein and Mae West. The spectacular, soaring arches are carved from New Jersey brownstone. Intricate details of death and resurrection, carved in Nova Scotia sandstone, are the handiwork of John Moffit.

The central branch of the **Brooklyn Public Library** (Grand Army Plaza, Prospect Heights, 1-718 230 2100) sits near Prospect Park's main entrance and the massive Civil War memorial arch at **Grand Army Plaza** (intersection of Flatbush Avenue, Eastern Parkway & Prospect Park West). The library's Brooklyn Collection includes thousands of artefacts and photos that trace the borough's history. Just around the corner are the tranquil **Brooklyn Botanic Garden** (*see p155*) and the recently spruced-up **Brooklyn Museum** (*see p155*), which has a renowned Egyptology collection and now a new glass façade and mesmerising fountain display that are worthy of it.

Enjoy green peace in **Brooklyn Botanic Garden**.

Brooklyn Botanic Garden
900 Washington Avenue, at Eastern Parkway,
Prospect Heights (1-718 623 7200/www.bbg.org).
Subway: B, Q, Franklin Avenue S to Prospect
Park; 2, 3 to Eastern Parkway-Brooklyn Museum.
Open *Apr-Sept* 8am-6pm Tue-Fri; 10am-6pm Sat,
Sun. *Oct-Mar* 8am-4.30pm Tue-Fri; 10am-4.30pm
Sat, Sun. **Admission** $5; $3 seniors and students;
free under-16s. Free Tuesday; Tue-Fri late Nov-Feb.
Credit MC, V.
Fifty-two acres of luscious greenery awaits you. In
spring, high-tail it out for the blooming of more than
220 cherry trees. The recently renovated Eastern
Parkway entrance and the Osborne Garden – an
Italian-style formal garden – are also worth a peek.

Brooklyn Museum
200 Eastern Parkway, at Washington Avenue,
Prospect Heights, Brooklyn (1-718 638 5000/www.
brooklynmuseum.org). Subway: 2, 3 to Eastern
Parkway-Brooklyn Museum. **Open** 10am-5pm
Wed-Fri; 11am-6pm Sat, Sun. First Saturday of the
month (except September) 11am-11pm. **Admission**
$8; $4 seniors and students; free under-12s (must
be accompanied by an adult). Free first Saturday
of the month (except September) 5-11pm.
Credit AmEx, MC, V.
Brooklyn's premier institution is a tranquil alternative to Manhattan's big-name spaces; it's rarely
crowded. Among the museum's many assets is a
rich, 4,000-piece Egyptian collection, which includes
a gilded-ebony statue of Amenhotep III and, on a

ceiling, a large-scale rendering of an ancient map of
the cosmos. You can even view a mummy preserved
in its original coffin.
Masterworks by Cézanne, Monet and Degas, part
of an impressive European painting and sculpture
collection, are displayed in the museum's skylight-
ed Beaux-Arts Court. On the fifth floor, American
paintings and sculptures include native son Thomas
Cole's *The Pic-Nic* and Louis Rémy Mignot's stunning *Niagara*. Don't miss the renowned Pacific
Island and African galleries.
Planned 2006 exhibitions: from March through
early June, Aminah Brenda Lynn Robinson's large-
scale compositions will focus on the collective memory of the African-American community, and in
October, 100 photographs by Annie Leibovitz will be
on display. Her subjects include a naked John Lennon
embracing Yoko Ono just days before his death.

Green-Wood Cemetery
Fifth Avenue, at 25th Street, Sunset Park (1-718
768 7300/www.green-wood.com). Subway: M, R to
25th Street. **Open** 8am-5pm daily. **Admission** free.

Fort Greene, Greenpoint & Williamsburg

Fort Greene, with its stately Victorian
brownstones and other grand buildings, has
undergone a major revival over the past decade.

The battle for Bed-Stuy

Gentrification is a loaded word in New York City these days, and especially in Brooklyn. Places like Williamsburg, Fort Greene, and even parts of Bushwick that were once beset by so many social ills, seem to be living proof that the grime and grunge of street culture is no match for the onslaught of cafés and baby strollers. But not every Brooklyn neighbourhood is calmly accepting the changes promised by gentrification. In one swathe of central Brooklyn known as Bedford-Stuyvesant, the debate over gentrification has become a matter of preserving the area's cultural and even ethnic character against an onslaught of uninvited change.

As one 15-year resident named Russell Frederick puts it, 'We know the British are coming. The future is going to be decided between those who think in terms of community and those who think in terms of maximum profit.' That pursuit of maximum profit is just what has some long-term Bed-Stuy residents worried the most. For years, the area was kept off the gentrification radar by its rough-and-tumble 'Bed-Stuy, Do or Die' motto. But with crime down 60 per cent in the

It has long been a centre of African-American life and business – Spike Lee, Branford Marsalis and Chris Rock have all lived here. **Fort Greene Park** (from Myrtle to DeKalb Avenues, between St Edwards Street and Washington Park) was conceived in 1846 at the behest of poet Walt Whitman (then editor of the *Brooklyn Daily Eagle*); its masterplan was fully realised by the omnipresent Olmsted and Vaux in 1867. At the centre of the park stands the Prison Ship Martyrs Monument, erected in 1909 in memory of 11,000 American prisoners who died on British ships that were anchored nearby during the Revolutionary War.

The **Lafayette Avenue Presbyterian Church** (85 South Oxford Street, at Lafayette Avenue, Fort Greene, 1-718 625 7515) was founded by a group of abolitionists; Abraham Lincoln's oldest son, Robert Todd Lincoln, broke ground for the church in 1860. Its subterranean tunnel once served as a stop on the Underground Railroad. The celebrated stained-glass windows created by Louis Comfort Tiffany are being restored.

A year after the church was established, the **Brooklyn Academy of Music** (*see p328*) was founded in Brooklyn Heights. It was later moved to its current site on Fort Greene's

southern border. BAM is America's oldest operating performing-arts centre. It once presented the likes of Edwin Booth and Sarah Bernhardt; now it's known for ambitious cultural performances of all kinds. In recent years, it has added several venues that show cutting-edge dance, theatre, music and film programmes and draw audiences from throughout the metropolitan area. From October through December, BAM hosts the Next Wave Festival (*see p265*). Also world-famous – though perhaps to a different audience – is the cheesecake at Junior's Restaurant (386 Flatbush Avenue, at DeKalb Avenue, 1-718 852 5257), just three blocks away. A slew of popular hangouts can be found nearby along **DeKalb Avenue**, including the funky South African i-Shebeen Madiba (No.195, at Carlton Avenue, 1-718 855 9190); lively bistro Chez Oskar (No.211, at Adelphi Street, 1-718 852 6250); and groovy bar and restaurant Liquors (No.219, between Adelphi & Clermont Streets, 1-718 488 7700), known for its killer Mojitos.

Williamsburg is further along in hipness than Fort Greene, especially if you're 22, in a band and well tattooed. Just one subway stop from the East Village (on the L line), **Bedford Avenue** is the neighbourhood's main action-

last 12 years, certain telltale signs of gentrification have come a-knocking: brownstones (Bed-Stuy has the largest stock of them in New York) that sold for $175,000 five years ago now command upwards of $700,000. Not only is the residential stock appreciating, but several new cafés and retail stores have opened to serve the growing population of young artists and professionals. Popping up amid the corner bodegas, hair salons and Chinese take-out joints that predominate the area's storefronts, these new businesses symbolise what many long-time residents, led by a vibrant, vocal art community, fear the most: that Bed-Stuy is threatening to become Brooklyn's latest gentrified, 'cool' neighbourhood. In response, a heated debate is growing about what these recent shifts along the residential and commercial frontier herald for the character of one of the country's largest black communities.

'Bed-Stuy is unique in that it is the last chance we have for a viable, predominantly black community in New York City that is oriented towards art and culture,' said a neighbourhood home-owner and artist known as TRUE (pictured). 'Harlem seems already lost because of gentrification, and we are taking steps to prevent that here.'

TRUE and his peers work to support open mics and chess competitions at black-owned cafés like Food 4 Thought (445 Marcus Garvey Boulevard, at McDonough, 1-718 443 4160), and sometimes talk about gentrification as a class, rather than a racial shift. They want a more wealthy Bed-Stuy, but one that maintains the current proportion of about 75 per cent of its 145,000 residents as black. But author Danny Simmons, the older brother of rap mogul Russell Simmons, says it will improve the quality of life for most residents, if Bed-Stuy becomes more economically and racially diverse. 'There is a lot of healing that needs to go on in the black community, but that doesn't happen just by keeping other people out,' he says. 'Besides,' he adds, 'services certainly improve when white people move into a neighbourhood. I know saying that puts me at odds with some people, but I don't give a damn.'

packed street. If you have a few hours to kill, hopping on the L train for ten minutes is worth the effort. You'll also find plenty of restaurants and nightspots along North 6th Street and Grand Avenue. During the day, Verb Café (218 Bedford Avenue, between North 4th & 5th Streets, 1-718 599 0977) is the nabe's prime slacker hangout; at night, the scene moves to eateries like the Thai palace SEA (see p210), funky Japanese Bozu (296 Grand Street, between Havemeyer & Roebling Streets, 1-718 384 7770) and the laid-back Diner (85 Broadway, at Berry Street, 1-718 486 3077). You'll also find the distinctly untrendy neighbourhood fixture and gustatory treasure Peter Luger (see p209), which grills what many people consider to be the best steak in the entire city.

The area also has dozens of art galleries, such as the local fave Pierogi (see p274). But the core of the art scene is the **Williamsburg Art & Historical Center** (135 Broadway, at Bedford Avenue, 1-718 4867372, www.wah center.org), in a landmark 1929 bank building. The performance and music scenes thrive, too; worth-a-trip spaces include Galapagos (see p316) and Northsix (see p320) and Pete's Candy Store (709 Lorimer Street, 1-718 302 3770).

Long before the hipster invasion, Billyburg's waterfront location made it ideal for industry; after the Erie Canal linked the Atlantic Ocean to the Great Lakes, in 1825, the area became an even more bustling port. Companies such as Pfizer and Domino Sugar started here. But by the late 20th century, businesses began to abandon the enormous industrial spaces – the landmark Domino refinery finally closed in 2004. Meanwhile, the beloved **Brooklyn Brewery** (79 North 11th Street, between Berry Street & Wythe Avenue, 1-718 486 7422, www.brooklynbrewery.com) is located in a former ironworks. Visit during happy hour on Friday evenings or take a tour on Saturday.

Williamsburg is one of New York's many curious multiethnic amalgams. To the south, Broadway divides a Latino neighbourhood from a lively community of Hasidic Jews, while the northern half extending into Greenpoint contains Polish and Italian settlements (with old-time delis and restaurants to match).

Bedford-Stuyvesant

Although Harlem gets props for being the cultural capital of black America, it's rivalled in size and architectural splendour by **Bed-Stuy**.

Walk this way: Brooklyn bound

Start: Brooklyn Bridge (Manhattan side)
Finish: Brooklyn Historical Society
Distance: About 2 miles
Time: 2 hours

Standing in City Hall Park, just outside the Brooklyn Bridge-City Hall subway entrance, face east (in the direction of the Brooklyn Bridge; pictured left). As you cross over Centre Street, to the bridge's pedestrian walkway, say goodbye to Manhattan. The 3,460ft suspension bridge you are walking on was the first to use steel for its stunning web of cable wires and was the longest suspension bridge in the world back on the day it opened – 24 May 1883. That day, more than 150,000 people paid one cent to stroll across the bridge and marvel at the Gothic towers that rise out of the East River. As you walk be sure to take a few minutes to read the panels that tell about the bridge's storied construction. As you near the Brooklyn side of the bridge the path splits; stay to the left and go down the stairs to the street. You'll come out on Cadman Plaza East. Turn left and cross over Prospect Street (Cadman Plaza becomes Washington Street here). Walk down the hill two blocks on Washington Street and

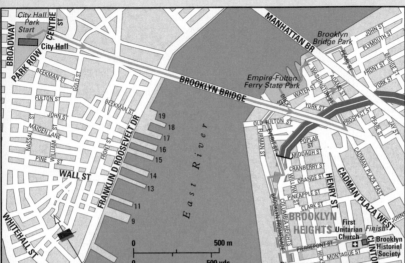

turn right on to Front Street. Welcome to
Dumbo (which is short for Down Under the
Manhattan Bridge Underpass). This hip little
enclave became a fashionable residential
area as artists took over warehouses that
were once part of the booming Fulton Ferry
commercial waterfront (which thrived starting
in 1814, when the steam-powered ferry came
on the scene). Nowadays, locals load up on
caffeine and art supplies at Dumbo General
Store (111 Front Street). Continue along Front
Street until you get to Pearl Street. Look up.
This is the Manhattan Bridge, which opened
in 1909. Turn left on Pearl Street and follow
it to the East River. At John Street, turn left
and head into Brooklyn Bridge Park. Follow
the gravel path along the water (past the
mini sandy beach). Exit the park at the
flagpole and cross over the pavement and
enter Empire-Fulton Ferry State Park – the
surrounding Fulton Ferry Landing dates back
to 1642. Curve your way around and exit
between the two Tobacco Warehouses
through the Dock Street gate. (Note: there's
a public toilet in the State Park office to the
left.) Turn right on Water Street. As the road
bends you'll pass the famous River Café,
Brooklyn Ice Cream Factory and Fulton Ferry

Water Taxi landing. Dog-leg over Old Fulton
Street and head up Everit Street (just east
of the gas station). Walk up the hill (here the
road becomes Columbia Heights). When you
reach Cranberry Street, in the distance you'll
spy the Statue of Liberty, standing tall in New
York Harbor. Stay to the right and head down
the ramp on to the Brooklyn Promenade
(pictured left), which abuts the charming
Brooklyn Heights, the city's first historic
district, dotted with wonderful Federal-style
homes erected in the 1820s and 1830s. As
you stroll don't forget to look back over your
shoulder to see the Empire State Building and
the Chrysler Building. Exit on Pierrepont Street
(a playground will be on your right where
public toilets are just inside the gate). Walk for
another five blocks, taking notice of the 1844
First Unitarian Church of Brooklyn (considered
a Gothic Revival masterpiece) at the corner of
Monroe Place. When you get to Clinton Street,
the Brooklyn Historical Society (128 Pierrepont
Street, *see p151*) will be on your right. Pop in
and learn more about this treasured borough.

To get back to Manhattan, walk one block
further west to Court Street, turn right and
walk two blocks to the Borough Hall subway
stations (2, 3, 4, 5 subways).

Join the annual **Brownstoners of Bedford-Stuyvesant Inc House Tour** (1-718 574 1979), held the third Saturday in October, rain or shine. The **Concord Baptist Church of Christ** (833 Gardner Boulevard, between Madison Street & Putnam Avenue, Bedford-Stuyvesant, 1-718 622 1818) offers gospel music from one of the largest African-American congregations in the United States. *See also p156* **The battle for Bed-Stuy**.

Brighton Beach & Coney Island

In the cultural stew that is New York City, **Brighton Beach** stands out for being unabashedly Russian. But this local borscht belt welcomes anyone in the mood for unfamiliar flavours, bargain shopping and seriously over-the-top entertainment. In the 1970s, an ageing population – mainly of Jews of Eastern European descent – moved or died out, leaving the neighbourhood marred by vacant storefronts. It was during those years that refugees from the Soviet Union began moulding the 'hood into what soon became known as Little Odessa. It may not have museums or galleries but it does have the ocean and lots of places to eat and drink. Brighton Beach Avenue, the main artery here, is packed with Russian-speaking shopkeepers hawking

glassware, caviar and DVDs from nearly every former Soviet Republic. Wander the aisles of M&I International Foods (249 Brighton Beach Avenue, between Brighton 2nd & 3rd Streets, 1-718 615 1011), a huge Russian deli and grocery. Most customers live nearby but many make weekly treks from as far away as Connecticut to stock up on various *kielbasas*, Russian breads and beers, several brands of *kefir* (a popular sour cultured-milk drink) and legendary butter from the Russian city of Vologda. Or make a reservation at a local nightclub, such as the National (273 Brighton Beach Avenue, at Brighton 2nd Street, 1-718 646 1225), where the dress is flashy, the food and vodka are plentiful, and the over-the-top burlesque shows are downright trippy.

Coney Island, on the peninsula just west of Brighton Beach, is a summertime destination. After decades of decay, the weirdly wonderful community – known for its amusement park, beach and boardwalk – has made a comeback. The biggest improvement is seaside KeySpan Park, home to the **Brooklyn Cyclones** (*see p335*), a minor-league baseball affiliate of the New York Mets. If you're a thrill-seeker, take a spin on the Cyclone at Astroland Amusement Park (*see p284*): a ride on the 79-year-old wooden rollercoaster lasts less than two minutes, but the first drop is nearly vertical, and the cars clatter along the 2,640 feet of track at speeds of up to 60 miles per hour.

A stroll along the boardwalk will take you to the **New York Aquarium** (*see p290*), where a family of beluga whales is in residence. Don't forget to look up: a recent wave of local artists has focused its creative energy on adding some colour to the local signage. The oddball Sideshows by the Seashore is put on by **Coney Island USA** (*see below*), an organisation that keeps the torch burning for early 20th-century Coney life – you won't want to miss a minute of the show, which includes legends like contortionist Ravi, Bendable Boy, snake charmer Princess Ananka and the heavily tattooed Tyler Fyre, who shows off his gift for sword-swallowing, among other talents.

The **Mermaid Parade** (*see p263*) and Nathan's Famous Fourth of July Hot Dog Eating Contest are two popular, quirky annual Coney Island events. In 2005 fifth-time winner Takeru Kobayashi, stuffed down 49 dogs – with buns – in 12 minutes, joining the likes of Lance Armstrong and Michael Jordan in the pantheon of enduring world champions. On Friday evenings throughout the summer, a fireworks display (9.30pm) is the perfect nightcap to a day of sandy adventures.

Coney Island USA

1208 Surf Avenue, at W 12th Street, Coney Island (1-718 372 5159/www.coneyislandusa.com). Subway: D, F, N, Q to Coney Island-Stillwell Avenue. **Open** *Call or visit website for schedule.* **Admission** *$5; $3 under-12s.*

Coney Island.

It happened here

In spite of all you hear about in-vitro fertilisation, artificial insemination and ovulation, the fact remains that in the down-and-dirty ins and outs of human intercourse, it's still a lot harder to copulate and not get pregnant than the other way around. While this is not exactly a news flash to the biologically aware, it started a revolution when Margaret Sanger opened America's first birth-control clinic in 1916. No doctor would join her crusade, so the facility, located at **46 Amboy Street** in Brooklyn's largely immigrant neighbourhood of Brownsville, was staffed by Sanger, her nurse sister Ethel and a translator. On opening day, women lined up around the block – and the clinic was shut down just nine days later; Sanger was arrested and sentenced to 30 days' detention for violating New York State law banning contraception. She spent her time in the pen advising fellow inmates about, yup, birth control, and went on to start what would become Planned Parenthood.

Queens

This unsung borough is the most culturally diverse in the city.

Queens is the sprawling north-eastern borough where New Yorkers go to catch a plane, a Mets game or a US Open tennis match. To the media elite and other Manhattan chauvinists, **Queens** is where you go for the punchline of a joke. From Archie Bunker and George Costanza to *The King of Queens* and *Entourage*, a Queens birthright signals arrested social development to denizens on the other side of the East River. But in the borough itself, they're saying, 'let 'em laugh'. Residents know that ungentrified, unyuppified, honest New York lives in Queens. If you're looking for an authentic city experience vibrant with ethnic colour and melting pot tradition, reserve a day to explore the many treasures of this dynamic borough.

You'll be in enlightened local company; a widening trickle of New Yorkers is opting out of ruinous Manhattan and Brooklyn rents and moving to Queens. Many city observers consider the Museum of Modern Art's 2002-4 relocation to Long Island City in western Queens the Big Bang of Queens's rediscovery. The museum has returned to Manhattan, but the art establishments that sprang up in factories and waterfront lots have remained, and with them a flourishing creative community.

This artistic revival has exposed the truth: that Queens is an affordable, interesting, even avant-garde place to live. Throughout the

Manhattan-view neighbourhoods of Long Island City, Astoria, Sunnyside, Woodside and Jackson Heights, row houses, lofts and art deco apartments are being staked out by open-minded rent refugees. Telltale signs are everywhere: bistros in Long Island City, strollers in Jackson Heights, endless craigslist.com apartment shares in Astoria.

Newly arrived professionals and painters are just two more demographic layers on the *mille-feuille* of Queens which claims the distinction of being the most ethnically diverse urban area on the planet. More than a third of its 2.3 million residents are foreign-born, and over a hundred languages are spoken here. Thanks to this staggering diversity, Queens boasts intense neighbourhood flavour and a global array of inexpensive ethnic restaurants and shops.

To kick off your Queens tour, hop on the 7 subway, a designated National Millennium Trail (like the Appalachian Trail). It is nicknamed the 'International Express' for the stunning variety of ethnic districts it passes through. From the first stop, Vernon Boulevard-Jackson Avenue in Long Island City, it's only a few blocks' walk to the historic waterfront. Its centrepiece is **Gantry Plaza State Park** (48th Avenue, at Center Boulevard), named after the hulking 19th-century railroad gantries that transferred cargo from ships to trains. Set directly across the East River from the United Nations, it flaunts postcard-worthy views of the skyline from every inch of its 2.5 acres, making it a superb perch for the 4 July fireworks. Just off to the right is a Queens landmark, the 1936 Pepsi-Cola sign in red neon script. Long Island City's scrappy dockside origins live on in the boxing-themed **Waterfront Crabhouse** (2-03 Borden Avenue, at 2nd Street, Long Island City, 1-718 729 4862), an old-time saloon and oyster bar. The nabe is also home to the **Museum for African Art** (*see p166*).

A few blocks east on Jackson Avenue is **PS 1 Contemporary Art Center** (*see p166*), a progressive cultural outpost affiliated with MoMA that highlights work of up-and-coming art stars and throws the deejayed Warm Up summer art parties on an 'urban beach', or its gravel-topped courtyard. Stop for a look at the 1904 English Renaissance-style **Long Island City Courthouse** (25-10 Court Square, at Thomson Avenue, Long Island City). Close by, a well-preserved block of 1800's row houses in every conceivable style – Flemish, Queen Anne, Federalist, ornate brownstone and modest wood-fronted – constitutes the **Hunters Point Historic District** (45th Avenue, between 21st & 23rd Streets).

Just past the second stop of the 7 train, Hunters Point Avenue, peer out the left windows to catch the marvellous graffiti-covered walls of 5 Pointz (www.5ptz.com), an outdoor graf-art gallery; moments later, you'll spy the Manhattan skyline through the elegant spans of the 59th Street Bridge (aka **Queensboro Bridge**). Completed in 1909, it signifies glamorous New York in everything from F Scott Fitzgerald's novel *The Great Gatsby* to Woody Allen's film *Manhattan* to Simon and Garfunkel's hit 'The 59th Street Bridge Song (Feelin' Groovy)'.

Back when Los Angeles was a sleepy orange grove, western Queens was America's film capital, and these days it buzzes with cinematic doings once more. The mounted 'Silvercup' sign visible from the Queensboro Plaza platform announces Silvercup Studios, once a bakery and today a TV- and film- production stage where *Sex and the City* and *The Sopranos* were made. WC Fields and the Marx Brothers clowned at Famous Players/Lasky Studios, now called Kaufman Astoria Studios. Movies, commercials and TV shows including *Sesame Street* are shot here. Kaufman Astoria also houses the **American Museum of the Moving Image** (*see 165*), which entices cinephiles with interactive exhibitions and screenings.

Astoria

At Queensboro Plaza, transfer to an N or W train and chug north to Astoria, a lively multi-ethnic neighbourhood favoured by post-grads sharing row-house digs. You can alight at Broadway for a visit to the indoor-outdoor **Noguchi Museum** (*see p166*), which shows works by the visionary Japanese sculptor and others. Nearby is **Socrates Sculpture Park** (*see p166*), a riverfront art space given to skateboard ramps, concerts and summer film screenings on Wednesday nights. At the end of the subway line (Astoria-Ditmars Boulevard), walk west to Astoria Park (from Astoria Park South to Ditmars Boulevard, between Shore Boulevard & 19th Street), for its dramatic views of two bridges: the **Triborough Bridge**, Robert Moses's automotive labyrinth connecting Queens, the Bronx and Manhattan; and the 1916 **Hell Gate Bridge**, a single-arch steel tour de force that was the template for the Sydney Harbour Bridge in Australia.

As New York's Greek-American stronghold, Astoria is known for Hellenic eateries specialising in impeccably grilled seafood.

Sightseeing

Don't miss Steinway & Sons

1 Steinway Place, 19th Avenue & 38th Street, Astoria (1-718 721 2600/ www.steinway.com/factory/tour). Travel: N, W, 7 to Queensboro Plaza or E, F, G, R to Queens Plaza, then take the Q101 bus to 20th Avenue.

Tours are conducted in Spring and Autumn. Call for tour information. Reservations required. **Admission** free.
This (roughly) 2.5-hour tour of how a Steinway grand piano is painstakingly pieced together (all 12,000 parts!) is simply amazing.

Local legend

During **Jackie Robinson**'s glory days at Ebbets Field in Brooklyn, his real home base was in Queens. The first African-American to play major-league baseball, in 1947, Robinson often took the Interboro Parkway from the Dodgers' stadium in Flatbush to his home at 112-40 177th Street, in the Addisleigh Park area of Saint Albans, an enclave that was also home to Lena Horne, Count Basie and Ella Fitzgerald. To honour the Hall of Fame second baseman, his former commuting route was renamed the Jackie Robinson Parkway in 1998.

Taverna Kyclades (33-07 Ditmars Boulevard, between 33rd & 35th Streets, 1-718 545 8666) offers a breezy Aegean atmosphere and a smoker-friendly patio. Dirt-cheap, 24-hour Uncle George's (33-19 Broadway, at 34th Street, 1-718 626 0593) is a beloved corner hangout. One of the city's few remaining Central European beer gardens, Bohemian Hall (29-19 24th Avenue, at 29th Street, 1-718 274 0043), hosts Czech-style dining and drinking; on weekends, New Yorkers gather around poker games in the oak-shaded courtyard. South of Astoria Boulevard, enjoy a (legal) hookah pipe with inky espresso in the Egyptian cafés along Steinway Street.

This thoroughfare is named after the Steinway family of piano lore, whose factory – one of a handful of manufacturing venues left in the city – still thrives (*see p163* **Don't miss**). Other factory tours highlight automation; the Steinway walkabout honours artistry and tradition. The 88-key Steinway masterpieces, priced from $49,000, are handcrafted the Old World way in a graceful red-brick 1871 plant.

Sightseeing (side tab)

Jackson Heights

Find your way back to a E, F, G, R or 7 train and ride to the 74th Street-Broadway stop. This is the crossroads of Jackson Heights, a dizzyingly multiculti neighbourhood even by Queens standards, and a cheap-eats paradise. Delhi Palace (37-73 74th Street, between Roosevelt & 37th Avenues, 1-718 507 0666) has an exceptional, inexpensive lunch buffet; Ashoka's all-you-can-eat is unfurled at lunch and dinner (74-14 37th Avenue, between 74th & 75th Streets, 1-718 898 5088). Shops selling saris, spices, Bollywood videos and intricate gold jewellery line 74th Street between Roosevelt and 37th Avenues.

Jackson Heights claims a roughly 30-square-block landmark district of notable Tudor and neo-Gothic-style co-op apartment buildings and attached houses characterised by tree-dotted lawns and park-like courtyards. Outstanding examples of these 1920s beauties are found on 70th Street, between 34th Avenue & Northern Boulevard, and on 34th Avenue, between 76th & 77th Streets and 80th & 81st Streets.

Jackson Heights and its adjoining neighbourhoods have welcomed successive waves of Latin American immigrants and their cuisines. Colombians and Argentinians are old school in these parts: get a taste of Buenos Aires at La Fusta, a convivial steakhouse (80-32 Baxter Avenue, between Broadway & Layton Street, Elmhurst, 1-718 429 8222). Sample sprightly Peruvian *ceviche* and fried seafood at La Pollada de Laura, decorated with Alianza Lima soccer banners (102-03 Northern Boulevard, at 102nd Street, Corona, 1-718 426 7818).

Flushing

At the end of the 7 train lies historic Flushing. Egalitarian Dutchmen staked their claim to 'Vlissingen' in the 1600s and were shortly joined by pacifist Friends, or Quakers, seeking religious freedom in the New World. These liberal settlers promulgated the Flushing Remonstrance, a groundbreaking 1657 edict extending 'the law of love, peace and liberty' to Jews and Muslims. It is now regarded as a forerunner of the US Constitution's First Amendment. Today, Flushing hosts prayer and meditation in churches, synagogues, mosques and temples. The plain wooden Friends Meeting House (137-16 Northern Boulevard, between Main & Union Streets, Flushing, 1-718 358 9636), built in 1694, remains.

Next door is **Kingsland Homestead** (*see p166*), a 1785 farmhouse that overlooks a cluster of centenarian trees in adjoining Weeping Beech Park. Kingsland is home to the Queens Historical Society, which holds regular exhibitions on local life; 2006's major show explores Queens landmarks.

Flushing Town Hall (*see p165*), built during the Civil War in the fanciful Romanesque Revival style, harbours local arts groups and hosts jazz concerts, chamber music and multimedia exhibits. Here, you can catch the **Queens Jazz Trail**, a monthly trolley tour of the homes of jazz legends who have resided in this musical borough, including Louis Armstrong, Count Basie, Ben Webster, Ella Fitzgerald, Dizzy Gillespie, Billie Holiday and John Coltrane. The tour's centrepiece is the **Louis Armstrong House** in Corona (*see p166*), a modest brick home in a working-class community that Satchmo never abandoned despite his global celebrity. (The house may also be visited on its own.)

Many visitors don't realise that Flushing houses Queens's museum row. The rambling **Flushing Meadows-Corona Park** (*see p165*), where the 1939 and 1964 World's Fairs were held, contains several museums. The destination includes the **Queens Zoo**, where natural environments include a lush parrot habitat; the late Philip Johnson-designed **Queens Theatre in the Park**, an indoor amphitheatre; the **New York Hall of Science** (*see p166*), an acclaimed interactive museum with a new exhibition wing; the **Queens Botanical Garden**, a 39-acre cavalcade of greenery; and the **Queens Museum of Art** (*see p166*), which houses a collection of Tiffany art glass, created in nearby Corona. The museum's mesmerising pièce de résistance is the *Panorama of the City of New York*, a 9,335-square-foot, 895,000-building scale model (1 inch equals 100 feet) of all five boroughs. The World Trade Center, however, has been replaced by a miniature version of *Tribute in Light*, the city's first memorial of September 11, 2001. The park also encompasses Shea Stadium, home base of the Mets baseball team (*see p335*); the USTA (United States Tennis Association) National Tennis Center, where the US Open raises a racket at summer's end; and the 140-ft-high Unisphere, a mammoth steel globe that became famous as the symbol of the 1964 World's Fair – and the final battle scene between humans and aliens in the *Men in Black* movie. (A few years back, borough native Donald Trump installed a scaled-down replica of this Queens icon in front of his hotel on Manhattan's Columbus Circle.)

The Queens Cultural Trolley takes tourists on a narrated 75-minute loop through the park and into nearby areas – for free. Stops include the Louis Armstrong House, Jackson Heights' Little India and Roosevelt Avenue, a pan-Latin

bazaar of a boulevard beneath the roaring 7 train. The trolley runs from the Queens Museum of Art at weekends, departing noon, 1, 2.30 and 4.30pm.

For New York life in the fast lane, consider Queens's alternating-season thoroughbred racetracks: **Aqueduct**, near JFK Airport, and the leafier **Belmont Park** (for both, *see p337*), just over the borough's eastern border. At celebrated, 100-year-old Belmont – the world's longest track – even the horses have that 'if you can make it here' NY confidence.

The website www.discoverqueensinfo.org is a good source of cultural and entertainment what's-on information.

American Museum of the Moving Image

35th Avenue, at 36th Street, Astoria, Queens (1-718 784 0077/www.ammi.org). Subway: G, R, V to Steinway Street. **Open** noon-5pm Wed, Thur; noon-8pm Fri; 11am-6.30pm Sat, Sun. **Admission** $10; $7.50 seniors and students; $5 5-18s; free under-5s. Free Fri 4-8pm. No strollers. **Credit** AmEx, MC, V.

Only a 15-minute subway ride from midtown Manhattan, Moving Image is one of the city's most dynamic institutions. Located in the restored complex that once housed the original Kaufman Astoria Studios, AMMI offers daily film and video programming. The museum also displays famous movie props and costumes, including the chariot driven by Charlton Heston in *Ben-Hur* and the Yoda puppet used in *Star Wars: Episode V – The Empire Strikes Back*.

Flushing Meadows-Corona Park

From 111th Street to Van Wyck Expressway, between Flushing Bay & Grand Central Parkway (1-718 760 6565/Queens Zoo 1-718-220-510/ www.queenszoo.com). Subway: 7 to Willets Point-Shea Stadium.

Most people come out to these parts to catch a game at Shea Stadium, home of the New York Mets, but don't overlook the 1964 World's Fair sculptures: definitely worth a peek.

Flushing Town Hall/Flushing Council on Culture & the Arts/Queens Jazz Trail

137-135 Northern Boulevard, at Linden Place, Flushing (1-718 463 7700/www.flushingtown hall.org). Subway: 7 to Main Street. **Open** 9am-5pm Mon-Fri; noon-5pm Sat, Sun. **Admission** *Exhibits* free. *Jazz Trail* $26; first Saturday of the month at 10am; reservations recommended. **Credit** AmEx, MC, V.

Jazz diehards will love the three-hour Queens Jazz Trail trolley tour that stops by neighbourhoods and haunts of such legendary jazz greats as Louis Armstrong, Ella Fitzgerald, Billie Holiday and Dizzy Gillespie. The 26 bucks also gets you a cool illustrated guide to take home.

Sightseeing

Kingsland Homestead/Queens Historical Society

143-135 37th Avenue, between Bowne Street & Parsons Boulevard, Flushing (1-718 939 0647 ext 17/www.queenshistoricalsociety.org). Subway: 7 to Flushing-Main Street. **Admission** $3; $2 seniors & students. **Tours** 2.30-4.30pm Tue, Sat, Sun, and by appointment. **No credit cards.**

Charming enough, especially if you are in the area, but no need to make a special trip.

Louis Armstrong House

34-56 107th Street, between 34th & 37th Avenues, Corona (1-718 478 8274/www.louisarmstrong house.org). Subway: 7 to 103rd Street-Corona Plaza. **Open** 10am-5pm Tue-Fri; noon-5pm Sat, Sun. **Tours** 10am-4pm Tue-Fri, on the hour; noon-4pm Sat, Sun, on the hour. **Admission** $8; $6 seniors and students; free under-4s. **Credit** MC, V ($15 minimum).

Jazz lovers will have to make the pilgrimage, but be warned: the tour may focus a tad too much on the decor and not the legendary life of Armstrong.

Museum for African Art

36-01 43rd Avenue, at 36th Street, 3rd floor, Long Island City, Queens (1-718 784 7700/www.africanart. org). Subway: 7 to 33rd Street. **Open** 10am-5pm Mon, Thur, Fri; 11am-5pm Sat, Sun. **Admission** $6; $3 seniors, students and children; free under-6s. **No credit cards.**

This institution, located in the now trendy art mecca of Long Island City, features exhibitions of African art that change about twice a year. The quality of the work – often on loan from private collections – is exceptional. The remarkable gift shop is filled with African art objects and crafts.

New York Hall of Science

47-01 111th Street, at 47th Avenue, Flushing Meadows-Corona Park, Queens (1-718 699 0005/www.nyscience.org). Subway: 7 to 111th Street. **Open** *Jul, Aug* 9.30am-5pm Mon-Fri; 10am-6pm Sat, Sun. *Sept-Jun* 9.30am-2pm Mon-Thur; 9.30am-5pm Fri; 10am-6pm Sat, Sun. **Admission** $11; $8 seniors, students & children. Free Fri Sept-Jun 2-5pm . *Science playground.* **Credit** AmEx, DC, Disc, MC, V.

The fun-for-all-ages New York Hall of Science, built for the 1964 World's Fair and recently expanded, demystifies its subject through colourful hands-on exhibits about biology, chemistry and physics, with topics such as Marvelous Molecules and The Realm of the Atom. Children can burn off their excess energy – and perhaps learn a thing or two – in the 30,000 sq ft outdoor science playground (summer only, $3 in addition to museum entry).

The Noguchi Museum

9-01 33rd Road, between Vernon Boulevard & 10th Street, Long Island City (1-718 204 7088/www. noguchi.org). Travel: N, W to Broadway, then bus Q104 to 11th Street; or 7 to Vernon Boulevard-Jackson Avenue, then Q103 bus to 10th Street. **Open** 10am-5pm Wed-Fri; 11am-6pm Sat, Sun. **Admission** $5; $2.50 seniors and students. No strollers. **No credit cards.**

In addition to his famous lamps, artist Isamu Noguchi (1904-88) designed stage sets for Martha Graham and George Balanchine, as well as large-scale sculptures of supreme simplicity and beauty. The museum is located in a 1920s-era factory in Queens; galleries surround a serene sculpture garden that was designed by Noguchi himself. The building, recently renovated (to the tune of $13.5 million), now stays open year-round. Look for the second-floor galleries devoted to Noguchi's interior design, a new café and a shop. A shuttle service from Manhattan is available on weekends (call the museum or see website for more information).

PS 1 Contemporary Art Center

22-25 Jackson Avenue, at 46th Avenue, Long Island City (1-718 784 2084/www.ps1.org). Subway: E, V to 23rd Street-Ely Avenue; G to 21st Street-Jackson Avenue; 7 to 45th Road-Court House Square. **Open** noon-6pm Mon, Thur-Sun. **Admission** suggested donation $5; $2 seniors & students. **Credit** AmEx, MC, V.

Cutting-edge shows and an international studio programme make each visit to this freewheeling contemporary-art space a treasure hunt, with artwork turning up in every corner, from the stairwells to the basement. In a distinctive Romanesque-Revival building that still bears some resemblance to the public school it once was, the MoMA affiliate mounts shows that appeal to adults and children.

Queens Museum of Art

New York City Building, park entrance on 49th Avenue, at 111th Street, Flushing Meadows-Corona Park (1-718 592 9700/www.queensmuseum.org). Subway: 7 to 111th Street. Walk south on 111th Street, then turn left on to 49th Avenue. Continue into the park and over Grand Central Parkway bridge. **Open** *26 June-5 Sept* 1-8pm Wed-Sun. *6 Sept-25 Jun* 10am-5pm Wed-Fri; noon-5pm Sat, Sun. **Admission** $5; $2.50 seniors and students; free under-5s. **No credit cards.**

Located on the grounds of the 1939 and 1964 World's Fairs, the QMA holds one of the area's most amazing sights: a 9,335-sq ft scale model of New York City accurate down to the square inch. The model, first a popular exhibit at the 1964 World's Fair, was last updated and carefully cleaned by its original builders in 1994, so some recent changes are not reflected. The World Trade Center, however, has been replaced by a miniature version of Tribute in Light, the city's first memorial of September 11, 2001.

Socrates Sculpture Park

Broadway, at Vernon Boulevard, Long Island City (1-718 956 1819/www.socratessculpturepark.org). Travel: N, W to Broadway, then take the Q104 bus to Vernon Boulevard. **Open** 10am-sunset daily, except on movie nights Jul-Aug. See website for schedule. **Admission** free.

The sweeping views of Manhattan across the East River make this well-worn park the perfect place for a picnic. The sculptures are fun, but the real draw is the summertime outdoor movie nights.

The Bronx

More than just baseball and beasts.

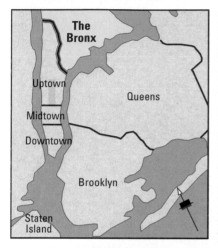

Because it boasts so many firsts, bests, biggests, mosts and onlys, the **Bronx** can be dubbed the borough of bravado. For starters, the northernmost borough is the city's greenest, with 24 per cent of it parkland. It is home to a world-famous baseball team that holds 26 World Series championships, more than any other team in history, and the nation's best high school, Bronx Science, which has produced more PhD's and Nobel Prize winners than any other college in the world. The Bronx also birthed hip hop and salsa dancing. Not bad for the old boondocks of booming New Amsterdam.

The area once belonged to the family of Jonas Bronck, a Swedish farmer who had a 500-acre homestead in what is now the southeastern Morrisania section. Back in the 1630s, it was called the 'the Broncks' farm' and the name stuck, though its spelling was altered. It is the only borough attached to the US mainland, and while it was originally part of Westchester county, the Bronx's soul was more city than suburb, and so, like the other boroughs, it was incorporated into New York City in 1898.

Throughout the early decades of the 20th century, the Bronx, like Queens and Brooklyn, drew much of its population from the ever-expanding pool of Irish, German, Italian and Eastern European Jewish immigrants who flocked to the area for its cheap rents and open

spaces. After World War II, as the borough grew more urbanised, the descendants of the European immigrants moved farther out to the suburbs of Long Island and Westchester, and fresh waves of newcomers, hailing from Central America, Puerto Rico, Albania and Russia, as well as Hispaniola and other points in the West Indies, took their places.

Along with the population shifts, the Bronx has probably witnessed more upheaval than the rest of the city combined. From the late 1940s until the early '70s, the borough felt the brunt of city planner Robert Moses's drastic remaking of the city as thousands of residents saw their apartment buildings razed to make room for the Whitestone and Throgs Neck Bridges, the east-to-west Cross Bronx Expressway and the north-to-south Bruckner Boulevard extension of the New England Thruway. Many neighbourhoods fell into neglect, a condition exacerbated by the economic and social downturns that plagued the entire city in the '60s and '70s.

These days, the Bronx is experiencing a long-awaited Renaissance, even in the formerly blighted South section. The one-time hotbed of crime, drugs and poverty, the South Bronx is now a burgeoning artist community, and some are even winkingly calling it SoBro. Those wanting a closer look at the up-and-coming arts scene should hop on the **Bronx Culture Trolley** (*see p170*), a free shuttle that visits the area's most happening galleries, performance spaces and museums.

Tucked in the south-eastern corner of the Bronx, **Hunts Point** looks like an industrial wasteland, but over the past decade it has become increasingly popular as a live-work destination for pioneering artists as well. In 1994, a group of artists and community leaders converted a 12,000-square-foot industrial building into the **Point Community Development Corporation** (940 Garrison Avenue, at Manida Street, 1-718 542 4139, www.thepoint.org), a performance space, gallery and business incubator. The Point also leads lively walking tours (call for reservations) like Mambo to HipHop, which covers the history of locally born music genres. Creative types stage performances at the nearby **Bronx Academy of Arts and Dance (BAAD)** (*see p170*), and more than a dozen painters and sculptors work in the academy's studios.

While the South continues its rebirth, the rest of the borough still draws sightseers for its long-standing gems. One of the Bronx's most recognizable landmarks is **Yankee Stadium**, (*see p335*) located at 161st Street and River Avenue. Baseball's most famous legends made history on its diamond, from Babe Ruth and Joe DiMaggio to A-Rod. When there isn't a day game, the Yankees organisation gives tours of the clubhouse, the dugout and the famous centre-field Monument Park. The coolest way to get to the game is by boat: the NY Waterway (*see p83*) will ferry you to the stadium (from Manhattan or New Jersey), aboard the *Yankee Clipper*. Enjoy it while you can: in 2009 the Yankees will move to their new home – a brand-new $800 million stadium smack across the street. When George Steinbrenner unveiled the plan in 2005, he put an end to years of threats of abandoning the borough for Manhattan or New Jersey, finally ensuring that the Bombers will remain in the Bronx.

A few blocks east lies the six-and-a-half mile **Grand Concourse**. Once the most prestigious drag in the Bronx, it's still a must for lovers of architecture. Engineer Louis Risse designed the boulevard, which stretches from 138th Street to Mosholu Parkway, in 1892, patterning it after Paris's Champs-Elysées. Starting at 161st Street and heading south, look for the permanent street plaques that make up the **Bronx Walk of Fame**, honouring famous Bronxites, from Regis Philbin to Colin Powell. The buildings heading north date mostly from the '20s to the early '40s and display the country's largest array of art deco housing. Erected in 1937 at the corner of 161st Street, 888 Grand Concourse has a concave entrance of gilded mosaic and is topped by a curvy metallic marquee. Inside, the mirrored lobby's central fountain and sunburst-patterned floor could rival those of any hotel on Miami's Ocean Drive. But the grandest building on the Concourse is the landmark **Andrew Freedman Home**, a 1924 French-inspired limestone palazzo between McClennan and 166th Streets. Freedman, a millionaire subway contractor, set aside the bulk of his $7 million estate to build a poorhouse for the rich – those who lost their fortunes, that is. It now houses the Family Preservation Center (FPC), a community-based social service agency. Across the street, the **Bronx Museum of the Arts** (*see p171*), established in 1971 and housed in a former synagogue, exhibits high-quality contemporary and historical works by Bronx-based artists, including many of African-American, Asian and Latino heritage.

Due north to Kingsbridge Road, lovers of literature will enjoy the **Edgar Allan Poe Cottage** (*see p171*), a small wooden farmhouse where the writer lived from 1846 to 1849 and penned the poem *Annabel Lee*. Moved to the Grand Concourse from its original spot on Fordham Road in 1913, the museum has period furniture and details about Poe and his work.

Many Manhattanites skip the more famous attractions and head straight to Bronx's **Little Italy**, centred around Arthur Avenue (www.arthuravenuebronx.com), which is lined with Italian delis, restaurants, markets and cafés. Browse and nibble at the Arthur Avenue Retail Market (Crescent Avenue, at 186th Street), an indoor bazaar built in the 1940s when former mayor Fiorello La Guardia campaigned to get pushcarts off the street. (The market is closed on Sundays.) Inside is Mike's Deli (2344 Arthur Avenue, between Crescent Avenue & E 186th Street, 1-718 295 5033), where you can try the trademark *schiacciata* (Italian for 'squashed') sandwich of grilled vegetables, or Big Mike's Combo, a roll loaded with Provolone cheese and Italian cold cuts like mortadella, prosciutto and salami. If you're in the mood for a full meal, we recommend old-style red-sauce joints Mario's (2342 Arthur Avenue, between Crescent Avenue & E 186th Street, 1-718 584 1188) and Dominick's (2335 Arthur Avenue, between Crescent Avenue & E 187th Street, 1-718 733 2807) – regulars love to argue about which place is the best.

Just a few miles from midtown Manhattan lie the serene 250 acres of the **New York Botanical Garden** (*see p171*) – a magical respite from cars and concrete comprising 48 gardens and plant collections, including the Rockefeller Rose Garden, the Everett Children's Adventure Garden and the last 50 original acres of a forest that once covered all of New York City. In springtime, the gardens are frothy with pastel blossoms as clusters of lilac, cherry, magnolia and crab-apple trees burst into bloom, followed in fall by vivid foliage in the oak and maple groves. On a rainy day, you can stay warm and sheltered inside the Enid A Haupt Conservatory, a striking glass-walled greenhouse built in 1902. It offers seasonal exhibits as well as the World of Plants, a series of environmental galleries that will send you on an ecotour through tropical rainforests, deserts and palm-tree oasis. The new high-tech Nolan Greenhouses, which are made up of 24 connected glass sheds, are used for public displays, botanical research and conservation projects. Just next door is the borough's most famous attraction, the **Bronx Zoo** (*see p171*), opened in 1899 by Theodore Roosevelt in an attempt to preserve game. At 265 acres, it's the largest urban zoo in the US. The zoo shuns cages in favour of indoor and outdoor environments that mimic the natural habitats of more than 4,000 mammals, birds, and reptiles. Nearly a hundred species, including monkeys, leopards and tapirs, live inside the lush, steamy Jungle World, a re-creation of an Asian rain forest inside a 37,000-square-foot building. The superpopular Congo Gorilla Forest has turned six and a half acres into a dramatic Central African rainforest habitat. A glass-enclosed tunnel winds through the forest, allowing visitors to get close to the dozens of primate families in residence, including 26 majestic western lowland gorillas. For those who prefer cats, Tiger Mountain has six adult Siberian tigers, who look particularly regal on snowy days. If you take the Bengali Express Monorail (which travels through the Wild Asia Encampment), try to grab a seat up front for prime viewing of antelope, Indian rhinos and Asian elephants. The zoo's newest additions include a butterfly garden, featuring 1,000 colourful flutterers, and the adjacent Bug Carousel, where children can claim their seat atop 64 insects, including a grasshopper, a ladybird and a honeybee.

Pelham Bay Park (the 6 train to Pelham Bay), in the borough's north-eastern corner, is NYC's biggest park. Take a car or a bike if you want to explore the park's 2,765 acres, once home to the Siwonay Indians. Get a map at the Ranger Nature Center, near the entrance on Bruckner Boulevard at Wilkinson Avenue. The **Bartow-Pell Mansion Museum** (*see p170*), in the park's south-eastern quarter, overlooks Long Island Sound. Finished in 1842, the elegantly furnished Greek Revival building faces a reflecting pool ringed by gardens. The park's 13 miles of coastline skirt the Hutchinson River to the west and the Long Island Sound and Eastchester Bay to the east. In summer, locals hit Orchard Beach; set up in the 1930s, it's a rare Robert Moses project loved by all.

VIP, RIP

New Yorkers spend their lives in pursuit of the right address, and more than 300,000 of them have made Woodlawn Cemetery in the North Bronx their oh-so-fashionable (permanent) place of residence. For many, it's the nicest place they've ever rested their bones. Although Brooklyn's Green-Wood Cemetery gets all the good press, stately, well-manicured Woodlawn is well worth a stop on the way to Wave Hill or Van Cortlandt Park. As you meander along graceful paths shaded by massive oak trees, the cemetery's 400 gently sloping acres, interspersed with flowering shrubs and emerald lawns, can feel something like Central Park – only quieter. Eloquent headstones pay homage, and money talks through elaborate mausoleums designed in neo-classical, Gothic, art deco and Egyptian styles by the reigning architects of the period.

A stroll through Woodlawn is a crash course in New York history. Opened during the Civil War, it welcomed fallen Union soldiers. Later, it became the final resting place for such Gilded Age moguls as Joseph Pulitzer, FW Woolworth, RH Macy and Jay Gould. Five New York City mayors, including Fiorello La Guardia, made their ultimate public appearance at Woodlawn. In 1912, Woodlawn took in seven unfortunates from the *Titanic*; nine victims of the World Trade Center attack were laid to rest here in 2001.

The extension of the subway into the Bronx in 1916 made non-sectarian Woodlawn the preferred destination of African-Americans prominent in the Harlem Renaissance. Madame CJ Walker (*see p145 **Local legend***), America's first black millionaire (thanks to her self-made hairdressing empire), arrived in 1919, and poet Countee Cullen capped his inkwell in 1946. Among jazz legends, Duke Ellington, Miles Davis, Coleman Hawkins, Milt Jackson, Illinois Jacquet and Lionel Hampton all came to rest here after they had played their last licks.

Aside from these musicians, Woodlawn's most visited graves belong to *Moby Dick* author Herman Melville, who died in obscurity in 1891; suffragist Elizabeth Cady Stanton; music maestro Irving Berlin; and Wild West icon Bat Masterson, whose gunslinging exploits were depicted in a top-rated TV series in the late 1950s.

To those who fall in love with the place, take note: the cemetery has enough burial space for the next 50 years. And you don't have to be a New Yorker to get in. At Woodlawn, you become one.

Woodlawn Cemetery

Entrance at Webster Avenue and E 233rd Street (1-718 920 0500). Subway: 4 to Woodlawn. **Open** *8.30am-5pm daily.* **Admission** *free. Maps and photo permits available at the visitors' entrance.*

Perhaps the leafiest neighbourhood is Riverdale, along the north-west coast of the Bronx. Huge homes perch on narrow, winding streets in this story-book town atop a hill overlooking the Hudson River. Theodore Roosevelt, Mark Twain and Arturo Toscanini have all lived in **Wave Hill House** (*see p171*), an 1843 stone mansion set on a former private estate that is now a cultural and environmental centre. The 28 acres of cultivated gardens and woodlands provide fine views of the river. The art gallery shows nature-themed exhibits, and the organisation presents year-round concerts and performances. If you need a day outdoors on foot or on bike, try the quiet pathways of the Hudson River-hugging **Riverdale Park**. Enter this swath of forest preserve along Palisade Avenue, between 232nd & 254th Streets.

The nearby 1,146-acre **Van Cortlandt Park** (entrance on Broadway, at 244th Street) often hosts cricket teams made up mostly of West Indians. You can hike through a 100-year-old forest, play golf on the nation's first municipal course or rent horses at stables in the park. **Van Cortlandt House Museum** (*see p171*), a fine example of pre-Revolutionary Georgian architecture, was built by Frederick van Cortlandt in 1748; it served as a headquarters for George Washington in the Revolutionary War. Donated to the city by the van Cortlandt family, it's the oldest building in the borough. Abutting the park is **Woodlawn Cemetery** (*see p169* **VIP, RIP**), which houses over 300,000 bodies, including Elizabeth Cady Stanton, Duke Ellington, Miles Davis, FW Woolworth and Damon Runyon. Maps are available at the visitors' entrance at Webster Avenue & E 233rd Street.

About five blocks south on Bainbridge Avenue, history buffs will also enjoy stopping in at the Bronx Historical Society's **Museum of Bronx History** (*see p171*), set in a lovely 1758 stone farmhouse, to brush up on local legends.

Old salts – and seafood fans – should stop at **City Island**. Located just east of Pelham Bay Park and ringed by the waters of Eastchester Bay and the Long Island Sound, City Island was settled in 1685 and was once a prosperous shipbuilding centre with a busy fishing industry, a history reflected in the streets lined with Victorian captains' houses. Nautical activity still abounds, especially in the summer, but recreational boating is the main industry now. The island's main drag, City Island Avenue, brims with art galleries and antique shops, while seafood restaurants, marine-themed bars, yacht clubs and sail makers crowd the docks. Join the warm-weather hordes at **Johnny's Famous Reef Restaurant** (2 City Island Avenue, at Belden Street, 1-718 885 2086)

for steamed clams, cold beer and great views. Few commercial fishermen remain, but you'd hardly know it at Rosenberg's Boat Livery (663 City Island Avenue, 1-718 885 1843), a bait-and-tackle shop that rents motorboats by the day. The Livery also doubles as a bustling bar (locals call it the Worm Hole). If it weren't for the crosstown bus running through, the enclave could pass for a sleepy New England village.

Bartow-Pell Mansion Museum

895 Shore Road North, at Pelham Bay Park (1-718 885 1461/www.bartowpellmansionmuseum.org). Travel: 6 to Pelham Bay Park, then take the Bee-Line bus 45 (ask driver to stop at the Bartow-Pell Mansion; bus does not run on Sunday), or take a cab from the subway station. **Open** noon-4pm Wed, Sat, Sun; 5.30-9.30pm first Fri of month. **Admission** $5; $3 seniors and students; free under-12s. Free Wed. **No credit cards**.

This stunning estate got its start in 1654, when Thomas Pell bought the land from the Siwanoy Indians. It was Robert Bartow who added the present day Grecian-style stone mansion. The grounds are simply stunning.

Bronx Academy of Arts & Dance (BAAD)

2nd Floor, 841 Barretto Street, between Garrison & Lafayette Avenues (1-718 842 5223/www.bronxacademyofartsanddance.org). Subway: 6 to Hunts Point Avenue. **Open** Check website for performances and prices.

A myriad dance, theatre and visual-art events including the borough's only fest celebrating works by lesbian, gay, bisexual and transgender artists during the month of June; the BlakTino Playwrights Showcase, presenting the works of black, Latino and playwrights of mixed race, in the autumn; and BAAD! ASS WOMEN, a cultural celebration of works by women.

Bronx Culture Trolley

The Bronx Council on the Arts (1-718 931 9500 ext 33/www.bronxarts.org). Subway: 2, 4, 5 to 149th Street-Grand Concourse. **Open** Feb-Jun, Oct-Dec first Wed of the month. Trolley picks up passengers from 5.30pm at Hostos Center for the Arts & Culture (450 Grand Concourse); leaves at 6pm. **Admission** free.

The trolley is a replica of an early 20th-century trolley that shuttles you (for nothing!) to a whole host of galleries and performing-arts venues. It also takes riders to the Artisans Marketplace – a giant craft fair with all sorts of attractive handmade stuff. Check out www.bronxarts.org for a current schedule of the seasonal event.

Bronx Museum of the Arts

1040 Grand Concourse, at 165th Street (1-718 681 6000/www.bxma.org). Subway: B, D, 4 to 161st Street-Yankee Stadium. **Open** noon-9pm Wed; noon-6pm Thur-Sun. **Admission** $5; $3 seniors and students; free under-12s. Free Wednesday. **No credit cards**.

This multicultural contemporary art museum shines a spotlight on 20th- and 21st-century artists of African, Asian and Latin American extraction. The museum has mounted several critically successful shows in recent years including *One Planet Under A Groove: Hip Hop and Contemporary Art* (2001) and *Urban Mythologies: The Bronx Represented Since the 1960s* (1999).

Bronx Zoo/Wildlife Conservation Society

Bronx Zoo.

Bronx River Parkway, at Fordham Road (1-718 367 1010/www.bronxzoo.org). Subway: 2, 5 to West Farms Square-East Tremont Avenue. **Open** *Apr-Oct* 10am-5pm Mon-Fri; 10am-5.30pm Sat, Sun, holidays. *Nov-Mar* 10am-4.30pm daily. **Admission** *Apr-Oct* $12; $9 seniors & children; free under-2s. *Nov-Mar* $8; $6 seniors & children; free under-2s. Voluntary donation Wed. (Some rides and exhibitions are extra.) **Credit** AmEx, DC, Disc, MC, V.

The elusive snow leopard wanders across the peaks of the Himalayan Highlands, and more than 30 species of rodent coexist in the Mouse House. Birds, giraffes, lions and reptiles abound in a zoo that is home to more than 4,500 creatures. For visitors who want a bird's-eye view, the Skyfari, an aerial tram ride over the zoo, is wonderful. Ground-crawlers can jump on the Zoo Shuttle, which provides rides (for a nominal few dollars) through the zoo (seniors can ride for free). On permanent display, you'll find: Tiger Mountain, a three-acre exhibit for Siberian tigers, the largest of the big cats. Highlights include an underwater viewing area; kiosks to educate visitors about tigers and conservation; and talks and demonstrations. The Butterfly Garden is perfect for children, with more than 1,000 colourful butterflies fluttering about in an enclosed habitat. **Photo** *right*.

Edgar Allan Poe Cottage

2640 Grand Concourse, at Kingsbridge Road (1-718 881 8900/www.bronxhistoricalsociety.org). Subway: B, D, 4 to Kingsbridge Road. **Open** 10am-4pm Sat; 1-5pm Sun. **Admission** $3; $2 seniors and students. **No credit cards**.

Pay homage to Poe in the very house where he wrote literary gems including *Annabel Lee* and *The Bells* and lived until his death in 1849. This was a bucolic idyll for the restless Poe and wife Virginia, with views as far as Long Island. Public outcry saved the charming home in 1902 from demolition. A presentation film and guided tour are available.

Museum of Bronx History

Valentine-Varian House, 3266 Bainbridge Avenue, between Van Cortlandt Avenue & E 208th Street (1-718 881 8900/www.bronxhistoricalsociety.org). Subway: D to Norwood-205th Street. **Open** 10am-4pm Sat; 1-5pm Sun. **Admission** $3; $2 seniors, students and children. **No credit cards**.

Operated by the Bronx County Historical Society, the Museum of Bronx History is located in the Valentine-Varian House, a Federal-style fieldstone residence built in 1758. The Society offers tours that explore the neighbourhoods and historic periods.

New York Botanical Garden

Bronx River Parkway, at Fordham Road (1-718 817 8700/www.nybg.org). Travel: D, 4 to Bedford Park Boulevard, then take the Bx26 bus to Garden gate; or Metro-North (Harlem Line local) from Grand Central Terminal to Botanical Garden. **Open** *Apr-Oct* 10am-6pm Tue-Sun, Mon federal holidays. *Nov-Mar* 10am-5pm Tue-Sun. **Admission** $6; $3 seniors and students; $1 children; free under-2s. Free Wed. **Credit** AmEx, DC, MC, V.

The basic $6 fee is for the grounds only; a $13 Garden Passport ($11 seniors and students, $5 children 2-12) allows entry to the Adventure Garden, the Haupt Conservatory and tram tours. If you're coming from Manhattan, a Getaway ticket (from Grand Central Terminal) buys a round trip on Metro-North's Harlem train and a Garden Passport. The winter holiday model-train show is super-festive.

Van Cortlandt House Museum

Van Cortlandt Park, entrance on Broadway, at 244th Street (1-718 543 3344/www.vancortlandthouse.org). Subway: 1 to 242nd Street-Van Cortlandt Park. **Open** 10am-3pm Tue-Fri; 11am-4pm Sat, Sun. **Admission** $5; $3 seniors and students; free under-12s. Free Wednesday. **No credit cards**.

Wave Hill House

W 249th Street, at Independence Avenue (1-718 549 3200/www.wavehill.org). Travel: Metro-North (Hudson Line local) from Grand Central Terminal to Riverdale. **Open** *15 Apr-31 May, 1 Aug-14 Oct* 9am-5.30pm Tue-Sun. *June, July* 9am-5.30pm Tue, Thur-Sun; 9am-9pm Wed. *15 Oct-14 Apr* 9am-4.30pm Tue-Sun. **Admission** $4; $2 seniors and students: free under-6s. Free Tue all day, 9am-noon Sat and Dec-Feb all times. **No credit cards**.

Staten Island

Hop on a ferry to find bosky tranquility and colonial splendour.

Sightseeing

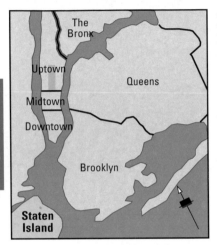

Staten Island has just about had it with its critics. When the soft-drink company Snapple made a recent jab at the borough with a Real Facts question (Q. What's the most recognisable smell in the world? A. No, it's not Staten Island – it's coffee), a councilman became so enraged he staged his own Boston-style tea party by ceremoniously dumping bottles of the drink down a drain by his office. Soon after, when radio station Z-100 aired a song with a line saying the borough 'reeks like gawbage', a resident retaliated by penning his own island-proud tune, which spurred the radio station to offer not only an apology, but free pizza and T-shirts at the Staten Island mall. The root of all this ribbing is the former Fresh Kills landfill, now in the process of being converted into parkland. So Islanders want everyone to get over it already. There's a lot more to the borough than its long-gone garbage dump.

First discovered by Giovanni da Verrazano in 1524, the island wasn't named until 1609, when Henry Hudson dubbed it *Staaten Eylandt* (Dutch for 'State's Island'). Early settlements were repeatedly wiped out by Native American resistance, but the Dutch eventually took hold in 1661. It then became a peaceful plot of land, with a shipping and manufacturing hub on the northern shore, and farms and small hamlets in the south. Despite being incorporated as one

of the five boroughs in 1898, the predominantly rural area didn't have much of a connection to the rest of the city until 1964, when the Verrazano-Narrows Bridge joined the island to Brooklyn's Bay Ridge neighbourhood.

The best-known link to the city, however, is the **Staten Island Ferry**, which passes the Statue of Liberty before sliding into the St George terminal. With so many attractions just steps away from the terminal, the view of Manhattan and the surrounding harbour are no longer the best things about the journey. On the Esplanade, next to the terminal, is *Postcards*, by Japanese architect Masayuki Sono. Dedicated in September 2004, the $2.7 million sculpture is a memorial to the 253 Staten Islanders lost on 9/11. Another addition to the Esplanade will be the **National Lighthouse Center & Museum** (1-718 556 1681, www.lighthousemuseum.org) scheduled to open in autumn 2005. The complex will include a restored lighthouse, a lightship, piers and exhibits just east of the ferry terminal.

Just along from Richmond Terrace lies the **Richmond County Savings Bank Ballpark**, home of the minor-league Staten Island Yankees (www.siyanks.com) and a great place to catch a game and a harbourside view. Across the street, look for the Borough Hall's (10 Richmond Terrace) distinctive clocktower and take a quick step inside for a peek at the Works Progress Administration murals depicting local history. Continuing north and then west along Richmond Terrace to Westervelt Avenue, then uphill two blocks to St Marks Place, you'll come upon the St George-New Brighton Historic District, a landmark neighbourhood full of Queen Anne and Colonial Revival buildings that date from the early 1830s. Continuing south to Bay Street near Victory Boulevard, vintage-fashion fans will enjoy the various thrift shops dotting the strip.

While the waterfront is easy to get to and has stunning views, inland areas also provide ample opportunities for exploration. You can spend an entire day looking around the 83-acre **Snug Harbor Cultural Center** (*see p174*), a short bus ride west along Richmond Terrace. Stately Greek Revival structures form the nucleus of the former maritime hospital and sailors' home dating from 1833. The centre was converted in the 1970s into a visual and performing arts complex that includes the **Art**

Take the **Staten Island Ferry** when the river runs mild. *See p172.*

Lab gallery, the **Noble Maritime Collection**, focusing on New York Harbor history, and the **Staten Island Botanical Garden**. Slightly further inland, the **Staten Island Zoo** (*see p174*), adjacent to the Clove Lakes Park, boasts one of the East Coast's largest reptile collections. The South American rainforest also makes it an appealing family destination.

Buses and the single-line Staten Island Railroad depart from St George for destinations along the eastern half of the island. Along Hylan Boulevard, one of Staten Island's major arteries, photographer **Alice Austen**'s house (*see p174*) is a 15-minute bus ride east of the ferry. The 18th-century cottage has breathtaking views of New York Harbor and 3,000 of Austen's glass negative photos. At the east end of Bay Street, historic **Fort Wadsworth** is one of the oldest military sites in the nation. There, visitors can explore the Civil War-era gun batteries or enjoy the views of the Verrazano Bridge and downtown Manhattan from one of the city's highest points. Further along the eastern coast, residents and tourists stroll along the two-mile boardwalk (which is apparently the fourth longest in the world) of **South Beach**. It's also a great area for picnicking.

In the centre of the island, on Lighthouse Avenue, many seek refuge at the **Jacques Marchais Museum of Tibetan Art** (*see p174*), a reproduction of a small Himalayan

temple with a tranquil meditation garden that also showcases a compact collection of Tibetan and Buddhist artefacts, artworks and religious items. Nearby, guides in period garb give tours of the 27 restored buildings of **Historic Richmond Town** (*see p174*), the island's one-time county seat. Take a look at Voorlezer's House, the nation's oldest former schoolhouse (circa 1695); there's also a general store, a blacksmith, a basket weaver and a working farm. Just a stone's throw away, **High Rock Park** (*see p174*) is the main access point for more than 30 miles of hiking trails.

On a summer day, a 40-minute ride on the S78 bus will take you to the island's south-eastern coast, where you can swim, picnic and even fish at **Wolfe's Pond Park** (Cornelia Avenue, at Hylan Boulevard, 1-718 984 8266). A little further south, tour the historic **Conference House**, the meeting place for a failed attempt at peace between American and British forces in 1776 and now a museum of colonial life. A short walk away, you can admire the passing sailboats from Tottenville Beach, at the very tip of the island.

Rich in history, cultural respites and parkland, these attractions make Staten Island a welcome escape from urban skyscrapers, congestion and sprawl. Add the city's low cost of living to the mix, and it's no wonder that this borough is booming, and brimming, with a justifiably renewed sense of self-esteem.

Alice Austen House

2 Hylan Boulevard, between Bay & Edgewater Streets (1-718 816 4506/www.aliceausten.org). Travel: From the Staten Island Ferry, take the S51 bus to Hylan Boulevard. **Open** *Mar-Dec* noon-5pm Thur-Sun (closed major holidays). **Admission** suggested donation $2. **No credit cards.**

History buffs will marvel at Austen's beautiful turn-of-the-century photographs. The restored house and grounds are lovely.

Conference House (Billopp House)

7455 Hylan Boulevard, at Craig Avenue (1-718 984 0415/www.theconferencehouse.org). Travel: From the Staten Island Ferry, take the S78 bus to Craig Avenue. **Open** *1 Apr-15 Dec* 1-4pm Fri-Sun. **Admission** $3; $2 seniors and children. **No credit cards.**

Britain's Lord Howe parleyed with John Adams and Benjamin Franklin in this 17th-century manor house in 1776, in an attempt to put the brakes on the American Revolution.

Fort Wadsworth

East end of Bay Street (1-718 354 4500). Travel: from the Staten Island Ferry, take the S51 bus to Fort Wadsworth on weekdays, Von Briesen Park on weekends. **Open** 10am-5pm Wed-Sun. **Tours** 2.30pm Wed-Fri; 10.30am, 2.30pm Sat, Sun. **Admission** free.

In spring and fall, the View From the Top tour not only takes you up into the lighthouse (which helped guide boats in the early 1900s) but down into the depths of the Fort – and it's free! Call for a schedule.

High Rock Park

200 Nevada Avenue, at Rockland Avenue (1-718 667 2165/www.sigreenbelt.org). Travel: From the Staten Island Ferry, take the S62 bus to Manor Road, then the S54 bus to Nevada Avenue. **Open** dawn-dusk daily. *Visitors' Center* 8.30am-5pm Mon-Fri. **Admission** free.

This 90-acre park is part of the Greenbelt, Staten Island's whopping 2,800 acres of parkland. Hike the mile-long Swamp Trail, climb Todt Hill or explore trails through forests, meadows and wetlands.

Historic Richmond Town

441 Clarke Avenue, between Richmond Road & St Patricks Place (1-718 351 1611/www.historic richmondtown.org). Travel: From the Staten Island Ferry, take the S74 bus to St Patrick's Place. **Open** *Sept-May* 1-5pm Wed-Sun. *Jun-Aug* 10am-5pm Wed-Sat; 1-5pm Sun. **Admission** $5; $4 seniors; $3.50 5-17s; free under-5s. **No credit cards.**

Get a taste of the old country right here in New York City. Fans of the PBS reality show *Colonial House* will enjoy stepping back in time at this colonial village.

Jacques Marchais Museum of Tibetan Art

338 Lighthouse Avenue, off Richmond Road, Staten Island (1-718 987 3500/www.tibetanmuseum.com). Travel: From the Staten Island Ferry, take the S74 bus to Lighthouse Avenue. **Open** 1-5pm Wed-Sun. **Admission** $5; $3 seniors and students; $2 under-12s. **Credit** AmEx, MC, V.

This tiny hillside museum contains a formidable Buddhist altar, lovely gardens and a large collection of Tibetan art that includes religious objects, bronzes and paintings. Every October, the museum hosts a Tibetan festival.

Staten Island Zoo

614 Broadway, between Glenwood Place & West Raleigh Avenue (1-718 442 3100/www.staten islandzoo.org). Travel: From the Staten Island Ferry, take the S48 bus to Broadway. **Open** 10am-4.45pm daily (closed major holidays). **Admission** $5; $4 seniors; $3 3-14s; free under-3s. Free 2-4.45pm Wed (suggested donation $2). **No credit cards.**

What they lack in big animals, they more than make up for in invertebrates, reptiles and amphibians, with one of the larger collections of such critters on the East Coast.

Snug Harbor Cultural Center

Art Lab

Snug Harbor Cultural Center, Building H (1-718 447 8667/www.artlab.info). **Open** 4-8pm Mon; 10am-8pm Tue-Thur; 10am-5pm Fri-Sun. **Admission** free.

This non-profit space offers classes in fine arts, crafts and photography for children and adults. The Art Lab Gallery exhibits the work of a different local artist each month.

Noble Maritime Collection

Snug Harbor Cultural Center, Building D (1-718 447 6490/www.noblemaritime.org). **Open** 1-5pm Thur-Sun. **Admission** $3; $2 seniors and students; free under-10s. **Credit** AmEx, MC, V.

The collection of works by noted maritime artist John A Noble also includes his houseboat studio, built with parts from larger boats.

Snug Harbor Cultural Center

1000 Richmond Terrace, between Snug Harbor Road & Tysen Street (1-718 448 2500/tickets 1-718 815 7684/www.snug-harbor.org). Travel: From the Staten Island Ferry, take the S40 bus to the north gate (tell the bus driver). **Open** *Galleries* 10am-5pm Tue-Sun. **Admission** $3; $2 seniors and under-12s. **Credit** AmEx, MC, V.

In addition to the venues listed here, Snug Harbor also houses a 400-seat auditorium, the city's oldest concert venue.

Staten Island Botanical Garden

Snug Harbor Cultural Center, Building H (1-718 273 8200/www.sibg.org). **Open** dawn-dusk daily. **Admission** *Chinese Scholar's Garden* $5; $4 seniors, students and children. *Grounds & other gardens* free. **Credit** AmEx, MC, V.

Stroll through more than 20 themed gardens and plantings, from the White Garden (based on Vita Sackville-West's creation at Sissinghurst Castle) and the tranquil, pavilion-lined Chinese Scholar's Garden to the delightful Secret Garden, which comes complete with a child-size castle, a maze and a secluded walled garden.

Eat, Drink, Shop

Features

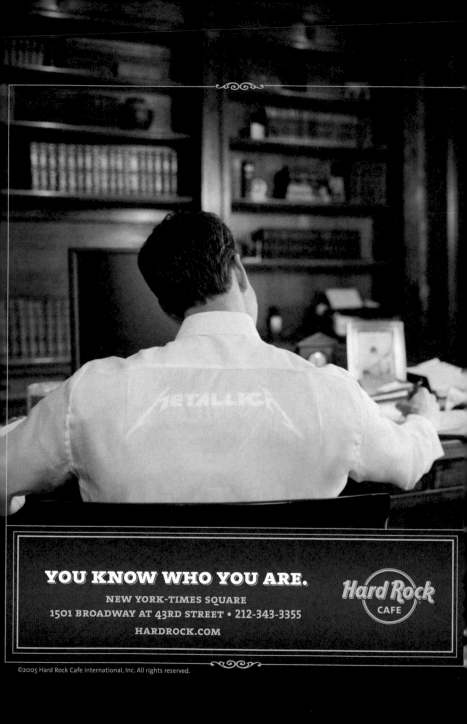

Restaurants & Cafés

The food capital of the world is currently facing stiff competition from in-form London. Which is best? There's really only one way to find out.

There seems to be a dichotomy on the New York restaurant scene: portions are getting smaller, while the restaurants themselves are getting bigger and bigger. These days, dining is more about going out – and staying out. New Yorkers, it seems, would rather dine on champagne and crostini at multiple spots around the city than sit down to a proper three-course meal at one restaurant. Take the hot new AvroKO-designed **Stanton Social** (*see p194*), for example, which opened last spring on the Lower East Side. The restaurant is massive – it's spread over three levels – but most of the 50 dishes on the menu are bite-sized (crispy Rockefeller oysters, mini-Kobe beefburgers). The same is true for **PS 450** (*see p204*), a new 4,000 square-foot lounge-restaurant in Murray Hill, where cocktails come in carafes, and a smattering of small plates, like duck confit taquitos and buffalo pops, are supposed to add up to a full meal. And at press time, two more sprawling eateries, Il Posto and Buddakan, are slated for a 2005 opening in two former warehouses in the Meatpacking District.

This year we saw another trend on the New York culinary scene: BBQ joints opening around town at a rapid-fire pace. In **BBQ Nation** (*see p202-3*), we tell you which spots are serving authentic 'cue from what regions (who would have known that a Kansas City platter has a whole different pedigree from the North Carolina stuff?). And since New Yorkers have reversed their aversion to carbs, we show you plenty of places to get those, too, in the form of good old-fashioned bagels (*see p208* **History in the round**). Of course, we realise that some of you are game for anything; for you, we recommend a new batch of flashy, fabulous venues (*see p194*).

Remember, NYC has more than 23,000 restaurants, bars and cafés, so we've outlined only a sampling of all the great eats the city has to offer. And it's constantly changing:

> ❶ Purple numbers given in this chapter correspond to the location of each restaurant and café as marked on the street maps. *See pp402-412.*

an average of five new restaurants open each week, while one will close its doors for good. You won't be able to conquer the city's culinary scene, but you can have some great meals trying.

PRACTICALLY SPEAKING
The hardest part about eating out in New York is the sheer choice; it's downright dizzying, even for locals. Snagging reservations can also be tough; always call ahead. Super trendy spots can be fully booked weeks in advance. Luckily, the vast majority require only a few days' notice or less. Most restaurants fill up between 7pm and 9pm. If you don't mind eating early or late, your chances of getting into somewhere popular will improve greatly.

In this rags-to-riches town, the dress code is all over the place, but some ultra-fancy eateries do require guys to don a jacket and tie. If in doubt, call ahead and ask.

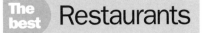 **The best Restaurants**

... for a taste of Old New York
Peter Luger (*see p210*), Lombardi's *p183*), Corner Bistro (*p191*).

... for celebrity sightings
Per Se (*see p206*), Bette (*p197*), Nobu 57 (*p201*).

... for outdoor dining
Pure Food & Wine (*see p199*), La Bottega (*p197*) and Falai (*p184*).

... for weekend brunch
Balthazar (*see p186*), Clinton Street Baking Company (*p184*) and @SQC (*p206*).

... for cheap eats
Empire Diner (*see p196*), Peanut Butter & Co (*p190*), Market Café (*p200*)

... for hangin' with hipsters
Freemans (*see p184*), SEA Thai Restaurant & Bar (*p210*), Café Habana (*p182*).

... for late-night grub
Blue Ribbon (*see p185*), Employees Only (*p193*) and Schiller's Liquor Bar (*p184*).

Eat, Drink, Shop

The winner is…

Every year *Time Out New York* magazine recognises the best offerings of the city's thousands of restaurants. The combination of the wisdom of our culinary experts and the votes of *Time Out New York* readers results in a list of outstanding eateries. Below, some of the winners from the 2005 awards:

Best presentation & Best new restaurant
Per Se. *See p206.*

Best pub fare
Spotted Pig. *See p193.*

Best comeback
Chef Laurent Tourondel, BLT Steak. *See p205.*

Worst-kept secret (food division)
Freemans. *See p184.*

Best reincarnation
Porcupine (formerly Mix It). *See p181.*

Most addictive new snack
Fried chickpeas at Tia Pol. *See p198.*

Downtown

Tribeca & south

American

Bouley Bakery & Market
130 West Broadway, at Duane Street (1-212 608 5829). Subway: A, C, 1, 2, 3 to Chambers Street. **Open** *Bakery* 7.30am-7.30pm daily. *Restaurant* 6-11pm Tue-Sat. **Main courses** $19. **Sandwich** $9. **Credit** AmEx, DC, Disc, MC, V. **Map** p402 E31 ❶
Chef David Bouley's new bakery has pastries, breads, sandwiches, salads and pizza on the ground floor; a cellar full of fresh seafood, produce, meats and cheeses; and on the first floor, a dining room with a sushi bar and cocktails by renowned bar chef Albert Trummer. Sidewalk seats appear in warm weather.

French

Landmarc
179 West Broadway, between Leonard & Worth Streets (1-212 343 3883). Subway: 1 to Franklin Street. **Open** noon-2am Mon-Fri;

11am-2am Sat, Sun. **Main courses** $23. **Credit** AmEx, DC, Disc, MC, V. **Map** p402 E31 ❷
Chef Marc Murphy has a great kids' menu – which buys the grown-ups time to to savour the good stuff: tender braised lamb shanks, steaks grilled in an open hearth, mussels steamed with chorizo and onions. An enticing bottles-only wine list is also served in half-bottle portions. The $3 tasting portions of desserts such as blueberry crumble and crème brûlée will please calorie-counters.

Le Zinc
139 Duane Street, between Church Street & West Broadway (1-212 513 0001). Subway: A, C, 1, 2, 3 to Chambers Street. **Open** 11.30am-11pm Tue, Wed; 11.30am-midnight Thur, Fri; 10am-midnight Sat; 10am-10pm Sun. **Main courses** $21. **Credit** AmEx, Disc, MC, V. **Map** p402 E31 ❸
This endearing restaurant is part French bistro (antique art posters, weathered mirrors) and part New York diner – the menu includes savoury staples like a bacon cheeseburger and mac and cheese. But it's the way the kitchen transforms ordinary dishes into something special that has made Le Zinc a Tribeca fixture. Specials like a silky butternut squash flan and a tender cured pork chop stuffed with goat's cheese, fennel and golden raisins elevate the menu beyond the norm.

Italian

Adrienne's Pizza Bar
54 Stone Street, between Mill Street & Coenties Alley (1-212 248 3838). Subway: A, C, E to Canal Street. **Open** 11am-11pm Mon-Thur; 11am-midnight Fri; 10.30am-midnight Sat, Sun. **Main courses** $20. **Credit** AmEx, DC, MC, V. **Map** p402 F33 ❹
A bright, modern pizzeria on a quaint, cobbled pedestrian street. You can get your pizza by the slice or thin-crust pie, and wolf it down at the standing-room bar, or more properly in the sit-down dining area. Dinner guests will find an extended menu of small plates and entrées, and plenty of outdoor seating.
Other locations: Bread, 20 Spring Street, between Elizabeth & Mott Streets (1-212 334 1015).

Lo Scalco
313 Church Street, between Lispenard & Walker Streets (1-212 343 2900). Subway: 1 to Franklin Street. **Open** 6.30-11pm Mon-Thur; noon-3pm, 6.30pm-midnight Fri; 6.30pm-midnight Sat. **Main courses** $27. **Credit** AmEx, DC, MC, V. **Map** p402 E31 ❺
In Renaissance Italy, the chef-maître d' to affluent families was called 'lo scalco'. Chef-owner Mauro Mafrici takes on this role at his gorgeous Tribeca restaurant. The setting is luxurious – grand arched ceilings, ceramic chandeliers – and the dishes aim to be too. Each is as carefully constructed as an entry in a cooking-school final: slices of salty duck prosciutto arranged in a fan around a perky stack of greens; a hunk of lightly seasoned branzino sitting on a golden ring of potato slices and a pile of wilted spinach. Mafrici's menu hones in on key ingredients,

Aroma. *See p188.*

"Minado is a slick, spacious, sophisticated, big city beauty with what seems like a mile-long buffet table loaded with sushi and sashimi, hot and cold entrees, salads and desserts."

-The New York Times, Richard J. Scholem

"Get ready to gorge at this "huge banquet-hall" like Murray Hiller offering an "eye-popping", "block-long", "all-you-can-eat buffet" of japanese fare; the "boatload" of sushi and such may not be "adventurous" but they are "surprisingly fresh" and given the "affordable" prices, what do you expect?"

-Zagat Survey 2005

6E 32nd Street New York, NY 10016
(between fifth and madison avenue)
t. 212. 725. 1333   f. 212. 725. 1925

www.minado.com

WEEKDAY LUNCH | $13.95
WEEKDAY DINNER | $23.95
WEEKEND LUNCH | $15.95
WEEKEND DINNER | $25.95

* HOURS AND PRICES ARE SUBJECT TO CHANGE WITHOUT NOTICE

japanese
seafood
buffet

WEEKDAY LUNCH | MON - FRI | 11:30AM - 2:30PM
WEEKDAY DINNER| MON - THURS | 6:00PM - 10:00PM | FRI. 5:30PM - 10:00PM
WEEKEND LUNCH | SAT & SUN | 11:30AM - 3:00PM
WEEKEND DINNER| SAT. 5:30PM - 10:00PM | SUN. 5:00PM - 9:00PM

Minado®
JAPANESE SEAFOOD BUFFET RESTAURANT
New York City's biggest and freshest buffet

offering three variations on artichokes, tomatoes, Dover sole, lamb, duck and more. Sample a few; tasting menus range from $48 to $64.

Japanese

Megu

62 Thomas Street, between Church Street & West Broadway (1-212 964 7777). Subway: A, C, 1, 2, 3 to Chambers Street. **Open** 11.30am-2.30pm, 5.30-11.30pm Mon-Fri; 5.30-11.30pm Sat, Sun. **Main courses** $30. **Credit** AmEx, DC, Disc, MC, V. **Map** p402 E31 ➏
Hot young chef-owner Koji Imai ha scertainly made a splash with his first New York restauran. He is obsessed with organic ingredients and orders only from local farmers. The results are on his eclectic menu: hand-harvested ginkgo nuts in an olive-oil bath, skewered shishamo fish cooked over hot coals, seared Kobe beef with karashi mustard. The decor is show-stopping, too: a vast space with columns made from porcelain rice bowls and saké bottles, and a lounge decorated with antique kimono fabrics.

Chinatown, Little Italy & Nolita

American

Barmarché

14 Spring Street, at Elizabeth Street (1-212 219 9542). Subway: N, R, W to Prince Street; 6 to Spring Street. **Open** 11am-11pm Mon, Sun;

11pm-midnight Tue-Thur; 10am-1am Fri, Sat. **Main courses** $15. **Credit** AmEx, MC, V. **Map** p403 F30 ➐
Peer inside this bright, white-on-white brasserie, and you'll be tempted to come in and join the party: the dining room is often filled with beautiful people and lively groups, and the kitchen keeps them happy and well fed with generous portions of reliable bistro hits. The menu is American in the melting-pot sense, covering all the greatest-hits, no-nonsense dishes from around the world: home-made fettuccine with pesto, thick gazpacho with a dollop of guacamole, tuna tartare with grated Asian pear and citrus ponzu, croques-monsieur and a made-in-the-USA juicy burger.

Porcupine

20 Prince Street, between Elizabeth & Mott Streets (1-212 966 8886). Subway: N, R, W to Prince Street; 6 to Spring Street. **Open** 11am-11pm Mon-Fri; 11am-11.30pm Sat, Sun. **Main courses** $20. **Credit** AmEx. **Map** p403 F29 ➑
Jacques Ouari is mixing things up once again: in early 2005 he closed his short-lived French brasserie, Mix It, and reopened it as a café-tavern called Porcupine, preparing audacious seasonal dishes from local artisanal ingredients. For lunch, you can try hearty sandwiches like a croque-madame with fried egg and vinegar radishes, or grilled leg of lamb with prune-hyssop butter and rocket. Dinners are meaty too: suckling pig with apple and celeriac, or mustard-braised veal with lemon pickles. Non-meat dishes could include Taylor Bay scallop and blackfish stew with almond milk and acorn squash.

Eclectic dishes and a ski-lodge vibe at **Freemans**. *See p184.*

On the tiles: a view of the loos at **Schiller's Liquor Bar**. *See p184.*

Chinese

Congee Village

100 Allen Street, between Broome & Delancey Streets (1-212 941 1818). Subway: F to Delancey Street; J, M, Z to Delancey-Essex Streets. **Open** 10.30am-2am daily. **Main courses** $12. **Credit** AmEx, MC, V. **Map** p403 F30 ❾

If you've never indulged in the starchy comfort of congee, this is a good place to be initiated. The rice porridge, cooked to bubbling in a clay pot over a slow fire, is best early in the day; pick a chunky version such as the treasure-laden seafood or sliced fish. Crab is impeccably fresh, as is the well-seasoned whole fish served over glistening Chinese broccoli. It may seem incongruous, but the Congee has a great pina colada – and it will only cost you $3 during the weekday happy hour (4-7pm).

Golden Bridge

50 Bowery, between Bayard & Canal Streets (1-212 227 8831). Subway: B, D to Grand Street; J, M, N, Q, R, W, Z, 6 to Canal Street. **Open** 9am-11pm daily. **Dim sum** $2. **Credit** AmEx, DC, Disc, MC, V. **Map** p402 F31 ❿

Dim sum devotees often pick Flushing, Queens, over Manhattan, but they should reconsider with this serious Cantonese venue above a Popeye's on the Bowery. An armada of carts offers fresh and flavourful standards like clams in black bean sauce and pillowy steamed pork buns, plus unusual items such as egg tarts with a soft taro crust. Look for the elusive cart bearing a mysterious wooden bucket; it's filled with an irresistible, lightly sweetened tofu.

Cuban

Café Habana

17 Prince Street, at Elizabeth Street (1-212 625 2001). Subway: N, R, W to Prince Street; 6 to Spring Street. **Open** 9am-midnight daily. **Main courses** $10. **Credit** AmEx, MC, V. **Map** p403 F29 ⓫

Hipsters storm this café day and night for its addictive grilled corn doused in butter and rolled in grated cheese and chilli powder. Other staples include crisp beer-battered catfish tortas with spicy mayo, and juicy marinated skirt steak with yellow rice and black beans. This year, the owners opened a second location in Greenpoint, Brooklyn.

Other locations: Café Habana to Go, 229 Elizabeth Street, between Houston & Prince Streets (1-212 625 2002).

Eclectic

Public

210 Elizabeth Street, between Prince & Spring Streets (1-212 343 7011). Subway: N, R, W to Prince Street; 6 to Spring Street. **Open** 6-11.30pm Mon-Fri; 6-12.30pm Sat; 6-10.30pm Sun. **Main courses** $20. **Credit** AmEx, MC, V. **Map** p403 F29 ⓬

This gorgeous industrial space, designed by AvroKo, is high on concept: machine-age glass lamps, pre-war office doors and a library card catalogue make sly references to public spaces. Chef Brad Farmerie, who worked at London's acclaimed Providores, has created the menu in tandem with Providores colleagues New Zealanders Anna

Hansen and Peter Gordon. Look for a Kiwi influence in dishes like grilled kangaroo on coriander falafel and New Zealand venison with pomegranates and truffles. Desserts are equally eclectic.

Pan-Asian

Kitchen Club
30 Prince Street, at Mott Street (1-212 274 0025). Subway: N, R, W to Prince Street; 6 to Spring Street. **Open** 12.30-4pm, 5.30-11.30pm Mon-Sat; 12.30-4pm, 5.30-10.30pm Sun. **Main courses** $21. **Credit** AmEx, MC, V. **Map** p403 F29 ⑬

Buzzworthy

Mark Ladner
Ladner has been one of Mario Batali's leading men for years, running the show at his phenomenal, and mega-popular, Thompson Street restaurant Lupa (*see p190*) and serving as Batali's trusted sous chef on the Food Network's *Iron Chef* battles. Now Ladner is in the spotlight in a bigger way, and this is no game. He's overseeing Batali's biggest, most spectacular restaurant ever – **Del Posto** (85 Tenth Avenue, at 16th Street, phone number unavailable at press time) in the Meatpacking District – serving a small town's worth of diners nightly and wowing them with perfectly roasted meats and dramatic tableside service. If you've ever seen Ladner on *Iron Chef*, you have a sense of how he's handling the pressure: calmly and gracefully, with a look on his face that suggests he's going to win.

The quasi host of this inviting pan-Asian spot is diminutive Chibi – a French bulldog who defers only to chef-owner Marja Samsom. Eclectic dishes with a Japanese tinge are carefully made and prettily presented. The dumplings are a justifiable source of pride, with tasty, inventive fillings including salmon tartare and tofu with chrysanthemum. And meat eaters will find sweet bliss in venison glazed with a spicy raspberry sauce and sprinkled with huckleberries.

Lovely Day
196 Elizabeth Street, between Prince & Spring Streets (1-212 925 3310). Subway: J, M, Z to Bowery; 6 to Spring Street. **Open** noon-11pm Mon-Thur; noon-midnight Fri; 11am-midnight Sat; 11am-11pm Sun. **Main courses** $10. **Credit** AmEx. **Map** p403 F30 ⑭
Tamarind appears in the shrimp summer roll's dressing, and again in the dressing for the flank steak served with rice and vegetables. But the spice isn't the only asset here: coconut curry noodles and pineapple fried rice are equally good. Slide into a booth and take your cue from the scents wafting from the tiny kitchen. Or come for brunch, which features crisp banana rolls (we're skipping straight to dessert here) and house-made carrot cake in a pool of steaming English custard.

Pizza

Lombardi's
32 Spring Street, between Mott & Mulberry Streets (1-212 941 7994). Subway: 6 to Spring Street. **Open** 11.30am-11pm Mon-Thur; 11.30am-midnight Fri, Sat; 11.30am-10pm Sun. **Large pizza** $15. **No credit cards**. **Map** p403 F30 ⑮
Lombardi's is the city's oldest pizzeria, established in 1905, and it offers pizza at it's best: made in a coal-fired oven and with a chewy, thin crust. The pepperoni is fantastic, as are the killer meatballs in tomato sauce. The setting is classic pizza-parlour – wooden booths, red-and-white checked tablecloths.

Vietnamese

Doyers Vietnamese Restaurant
11 Doyers Street, between Bowery & Pell Street (1-212 513 1521). Subway: J, M, N, Q, R, W, Z, 6 to Canal Street. **Open** 11am-10pm Mon-Thur, Sun; 11am-11pm Fri, Sat. **Main courses** $8. **Credit** AmEx. **Map** p402 F31 ⑯
The search to find this restaurant is part of the fun: it's tucked away in a basement on a zigzagging Chinatown alley. The 33 appetisers include balls of grilled minced shrimp wrapped around sugarcane sticks and a delicious Vietnamese crêpe filled with shrimp and pork. Hot pot soups, served on a table-top stove, are made with an exceptional fish-broth base and brim with vegetables. For maximum enjoyment, come with a six-pack of Singha in tow (the restaurant is BYOB).

Lower East Side

American creative

Clinton Street Baking Company

4 Clinton Street, between Houston & Stanton Streets (1 646 602 6263). Subway: F to Delancey Street; J, M, Z to Delancey-Essex Streets. **Open** 8am-11pm Mon-Fri; 10am-4pm, 6-11pm Sat; 10am-4pm Sun. **Main courses** $13. **Credit** AmEx, DC, MC, V. **Map** p403 G29 ⑰

The warm buttermilk biscuits here are reason enough to face the brunchtime crowds; if you want to avoid the onslaught, however, the homey Lower East Side spot is just as reliable at lunch and dinner, when locals drop in for fish tacos, grilled pizzas and a daily $10 beer-and-burger special: eight ounces of Black Angus topped with Swiss cheese and caramelised onions, served with a Brooklyn lager. Pssst – to better your odds for getting a table at brunch (the best in town), show up between 9 and 10am, when coffee and pastries are served before the rest of the kitchen opens.

Freemans

2 Freeman Alley, off Rivington Street between Bowery & Chrystie Street (1-212 420 0012). Subway: F, V to Lower East Side-Second Avenue; J, M, Z to Bowery. **Open** 5pm-midnight Mon-Fri; 11am-4pm, 6pm-midnight Sat, Sun. **Main courses** $22. **Credit** AmEx, DC, Disc, MC, V. **Map** p403 F29 ⑬

Once you find this secret restaurant (hidden at the end of Freeman Alley; *see p100* **Alley cat**) you'll feel as though you've stepped into a ski lodge on a mountaintop in Aspen. Those in the know feast on affordable dishes like juicy trout, warm artichoke dip, rich wild-boar terrine, and perfect batches of mac and cheese, plus a few retro oddities like 'devils on horseback' (prunes stuffed with blue cheese and wrapped in bacon), all served under the gaze of mounted animal heads. Brunch, when raised waffles with banana-maple syrup are served and the sun streams through the front windows, is rather more tranquil. **Photo** *p181*.

Cafés

Brown

61 Hester Street, between Essex & Ludlow Streets (1-212 477 2427). Subway: F to East Broadway. **Open** 9am-11pm Tue-Sat; 9am-6pm Sun. **Main courses** $12. **Credit** AmEx. **Map** p403 G30 ⑲

Owner Alejandro Alcocer opened this small café to compensate for the lack of a decent cup of joe in the hood. Not only can you get a mean latte here, but now you can also choose from more than 20 entrées based on organic ingredients. Daily specials, scribbled on the front-door glass, usually include a soup, a frittata and a cheese-and-fruit plate. Alcocer recently started serving beer and wine and a dinner menu. Sculpted wooden plank tables, benches and stumplike stools give the place the feel of an afternoon picnic straight from the glossy pages of *Surface*.

Eclectic

Schiller's Liquor Bar

131 Rivington Street, at Norfolk Street (1-212 260 4555). Subway: F to Delancey Street; J, M, Z to Delancey-Essex Streets. **Open** 11am-4am Mon-Fri; 10am-4am Sat, Sun. **Main courses** $12. **Credit** AmEx, MC, V. **Map** p403 G29 ⑳

Decorated with old mirrors and antique subway tiles, Keith McNally's latest is a playful all-day bohemian hangout that attracts a variety show of a clientele, from suits to drag queens and artfully tousled locals. No dish, except steak, costs more than $16. The menu is a mix of French bistro (steak-frites), British pub (Welsh rarebit) and Louisiana lunch counter (oyster po'boys). Traversing the wine list is a cinch: it's a mere six bottles long, designated 'cheap', 'decent' or 'good'. Desserts are mandatory; best is the sticky toffee pudding. **Photo** *p182*.

Stanton Social

See p194 **Get your chic on**. **Map** p403 F29 ㉑

French

Le Père Pinard

175 Ludlow Street, between Houston & Stanton Streets (1-212 777 4917). Subway: F to Delancey Street; J, M, Z to Delancey-Essex Streets. **Open** 5pm-midnight Mon-Wed; 5pm-1am Thur; 5pm-2am Fri, Sat; 5-11pm Sun. **Main courses** $17. **Credit** AmEx. **Map** p403 F29 ㉒

Just by walking by, you can tell the patrons of this bistro/wine bar are having fun. That's because they're mopping up heavenly garlic-butter broth from plates of perfect mussels; spreading homemade pâtés on to slices of fresh baguette; or digging into unsticky duck à l'orange. Take advantage of the early evening three-course *prix fixe* for just $14. In warm weather, the fun continues in the garden.

Italian

Falai

see p194 **Get your chic on**. **Map** p403 G29 ㉓
Photo *p185*.

Japanese

Cube 63

63 Clinton Street, between Rivington & Stanton Streets (1-212 228 6751). Subway: F to Delancey Street; J, M, Z to Delancey-Essex Streets. **Open** 5pm-midnight Mon-Thur, Sun; 5pm-1am Fri, Sat. **Sushi meal** $19. **Credit** MC, V. **Map** p403 G29 ㉔

This glowing lime-green dining room is tiny, but the inventive flavours created by sushi chefs Ben and Ken Lau (brothers who worked at Bond Street) are bigger than you'll find just about anywhere. Jumbo speciality rolls are the main draw: shrimp tempura hooks up with eel, avocado, cream cheese and caviar

Eat, Drink, Shop

in the Tahiti roll; the Volcano is crab and shrimp topped with spicy lobster salad then set aflame with a blowtorch in an eruption of melding flavours.

Seafood

Tides

102 Norfolk Street, at Delancey Street (1-212 254 8855). Subway: F, J, M, Z to Delancey-Essex Streets. **Open** 11am-3pm, 6-11pm Mon-Fri; 10am-2pm, 5-10pm Sat, Sun. **Main courses** $20. **Credit** AmEx, MC, V. **Map** p403 G30 ❷⑤

In July 2005, Allen Leung and Bobby Yee opened this sleek seafood restaurant in an intimate Lower East Side space, with custom-designed booths, chairs and tables made from different bamboos. Chef Judy Seto knows her seafood beyond the fish-fry tradition: she pairs mussels with fennel and cream broth and serves grilled shrimp with wild mushroom and chestnut spaetzle. Whole lobster, seared scallops and a lobster roll for every season are available for purists.

Spanish

Oliva

161 E Houston Street, at Allen Street (1-212 228 4143). Subway: F, V to Lower East Side-Second Avenue. **Open** 5.30pm-midnight Mon-Thur; 5.30pm-1am Fri; 11.30am-3.30pm, 5.30pm-1am Sat, Sun. **Main courses** $17. **Tapas** $5. **Credit** AmEx. **Map** p403 F29 ❷⑥

A bright red *toro* is stencilled on each table at Oliva. Young downtowners read the daily selections from an inscribed mirror over the bar; pintxos change daily. Serrano ham croquettes or tortilla are a tasty prelude to heartier dishes, such as seafood-heavy paella. On Wednesday and Sunday sangria flows freely while a Latin band keeps the place jumping.

Suba

109 Ludlow Street, between Delancey & Rivington Streets (1-212 982 5714). Subway: F to Delancey Street; J, M, Z to Delancey-Essex Streets. **Open** 6pm-2am Mon-Thur; 6pm-4am Fri-Sat; 6pm-midnight Sun. **Main courses** $24. **Credit** AmEx, MC, V. **Map** p403 G30 ❷⑦

Down the suspended steel staircase from the loud ground-floor tapas bar is another scene entirely. Suba's acclaimed chef, Alex Ureña, fuses traditional Spanish dishes with modern techniques. Duck breast with white-peach coulis and cinnamon sauce is undeniably sexy, especially when followed by the sultry dark-chocolate almond cake or a lime-pie cocktail.

Soho

American

Blue Ribbon

97 Sullivan Street, between Prince & Spring Streets (1-212 274 0404). Subway: C, E to Spring Street. **Open** 4pm-4am Tue-Sun. **Main courses** $22. **Credit** AmEx, DC, MC, V. **Map** p403 E30 ❷⑧

Falai. *See p184.*

Since 1992, this Soho fixture has continuously attracted global foodies and off-the-clock chefs from the neighbourhood, who come for the pristine raw bar, excellent blue-cheese burgers and beef marrow with oxtail marmalade. Open until 4am, the restaurant lures the fabulous for a late-night nosh, which usually means oysters and champagne.

Other locations: Blue Ribbon Brooklyn, 280 Fifth Avenue, between Garfield Place & First Street, Park Slope, Brooklyn (1-718 840 0404).

Fanelli's Café

94 Prince Street, at Mercer Street (1-212 226 9412). Subway: N, R, W to Prince Street. **Open** 10am-2.30am Mon-Thur; 10am-3am Fri, Sat; 11am-12.30am Sun. **Main courses** $10. **Credit** AmEx, MC, V. **Map** p403 E29 ❷

Deemed the second-oldest restaurant in New York, Fanelli's has stood at this cobblestoned intersection since 1847, and local artists and worldly tourists pour into the lively landmark for perfectly charred beef patties on toasted onion rolls. The long bar, prints of boxing legends and check tablecloths add to the charm. Specials, such as pumpkin ravioli or grilled mahimahi with lime and coriander, are surprisingly good offerings in a sea of pub grub.

French

Balthazar

80 Spring Street, between Broadway & Crosby Street (1-212 965 1414). Subway: N, R, W to Prince Street; 6 to Spring Street. **Open** 7.30-11.30am, noon-5pm, 6pm-1am Mon-Wed; 7.30-11.30am, noon-5pm, 6pm-1.30am Thur; 7.30-11.30am, noon-5pm, 6pm-2am Fri; 10am-4pm, 6pm-2am Sat; 10am-4pm, 5.30pm-midnight Sun. **Main courses** $21. **Credit** AmEx, MC, V. **Map** p403 E30 ❸

Now heading for its tenth birthday, this authentic French brasserie is still a scene – especially for the Saturday and Sunday brunch, when the room is packed with media executives, rail-thin lookers and trendy boys in chic hoodies. A three-tiered seafood platter (a house special) casts the most impressive shadow of any appetiser in town. Frisée aux lardons is exemplary, as is roasted chicken on mashed potatoes for two, and skate with brown butter and capers.

Félix

340 West Broadway, at Grand Street (1-212 431-0021). Subway: A, C, E, 1 to Canal Street. **Open** noon-midnight daily. **Main courses** $19. **Credit** AmEx. **Map** p403 E30 ❸

Antique ads, large glass doors that open on to the sidewalk and a pressed-tin ceiling provide a timeless backdrop for a modish scene (you'll recognise it from films like *Iggby Goes Down*). The food has actually improved over Félix's 13-year tenure. You come here to eat steak-frites – choose among peppercorn, béarnaise or Roquefort sauces to accompany a very tender piece of meat and golden frites. Félix is most frenzied at weekend brunch, when patrons spill out of the front door with Caipirinhas in hand.

Aroma.
See p188.

Italian

Ama

48 MacDougal Street, between Houston & Prince Streets (1-212 358 1707). Subway: C, E to Spring Street. **Open** 11am-3pm, 5-11pm daily. **Main courses** $19. **Credit** AmEx, Disc, MC, V. **Map** p403 E29 ㉜

Although Donatella Arpaia gave her name to the uptown restaurant she runs with chef David Burke – davidburke & donatella – her heart seems to be here, at this much smaller, much homier new Soho spot. She named the place after the Italian word fo love; it is indeed a lovely little restaurant. The food is a tribute to the cuisine of her mom's native Puglia. Chef Turibio Girardi serves rustic fare with upscale twists, such as rabbit stuffed with chestnuts, and cod with cream of fava beans and wild chicory. If you don't have time for dinner, stop by the bar for an espresso and a plate of home-made almond cookies.

Thai

Kittichai

Thompson Hotel, 60 Thompson Street, between Broome & Spring Streets (1-212 219 2000). Subway: C, E to Spring Street. **Open** 5.30-11pm daily. **Main courses** $22. **Credit** AmEx, DC, Disc, MC, V. **Map** p403 E30 ㉝

The experience of Kittichai at the Thompson Hotel begins when you enter. If enchanting orchids submerged in dramatic bottles don't capture your attention, the beautiful people sipping cocktails made with coconut milk or fresh juices will. The space, made over from the old Thom by the Rockwell Group features orange-hued lighting that bounces off fabric dividers and candles floating in a pool strewn with orchids. Chef Ian Chalermkittichai, formerly of the Four Seasons in Bangkok, prepares exceptional modern Thai dishes such as Thai marinated beef salad with Chinese long beans, and tender green-curry braised short ribs.

Turkish

Antique Garage

41 Mercer Street, between Broome & Grand Streets (1-212 219 1019). Subway: J, M, N, Q, R, W, Z, 6 to Canal Street. **Open** noon-midnight daily. **Main courses** $11. **Credit** AmEx, MC, V. **Map** p403 E30 ㉞

Formerly an auto-repair shop, the Antique Garage has good acoustics and ample Turkish carpeting to control the volume of its garrulous crowd, which comes for the live music as well as the food. Other assets: faded paintings and peeling mirrors on the walls, heirloom plates and antique chandeliers – all of which are for sale. The kitchen manages to live up to the decor with decent portions of borek (feta-stuffed filo), creamy houmous with fried toast points, and seared tuna doused in red-pepper purée.

East Village

American creative

Smoked

103 Second Avenue, at E 6th Street (1-212 388 0388). Subway: 6 to Astor Place. **Open** 5pm-midnight Mon-Wed; 5pm-1am Thur, Fri; 11am-1am Sat, Sun.* **Main courses** $11. **Credit** AmEx, DC, Disc, MC, V. **Map** p403 F28 ㉟

Smoked is like a set designer's take on a college campus restaurant: there's a big metal sign shaped like a flame, a DJ playing music by REM and Live and long cafeteria-like rows of tables. The 'cue here is fantastic and the kitchen sticks to what it does best: long, slow smoking, resulting in succulent short ribs and piles of tender pulled pork served on a warm bun with caramelised onions. The sides hold their own, too, like sweet cornbread baked in an iron skillet and hot fries dusted with addictive Cajun spices.

Cuban

Cafecito

185 Avenue C, at 12th Street (1-212 253 9966). Subway: L to First Avenue. **Open** 6-10pm Tue, Thur, Sun; 6pm-2am Fri, Sat. **Main courses** $12. **No credit cards**. **Map** p403 G28 ㊱

The relaxed outdoor bar is just one of the authentic touches at Cafecito ('tiny coffee'). You can sip a Mojito and nibble on green plantain chips as you contemplate menu choices: the aborcito de Cuba gives you a taste of each of the small hot appetisers – the best of which are the bollos, corn and black-bean fritters. In addition to blackboard specials like char-grilled skirt steak with chimichurri sauce, the perfectly pressed Cuban sandwich is spot on.

Eclectic

Ludo

42 E 1st Street, between First & Second Avenues (1-212 777 5617). Subway: F, V to Lower East Side-Second Avenue. **Open** 6-11pm daily. **Main courses** $22. **Credit** AmEx, MC, V. **Map** p403 F29 ㊲

The space formerly known as Chez es Saada has reopened as Ludo, an equally sensuous restaurant and lounge with blue lighting that ripples off stone walls, mimicking the movement of water. The name means 'I play' in Latin, and chef Einat Adimony has created a menu of global meze plates to reflect that idea. Cantaloupe gelato is encrusted with almonds and wrapped in prosciutto. Pork-belly spring rolls come with a tangy tamarind dipping sauce. Descending the steps from the ground-level bar to the grotto-like dining area is still a thrill.

Share

406 E 9th Street, between First Avenue & Avenue A (1-212 777 2425). Subway: L to First Avenue. **Open** 5.30-10.30pm Tue-Sat. **Main courses** $12. **Credit** Disc, MC, V. **Map** p403 F28 ㊳

Eat, Drink, Shop

All Winston Shih wanted was a makeover on *Queer Eye for the Straight Guy*. After he told the show's producers that he was opening a restaurant with his girlfriend, former *Real Simple* food editor Kay Chun, the Fab Five gave the couple the full treatment. They helped design the space and reworked Shih's wardrobe. The results include a tiny upstairs lounge and a dining room where you can share French-inspired dishes and sip interesting wines. Choose from sage-roasted fresh bacon with lentils and crisp pancetta or pan-roasted black cod in a shallot beurre blanc with flowering chives and French beans.

French

Jules Bistro

65 St Marks Place, between First & Second Avenues (1-212 477 5560). Subway: L to First Avenue. **Open** 11am-4pm, 5pm-1am Mon-Fri; 10am-4pm, 5pm-1am Sat, Sun. **Main courses** $14. **Credit** AmEx. **Map** p403 F28 **39**

Habitués at this chic enclave may have scored high-paying jobs uptown, but they still prefer to play downtown-style. Candles flicker, tables are separated by groovy beaded partitions and the live jazz has a swinging, loungey feel (lively groups like to sit near the bar; quieter diners head for the narrow back room). The kitchen turns out exceedingly good bistro fare: beef stew simmered in red wine or spiced lamb shanks with figs; veal scaloppine comes with gnocchi bathed in gorgonzola and truffle oil.

Indian

Spice Cove

326 E 6th Street, between First & Second Avenues (1-212 674 8884). Subway: F, V to Lower East Side-Second Avenue. **Open** 11.30am-midnight Mon-Fri; 11.30am-12.30am Sat, Sun. **Main courses** $12. **Credit** AmEx, DC, Disc, MC, V. **Map** p403 F28 **40**

Curry Row is looking less rough around the edges, as new restaurants like this one, with snazzy decor and a refined menu, replace the old garish curry houses. Bright orange walls, stone archways and candles provide a seductive setting; St Germain stands in for sitar music; and in place of an all-you-can-eat buffet are chef Muhammed Ahmed Ali's specialities. Expect properly spiced dishes such as chickpeas stir-fried with coriander, cumin and cinnamon and fenugreek-scented Atlantic salmon crowned with tomato masala.

Italian

Aroma

36 E 4th Street, between Bowery & Lafayette Street (1-212 375 0100). Subway: 6 to Astor Place. **Open** 6pm-midnight Tue-Thur; 6pm-2am Fri; 12.30am-3.30pm, 6pm-2am Sat; 12.30am-3.30pm, 6pm-midnight Sun. **Main courses** $18. **Credit** AmEx, DC, MC, V. **Map** p403 F29 **41**

This slender wine bar has been carved out of a former streetwear boutique, and the result is enchanting: raindrop crystal chandeliers hang from the ceiling, olives are laid out single file in porcelain vessels, and a long brick wall displays the Italian wines (including Gragnano, a rare sparkling red). Chef Christopher Daly's dishes are carefully conceived: a duck salad is loaded with lardons, wild chicory and a soft-poached egg. The excellent 'lamb three ways' consists of a tower of braised shoulder, a patty of neck meat, pine nuts, raisins and capers, and a juicy, rosemary-rubbed chop. **Photos** *p179, p186.*

Poetessa

92 Second Avenue, between 5th & 6th Streets (1-212 387 0065). Subway: F, V to Lower East Side-Second Avenue; 6 to Astor Place. **Open** 5-11pm Mon-Thur; 12-4.30pm, 5pm-2am Fri, Sat; 5-10pm Sun. **Main courses** $18. **Credit** AmEx, Disc, MC, V. **Map** p403 F28 **42**

Chef Pippa Calland has been working in the food biz since she was 14, and now she's taken over the East Post space to share what she's learned. The dining room is comfortably familiar – exposed brick walls, wood furniture, ceiling fans. And Calland follows through with flavourful Italian dishes: Parmesan-battered soft-shell crab with courgettes and fresh peas; sizzling home-made pork meatballs; and plenty of hearty pasta dishes.

Mexican

Mercadito

179 Avenue B, between 11th & 12th Streets (1-212 529 6493). Subway: 6 to Astor Place. **Open** 5pm-midnight Mon-Thur; noon-4pm, 5pm-1am Fri; 11.30am-4pm, 5pm-1am Sat; 11.30am-4pm, 5-11pm Sun. **Main courses** $11. **Credit** AmEx, MC, V. **Map** p403 G28 **43**

This Mexican newcomer features wood, tile and stucco from Mexico, a thatched roof inside the dining room and an elaborate hacienda-style courtyard outside. In the kitchen, chef Patricio Sandoval creates dishes inspired by the cuisine of southern Mexico, like smoked mahimahi ceviche, rib-eye steak with cactus salad and tomatillo-avocado chimichurri, plus six kinds of tacos sold by weight. At brunch, breakfast tacos and Mexican sausage are a welcome break from bacon and eggs.

Seafood

Jack's Luxury Oyster Bar

246 E 5th Street, between Second & Third Avenues (1-212 673 0338). Subway: F, V to Lower East Side-Second Avenue; 6 to Astor Place. **Open** 6-11pm Mon-Sat. **Four-course prix fixe** $75. **Credit** AmEx, DC, Disc, MC, V. **Map** p403 F29 **44**

Jack and Grace Lamb, who revealed themselves as obsessively detail-oriented with Jewel Bako, have transformed the first two floors of their romantic Fifth Street townhouse into a doll's house of a restaurant. The real magic unfolds in the tiny upstairs

Buzzworthy

Zak Pelacchio

A few years ago, Pelacchio was cooking with a toaster oven at a beloved but short-lived Williamsburg restaurant, Chickenbone Café. Now he's a headliner chef in the Meatpacking District, running the kitchen at the buzzing townhouse restaurant **5 Ninth** (see p193) and serving soulful, more casual Southeast Asian grub like Malaysian chicken wings and Singaporean chilli crab at **Fatty Crab** (643 Hudson Street, between Horatio & Gansevoort Streets, 1-212 352 3590). If you get a thrill out of seeing culinary superstars in person, you'll have a good chance of spotting Pelacchio in the neighbourhood: he dashes between the two restaurants on foot.

dining room, where a mere dozen or so guests settle in near a fireplace for each night's dinner party, a phenomenal five-course feast by chef Maxime Bilet. On the menu, you might find decadent lobster Newburg or pan-seared halibut in a vermouth-camomile sauce with chive blossoms. **Photo** *p191*.

Mermaid Inn

96 Second Avenue, between 5th & 6th Streets (1-212 674 5870). Subway: F, V to Lower East Side-Second Avenue. **Open** 5.30-11pm Mon-Thur; 11.30pm-midnight Fri, Sat; 5pm-10pm Sun. **Main courses** $20. **Credit** AmEx, DC, Disc, MC, V. **Map** p403 F28 ⓐ
The fabulous, well-stuffed lobster roll, which eschews the usual hot-dog bun for toasted brioche, rivals those at stalwarts like the Pearl Oyster Bar (*see p196*). The menu changes seasonally, but

spaghetti with shrimp, scallops and calamari in a spicy marinara sauce topped with rocket is another constant. Everything's even better in the summer, when you can idle in the pleasant back garden.

Thai

Pukk

71 First Avenue, between 4th & 5th Streets (1-212 253 2740). Subway: F, V to Lower East Side-Second Avenue. **Open** 11am-11pm daily. **Main courses** $7. **Credit** MC, V. **Map** p403 F29 ⓐ
Strip this groovy little hole in the wall of its East Village clientele and you might mistake it for an empty pool: some of the stools and tables are crafted from concrete and small circular tiles (they grow out of the walls like pool steps), and the space basks in a mysterious yellow-green glow. The folks behind Highline and Peep have opened this third spot with a twist: they're cooking only vegetarian Thai dishes. So instead of pork and duck, you'll get your thrills from sweet breaded and fried tofu, seriously spicy tom yum soup, linguine in yellow curry and more.

Vegetarian & Organic

Onju

108 E 4th Street, between First & Second Avenues (1-212 228 3880). Subway: F, V to Lower East Side-Second Avenue. **Open** 5.30-11pm Mon-Thur; 5.30pm-midnight Fri; noon-3.30pm, 3.30pm-midnight Sat, Sun. **Main courses** $18. **Credit** MC, V. **Map** p403 F29 ⓐ
Eating conscientiously is rarely a pleasure. But dinner at Onju is an exception: the menu is 100% organic, dotted with inspired vegan and vegetarian dishes – chanterelle ravioli with tofu cream, or lavender-hued gnocchi made with purple potatoes – but also meaty entrées, such as spaghetti with carbonara sauce and pancetta. PC diners may protest the veal but should note that owner Onju Ha uses fair-trade ingredients, including coffee beans and tropical fruit on the brunch menu.

Venezuelan

Caracas Arepa Bar

91 E 7th Street, at First Avenue (1-212 228 5062). Subway: F, V to Lower East Side-Second Avenue; 6 to Astor Place. **Open** noon-11pm Tue-Sat; noon-10pm Sun. **Arepa** $4. **Credit** AmEx, DC, Disc, MC, V. **Map** p403 F28 ⓐ
This endearing little Venezuelan spot, with flower-patterned, vinyl-covered tables, zaps you straight to South America. The secret is in the home-made arepas: each golden patty is made from scratch daily. The golden pitta-like pockets are stuffed with a choice of 18 fillings, such as chicken and avocado or mushrooms with tofu. The simplest ones, like plain butter or nata (Venezuelan sour cream), are

Eat, Drink, Shop

the best. Top off your snack with a cocada, a thick and creamy milkshake made with freshly grated coconut and cinnamon.

Greenwich Village/Noho

American

Jane
100 W Houston Street, between La Guardia Place & Thompson Street (1-212 254 7000). Subway: C, E to Spring Street; 1 to Houston Street. **Open** 11.30am-midnight Mon-Sat; 11am-11pm Sun. **Main courses** $19. **Credit** AmEx, MC, V. **Map** p403 E29 **49**

One visit, and you too will suffer a Jane's addiction. This popular neighbourhood spot has warm lighting, plush banquette seating and sunny sidewalk tables; they all match well with the good vibe and pleasant menu. A flavourful bouquet of baby rocket, blue cheese and pear is sprinkled with dried cranberries and toasted pumpkin seeds; fluffy pillows of ricotta gnocchi sit in a rich pool of white-truffle and Parmesan sauce. And at brunch, hollandaise-glossed poached eggs top delicious crab and crawfish cakes.

American creative

Blue Hill
75 Washington Place, between Washington Square West & Sixth Avenue (1-212 539 1776). Subway: A, B, C, D, E, F, V to W 4th Street. **Open** 5.30-11pm Mon-Sat; 5.30-10pm Sun. **Main courses** $25. **Credit** AmEx, DC, MC, V. **Map** p403 E28 **50**

This beloved gourmand destination has a knack for scoring the best local produce all year round. Chefs Dan Barber and Michael Anthony succeed so consistently with their dishes because of their solid foundation in classical French cooking. When in season, Blue Hill's strawberries have more berry flavour, and its heirloom tomatoes are juicier, than anyone else's. The poached foie gras, duck breast in beurre blanc, tender roasted chicken and mango sorbet are sublime.

Cafés

Peanut Butter & Co
240 Sullivan Street, between Bleecker & W 3rd Streets (1-212 677 3995). Subway: A, B, C, D, E, F, V to W 4th Street. **Open** 11am-9pm Sun-Thur; 11am-10pm Fri, Sat. **Credit** AmEx, DC, Disc, MC, V. **Map** p403 E29 **51**

To Americans, nothing brings on an attack of 'happy childhood' nostalgia like a peanut-butter sandwich. Every day, the staff at Peanut Butter & Co grinds out a fresh batch of peanut butter, which is used to create gooey mood-pacifiers like the popular Elvis – the King's infamous grilled favourite of peanut butter, banana and honey. Owner Lee Zalben confesses to a weakness for the warm sandwich

of cinnamon-raisin peanut butter, vanilla cream cheese and tart apple slices. Goober-free menu items, like tuna melts and bologna sandwiches, continue the brown-bag theme.

Italian

Il Buco
47 Bond Street, between Lafayette Street & Bowery (1-212 533 1932). Subway: B, D, F, V to Broadway-Lafayette Street; 6 to Bleecker Street. **Open** 6pm-midnight Mon; noon-4pm, 6pm-midnight Tue-Thur; noon-4pm, 6pm-1am Fri, Sat; 5pm-midnight Sun. **Main courses** $28. **Credit** AmEx, MC, V. **Map** p403 F29 **52**

The old-world charm of well-worn communal tables and flickering lamps may help explain why a 12-year-old restaurant is still tough to get into on a Saturday night. Seasonal produce shapes the menu of chef Ed Witt (Daniel, River Café). Dunk the warm country bread in Umbrian olive oils produced exclusively for Il Buco. *Primi* include a thin-crust pizza with fresh porcini, shallots and aged Asturian goat's cheese; entrées include an excellent suckling pig snuggled into warm polenta. Book a table in the candlelit wine cellar – you'll be lent the same inspiration that prompted Edgar Allen Poe to write 'The Cask of Amontillado'.

La Lanterna di Vittorio
129 MacDougal Street, between Third & 4th Streets (1-212 529 5945). **Open** 10am-3am Mon-Thur, Sun; 10am-4am Fri, Sat. **Main courses** $28. **Credit** AmEx, DC, Disc, MC, V. **Map** p403 E29 **53**

Woo your darling by the fire or under the stars at a romantic Village spot that has been helping to smooth the course of true love for 28 years. The 200-year-old garden was once owned by Aaron Burr; its history is heard in the wind rustling through the dense green canopy of apple and cherry trees and the worn walls are strung with ivy. (In wintertime, four fireplaces spark your courting.) Choose a bottle from the extensive wine list to go with light café eats like panini, crostini, smoked duck breast with salad, or thin-crust pizza.

Lupa
170 Thompson Street, between Bleecker & Houston Streets (1-212 982 5089). Subway: A, B, C, D, E, F, V to W 4th Street. **Open** noon-3pm, 5-11.30pm Mon-Fri; 11.30am-2.30pm, 5-11.30pm Sat, Sun. **Main courses** $14. **Credit** AmEx, MC, V. **Map** p403 E29 **54**

Fans of this 'poor man's Babbo' (celeb-chef Mario Batali's pricier restaurant around the corner) keep reclaiming their seats. Here's the ritual they recommend: first, a cutting board of fatty-delicious cured meats like tender prosciutto and spirited coppi. Move on to sublime pasta, like the ricotta gnocchi with sausage and fennel. Then choose a meaty main, like oxtail alla vaccinara or a classic saltimbocca. By the time the panna cotta with apricot arrives, you'll be ready to become a regular, too.

Jack's Luxury Oyster Bar: a doll's house of a restaurant. *See p188.*

Steakhouse

Strip House

13 E 12th Street, between Fifth Avenue & University Place (1-212 328 0000). Subway: L, N, Q, R, W, 4, 5, 6 to 14th Street-Union Square. **Open** 5-11.30pm Mon-Thur; 5pm-midnight Fri, Sat; 5-11pm Sun. **Main courses** $32. **Credit** AmEx, DC, Disc, MC, V. **Map** p403 E28 ⑤⑤

Strip House cultivates a retro-sexy vibe with its suggestive name, red furnishings and vintage pin-ups. But it's still a modern meat shrine flaunting French influences. Executive chef David Walzog makes sure his New York strips arrive at your table still sizzling, seasoned with sea salt and peppercorns – they're a sublime combination of a perfectly charred outside with a luscious rare-red inside. Don't miss the black-truffle creamed spinach, one of several gourmet takes on classic steak sides.

Thai

Prem-On Thai

138 W Houston Street, between Sullivan & MacDougal Streets (1-212 353 2338). Subway: C, E to Spring Street. **Open** noon-11.30pm

Mon-Fri; noon-midnight Sat, Sun. **Main courses** $17. **Credit** AmEx, DC, MC, V. **Map** p403 E29 ⑤⑥

In one of several stylish rooms, you'll watch in awe as dramatically plated Thai dishes and cocktails are carried through the dining room. Prem-On doesn't hold back with the seasoning either: a whole fried sea bass fillet is served upright and loaded with basil and roasted-chilli-paste sauce. Red snapper is smothered with a pineapple and lychee sauce, and pork hand rolls are an impressive trio of towers with a punchy sesame-chilli rice-vinegar sauce.

West Village & Meatpacking District

American

Corner Bistro

331 W 4th Street, at Jane Street (1-212 242 9502). Subway: A, C, E to 14th Street; L to Eighth Avenue. **Open** 11.30am-4am daily. **Burgers** $5. **No credit cards. Map** p403 D28 ⑤⑦

There's only one reason to come to this legendary pub: you'll find one of the city's best burgers – and beer is just $2 a mug (well, that makes two reasons.)

Employees Only. *See p193.*

The patties here are cheap, delish and no-frills, served on a flimsy paper plate. To get your hands on one, you may have to queue for a good hour, especially on weekend nights. Fortunately, the game is on the tube, and a jukebox covers everything from Calexico to Coltrane.

The Place

310 W 4th Street, between Bank & W 12th Streets (1-212 924 2711). Subway: A, C, E to 14th Street; L to Eighth Avenue. **Open** 6-10pm Mon-Wed; 6-10.30pm Thur, Fri; 5.30-10.30pm Sat; 5.30-10pm Sun. **Main courses** $19. **Credit** AmEx, MC, V. **Map** p403 D28 ❻

On a summer evening, a table on the sidewalk terrace of this endearing little West Village restaurant is a perfect place to be. A tiny bar up front lures locals for a glass of wine and small plates such as char-grilled calamari and tiger shrimp with fresh mango salsa. Couples tend to gravitate towards the candlelit back room with low wooden beams and stone walls for more serious dining, which could include the likes of delicately pan-roasted cod with Jersey corn, asparagus and sugar-snap peas in a saffron beurre blanc, or fresh pappardelle with braised duck and baby artichokes.

American regional

RIB

357 West Street, between Leroy & Clarkson Streets (1-212 336 9330). Subway: 1 to Christopher Street-Sheridan Square. **Open** 11am-11pm Mon-Sat; 10am-4.30pm Sun. **Main courses** $15. **Credit** AmEx, MC, V. **Map** p403 D29 ❺

You'll need a few napkins to get through your meal at RIB, set in a 1950s diner car. Three versions of the namesake meaty slabs appear on the menu – including one bathed in a bourbon-molasses sauce. Chef Christopher Remaley prepares corn fritters and other Southern dishes with key indigenous ingredients, like iceberg salad with cracklings and blue cheese made by Clemson students, and peach cobbler with fruit from Chilton County, Alabama.

Chinese

Yumcha

29 Bedford Street, at Downing Street (1-212 524 6800). Subway: A, B, C, D, E, F, V to W 4th Street; 1 to Houston Street. **Open** 6pm-2am Mon-Fri; 11.30am-midnight Sat, Sun. **Main courses** $23. **Credit** AmEx, DC, Disc, MC, V. **Map** p403 D29 ❻

Angelo Sosa, a Jean-Georges protégé, is preparing haute Chinese food in this slick black-and-red dining room with a long open kitchen. Many of the menu items are infused with tea – from smoked chicken to Martinis. Chilli frog legs are properly spicy, and exceptional ginger-lacquered veal cheeks are heartbreakingly tender. Late-nighters can sip green-tea Martinis or green-tea ice cream until 2am from Monday to Friday.

Eclectic

Employees Only

510 Hudson Street, between Christopher & W 10th Streets (1-212 242 3021). Subway: 1 to Christopher Street-Sheridan Square. **Open** 6pm-4am daily. **Main courses** $22. **Credit** AmEx, Disc, MC, V. **Map** p403 C28 ❻

The psychic palm reader in the window is part of the high-concept decor, inspired by the speakeasies of yore. Peek behind the purple curtain in the foyer and you'll see mahogany walls, a working fireplace, a shiny tin ceiling and a collection of vintage cocktail books and bottles – inspiration for co-owner Jason Kosmas's interesting drinks. The 'rustic European' menu features butternut-squash rigatoni and house-cured gravalax. Swing by late at night, and you can nosh on oysters, baked brie and veal goulash until 4am. **Photo** *p192*.

Five Ninth

5 Ninth Avenue, between Gansevoort & Little W 12th Streets (1-212 929 9460). Subway: A, C, E, L to 14th Street. **Open** 5.30pm-midnight Mon-Thur; 5.30pm-1am Fri, Sat; 11am-midnight Sun. **Main courses** $15. **Credit** AmEx, MC, V. **Map** p403 C28 ❻

This spare, brick-walled duplex of dining rooms has a hotter-than-hot location smack dab in the middle of the Meatpacking District. Chef Zak Pelaccio's Asian-inflected instincts are as sharp as ever: thick chips of bacon teeter atop four tiny oysters, each on a spoonful of vivid-green sweet-pea purée. Poached lobster in a ginger beurre blanc and the kobe rib eye in chunky coconut chutney are too good to share. In the summer, sip a cocktail on the peaceful back deck.

Spotted Pig

314 W 11th Street, at Greenwich Street (1-212 620 0393). Subway: A, C, E to 14th Street; L to Eighth Avenue. **Open** noon-2am Mon-Fri; 11am-2am Sat, Sun. **Main courses** $15. **Credit** AmEx, MC, V. **Map** p403 D28 ❻

Brick archways, a pressed-tin ceiling and retro farm-animal pictures make this perpetually jammed two-room pub feel like a piece of England. Most of the beer is brewed in Brooklyn, and the menu, well, it's actually quite Italian, thanks to consultant Mario Batali and chef April Bloomfield, a British import from London's highly regarded, Italian-inspired River Café. The small menu changes daily but always includes Bloomfield's melt-in-your-mouth ricotta gnudi and rich smoked-haddock chowder, as well as a handful of heartier dishes like pork sausages with polenta – a sly spin on bangers and mash.

French

Metropol

234 W 4th Street, at W 10th Street (1-212 206 8393). Subway: 1 to Christopher Street-Sheridan Square. **Open** 5.30pm-3am Mon-Fri; 11am-3am Sat, Sun. **Main courses** $16. **Credit** Disc, MC, V. **Map** p403 C28 ❻

Get your chic on

Last year we saw a brigade of massive, splashy restaurants open, with prices geared towards the expense-account set and enough seats to host a U2 concert. This year, the chic trend continues, but the pretty packages come in all sizes. And lucky for us, the prices are surprisingly low for such high-design spots. If you don't have time for a full meal, we recommend just stopping into the bar for a well-mixed Martini: the show-stopping surroundings will elevate your buzz.

Of all the new chic restaurants this year, the most stunning (and priciest) is **Alto** (520 Madison Avenue, at 53rd Street, 1-212 308 1099). Acclaimed chef Scott Conant, of L'Impero fame, has a jaw-dropping stage for his modern Italian menu: oversized white lampshades hang in the corners, menus are encased in sleek white leather books and the walls of the main dining room double as a dramatically backlit 7,000-bottle wine cellar. At the entrance trees festooned with twinkling lights frame a walkway that incorporates a piece of the Berlin Wall. The food combines Conant's ingenious ingredient pairings with influences from all over Europe: pumpernickel ravioli with porcini filling and sauerkraut, smoked Tasmanian trout with horseradish froth and potato blini, and smoked goose-liver carpaccio with green-tomato mustard, fig vinegar and herbed bread sticks.

Edgy and divey may be the usual style in the Lower East Side, but **Stanton Social** (99 Stanton Street, at Ludlow Street, 1-212 995 0099; pictured) breaks the mould. Gorgeous chandeliers, lizard-skin banquettes and retro rounded booths only hint at the 1940s-inspired elegance of the three-level AvroKo-designed restaurant. The ground floor has a masculine feel, with dark fringe-covered walls and belt-strapped pillows, while the prettier upstairs lounge is dotted with feminine elements like handpainted Japanese floral screens, tea lights and antique hand mirrors. Chef Chris Santos has created 40 shareable, international dishes, all of which receive special treatment. French onion soup comes in dumpling form; Kobe beef burgers and lobster rolls come bite-sized; and red-snapper tacos are covered with an irresistibly fiery mango and avocado salsa.

Nearby on the Lower East Side's restaurant row, **Falai** (68 Clinton Street, between Rivington & Stanton Streets; 1-212 253 1960) is a tiny restaurant that makes a big impression. The precious little spot has just 40 seats and a white-on-white design theme: white walls, white floors, white tables and chairs, and a brigade of tiny white candles that gives the room a soft glow at night. The obsession with white continues in the back garden (open May to October), which feels more like a beach house in the Hamptons than the patio of a tenement. Chef Iacopo Falai, who previously worked as the pastry chef at Le Cirque 2000, prepares everything 'fatto in casa', or 'made in-house' – including bread, chocolate, and pastas like green-pea pappardelle. But desserts are his rightful domain, and the menu divides them between 'classici' (cannoli, zeppole) and 'non-classici' (panna cotta with asparagus foam and balsamic vinaigrette). Falai's recruited a sommelier from Florence's famed Enoteca Pinchiorri to oversee the all-Italian list, featuring – surprise, surprise – ten dessert wines by the glass.

We've heard of secret restaurants before, but we've never seen anything like **La Esquiña** (106 Kenmare Street, at Cleveland Place, 1-646 613 1333), a former cabbie pit stop turned taco stand-speakeasy. It's the first of its kind – and one that's hardly replicable. Serge Becker, who designed Lure Fishbar and owns Joe's Pub, together with restaurant consultant James Gersten, architect Derek Sanders and nightlife promoter Cordell Lochin collaborated to buy the former Corner Deli and transform it into three separate dining and drinking areas. First there's the corner chrome taqueria, reminiscent of a 1970s diner with faux-wood panelled walls, stationary bar stools and a short-order menu of fish tacos and Mexican tortas. Around the corner is the casual 30-seat café, with rough-cut wood walls and shelves stocked with books and old vinyl. Lastly – and most spectacularly – there's a grotto-like basement restaurant and lounge accessible through a door in the taqueria, which is guarded by a woman with a clipboard (you'll have to confirm that you have a reservation to be granted entrance). It's worth the hassle: an underground world of fine tequilas, Mexican tiled murals and an expanded menu that features huitlacoche quesadillas and lump blue-crab tostadas awaits you.

If Edith Piaf and the Cure opened a restaurant, it would probably look like this place, which lends a 1980s rock edge to a worn French bistro. The decor is bistro-plus: black leather banquettes, photos of Edie Sedgwick, giant globe lights and pressed-tin ceilings. A good-looking crowd feasts on moules frites, lobster salad and filet mignon au poivre with long strips of golden fries until 3am.

Italian

Barbuto

775 Washington Street, between Jane & W 12th Streets (1-212 924 9700). Subway: A, C, E to 14th Street; L to Eighth Avenue. **Open** noon-11pm Mon-Fri; noon-midnight Sat; noon-10pm Sun. **Main courses** $18. **Credit** AmEx, Disc, MC, V. **Map** p403 D28 ⊕

For such an industrial-chic space (housed in a former garage), this bright corner restaurant serves surprisingly rustic food. Owner Fabrizio Ferri (who runs the Industria Superstudio complex upstairs) teamed with chef Jonathan Waxman to create a seasonal kitchen anchored by both a brick and a wood oven. Marvellously light calamari comes in lemon-garlic sauce; chitarra all'aia mixes pasta with crushed walnuts, garlic, olive oil and Parmesan; Vermont veal is perfectly fried. In summer, the garage doors go up and a breeze sweeps through the airy dining room.

Gusto Ristorante e Bar Americano

60 Greenwich Avenue, at Perry Street (1-212 924 8000). Subway: 1, 2, 3 to 14th Street. **Open** noon-3pm, 6-11pm Mon-Fri; noon-4pm, 6-11pm Sat, Sun. **Main courses** $23. **Credit** AmEx, DC, Disc, MC, V. **Map** p403 D28 ⊕

This new addition to Greenwich Avenue has no pretence – just simple, tasty Italian food served in an attractive dining room with white tiles, sexy black velvet banquettes and a dramatic Viennese chandelier. Chef Jody Williams shows off what she learned while cooking in Italy: tender grilled octopus, a heap of perfect fritto misto, whole grilled branzino doused with peppery olive oil, and plump, rich gnocchi.

Japanese

EN Japanese Brasserie

435 Hudson Street, at Leroy Street (1-212 647 9196). Subway: 1 to Houston Street. **Open** 5pm-2am Mon-Sat; 5pm-midnight Sun. **Main courses** $15. **Credit** AmEx, DC, Disc, MC, V. **Map** p403 D29 ⊕

On the main floor of the multi-level space, Bunkei and Reika Yo have built tatami-style rooms; on the mezzanine level, they've recreated the living room, dining room and library of a Japanese home from the Meiji era (1868-1912). Chef Koji Nakano runs with the theme by offering handmade miso paste, tofu and yuba (soy-milk skin) in dishes like Berkshire pork belly braised in sansho miso; foie gras and poached daikon steak with white miso vinegar.

Seafood

Pearl Oyster Bar

18 Cornelia Street, between Bleecker & W 4th Streets (1-212 691 8211). Subway: A, B, C, D, E, F, V to W 4th Street. **Open** noon-2.30pm, 6-11pm Mon-Fri; 6-11pm Sat. **Main courses** $22. **Credit** MC, V. **Map** p403 D29 ⊕

Thanks to a recently added dining room, Pearl is now twice its original size. But you'll still have to queue to enjoy chef Rebecca Charles's straightforward New England-style seafood. The gussied-up lobster roll – with chunky lobster salad spilling out of a toasted, butter-drenched hot-dog bun – is her signature dish. Other fishy favourites include fresh steamers, clam chowder accented with smoky bacon, pan-roasted oysters and boiled or grilled whole lobster.

Chelsea

American

Empire Diner

210 Tenth Avenue, at 22nd Street (1-212 243 2736). Subway: C, E to 23rd Street. **Open** 24hrs daily. **Main courses** $13. **Credit** Disc, MC, V. **Map** p404 C26 ⊕

It's 3am and you're hungry – do you know where your middle-of-the-night grub is? This Fodero-style diner is the answer for those who find themselves in Chelsea and in need of sustenance. It looks like a

EN Japanese Brasserie.

Tax & tipping

Most New York restaurants don't add a
service charge to the bill unless there are
six or more people in your party. So it's
customary to give 15 to 20 per cent of the
total bill as a tip. The easiest way to figure
out the amount is to double the 8.625 per
cent sales tax. Complain – preferably to a
manager – if you feel the service is under
par, but only in the most extreme cases
should you completely withhold a tip.
Remember that servers are paid far below
minimum wage and rely on tips to pay the
rent. Bartenders get tipped, too; $1 a drink
should ensure friendly pours until last call.

classic – gleaming stainless-steel walls and rotating
stools – but few other hash houses have candlelight,
sidewalk café tables and a pianist playing dinner
music. Fewer still attempt dishes such as sesame
noodles with chicken, and linguine with smoked
salmon, watercress and garlic. The more standard
platters are terrific – like massive omelettes and a
juicy blue-cheese steak burger.

Red Cat

*227 Tenth Avenue, between 23rd & 24th Streets
(1-212 242 1122). Subway: C, E to 23rd Street.*
Open 5.30-11pm Mon-Thur; 5.30pm-midnight
Fri, Sat; 5-10pm Sun. **Main courses** $21. **Credit**
AmEx, DC, MC, V. **Map** p404 C26 ⑩
Art-world luminaries and London Terrace residents descend on this comfortable, reliable, handsome eaterie, which is done out with red walls
and crisp white tablecloths. Although the kitchen
gives almost every dish an intriguing twist, do not
attempt to eat lightly here. The Red Cat specialises
in all that's hearty: gargantuan pork chops,
Parmesan-covered french fries, extra-juicy shell
steak, along with big-time sweets like banana splits
and apple tarts.

American creative

Bette

*461 W 23rd Street, at Tenth Avenue (1-212 366
0404). Subway: C, E to 23rd Street.* **Open** 6-11.30pm
Mon-Sat. **Main courses** $25. **Credit** AmEx, MC, V.
Map p404 C21 ⑪
Amy Sacco, the beauty and brains behind Bungalow
8 and Lot 61, has opened a serious restaurant in
Chelsea. The space is relatively small, but tastefully
decorated with designer touches: art by Richard
Phillips and stemware from Lalique. Executive chef
Tom Dimarzo – a Jean-Georges protégé – serves
lofty fare like lobster gazpacho and seared tuna with
basil, capers and tapenade. **Photo** *p205.*

Cafés

Wild Lily Tea Room

*511 W 22nd Street, between Tenth & Eleventh
Avenues (1-212 691 2258). Subway: C, E to 23rd
Street.* **Open** noon-9pm Tue-Sun. **Main courses**
$11. **Credit** AmEx, MC, V. **Map** p404 C26 ⑫
Goldfish swim among floating candles in a round
stone pool at the front of this spare, peaceful tri-level
space. The food is precious pan-Asian and often
incorporates tea: black sticky-rice risotto with mas-
carpone cheese shares space with steamed turbot
and shiitake mushrooms in a slightly sweet jasmine-
tea broth; a shrimp salad is delicately flavoured with
a lavender-mint dressing. The $25 tasting of five
carefully chosen, well-described sakés is a bargain.

Eclectic

Biltmore Room

*290 Eighth Avenue, between 24th & 25th Streets
(1-212 807 0111). Subway: C, E to 23rd Street.*
Open 5.30-10.30pm Mon-Thur; 5.30-11.30pm Fri,
Sat; 5.30-10pm Sun. **Main courses** $28. **Credit**
AmEx, DC, MC, V. **Map** p404 D26 ⑬
Named after a legendary hotel, the Biltmore Room
lives up to the swank implicit in its name. The dining room shimmers with crystal chandeliers, mirrors, brass doors, and marble floors and columns.
The Asian-influenced dishes combine bold and brac-
ing flavours: Goan-spiced rack of lamb, giant
prawns wrapped in crispy noodles and Indian-
spiced Alaskan salmon.

Italian

La Bottega

*Maritime Hotel, 88 Ninth Avenue, at 17th Street
(1-212 243 8400). Subway: A, C, E to 14th Street;
L to Eighth Avenue.* **Open** 7-11.30am, 5pm-1am
Mon, Tue; 7-11.30am, 5pm-2am Wed, Thur; 7-
11.30am, 5pm-3am Fri; 11am-4pm, 5pm-3am Sat;
11am-4pm, 5pm-1am Sun. **Main courses** $18.
Credit AmEx, DC, Disc, MC, V. **Map** p403 C27 ⑭
Given how popular this place is – especially during
summer, when the vast lantern-lit terrace is jammed
with a fashionable Euro crowd – the reasonably
priced chow is much better than it needs to be. La
Bottega has the classic trattoria mix: pasta, meat,
fish and pizzas. Truffle oil is liberally sprinkled on
starters, from a wet, tangy version of beef carpaccio
to a tower of shredded artichoke.

Pan-Asian

Rickshaw Dumpling Bar

*61 W 23rd Street, between Fifth & Sixth Avenues
(1-212 924 9220). Subway: F, N, R, V, W to 23rd
Street.* **Open** 11.30am-9.30pm Mon-Sat; 11.30am-
8.30pm Sun. **Dumplings** $5 (6). **Credit** AmEx, MC,
V. **Map** p404 E26 ⑮

Annisa chef Anita Lo has designed a simple menu consisting of six different dumplings, each inspired by an Asian cuisine and matched with its own dipping sauce: classic Chinese pork and chive with a soy vinegar, for instance, or Thai chicken with peanut satay. If you're hungry enough for a full meal, you can pair your dumplings with a big bowl of noodle soup, then top it all off with a green-tea milkshake or a dessert dumpling of molten chocolate in a mochi wrapper.

Sapa

43 W 24th Street, between Broadway & Sixth Avenue (1-212 929 1800). Subway F, N, R, V, W to 23rd Street. **Open** 5.30-11.00pm Mon-Thur; 5.30-11.30am Fri, Sat; 5.30-10.30pm Sun. **Main courses** $24. **Credit** AmEx, Disc, MC, V. **Map** p404 E26 ⑯

This savvy AvroKo-designed dining room is a perfect setting for inventive cocktails like a yellow-tomato version of a Bloody Mary, and a French-Vietnamese menu by chef Patricia Yeo. Sapa's roll bar serves variations on spring and summer rolls, including ones with raw wild salmon and cucumber, or foie gras and duck. Among the adventurous main dishes are cider-braised monkfish, and scallops marinated in cane sugar.

Spanish

Tia Pol

205 Tenth Avenue, between 22nd & 23rd Streets (1-212 675 8805). Subway: C, E to 23rd Street. **Open** noon-3pm, 5pm-midnight Mon-Thur; noon-3pm, 5pm-1am Fri, Sat; 11am-3pm, 6pm-midnight Sun. **Small plate** $7. **Credit** AmEx, MC, V. **Map** p404 C26 ⑰

This tiny tapas restaurant keeps things simple with traditional tapas like sautéed cockles and razor clams. Other dishes showcase unlikely combinations: tomato-covered bread with lima-bean purée and chorizo and chocolate on bread rounds. The all-Spanish wine list is well priced, with selections that pair well with the spicy food.

Gramercy & Flatiron

American creative

Craftbar

900 Broadway, at 20th Street (1-212 461 4300). Subway: N, R, W, 6 to 23rd Street. **Open** noon-11pm Mon-Thur, Sun; noon-midnight Fri, Sat. **Main courses** $25. **Credit** AmEx, DC, Disc, MC, V. **Map** p403 E27 ⑱

Tom Colicchio's flashy spin-off of his upscale restaurant Craft recently moved to a bigger and brighter space around the corner from the original Craftbar. The dining room is still positively raucous, and the busy bar is jammed with chatty, wine-swigging groups. Appetisers rate highest, especially a lavish platter of Italian, Spanish and house-cured meats

and the addictive pork-stuffed sage leaves. Desserts like chocolate pot de crème and steamed lemon pudding are sheer heaven.

Other locations: Craft, 43 E 19th Street, between Broadway & Park Avenue South (1-212 780 0880); 'wichcraft, 49 E 19th Street, between Broadway & Park Avenue South (1-212 780 0577).

Eclectic

Komegashi

928 Broadway, between 21st & 22nd Streets (1-212 475 3000). Subway: F, V, R, W to 23rd Street. **Open** 11.30am-11pm Mon-Fri; 5.30-10.30pm Sat. **Main courses** $17. **Credit** AmEx, MC, V. **Map** p404 E26 ⑲

This jazzy, modern 4,000sq ft fusion restaurant features a long sushi counter, cabana-like booths and tilework that incorporates the Komegashi restaurant logo. Atsushi Yokota (who has worked at Sono, Brasserie 360 and Atelier) merges Japanese and French cooking with dishes such as a frothy miso cappuccino, terrine of foie gras and teriyaki chicken, and other hybrids – all of which are as interesting as they are flavourful.

French

Le Express

249 Park Avenue South, at 20th Street (1-212 254 5858). Subway: 6 to 23rd Street. **Open** 24hrs daily. **Main courses** $13. **Credit** AmEx, MC, V. **Map** p403 E27 ⑳

It's 3am and, if you want to dodge that hangover, you'd better eat something. So why not consider this bustling bistro, which stays open 24 hours a day, seven days a week? You are likely to find it as crowded in the wee hours as it is at 8pm. Bistro standards like steak au poivre, seared tuna steak, along with monkfish and chorizo brochettes, are satisfying at any hour.

Indian

Dévi

8 E 18th Street, at Fifth Avenue (1-212 691 1300). Subway: N, R, W, 6 to 23rd Street. **Open** noon-2.30pm, 5.30-10.30pm Mon-Thur; noon-2.30pm, 5.30-11pm Fri, Sat; 5.30-10.30pm Sun. **Main courses** $21. **Credit** AmEx, Disc, MC, V. **Map** p403 E27 ㉛

Dangling from the ceiling like clusters of shiny hard candies, ornate multicoloured lanterns cast a warm glow over diners, who are surrounded by gauzy saffron draperies in the bi-level dining room. Start your evening with a citrusy Dévi Fizz cocktail, nibble some crisp samosas, then pamper yourself with inspired Indian dishes like velvety yam dumplings in a spiced tomato gravy; stuffed baby aubergine bathed in spicy peanut sauce; or moist chunks of chicken with pistachios, cilantro (coriander) and green chillies.

Vegetative state

This tough-talking, hot-dog-chomping city has become increasingly veg-friendly in the last few years. And instead of a blissed-out, ponytailed dude slopping houmous behind a counter, many of the new and stylish destinations come with pedigreed celeb chefs and organic-wine lists.

At **Pure Food & Wine** (54 Irving Place, between 17th & 18th Streets, 1-212 477 1010), the city's first upscale raw eatery, chefs Matthew Kenny and Sarma Melngailis create standout uncooked dishes like ginger-spiked avocado rolls and lasagna layered with basil-pistachio pesto. On Tuesday nights, the East Village's chic little **Counter** (105 First Avenue, between 6th & 7th Streets, 1-212 982 5870) goes raw, with chef Michele Thorne whipping up special tasting menus. On other evenings, the kitchen turns out a

delectable mix of raw and cooked items. Much of the produce used is grown in the owners' rooftop garden, and the wine list is strictly organic.

A stand-out among the interchangeable Indian restaurants in Curry Hill, **Saravanaas** (81 Lexington Avenue, at 26th Street, 1-212 679 0204) is no typical steam-table-buffet joint. At this first US outpost of a popular South Indian chain, six chefs make everything to order, including two-foot long dosas, spicy rice dishes and house-made breads.

Candle 79 (154 E 79th Street, at Lexington Avenue, 1-212 537 7179) dishes up its elegant, globally inspired vegetarian fare in an earth-toned duplex with cushy mocha-toned banquettes. The menu offers spiced edamame, porcini stroganoff and dark chocolate cake with peanut-butter mousse.

Spanish

Casa Mono/Bar Jamón

Casa Mono, 52 Irving Place, at 17th Street; Bar Jamón, 125 E 17th Street at Irving Place (1-212 253 2773). Subway: L to Third Avenue; N, Q, R, W, 4, 5, 6 to 14th Street-Union Square. **Open** *Casa Mono* noon-midnight daily. *Bar Jamón* 5pm-2am Mon-Fri; noon-2am Sat, Sun. **Small plate** $9. **Credit** AmEx, MC, V. **Map** p403 F27 ⊕

Part of Mario Batali's ever-expanding restaurant spread, this busy and tiny tapas restaurant (Bar

Jamón is the equally teeny wine bar around the corner) specialises in making 'difficult' meats irresistible. Fried sweetbreads in a nutty batter, oxtail-stuffed piquillo peppers, baby squid with plump white beans, tripe with sausage: it's all good, especially with a glass of wine or sherry from the extensive Iberian-focused list.

Vegetarian & organic

Pure Food & Wine

See above **Vegetative state**. **Map** p403 F27 ⊕

Midtown

Midtown West

American

Burger Joint

Le Parker Meridien Hotel, 119 W 56th Street, between Sixth & Seventh Avenues (1-212 245 5000). Subway: F, N, Q, R, W to 57th Street. **Open** 11am-11pm Mon-Sat. **Burgers** $5. **No credit cards. Map** p405 D22 ❷❹
Kitsch and chichi mingle at this tiny, hidden spot in the posh Parker Meridien. It's a perfectly recreated burger emporium circa 1972, down to the 'wood' panelling, vinyl booths and Def Leppard posters. The burgers are picture-perfect too – juicy and flavourful, with an excellent char. Fries and thick, creamy shakes round out the deal.

Market Café

496 Ninth Avenue, between 37th & 38th Streets (1-212 967 3892). Subway: C, E to 34th Street. **Open** 11am-11pm daily. **Empanada** $2. **No credit cards. Map** p404 C24 ❻❺
Market has been a beacon in the gritty shadow of Port Authority for ten years now. Park yourself at one of the gleaming Formica tables and prepare to eat downright delicious seasonal food, and plenty of it. First courses are the secret weapon: home-made gnocchi are bathed in chunky tomato sauce with peas, ham and fresh ricotta; plump seared scallops sit on a bed of whipped potatoes drizzled with brown butter; and some of the best houmous in town comes with triangles of char-grilled flatbread.

American creative

Bar Room at Modern

9 W 53rd Street, between Fifth & Sixth Avenues (1-212 333 1220). Subway: E, V to Fifth Avenue-53rd Street. **Open** noon-2.15pm, 6-9.30pm Mon-Thur; noon-2.15pm, 5.30-10.30pm Fri; 5.30-10.30pm Sat. **Small plate** $12. AmEx, DC, Disc, MC, V. **Map** p404 E23 ❻❻
The main culinary attraction at the new MoMA opened a little after the museum, but to fans of chef Gabriel Kreuther, the Modern was worth the wait. Those who can't afford to drop a pay cheque at the formal dining room should drop into the equally stunning and less pricey bar room (which shares the same kitchen). Standouts include Arctic char tartare and sweetbread ravioli in a balsamic-sage sauce.

American regional

Bar Americain

152 W 52nd Street, between Sixth & Seventh Avenues (1-212 265 9700). Subway: 1 to 50th Street; N, R to 49th Street. **Open** noon-11pm daily. **Main courses** $28. **Credit** AmEx, DC, Disc, MC, V. **Map** p404 D23 ❻❼

Bobby Flay, the high-spirited, redheaded grill guy from the Food Network, opened this flashy eaterie in April 2005, 14 years after he opened his last NYC restaurant, Mesa Grill. The menu is a good ol' boy's take on a traditional European brasserie: rack of pork comes with apple-ginger chutney, creamed corn and sour mash; barbecued lamb gets hominy flecked with yellow peppers. While you're waiting for a table, you can take a seat at the bar and sip one of 50 classic cocktails.

Argentine

Mama Empanada

763 Ninth Avenue, at 51st Street (1-212 698 9008). Subway: C, E to 50th Street. **Open** 9am-midnight daily. **Empanada** $2. **Credit** MC, V. **Map** p404 C23 ❻❽
This vibrant South American spot serves 40 varieties of empanadas. Fillings range from traditional (mozzarella in a corn-flour empanada) to more creative versions like Cuban and cheese steak. The Elvis comes with peanut butter and bananas, and the Viagra with prawns, crab and scallops.

French

Marseille

630 Ninth Avenue, at 44th Street (1-212 333 3410). Subway: A, C, E to 42nd Street-Port Authority. **Open** noon-3pm, 5.15-11.30pm Mon-Fri; 11am-3pm, 5.15-11.30pm Sat; 11am-3pm, 5.15-10pm Sun. **Main courses** $23. **Credit** AmEx, MC, V. **Map** p404 C24 ❻❾
This bustling corner restaurant with floor-to-ceiling windows, proscenium arches, a weathered bar and damask wallpaper will instantly transport you to the notorious port city. While chef Alex Urena's version of bouillabaisse is not textbook, it is undeniably tasty: haddock, skate, cod and mussels are cooked separately, then added to a light broth with a generous dose of garlic. Sipping and snacking are encouraged in the bustling bar: you can order every meze on the menu for only $24.

Seppi's

123 W 56th Street, between Sixth & Seventh Avenues (1-212 708 7444). Subway: F, N, Q, R, W to 57th Street. **Open** noon-2am Mon-Sat; 10.30am-2am Sun. **Main courses** $21. **Credit** AmEx, DC, Disc, MC, V. **Map** p405 D22 ❾❶
We can't decide what we like best about this classic French bistro: the decor is spot on (black-and-white booths, pressed-tin ceilings); the hours are rare for midtown (order until 2am nightly); the steak au poivre is properly peppery; and then there's Bob Baxter, an 85-year-old suspenders-sportin' magician who stops by your table late at night. Chocoholics come on Sundays to indulge in the divine $24 prix-fixe chocolat brunch, which starts with a chocolate mimosa and follows with a buffet of chocolate delicacies.

Italian

Abboccato

*138 W 55th Street, between Sixth & Seventh Avenues
(1-212 265 4000). Subway: F, N, Q, R, W to 57th
Street.* **Open** 6.30-10.30am, noon-3pm, 5.30-10pm
Mon; 6.30-10.30am, noon-3pm, 5.30-11pm Tue-Thur;
6.30-10.30am, noon-3pm, 5.30-midnight Fri, Sat; 6.30-
10.30am, noon-10pm Sun. **Main courses** $28. **Credit**
AmEx, DC, Disc, MC, V. **Map** p405 D22 **91**

Buzzworthy

Josh DeChellis

In his breakout role at the West Village
restaurant Sumile, DeChellis thrilled critics
and food enthusiasts with his truly daring,
truly delicious take on Japanese-themed
cuisine. While other restaurants were
jumping on the trend of serving overpriced
Texas Kobe beef and gimmicky sushi rolls,
DeChellis was topping daikon with tea-
smoked eel, stocking ethereal custards
with snails and serving headcheese
with duck tongue. Now the gutsy chef is
putting the same inspired touch on Italian
cuisine at his brand new Upper East Side
restaurant, Jovia (135 E 62nd Street,
at Lexington Avenue, phone number
unvailable at press time). It's a much
bigger stage for DeChellis, and,
considering his recurring role on the
Discovery Channel's goofy cooking
show, *Go Ahead, Make My Dinner*,
a much more fitting one, too.

Each dish at Jim Botsacos' new Sinatra-esque restaurant (low ceilings, circular leather banquettes) is
associated with a region of Italy: there's Umbrian-
style quail, and octopus with Sicilian oregano.
Carbonara subs in flavourful duck eggs for a richer
sauce. His vaniglia e cioccolato, meanwhile, combines
two classic dishes into one: vanilla-scented veal
cheeks and wild boar stewed in red wine, spices and
chocolate. It's dinner and dessert rolled into one.

Japanese

Koi

*Bryant Park Hotel, 40 W 40th Street, between Fifth
& Sixth Avenues (1-212 642 2100). Subway: B, D,
F, V to 42nd Street-Bryant Park; 7 to Fifth Avenue.*
Open noon-2.30pm, 6-10pm Mon, Sun; noon-2.30pm,
5.30-11pm Tue-Sat. **Main courses** $23. **Credit**
AmEx, Disc, MC, V. **Map** p404 E24 **92**
The newly opened Koi is a spin-off of the sceney LA
Japanese restaurant. The decor embodies the four
elements of feng shui: earth (bamboo stalks), wind
(a ceiling installation modelled after a fluttering fish-
net), fire (chandeliers of amber glass) and water (a
fountain at the entrance). Chef Sal Sprufero, who
worked at Ilo, put his own spin on Koi's menu,
adding a white asparagus salad with crab, osetra
and watercress pesto, rock shrimp tempura and
duck breast with green-tea soba. **Photo** *p206.*

Nobu 57

*40 W 57th Street, between Fifth & Sixth Avenues
(1-212 757 3000). Subway: F to 57th Street; N, R,
W to Fifth Avenue-59th Street.* **Open** 11.45am-
2.15pm, 5.45-10.15pm Mon-Fri; 5.45-10.15pm Sat,
Sun. **Main courses** $23. **Sushi roll** $6. **Credit**
AmEx, DC, Disc, MC, V. **Map** p405 E22 **93**
Tables at this soaring new midtown location of the
venerable Tribeca mothership are just as hard to
come by any night of the week. Chef Nobu
Matsuhisa continues his sushi revolution with
paper-thin slices of seared fish with a hint of yuzu.
The salmon-skin roll is as stellar as its reputation:
slices of cucumber enfold salty salmon skin and bits
of fish along with avocado, pickled burdock, shiso
and rice so fresh it has a translucent sheen. A heap-
ing bowl of rock-shrimp tempura with ponzu or
Nobu's special creamy, spicy dipping sauce proves
irresistible. If you can't get a table here, you can
always try your luck at the downtown Next Door
Nobu, the no-reservations sibling (105 Hudson
Street, at Franklin Street, 1-212 334 4445).

Thai

Breeze

*661 Ninth Avenue, between 45th & 46th Streets
(1-212 262 7770). Subway: A, C, E to 42nd Street/
Port Authority.* **Open** 11.30am-11.30pm Mon-Wed;
11.30am-12.30am Thur, Fri; 10.30am-12.30am Sat;
10.30am-11.30pm Sun. **Main courses** $17. **Credit**
AmEx, DC, MC, V. **Map** p404 C23 **94**

BBQ nation

The city's latest batch of barbecue joints has got the country covered.

Like politics and religion, barbecue is not a topic for polite discussion. The great debates will never end: vinegar or no vinegar? Memphis or Kansas City? Chopped pork or pulled? Anyone who doubts the passion New Yorkers have for regional barbecue need only visit the myriad barbecue joints that have opened here. Each spot has its own style and regional influence, so we've put together a tasting map to the city's best 'cue. We'll get out of the way of the sauce-slinging and leave the final verdict, on which region rules, to you.

Kansas City

Speciality: Fatty spare ribs slathered with sweet, tomatoey sauce; and burned ends (well-done pieces of brisket). **Get the goods**: At **Spankys BBQ** (127 W 43rd Street, between Broadway & Sixth Avenue, 1-212 575 5848) you'll find spare ribs with streaks of fat and a sweet, tangy sauce.

Texas

Speciality: Cowboy-sized beef ribs and brisket. Texans let the smoke impart most of the flavour, adding a light dusting of salt, pepper and chilli powder on the meat. The meat is often defined by a red ring near the surface, the product of barbecue cooked over raw wood. **Get the goods**: **Rangers Texas Barbecue** (Legends, 71-04 35th Avenue, at 71st Street, Jackson Heights, Queens; 1-718 779 6948) serves lightly seasoned, quality beef ribs – just the kind of chewy, smoky meat that Texans love.

Memphis

Speciality: Lean baby back ribs, served one of two ways: dry-rubbed ribs seasoned with salts, hot pepper and other spices, or wet ones made with thick tomatoey sauces. **Get the goods**: **Smoked** (103 Second Avenue, at 6th Street, 1-212 388 0388) doesn't stake claim on a particular region, but Southern chef Kenneth Collins's hybrid style captures the Memphis spirit. The smoky meat barely clings to the bone and is slathered with a thick, just-sweet-enough tomato-based sauce.

Eastern North Carolina

Speciality: Pulled pork from the whole pig (ideally cooked 15-18 hours over wood) with a strict no-tomato policy – just tangy, peppery vinegar sauce.

Get the goods: **Bar BQ** (689 Sixth Avenue, at 20th Street, Park Slope, Brooklyn, 1-718 499 4872). The flavourful, freshly pulled pig meat is served in sandwiches or in paper containers.

Manhattan

Speciality: OK, we're not exactly known for barbecue, but we kick ass with our pastrami.

Get the goods: For all the hype over **RUB** (208 W 23rd Street, between Seventh & Eighth Avenues, 1-212 524 4300), it's shocking that the best piece of meat in the house is the pastrami. The moist, smoked version is extraordinary and beats the heck out of the brisket.

Western North Carolina

Speciality: Pulled pork with a tomatoey vinegar sauce.

Get the goods: **Bone Lick Park** (75 Greenwich Avenue, at Seventh Avenue South, 1-212 647 9600). The pork is delicious, cooked for 14 hours over apple, hickory and cherry wood. But purists might take issue; the house sauce is tomatoey and laced with roasted fresh poblano and chipotle peppers.

South Carolina

Speciality: Pulled pork with a slight mustard tinge.

Get the goods: None of the new spots serve this variety; however, **Daisy May's** (623 Eleventh Avenue, at 46th Street, 1-212 977 1500) has it (Adam Perry Lang mixes up a mean mustard-based sauce with molasses and vinegar for his pulled pork.

Breeze sails past the other Thai contenders with tangerine walls, triangular mirrors, a long backlit bar and a menu – printed on old 45s and CD cases – that doesn't stick to tradition. Chef Jeff Hardinger melds haute French techniques with Thai ingredients, and the outcome is spellbinding: fried mushroom dumplings cradle wild mushrooms and caramelised onions in a soy-black truffle foam; succulent braised short ribs appear in a cinnamon-anise broth with celery hearts and fresh rice noodles.

Midtown East

American

PS 450

450 Park Avenue South, between 30th & 31st Streets (1-212 532 7474). Subway: 6 to 33rd Street. **Open** *11.30am-4am daily.* **Main courses** *$15.* **Credit** *AmEx, MC, V.* **Map** *p404 E25* ⓰
This is what happens when a distinctly unsexy, quiet neighbourhood gets a big new playground: the place is packed. An admirable selection of finger food pairs nicely with cocktails, including tasty duck-confit taquitos with tomatillo and pear salsa, tender pulled-pork sliders, and satisfying entrées such as a wood-grilled hangar steak sliced over chorizo hash with lobster butter. Chef Dominic Giuliano's food is better than what you'd find at most lounges and clubs – just don't plan on enjoying a quiet meal.

Cafés

Penelope

159 Lexington Avenue, at 30th Street (1-212 481 3800). Subway: 6 to 28th Street. **Open** *8am-11pm daily.* **Main courses** *$9.* **No credit cards.** **Map** *p404 F25* ⓰
This pretty little café and wine bar is the last thing you'd expect to find in Curry Hill, with its generic hot-table curry houses. The kitchen here cranks out dishes with care: creamy houmous with toast, chicken potpies and a terrific grilled cheese are just a few of the homespun dishes. The soup of the day is listed on a chalkboard and is served with chunks of good, earthy bread; the skins are left on the hand-cut french fries.

Egyptian

Casa La Femme North

1076 First Avenue, between 58th & 59th Streets (1-212 505 0005). Subway: N, R, W to Lexington Avenue-59th Street; 4, 5, 6 to 59th Street. **Open** *5pm-midnight Mon-Thur, Sun; 5pm-3am Fri, Sat.* **Main courses** *$21.* **Credit** *AmEx, MC, V.* **Map** *p405 F22* ⓰
North isn't a new branch but the relocation of Soho's long-standing seduction spot, along with its flashy belly dancers and fabric-partitioned, pillow-backed

kissing tents. The multi-course prix fixe ($55) commences promisingly with thick, peppery houmous. Next, savour crabmeat and pine-nut kofta, an Arabic crab cake. Samek fil forne, a sweet, moist oven-roasted snapper, is worth the $5 entrée supplement it carries. Optional: a go at the ornate hookah the waiter plants on your table.

French

Artisanal

2 Park Avenue, at 32nd Street (1-212 725 8585). Subway: E, V to Lexington Avenue-53rd Street; 6 to 51st Street. **Open** *noon-11pm Mon-Thur; noon-midnight Fri, Sat; 11am-10pm Sun.* **Main courses** *$28.* **Credit** *AmEx, DC, Disc, MC, V.* **Map** *p404 E25* ⓰
At Artisanal, 250 varieties of cheese are displayed as if they were prize orchids (cheese is big and getting bigger in this town). Chef-owner Terrance Brennan nods to Alsace with his boudin blanc, rillettes and rabbit in riesling with shredded-rutabaga sauerkraut. Crisp skate takes to its blood-orange sauce like a party girl to a Cosmo. Still, Artisanal is really the place to discover just how much cheese you can really handle. An appetiser of raclette? A basket of puffy gougères? Or how about a cheese plate for dessert?

Brasserie

100 E 53rd Street, between Park & Lexington Avenues (1-212 751 4840). Subway: 6 to 33rd Street. **Open** *7am-midnight Mon-Thur; 7am-1am Fri; 11am-1am Sat; 11am-10pm Sun.* **Main courses** *$23.* **Credit** *AmEx, Disc, DC, MC, V.* **Map** *p404 E23* ⓰
The trouble with cutting-edge design is that it soon becomes passé. Such is the case with Brasserie's high-concept interior. The curved pear-wood ceiling and plush booths still look coolly modern, but the monitors above the bar, displaying blurry photos of entering diners, now seem little more than senseless techno-fiddling. So it's a good thing that the food holds its own. Old-school French classics (steak-frites, escargots) never go out of style, and mix well with more inventive dishes, like an appetiser of tuna tartare with mango-chilli marmalade. The days when Brasserie stayed open all night are long gone, but at least it still serves food after most of the neighbourhood has shut down. *See also p220*, for Brasserie's popular bar.

Mexican

Pampano

209 E 49th Street, between Second & Third Avenues (1-212 751-4545). Subway: E, V to Lexington Avenue-53rd Street; 6 to 51st Street. **Open** *11.30am-3pm, 5-10pm Mon-Wed; 11.30am-3pm, 5-11pm Thur, Fri; 5-11pm Sat; 5-9.30pm Sun.* **Main courses** *$23.* **Credit** *AmEx, MC, V.* **Map** *p404 F23* ⓰

Bette: small space, serious food. *See p197.*

Maya's Richard Sandoval is one of the city's most creative Mexican chefs, and this classy seafood outpost is a midtown favourite. Mini lobster tacos taste as if the tender meat and fresh tortillas had been grilled beachside; striped bass is carefully steamed in a banana leaf, with plantain and bell pepper.

Pan-Asian

Tao
42 E 58th Street, between Madison & Park Avenues (1-212 888 2288). Subway: N, R, W to Fifth Avenue-59th Street. **Open** 11.30am-midnight Mon, Tue; 11.30am-1am Wed-Fri; 5pm-1am Sat; 5pm-midnight Sun. **Main courses** $22. **Credit** AmEx, DC, MC, V. **Map** p405 E22

A magnificent, scenic palace, Tao is packed with glowing Chinese lanterns, wealthy businesspeople, trendy Manhattanites and intrepid tourists. The bar (*see p221*) is always thronged, and the stunning dining room has an over-the-top Far Eastern vibe, thanks to curly bamboo, Asian art and a 16ft stone Buddha. The menu offers generic small plates (dumplings, satay) and decent entrées. Tao is one of New York's first restaurants to serve Kobe beef, and it's worth ponying up for the buttery pleasure of a few ounces, which you cook at your table on a hot stone.

Steakhouse

BLT Steak
106 E 57th Street, between Park & Lexington Avenues (1-212 752 7470). Subway: N, R, W to Lexington Avenue-59th Street; 4, 5, 6 to 59th Street. **Open** 11.45am-2.30pm, 5.30-11pm Mon-Thur; 11.45am-2.30pm, 5.30-11.30pm Fri; 5.30-11.30pm Sat. **Main courses** $32. **Credit** AmEx, DC, Disc, MC, V. **Map** p405 E22

BLT (Bistro Laurent Tourondel) Steak is an interpretation of an American steakhouse, in an elegant room with ebony tables and walnut floors. There's Caesar salad or shrimp cocktail to start, or trust Tourondel's whims and try beef carpaccio with lemon and rocket, or tuna tartare with soy-lime dressing. The meats are marvellous, if modest – only the 40oz porterhouse for two was really humungous – but no one can complain about the selection of sides: eight takes on potato; ten additional vegetables and starches (don't miss the heavenly onion rings).

Uptown

Upper West Side

American creative

@SQC
270 Columbus Avenue, between 72nd & 73rd Streets (1-212 579 0100). Subway: B, C, 1, 2, 3 to 72nd Street. **Open** 11.30am-11pm Mon-Thur; 11.30am-midnight Fri; 10am-midnight Sat; 10am-11pm Sun. **Main courses** $22. **Credit** AmEx, DC, Disc, MC, V. **Map** p405 C20

Chef-owner Scott Campbell likes to do things his own way. He cranks out an $18 truffled matzo-ball soup with poached foie gras for Passover, and sticks popcorn into a tower of tuna sashimi and avocado. Stylish entrées like miso cod with asparagus and soy beans in a lemon-soy vinaigrette keep fashionable locals coming back. But sometimes simpler is better: a big cup of crisp calamari rings with a lemongrass dipping sauce is the house speciality.

Ouest
2315 Broadway, at 84th Street (1-212 580 8700). Subway: 1 to 86th Street. **Open** 5-11pm Mon-Thur; 5pm-midnight Fri, Sat; 5-10pm Sun. **Main courses** $24. **Credit** AmEx, DC, Disc, MC, V. **Map** p406 C19

The friendly servers are all pros; the kitchen is open to the dining room; tables and chairs are immensely comfortable, and the round red booths are reminiscent of Tilt-A-Whirl fairground rides. Tom Valenti adds some marvellously unexpected twists to the food. Sautéed baby calamari in a spicy tomato soppressata sauce delivers the promised heat. Potato gnocchi shares a bowl with 'hen of the woods' mushrooms, artichoke and prosciutto.

Cafés

Alice's Tea Cup

102 W 73rd Street, at Columbus Avenue (1-212 799 3006). Subway: B, C, 1, 2, 3 to 72nd Street. **Open** 8am-8pm Mon-Thur; 8am-10pm Fri; 10am-10pm Sat; 10am-8pm Sun. **Sandwich** $8. **Credit** AmEx, Disc, MC, V. **Map** p405 C20

Wander into this basement and you'll be transported to the end of rabbit hole. This quirky *Alice in Wonderland*-themed boutique-cum-bake-shop is the perfect refuge for afternoon tea. Choose from scrumptious scones and muffins, overstuffed sandwiches like curried chicken salad and croque monsieur, and sprightly salads like warm lentil with ginger dressing. Or you can have the full teatime treatment (dubbed the Mad Hatter) for $27 ($7 extra to share).

Eclectic

Per Se

4th floor, Time Warner Center, 10 Columbus Circle, at Broadway (1-212 823 9335). Subway: A, B, C, D, 1 to 59th Street-Columbus Circle. **Open** 5.30-10pm Mon-Thur; 11.30am-1.30pm, 5.30-10.30pm Fri, Sat; 11.30am-1.30pm, 5.30-10pm Sun. **Prix fixe** $125-$150. **Credit** AmEx, MC, V. **Map** p405 D22 106

Even though getting one of the 74 seats in Thomas Keller's luxurious restaurant in the Time Warner Center can take hours of speed-dialling (reservations are taken two months in advance), you're very likely to have one of the greatest (and longest) meals of your

life. Each dish in the lengthy procession of plates is a jewel of just a few bites, from the initial 'salmon cone' (a crisp sesame tuile filled with crème fraîche and salmon tartare) through delights like caviar-topped cauliflower panna cotta and butter-poached lobster, followed by whimsical desserts like 'coffee and doughnuts', a warm, sugar-coated beignet served with coffee semifreddo. Brace yourself for the bill.

French

Aix

2398 Broadway, at 88th Street (1-212 874 7400). Subway: 1 to 86th Street. **Open** 5.30-10.30pm Mon-Thur; 5.30-11pm Fri, Sat; 11.30am-2.30pm, 5.30-10.30pm Sun. **Main courses** $32. **Credit** AmEx, DC, MC, V. **Map** p406 C18 107

Didier Virot was the talk of the food world when he went up Broadway to open Aix a few years back. His (now-loyal) local crowd appreciates his experimentation with flavour: tender grilled calamari is tangled with refreshing slivers of fresh ginger, and served over a bed of spinach fettuccine; a halibut steak is paired with an oatmeal and porcini patty and a hill of green beans; and fluffy gnocchi lies in a cream sauce with Jerusalem artichokes. The truly creative station is the pastry chef's, where Jehangir Mehta slips rosemary into his apple brioche and pairs a Provençal cake with violet-nougat parfait.

Greek

Onera

222 W 79th Street, between Broadway & Amsterdam Avenue (1-212 873 0200). Subway: B, C to 81st Street-Museum of Natural History. **Open** noon-3pm, 5-10pm Tue-Thur, Sun; noon-3pm, 5-11.30pm Fri, Sat. **Main courses** $24. **Credit** AmEx, DC, Disc, MC, V. **Map** p405 C19 108

Offal is made more than palatable at Onera, an upscale Greek restaurant where chef-owner Michael Psilakis offers a five-course $75 offal tasting (it requires 48 hours' notice). When you arrive, Psilakis describes every delicious dish himself, proudly explaining how the headcheese is made from boiled pig head and feet, why the goat-kidney and pig-tripe salad is a deconstructed Greek classic, and why everyone should indulge in the likes of pan-seared calf brain and braised tongue.

Japanese

Haku

2425 Broadway, between 89th & 90th Streets (1-212 580 2566). Subway: 1 to 86th Street. **Open** 5-11pm Mon-Thur, Sun; 5pm-midnight Fri, Sat. **Main courses** $20. **Credit** AmEx, DC, Disc, MC, V. **Map** p406 C18 109

The Upper West Side has hosted sushi joints for decades, but it hasn't seen anything like this. Red spiky sculptures adorn the walls and dozens of rod-

Looks count at **Koi**. *See p201.*

like lights hang from the ceiling. Chef Hajime Ito adds modern twists to the food: a jellyfish roll comes with fig miso and cilantro (coriander), and crisp-fatty smoked duck breast is paired with a luscious blackcurrant sauce. To make sure that you leave on a bright note, Ito delivers petits fours (yuzu squares, sesame cookies) to your table.

Mexican

Rosa Mexicano
61 Columbus Avenue, at 62nd Street (1-212 977 7700). Subway: 1 to 66th Street-Lincoln Center. **Open** noon-3pm, 5-10pm Mon-Fri; 5-10pm Sat; noon-3pm, 4-10pm Sun. **Main courses** $23. **Credit** AmEx, DC, Disc, MC, V. **Map** p405 C21 ⑩
The jazzy technicolour journey up vivid terrazzo steps to the cavernous dining room is worth the trip uptown. But the famous guacamole is still the main draw, smashed to order at your table. As the waiter unwraps a parchment package of braised lamb shank, the rich aroma of chilli, cumin and clove envelopes the table. Veracruz-style red snapper is stuffed with crab and brightened with a punchy sauce of tomatoes, olives and capers.
Other locations: 1063 First Avenue, at 58th Street (1-212 753 7407).

Thai

Land Thai Kitchen
450 Amsterdam Avenue, at 82nd Street (1-212 501 8121). Subway: 1 to 79th Street. **Open** noon-11pm Mon-Sat; noon-10.30pm Sun. **Main courses** $12. **Credit** AmEx, DC, MC, V. **Map** p405 C19 ⑪
Thai restaurants are seldom known for practising restraint with spices, but chef David Bank, who's a veteran of Jean-Georges Vongerichten's Mercer Kitchen, promises simple flavours at his restaurant. The subtlety starts in the 30-seat dining room, which is lined with beige panelling and exposed brick. In addition to lamb, chicken and beef stir-fries, you'll find plenty of seafood dishes on offer, including snapper and salmon.

Vietnamese

Monsoon
435 Amsterdam Avenue, at 81st Street (1-212 580 8686). Subway: B, C to 81st Street-Museum of Natural History; 1 to 79th Street. **Open** 11.30am-11.30pm Mon-Thur, Sun; 11.30am-midnight Fri, Sat. **Main courses** $15. **Credit** AmEx, MC, V. **Map** p405 C19 ⑫
Ceiling fans, bamboo shades and a lush garden mural create a pleasant space for locals to satisfy their cravings for lemongrass, ginger, gingko and aromatic fresh herbs. The ample selections start with a long list of dim sum and unusual summer rolls. Chicken-mango rolls with wasabi-jalapeño sauce are delicious, as is beef bun with bean sprouts,

scallions and nuoc cham. Ginger sneaks in everywhere, but is best at dessert, where big, pungent chunks are buried in the ice-cream.

Upper East Side

American

Lexington Candy Shop
1226 Lexington Avenue, at 83rd Street (1-212 288 0057). Subway: 4, 5, 6 to 86th Street. **Open** 7am-7pm Mon-Sat; 9am-6pm Sun. **Main courses** $9. **Credit** AmEx, MC, V. **Map** p405 E19 ⑬
You won't find much candy for sale at Lexington Candy Shop. Instead, you'll find a preserved retro diner, lined with chatty locals digging into gigantic chocolate malteds or peanut butter and bacon sandwiches. The shop was founded in 1925 and has appeared in numerous films, including the Robert Redford classic *Three Days of the Condor*.

American creative

davidburke & donatella
133 E 61st Street, between Park & Lexington Avenues (1-212 813 2121). Subway: N, R, W to Lexington Avenue-59th Street; 4, 5, 6 to 59th Street. **Open** noon-2.30pm, 5-10pm Mon-Fri; 5-10.30pm Sat; 11am-2.30pm, 4.30-9pm Sun. **Main courses** $30. **Credit** AmEx, DC, Disc, MC, V. **Map** p405 E22 ⑭
Don't let the play-with-your-food gimmicks of culinary merry prankster David Burke fool you: this guy knows how to cook. His food runs the gamut from the merely fine (handmade garganelli with seafood) via the fantastic (the Bronx-style filet mignon of veal) and then right through to the fabulously silly (a cheesecake-lollipop 'tree' with bubblegum whipped cream). Donatella's surname is not Versace but rather Arpaia; she's a lawyer-turned-restaurateur who manages the vibrant and occasionally overwhelming social scene in the front of the house.

Austrian

Café Sabarsky
Neue Galerie, 1048 Fifth Avenue, at 86th Street (1-212 288 0665). Subway: 4, 5, 6 to 86th Street. **Open** 9am-6pm Mon, Wed; 9am-9pm Thur-Sun. **Main courses** $14. **Credit** AmEx, MC, V. **Map** p406 E18 ⑮
Nearby museum-goers come to this elegant Viennese café on Fifth Avenue for lunch plates such as smoked trout and goulash with spaetzle. But the savoury stuff is little more than a prelude to the real works of art that come after – apple strudel in crackling golden pastry, feather-light quark cheesecake, luscious Sachertorte and magnificent cream-topped (mit schlag) coffee. Breakfast is a particularly serene moment for appreciating the beautifully carved darkwood walls and the leafy park views.

Arts & Entertainment

French

Le Bilboquet

25 E 63rd Street, between Madison & Park Avenues (1-212 751 3036). Subway: F to Lexington Avenue-63rd Street. **Open** noon-11pm daily. **Main courses** $22. **Credit** AmEx, MC, V. **Map** p405 E21 ⑯

It's hard to believe that the skinny, skin-baring beauties who flock here on a Friday night can put away the portions this tiny bistro dishes out. With its loud, flirty rock 'n' roll ambience, Le Bilboquet knows how to get sexy and raw. Thick chunks of fresh tuna teeter between layers of lightly fried won ton skins; rich, piquant steak tartare comes with a tower of crisp frites. The unmarked entrance makes this feel like an upscale speakeasy.

Italian

Spigolo

1561 Second Avenue, at 81st Street (1-212 744 1100). Subway: 4, 5, 6 to 86th Street. **Open** 5pm-2am Mon-Sat. **Main courses** $19. **Credit** AmEx, DC, Disc, MC, V. **Map** p405 F19 ⑰

History in the round

Like many New Yorkers, bagels travelled from afar to make this metropolis their home. When Jewish Eastern European immigrants began arriving in New York City in the late 19th century, they brought with them a taste for dense, chewy breads, including a ring-shaped roll known by the Yiddish word *beygl*, derived from the German word *beugel*, meaning 'bracelet' or 'ring'.

Peddlers walked the crowded, tenement-lined streets of the Lower East Side (a common destination for Jewish newcomers), brandishing long sticks stacked with fresh bagels. Competition was fierce, and in 1907 a very exclusive bagel bakers' union formed in New York City. (One of its rules stipulated that only the sons of members could become apprentices.) The union knew the real secret of making a fine bagel – give it a quick bath

in boiling water before baking. This brief dunk is responsible for the bagel's signature shiny crust and chewy interior.

As Jews in New York began moving out of the Lower East Side, they took their culinary traditions with them. Bagels, which became a standard offering in delicatessens throughout the city, were typically flavoured with onions or poppy seeds and topped with a thick 'schmear' of cream cheese and a piece of the salty smoked salmon known as lox. As Jewish humour and traditions became part of the city's cultural fabric, so did bagels. For Jews and gentiles alike, weekend brunch just isn't complete without bagels, coffee and the plump Sunday edition of the *New York Times*.

Although bagels can be found everywhere from Starbucks to McDonald's these days, tracking down the traditional boiled and baked version can be tough. Most bakeries use mechanised ovens that steam-mist the dough instead of boiling it, which results in soft, puffy rolls without the classic chewy crust.

For a taste of the real, old-fashioned thing, visit the legendary **H&H Bagels**, from either the Upper West Side shop (2239 Broadway, at 80th Street, 1-212 595 8003) or the big factory in Hell's Kitchen (639 W 46th Street, between Eleventh & Twelfth Avenues, 1-212 595 8000), across from the Intrepid Sea-Air-Space Museum. Both are open 24/7.

While H&H's creations are the perfect snack, just one roll from **Ess-a-Bagel** (359 First Avenue, at 21st Street, 1-212 980 1010; 831 Third Avenue, at 51st Street, 1-212 980 4315) could easily be a meal for two or three. Since 1976, this family-run operation has been making monstrously big bagels with exceptional texture and flavour. Just be sure to come early on weekends, or you risk waiting in a line that snakes out the door.

Scott and Heather Fratangelo met in the kitchen at Union Square Café. The two talented chefs decided to move uptown in 2005. In passing, you might mistake the brick-walled place for just another pasta-slinging joint. It's not. Fat slices of grilled cotechino sausage marinated in red wine burst with flavour, and a brick-roasted baby chicken competes for top menu billing with a wild-mushroom sauce and side of soft polenta. Heather handles desserts; her caramel affogato and bombolini puts your regular coffee and doughnuts to shame.

Uva

1486 Second Avenue, at 77th Street (1-212 472 4552). Subway: 6 to 77th Street. **Open** noon-1am Mon-Thur, Sun; noon-2am Fri, Sat. **Main courses** $15. **Credit** AmEx, MC, V ($30 minimum). **Map** p405 F19 ⓲

Although the Upper East Side has plenty of rustic Italian restaurants, the neighbourhood could still use a few more wine bars. Luigi Lusardi and his brother Mauro opened Uva to fill the void. A 200-year-old wooden floor and antique couches give the place a warm, worn-in feel, and as per the wine-bar formula, you can take your pick of cured meats and cheeses to pair with most Italian wines (30 are available by the glass).

Pan-Asian

Geisha

33 E 61st Street, between Madison & Park Avenues (1-212 813 1112). Subway: N, R, W to Fifth Avenue-59th Street; 4, 5, 6 to 59th Street. **Open** noon-3.30pm, 5.30pm-midnight Mon-Sat. **Main courses** $24. **Credit** AmEx, DC, MC, V. **Map** p405 E22 ⓳

Leggy young blondes and older men jockey for prime seating in the posh lounge downstairs or the main dining room upstairs – each beautifully designed by David Rockwell. The menu, crafted by Eric Ripert (of Le Bernadin fame), is predominantly Japanese, but several dishes reveal other influences. Besides the seriously fresh sushi, starters include the likes of mussels in Thai red-curry broth, and grilled shrimp lollipops with a dipping sauce of sesame oil, Indonesian sweet soy sauce, white vinegar and chilli.

Above 116th Street

American

Kitchenette Uptown

1272 Amsterdam Avenue, between 122nd & 123rd Streets (1-212 531 7600). Subway: 1 to 125th Street. **Open** 8am-11pm daily. **Main courses** $16. **Credit** AmEx, DC, MC, V. **Map** p407 C14 ⓴

Riding the wave of South Harlem gentrification, Kitchenette Uptown brings Tribeca-style country dining to a sunlit space in Morningside Heights. At brunch, order the BLT on challah – it does cartwheels around the egg dishes. Cheese grits with home-made turkey sausage also makes a great meal, followed by a down-home slice of cherry pie. All-day

breakfast and weekend brunch attract a lively group of university types, as does the BYOB dinner with chicken potpie and four-cheese macaroni.
Other locations: Kitchenette, 80 West Broadway at Warren Street (1-212 267 6740).

American regional

Miss Maude's Spoonbread Too

547 Malcolm X Boulevard (Lenox Avenue), between 137th & 138th Streets (1-212 690 3100). Subway: B, C to 135th Street. **Open** 11.30am-9.30pm Mon-Sat; 11am-8pm Sun. **Main courses** $12. **Credit** AmEx, MC, V. **Map** p407 D11 ㉑

Norma Jean Darden knows that sometimes nothing will do but real home cookin'. The three-year-old off-shoot of Darden's original Morningside Heights spot makes everything from scratch. Get a load of fall-off-the-bone short ribs, flaky cornmeal-crusted catfish, or thick-cut pork chops smothered in creamy gravy, and dig into sides like smoky collard greens. Weekends brunch includes nap-inducing favourites like pecan waffles, fried fish and biscuits.

Pizza

Patsy's

2287 First Avenue, between 117th & 118th Streets (1-212 534 9783). Subway: 6 to 116th Street. **Open** 11am-11pm Mon-Sat; 1-10pm Sun. **No credit cards.** **Map** p407 F14 ㉒

This is East Harlem's favourite parlour, and with good reason. Sit down for a pie or stand up for a slice at the 71-year-old uptown joint.

Brooklyn

American

Applewood

501 11th Street, at Seventh Avenue, Park Slope, Brooklyn (1-718 768 2044). Subway: F to Seventh Avenue. **Open** 5-11pm Tue-Sat; 10am-3pm Sun. **Main courses** $20. **Credit** AmEx, Disc, MC, V. **Map** p410 T12 ㉓

David and Laura Shea met at the Culinary Institute of America and then returned to New York to open this charming eatery with country style and organic produce. Tables are adorned with bundles of fresh herbs, there's a working fireplace, and many ingredients come from a friend's upstate farm. On the opening menu: ricotta dumplings with braised pork shoulder, roasted chicken with chanterelle-sage gravy, and wild striped bass with roasted corn and curried mussel chowder.

Schnäck

122 Union Street, at Columbia Street, Carroll Gardens, Brooklyn (1-718 855 2879). Subway: F, G to Carroll Street. **Open** 11am-1am daily. **Burgers** $5. **No credit cards.** **Map** p410 S10 ㉔

A greasy spoon with a sense of humour, Schnäck has a knack for burgers: you can order up to five small patties stacked on a single bun, with a full array of toppings ('schnäck sauce', spicy onions, chilli, kraut, etc). The $2 quickie – a mini burger with a 'children's portion' of beer – is one of the best deals in Brooklyn. Buttermilk-soaked onion rings fry up flaky-crisp and are sprinkled with salt and parsley seasoning. The award-winning beer milkshake tastes just like a regular milkshake, but has a buzz.

American creative

DuMont

432 Union Avenue, between Devoe Street & Metropolitan Avenue, Williamsburg, Brooklyn (1-718 486 7717). Subway: G to Metropolitan Avenue; L to Lorimer Street. **Open** 11am-3pm, 6-11pm daily. **Main courses** $12. **Credit** MC, V. **Map** p411 V8 **125**

DuMont is the kind of place where Byron, Shelley and Keats might have gathered for a drink – a gently worn joint with pressed-tin ceilings, a wenge-wood bar, retro brown leather booths and plenty of candles. A private den in the back doubles as a bar and holding pen for those who are waiting to dig into excellent seasonal American dishes like frothy lobster bisque with a dollop of curry butter, or braised duck leg risotto. Lucky for all of us, the lardon-laced macaroni and cheese never disappears.

Italian

DOC Wine Bar

83 North 7th Street, at Wythe Avenue, Williamsburg, Brooklyn (1-718 963 1925). Subway: L to Bedford Avenue. **Open** 6pm-midnight Mon-Thur; 6pm-1am Fri-Sun. **Small plate** $7. **No credit cards.** **Map** p411 U7 **126**

Tucked on a quiet side street, this unpretentious spot charms with brown-paper-covered tables and menus held together with wooden spoons. Peruse the list of 70 Italian wines, and a menu of small plates: vegetarian carpaccio serves up as a mound of thin, perfectly rolled slices of carrot and courgette topped with Parmesan shavings. Pistokku – traditional flatbread from the region of Sardinia – is served pizza-style, warm and crisp with toppings such as bresaola (air-cured beef), goat's cheese and rocket.

Mexican

Alma

187 Columbia Street, at DeGraw Street, Cobble Hill, Brooklyn (1-718 643 5400). Subway: F, G to Carroll Street. **Open** 5.30-10pm Mon-Fri; 6-11pm Sat, Sun. **Main courses** $15. **Credit** MC, V. **Map** p410 S10 **127**

From the subway, it's a long walk west (when you get to the far side of the BQE overpass, you're almost there), but if you want to chill with local Margarita-lovin' arty types, head over to this sexy Mexi spot. Have a drink at the ground-floor bar, B61, then head upstairs to Alma's colourful dining room. In good weather, snag a table on the rooftop deck, which has

industrial-chic views of the Brooklyn waterfront and the downtown Manhattan skyline. Citrusy ceviche of shrimp, scallop and bass has a hint of jalapeño; a side of black beans with sticky, luscious sautéed plantains is pure south-of-the-border comfort.

Steakhouse

Peter Luger

178 Broadway, at Driggs Avenue, Williamsburg, Brooklyn (1-718 387 7400). Subway: J, M, Z to Marcy Avenue. **Open** 11.30am-10pm Mon-Thur, Sun; 11.30am-11pm Fri, Sat. **Steak for two** $65. **No credit cards.** **Map** p411 U7 **128**

Does this Williamsburg landmark deserve its rep as one of the best steakhouses in America? A four-star experience this isn't, but the quality of the beef may make you forgive any shortcomings. Established as a German beer hall in 1887, the restaurant serves only one cut: a porterhouse that's char-broiled black on the outside, tender and pink on the inside. Service is slow, provided by crusty waiters who would rather give out wisecracks than water. Remember to stuff your wallet before you stuff your face; Luger's doesn't take credit cards (although it will accept US debit cards).

Thai

SEA Thai Restaurant and Bar

114 North 6th Street, at Berry Street, Williamsburg, Brooklyn (1-718 384 8850). Subway: L to Bedford Avenue. **Open** 11.30am-12.30am Mon-Thur, Sun; 11.30am-1.30am Fri, Sat. **Main courses** $9. **Credit** AmEx, MC, V. **Map** p411 U7 **129**

You may mistake SEA for a nightclub, given the reverberating dance music and a mod lounge complete with bubble-chair swing. Get a table by the reflecting pool and flip through the campy postcard menu. For a place so stylin', prices are cheap and the food good. Stuffed with shrimp and real crab, jade seafood dumplings come with a nutty Massaman sauce, while Queen of Siam beef with basil and red chilli is best when you ask the kitchen to fire it up. **Other locations**: SEA, 75 Second Avenue, between 4th & 5th Streets (1-212 228 5505).

American creative

Angie's

41-46 54th Street, between Roosevelt Avenue & Queens Boulevard, Woodside, Queens (1-718 651 2277). Subway: 7 to 52nd Street. **Open** 2-11pm Mon-Fri; 9am-11pm Sat, Sun. **Main courses** $16. **Credit** AmEx, MC, V. **Map** p412 X5 **130**

Chef-owner Angel Hernandez turns out sophisticated dishes with Latin twists – like crisp duck breast with a chestnut ragout and pan-seared sea scallops with vanilla beurre blanc. The duck breast perches on earthy corn pancakes, and an entrée of garlic shrimp

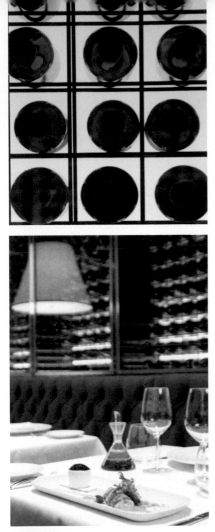

arrives with creamy coconut rice and fried plantains. At brunch, served daily, you can indulge in the likes of pressed Cuban sandwiches.

French

Le Sans Souci

44-09 Broadway, at 44th Street, Astoria, Queens (1-718 728 2733). Subway: R, V to 46th Street. **Open** noon-10pm Tue-Sun. **Main courses** $9. **Credit** AmEx, Disc, MC, V. **Map** p412 X4 ⑬①

A busy commercial stretch in Astoria is the last place you'd expect to stumble upon a sweet European-style café, but this one is a fully French operation. The menu focuses on owner Le Pape's native Brittany: pork tenderloin with scallion mashed potatoes and a Calvados cream sauce; baguettes stuffed with merguez sausage and harissa mayonnaise. The stone-walled dining room is equipped with a piano and a chess table, in case you want to stay a while. Early birds can drop in at 7am for a breakfast of pain au chocolat on weekdays.

Greek

Philoxenia

26-18 23rd Avenue, between 26th & 27th Streets, Astoria, Queens (1-718 626 9162). Subway: N, W to Astoria-Ditmars Boulevard . **Open** 5pm-midnight Tue-Sat; 2pm-midnight Sun. **Main courses** $12. **No credit cards. Map** p412 X3 ⑬②

Some restaurateurs use mom's old recipes; Nancy Gavoboulou did one better and put mom in the kitchen. Momma Dionysia cooks meat dishes from her native north-central Greece and seafood dishes from the Aegean coast. Feta-stuffed squid, an appetiser special, comes with a tomato sauce and an unlikely hit of orange. Splurge on meat for an entrée, like pork sausages, garlicky loukanika lamb links or cumin-laced beef meatballs, fried or char-broiled.

Bronx

French

Riverdale Garden

4574 Manhattan College Parkway, near W 242nd Street, Bronx (1-718 884 5232). Subway: 1 to 242nd Street. **Open** 11.30am-2.30pm, 5-11pm Mon, Wed-Fri; 10.30am-2.30pm, 5-11pm Sat, Sun. **Main courses** $22. **Credit** AmEx, DC, Disc, MC, V.

There really is a garden at the recently opened Riverdale Garden, along with a backyard patio; both offer a little taste of the country life. The menu changes daily, but the chef has a fondness for game, including succulent venison with mashed potatoes and asparagus. For dessert, try the molten chocolate lava cake or just-like-mom-made-it peach cobbler.

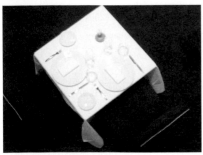

High design at **Alto**. *See p194.*

Bars

Lounge lizards and bar crawlers start here. And just keep on going.

The **Flatiron Lounge**. *See p218.*

In a city where bars open as early as 8am and keep the suds going until dawn, you'll have no problem wetting your whistle. The dilemma will be choosing where to raise a glass: nearly 5,000 bars, pubs and clubs keep the booze, whether lychee Martinis or bottles of Bud, flowing 'till last call.

Our 'average drink' price covers a standard well drink (spirit) plus mixer, or equivalent.

Downtown

Tribeca & around

Another Room

249 West Broadway, between Beach and North Moore Streets (1-212 226 1418). Subway: A, C, E to Canal Street. **Open** 5pm-4am daily. **Average drink** $7. **No credit cards**. **Map** p402 E31 **❶**
Like its siblings, this sleek and civilised bar doubles as an art gallery. You won't find any hard liquor, but the selection of fine beer and wine is varied and vast and the crowd – gay, straight, fashionistas, 9-to-5 execs – interesting. If the weather is decent, sit at the picnic table out front.

Other locations: The Other Room, 143 Perry Street between Greenwhich and Washington Streets (1-212 645 9758); The Room, 144 Sullivan Street, between Houston & Prince Streets (1-212 477 2102).

Brandy Library

25 North Moore Street, at Varick Street (1-212 226 5545). Subway: 1 to Franklin Street. **Open** 4pm-4am daily. **Average drink** $12. **Credit** AmEx, MC, V. **Map** p402 E31 **❷**
Cocktail connoisseurs and spirit snobs will find themselves at home inside this handsome cognac-coloured liquor lounge. As the name implies, the place is set up like a library: bottles of booze line the shelves from floor to ceiling. Wood panelling, low couches, a long bar and blue-note jazz create an atmosphere that begs for a smoking jacket (you can smoke cigars on the heated terrace out front). The fat leather-bound menu lists a good hundred classic cocktails – among them the Rob Roy and the Moscow Mule – and still more bottles of whiskies, rums and brandies, along with a range of seasonal drinks such as grog.

Dekk

134 Reade Street, between Greenwich & Hudson Streets (1-212 941 9401). Subway:1, 2, 3 to Chambers Street. **Open** 11am-4am Mon-Fri; 10am-4am Sat, Sun. **Average drink** $8. **Credit** AmEx, MC, V. **Map** p402 E31 **❸**
Decorated with antique Parisian subway seats and French doors, Dekk has a screening room in the back that shows depraved films like *Cecil B Demented* and *Tromeo and Juliet*. A long list of wines by the glass complements a menu of thin crust pizzas and northern Italian pastas.

Megu Kimono Lounge

See p181 for listing. **Map** p402 E31 **❹**
The lounge of this high-end, high-profile Japanese restaurant is show-stopping: white columns are fashioned from porcelain rice bowls and saké bottles and kimono fabrics abound. Kimono's cocktails are simimlarly fancy: Autumn Rain is a refreshing blend of citrus vodka, elderflower syrup, Asian-pear purée and ginger.

Chinatown, Little Italy & Nolita

Odea

389 Broome Street, at Mulberry Street (1-212 941 9222). Subway: J, M, Z to Bowery; 6 to Spring Street. **Open** 6pm-2am Mon-Wed, Sun; 6pm-4am Thur-Sat. **Average drink** $10. **Credit** AmEx, DC, Disc, MC, V. **Map** p403 F30 **❺**

Eat, Drink, Shop

This sleek AvroKO-designed lounge nails the industrial-chic look – high ceilings, wood beams and brick walls painted black – but also includes some old-fashioned touches that soften the room. Stay long enough, and you'll find yourself nibbling on tasty tapas such as aubergine mousse or figs wrapped in prosciutto.

Palais Royale

173 1/2 Mott Street, between Broome & Grand Streets (1-212 941 6112). Subway: J, M, Z to Bowery; 6 to Spring Street. **Open** 1pm-2am Mon-Wed; 1pm-4am Thur-Sun. **Average drink** $6. **Credit** AmEx, MC, V. **Map** p403 F30 ❻

Palais Royale might be the city's first haute dive bar. The owners, who also run Double Happiness and Orchard Bar, are serious about booze – they're serving 30 types of bourbon – but they're having fun with the menu: Hungry-Man and Lean Cuisine microwaveable meals. A pool table and televisions above the bar add to the 'dive' quotient.

Xicala Wine & Tapas Bar

151B Elizabeth Street, between Broome & Kenmare Streets (1-212 219 0599). Subway: J, M, Z to Bowery. **Open** 5pm-2am daily. **Average drink** $8. **Credit** AmEx, MC, V. **Map** p403 F30 ❼

Everything about this Spanish spot, located on an ungentrified block, is incongruous. A bright neon sign leads to a dark, tiny space. Classic tapas – chorizo, codfish, olives – coexist with chocolate fondue, and powerhouse wines are properly chilled and generously poured. Full capacity is 20 people, so in warm weather patrons spill out on to the pavement.

Lower East Side

Barrio Chino

253 Broome Street, between Ludlow & Orchard Streets (1-212 228 6710). Subway: F to Delancey Street; J, M, Z to Delancey-Essex Streets. **Open** 6pm-2am Mon-Thur, Sun; 6pm-4am Fri, Sat. **Average drink** $8. **Credit** MC, V. **Map** p403 G30 ❽

Neighbourhood cool kids have taken up positions at Barrio Chino's rough-hewn wooden bar. Owners Patrick Durocher and Dylan Dodd aim to 'give tequila credibility as a sipping liquor, like Scotch'. Fifty tequilas are available, at $6 to $25 per shot. Each comes with a slice of mango and a glass of Sangrita, a tomato-citrus palate-cleanser. There's also a list of unusual but delicious Margaritas.

Café Charbon

100C Forsyth Street, between Broome & Grand Streets (1-212 625 3444). Subway: B, D to Grand Street. **Open** 6pm-2am Mon-Sat. **Average drink** $8. **Credit** AmEx, Disc, MC, V. **Map** p403 F30 ❾

The romance of Paris on Rue d'Orchard? This *bar-tabac-épicerie* features ten well-priced wines by the glass, a fine selection of Belgian beers and fresh downbeats every night. If hunger strikes, the full menu from the attached bistro, Epicerie, is available.

Delancey

168 Delancey Street, at Clinton Street (1-212 254 9920). Subway: F to Delancey Street; J, M, Z to Delancey-Essex Streets. **Open** 4pm-4am daily. **Average drink** $6. **Credit** MC, V. **Map** p403 G30 ❿

The tropical-themed rooftop is what keeps luring the cool crowd – a wood deck lined with potted palms and equipped with a fishpond, a bar and a Margarita machine. When the alfresco party ends at midnight, you can head down to the main floor for DJ music or into the basement to catch a live show.

East Side Company Bar

49 Essex Street, at Grand Street (1-212 614 7408). Subway: F to Delancey Street; J, M, Z to Delancey-Essex Streets. **Open** 8pm-4am daily. **Average drink** $8. **Credit** AmEx, MC, V. **Map** p403 G30 ⓫

If you still can't get into Milk & Honey (the exclusive reservation-only bar owned by Sasha Petraske), you'll fare much better at his new Lower East Side spot: the phone number is listed, and you can also walk in off the street. This snug new space also has a 1940s-era vibe (leather booths, classic cocktails), as well as a few additions, such as a raw bar.

'inoteca

98 Rivington Street, at Ludlow Street (1-212 614 0473). Subway: F to Delancey Street; J, M, Z to Delancey-Essex Streets. **Average drink** $8. **Credit** AmEx, MC, V. **Map** p403 G29 ⓬

Where chefs drink, their partisans follow. So Jason Denton and his partners at the microscopic wine bar 'ino opened a bigger space across town. Same warm atmosphere, same foodie crowd, but there's also a menu of great pan-Italian share-plates and enough space to give your glass a proper swirl. The downstairs wine cellar is more conversation friendly.

Punch and Judy

26 Clinton Street, between Houston & Stanton Streets (1-212 982 1116). Subway: F to Delancey Street; J, M, Z to Delancey-Essex Streets. **Open** 6pm-2am Mon-Wed, Sun; 6pm-4am Thur-Sat. **Average drink** $10. **Credit** AmEx, MC, V. **Map** p403 G29 ⓭

This stylish, modern wine bar and lounge, furnished with 1930s theatre seats and red couches, offers 150 wines that pair beautifully with nibbles like a lobster club sandwich, cheese plates or a caprese salad in which the ingredients are rolled up sushi-style.

Schiller's Liquor Bar

See p184 for listing. **Map** p403 G29 ⓮

Keith McNally's downtown bar attracts the hep cats with decidedly unsnobbish wine-list categories ('cheap', 'decent' and 'good').

❶ Pink numbers given in this chapter correspond to the location of each bar as marked on the street maps. *See pp402-412.*

Eat, Drink, Shop

Soho

Fanelli's Café

94 Prince Street, at Mercer Street (1-212 226 9412). Subway: N, R, W to Prince Street. **Open** 10am-1.30am Mon-Thur, Sun; 10am-3.30am Fri, Sat. **Average drink** $5. **Credit** AmEx, MC, V. **Map** p403 E29 ⓱

On a lovely cobblestoned corner, this 1847 joint claims to be the second-oldest continuously operating bar and restaurant in the city. Prints of boxing legends and one of the city's best burgers add to the easy feel. The banter of locals and the merry clinking of pint glasses sound just like the old days.

Fiamma Osteria

206 Spring Street, between Sixth Avenue & Sullivan Street (1-212 653 0100). Subway: C, E to Spring Street. **Open** noon-2.30pm, 5.30-11pm Mon-Thur; noon-2.30pm, 5.30pm-midnight Fri; 5.30pm-midnight Sat; 5.30-11pm Sun. **Average** *Main course* $20. **Credit** AmEx, Disc, MC, V. **Map** p403 E30 ⓰

After a short glass-elevator ride up to the second floor, you find a hidden lounge that looks like an upscale building-material showroom: stone walls, hardwood floors, leather banquettes and a brigade of tealights. Regulars get giddy over the smooth Cappuccino Martini, but wine aficionados come for a sampling of one of the city's best wine lists.

Grand Bar & Lounge

SoHo Grand Hotel, 310 West Broadway, between Canal & Grand Streets (1-212 965 3000). Subway: A, C, E, 1 to Canal Street. **Open** noon-1.30am Mon-Wed, Sun; noon-2.30am Thur-Sat. **Average drink** $12. **Credit** AmEx, DC, Disc, MC, V. **Map** p403 E30 ⓱

They're been around for a while, but the second-floor bar and lounge still draw a media-industry crowd. The two spaces – a wood-panelled bar and a plush lounge drenched in chocolate hues – are linked by a long corridor. Sip a pricey cocktail or glass of wine while you take in evening sessions of newly released lounge imports. Hungry drinkers can order grilled salmon BLTs or truffled turkey burgers.

MercBar

151 Mercer Street, between Houston & Prince Streets (1-212 966 2727). Subway: B, D, F, V to Broadway-Lafayette Street; N, R, W to Prince Street; 6 to Bleecker Street. **Open** 5pm-2am Mon, Tue, Sun; 5pm-2.30am Wed; 5pm-3am Thur; 5pm-4am Fri, Sat. **Average drink** $9. **Credit** AmEx, MC, V. **Map** p403 E29 ⓲

Need a sharp-looking place to try on your blind date for size? Head to the MercBar, where the well-coiffed after-work crowd comes to engage in polite conversation and avoid mingling. The interior (soft lighting, log-cabin-like walls, landscape paintings and a canoe hanging above the sleek wooden bar) feels like your rich friend's parents' mountain lodge, but the drinks are city-sleek – the Concorde blends apple schnapps, Bacardi Limón and grape juice.

Milady's

160 Prince Street, at Thompson Street (1-212 226 9340). Subway: C, E to Spring Street; N, R to Prince Street. **Open** 11am-4am daily. **Average drink** $5. **Credit** AmEx, DC, Disc, MC, V. **Map** p403 E29 ⓳

Pretty quickly, you get it: the area has changed, but one little corner dive hasn't. Drinks are outer-borough cheap and the buy-back ethos is one of the best in town, and strictly adhered to across the bartending staff. Patrons spanning all ages and careers down everything from pina coladas in pint glasses to whiskey shots. The lone pool table sees more action than the star quarterback at the senior prom, and the rock-ruled jukebox gets props as well.

East Village

Baraza

133 Avenue C, between 8th & 9th Streets (1-212 539 0811). Subway: L to First Avenue; 6 to Astor Place. **Open** 7.30pm-4am daily. **Average drink** $5. **No credit cards. Map** p403 G28 ⓴

One of the pioneers on Avenue C, this lively Latin spot is famous for its good $5 Caipirinhas and Mojitos, which continuously draw a sleek boho crowd (the place is always packed). In the candlelit lounge past the bar, patrons puzzle over the Barbie aquarium, in which the plastic diva and Ken enjoy a lovely beach scene.

DBA

41 First Avenue, between 2nd & 3rd Streets (1-212 475 5097). Subway: F, V to Lower East Side-Second Avenue. **Open** 1pm-4am daily. **Average drink** $6. **Credit** AmEx, DC, Disc, MC, V. **Map** p403 F29 ㉑

DBA is a true beer hall for the true beer connoisseur – 130 brews (20 or so on tap), from the expensive (Belgian wheat drafts) to the unpronounceable (Schlenkerla Rauchbier). If you're not already paralysed by indecision, add more than 130 single malts and 50 tequilas to muddy your thinking. There's even a garden in the back, where you can enjoy your brew alfresco in warmer months.

11th Street Bar

510 E 11th Street, between Avenues A & B (1-212 982 3929). Subway: L to First Avenue; 6 to Astor Place. **Open** 4pm-4am daily. **Average drink** $5. **Credit** AmEx, MC, V. **Map** p403 G28 ㉒

In a city where comfortable living rooms are at a premium, the 11th Street Bar serves an important purpose: giving patrons a stress-free place to lounge and drink in peace (there's even a cat). The warm, old-timey space with exposed-brick walls and a pressed-tin ceiling; the back room holds the bulk of the tables – and poetry readings every other Monday night.

In Vino

215 E 4th Street, between Avenues A & B (1-212 539 1011). Subway: F, V to Lower East Side-Second Avenue. **Open** 5.30pm-midnight Mon-Thur, Sun; 5.30pm-1am Fri, Sat. **Average drink** $8. **Credit** MC, V. **Map** p403 G29 ㉓

The **Ava Lounge**. *See p219.*

Come to savour southern Italian vinos: the small cave-like space offers hundreds of regional wines that can accommodate such tasty, rustic appetisers as tomato-and-truffle crostini.

Le Souk
47 Avenue B, between 3rd & 4th Streets (1-212 777 5454). Subway: F, V to Lower East Side-Second Avenue. **Open** 6pm-4am daily. **Average drink** $9. **Credit** MC, V. **Map** p403 G29 **24**
In the early evening, the muted lighting and *shishas* (what Egyptians call hookahs) give this two-room lounge the feel of a North African teahouse; a few hours on, it's a bump-and-grind bar; later still, when the tables and chairs are cleared away, it seems like a private after-hours party. Le Souk is an absolute hit every night, whether for weeknight belly dancing, the weekend's Arabic-infused house beats or Sunday night's legendary progressive house party.

McSorley's Old Ale House
15 E 7th Street, between Second & Third Avenues (1-212 473 9148). Subway: N, R, W to 8th Street-NYU; 6 to Astor Place. **Open** 11am-midnight Mon-Sat. **Average drink** $2. **No credit cards**. **Map** p403 F28 **25**
It would take days to read the newspaper clips on the walls of this 1854 drinking landmark. Order a house beer – Dark Ale (sweet and smooth) or Light Ale (smooth with a bite) – and the veteran Irish waiters will bring you double mugs of suds. The sawdusted floor and never-dusted chandelier add to the old-time feel. Look up bartender-poet Geoffrey Bartholomew's *The McSorley Poems* before stopping by.

Butting in

Despite the strict citywide smoking ban of 2003, there are still a few places where you can legally light up:
Circa Tabac, 32 Watts Street, between Sixth Avenue & Thompson Street (1-212 941 1781).
Club Macanudo, 26 E 63rd Street, between Madison & Park Avenues (1-212 752 8200).
Karma, 51 First Avenue, between 3rd & 4th Streets (1-212 677 3160).
Velvet Cigar Lounge, 80 E 7th Street, at 1st Avenue (1-212 533 5582).

At press time, smoking was still permitted at many (but not all) outdoor patios and roof decks. If the weather is nice, you'll enjoy lighting up at:
Ava Lounge (*see p218*).
Central Park Boathouse (*see p221*).
Glass 287 Tenth Avenue, between 26th & 27th Streets (1-212 904 1580).

Sutra Lounge
16 First Avenue, between 1st & 2nd Streets (1-212 677 9477). Subway: F, V to Second Avenue-Lower East Side. **Open** 9pm-4am daily. **Average drink** $8. **Credit** AmEx, MC, V. **Map** p403 **26**
Sutra wants to put you in the mood: you're seduced with incense and warm amber lighting the moment you enter. A downstairs cave is preserved as an old Turkish gentlemen's club, and an upstairs bar and billiards room is lined with red velvet banquettes and bordello-style lamps. You can nibble on delicacies such as chocolate-covered strawberries and sip concoctions like the Sutra Martini, with vodka, vermouth and crème de cassis.

Greenwich Village & Noho

Bar Next Door
129 MacDougal Street, between 3rd & 4th Streets (1-212 529 5945). Subway: A, B, C, D, E, F, V to W 4th Street. **Open** 6pm-2am Mon-Thur, Sun; 6pm-3am Fri, Sat. **Average drink** $7. **Cover** $5 (Tue-Thur, Sun). **Credit** AmEx, DC, Disc, MC, V. **Map** p403 E29 **27**
Hidden in the basement of a beautifully restored townhouse, Bar Next Door feels like a special secret you're lucky to know about. The romantic nook evokes old New York, as well as owner Vittorio Antonini's hometown on the Italian Riviera. Low ceilings, exposed brick and stone walls provide superb acoustics for the regularly scheduled live jazz performances (Tuesday through Sunday). If you'd like something to nibble, a full menu is offered until 2am (3am on weekends) from the adjacent trattoria, La Lanterna di Vittorio.

Marion's Continental Restaurant & Lounge
354 Bowery, between Great Jones & E 4th Streets (1-212 475 7621). Subway: B, D, F, V to Broadway-Lafayette Street; 6 to Bleecker Street. **Open** 5.30pm-2am daily. **Average drink** $7. **Credit** AmEx, DC, Disc, MC, V. **Map** p403 E29 **28**
Marion's hasn't been serving old-fashioned cocktails forever, but it sure feels that way. Decorated with thrift-shop paintings and bric-a-brac, this retro shrine to 1950s New York nightlife assumes the air of a festive but down-to-earth supper club, with fabulous music that varies from lounge and Latin to lovely soul.

Table 50
See p295 for listing. **Map** p403 E29 **29**
It's always cool in this basement bar, and it would feel Zen-like if the techno weren't so loud. Grab a candlelit nook and sink into a leather banquette, but do try to stay away from the seemingly guileless Painkiller (a concoction of coconut, rum and orange juice). One too many of those, and the hall of mirrors leading to the blood-red bathroom might start to look more like a terrifying carnival maze than a playful remnant of the space's smutty heyday as an S&M bar.

Eat, Drink, Shop

Von Bar

3 Bleecker Street, between Bowery & Elizabeth Street (1-212 473 3039). Subway: B, D, F, V to Broadway-Lafayette Street; 6 to Bleecker Street. **Open** 5pm-2am Mon-Wed, Sun; 5pm-4am Thur-Sat. **Average drink** $7. **Credit** AmEx, MC, V. **Map** p403 F29 ③⓪

This low-key two-room lair, all candlelit dark wood and exposed brick, is a perfect first-date spot. A large blackboard trumpets an extensive selection of (mostly French) wines by the glass, but the bar also has a full liquor licence. Pick a full-bodied red, like the Vacqueyras, take your friend by the hand, and head for one of the benches in the back room.

West Village & Meatpacking District

APT

See p295 for listing. **Map** p403 C27 ③①
By shifting its focus from door attitude to DJs, APT lives up to India Mahdavi's sleek, polished design.

Arthur's Tavern

57 Grove Street, between Bleecker Street & Seventh Avenue South (1-212 675 6879). Subway: 1 to Christopher Street-Sheridan Square. **Open** 7pm-4am daily. **Average drink** $8 (two-drink minimum). **No credit cards.** **Map** p403 D28 ③②

For about 60 years, this no-nonsense dive with year-round Christmas decorations and cheap suds has attracted tourists, old Village bohemians, fans of Dixieland jazz and the odd drag queen. Free live jazz and blues often make the two-drink minimum worthwhile. Best bet: Thursday through Saturday, the early evening piano slot with Eri Yamamoto.

Blind Tiger Alehouse

518 Hudson Street, at 10th Street (1-212 675 3848). Subway: 1 to Christopher Street-Sheridan Square. **Open** noon-4am Mon-Fri; 1pm-4am Sat, Sun. **Average drink** $4. **Credit** AmEx, MC, V. **Map** p403 D28 ③③

Here's the place to learn the difference between ales and lagers. Home to brews of all nations, the Blind Tiger offers a large wooden bar amply stocked with chips, nuts, television – and beer. Wednesday is 'you cut the cheese' day: six to 15 beers of a particular style are put on tap, and five farmhouse cheeses are offered for complimentary (and complementary) snacking. On Saturdays and Sundays, the bagels are on the house.

Chumley's

86 Bedford Street, between Barrow & Grove Streets (1-212 675 4449). Subway: 1 to Christopher Street-Sheridan Square. **Open** 4pm-midnight Mon-Thur; 4pm-2am Fri; noon-2am Sat, Sun. **Average drink** $6. **No credit cards.** **Map** p403 D29 ③④

The two unmarked entrances to Chumley's reflect its speakeasy roots. Since its opening in 1922, the place has poured pints for its share of famous authors; notice the countless book covers displayed on the walls. A working fireplace, free-roaming Labradors and sawdusted floors maintain the scruffy yet genteel sensibility.

Double Seven

418 W 14th Street, between Ninth & Tenth Avenues (1-212 981 9099). Subway: A, C, E to 14th Street; L to Eighth Avenue. **Open** 6pm-4am Mon-Fri; 8pm-4am Sat. **Average drink** $16. **Credit** AmEx, MC, V. **Map** p403 C27 ③⑤

Eventually, club kids have to grow up, and Lotus owner David Rabin has just the place for them when they do at his new cocktail lounge across the street from his sceney Meatpacking District den. It's small – just 75 seats – and built for conversation rather than craziness. Drinks (by consultant Sasha Petraske of Milk & Honey) are a whopping $16, but each one is served with Debauve & Galais chocolates. There's no need to queue: the place takes reservations for parties of four or more.

5 Ninth

See p193 for listing. **Map** p403 C28 ③⑥
The bar inside the rustic restaurant, in a charming three-storey 1848 house, vibrates with speakeasy charm; old-school Scotches, cognacs and whiskeys are the main ingredients of heady cocktails (like the fizzy Floridora) named after Broadway shows. Fireplaces, exposed brick and one of the city's loveliest gardens contribute to the intimacy, which encourages chatting up strangers.

Little Branch

20-22 Seventh Avenue South, at Leroy Street (1-212 929 4360). Subway: 1 to Houston Street. **Open** 7pm-3am Mon-Fri; 9pm-3am Sat. **Average drink** $9. **No credit cards.** **Map** p403 D29 ③⑦

Milk & Honey owner Sasha Petraske is letting commoners into this candlelit, subterranean spot to sample his legendary cocktails. No reservations needed.

Spice Market

403 W 13th Street, at Ninth Avenue (1-212 675 2322). Subway: A, C, E to 14th Street; L to Eighth Avenue. **Open** 6pm-2am daily. **Average drink** $12. **Credit** AmEx, DC, MC, V. **Map** p403 D29 ③⑧

Glide down the dramatic staircase and enter a glamorous world where votives flicker over a fashionable crowd that comes for the scene, the fruity cocktails and the street-market-inspired dishes.

Turks & Frogs

323 West 11th Street, between Greenwich & Washington Streets (1-212 691 8875). Subway: A, C, E to 14th Street; L to Eighth Avenue. **Open** 5pm-4am daily. **Average drink** $7. **Credit** AmEx, MC, V. **Map** p403 C28 ③⑨

Owner Osman Cakir has operated this antiques shop for three years but has now decided it'll do double duty as a wine bar and restaurant. In addition to the Turkish and French pottery doing decoration duty, visitors will find 50 wines (including

Eat, Drink, Shop

some from Cakir's native Turkey) and a small menu of prepared foods (there's no oven on the premises) made with aubergine, cheese, grape leaves and other Mediterranean ingredients. Cakir has managed to pack an antique couch, a small bar and a few tables into the 800sq ft place. It makes for a nice getaway from the Meatpacking crowd.

Ye Waverly Inn

16 Bank Street, at Waverly Place (1-212 929 4377). Subway: 1, 2, 3 to 14th Street. **Open** 5pm-4am daily. **Average drink** $8. **Credit** AmEx, DC, Disc, MC, V. **Map** p403 D28 ⓪

Ignore the hokey connotations of the 'Ye'; this one's for real. Not many places are more typical of old Greenwich Village than this former tavern, nestled in a 160-year-old brownstone. The tiny bar seats a handful of patrons and offers wines by the glass, a stellar selection of single malts and Charles Mingus on the speakers, all of which combine to make it a fine place to round out a date. Grab a seat near the same flickering fireplace Robert Frost once wrote beside, and wax poetic.

Midtown

Chelsea & Flatiron

Bar Veloce

176 Seventh Avenue, between 20th & 21st Streets (1-212 629 5300). Subway: 1 to 18th Street. **Open** 5pm-3am daily. **Average drink** $8. **Credit** AmEx, MC, V. **Map** p403 D27 ⓪

This new outpost of the popular East Village Italian wine bar has a similar layout: a long wood bar and wine bottles stacked horizontally on artfully designed racks. The all-Italian wines pair well with an assortment of panini, bruschetta and meat and cheese plates.

Flatiron Lounge

37 W 19th Street, between Fifth & Sixth Avenues (1-212 727 7741). Subway: F, N, R, V, W to 23rd Street; 1 to 18th Street. **Open** 5pm-2am Mon-Wed, Sun; 5pm-4am Thur-Sat. **Average drink** $10. **Credit** AmEx, MC, V. **Map** p403 E27 ⓪

To get to the 30ft mahogany bar (built in 1927), follow an arched hallway warmed by the soft glow of candles. You'll find an art deco space with red leather booths, round glass tables, flying-saucer-shaped lamps and an imaginative cocktail menu. Co-owner Julie Reiner is the mistress of mixology: the Persephone, for instance, is a subtle pomegranate Martini named for the queen of Hades. **Photo** *p212*.

Hiro

Maritime Hotel, 371 W 16th Street, at Ninth Avenue (1-212 727 0212). Subway: A, C, E to 14th Street; L to Eighth Avenue. **Open** 10pm-4am daily. **Average drink** $12. **Credit** AmEx, MC, V. **Map** p403 C27 ⓪

Past the guard at the speakeasy window is a vast, vaulted room lined with backlit paper screens. The place is often filled with girls in tube tops and the banker types who love them, as well as an occasional Rolling Stones heiress (Elizabeth Jagger, Theodora Richards). Signature cocktails, such as the Sakenade

The **Boogaloo**. *See p222.*

(saké, fresh ginger and lemon juice), are the kinds of delicious drinks that taste benign but quickly kick your ass – as they should, for $12.

Opus 22 Turntable Lounge

559 W 22nd Street, at Eleventh Avenue (1-212 243 1851). Subway: C, E to 23rd Street. **Open** 5pm-2am daily. **Average drink** $7. **Credit** AmEx, MC, V. **Map** p404 C26 ④

Sunsets over the Hudson remain the draw at this sleek space off the West Side Highway. But new owner Eddie Lee brought in a menu of upscale eats, like macaroni au gratin with ham and parmesan, and cream of melon soup with pepper and mint. Lee has revamped the open-air room, covering the space in Brazilian cherry wood and charcoal-grey upholstery. A custom-designed sound system and DJ booth lure aspiring artists during open-turntable sessions.

Park Bar

15 E 15th Street, between Fifth Avenue & Union Square West (1-212 367 9085). Subway: L, N, Q, R, W, 4, 5, 6 to 14th Street-Union Square. **Open** 3pm-5am daily. **Average drink** $7. **Credit** AmEx, MC, V. **Map** p403 E27 ④

What's small, dark and packed all over? Park Bar's dusky den of a room might be teensier than the average studio apartment, but for all that it has charm to spare. You'll need to arrive early to have any hope of a seat at the bar. Hungry drinkers often order pizza from nearby Giorgio's.

Passerby

436 W 15th Street, between Ninth & Tenth Avenues (1-212 206 7321). Subway: A, C, E to 14th Street; L to Eighth Avenue. **Open** 6pm-2am Mon-Sat. **Average drink** $8. **Credit** AmEx, MC, V. **Map** p403 C27 ④

The unmarked Passerby is a sort of clubhouse for arty types. Flashing coloured floor panels, created by artist Piotr Uklansky, pulse with the DJ's beats and lend an ambient glow. Early evening, this is a civilised place for a drink; later, things can get deliciously raucous.

Sapa

43 W 24th Street, between Fifth & Sixth Avenues (1-212 929 1800). Subway: N, R, W, 6 to 23rd Street. **Open** 5.30pm-1am Mon-Thur, Sun; 5.30pm-2am Fri, Sat. **Average drink** $9. **Credit** AmEx, DC, Disc, MC, V. **Map** p404 E26 ④

The savvy AvroKO design team has come up with another thrilling bar and restaurant: a gorgeous minimalist lounge with walnut floors, onyx tabletops and six private restrooms surrounding a pool of water. A French-Vietnamese menu by chef Kenneth Tufo includes spring and summer rolls, as well as more adventurous main dishes like cider-braised monkfish with salsify. Inventive cocktails such as the Pegu (Tangueray, *calamansi*-lime juice, Cointreau and orange bitters) are available to match.

Midtown West

Ava Lounge

Majestic Hotel, 210 W 55th Street, between Seventh Avenue & Broadway (1-212 956 7020). Subway: N, Q, R, W to 57th Street. **Open** 5pm-3am Mon, Tue; 5pm-4am Wed-Fri; 6pm-4am Sat; 6pm-3am Sun. **Average drink** $9. **Credit** AmEx, Disc, MC, V. **Map** p405 D22 ④

The top of the Majestic Hotel has been transformed into a penthouse lounge and rooftop deck with views of both the twinkling cityscape and the blondes in black who serve Key lime Martinis and Flirtinis. Modern, chic and slick but not overdesigned, the space is often used for private parties, and the outdoor patio is a lure for smokers. **Photo** *p215*.

Hudson Bar

The Hudson, 356 W 58th Street, between Eighth & Ninth Avenues (1-212 554 6343). Subway: A, B, C, D, 1 to 59th Street-Columbus Circle. **Open** 4pm-2am Mon-Sat; 4pm-1am Sun. *Library bar* noon-2am Mon-Sat; noon-1am Sun. **Average drink** $10. **Credit** AmEx, DC, Disc, MC, V. **Map** p405 C22 ④

Like a lime-green stairway to heaven, an escalator leads to the lobby of Ian Schrager's Hudson hotel, where you'll find three separate bars. Most dazzling is the postmodern Hudson Bar, with a backlit glass floor. The Library bar marries class (leather sofas) and kitsch (photos of cows in pillbox hats). If that's too cute, then get some air in the seasonal Private Park (open April to November), the leafy, cigarette-friendly outdoor bar lit by candle chandeliers.

Kemia Bar

630 Ninth Avenue, at 44th Street (1-212 582 3200). Subway: A, C, E to 42nd Street-Port Authority. **Open** 6pm-1am Tue-Fri; 8pm-2am Sat. **Average drink** $8. **Credit** AmEx, MC, V. **Map** p404 C24 ⑤

Descending into this lush Middle Eastern oasis is like penetrating the fourth wall of a brilliant stage set. Gossamer fabric billows from the ceiling, ottomans are clustered around low tables, and dark-wood floors are strewn with rose petals. A soulful DJ helps, as do the luscious libations.

Marseille

630 Ninth Avenue, at 44th Street (1-212 333 3410). Subway: A, C, E to 42nd Street-Port Authority. **Open** noon-1am daily. **Average drink** $9. **Credit** AmEx, MC, V. **Map** p404 C24 ⑤

Oenophiles line up at this slice of Paris, eager to taste selections from the 300 varieties kept in a cellar that once served as a bank vault. Wine director Sterling Roig has received accolades for putting together an eclectic list with overlooked vintages from France's Languedoc-Roussillon and Loire regions, as well as Sardinia and Sicily, in Italy. More than a dozen wines are sold by the glass.

Oak Bar

The Plaza Hotel, 768 Fifth Avenue, at Central Park South (1-212 546 5320). Subway: N, R, W to Fifth Avenue-59th Street. **Open** 11.30am-1.30am Mon-Sat;

11.30am-midnight Sun. **Average drink** $10. **Credit** AmEx, DC, Disc, MC, V. **Map** p405 E22 **52**

Small wonder Gloria Steinem once refused to leave this stunning classic, formerly open to men only, even after the manager removed her table. Study the Ashcan School murals by Everett Shinn while sipping a single malt ($13 to $24 per glass), and bend an elbow where Diamond Jim Brady and George M Cohan once tippled.

Single Room Occupancy

360 W 53rd Street, between Eighth & Ninth Avenues (1-212 765 6299). Subway: B, D to Seventh Avenue; C, E to 50th Street. **Open** 7.30pm-2am Mon, Tue; 7.30pm-4am Wed-Sat. **Average drink** $8. **Credit** AmEx. **Map** p405 C23 **53**

It's hard to overstate the importance of feeling like a New York insider. At this wine and beer speakeasy, where you must ring the doorbell to enter, you'll be deliciously in the know. SRO comfortably fits 20 or so, but more have been known to squeeze into the cave-like medieval-modern space. Locals think of owner Markos as the host of their favourite nightly party, and on one random evening a month, he rewards them with go-go dancers.

Town

Chambers, 15 W 56th Street, between Fifth & Sixth Avenues (1-212 582 4445). Subway: F to 57th Street; N, R, W to Fifth Avenue-59th Street. **Open** noon-1am daily. **Average drink** $12. **Credit** AmEx, DC, Disc, MC, V. **Map** p405 E22 **54**

Monied drinkers in their middle years pick from four designated drinking areas: the narrow bar at the head of the passageway leading to the restaurant; the spacious back balcony bar; the hotel's lofty lobby bar; and the mezzanine bar. There's a pricey wine list, but you might prefer a sassy house cocktail like the Town Plum, made with plum nectar and the premium French grape vodka Cîroc.

Trousdale

226 W 50th Street, between Broadway & Eighth Avenue (1-212 262 4070). Subway: C, E to 50th Street. **Open** 4pm-1am Mon-Thur; 4pm-2am Fri, Sat; 1.30-11pm Sun. **Average drink** $8. **Credit** AmEx, Disc, MC, V. **Map** p404 D23 **55**

Slick and sophisticated, the venue (designed by Jeffrey Goodman and Steven Charlton) is so unapologetically upscale – leather couches, Jonathan Adler throw pillows – that there's no beer on tap. After all, you don't want to be seen chugging a pint. Speciality Martinis are featured, and your sweet tooth will thank you for the Olé au Lait, a creamy cocktail of Stoli Vanil, Kahlúa, crème de cacao and milk.

Midtown East

Artisanal

See p204 for listing. **Map** p404 E25 **56**

Wine and cheese move into the realm of art at this restaurant's boisterous bar. There are 150-plus wines by the glass, and 250 or so cheeses – enough

permutations that you can forever swear off chardonnay and Brie. (Pairing flights can help the uninitiated.) The bar area is packed at dinner, when fondue-craving hordes await their tables.

Brasserie

See p204 for listing. **Map** p404 E23 **57**

Take an architectural tour: this striking spot, in the basement of Mies van der Rohe's much-lauded Seagram Building, was outfitted by Diller + Scofidio. It features backlit bottles stored horizontally behind opaque glass, a long granite bar and curved walls made of pear wood. You can spy on new arrivals via stop-motion images on screens mounted above the bar.

PJ Clarke's

915 Third Avenue, at 55th Street (1-212 317 1616). Subway: E, V to Lexington Avenue-53rd Street; 6 to 51st Street. **Open** 11.30am-4am daily. **Average drink** $7. **Credit** AmEx, DC, Disc, MC, V. **Map** p405 F22 **58**

PJ Clarke's has been a beloved saloon since 1884, but the storied, hard-drinking hacks, pols, molls and palookas of yore have been supplanted by briefcase-toting execs, cashmere-clad couples and baseball-capped buddies. Recently restored to vintage perfection, Clarke's draws the likes of Johnny Depp and Bill Murray. Bartenders are polite and the pours generous. Must-peeks: the Tiffany stained glass in

The winner is...

Every year *Time Out New York* magazine recognises the best offerings of the city's bars. The combination of our expert imbibers and the votes of *Time Out* readers results in a list of outstanding bars chosen by those in the know. Below we've selected some of the winners from the 2005 awards. Get out there and raise a glass!

Best wine bar
'inoteca. *See p213.*

Best new cocktail list
5 Ninth. *See p217.*

Best beer garden
Bohemian Hall and Beer Garden. *See p222.*

Best bathroom
Schiller's Liquor Bar. *See p213.*

Worst-kept secret (drink division)
East Side Company Bar. *See 213.*

the men's room and the cosy dining alcove where Renée Zellweger and Salma Hayek order steak to amp up their real-girl cred.

Sakagura

211 E 43rd Street, between Second & Third Avenues (1-212 953 7253). Subway: 42nd Street S, 4, 5, 6, 7 to 42nd Street-Grand Central. **Open** noon-2.30pm, 6pm-midnight Mon-Thur; noon-2.30pm, 6pm-1am Fri; 6pm-1am Sat; 6-11pm Sun. **Average drink** $7. **Credit** AmEx, DC, Disc, MC, V. **Map** p404 F24 ⑤⑨

At Sakagura, you'll have to do a little work: walk through the unmarked lobby of an office building, down a few stairs and along a basement corridor. Finally, enter a quiet room of bamboo and blond wood and prepare to learn about saké. The 200 kinds available here, categorised by region, are served in delicate handblown-glass vessels. If you can't decide, try a Sakagura Tasting Set, which teams an appetizer, entrée and dessert with three corresponding sakés. Check out the candlelit restrooms, cleverly fashioned from giant saké casks.

Tao

See p205 for listing. **Map** p405 E22 ⑥⓪

This sceney palace is forever packed with suits and skirts; a 16ft stone Buddha towers over the dining room. Drinks include many, many sakes and a list of appealing Asian-inflected cocktails.

Uptown

Upper West Side

Bin 71

237 Columbus Avenue, at 71st Street (1-212 362 5446). Subway: B, C to 72nd Street. **Open** 5pm-midnight Mon, Tue; 11am-1am Wed-Sun. **Average drink** $8. **Credit** AmEx, Disc, MC, V. **Map** p405 C20 ⑥①

This classy new wine bar from father and son Anselmo and Lawrence Bondulich helps fill the neighbourhood's 'inoteca void. Anselmo is coming out of retirement to create dishes like pink-snapper sashimi with garlic oil, and meatballs braised in white wine, lemon and bay leaves. Snackers can share antipasto platters or cheese plates, paired with wines from California, Italy, France and Spain. Of course, there's plenty of fine beer too.

Café del Bar

945 Columbus Avenue, between 106th & 107th Streets (1-917 741 0270). Subway: B, C to 103rd Street. **Open** 6pm-2am Tue-Sat; 8pm-2am Sun. **Average drink** $4. **Credit** AmEx, MC, V. **Map** p406 C16 ⑥②

If you can't get to Jamaica, Red Stripes here are $4 and the soundtrack is pure reggae-runs-the-world. Located next door to the tiny French-Caribbean bistro A, the bar specialises in island drinks like a potent Dark and Stormy, made with ginger beer and spiced rum, or a Sorrel-a-Go-Go, made with rum, Cointreau and sorrel.

Upper East Side

Barbalùc Wine Bar

135 E 65th Street, between Park & Lexington Avenues (1-212 774 1999). Subway: F to Lexington Avenue-63rd Street; 6 to 68th Street-Hunter College. **Open** 6pm-midnight Mon-Sat. **Credit** AmEx, DC, MC, V. **Map** p405 E21 ⑥③

The kitchen emphasises food from the north-eastern Italian region of Friuli, and the upstairs bar follows through with perhaps the city's most extensive list of Friulian wine, including two dozen by the glass. The mood is quite civil, and on Fridays a pleasant jazz trio softens the stark white-on-white decor.

Central Park Boathouse

Central Park Lake, Park Drive North, at 72nd Street (1-212 517 2233). Subway: 6 to 68th Street-Hunter College. **Open** noon-4pm, 5.30-9.30pm Mon-Fri; 9.30am-4pm, 6-9.30pm Sat, Sun. **Average drink** $7. **Credit** AmEx, DC, MC, V. **Map** p405 D20 ⑥④

The view from the tree-shaded deck bordering the boat-freckled lake looks like a shot framed by Woody Allen. Step into the film at the outdoor bar after Sunday brunch (the Bloody Marys are mighty powerful). Plush leather armchairs near the fireplace beckon in winter. A Boathouse Martini (Bacardi Limón, triple sec and a splash each of lime and cranberry juices) will make you smile all year long.

Lexington Bar & Books

1020 Lexington Avenue, at 73rd Street (1-212 717 3902). Subway: 6 to 77th Street. **Open** 5pm-3am Mon-Wed, Sun; 5pm-4am Thur-Sat. **Average drink** $10. **Credit** AmEx, DC, MC, V. **Map** p405 E20 ⑥⑤

Order a drink, and the barman offers you an ashtray. Yes, it's a legal cigar bar – and one with class: walls are lined with books and fine brandies, beer and Martini glasses are frosted, and the selection of single-malt Scotches and cognacs is top flight. If James Bond was an East Sider, you would find him here.

Uva

1486 Second Avenue, at 77th Street (1-212 472 4552). Subway: 6 to 77th Street. **Open** noon-2am Mon-Thur, Sun; noon-3am Fri, Sat. **Average drink** $9. **Credit** AmEx, MC, V ($30 minimum). **Map** p405 F19 ⑥⑥

The Upper East Side has plenty of rustic Italian restaurants but it could use a few more wine bars. A 200-year-old wooden floor and antique couches give this one a warm, worn-in feel. You can take your pick of cured meats and cheeses to pair with many Italian wines (30 are available by the glass).

Above 116th Street

Den

2150 Fifth Avenue, between 131st & 132nd Streets (1-212 234 3045). Subway: 2, 3 to 135th Street. **Open** 6pm-1am Mon-Thur; 6pm-4am Fri, Sun. **Average drink** $9. **Credit** AmEx, Disc, MC, V. **Map** p407 E12 ⑥⑦

Eat, Drink, Shop

Under the glow of a classic old streetlamp, a dapper doorman tips his derby and welcomes visitors to a subterranean lounge set in a Harlem brownstone. Designer Carlos Jimenez, whose resumé includes industry (food) and Flow, has cast a lush red haze over the 1920s-era room, which is lined with exposed brick and accented by a copper-topped bar.

Lenox Lounge

288 Malcolm X Boulevard (Lenox Avenue), between 124th & 125th Streets (1-212 427 0253). Subway: 2, 3 to 125th Street. **Open** noon-4am daily. **Average drink** $5 (cover varies). **Credit** AmEx, DC, MC, V. **Map** p407 D13 **69**

This is where a street hustler named Malcolm worked before he got religion and added an X to his name. Now the famous Harlem bar, lounge and jazz club welcomes a mix of old-school cats and unobtrusive booze hounds. Settle into the refurbished art deco area at the front or take a table in the zebra-papered back room, then tune in to the haunting presence of Billie Holiday and Miles Davis.

Brooklyn

Bembe

81 South 6th Street, at Berry Street, Williamsburg (1-718 387 5389). Subway: J, M, Z to Marcy Avenue; L to Bedford Avenue. **Open** 7.30pm-4am Mon-Thur; 7pm-4am Fri-Sun. **Average drink** $5. **No credit cards. Map** p411 U8 **69**

At an unmarked hideaway under the Williamsburg Bridge, the swinging clientele dances by candlelight to Latin beats laid down by sexy DJs. Take a breather from the salsa and refuel with tequila shots at the sleek wooden bar. Regulars swear by the post-shot practice of sucking the lime after dipping one side in fresh-ground coffee and the other in sugar.

Boogaloo

168 Marcy Avenue, between Broadway & South 5th Street, Williamsburg (1-718 599 8900). Subway: J, M, Z to Marcy Avenue. **Open** 7pm-4am Tue-Thur; 8pm-4am Fri-Sun. **Average drink** $6. **Credit** AmEx, Disc, MC, V. **Map** p411 U8 **70**

This sleek white hideaway oozes *Barbarella* cool. A long, narrow front room leads to a small dancefloor and DJ station (Latin, house, hip hop and funk); the rooftop space is open in warm weather. Rum is a speciality (some 50 varieties), but bartenders can fix any number of exotic combos. None is especially cheap, but that seems to suit Boogaloo's patrons – a mix of Bedford Avenue habitués, slightly older sophisticates and Pratt students – just fine. **Photo** *p218.*

Brooklyn Social

335 Smith Street, between Carroll & President Streets, Carroll Gardens (1-718 858 7758). Subway: F, G to Carroll Street. **Open** 6pm-2am Mon-Thur; 6pm-4am Fri, Sat; 5pm-2am Sun. **Average drink** $6. **No credit cards. Map** p410 S10 **71**

When Matt Dawson heard that Società Riposto was closing, he thought the old Sicilian social club would make an ideal hipster watering hole. So he gutted

the bland card-playing room and installed designer touches, right? Fuhgeddaboudit. He kept every detail he could and even hung photographs of the original members on the walls. The bar has been kept simple (and prices, reasonable), but there's one significant add-on: a backyard with a patio.

Galapagos

See p316 for listing. **Map** p411 U7 **72**

This perennial Williamsburg fave doubles as a performance space for all kinds of art.

Moto

394 Broadway, at Hooper Street, Williamsburg (1-718 599 6895). Subway: J, M to Hewes Street. **Open** 6pm-2am Mon-Thur, Sun; 6pm-3am Fri, Sat. **Average drink** $6. **No credit cards. Map** p411 V8 **73**

Owners Billy Phelps and John McCormick have somehow created a café-bar evocative of 1930s Paris in a former check-cashing store beneath the J-M elevated tracks. (The film *Eat This New York* captured Moto's rocky transformation on celluloid.) However, the menu is Italian, the wines are handpicked and the beers include Belgian Corsendonk. The pan-Euro attitude, easy subway access, and good food and drink in an intimate triangular room make Moto a Williamsburg must-go.

Superfine

126 Front Street at Pearl Street, Dumbo (1-718 243 9005). Subway: A, C to High Street; F to York Street. **Open** 11.30am-3pm, 6pm-1am Tue-Thur; 11.30am-3pm, 6pm-4am Fri; 2pm-4am Sat; 11am-3pm, 6-10pm Sun. **Average drink** $6. **Credit** AmEx, MC, V. **Map** p411 T9 **74**

Praised for its weekend Southwestern Chili Brunch, this eaterie is also a fine place for drinks any evening of the week (there's also a tiny art gallery and scruffy types in smart-guy glasses). The worn-in mix-and-match furniture is usually occupied by young, suited professionals downing Cosmos, or arty locals who hang at the pool table. You might even see regulars from the Federation of Black Cowboys, who hitch their horses at the door before they take their usual seats at the bar.

Queens

Bohemian Hall & Beer Garden

29-19 24th Avenue, between 29th & 31st Streets, Astoria (1-718 274 0043). Subway: N, W to Astoria Boulevard. **Open** 5pm-2am Mon-Fri; noon-3am Sat, Sun. **Average drink** $4. **Credit** MC, V ($10 minimum). **Map** p412 X3 **75**

Echt Mitteleuropa in the Greek precinct of Astoria? Czech! This authentic (circa 1910) beer hall is a throwback to the time when hundreds of such places dotted the town; the vibe manages to combine the ambience of that era with the youthful spirit of a junior year in Prague. Go for the cheap, robust platters of Czech sausage, $4 Stolis, Spaten Oktoberfests and the rockin' juke. In summer, the huge, tree-canopied beer garden beckons.

Off the beaten path

While New York's size makes it a natural cultural magnet, it can be difficult to sustain smaller, edgy venues in a city this large. Astronomical rents, competition from more established spots and ever-shifting tastes make short work of many hip scenes, leaving the most stridently unique at risk of closure.

With any luck, **Cake Shop** (152 Ludlow Street, between Rivington & Stanton Streets, 1-212 253 0036, www.cake-shop.com), a café-cum-record-store-and-rock-club-bar, will preserve its DIY aesthetic on trendy Ludlow Street. A young, hip crowd packs the sloping downstairs bar for raucous indie bands, while gently dishevelled shoppers browse the wares upstairs. The folks over at **Happy Ending** (302 Broome Street, between Forsyth & Eldridge Streets, 1-212 334 9676; pictured) are always cooking up something seedy in the lounge and former steam rooms of the ex-massage parlour, best visited late on.

On the other side of the East River, in Williamsburg, **Monkey Town** (58 North 3rd Street, between Kent & Wythe Avenues, 1-718 384 1369, www.monkeytownhq.com), which debuted its 32-seat location in the summer of '05, after a year-long hiatus, serves a full plate of audio, visual and culinary experimentation – curators and performers have ranged from the director Miranda July to local noisemakers Black Dice. In an inspired take on dinner theatre, contemporary films are projected (sometimes simultaneously) on four screens while Chanterelle and Alain Ducasse alumni prepare yummy eats. An avant Swedish video installation, for example, might be paired with crêpes and crawfish. Despite the caliber of the kitchen, don't expect anything hoity-toity. 'We're keeping it Brooklyn,' says founder Montgomery Knott.

At **Glass House Gallery** (38 South 1st Street, between Kent & Wythe Avenues, Williamsburg, Brooklyn), you're invited to give as much as you take: the combination of common-use art supplies, cheap beer and carte blanche to draw wherever you like has transformed the walls into an anarchic palimpsest backdrop for the mainly art-punk bands that take its small stage. Since Glass House has neither website nor phone number, check local scene maker Todd P's show list (toddpnyc.com) for upcoming events, most of which he has a hand in putting together. His efforts supply the neighbourhood's underground music scene – cobbled together from warehouse parties, art collectives and old Polish bars – a rare centre of gravity.

Eat, Drink, Shop

Shops & Services

Shop 'til you drop. Rest. Repeat.

Sure, the museums and cultural offerings of the city are impressive but, let's face it, the shopping is truly staggering. You can find just about anything you'd ever want here – the challenge is narrowing down your many options (oh, and paying for your finds). Here's how to navigate the complicated world of NY shopping like a pro, whether your taste leans towards Fifth Avenue glam or thrift-store grunge.

SHOP AROUND

Shopping events such as Barneys' ever-popular twice yearly warehouse sales and designers' frequent sample sales are excellent sources for reduced-price clothing by fashion's biggest names. To find out who's selling where during any given week, consult the Check Out section of *Time Out New York*. Top Button (www.topbutton.com) and the SSS Sample Sales hotline (1-212 947 8748, www.clothingline.com) are also great discount resources. Sales are usually held in the designers' shops or in rented loft spaces. Typically, loft sales are not equipped with changing rooms, so bring a courageous spirit with you (and plenty of cold, hard cash!) and remember to wear appropriate undergarments.

Harlem, the Meatpacking District and Brooklyn's Williamsburg are the city's newest fashion foundations, albeit a bit more far flung than some fashionistas are willing to travel. Serious shoppers agree that the most cutting-edge young labels are found in the **Lower East Side**, along Ludlow Street, although the

uptown's **Fifth Avenue** (between 42nd and 59th Streets) is difficult to beat. Over on the west side of the island, the West Village's **Bleecker Street** has become hot property seemingly overnight, touting the likes of Intermix, LuLu Guinness, Cynthia Rowley, two Ralph Lauren stores (one for men and one for women) and no fewer than *three* Marc Jacobs stores. Now you can window-shop like you're uptown with a cupcake from Magnolia Bakery. To find out the latest stores and hotspots making waves on New York's design scene, visit the TONY website (www.timeoutny.com), click on Check Out and scan the archives.

Pressed for time? Head to one of New York's shopping malls... yes, we said *shopping mall*. You won't get the best deal or the uniqueness of a boutique, but the **Manhattan Mall** (Sixth Avenue, at 33rd Street), the **Shops at Columbus Circle** (Time Warner Center, 10 Columbus Circle, at 59th Street), and the myriad stores in **Trump Tower** (Fifth Avenue, at 56th Street), **Grand Central Terminal** (42nd Street, at Park Avenue) and South Street Seaport's cobblestoned **Pier 17** (Fulton Street, at the East River) are convenient options.

Thursday is the universal – though unofficial – shop-after-work night; most stores remain open until at least 7pm. Stores downtown generally stay open an hour or so later than those uptown. Certain businesses have multiple locations. For shops that have more than two branches, check the business pages in the phone book for additional addresses.

The winner is...

Every year *Time Out New York* recognises the best of the city's shops. The combination of our seasoned retail experts (we're talking major shopaholics) plus the votes of *Time Out* readers results in a must-go-to list of outstanding shops. Below, some of the winners from the 2005 awards.

Best spot for co-ed shopping
Barneys New York. *See p225.*

Best sneakers
Classic Kicks. *See p237.*

Stock most likely to cause fisticuffs
A Bathing Ape. *See p235.*

Best sex shop for prudes
Myla. *See p257.*

Best tech
The **Apple Store**. *See p253.*

Most stylish kids' togs
Calypso Enfant. *See p232.*

One-stop Shopping

Department stores

Barneys New York

660 Madison Avenue, at 61st Street (1-212 826 8900/www.barneys.com). Subway: N, R, W to Fifth Avenue-59th Street; 4, 5, 6 to 59th Street. **Open** 10am-8pm Mon-Fri; 10am-7pm Sat; 11am-6pm Sun. **Credit** AmEx, MC, V.

The top designers are represented at this bastion of New York style. At Christmas time, Barneys has the most provocative windows in town (*see p246* **So you know, it's Christmas**). Its co-op branches carry young designers as well as secondary lines from heavies like Marc Jacobs and Theory. Every February and August, the Chelsea co-op hosts the Barneys Warehouse Sale, in which prices are reduced by 50% to 80%.
Other locations: throughout the city.

Bergdorf Goodman

754 Fifth Avenue, at 57th Street (1-212 753 7300/www.bergdorfgoodman.com). Subway: E, V to Fifth Avenue-53rd Street; N, R, W to Fifth Avenue-59th Street. **Open** 10am-7pm Mon-Wed, Fri, Sat; 10am-8pm Thur; noon-6pm Sun. **Credit** AmEx, DC, MC, V.

Barneys aims for a young, trendy crowd; Bergdorf's is dedicated to an elegant, understated clientele that has plenty of disposable income. Luxury clothes, accessories and even stationery are found here, along with an over-the-top Beauty Level. The famed men's store is across the street (745 Fifth Avenue).

Bloomingdale's

1000 Third Avenue, at 59th Street (1-212 705 2000/www.bloomingdales.com). Subway: N, R, W to Lexington Avenue-59th Street; 4, 5, 6 to 59th Street. **Open** 10am-8.30pm Mon-Fri; 10am-7pm Sat; 11am-7pm Sun. **Credit** AmEx, MC, V.

Bloomies is a gigantic, glitzy department store offering everything from handbags and cosmetics to furniture and designer duds. Brace yourself for the crowds – this store ranks among the city's most popular tourist attractions, right up there with the Empire State Building. Check out the cool new little-sister branch in Soho.
Other locations: 504 Broadway, between Broome & Spring Streets (1-212 279 5900).

Henri Bendel

712 Fifth Avenue, at 56th Street (1-212 247 1100/www.henribendel.com). Subway: E, V to Fifth Avenue-53rd Street; N, R, W to Fifth Avenue-59th Street. **Open** 10am-8pm Mon-Sat; noon-7pm Sun. **Credit** AmEx, DC, Disc, MC, V.

Bendel's lavish quarters resemble an opulently appointed townhouse. Naturally there are elevators – no one expects you to walk; this is Fifth Avenue – but it's nicer to saunter up the elegant, winding staircase. Prices are comparable to those of other upscale

Barneys New York.

stores, but the merchandise somehow seems more desirable here – we guess it must be those darling brown-striped shopping bags.

Jeffrey New York

449 W 14th Street, between Ninth & Tenth Avenues (1-212 206 1272). Subway: A, C, E to 14th Street; L to Eighth Avenue. **Open** 10am-8pm Mon-Wed, Fri; 10am-9pm Thur; 10am-7pm Sat; 12.30-6pm Sun. **Credit** AmEx, MC, V.

Jeffrey Kalinsky, a former Barneys shoe buyer, was a Meatpacking District pioneer with his namesake shop, a branch of the Atlanta, Georgia, original. Designer clothing abounds here – Lang, Versace and Saint Laurent among other brands. But the centrepiece is the shoe salon, which features Manolo Blahnik, Prada and Robert Clergerie.

Lord & Taylor

424 Fifth Avenue, between 38th & 39th Streets (1-212 391 3344). Subway: B, D, F, V to 42nd Street-Bryant Park; 7 to Fifth Avenue. **Open** 10am-8.30pm Mon-Fri; 10am-7.30pm Sat; 11am-7pm Sun. **Credit** AmEx, Disc, MC, V.

Classic is the word at Lord & Taylor, in both the clothing stocked and the presentation; this is where the tradition of dramatic Christmas window displays began. Check out two recent dining additions: An American Place and the Signature Café, run by celebrity chef Larry Forgione.

Macy's

151 W 34th Street, between Broadway & Seventh Avenue (1-212 695 4400/www.macys.com). Subway: B, D, F, N, Q, R, V, W to 34th Street-Herald Square; 1, 2, 3 to 34th Street-Penn Station. **Open** 10am-9pm Mon-Sat; 11am-8pm Sun. **Credit** AmEx, MC, V.

Behold the real miracle on 34th Street. Macy's has everything: designer labels and lower-priced knock-offs, a pet-supply shop, a restaurant in the Cellar (the

Eat, Drink, Shop

Baby blues

It's official: the New Yorker uniform is denim and New York has beome the centre of the ever-expanding jeans universe. Here are some of the hippest hip-hugger brands.

CK39
Making good on the decades-old decree that nothing gets between you and your Calvins, designer Calvin Klein has rolled out a spankin' new premium denim collection with classic, clean-lined styles for girls and guys.
● *SCK39 black bootcut jeans, $185, from Calvin Klein, 654 Madison Avenue, at 60th Street (1 212 292 9000).*

Edun
Designer Ali Hewson and her husband, U2 singer Bono, have joined up with super-hip label Rogan to produce Edun, a clothing line that was set up to create sustainable employment in developing areas. Desirable designs include super-stylish men's and women's jeans made in countries including Tunisia and Peru.
● *Edun slash-pocket bootcut Sphinx jeans in Elven wash, $170, from Saks Fifth Avenue (see p226).*

Ødyn
This ladies' premium denim line, inspired by Scandinavian folklore, offers intricately detailed pieces named after a Danish fairy-tale characters. They come with silk tags bearing drawings inspired by their namesake.
● *Ødyn Thumbelina jeans, $140, from Zabari, 506 Broadway, between Broome & Spring Streets (1-212 431 7980).*

Stitch's Jeans
Named largely after Native American tribes, the rugged styles from this new Old West-themed line are made of denim aged in antique redwood barrels, resulting in dungarees that look like they were broken in on the back of a horse.
● *Stitch's Jeans Feather, $275, from Barneys New York (see p224).*

Ü Denim
From the folks behind dungaree-world darling Yanük comes this wallet-friendly women's collection, which boasts fine fabric finishes, flattering cuts and high-quality denim.
● *Ü Denim five-pocket graphite Slim Flare jeans, $88, at Lord & Taylor (see p225).*

housewares section), a Metropolitan Museum of Art gift shop and – gulp – a McDonald's on the kids' floor. The store also offers Macy's by Appointment, a free service that allows shoppers to order goods or clothing over the phone and have them shipped anywhere in the world (1-800 343 0121).

Saks Fifth Avenue
611 Fifth Avenue, at 50th Street (1-212 753 4000). Subway: E, V to Fifth Avenue-53rd Street. **Open** 10am-7pm Mon-Wed, Fri, Sat; 10am-8pm Thur; noon-6pm Sun. **Credit** AmEx, DC, Disc, MC, V.

Although Saks maintains a presence in 24 states, the Fifth Avenue location is the original, established in 1924 by New York retailers Horace Saks and Bernard Gimbel. The store features all the big names in women's fashion, from Armani to Yves St Laurent, plus an excellent menswear department and a children's section. There are also fine household linens, La Prairie skincare and attentive customer service. New management is exploring the possibility of a major overhaul this year; at press time, Frank Gehry's name had made the rumour mill as the architect.

The winner is...

The days are gone when jeans were just jeans and a single style saw you through all occasions. *Time Out New York* helps you find denims to fill every wardrobe niche.

Instant old favourite
Paper Denim & Cloth 'LTD Old School' men's relaxed bootcut jeans, $198, at Barneys New York (*see p225*) and Scoop (*see p231*).

Best bang for your buck
Levi's Red Tab 501s in rusted wash, $54, *at the Levi's Store, 536 Broadway, between Prince & Spring Streets (1-646 613 1847).*

Coolest curve-huggers
James premium five-pocket bootleg in Phantom, $180, at Scoop (*see p231*).

Greatest butt (men's division)
SALT Works Bedford Street jeans in Anger wash, $136, at Bloomingdale's (*see p225*).

Greatest butt (women's division)
Paige Laurel Canyon five-pocket jeans in medium clean wash, $169, Bergdorf Goodman (*see p225*).

Best rigid denim
Nudie regular Ralf jeans in dry selvedge denim, $265, at Atrium, 644 Broadway, at Bleecker Street (1-212 473 9200).

Best skinny-leg jean
The Nomad Tribe stretch skinny Saigon jeans, $128, at Atrium (*see above*).

Takashimaya
693 Fifth Avenue, between 54th & 55th Streets (1-212 350 0100). Subway: E, V to Fifth Avenue-53rd Street. **Open** 10am-7pm Mon-Sat; noon-5pm Sun. **Credit** AmEx, DC, MC, V.
Step out of the Fifth Avenue hustle-bustle and into Takashimaya to experience the Zen garden of the retail world. Explore floor by floor, indulging your senses as you pass beauty essentials, furniture and the men's and women's signature clothing collections. A cup of tea in the basement Tea Box makes the perfect end to a trip to consumer nirvana.

National chains

National chains
Many New Yorkers regard chain stores as unimaginative places to shop, but that doesn't mean you won't have to stand behind a long line of locals while waiting at the register. Stores such as American Apparel, Anthropologie, Banana Republic, Express, H&M, Old Navy, Target and Urban Outfitters abound. To find the nearest location of your favourite chain, refer to the phone book.

Fashion

Flagships
These big-name designers have clothes horses chomping at the bit for new designs and seasonal collections.

Alexander McQueen
417 W 14th Street, between Ninth & Tenth Avenues (1-212 645 1797/www.alexandermcqueen.com). Subway: A, C, E to 14th Street; L to Eighth Avenue. **Open** 11am-7pm Mon-Sat; 12.30-6pm Sun. **Credit** AmEx, DC, Disc, MC, V.
A barrel-vaulted ceiling and serene lighting make the rebellious Brit's Meatpacking District store feel like a religious retreat. But the top-stitched denim skirts and leather jeans are far from monastic.

Bottega Veneta
699 Fifth Avenue, between 54th & 55th Streets (1-212 371 5511/www.bottegaveneta.com). Subway: E, V to Fifth Avenue; N, R, W to Fifth Avenue-59th Street. **Open** 10am-6.30pm Mon-Wed, Fri, Sat; 10am-7pm Thur; noon-5pm Sun. **Credit** AmEx, DC, Disc, MC, V.
At this luxe Italian label's largest store worldwide, a dramatic leather-and-steel staircase links the ground floor with a mezzanine. The gargantuan emporium stocks the complete line of shoes and handbags, along with men's and women's apparel available only here.

Burberry
9 E 57th Street, between Fifth & Madison Avenues (1-212 407 7100/www.burberry.com). Subway: E, V to Fifth Avenue-53rd Street; N, R, W to Fifth Avenue-59th Street. **Open** 9.30am-7pm Mon-Fri; 9.30am-6pm Sat; noon-6pm Sun. **Credit** AmEx, DC, Disc, MC, V.
Now that Burberry has ballooned into this six-storey tower, it can peddle more of its trademark tartan-plaid wares, plus baby and home accessory lines. **Other locations**: 131 Spring Street, between Greene & Wooster Streets (1-212 925 9300).

Chanel
15 E 57th Street, between Fifth & Madison Avenues (1-212 355 5050/www.chanel.com). Subway: E, V to Fifth Avenue-53rd Street; N, R, W to Fifth Avenue-

Eat, Drink, Shop

59th Street. **Open** 10am-6.30pm Mon-Wed, Fri; 10am-7pm Thur; 10am-6pm Sat; noon-5pm Sun. **Credit** AmEx, DC, MC, V.

With a façade that resembles the iconic Chanel No.5 perfume bottle, the brand's flagship conjures the spirit of Madame Coco herself. Fashion architect Peter Marino recently redesigned and enlarged the space for this haul of divine Frenchness. Drop in at Chanel Fine Jewelry (733 Madison Avenue, at 64th Street, 1-212 535 5828) for correspondingly elegant baubles and beads.

Other locations: 139 Spring Street, at Wooster Street (1-212 334 0055); 737 Madison Avenue, at 64th Street (1-212 535 5505).

Diane von Furstenberg, the Shop

385 W 12th Street, between Washington Street & West Side Highway (1-646 486 4800/www. dvf.com). Subway: A, C, E to 14th Street; L to Eighth Avenue. **Open** 11am-6pm Mon-Wed, Fri; 11am-8pm Thur; 11am-5pm Sat; noon-5pm Sun. **Credit** AmEx, Disc, MC, V.

Although she's known for her classic wrap dress (she sold 5 million of them in the 1970s), indefatigable socialite Diane von Furstenberg has installed much more at this *soigné* space, which resembles the inside of a glittery jewel box. Whether you go for ultra-feminine dresses or sporty knits, you'll emerge from the changing room feeling like a princess.

Dolce & Gabbana

825 Madison Avenue, between 68th & 69th Streets (1-212 249 4100/www.dolcegabbana.it). Subway: 6 to 68th Street-Hunter College. **Open** 10am-6pm Mon-Wed, Fri, Sat; 10am-7pm Thur. **Credit** AmEx, DC, MC, V.

The Italian design team of Domenico Dolce and Stefano Gabbana gives love to uptowners and downtowners alike. Visit the tonier Madison Avenue locale (and see for yourself how close the Canal Street knock-offs come to the real thing), or shop the West Broadway store for the lower-priced D&G line. **Other locations**: D&G, 434 West Broadway, between Prince & Spring Streets (1-212 965 8000).

Donna Karan New York

819 Madison Avenue, between 68th & 69th Streets (1-212 861 1001/www.donnakaran.com). Subway: 6 to 68th Street-Hunter College. **Open** 10am-6pm Mon-Wed, Fri, Sat; 10am-7pm Thur; noon-6pm Sun. **Credit** AmEx, DC, MC, V.

Created around a central garden with a bamboo forest, Donna Karan's upscale flagship caters to men, women and the home. Check out the organic café at the nearby DKNY store, as well as Donna-approved reads, clothing, shoes and vintage furniture. **Other locations**: DKNY, 655 Madison Avenue, at 60th Street (1-212 223 3569).

Gucci

685 Fifth Avenue, at 54th Street (1-212 826 2600/www.gucci.com). Subway: E, V to Fifth Avenue-53rd Street. **Open** 10am-6.30pm Mon-Wed, Fri; 10am-7pm Thur; Sat; noon-6pm Sun. **Credit** AmEx, DC, Disc, MC, V.

The abstract decadent vibe pulsing through this five-storey temple of fashion hasn't faded with the departure of Tom Ford, who designed the store. Men's and women's shoes are spread out on their own floors, and even if you're not in the market, the jewels on the ground level are worth a gander. **Other locations**: 840 Madison Avenue, between 69th & 70th Streets (1-212 717 2619).

Jill Stuart

100 Greene Street, between Prince & Spring Streets (1-212 343 2300/www.jillstuart.com). Subway: N, R, W to Prince Street; 6 to Spring Street. **Open** 11am-7pm Mon-Sat; noon-6pm Sun. **Credit** AmEx, MC, V.

Vintage mixes with vixen at Stuart's cavernous boutique. Womenswear and accessories (including shoes, handbags, casual and cocktail clothes) for the young and modern make their home upstairs; head downstairs to find a boudoir-like setting – complete with antique armoire and Victorian garment rack – devoted to a handpicked vintage collection.

Louis Vuitton

1 E 57th Street, at Fifth Avenue (1-212 758 8877/www.vuitton.com). Subway: F to 57th Street; N, R, W to Fifth Avenue-59th Street. **Open** 10am-7pm Mon-Wed, Fri, Sat; 10am-8pm Thur; noon-6pm Sun. **Credit** AmEx, DC, Disc, MC, V.

Vuitton's flagship was recently relocated and revamped to celebrate the company's 150th anniversary. The four-storey, glass-encased retail cathedral certainly gives cause for jubilation: crane your neck to view the three-floor-high LED wall screen and antique Vuitton trunks suspended from the ceiling. The much-coveted bags and ready-to-wear collection are here as well. **Other locations**: 116 Greene Street, between Prince & Spring Streets (1-212 274 9090).

Marc Jacobs

163 Mercer Street, between Houston & Prince Streets (1-212 343 1490/www.marcjacobs.com). Subway: B, D, F, V to Broadway-Lafayette Street; N, R, W to Prince Street; 6 to Bleecker Street. **Open** 11am-7pm Mon-Sat; noon-6pm Sun. **Credit** AmEx, DC, Disc, MC, V.

Men and women get fashion parity at Jacobs's Soho boutique. A separate-but-equal policy rules on the designer's Bleecker Street strip, where a trio of stores – men's, women's and accessories – keeps the West Village well outfitted. **Other locations**: Marc by Marc Jacobs, 403-405 Bleecker Street, at 11th Street (1-212 924 0026); Marc Jacobs Accessories, 385 Bleecker Street, at Perry Street (1-212 924 6126).

Prada

575 Broadway, at Prince Street (1-212 334 8888/www.prada.com). Subway: N, R, W to Prince Street. **Open** 11am-7pm Mon-Sat; noon-6pm Sun. **Credit** AmEx, Disc, MC, V.

The Rem Koolhaas-designed Soho flagship cemented Prada's status as the label of choice for New York's fashion fleet (yes, you still have to put your name on a waiting list to buy the latest shoe styles).

The giant wood Wave structure is the store's focal point. If you're interested only in accessories, then skip the crowds at the two larger shops and stop by the small Fifth Avenue location.
Other locations: 724 Fifth Avenue, at 57th Street (1-212 664 0010); 841 Madison Avenue, at 70th Street (1-212 327 4200).

Ralph Lauren

867 Madison Avenue, at 72nd Street (1-212 606 2100/www.polo.com). Subway: 6 to 68th Street-Hunter College. **Open** 10am-7pm Mon-Wed, Fri, Sat; 10am-8pm Thur; noon-5pm Sun. **Credit** AmEx, DC, Disc, MC, V.
Ralph Lauren spent $14 million turning the old Rhinelander mansion into an Ivy League dream of a superstore: it's filled with oriental rugs, English paintings, riding whips, leather club chairs, old mahogany and fresh flowers. The young homeboys, skaters and bladers who've adopted Ralphie's togs head straight to Polo Sport across the street.
Other locations: Ralph Lauren Boutique, 380 Bleecker Street, between Charles & Perry Streets (1-212 645 5513); Polo Sport, 381 Bleecker Street, between Charles & Perry Streets (1-646 638 0684).

Stella McCartney

429 W 14th Street, between Ninth & Tenth Avenues (1-212 255 1556/www.stellamccartney. com). Subway: A, C, E to 14th Street; L to Eighth Avenue. **Open** noon-7pm Mon-Sat; 12.30-6pm Sun. **Credit** AmEx, DC, Disc, MC, V.
Celeb designer McCartney, who won acclaim for her rock-star collections for Chloé, now showcases pricey lines of glam-sprite womenswear, shoes and accessories at her first-ever store.

Boutiques

Bird

430 Seventh Avenue, between 14th & 15th Streets, Park Slope, Brooklyn (1-718 768 4940). Subway: F to 15th Street-Prospect Park. **Open** 11.30am-7pm Mon-Sat; noon-6pm Sun. **Credit** AmEx, Disc, MC, V.
Park Slope's Bird has always been a favourite of neighbourhood girls looking for designer dresses and tees, but new owner Jennifer Mankins recently made it the spot in brownstone Brooklyn for jeans, stocking Chip & Pepper, James Jeans and Wrangler, to name just a few.

Bond 07

7 Bond Street, between Broadway & Lafayette Street (1-212 677 8487). Subway: B, D, F, V to Broadway-Lafayette Street; 6 to Bleecker Street. **Open** 11am-7pm Mon-Sat; noon-7pm Sun. **Credit** AmEx, MC, V.
Selima Salaun, of the famed Le Corset by Selima (*see p232*) and Selima Optique (*see p238*), has branched out from undies and eyewear to embrace an eclectic mix of clothing (Alice Roi, Colette Dinnigan, etcetera), accessories and French furniture. Vintage eyewear and bags are also available.

Calypso Christiane Celle

654 Hudson Street, between Gansevoort & W 13th Streets (1-646 638 3000/www.calypso-celle.com). Subway: A, C, E to 14th Street; L to Eighth Avenue. **Open** 11am-7pm Mon-Sat; noon-7pm Sun. **Credit** AmEx, DC, MC, V.
Christiane Celle has created a Calypso empire, of which this new outpost in the Meatpacking District is the crown jewel. Stop by any of the shops for gorgeous slip dresses, suits, sweaters and scarves, many from little-known French designers.
Other locations: throughout the city.

Cantaloup

1036 Lexington Avenue, at 74th Street (1-212 249 3566). Subway: 6 to 77th Street. **Open** 11am-7pm Mon-Sat; noon-6pm Sun. **Credit** AmEx, MC, V.
Finally, a boutique that gives UES girls a reason to skip the trip down to Nolita. Cantaloup is chock-full of emerging labels such as James Coviello and Chanpaul, and it's less picked over than the below-Houston boutiques. A sister store is stocked with jeans from elite labels like Loomstate and Tsubi.
Other locations: 1359 Second Avenue, at 74th Street (1-212 288 3569).

Comme des Garçons

520 W 22nd Street, between Tenth & Eleventh Avenues (1-212 604 9200). Subway: C, E to 23rd Street. **Open** 11am-7pm Tue-Sat; noon-6pm Sun. **Credit** AmEx, DC, Disc, MC, V.
In this austere store devoted to Rei Kawakubo's architectural designs for men and women, clothing is hung like art in an innovative space that feels like a gallery – well placed in Chelsea.

Elizabeth Charles

639 1/2 Hudson Street, between Gansevoort & Horatio Streets (1-212 243 3201/www.elizabeth-charles.com). Subway: A, C, E to 14th Street; L to Eighth Avenue. **Open** noon-7.30pm Tue-Sat; noon-6.30pm Sun. **Credit** AmEx, MC, V.
Oz native Elizabeth Charles transferred her eponymous shop from the West Village to the fashion nexus of the Meatpacking District last year, allowing for an even greater selection of flirty clothes from down under designers. Most labels are exclusive to the store, so chances are you won't see your outfit on anyone else – unless you go to Australia.

Girlshop

819 Washington Street, between Gansevoort & Little W 12th Streets (1-212 255 4985/www.girlshop. com). Subway: L to Eighth Avenue. **Open** 11am-7pm Mon-Wed; 11am-8pm Thur-Sat; noon-7pm Sun. **Credit** AmEx, MC, V.
Girlshop.com's bricks-and-mortar sibling offers instant gratification to shoppers who can now try on hot numbers available online by Keanan Dufty, Cigana, or any of the myriad labels – the perfect alternative for those who are short of patience, fall between two sizes or just have bad relationships with their FedEx men.

It's a girl's world at whimsical **Rebecca Taylor**. *See p231.*

Hotel Venus by Patricia Field

382 West Broadway, between Broome & Spring Streets (1-212 966 4066/www.patriciafield. com). Subway: C, E to Spring Street. **Open** 11am-8pm Mon-Fri, Sun; 11am-9pm Sat. **Credit** AmEx, Disc, MC, V.

Patricia Field is a virtuoso at blending eclectic club and street styles (she assembled the costumes for *Sex and the City*). Her idiosyncratic mix of jewellery, make-up and cool clothing proves it.

Kirna Zabete

96 Greene Street, between Prince & Spring Streets (1-212 941 9656/www.kirnazabete.com). Subway: C, E to Spring Street; R, W to Prince Street. **Open** 11am-7pm Mon-Sat; noon-6pm Sun. **Credit** AmEx, MC, V.

The Nick Dine-designed, futuristic-feeling store stocks avant-garde yet wearable women's clothing and shoes from haute designers like Jean Paul Gaultier and Balenciaga, along with a range of fragrances, and the kind of jeans you probably won't want to do the decorating in.

Opening Ceremony

35 Howard Street, between Broadway & Lafayette Street (1-212 219 2688). Subway: J, M, N, Q, R, W, Z, 6 to Canal Street. **Open** 11am-8pm Mon-Sat; noon-7pm Sun. **Credit** AmEx, MC, V.

Opening Ceremony offers a stylish trip around the world, in a warehouse-size space gussied up with grape-coloured walls and crystal chandeliers. The boutique presents fashions by country (2005 kicked off with Germany, and the UK swoops in next). Buyers cull from couture labels, independent designers, mass-market brands and open-air markets.

Pieces

671 Vanderbilt Avenue, at Park Place, Prospect Heights, Brooklyn (1-718 857 7211/www.piecesof bklyn.com). Subway: 2, 3 to Grand Army Plaza. **Open** 10am-7pm Tue-Thur; 10am-8pm Fri, Sat; 11am-6pm Sun. **Credit** AmEx, MC, V.

At this husband-and-wife-owned store, white-washed brick walls are the backdrop for vibrant coed clothing and accessories along the lines of Pretty Punk mini skirts, Ant pinstriped dress shirts and Anja Flint clutches.

Other locations: Pieces of Harlem, 228 W 135th Street, between Adam Clayton Powell Jr Boulevard (Seventh Avenue) & Frederick Douglass Boulevard (Eighth Avenue) (1-212 234 1725).

Rebecca Taylor

260 Mott Street, between Houston & Prince Streets (1-212 966 0406/www.rebeccataylor.com). Subway: B, D, F, V to Broadway-Lafayette Street; N, R, W to Prince Street; 6 to Bleecker Street. **Open** noon-6pm daily. **Credit** AmEx, MC, V.

This New Zealand designer's shop is adorned with murals of fairy worlds and butterflies – arguably the source of inspiration for her whimsical, kittenish dresses and jackets. **Photo** *p230*.

Scoop

861 Washington Street, between 13th & 14th Streets (1-212 691 1905/www.scoopnyc.com). Subway: A, C, E to 14th Street; L to Eighth Avenue. **Open** 11am-8pm Mon-Fri; 11am-7pm Sat; noon-6pm Sun. **Credit** AmEx, DC, Disc, MC, V.

Scoop is the ultimate fashion editor's closet. Clothing from the likes of Juicy Couture, Diane von Furstenberg, Philosophy and others is arranged by hue, not label. The newest outposts, in the Meatpacking District, have fab finds for both genders at neighbouring stores; hit the Soho shop for women only, uptown if you're after a more classic look for guys and gals.

Other locations: 532 Broadway, between Prince & Spring Streets (1-212 925 2886); 1275 Third Avenue, between 73rd and 74th Streets (1-212 535 5577).

Steven Alan

103 Franklin Street, between Church Street & West Broadway (1-212 343 0692/www.stevenalan. com). Subway: 1 to Franklin Street. **Open** 11.30am-7pm Mon-Wed, Fri, Sat; 11.30am-8pm Thur. **Credit** AmEx, MC, V.

Decorated like an old-school general store, this roomy shop leans slightly in favour of the ladies – the front section is earmarked for hot-chick labels such as Botkier, Christopher Deane and, of course, Steven Alan. The back area does right by the gents, though, with Rogan jeans and items from Filson, an outdoorsmen's line. Don't skip the jewellery up front.

Other locations: 465 Amsterdam Avenue, between 82nd & 83rd Streets (1-212 595 8451).

TG-170

170 Ludlow Street, between Houston & Stanton Streets (1-212 995 8660/www.tg170.com). Subway: F to Delancey Street; J, M, Z to Delancey-Essex Streets. **Open** noon-8pm daily. **Credit** AmEx, MC, V.

Terri Gillis has an eye for emerging designers: she was the first to carry Built by Wendy and Pixie Yates. Nowadays, you'll find Jared Gold and Liz Collins pieces hanging in her newly expanded store.

Bargains

Century 21

22 Cortlandt Street, between Broadway & Church Street (1-212 227 9092/www.c21stores.com). Subway: R, W to Cortlandt Street. **Open** 7.45am-8pm Mon-Wed, Fri; 7.45am-8.30pm Thur; 10am-8pm Sat; 11am-7pm Sun. **Credit** AmEx, MC, V.

A white Gucci men's suit for $300? A Marc Jacobs cashmere sweater for less than $200? Roberto Cavalli sunglasses for a scant $30? You're not dreaming – you're shopping at Century 21. The score is rare but intoxicating: savings are usually between 25% and 75% off regular retail prices.

Other locations: 472 86th Street, between Fourth and Fifth Avenues, Bay Ridge, Brooklyn (1-718 748 3266).

Find Outlet

229 Mott Street, between Prince & Spring Streets (1-212 226 5167). Subway: N, R, W to Prince Street; 6 to Spring Street. **Open** noon-7pm daily. **Credit** MC, V.

Skip the sample sales and head to Find Outlet instead. High-fashion samples and overstock are at drastically reduced prices (50% off, on average), so you can you dress like a fashion editor on an editorial assistant's budget.

Other locations: 361 W 17th Street, between Eighth and Ninth Avenues (1-212 243 3177).

The Market NYC

268 Mulberry Street, between Houston & Prince Streets (1-212 580 8995/www.the marketnyc.\om). Subway: B, D, F, V to Broadway-Lafayette Street; N, R, W to Prince Street; 6 to Bleecker Street. **Open** 11am-7pm Sat, Sun. **No credit cards**.

Yes, it's housed in the gymnasium of a church's youth centre, but it's no small shakes. Every Saturday, contemporary fashion and accessory designers hawk their (usually unique) wares here. Open weekends only.

Eat, Drink, Shop

Children's clothing

Babybird
428 Seventh Avenue, between 14th & 15th Streets, Park Slope, Brooklyn (1-718 788 4506). Subway: F to Seventh Avenue. **Open** 10.30am-6.30pm Mon-Sat; noon-6pm Sun. **Credit** AmEx, MC, V.
An offshoot of the neighbouring Bird (an ultra cool store for grown-up girls; *see p229*), Babybird is filled with comfy basics in stylish colours. We love the fish tank built into the register counter.

Calypso Enfant
426 Broome Street, between Crosby & Lafayette Streets (1-212 966 3234/www.calypso-celle.com). Subway: 6 to Spring Street. **Open** 11am-7pm Mon-Sat; noon-7pm Sun. **Credit** AmEx, MC, V.
Fans of Calypso Christiane Celle (*see p229*) adore this Francophile children's boutique: the tiny wool coats look as if they could have been lifted straight from the pages of the *Madeline* books.

Sam & Seb
208 Bedford Avenue, between North 5th & 6th Streets, Williamsburg, Brooklyn (1-718 486 8300/www.samandseb.com). Subway: L to Bedford Avenue. **Open** noon-7pm Mon-Wed; noon-8pm Thur, Fri; 11am-8pm Sat; 11am-7pm Sun. **Credit** AmEx, DC, Disc, MC, V.
For style-conscious procreators who wouldn't dream of clothing their offspring in generic baby clothes, Williamsburg's groovey Sam & Seb delivers 1960s-and '70s-inspired play clothes and funky consignment pieces by local designers, along with silk-screened Jimi Hendrix and Bob Marley mini Ts.

Yoya
636 Hudson Street, between Horatio & Jane Streets (1-646 336 6844/www.yoyashop.com). Subway: A, C, E to 14th Street; L to Eighth Avenue. **Open** 11am-7pm Mon-Sat. **Credit** AmEx, Disc, MC, V.
Various Village sensibilities – European, bohemian, and hip – come together in this store, which is aimed at infants to six-year-olds. Labels such as Erica Tanov, Temperley for Little People, and Imps & Elves are available, as well as tiny-size (but not tiny-priced) Diesel Ts.

Lingerie & swimwear

Most department stores have comprehensive lingerie and swimwear sections, and Victoria's Secret shops abound, but these spots are special places to go for extra-beautiful bedroom and beachside wear.

Agent Provocateur
133 Mercer Street, between Prince & Spring Streets (1-212 965 0229/www.agentprovocateur.com). Subway: B, D, F, V to Broadway-Lafayette Street; N, R, W to Prince Street; 6 to Spring Street. **Open** 11am-7pm Mon-Sat; noon-6pm Sun. **Credit** AmEx, MC, V.

Looking for something to rev up your sweetie's heartbeat? Then check out this patron saint of provocative panties. Va-va-voomy bras, garters and bustiers are dubbed with Bond-girl names. **Photo** *p233.*

Catriona MacKechnie
400 W 14th Street, between Ninth & Tenth Avenues (1-212 242 3200). Subway: A, C, E to 14th Street. **Open** 11am-7.30pm Mon-Sat; noon-6pm Sun. **Credit** AmEx, MC, V.
Glasgow-born Catriona MacKechnie has turned lingerie into haute couture with her dramatically decked-out eponymous shop. Along with exclusive UK labels and the proprietor's own line, MacKechnie offers custom knicker fittings.

Le Corset by Selima
80 Thompson Street, between Broome & Spring Streets (1-212 334 4936). Subway: C, E to Spring Street. **Open** 11am-7pm Mon-Fri; noon-8pm Sat; noon-7pm Sun. **Credit** AmEx, DC, Disc, MC, V.
In addition to Selima Salaun's slinky designs, this boudoir-like boutique stocks antique camisoles, vintage silk kimonos, comely lingerie and Victorian- and Edwardian-inspired corsets.

Erès
621 Madison Avenue, between 58th & 59th Streets (1-212 223 3550/www.eres.fr). Subway: N, R, W to Fifth Avenue-59th Street. **Open** 10am-6pm Mon-Sat. **Credit** AmEx, DC, Disc, MC, V.
Paris's reigning queen of sophisticated bathing togs fits in swimmingly on New York's toniest avenue. Sunny white walls and serene blond-wood floors and counters give the merchandise the pedestal treatment. Precious intimates and colourful bathing suits are displayed on custom-made hangers, fabric busts and mannequins.
Other locations: 98 Wooster Street, between Prince & Spring Streets (1-212 431 7300).

Malia Mills
199 Mulberry Street, between Kenmare & Spring Streets (1-212 625 2311/www.maliamills.com). Subway: 6 to Spring Street. **Open** noon-7pm Mon-Sat; noon-6pm Sun. **Credit** AmEx, MC, V.
Ever since one of her designs made the cover of *Sports Illustrated*'s swimsuit issue a dozen years ago, Malia Mills's swimwear has been a staple for St Bart's bathing beauties. Flip-flops and long, luxurious terry-cloth robes are provided for ladies trying on bikini separates.
Other locations: Malia Mills Outlet, 16th floor, 263 W 38th Street, between Seventh & Eighth Avenues (1-212 354 4200, ext 214).

Mixona
262 Mott Street, between Houston & Prince Streets (1-646 613 0100/www.mixona.com). Subway: B, D, F, V to Broadway-Lafayette Street; N, R, W to Prince Street; 6 to Bleecker Street. **Open** 11am-7.30pm Mon-Fri, Sun; 11am-8pm Sat. **Credit** AmEx, MC, V.

Frills and thrills at **Agent Provocateur**. *See p232.*

Luxurious under-things by 30 designers are found here, including Christina Stott's leather-trimmed mesh bras and Passion Bait's lace knickers.

Vilebrequin

1070 Madison Avenue, at 81st Street (1-212 650 0353/www.vilebrequin.com). Subway: 6 to 77th Street. **Open** 10am-7pm daily. **Credit** AmEx, DC, MC, V.

Boxer-style swimming trunks (men's only) in five adult styles (plus one for boys) are the mainstay of this Saint-Tropez-based company's shop. Styles and patterns include seahorses and pin stripes.
Other locations: 436 West Broadway, at Prince Street (1-212 431 0673).

Maternity wear

Cadeau

254 Elizabeth Street, between Houston & Prince Streets (1-212 994 1801/www.cadeau maternity.com). Subway: F, V to Lower East Side-Second Avenue. **Open** 11am-7pm Mon-Sat; noon-6pm Sun. **Credit** AmEx, MC, V.

Meant to celebrate rather than camouflage the pregnant belly, Cadeau ('gift' in French) offers sleek, sophisticated maternity wear. Armoires and free-standing mirrors lend the shop a residential feel.

Liz Lange Maternity

958 Madison Avenue, between 75th & 76th Streets (1-212 879 2191/www.lizlange.com). Subway: 6 to 77th Street. **Open** 10am-7pm Mon-Fri; 10am-6pm Sat; noon-5pm Sun. **Credit** AmEx, MC, V.

Former *Vogue* editor Liz Lange is the mother of hip maternity wear; high-profile moms like Catherine Zeta-Jones and Iman are among her customers.

Veronique

1321 Madison Avenue, at 93rd Street (1-212 831 7800/www.veroniquematernity.com). Subway: 6 to 96th Street. **Open** 10am-7pm Mon-Thur; 10am-6pm Fri, Sat; noon-5pm Sun. **Credit** AmEx, MC, V.

Veronique is dedicated to providing maternity clothes just as cool as your regular duds. Try a pair of sexy, low-cut Seven jeans, plus styles by Nicol Caramel, Amy Zoller and Cadeau.

Menswear

A

125 Crosby Street, between Houston & Prince Streets (1-212 941 8435). Subway: N, R, W to Prince Street. **Open** 11am-7pm Mon-Fri; noon-7pm Sat; noon-6pm Sun. **Credit** AmEx, DC, MC, V.

When A Atelier dropped women's clothes from its racks last year, it also dropped 'atelier' from its name. Now a sophisticated men's-only store, A distinguishes itself from the high-fashion Soho pack with rarefied labels such as Balenciaga, Cloak and Les Hommes. Score one for the boys.

The Soho shopping scene offers so many boutique treats...

agnès b homme

79 Greene Street, between Broome &
Spring Streets (1-212 431 4339/www.agnesb.
com). Subway: N, R, W to Prince Street; 6 to
Spring Street. **Open** 11am-7pm daily. **Credit**
AmEx, DC, Disc, MC, V.
French New Wave cinema from the 1960s is clearly
an inspiration for agnès b's designs. Men's basics
include her classic snap-button cardigan sweater
and striped, long-sleeved T-shirts.

Comme des Garçons

For review, *see p229.*

Duncan Quinn

8 Spring Street, between Bowery & Elizabeth Street
(1-212 226 7030/www.duncanquinn.com). Subway:
J, M, Z to Bowery. **Open** noon-8pm Tue-Sun. **Credit**
AmEx, DC, Disc, MC, V.
Young Brit Duncan Quinn aims to clean up scruffy
boys by decking them out in old-fashioned tailored
suits combined with shirts in eye-popping colours
and prints. His namesake shop stocks slim-fitting
button-downs in windowpane checks and candy-
coloured stripes, along with flamboyant silk ties and
narrow-cut suits.

Foley & Corinna Men

For review, *see p238* **Foley & Corinna.**

INA Men

262 Mott Street, between Houston & Prince
Streets (1-212 334 2210). Subway: B, D, F, V
to Broadway-Lafayette Street; N, R, W to Prince
Street. **Open** noon-7pm Mon-Thur, Sun; noon-8pm
Fri, Sat. **Credit** AmEx, MC, V. For review, *see p238.*

Jack Spade

For review, *see p238* **Kate Spade.**

Odin

328 E 11th Street, between First & Second Avenues
(1-212 475 0666). Subway: L to First Avenue. **Open**
noon-8pm daily. **Credit** AmEx, MC, V.
Gentlemen prefer one-stop shopping, and so favour
this East Village guys' emporium, which toes the
line between boys' street-savvy threads and men's
tailored attire – all with an edge, of course.

Paul Smith

108 Fifth Avenue, between 15th & 16th Streets
(1-212 627 9770/www.paulsmith.co.uk). Subway: L,
N, Q, R, W, 4, 5, 6 to 14th Street-Union Square.
Open 11am-7pm Mon-Wed, Fri, Sat; 11am-8pm
Thur; noon-6pm Sun. **Credit** AmEx, MC, V.
Paul Smith devotees love this store's raffish English-
gentleman look. They're even more partial to the
designs and accessories that combine elegance, quality and wit (and some serious price tags).

... that everybody deserves a little sit-down.

Scoop Men

*873 Washington Street, between 13th & 14th Streets
(1-212 929 1244); 1275 Third Avenue, between
73rd & 74th Streets (1-212 535 5577). Subway: A,
C, E to 14th Street; L to Eighth Avenue.*
For review, *see p231* **Scoop.**

Seize sur Vingt

*243 Elizabeth Street, between Houston &
Prince Streets (1-212 343 0476/www.16sur20.
com). Subway: B, D, F, V to Broadway-Lafayette
Street; N, R, W to Prince Street; 6 to Bleecker
Street.* **Open** *11am-7pm Mon-Sat; noon-6pm Sun.*
Credit *AmEx, Disc, MC, V.*
Ready-to-wear men's shirts are available, but the real
draws are the bespoke suits and custom-cut button-
downs. Shirts come in Wall Street pinstripes and prep-
py gingham, with mother-of-pearl buttons and short,
square collars. Check out the fine handkerchiefs.

Steven Alan

For review, *see p231.*

Thomas Pink

*520 Madison Avenue, at 53rd Street (1-212 838
1928/www.thomaspink.co.uk). Subway: E, V to Fifth
Avenue-53rd Street.* **Open** *10am-7pm Mon-Wed, Fri;
10am-8pm Thur; 10am-6pm Sat; noon-6pm Sun.*
Credit *AmEx, DC, MC, V.*

Thomas Pink's shirts are made in bold, dynamic
colours that animate conservative suits. But the
shop is no longer strictly for men: the women's
department includes accessories, jewellery and – of
course – shirts.
Other locations: 1155 Sixth Avenue, at 44th Street
(1-212 840 9663).

Streetwear

A Bathing Ape

*91 Greene Street, between Prince & Spring
Streets (1-212 925 0222). Subway: N, R to
Prince Street.* **Open** *noon-7pm Mon-Sat;
noon-6pm Sun.* **Credit** *AmEx, MC, V.*
The cult streetwear label created by Japanese
designer Nigo planted its first US flagship in Soho
last spring. Nigo, who has collaborated with Adidas
and NERD frontman Pharrell Williams, among others, devotes most of his shop to BAPE threads, while
an upstairs shoe salon housing BAPEsta kicks has
made the city's sneaker-hungry masses go ape.

Autumn

*436 E 9th Street, between First Avenue & Avenue A
(1-212 677 6220/www.autumnskateboarding.com).
Subway: L to First Avenue; 6 to Astor Place.* **Open**
noon-8pm daily. **Credit** *AmEx, Disc, MC, V.*

Thinking inside the box at **Adidas**. *See p237.*

Proprietor and amateur skateboarder David Mimms and his wife, Kristen Yaccarino, stock DVS, Emerica, Etnies, iPath, Lakai and Vans for your half-pipe pleasure. Ts and jeans, not to mention scores of boards, are available too.

Brooklyn Industries

162 Bedford Avenue, at North 8th Street, Williamsburg, Brooklyn (1-718 486 6464/www. brooklynindustries.com). Subway: L to Bedford Avenue. **Open** 11am-9pm Mon-Sat; noon-8pm Sun. **Credit** AmEx, Disc, MC, V.
Bags sporting the skyline label and zippered sweatshirt hoodies with Brooklyn emblazoned across the chest are just the tip of the iceberg here.
Other locations: 286 Lafayette Street, between Prince & Spring Streets (1-212 219 0862); 206 Fifth Avenue, at Union Street, Park Slope, Brooklyn (1-718 789 2764); 100 Smith Street, at Atlantic Avenue, Boerum Hill, Brooklyn (1-718 596 3986); 184 Broadway, at Driggs, Williamsburg, Brooklyn (1-718 218 9166).

Dave's Quality Meat

7 E 3rd Street, between Bowery & Second Avenue (1-212 505 7551/www.davesqualitymeat.com). Subway: F, V to Lower East Side-Second Avenue. **Open** noon-7pm Mon-Sat; noon-6pm Sun. **Credit** AmEx, Disc, MC, V.
Dave Ortiz – formerly of urban-threads label Zoo York – and professional skateboarder Chris Keefe stock top-shelf streetwear in their wittily designed shop, it decor complete with meat hooks and mannequins sporting butcher's aprons. Home-made graphic-print Ts are wrapped in plastic and displayed in a deli case.

Phat Farm

129 Prince Street, between West Broadway & Wooster Street (1-212 533 7428/www.phatfarm store.com). Subway: C, E to Spring Street; N, R, W to Prince Street. **Open** 11am-7pm Mon-Sat; noon-6pm Sun. **Credit** AmEx, Disc, MC, V.

Find Def Jam impresario Russell Simmons's classy, conservative take on hip-hop couture: phunky-phresh baggy clothing for guys, and for gals, the curvy Baby Phat line.

Prohibit NYC

269 Elizabeth Street, between Houston & Prince Streets (1-212 219 1469/www.prohibitnyc.com). Subway: F, V to Lower East Side-Second Avenue. **Open** noon-8pm daily. **Credit** AmEx, MC, V.
City guys can get all the necessities at this spare, polished upscale streetwear boutique, from well-made threads and special-edition sneakers to haircuts (with hot-towel treatment, $30) while seated in an apple-red vintage barber's chair.

Recon

237 Eldridge Street, between Houston & Stanton Streets (1-212 614 8502). Subway: F, V to Lower East Side-Second Avenue. **Open** noon-7pm Mon-Sat; noon-6pm Sun. **Credit** AmEx, MC, V.
The joint venture of one-time graffiti artists Stash and Futura, Recon offers graf junkies a chance to wear the work on clothing and accessories.

Stüssy

140 Wooster Street, between Houston & Prince Streets (1-212 274 8855). Subway: N, R, W to Prince Street. **Open** noon-7pm Mon-Fri; 11am-7pm Sat; noon-6pm Sun. **Credit** AmEx, MC, V.
Tricky isn't the only one who wants to be dressed up in Stüssy. Come here for all the skate and surf wear that made Sean Stüssy famous, as well as utilitarian Japanese bags from Headporter.

Supreme

274 Lafayette Street, between Jersey & Prince Streets (1-212 966 7799). Subway: B, D, F, V to Broadway-Lafayette Street; N, R, W to Prince Street; 6 to Spring Street. **Open** 11.30am-7pm Mon-Sat; noon-6pm Sun. **Credit** AmEx, MC, V.

Filled mostly with East Coast brands such as Chocolate, Independent and Zoo York, this skatewear store also stocks its own line. Look for pieces by Burton and DC Shoe – favourites of skaters like Colin McKay and Danny Way.

Triple Five Soul

290 Lafayette Street, between Houston & Prince Streets (1-212 431 2404/www.triple5soul.com). Subway: B, D, F, V to Broadway-Lafayette Street; N, R, W to Prince Street; 6 to Bleecker Street. **Open** 11am-7pm Mon-Thur, Sun; 11am-7.30pm Fri, Sat. **Credit** AmEx, Disc, MC, V.
Although the label is no longer exclusive to New York, the city can still boast the brand's sole stores. Find the very necessary hooded sweatshirts and Ts stamped with the Triple Five logo at this Soho spot. **Other locations**: 145 Bedford Avenue, at North 9th Street, Williamsburg, Brooklyn (1-718 599 5971).

Unis

226 Elizabeth Street, between Houston & Prince Streets (1-212 431 5533). Subway: B, D, F, V to Broadway-Lafayette Street; N, R, W to Prince Street; 6 to Bleecker Street. **Open** noon-7pm Mon-Wed, Sun; noon-7.30pm Thur-Sat. **Credit** AmEx, Disc, MC, V.
Korean-American designer Eunice Lee's structured streetwear used to be for boys only, but she let the girls in on the fun in 2003. Both collections are featured in her sleek Nolita boutique, along with Botkier bags and other accessories.

VICE

252 Lafayette Street, between Prince & Spring Streets (1-212 219 7788/www.viceland.com). Subway: N, R, W to Prince Street; 6 to Spring Street. **Open** noon-8pm Mon-Sat; noon-7pm Sun. **Credit** AmEx, MC, V.
Magazine and clothier extraordinaire VICE dictates downtown fashion. Peruse racks of Brooklyn Industries, Ben Sherman, Crypto, Religion and (of course) VICE, among other style superstars.

Sneakers

Adidas

610 Broadway, at Houston Street (1-212 529 0081). Subway N, R, W to Prince Street, **Open** 10am-10pm Mon-Sat; 11am-7pm Sun. **Credit** AmEx, DC, MC, V.
Inside this 29,500sqft Soho space – decorated with giant images of athletes – you'll find every imaginable garment associated with the brand, including sportster threads Stella McCartney. **Photo** *p236.*

Alife Rivington Club

158 Rivington Street, between Clinton & Suffolk Streets (1-212 375 8128). Subway: F to Delancey Street; J, M, Z to Delancey-Essex Streets. **Open** noon-7pm daily. **Credit** AmEx, MC, V.
'Sneakers' equal 'religion' in this tiny, out-of-the-way shop, which is arguably the city's main hub for hard-to-get shoes. The store, like its wares, has a rather exclusive vibe: there's no sign, no street number, no

indication the joint even exists from the outside. Look closely and ring the bell to check out the rotating selection of 60 or so styles.

Classic Kicks

298 Elizabeth Street, between Houston & E 1st Streets (1-212 979 9514). Subway: B, D, F, V to Broadway-Lafayette; 6 to Bleecker Street. **Open** noon-7pm Mon-Sat; noon-6pm Sun. **Credit** AmEx, MC, V.
One of the more female-friendly sneaker shops, Classic Kicks stocks mainstream and rare styles of Converse, Lacoste, Puma and Vans, to name but a few, for both boys and girls, along with a decent selection of clothes.

Clientele

267 Lafayette Street, at Prince Street (1-212 219 0531). Subway: N, R, W to Prince Street; 6 to Spring Street. **Open** noon-8pm Mon-Sat; noon-7pm Sun. **Credit** AmEx, MC, V.
Set up like an art-gallery display, the kicks line one wall of the minimalist store, and patrons sit on a long wooden bench to admire them.

Vintage & thrift

Goodwill and the Salvation Army are great for vintage finds, but it can take hours of digging to discover a gem. Enter thrift boutiques, where the digging has been done for you. We've listed a wide range here, from the more extravagant shops that cherry-pick vintage YSL and Fiorucci for their racks to your general T-shirt havens, as well as a few that fall in between.

Allan & Suzi

416 Amsterdam Avenue, at 80th Street (1-212 724 7445/www.allanandsuzi.net). Subway: 1 to 79th Street. **Open** 12.30-7pm Mon-Sat; noon-6pm Sun. **Credit** AmEx, Disc, MC, V.
Models and celebs drop off worn-once Gaultiers, Muglers, Pradas and Manolos here. The platform shoe collection is flashback-inducing and incomparable, as is the selection of vintage jewellery.

Beacon's Closet

88 North 11th Street, between Berry Street & Wythe Avenue, Williamsburg, Brooklyn (1-718 486 0816). Subway: L to Bedford Avenue. **Open** noon-9pm Mon-Fri; 11am-8pm Sat, Sun. **Credit** AmEx, Disc, MC, V.
At this Brooklyn fave, the prices are great, and so is the Williamsburg-appropriate clothing selection. **Other locations**: 220 Fifth Avenue, between President & Union Streets, Park Slope, Brooklyn (1-718 230 1630).

D/L Cerney

13 E 7th Street, between Second & Third Avenues (1-212 673 7033). Subway: N, R, W to 8th Street-NYU; 6 to Astor Place. **Open** noon-7.30pm daily. **Credit** AmEx, MC, V.
Specialising in timeless, original designs for stylish fellows, the store also carries menswear from the

Eat, Drink, Shop

1940s to the '60s. Mint-condition must-haves include hats (some pristine fedoras), ties and shoes. An adjacent shop carries D/L Cerney's new women's line.

Edith & Daha

104 Rivington Street, between Essex & Ludlow Streets (1-212 979 9992). Subway: F to Delancey Street; J, M, Z to Delancey-Essex Streets. **Open** 1-8pm Mon-Fri; noon-8pm Sat, Sun. **Credit** AmEx, MC, V.

Check out one of the city's best collections of (mostly) fine leather bags, not to mention an army of shoes, at this slightly below-street-level shop. There's no trash here – only the cream of the vintage crop. The front rack displays Edith & Daha's own line of clothing.

Foley & Corinna

108 Stanton Street, between Essex & Ludlow Streets (1-212 529 2338/www.foleyandcorinna.com). Subway: F to Delancey Street; J, M, Z to Delancey-Essex Streets. **Open** noon-8pm Mon-Sat; noon-7pm Sun. **Credit** AmEx, MC, V.

Vintage-clothing fiends like Liv Tyler and Donna Karan know they can have it both ways: shoppers freely mix old (Anna Corinna's vintage finds) with new (Dana Foley's original creations, including lace tops, leather-belted pants and sheer wool knits) to compose a truly one-of-a-kind look. Encourage the boy in your life to spiff up at the men's store, just around the corner.

Other locations: Foley & Corinna Men, 143 Ludlow Street, between Rivington & Stanton Streets (1-212 529 5043).

INA

101 Thompson Street, between Prince & Spring Streets (1-212 941 4757). Subway: C, E to Spring Street. **Open** noon-7pm Mon-Thur, Sun; noon-8pm Fri, Sat. **Credit** AmEx, MC, V.

For the past 11 years, INA on Thompson Street has reigned over the downtown consignment scene. The Soho location features drastically reduced couture pieces, while the Nolita shop, on Prince Street, carries trendier clothing. Guys: be sure to drop into the men's store (*see p234*).

Other locations: 21 Prince Street, between Elizabeth & Mott Streets (1-212 334 9048); 208 E 73rd Street, between Second & Third Avenues (1-212 249 0014).

Marmalade

172 Ludlow Street, between Houston & Stanton Streets (1-212 473 8070). Subway: F, V to Lower East Side-Second Avenue. **Open** noon-8.30pm Mon-Thur, Sun; noon-9.30pm Fri, Sat. **Credit** AmEx, MC, V.

Marmalade, one of the cutest vintage-clothing stores on the Lower East Side, has some of the hottest 1970s and '80s threads to be found below Houston Street. That slinky cocktail dress or ruffled blouse is tucked amid a selection of well-priced, well-cared-for items. Accessories, vintage shoes and a small selection of men's clothing are also available.

Fashion accessories

Eyewear

Fabulous Fanny's

335 E 9th Street, between First & Second Avenues (1-212 533 0637/www.fabulousfannys.com). Subway: L to First Avenue; 6 to Astor Place. **Open** noon-8pm daily. **Credit** AmEx, MC, V.

The city's premier source of period eyeglasses for more than 17 years, this former booth at the 26th Street flea market now calls the East Village home. You'll find more than 10,000 pairs of spectacles, everything from WWII-era aviator goggles to '70s rhinestone-encrusted Versace shades.

Selima Optique

59 Wooster Street, at Broome Street (1-212 343 9490/www.selimaoptique.com). Subway: C, E to Spring Street. **Open** 11am-8pm Mon-Sat; noon-7pm Sun. **Credit** AmEx, Disc, MC, V.

Selima Salaun's wear-if-you-dare frames are popular with such famous four-eyes as Lenny Kravitz and Sean Lennon (both of whom have styles here named after them).

Other locations: throughout the city.

Sol Moscot Opticians

118 Orchard Street, at Delancey Street (1-212 477 3796/www.moscots.com). Subway: F to Delancey Street; J, M, Z to Delancey-Essex Streets. **Open** 10am-6pm Mon-Sat; 9am-5pm Sun. **Credit** AmEx, DC, Disc, MC, V.

This 84-year-old family-run emporium offers the same big names you'll find uptown – for about 20% less. It also carries vintage frames, Chanel and Gucci sunglasses, and bifocal contacts.

Other locations: 69 W 14th Street, at Sixth Avenue (1-212 647 1550); 107-20 Continental Avenue (71st Avenue), between Austin Street & Queens Boulevard, Forest Hills, Queens (1-718 544 2200).

Handbags

Destination

32-36 Little W 12th Street, between Ninth Avenue & Washington Street (1-212 727 2031). Subway: A, C, E to 14th Street; L to Eighth Avenue. **Open** 10.30am-8pm Mon-Sat; noon-7pm Sun. **Credit** AmEx, MC, V.

Manhattan's largest accessories boutique is in the Meatpacking District. The bags, shoes, hats and jewellery, from more than 30 designers, include Vegas-worthy baubles and handbags crafted from Vietnamese film strips.

Kate Spade

454 Broome Street, at Mercer Street (1-212 274 1991/www.katespade.com). Subway: N, R, W to Prince Street; 6 to Spring Street. **Open** 11am-7pm Mon-Sat; noon-6pm Sun. **Credit** AmEx, Disc, MC, V.

Popular handbag designer Kate Spade sells her classic boxy tote, as well as other smart numbers, in this

bright store, plus shoes, pyjamas and rain slickers. Men's accessories are sold at Jack Spade.
Other locations: Jack Spade, 56 Greene Street, between Broome & Spring Streets (1-212 625 1820).

Ro
150 W 28th Street, between Sixth & Seventh Avenues (1-212 477 1595/www.gotoro.com). Subway: 1 to 28th Street. **Open** By appointment only. **Credit** AmEx, Disc, MC, V.
Gene Miao and Yvonne Roe's signature travel accoutrements, such as sleek suitcase-shaped wallets, hang on pegs in the foyer-size store. In an era of overly fussy accessories, Ro's streamlined satchels are an appealing contrast.

Jewellery

Agatha
611 Madison Avenue, at 58th Street (1-212 758 4301/www.agatha.fr). Subway: N, R, W to Fifth Avenue-59th Street; 4, 5, 6 to 59th Street. **Open** 10am-7pm Mon-Sat; noon-6pm Sun. **Credit** AmEx, Disc, MC, V.
The queen of the costume-jewellery joints, Agatha stocks low-priced trinkets that look like a million bucks. Jumbo pearls, oversize rings and graphic, modern designs abound.
Other locations: 159A Columbus Avenue, between 67th & 68th Streets (1-212 362 0959).

Alexis Bittar
465 Broome Street, between Greene & Mercer Streets (1-212 625 8340). Subway: N, R, W to Prince Street; 6 to Spring Street. **Open** 11am-7pm Mon-Sat; noon-6pm Sun. **Credit** AmEx, MC, V.
A Brooklyn-based designer known for his chunky Lucite and semi-precious-stone accessories, Bittar adorned his recently opened boutique with vintage wallpaper and a Victorian lion's-paw table.

Doyle & Doyle
189 Orchard Street, between Houston & Stanton Streets (1-212 677 9991/www.doyledoyle.com). Subway: F, V to Lower East Side-Second Avenue. **Open** 1-7pm Tue, Wed, Fri; 1-8pm Thur; noon-7pm Sat, Sun. **Credit** AmEx, Disc, MC, V.
Whether your taste is art deco or nouveau, Victorian or Edwardian, gemologist sisters Pam and Elizabeth Doyle, who specialise in estate and antique jewellery, will have that intimate, one-of-a-kind piece you're looking for, including engagement rings and eternity bands.

Fragments
116 Prince Street, between Greene & Wooster Streets (1-212 334 9588/www.fragments.com). Subway: B, D, F, V to Broadway-Lafayette Street; N, R, W to Prince Street. **Open** 11am-7pm Mon-Sat; noon-6pm Sun. **Credit** AmEx, DC, Disc, MC, V.
Over two decades, Fragments owner Janet Goldman has assembled a stable of more than 100 pet jewellery designers, who offer their creations to her before selling them to major stores such as Barneys.

Tiffany & Co
727 Fifth Avenue, at 57th Street (1-212 755 8000/www.tiffany.com). Subway: E, V to Fifth Avenue-53rd Street; F to 57th Street; N, R, W to Fifth Avenue-59th Street. **Open** 10am-7pm Mon-Fri; 10am-6pm Sat; noon-5pm Sun. **Credit** AmEx, DC, Disc, MC, V.
The heyday of Tiffany's was at the turn of the 20th century, when Louis Comfort Tiffany, the son of founder Charles Lewis Tiffany, took the reins and began to create sensational art nouveau jewellery. Today the design stars are the no-less august Paloma Picasso and Elsa Peretti. Three floors are stacked with precious jewels, silver, watches, porcelain and the classic Tiffany engagement rings. FYI: breakfast is not served.

Shoes

Camper
125 Prince Street, at Wooster Street (1-212 358 1842/www.camper.es). Subway: N, R, W to Prince Street. **Open** 11am-8pm Mon-Sat; noon-6pm Sun. **Credit** AmEx, DC, MC, V.
Dozens of styles from the Spanish-made line of casual shoes are stocked in this large corner store.

Christian Louboutin
941 Madison Avenue, between 74th & 75th Streets (1-212 396 1884). Subway: 6 to 77th Street. **Open** 10am-6pm Mon-Sat. **Credit** AmEx, MC, V.
Serious shoe-hounds should plan to drop several C-notes on a pair of Christian Louboutin's irresistibly sexy kicks, distinguished by their vertiginous heels and signature scarlet soles. The racy footwear could easily convince you to walk on water. Don't try it – and don't try hobbling more than a block or two in these fierce spikes, either.
Other locations: 59 Horatio Street, at Greenwich Street (1-212 255 1910).

Chuckies
1073 Third Avenue, between 63rd & 64th Streets (1-212 593 9898). Subway: F to Lexington Avenue- 63rd Street. **Open** 10.45am-7.45pm Mon-Fri; 10.45am-7.30pm Sat; 12.30-7pm Sun. **Credit** AmEx, DC, Disc, MC, V.
An alternative to department stores, Chuckies carries high-profile labels for men and women. Its stock ranges from old-school Calvin Klein to up-and-coming Ernesto Esposito.

Jimmy Choo
645 Fifth Avenue, at 51st Street (1-212 593 0800/www.jimmychoo.com). Subway: E, V to Fifth Avenue-53rd Street. **Open** 10am-6pm Mon-Wed, Fri, Sat; 10am-7pm Thur; noon-5pm Sun. **Credit** AmEx, MC, V.
Jimmy Choo, famed for conceiving Princess Diana's custom-shoe collection, has conquered America with his six-year-old emporium, which features chic boots, sexy stilettos, curvaceous pumps and kittenish flats. Prices start at $450.

Manolo Blahnik

*31 W 54th Street, between Fifth & Sixth Avenues
(1-212 582 3007). Subway: E, V to Fifth Avenue-
53rd Street.* **Open** 10.30am-6pm Mon-Fri; 10.30am-
5.30pm Sat. **Credit** AmEx, MC, V.

The high priest of timelessly glamorous shoes will
put style in your step, kudos on your tootsies – and
a deep, deep dent in your wallet.

Otto Tootsi Plohound

*137 Fifth Avenue, between 20th & 21st
Streets (1-212 460 8650). Subway: N, R,
W to 23rd Street.* **Open** 11.30am-8pm Mon-Fri;
11am-8pm Sat; noon-7pm Sun. **Credit** AmEx,
DC, Disc, MC, V.

One of the best places for the latest shoe styles,
Tootsi has a big selection of trendy (and slightly
overpriced) imports for women and men.
Other locations: throughout the city.

Food & Drink

There are more than 20 open-air 'greenmarkets',
sponsored by city authorities, in various
locations on different days. The largest and
best known is at Union Square, where small
producers of cheese, flowers, herbs, fruits and
vegetables hawk their goods on Mondays,
Wednesdays, Fridays and Saturdays (8am-
6pm). Arrive early, before the prime stuff sells
out. For other venues, check with the Council
on the Environment of NYC (1-212 788 7476,
www.cenyc.org).

Bakeries & cupcakes

Thanks to Magnolia bakery, cupcakes have
become a portable obsession among New
Yorkers in recent years; here's where to grab
your sugar fix.

Amy's Bread

*672 Ninth Avenue, between 46th & 47th Streets
(1-212 977 2670/www.amysbread.com). Subway:
C, E to 50th Street; N, R, W to 49th Street.* **Open**
7.30am-11pm Mon-Fri; 8am-11pm Sat; 9am-6pm Sun.
No credit cards.

Whether you want sweet (chocolate-chubbie cookies) or savoury (semolina-fennel bread, hefty French
sourdough boules), Amy's never disappoints.
Other locations: Chelsea Market, 75 Ninth Avenue,
between 15th & 16th Streets (1-212 462 4338).

Billy's Bakery

*184 Ninth Avenue, between 21st & 22nd
Streets (1-212 647 9956/www.billysbakerynyc.
com). Subway: C, E to 23rd Street.* **Open**
9am-11pm Mon-Thur, Sun; 9am-12.30am
Fri, Sat. **Credit** AmEx, DC, Disc, MC, V.

Amid super-sweet retro delights such as coconut
cream pie, Hello Dollies and Famous Refrigerator
Cake, you'll find friendly service in a setting that will

remind you of Grandma's kitchen – or, at least, it
will if your grandmother was Betty Crocker.

Magnolia Bakery

*401 Bleecker Street, at 11th Street (1-212 462
2572). Subway: 1 to Christopher Street.* **Open** noon-
11.30pm Mon; 9am-11.30pm Tue-Thur; 9am-12.30am
Fri; 10am-12.30am Sat; 10am-11.30pm Sun. **Credit**
AmEx, Disc, MC, V.

Part sweet market, part meet market, Magnolia
skyrocketed to fame thanks to *Sex and the City*. The
pastel-iced cupcakes are much vaunted, but you can
also pick up a cup of custardy, Southern-style
banana pudding (Brits: think trifle) or point yourself
out a scoop from the summertime ice-cream cart.
Then, sweetmeat in hand, join the other happy
eaters clogging nearby apartment stoops.

Chocolatiers

Jacques Torres Chocolate Haven

*350 Hudson Street, between Charlton
& King Streets, entrance on King Street
(1-212 414 2462/www.jacquestorres.com).
Subway: 1 to Houston Street.* **Open** 9am-7pm
Mon, Wed-Fri; 10am-8pm Sat; 11am-7pm Sun.
Credit AmEx, MC, V.

Walk into Jacques Torres's new glass-walled shop
and café, and you'll be surrounded by a Willy
Wonka-esque chocolate factory that turns raw cocoa
beans into luscious goodies before your very eyes.
Sweets for sale range from the sublime (deliciously
rich hot chocolate, steamed to order) to the ridicu-
lous (chocolate-covered fortune cookies).
Other locations: Jacques Torres Chocolate, 66
Water Street, between Dock & Main Streets, Dumbo,
Brooklyn (1-718 875 9772).

La Maison du Chocolat

*1018 Madison Avenue, between 78th & 79th Streets
(1-212 744 7117/www.lamaisonduchocolat.com).
Subway: 6 to 77th Street.* **Open** 10am-7pm Mon-Sat;
noon-6pm Sun. **Credit** AmEx, MC, V.

This suave cocoa-brown boutique, the creation of
Robert Linxe, packages refined (and pricey) examples of edible Parisian perfection like fine jewellery.
A small café serves hot and cold chocolate drinks
and a selection of sweets.
Other locations: 30 Rockefeller Plaza, 49th Street,
between Fifth & Sixth Avenues (1-212 265 9404).

Richart

*7 E 55th Street, between Madison & Fifth
Avenues (1-888 742 4278/www.richart-
chocolates.com). Subway: E, V to Fifth
Avenue-53rd Street.* **Open** 10am-7pm Mon-Fri;
10am-6pm Sat. **Credit** AmEx, MC, V.

French master-chocolatier Michel Richart is an intellectual sensualist, one who's as likely to fill a bon-
bon with green-tea essence or basil ganache as with
the more expected coffee or hazelnuts. His precisely
geometric squares are topped with cool graphic
patterns – swirls, bubbles, even leopard prints – to
indicate the fillings within.

Scharffen Berger

*473 Amsterdam Avenue, at 83rd Street
(1-212 362 9734/www.scharffenberger.com).
Subway: 1 to 86th Street.* **Open** 10am-8pm
Mon-Thur; 10am-9pm Fri, Sat; 11am-7pm Sun.
Credit AmEx, Disc, MC, V.
At this bite-sized boutique from the artisanal chocolate maker from Berkeley, California, you'll find gift
boxes of remarkable dark ganache-filled treats (in
flavours like fresh lemon and sea-salt caramel), jars
of chocolate sauce and chocolate-mint lip balm.

Stores

Dean & DeLuca

*560 Broadway, at Prince Street (1-212 431 1691/
www.deananddeluca.com). Subway: N, R, W to
Prince Street.* **Open** 10am-8pm Mon-Sat; 10am-7pm
Sun. **Credit** AmEx, Disc, MC, V.
Dean & DeLuca's flagship store (one of only two that
offer more than just a fancy coffee bar) provides the
most sophisticated (and pricey) selection of speciality food items in the city.
Other locations: throughout the city.

Whole Foods

*Concourse level, Time Warner Center, 10 Columbus
Circle, at Broadway (1-212 823 9600/www.whole
foods.com). Subway: A, B, C, D, 1 to 59th Street-
Columbus Circle.* **Open** 8am-10pm daily. **Credit**
AmEx, Disc, MC, V.
You'll feel healthier just walking around this veri-
table cornucopia of fresh food. Gorgeous as well as
good for you, Whole Foods is the city's best bet for
organic offerings. Take advantage of the well-
stocked wine store seven days a week.
Other locations: 4 Union Square South, between
Broadway & University Place (1-212 673 5388); 250
Seventh Avenue at 24th Street (1-212 924 5969).

Zabar's

*2245 Broadway, at 80th Street (1-212 787 2000/
www.zabars.com). Subway: 1 to 79th Street.* **Open**
8am-7.30pm Mon-Fri; 8am-8pm Sat; 9am-6pm Sun.
Credit AmEx, MC, V.
Zabar's is more than just a market – it's a New York
City landmark. You might leave the place feeling a
little light in the wallet, but you can't beat the top-
flight prepared foods. Besides the famous smoked
fish and rafts of Jewish delicacies, Zabar's has fabulous selections of bread, cheese and coffee – and an
entire floor of well-priced gadgets and housewares.

Sundries

Guss' Pickles

*85-87 Orchard Street, between Broome &
Grand Streets. Subway: F to Delancey Street;
J, M, Z to Delancey-Essex Streets.* **Open** 9.30am-
6.30pm Mon-Thur; 9.30am-4pm Fri; 10am-6pm
Sun. **Credit** AmEx, MC, V.
After moving twice in recent years, the Pickle King
has settled down, and the complete, delicious array

of sours and half-sours, pickled peppers, watermelon
rinds and sauerkraut is available to grateful New
Yorkers once again.

Russ & Daughters

*179 E Houston Street, between Allen & Orchard
Streets (1-212 475 4880/www.russanddaughters.
com). Subway: F, V to Lower East Side-Second
Avenue.* **Open** 9am-7pm Mon-Sat; 8am-5.30pm Sun.
Credit AmEx, Disc, MC, V.
Russ & Daughters, open since 1914, sells eight kinds
of smoked salmon and many Jewish-inflected
Eastern European delectables, along with dried
fruits, chocolates, and Russian and Iranian caviar.

Health & Beauty

Beauty & cosmetics

Alcone

*235 W 19th Street, between Seventh & Eighth
Avenues (1-212 633 0551/www.alconeco.com).
Subway: 1 to 18th Street.* **Open** 11am-6pm Mon-Sat.
Credit AmEx, MC, V.
Frequented by make-up artists on the prowl for the
German brand Kryolan and for kits of fake blood
and bruises, this shop also attracts mere mortals
looking to score the shop's own line of sponges and
pre-made palettes – trays of a dozen or more eye, lip
and cheek colours.

Gorgeous **Guss'**, Pickle King (and queen).

Face Stockholm

110 Prince Street, at Greene Street (1-212 966 9110/www.facestockholm.com). Subway: N, R, W to Prince Street. **Open** 11am-7pm Mon-Sat; noon-6pm Sun. **Credit** AmEx, MC, V.

In addition to a full line of eyeshadows, lipsticks, blushes and tools, Face offers make-up application and lessons to help improve your own technique. **Other locations**: 226 Columbus Avenue, between 70th & 71st Streets (1-212 769 1420).

John Masters Organics

77 Sullivan Street, between Spring & Broome Streets (1-212 343 9590/www.johnmasters.com). Subway: C, E to Spring Street; N, R, W to Prince Street. **Open** 11am-7pm Mon-Sat. **Credit** AmEx, MC, V.

Organic doesn't get more orgasmic than it is in John Masters's chic apothecary line. Blood orange and vanilla body wash and lavender and avocado intensive conditioner are just two of the good-enough-to-eat products that you can get to go. **Photos** *p243.*

Kiehl's

109 Third Avenue, between 13th & 14th Streets (1-212 677 3171/www.kiehls.com). Subway: L to Third Avenue; N, Q, R, W, 4, 5, 6 to 14th Street-Union Square. **Open** 10am-7pm Mon-Sat; noon-6pm Sun. **Credit** AmEx, DC, MC, V.

Although it is 154 years old and has recently expanded, this New York institution is still a mob scene. Check out the Motorcycle Room, full of vintage Harleys (the owner's obsession). Try one dab of Kiehl's moisturiser, lip balm or body lotion from the plentiful free samples, and you'll be hooked. **Other locations**: 150 Columbus Avenue, between 66th & 67th Streets (1-212 799 3438).

MAC

113 Spring Street, between Greene & Mercer Streets (1-212 334 4641/www.maccosmetics.com). Subway: C, E to Spring Street. **Open** 11am-7pm Mon-Wed; 11am-8pm Thur-Sat; noon-7pm Sun. **Credit** AmEx, DC, Disc, MC, V.

Makeup Art Cosmetics is famous for lipsticks and eyeshadows in must-have colours and for offbeat celebrity spokesmodels like RuPaul and kd lang. **Other locations**: throughout the city.

Make Up Forever

409 West Broadway, between Prince & Spring Streets (1-212 941 9337/www.makeupforever.com). Subway: C, E to Spring Street; N, R, W to Prince Street. **Open** 11am-7pm Tue-Sat; noon-6pm Sun. **Credit** AmEx, MC, V.

MUF's line of French cosmetics is popular with glam women and drag queens. Colours range from bold purples and fuchsias to muted browns and soft pinks. The mascara is essential.

Ricky's

509 Fifth Avenue, between 42nd & 43rd Streets (1-212 949 7230/www.rickys-nyc.com). Subway: B, D, F, V to 42nd Street-Bryant Park; 7 to Fifth Avenue. **Open** 8am-9pm Mon-Fri; 10am-8pm Sat; 10am-7pm Sun. **Credit** AmEx, Disc, MC, V.

Stock up on tweezers, cheap travel containers and make-up cases that look like souped-up fishing tackle boxes at this mecca for make-up. Ricky's in-house make-up line, Mattése, includes fake eyelashes and glitter nail polish. **Other locations**: throughout the city.

Santa Maria Novella

285 Lafayette Street, between Jersey & Prince Streets (1-212 925 0001/www.lafcony.com). Subway: B, D, F, V to Broadway-Lafayette Street; N, R, W to Prince Street; 6 to Bleecker Street. **Open** 11am-7pm Mon-Wed, Fri, Sat; 11am-8pm Thur; noon-6pm Sun. **Credit** AmEx, MC, V.

The 470 skin creams and fragrances at this retail outlet for the hard-to-find Florentine toiletries are produced at the Italian monastery where they were conceived in the year 1210.

Three Custom Color Specialists

3rd floor, 54 W 22nd Street, at Sixth Avenue (1-888 262 7714/www.threecustom.com). Subway: F, V to 23rd Street. **Open** By appointment only. **Credit** AmEx, MC, V.

Beauty-industry veterans Trae Bodge, Scott Catto and Chad Hayduk have been blending custom lipsticks, cream blushes and eyeshadows since 1997. They offer a ready-to-wear line at their new minimalist white-and-silver studio.

Nails

Jin Soon Natural Hand & Foot Spa

56 E 4th Street, between Bowery & Second Avenue (1-212 473 2047). Subway: F, V to Lower East Side-Second Avenue; 6 to Bleecker Street. **Open** 11am-8pm daily. **Credit** MC, V.

Most mani and pedi salons feel more like factory assembly lines than places to be pampered. Not Jin Soon, which has private rooms and a tranquil Zen vibe. Basic manicures ($15) and pedicures ($30) are refreshingly affordable. Nail treatments are meticulously administered, and the floating foot-tub specials include season-specific ingredients like spring flowers or spiced orange. **Other locations**: 23 Jones Street, between Bleecker & W 4th Streets (1-212 229 1070).

Rescue Beauty Lounge

2nd floor, 34 Gansevoort Street, between Greenwich & Hudson Streets, second floor (1-212 206 6409/www.rescuebeauty.com). Subway: A, C, E to 14th Street; L to Eighth Avenue. **Open** 11am-8pm Tue-Fri; 10am-6pm Sat, Sun. **Credit** AmEx, MC, V.

Rescue doesn't look overly posh, but it doesn't skimp on luxury: manicures start at $23 and pedicures at $43. The stylishly minimalist salon is also well stocked with high-end beauty products – tony moisturisers from La Mer, Go Smile tooth whitener, and Dr Hauschka lotions and oils. **Other locations**: 8 Centre Market Place, at Grand Street (1-212 431 0449).

Luscious luxuries at **John Masters Organics**. *See p242.*

Sweet Lily

222 West Broadway, between Franklin & North Moore Streets (1-212 925 5441/www.sweetlily spa.com). Subway: A, C, E to Canal Street; 1 to Franklin Street. **Open** *11am-8pm Mon-Fri; 10am-6pm Sat.* **Credit** AmEx, MC, V (gratuities in cash only).
Although it's in trendy Tribeca, this spa's shabby-chic decor gives it the feel of a country cottage. Sweet Lily further sweetens the deal by replacing generic salon chairs with giant, overstuffed floral armchairs. Seasonal pedis include grapefruit and mint in summer, and apple, brown sugar and cinnamon in the fall.

Perfumeries

Bond No.9

9 Bond Street, between Broadway & Lafayette Street (1-212 228 1940). Subway: B, D, F, V to Broadway-Lafayette Street; 6 to Bleecker Street. **Open** *11am-8pm Mon-Sat; noon-6pm Sun.* **Credit** AmEx, MC, V.
Custom-blended bottles of bliss and scents that pay olfactory homage to New York City – Wall Street, Nouveau Bowery, New Harlem – are available here. Don't worry, there's no Chinatown Sidewalk.

Different strokes

NY's spas have a bounty of new and surprising Itreatments.

GUA SHA

We have no problem with the no-pain, no-gain notion, but the Gua Sha technique takes the concept further than one might guess. It is potentially so jarring and so bruising that you have to sign a consent form. During the $80, hour-long session of this Chinese healing process, a masseuse works oil into your entire body, then whips out a five-inch-long, flat plank made from a bull's horn. With this device, she scrapes your back using quick, short strokes – a process that may leave small red welts on the skin. The treatment ends with a warm, wet towel on the back. (You'll feel like melting!) When it's over, you may feel dizzy and groggy, but mysteriously cleansed. Perhaps you'll even buy into the theory: with the movement of the blood comes greater dispersion of nutrients, resulting in more balanced lymphatic and circulatory systems. But you may have some explaining to do when you get home.

Graceful Services

Second Floor, 1097 Second Avenue, between 57th & 58th Streets (1-212 593 9904/www.gracefulservices.com). Subway: N, R, W to Lexington Avenue to 59th Street; 4, 5, 6 to 59th Street. **Basic massage** *$50.* **Credit** *AmEx, MC, V. Pictured.*

BELLYWORKS

The words pain and exertion aren't generally associated with a spa visit, but, designed for couch potatoes, the new Bellyworks treatment ($89, 60 minutes) requires a little of both. The personal trainer-cum-therapist starts gently enough, demonstrating a simple exercise that combines deep breathing with the rhythmic tightening and relaxing of tummy muscles; she then wraps your unruly gut in heated, seaweed-soaked elastic bandages. The quick succession of crunches and leg lifts that follow will no doubt leave you panting, but you'll feel the kelp corset concentrating your efforts on reluctant abs. Before it's all over, your aching belly is rubbed with toning gel and a sharp-smelling juniper-, pine- and peppermint-infused anti-cellulite oil. If you keep up the torso-clenching exercises that spare tyre is bound to deflate some.

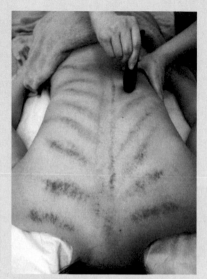

Dorit Baxter Day Spa

Third Floor, 47 W 57th Street, between Fifth and Sixth Avenues (1-212 371 4542/ www.newyorkdayspa.com). Subway: F to 57th Street; N, R, W to Fifth Avenue to 59th Street. **Facial** *basic $68;* **massage** *basic $78.* **Credit** *AmEx, MC, V.*

SOUND THERAPY

In New York, most people try to escape the constant din to relax; but the new, imported-from-Japan Sound Therapy treatment ($50 for 30 minutes, $95 for 60 minutes, $145 for 80 minutes) actually uses noise to help clear the mind and relax the muscles. The Bodysonic Relaxation System is a small metal box with a CD player, headphones and a palm-sized massage pad plugged into it. As you lie face down, the therapist applies the pad – which vibrates at a low frequency in time with the (cheesy) New Age music – along your back, neck, legs and scalp. You might not think the treatment does much until it's time to sit up – and discover your body feels like a wet noodle. After you're out the door, you'll feel remarkably less stressed – and it will last a while, too.

Olive Leaf Wholeness Center

145 E 23rd Street, between Lexington & Third Avenues (1-212 477 0405/www.olwcnyc. com). Subway: 6 to 23rd Street. **Facial** *basic $95.* **Massage** *basic $95.* **Credit** *AmEx, MC, V.*

Other locations: 680 Madison Avenue, at 61st Street (1-212 838 2780); 897 Madison Avenue, at 73rd Street (1-212 794 4480).

CB I Hate Perfume

93 Wythe Avenue, between North 10th & 11th Streets, Williamsburg, Brooklyn (1-718 384 6890). Subway: L to Bedford. **Open** noon-6pm Tue-Sat. **Credit** MC, V.
Contrary to his shop's name, olfactory genius Christopher Brosius doesn't hate what he sells, he just despises the concept. Collaborate with the olfactory genius on a signature scent of your own, or pick up a ready-made splash of quirky scents like Crayon and Rubber Cement.

Jo Malone

949 Broadway, at 22nd Street (1-212 673 2220/ www.jomalone.com). Subway: N, R, W to 23rd Street. **Open** 10am-8pm Mon-Sat; noon-6pm Sun. **Credit** AmEx, DC, Disc, MC, V.
British perfumer Jo Malone champions the 'layering' of scents as a way of creating a personalised aroma. Along with perfumes and colognes, her Flatiron District boutique offers candles, skin-care products and super-pampering facials. Both treatments and products hit the mark.
Other locations: 946 Madison Avenue, between 74th & 75th Streets (1-212 472 0074).

Salons

New York is the city of fresh starts; what better way to begin anew than with your hair? Whether you want a full-out makeover, a rock 'n' roll do, or just a trim, there's a salon for you. The stylin' superstars at Frédéric Fekkai Beauté de Provence (1-212 753 9500) and Louis Licari (1-212 758 2090) are top-notch, but they charge hair-raising prices. The following salons offer specialised services – budget, rocker, ethno-friendly – and unique settings for your special NYC cut.

Astor Place Hair Stylists

2 Astor Place, at Broadway (1-212 475 9854). Subway: N, R, W to 8th Street-NYU; 6 to Astor Place. **Open** 8am-8pm Mon-Sat; 9am-6pm Sun. **No credit cards.**
An army of barbers does everything from neat trims to shaved designs. You can't make an appointment; just take a number and wait outside with the crowd. Sunday mornings are quiet. Cuts start at $12; blow-drys, $20; dreads, $75.

Blow Styling Salon

342 W 14th Street, between Eighth & Ninth Avenues (1-212 989 6282). Subway A, C, E to 14th Street. **Open** 8am-8pm Mon-Fri; 10am-8pm Sat; noon-6pm Sun. **Credit** AmEx, Disc, MC, V.
Owners Jennifer Denton and Vigdis Boulton's Meatpacking District spot is scissor-free, focusing instead on pampering head massages and expertly executed blow-outs.

John Masters Organics

For listings, *see p242.*
It's like visiting an intoxicating botanical garden: the organic scalp treatment will send you into relaxed oblivion, and ammonia-free, herbal-based colour treatments will appeal to your inner purist. Cuts or colouring start at $90. **Photos** p243.

Laicale

129 Grand Street, between Broadway & Crosby Street (1-212 219 2424). Subway: J, M, N, Q, R, W, Z, 6 to Canal Street. **Open** 11am-8pm Mon-Fri; 10am-6pm Sat; noon-6pm Sun. **Credit** AmEx, MC, V (gratuities accepted in cash only).
Get your locks chopped at this industrial chrome-and-glass hair mecca while the shop's own DJ spins the tunes. Most of the stylists here also work for magazines and runway shows. Cuts start at $75; highlights, $145.

Miwa/Alex Salon

24 E 22nd Street, between Broadway & Park Avenue South (1-212 228 4422/www.miwaalex.com). Subway: N, R, W, 6 to 23rd Street. **Open** 8.30am-5.30pm Mon; 8.30am-7pm Tue-Fri. **Credit** MC, V.
Tucked inside a posh, friendly space in the Flatiron District, Miwa/Alex delivers the sort of smart and unique cut you expect in New York. Cuts start at $65 for women; $50 for men.

Mudhoney

148 Sullivan Street, between Houston & Prince Streets (1-212 533 1160). Subway: C, E to Spring Street. **Open** noon-8pm Tue-Fri; noon-6pm Sat. **No credit cards.**
Don't be surprised if the stylist never removes his orange-tinted sunglasses; you're in the city's premier rock 'n' roll salon. The decor alone – a torture chair, lascivious stained glass – will make the time in this tiny, attitude-packed place fly by. Cuts start at $75, and attract just as much attention as you want.
Other locations: 7 Bond Street, between Broadway & Lafayette Street (1-212 228 8128).

Spas

Amore Pacific

114 Spring Street, between Greene & Mercer Streets (1-212 966 0400). Subway: N, R, W to Prince Street; 6 to Spring Street. **Open** 11am-7pm daily. **Credit** AmEx, DC, MC, V.
This is the only US outlet for the super-swanky product line AP, a Korean company. The skincare system uses botanicals (red ginseng, bamboo sap) in conjunction with a high-tech process so that treatments quickly penetrate and revitalise the skin. Reflexology and massage are also available.

Juvenex

5th floor 25 W 32nd Street, between Broadway & Fifth Avenue (1-646 733 1330/www.juvenex spa.com). Subway: B, D, F, N, Q, R, V, W to 34th Street-Herald Square. **Open** 24hrs daily. **Credit** AmEx, Disc, MC, V.

So you know, it's Christmas

New York is the world's favourite Christmas shopping stop-off, with ever-growing numbers of everyday Santas dropping in every year from the US and, increasingly, Britain. And with good reason: add some of the world's best shopping to a flair for cold-weather comforts and seasonal cheer, and you've got yourself a fair old winter wonderland.

Eat, Drink, Shop

Fair trade

Sweater for your mom at Bloomingdale's? Check. Stuffed animal for your niece from FAO Schwartz? Got it. But what about your cat-obsessed cousin? Sometimes regular old department stores and boutiques just won't cut it when it comes to buying gifts. That's where the city's holiday bazaars come in. These sprawling temporary shops are filled with offbeat toys, handmade crafts, and more soap and candles than you ever thought existed. But they can also be intimidatingly crowded and stocked with cheap junk. Sales tend to take place between Thanksgiving and New Year; check the Around Town section of *Time Out New York* for information.

Holiday Market at Union Square

The goods: lots of candles and soap, plus toys, ties, clocks and crèche sets. Most items are reasonably priced, though some jewellery and imported goods can be quite expensive.
The crowds: this 11-year-old bazaar is probably the city's best known; as a result, it tends to be the most packed, particularly at weekends.
The vibe: competition for customers is fierce, so vendors are aggressive. Frustration can run high when a group stops in front of a booth, easily causing a bottleneck in the narrow walkways with few escape routes.
Worth a visit? If you can tolerate the crowds, you may find treasures buried here.

Grand Central Terminal Holiday Fair

The goods: you'll find lots of jewellery incorporating silver and/or turquoise at this indoor fair, as well as booths housing unusual (and pricey) gifts from Our Name is Mud, the Czechoslovak-American Puppet Theatre and the American Folk Art Museum. But the biggest draw is a huge selection of Christmas-tree ornaments.
The crowds: rush hour can be busy here, and many browsers will be dragging bulky suitcases.
The vibe: live musicians playing over-the-top Christmas tunes, but the crowd is low-key.
Worth a visit? Definitely go if you want to fill your tree with cool, handmade ornaments.

Holiday Market at Columbus Circle

The goods: this one's from the same people who put on the Union Square Market, but it seems to have more diverse merchandise – though the air still hangs thick with the scent of soap and candles.
The crowds: narrow, clog-prone walkways mean mobs.
The vibe: lots of no-nonsense shopping.
Worth a visit? Yes. After shopping, treat yourself to a crêpe at Chez Madeleine.

Window wonderlands

Come the winter holidays, these megashops compete for our attention – and our cash – by tarting themselves up with over-the-top spectacles of lights, wreaths and other Yuletide fanfare. Generally between Thanksgiving and the first week of the new year.

Barneys New York
660 Madison Avenue, at 61st Street (1-212 826 8900). Subway: N, R, W to Fifth Avenue-59th Street; 4, 5, 6 to 59th Street.

Bergdorf Goodman
754 Fifth Avenue, at 57th Street (1-212 753 7300). Subway: N, R, W to Fifth Avenue-59th Street.

Bloomingdale's
1000 Third Avenue, at 59th Street (1-212 705 2000). Subway: N, R, W to Lexington Avenue-59th Street; 4, 5, 6 to 59th Street.

Henri Bendel
712 Fifth Avenue, at 56th Street (1-212 247 1100). Subway: E, V to Fifth Avenue-53rd Street; N, R, W to Fifth Avenue-59th Street.

Macy's
151 W 34th Street, between Broadway & Seventh Avenue (1-212 695 4000). Subway: B, D, F, N, Q, R, V, W to 34th Street-Herald Square; 1, 2, 3 to 34th Street-Penn Station.

Saks
611 Fifth Avenue, at 50th Street (1-212 753 4000). Subway: B, D, F, V to 47th-50th Streets-Rockefeller Center.

Wrap it up

Looking for great gift wrapping ideas? Check out these stores selling paper and more.

Kate's Paperie
561 Broadway, between Prince & Spring Streets (1-212 941 9816/ www.katespaperie.com).
The last word on all things paper, Kate's never fails to delight and fascinate. Gift-wrapping services available. *See also p257.* **Other locations**: throughout the city.

Papercuts New York
27 W 20th Street, between Fifth & Sixth Avenues (1-212 620 0163/ www.papercutsnewyork.com). Subway: N, R, W to 23rd Street. **Open** 9am-6pm Mon-Fri. **Credit** AmEx, MC, V.

This speciality shop features animal patterns and novelty papers. Gift-wrapping services available.

Pearl Paint
308 Canal Street, between Broadway & Church Street (1-212 431 7932/ www.pearlpaint.com).
This massive art store brims with all sorts of goodies to gussy up gifts. *See also p258.*

This formerly girls-only 24-hour spa gained a cult following among post-partyers seeking communal detox in its jade igloo sauna. But boys can finally join the fun every night after 9pm. Treatments (unlike the sauna) are private; facials include the Oxygen ($130 for 75 minutes) and the Energizing Ginseng ($105 for 60 minutes). Massages from $95.

Nickel

77 Eighth Avenue, at 14th Street (1-212 242 3202/www.nickelformen.com). Subway: A, C, E to 14th Street; L to Eighth Avenue. **Open** 1-9pm Mon, Sun; 11am-9pm Tue-Fri; 10am-9pm Sat. **Credit** AmEx, Disc, MC, V.

New York's official temple of male grooming offers facials, waxing, massages, manicures and pedicures. The product line includes Washing Machine shower gel and Fire Insurance aftershave, as well as Self-Absorbed suntan oil – for the Narcissus in all of us.

Oasis Day Spa

2nd floor, 108 E 16th Street, between Union Square East & Irving Place, second floor (1-212 254 7722/www.oasisdayspanyc.com). Subway: L, N, Q, R, W, 4, 5, 6 to 14th Street-Union Square. **Open** 10am-10pm Mon-Fri; 9am-9pm Sat, Sun. **Credit** AmEx, Disc, MC, V.

The flagship location of this posh wellness sanctuary features everything from hair styling and detoxifying mud wraps to acupuncture. Stressed-out travellers can stop at the JFK branch (Jet Blue Terminal 6, 1-212 254 7722) for manicures, hot shaves or even full-body massages. **Other locations**: throughout the city.

Spa at Chelsea Piers

The Sports Center at Chelsea Piers, Pier 60, 23rd Street, at Twelfth Avenue (1-212 336 6780/www. chelseapiers.com). Subway: C, E to 23rd Street. **Open** 10am-9pm Mon-Fri; 10am-7pm Sat, Sun. **Credit** AmEx, Disc, MC, V.

Treat yourself to a massage ($95 and up), facial ($90 and up) and more at this intimate, full-service spa inside the mammoth Chelsea Piers Sports Center, and get a free day pass to the exercise club, where you can try yoga or rock-climbing, have a dip in the pool or grab a smoothie. Then head to the riverfront deck for a well-deserved nap in the sun.

Home & Gifts

Children's toys

Geppetto's Toy Box

10 Christopher Street, between Greenwich Avenue & Gay Street (1-212 620 7511). Subway: 1 to Christopher Street. **Open** 11.30am-7pm Mon-Sat; 12.30-5.30pm Sun. **Credit** AmEx, Disc, MC, V.

Like all good toys-for-tots stores, Geppetto's focuses on constructive, non-confrontational diversions. We particularly like the wooden make-your-own Empire State Building kit.

Kidding Around

60 W 15th Street, between Fifth & Sixth Avenues (1-212 645 6337). Subway: F, V to 14th Street; L to Sixth Avenue. **Open** 10am-7pm Mon-Sat; 11am-6pm Sun. **Credit** AmEx, Disc, MC, V.

Loyal customers frequent this quaint shop for clothing and learning toys for the brainy baby. The play area in the back will keep your little one occupied while you shop.

Scholastic Store

557 Broadway, between Prince & Spring Streets (1-212 343 6166). Subway: B, D, F, V to Broadway-Lafayette Street; N, R, W to Prince Street; 6 to Bleecker Street. **Open** 10am-7pm Mon-Sat; noon-6pm Sun. **Credit** AmEx, Disc, MC, V.

After checking out the huge selection of Scholastic books, move along to the toy section. This is the city's Harry Potter headquarters.

Toys 'R' Us Times Square

1514 Broadway, between 44th & 45th Streets (1-800 869 7787). Subway: N, Q, R, W, 42nd Street S, 1, 2, 3, 7 to 42nd Street-Times Square. **Open** 9am-10pm Mon-Sat; 11am-6pm Sun. **Credit** AmEx, Disc, MC, V.

The chain's flagship location is the world's largest toy store – big enough for a 60ft-high Ferris wheel inside and an animatronic tyrannosaur to greet you at the door. Brands rule here: a two-storey Barbie doll's house and a café with its very own sweetshop, Candy Land, designed to look like the board game. **Other locations**: throughout the city.

Flea markets

Among bargain-hungry New Yorkers, flea-market rummaging is pursued with religious devotion. What better way to walk off that overstuffed omelette and Bloody Mary from brunch than to explore aisles of old vinyl records, unusual tchotchkes, vintage linens and funky furniture?

The Garage

112 W 25th Street, between Sixth & Seventh Avenues (1-212 647 0707). Subway: F, V to 23rd Street. **Open** sunrise-sunset Sat, Sun. **No credit cards.**

Designers (and the occasional dolled-down celebrity) hunt regularly – and early – at this flea market inside an emptied parking garage. This spot specialises in old prints, vintage clothing, silver and linens; there's lots of household paraphernalia, too.

Hell's Kitchen Flea Market

39th Street, between Ninth and Tenth Avenues (1-212 243 5343). Subway: A, C, E to 34th Street-Penn Station. **Open** sunrise-sunset Sat, Sun. **No credit cards.**

The once-expansive Annex Antiques Fair & Flea Market on 26th Street lost its lease to a property developer, so many of the vendors packed up and moved to this stretch of road in Hell's Kitchen. Anyone familiar with the mind-boggling array of goods on offer at the former site may likely feel a bit cheated in the new space, but there are treasures to be found and momentum is still growing.

Greenflea
Intermediate School 44, Columbus Avenue, at 76th Street. Subway: B, C to 72nd Street; 1 to 79th Street. **Open** 10am-5.30pm Sun. **No credit cards**.
Greenflea is an extensive market that offers rare books, African art, antiques, handmade jewellery, crafts and eatables like vegetables and spiced cider (hot or cold, depending on the season). Visit both the labyrinthine interior and the schoolyard.

Gift shops

Auto
805 Washington Street, between Gansevoort & Horatio Streets (1-212 229 2292). Subway: A, C, E to 14th Street; L to Eighth Avenue. **Open** noon-7pm Mon-Sat; noon-6pm Sun. **Credit** AmEx, MC, V.
A cool gallery vibe makes this white-walled shop inviting. The owners buy from gifted artisans who produce everything from handblown-glass pieces and personalised ceramic Shrinky Dink necklaces to paintings and bedding.

Love Saves the Day
119 Second Avenue, at 7th Street (1-212 228 3802). Subway: 6 to Astor Place. **Open** noon-9pm daily. **Credit** AmEx, MC, V.
Yoda dolls, Elvis lamps, ant farms, lurid machine-made tapestries of Madonna, glow-in-the-dark crucifixes, collectable toys and Mexican Day of the Dead statues: kitsch reigns. Vintage clothing is peppered throughout the store.

Metropolitan Opera Shop
136 W 65th Street, at Broadway (1-212 580 4090/www.metguild.com/shop). Subway: 1 to 66th Street-Lincoln Center. **Open** 10am-10pm Mon-Sat; noon-6pm Sun. **Credit** AmEx, Disc, MC, V.
This shop in the Metropolitan Opera House at Lincoln Center sells CDs and cassettes, opera books, memorabilia and DVDs. Kids aren't forgotten, either: there are plenty of educational CDs.

Move Lab
803 Washington Street, between Gansevoort & Horatio Streets (1-212 741 5520). Subway: A, C, E to 14th Street; L to Eighth Avenue. **Open** noon-7pm Tue-Sat; noon-6pm Sun. **Credit** AmEx, MC, V.
Quirky, modern-looking objects bear visible marks of craftsmanship and a sense of history. Move Lab boasts an exciting blend of furniture, jewellery (including Braille-inscribed rings) and other baubles.

Mxyplyzyk
125 Greenwich Avenue, at 13th Street (1-212 989 4300/www.mxyplyzyk.com). Subway: A, C, E to 14th Street; L to Eighth Avenue. **Open** 11am-7pm Mon-Sat; noon-5pm Sun. **Credit** AmEx, MC, V.

The name doesn't mean anything, though it's reminiscent of a *Superman* character. Mxyplyzyk offers cool gifts, lighting, furniture, housewares, stationery, toys, pet gear and lots of novelty books – on important topics such as taxi drivers' words of wisdom.

Pearl River Mart
477 Broadway, between Broome & Grand Streets (1-212 431 4770/www.pearlriver.com). Subway: J, M, N, Q, R, W, Z to Canal Street; 6 to Spring Street. **Open** 10am-7.20pm daily. **Credit** AmEx, Disc, MC, V.
This browse-worthy downtown emporium is crammed with all things Chinese: slippers, clothing, gongs, groceries, medicinal herbs, stationery, teapots and all sorts of fun trinkets and gift items.

Home design

ABC Carpet & Home
888 Broadway, at 19th Street (1-212 473 3000/ www.abchome.com). Subway: L, N, Q, R, W, 4, 5, 6 to 14th Street-Union Square. **Open** 10am-8pm Mon-Thur; 10am-6.30pm Fri, Sat; noon-6pm Sun. **Credit** AmEx, Disc, MC, V.
At this shopping landmark, the selection of accessories, linens, rugs, and reproduction and antique furniture (Western and Asian) is unbelievable; so are the mostly steep prices. For bargains, head to ABC's warehouse outlet in the Bronx. **Photos** *p251*.
Other locations: 20 Jay Street, at Plymouth Street, Dumbo, Brooklyn (1-718 643 7400); ABC Carpet & Home Warehouse, 1055 Bronx River Avenue, between Bruckner Boulevard & Westchester Avenue, Bronx (1-718 842 8772).

Area ID Moderne
262 Elizabeth Street, between Houston & Prince Streets (1-212 219 9903). Subway: B, D, F, V to Broadway-Lafayette Street; 6 to Bleecker Street. **Open** noon-7pm Mon-Fri; noon-6pm Sat, Sun. **Credit** AmEx, MC, V.
Home accessories and furniture from the 1950s, '60s and '70s, both vintage and reproduction, are this shop's métier, but the furniture has been reupholstered in luxurious fabrics. You'll also find a wide selection of fur throws and rugs.

Butter & Eggs
83 West Broadway, at Warren Street (1-212 676 0235/www.butterandeggs.com). Subway: A, C, E, 1, 2, 3 to Chambers Street. **Open** 11am-6pm Mon-Wed, Fri, Sat; noon-8pm Thur; noon-5pm Sun. **Credit** AmEx, MC, V.
Warren Street was the hub of NYC's butter and egg business in the 1800s. Nowadays, eclectic home emporium Butter & Eggs sells wares such as Saké sets and handmade pillows.

Conran Shop
407 E 59th Street, between First & York Avenues (1-212 755 9079). Subway: N, R, W to Lexington Avenue-59th Street; 4, 5, 6 to 59th Street. **Open** 11am-8pm Mon-Fri; 10am-7pm Sat; noon-6pm Sun. **Credit** AmEx, DC, MC, V.

Sir Terence Conran's shop, nestled beneath the Queensboro Bridge, stocks a vast selection of trendy products – new and vintage – for every room of the house: the range includes cabinets, dishes, lighting, rugs, sofas, draperies, beds, linens, kitchen gadgets and much, much more.

Las Venus
163 Ludlow Street, between Houston & Stanton Streets (1-212 982 0608). Subway: F, V to Second Avenue. **Open** noon-8pm Mon-Sat; noon-7pm Sun. **Credit** AmEx, Disc, MC, V.
Local hipsters all head to the epicentre of 20th-century pop culture to feed their kitsch furniture fixes. Vintage pieces by the greats – Miller, McCobb, Kagan among others – are flanked by reproductions, the overall collection creating an artfully cluttered reservoir of affordable finds. **Photos** *pp252-3.*
Other locations: Las Venus at ABC, 888 Broadway, at 19th Street (1-212 473 3000 ext 519).

MoMA Design Store
44 W 53rd Street, between Fifth & Sixth Avenues (1-212 767 1050/www.momastore. org). Subway: E, V to Fifth Avenue-53rd Street. **Open** 10am-6.30pm Mon-Thur, Sat, Sun; 10am-8pm Fri. **Credit** AmEx, MC, V.
The store is as wide-ranging as the museum's collection. State-of-the-art home items on display include casseroles, coffee tables, high-design chairs, lighting, office workstations, kids' furniture, jewellery, calendars and lots of Christmas ornaments. **Other locations**: 81 Spring Street, at Crosby Street (1-646 613 1367).

Moss
146 Greene Street, between Houston & Prince Streets (1-212 204 7100). Subway: B, D, F, V to Broadway-Lafayette Street; N, R, W to Prince Street; 6 to Bleecker Street. **Open** 11am-7pm Mon-Sat; noon-6pm Sun. **Credit** AmEx, Disc, MC, V.
Proprietor Murray Moss has curated perhaps the most impressive collection of high-design items in the city. Many of the streamlined clocks, curvy sofas and funky flatware are kept protected under glass at this temple of contemporary home design. For creativity on a larger scale, stop by his newly opened 'museum' adjacent to the store.

Leisure

Bookstores

Chain stores

Barnes & Noble has a number of megastores, and several feature readings by authors. The smaller **Borders** chain also provides under-one-roof browsing. Check the phone book for the location nearest you, and pick up *Time Out New York* for listings of readings at bookstores and other venues. *See also p276* **Books & Poetry**.

General interest

Coliseum Books
11 W 42nd Street, between Fifth & Sixth Avenues (1-212 803 5890/www.coliseumbooks. com). Subway: B, D, F, V to 42nd Street-Bryant Park; 7 to Fifth Avenue. **Open** 8am-8.30pm Mon-Fri; 11am-8.30pm Sat; noon-7pm Sun. **Credit** AmEx, DC, Disc, MC, V.
Coliseum is something of a miracle: in 2002, the beloved haunt of bibliophiles was forced out of its 57th Street location by a rent hike. A year later, it magically resurfaced 15 blocks south, with many of the same staffers and fixtures.

192 Books
192 Tenth Avenue, between 21st & 22nd Streets (1-212 255 4022/www.192books.com). Subway: C, E to 23rd Street. **Open** noon-6pm Mon, Sun; 11am-7pm Tue-Sat. **Credit** AmEx, MC, V.
In an era when many an indie bookshop has closed its doors, this youngster, opened in 2003, is proving that quirky boutique booksellers can make it after all. Owned and 'curated' by art dealer Paula Cooper and her husband, editor Jack Macrae, 192 offers a strong selection of art books and literature, as well as sections on gardening, history, politics, design, music and memoirs.

St Mark's Bookshop
31 Third Avenue, between 8th & 9th Streets (1-212 260 7853/www.stmarksbookshop.com). Subway: N, R, W to 8th Street-NYU; 6 to Astor Place. **Open** 10am-midnight Mon-Sat; 11am-midnight Sun. **Credit** AmEx, Disc, MC, V.
Students, academics and art professionals gravitate to this East Village bookseller, which maintains strong inventories on cultural theory, graphic design, poetry and film studies, as well as numerous avant-garde journals and zines.

Second-hand books

Housing Works Used Book Café
126 Crosby Street, between Houston & Prince Streets (1-212 334 3324/www.housingworksubc.com). Subway: B, D, F, V to Broadway-Lafayette Street; N, R, W to Prince Street; 6 to Bleecker Street. **Open** 10am-9pm Mon-Fri; noon-9pm Sat; noon-7pm Sun. **Credit** AmEx, MC, V.
Housing Works bookstore is extraordinarily endearing. The two-level Soho space – which stocks literary fiction, non-fiction and collectibles – is a peaceful spot for solo relaxation or for meeting friends over coffee or wine. All proceeds go to support services for homeless people living with HIV/AIDS.

Labyrinth Books
536 W 112th Street, between Amsterdam Avenue & Broadway (1-212 865 1588/www.labyrinthbooks. com). Subway: 1 to 110th Street-Cathedral Pkwy. **Open** 9am-10pm Mon-Fri; 10am-8pm Sat; 11am-7pm Sun. **Credit** AmEx, Disc, MC, V.

Eat, Drink, Shop

The near-legendary
ABC Carpet & Home. *See p249*.

The academic crowd thrives in Labyrinth's rarefied air. You may find remaindered copies of *Heidegger, Coping, and Cognitive Science* or a coffee-table book entitled *Black Panthers 1968*.

Strand Book Store

828 Broadway, at 12th Street (1-212 473 1452/ www.strandbooks.com). Subway: L, N, Q, R, W, 4, 5, 6 to 14th Street-Union Square. **Open** 9.30am-10.30pm Mon-Sat; 11am-10.30pm Sun. **Credit** AmEx, DC, Disc, MC, V.

Owned by the Bass family since 1927, the legendary Strand – with its '18 miles of books' – offers incredible deals on new releases, loads of used books, plenty of hard-to-finds and the New York City's largest rare-book collection. Staff are pretty good at pointing you in the right direction. **Photo** *p254.* **Other locations**: Strand , 95 Fulton Street, between Gold & William Streets (1-212 732 6070); Strand Kiosk, Central Park, Fifth Avenue, at 60th Street (1-646 284 5506).

Speciality stores

Books of Wonder

18 W 18th Street, between Fifth & Sixth Avenues (1-212 989 3270/www.booksofwonder.com). Subway: F, V to 14th Street; L to Sixth Avenue; 1 to 18th Street. **Open** 10am-7pm Mon-Sat; noon-6pm Sun. **Credit** AmEx, Disc, MC, V.

It recently moved two doors down and combined forces with the Cupcake Café in late 2004, but the city's only independent children's bookstore still features both the very new (the staff hosted a midnight-madness party to celebrate the release of the last *Harry Potter*) and the very old (rare and out-of-print editions), plus foreign-language and reference titles, and a special collection of Oz books.

East West

78 Fifth Avenue, between 13th & 14th Streets (1-212 243-5994/www.eastwest.com). Subway: L, N, Q, R, W, 4, 5, 6 to 14th Street-Union Square. **Open** 10am-7.30pm Mon-Sat; 11am-6.30pm Sun. **Credit** AmEx, Disc, MC, V.

This spiritual title-holder devotes equal space to Eastern and Western traditions, from alternative health and yoga to philosophy.

Forbidden Planet

840 Broadway, at 13th Street (1-212 475 6161/ www.fpnyc.com). Subway: L, N, Q, R, W, 4, 5, 6 to 14th Street-Union Square. **Open** 10am-10pm Mon, Tue, Sun; 10am-midnight Wed-Sat. **Credit** AmEx, Disc, MC, V.

Embracing both the pop-culture mainstream and the cult underground, the Planet takes all comics seriously. You'll find graphic novels (Neil Gaiman's *Sandman*, Craig Thompson's *Blankets*), serials (*Asterix, Batman*), and film and TV tie-ins.

Hue-man Bookstore & Café

2319 Frederick Douglass Boulevard (Eighth Avenue), between 124th & 125th Streets (1-212 665 7400/ www.huemanbookstore.com). Subway: A, B, C, D to 125th Street. **Open** 10am-8pm Mon-Sat; 11am-7pm Sun. **Credit** AmEx, Disc, MC, V.

Las Venus. See p250.

Focusing on African-American non-fiction and fiction, this superstore-size Harlem indie also stocks bestsellers and general-interest books.

Mysterious Bookshop
129 W 56th Street, between Sixth & Seventh Avenues (1-212 765 0900/www.mysterious bookshop.com). Subway: F, N, Q, R, W to 57th Street. **Open** 11am-7pm Mon-Sat. **Credit** AmEx, DC, Disc, MC, V.
Devotees of mystery, crime and spy genres will know owner Otto Penzler, both as an editor and from his book recommendations on Amazon.com. His shop holds a wealth of paperbacks, hardcovers and autographed first editions.

Cameras & electronics

When buying expensive electronic gear, it pays to go to a well-known store, where you'll get reliable advice about a device's compatibility with systems in the country in which you plan to use it. For specialised photo processing, we recommend Duggal (www.duggal.com).

Apple Store
103 Prince Street, at Greene Street (1-212 226 3126/store.apple.com). Subway: N, R, W to Prince Street. **Open** 10am-8pm Mon-Sat; 11am-7pm Sun. **Credit** AmEx, DC, Disc, MC, V.
Maybe it's the bright-white high-design interior, or maybe it's the chance to try out just about every shiny, nifty innovation. Perhaps it's the free seminars

or the friendly troubleshooters behind the Genius Bar. Whatever the reason, buying or repairing high-tech gear here – or just gawking – is fun.

B&H
420 Ninth Avenue, at 34th Street (1-212 444 5040/www.bhphotovideo.com). Subway: A, C, E to 34th Street-Penn Station. **Open** 9am-7pm Mon-Thur; 9am-2pm Fri; 10am-5pm Sun. **Credit** AmEx, Disc, MC, V.
B&H is the ultimate one-stop shop for all your photographic, video and audio needs (including professional audio equipment and discounted Bang & Olufsen products). Note that B&H is closed Friday afternoon, all day Saturday and on Jewish holidays.

Harvey
2 W 45th Street, between Fifth & Sixth Avenues (1-212 575 5000). Subway: B, D, F, V to 42nd Street-Bryant Park; 7 to Fifth Avenue. **Open** 10am-7pm Mon-Wed, Fri; 10am-8pm Thur; 10am-6pm Sat; noon-5pm Sun. **Credit** AmEx, MC, V.
Although Harvey is known mainly for its huge selection of high-end electronics, it stocks plenty of realistically priced items and stereo furniture too.
Other locations: ABC Carpet & Home, mezzanine level, 888 Broadway, at 19th Street (1-212 228 5354).

J&R Music and Computer World
23 Park Row, between Ann & Beekman Streets (1-212 238 9000/1-800 221 8180/www.jr.com). Subway: A, C to Broadway-Nassau Street; J, M, Z, 4,

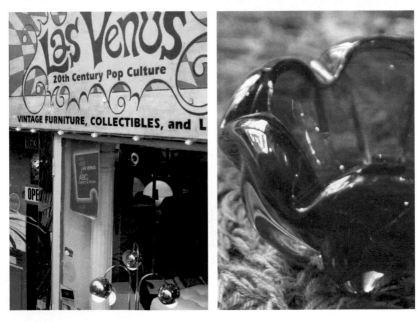

5 to Fulton Street; 2, 3 to Park Place. **Open** 9am-7.30pm Mon-Sat; 10.30am-6.30pm Sun. **Credit** AmEx, Disc, MC, V.
Every electronic device you'll ever need (PCs, TVs, CD players... and battery-powered nose-hair trimmers) can be found at this block-long shop.

Gadget repairs

Computer Solutions Provider
45 W 21st Street, between Third & Fourth Avenues (1-212 673 8400/www.phototech.com). Subway: F, N, R, V, W to 23rd Street. **Open** 9am-6pm Mon-Fri. **Credit** AmEx, MC, V.
It might not be a sexy name but it delivers exactly what you want, when you want it: specialists in Macs, PCs and related peripherals, these techies can recover lost data and help you through other computer disasters; they even make house calls.

Photo-Tech Repair Service
110 E 13th Street, between Third & Fourth Avenues (1-212 673 8400/www.phototech. com). Subway: L, N, Q, R, W, 4, 5, 6 to 14th Street-Union Square. **Open** 8am-4.45pm Mon, Tue, Thur, Fri; 8am-6pm Wed; 10am-3pm Sat. **Credit** AmEx, Disc, MC, V.
This shop has 18 on-site technicians and guarantees that it can fix your camera regardless of the brand. Rush service is also available.

The inimitable **Strand Book Store**. *See p252.*

Music

Classical

Westsider Records
233 W 72nd Street, between Broadway & West End Avenue (1-212 874 1588). Subway: 1, 2, 3 to 72nd Street. **Open** 11am-8pm daily. **Credit** MC, V.
This solidly classical store has traditionally stocked vinyl only, but the 21st century has swept in a wave of CDs. It also carries a sprinkling of jazz records and drama and film books.

Electronica

Dance Tracks
91 E 3rd Street, at First Avenue (1-212 260 8729/www.dancetracks.com). Subway: F, V to Lower East Side-Second Avenue. **Open** noon-9pm Mon-Fri; noon-8pm Sat; noon-7pm Sun. **Credit** AmEx, Disc, MC, V.
European imports hot off the plane make this store a must. But it also has racks of domestic house, enticing bins of Loft/Paradise Garage classics and private decks on which to sample.

Hip hop & R&B

Beat Street Records
494 Fulton Street, between Bond Street & Elm Place, Brooklyn (1-718 624 6400/www.beatst.com). Subway: A, C, G to Hoyt-Schermerhorn; 2, 3, 4, 5 to Nevins Street. **Open** 10am-7pm Mon-Wed; 10am-7.30pm Thur-Sat; 10am-6pm Sun. **Credit** AmEx, Disc, MC, V.
In a block-long basement with two DJ booths, Beat Street proffers the latest vinyl. CDs run from dancehall to gospel, but the 12in singles and new hip-hop albums make this the first stop for local DJs seeking killer breakbeats and samples.

Fat Beats
Second floor, 406 Sixth Avenue, between 8th & 9th Streets (1-212 673 3883/www.fatbeats.com). Subway: A, B, C, D, E, F, V to W 4th Street. **Open** noon-9pm Mon-Sat; noon-6pm Sun. **Credit** MC, V.
Everyone – Beck, DJ Evil Dee, DJ Premier, Mike D, Q-Tip – shops at this tiny Greenwich Village shrine to vinyl for treasured hip-hop, jazz, funk and reggae releases; underground magazines (*Wax Poetics*); and cult flicks (*Wild Style*).

Jazz

Jazz Record Center
Room 804, 236 W 26th Street, between Seventh & Eighth Avenues (1-212 675 4480/www.jazzrecord center.com). Subway: C, E to 23rd Street; 1 to 28th Street. **Open** 10am-6pm Mon-Sat. **Credit** Disc, MC, V.
The city's best jazz store stocks current and out-of-print records, books, videos and other jazz-related merchandise. Worldwide shipping is available.

On the record

DJ culture has sparked a revival in the popularity of vinyl records, but for many New Yorkers, the format never faded, thanks to the city's thriving club scene. While CDs – and, later, downloads – took over the music industry, celebrity DJs kept vinyl on the radar. In the early and mid 1980s, club kids would leave hot spots like Paradise Garage in the morning and immediately make the short trek to **Vinylmania** (60 Carmine Street, between Bedford Street & Seventh Avenue South, 1-212 924 7223, www.vinylmania.com) to pick up copies of whatever the DJ had spun the night before. Today, the city even boasts its own trade school for all things vinyl: **Scratch DJ Academy** (434 Sixth Avenue, between 9th & 10th Streets, 1-212 529 1599, www.scratch.com), where wannabe turntablists can take private lessons in mixing, beat-matching and scratching.

The high demand for vinyl means that good records are hard to find at reasonable prices (we're looking at you, Bleecker Bob's), especially in Manhattan. But an hour north of midtown, **Mooncurser Records** (229 City Island Avenue, between Centre & Schofield Streets, City Island, Bronx, 1-718 885 0302) is a terrific repository of 100,000 LPs, 45s and 78s, ranging from big band and new wave to children's music and soul-country. Hours vary, so be sure to call before making the trip.

The only store in the city to beat Mooncurser in terms of sheer stock, the semi-legendary **The Thing** (1001 Manhattan Avenue, between Green & Huron Streets, Greenpoint, Brooklyn, 1-718 349 8234) hoards at least 150,000 albums in its musty, fluorescent-lit basement – haphazardly lining the walls, stacked in makeshift piles, spilling on to the floor and costing an unheard-of $2 a

disc. A recent trip unearthed vintage Randy Newman, Heaven 17 and Curtis Mayfield LPs, rare disco singles and a Teenage Mutant Ninja Turtles 12-in. Walk down the street to **The Vortex** (1084 Manhattan Avenue, between Dupont & Eagle Streets, Greenpoint, Brooklyn, 1-718 609 6066), which is run by Dawn Babbush, Thing owner Larry Fisher's wife. Its inexpensive, eclectic selection of '60s soul and psych-rock records is arranged alphabetically and by genre.

Halcyon (57 Pearl Street, between Plymouth & Water Streets, Dumbo, Brooklyn, 1-718 260 9299, www.halcyonline.com), another Brooklyn institution, has been a club-scene fixture since 1999, selling new and used wax – plus top-of-the-line DJ gear, indie designer clothes, books and art – to the audiophile hipsters who scour the bins for underground electronica, hip hop and dub.

Pricey but worth the expense, **A-1 Records** (439 E 6th Street, between First Avenue & Avenue A, 1-212 473 2870; pictured) carries some of the most obscure hip-hop and funk records in the city. Want proof? Check out the Polaroids of big-name DJs and producers who've stopped by, from Fatboy Slim to Kurtis Blow. Four turntables allow you to test-drive a twelve-inch before buying.

In June and December **The ARChive of Contemporary Music** (54 White Street, between Broadway & Church Street, 1-212 226 6967, www.arcmusic.org), a vast music library and research centre, unloads more than 10,000 extras from its encyclopedic collection of 20th-century popular music in twice-yearly, week-long sales. Gems old and new go for next to nothing. Be sure to spend generously – it's a small price to pay to keep vinyl alive in the iPod age.

Creature comforts

Spoiled pets are nothing new. And, in a city that found takers for a $19 hot dog (at the Old Homestead Steakhouse), it should come as no surprise that for about 1,400 bucks, you can swing by Hermès and pick out a crocodile-and-calfskin leather leash and collar for your four-legged friend. Still, is it just us or have creature comforts here gone to the dogs? Over at **Happy Paws** (316 Lafayette Street, at Houston Street, 1-212 431 6898), travel-bound New Yorkers or visitors with pet-unfriendly lodgings can shell out $115 a night for a doggie suite – replete with a bed, couch and TV with DVD player. That's right, Fido can jump on the bed, or just kick back and enjoy a personal screening of *101 Dalmatians*.

Mini pearl necklaces ($75) and shearling coats ($250) can be had for your Madison Avenue mutt at the Upper East Side's tony **Canine Style** (830 Lexington Avenue, between 63 & 64th Streets, 1-212 838 2064). For the politically correct pet, faux fur coats are for sale at **Karen for People + Pets** (1195 Lexington Avenue, between 81st & 82nd Streets, 1-212 472 9440). At the **Dog Run** (136 Ninth Avenue, 1-212 414 2500, between 18th & 19th Streets; pictured) harried pups can doggie-paddle away the stress of city living in the lap pool. If social calls are in order, perhaps a dog run will fit the bill: there are at least 49 of these gigantic puppy playpens throughout the city's parks. And forget those arcane trips to the vet. Our cosmopolitan hounds have chiropractors, acupuncturists and massage therapists. Just stop in at **Whiskers** (235 E 9th Street, 1-212 979 2532, between Stuyvesant & 2nd Streets) and see the myriad holistic pet products, herbal remedies and dietary supplements packing the shelves.

Multigenre

Bleecker Bob's

118 W 3rd Street, between MacDougal Street & Sixth Avenue (1-212 475 9677/www.bleecker bobs.com). Subway: A, B, C, D, E, F, V to W 4th Street. **Open** 11am-1am Mon-Thur, Sun; 11am-3am Fri, Sat. **Credit** AmEx, MC, V.
Come to Bleecker Bob's for hard-to-find new and used music, especially on vinyl. An online ordering service is due imminently.

Etherea

66 Avenue A, between 4th & 5th Streets (1-212 358 1126/www.ethereaonline.com). Subway: F, V to Lower East Side-Second Avenue. **Open** noon-10pm Mon-Thur, Sun; noon-11pm Fri, Sat. **Credit** AmEx, Disc, MC, V.
Etherea stocks mostly electronic, experimental, house, indie and rock CDs.

Mondo Kim's

6 St Marks Place, between Second & Third Avenues (1-212 598 9985/www.kimsvideo.com). Subway: 6 to Astor Place. **Open** 9am-midnight daily. **Credit** AmEx, MC, V.
Each branch of this movie and music mini chain has a slightly different name (see the website for locations) but all offer a great selection for collector

geeks: electronic, indie, krautrock, prog, reggae, soul, soundtracks and used CDs.
Other locations: throughout the city.

Other Music

15 E 4th Street, between Broadway & Lafayette Street (1-212 477 8150/www.othermusic.com). Subway: N, R, W to 8th Street-NYU; 6 to Astor Place. **Open** noon-9pm Mon-Fri; noon-8pm Sat; noon-7pm Sun. **Credit** AmEx, MC, V.
This wee audio temple is dedicated to small-label, often imported new and used CDs and LPs. It organises music by arcane categories (for instance, 'La Decadanse' includes lounge, Moog and slow-core soundtracks) and sends out a free weekly email with staffers' reviews of their favourite new releases.

St Marks Sounds

20 St Marks Place, between Second & Third Avenues (1-212 677 2727/1-212 677 3444). Subway: 6 to Astor Place. **Open** noon-9pm Mon-Thur, Sun; noon-10pm Fri, Sat. **No credit cards**.
Housed in two neighbouring storefronts, Sounds is the best bargain on the block for new and used music. The shop at 20 St Marks Place specialises in jazz and international recordings.

Subterranean Records

5 Cornelia Street, between Bleecker & W 4th Streets (1-212 463 8900). Subway: A, B, C, D, E, F, V to W

4th Street. **Open** noon-8pm Mon-Wed; noon-10pm Thur-Sat; noon-7pm Sun. **Credit** MC, V.
Just off Bleecker Street, this shop carries new, used and live recordings, as well as a large selection of imports. Vinyl LPs and 45s fill the basement.

Superstores

J&R Music and Computer World
For listing and review, *see p253.*

Tower Records
692 Broadway, at 4th Street (1-212 505 1500/ 1-800 648 4844/www.towerrecords.com). Subway: N, R, W to 8th Street-NYU; 6 to Astor Place. **Open** 9am-midnight daily.
Credit AmEx, Disc, MC, V.
Tower has all the current sounds on CD and tape.
Other locations: throughout the city.

Virgin Megastore
52 E 14th Street, at University Place (1-212 598 4666/www.virginmega.com). Subway: L, N, Q, R, W, 4, 5, 6 to 14th Street-Union Square. **Open** 9am-1am Mon-Sat; 10am-midnight Sun.
Credit AmEx, Disc, MC, V.
Besides a huge selection of every genre of music, Virgin Megastore has in-store performances and a great selection of CDs from the UK. Books, DVDs and videos are also available.
Other locations: 1540 Broadway, between 45th & 46th Streets (1-212 921 1020).

World music

World Music Institute
Suite 903, 49 W 27th Street, between Broadway & Sixth Avenue (1-212 545 7536/www.world musicinstitute.org). Subway: N, R, W to 28th Street. **Open** 10am-6pm Mon-Fri. **Credit** AmEx, MC, V.
The shop is small, but if you can't find what you're looking for, then WMI's expert, helpful employees can order sounds from the remotest corners of the planet and have them shipped to you, usually within two to four weeks.

Sex shops

Leather Man
111 Christopher Street, between Bleecker & Hudson Streets (1-212 243 5339/www.theleatherman.com). Subway: 1 to Christopher Street. **Open** noon-10pm Mon-Sat; noon-8pm Sun. **Credit** AmEx, Disc, MC, V.
Cock rings, padlocks and sturdy handcuffs beckon from wall-mounted cabinets on the first floor, while the basement (of course) is where serious bondage apparel is hung. There are also fake penises of every imaginable (and unimaginable) description.

Myla
20 E 69th Street, between Fifth & Madison Avenues (1-212 570 1590) Subway: 6 to 68th Street Hunter College. **Open** 10am-6pm Mon-Sat.
Credit AmEx, Disc, MC, V.

London-based naughty-nighties emporium Myla sells elegant boudoir accessories, including tasteful (yet nipple-exposing) 'peephole' bras, silk wrist-ties and blindfolds, plus a handful of sculptural, Brancusi-esque vibrators.

Toys in Babeland
94 Rivington Street, between Ludlow & Orchard Streets (1-212 375 1701/www.babeland.com). Subway: F, V to Lower East Side-Second Avenue. **Open** noon-10pm Mon-Sat; noon-7pm Sun.
Credit AmEx, MC, V.
At this friendly sex-toy boutique – run by women and skewed towards women, although everyone is welcome if the attitude is right – engrossed browsers are encouraged to handle all manner of buzzing, wriggling and bendable playthings. The ladies at Babeland also host frank sex-ed classes (open to all genders and sexualities), whose subjects include, for example, 'Strap-On Seductions'.
Other locations: 43 Mercer Street, between Broome & Grand Streets (1-212 966 2120).

Specialities & eccentricities

Jerry Ohlinger's Movie Material Store
242 W 14th Street, between Seventh & Eighth Avenues (1-212 989 0869/www.movie materials.com). Subway: A, C, E, 1, 2, 3 to 14th Street; L to Eighth Avenue. **Open** 1-7.45pm daily. **Credit** AmEx, Disc, MC, V.
On the premises: the city's most extensive stock of 'paper material' from movies past and present, including photos, posters, programmes and fascinating celebrity curios.

Kate's Paperie
561 Broadway, between Prince & Spring Streets (1 212 941-9816/www.katespaperie. com). Subway: N, R, W to Prince Street; 6 to Spring Street. **Open** 10am-7.30pm daily.
Credit AmEx, Disc, MC, V.
Kate's is the ultimate paper mill. Choose from more than 5,000 kinds of paper by mining the rich vein of stationery, custom-printing services, journals, photo albums and creative, amazingly beautiful gift wrap. Definitely something to write home about.
Other locations: throughout the city.

Nat Sherman
500 Fifth Avenue, at 42nd Street (1-212 764 5000/www.natsherman.com). Subway: B, D, F, V to 42nd Street-Bryant Park; 7 to Fifth Avenue. **Open** 10am-8pm Mon-Fri; 10am-7pm Sat; 11am-5pm Sun. **Credit** AmEx, C, MC, V.
Just across the street from the New York Public Library, Nat Sherman offers its own brand of slow-burning cigarettes, as well as cigars and related accoutrements, for your smoking pleasure. Flick your Bic in the upstairs smoking room.

Eat, Drink, Shop

Pearl Paint

308 Canal Street, between Broadway & Church Street (1-212 431 7932/www.pearlpaint.com). Subway: J, M, N, Q, R, W, Z, 6 to Canal Street. **Open** 9am-7pm Mon-Fri; 10am-6.30pm Sat; 10am-6pm Sun. **Credit** AmEx, Disc, MC, V.

This huge art- and drafting-supply commissary sells everything you could possibly need to create your own masterpiece.

Other locations: 207 E 23rd Street, between Second and Third Avenues (1-212 592 2179).

Quark International

240 E 29 Street, between Second & Third Avenues (1-212 889 1808). Subway: 6 to 33rd Street. **Open** 10am-6.30pm Mon-Fri; noon-5pm Sat. **Credit** AmEx, DC, Disc, MC, V.

Spy wannabes and budding paranoids can buy body armour or high-powered bugs here. The store will also custom-bulletproof your favourite jacket.

Sam Ash Music

160 W 48th Street, between Sixth & Seventh Avenues (1-212 719 2299/www.samash music.com). Subway: B, D, F, V to 47th-50th Streets-Rockefeller Center; N, R, W to 49th Street. **Open** 10am-8pm Mon-Sat; noon-6pm Sun. **Credit** AmEx, MC, V.

This octogenarian musical-instrument emporium dominates its midtown block with four contiguous shops. New, vintage and custom guitars of all varieties are available, along with amps, DJ equipment, drums, keyboards, recording equipment, turntables and an array of sheet music.

Other locations: throughout the city.

Sports

Blades, Board & Skate

659 Broadway, between Bleecker & Bond Streets (1-212 477 7350/www.blades.com). Subway: B, D, F, V to Broadway-Lafayette Street; 6 to Bleecker Street. **Open** 10am-9pm Mon-Sat; 11am-7pm Sun. **Credit** MC, V.

The requisite clothing and gear is sold alongside in-line skates, skateboards and snowboards.

Other locations: throughout the city.

Gerry Cosby & Co

3 Pennsylvania Plaza, Madison Square Garden, Seventh Avenue, at 32nd Street (1-212 563 6464/ 1-877 563 6464/www.cosbysports.com). Subway: A, C, E, 1, 2, 3 to 34th Street-Penn Station. **Open** 9.30am-7.30pm daily. **Credit** AmEx, Disc, MC, V.

Cosby has a huge selection of official team wear and other sporting necessities. The store is open during – and until 30 minutes after – evening Knicks and Rangers games, in case you feel like celebrating.

Paragon Sporting Goods

867 Broadway, at 18th Street (1-212 255 8036/ www.paragonsports.com). Subway: L, N, Q, R, W, 4, 5, 6 to 14th Street-Union Square. **Open** 10am-8pm Mon-Sat; 11.30am-7pm Sun. **Credit** AmEx, DC, Disc, MC, V.

Three floors of equipment and clothing for almost every activity (at every level of expertise) make this the New York sports-gear mecca.

Tattoos & piercing

Tattooing was made legal in New York in 1998; piercing, however, remains relatively unregulated, so mind your nipples.

New York Adorned

47 Second Avenue, between 2nd & 3rd Streets (1-212 473 0007/www.newyorkadorned.com). Subway: F, V to Lower East Side-Second Avenue. **Open** 1-9pm Mon-Thur, Sun; 1-10pm Fri, Sat. **Credit** AmEx, MC, V (cash only for tattoos).

Proprietor Lori Leven hires world-class tattoo artists to wield the needles at her eight-year-old gothic-elegant establishment. Those with low pain thresholds can go for gentler body decorations such as henna tattoos, finery like ethereal white-gold cluster earrings, crafted by Leven, or pieces by a group of emerging body-jewellery designers.

Venus Modern Body Arts

199 E 4th Street, between Avenues A & B (1-212 473 1954). Subway: F, V to Lower East Side-Second Avenue. **Open** 1-9pm Mon-Thur, Sun; 1-10pm Fri, Sat. **Credit** AmEx, Disc, MC, V.

Venus has tattooed and pierced New Yorkers since 1992 – before body art became de rigueur. It also offers a positively enormous selection of jewellery, so you can put diamonds in your navel and platinum in your tongue.

Travel & luggage

Coach

595 Madison Avenue, at 57th Street (1-212 754 0041/www.coach.com). Subway: N, R, W to Fifth Avenue-59th Street. **Open** 10am-8pm Mon-Sat; 11am-6pm Sun. **Credit** AmEx, DC, Disc, MC, V.

Coach's butter-soft leather briefcases, wallets and handbags have always been exceptional, but the Manhattan Coach stores also stock the label's luxurious outerwear collection.

Other locations: throughout the city.

Flight 001

96 Greenwich Avenue, between Jane & W 12th Streets (1-212 691 1001/www.flight 001.com). Subway: A, C, E to 14th Street; L to Eighth Avenue. **Open** 11am-8.30pm Mon-Fri; 11am-8pm Sat; noon-6pm Sun. **Credit** AmEx, DC, Disc, MC, V.

Forget something – or taken greater advantage of New York's shopping than your bags can handle? This one-stop West Village shop carries guidebooks and chic luggage, along with fun travel products such as pocket-size aromatherapy kits. Flight 001's 'essentials' wall features packets of Woolite, mini-dominoes and everything in between.

Arts & Entertainment

Features

Festivals & Events

24-hour party people – New Yorkers love to celebrate.

New York may be known as the city that never sleeps, but it might be more appropriate to consider it the city that never even sits down. No matter what day of the week or time of year, there's always something to do here. What follows is but a sampling of the plethora of annual and seasonal events, fairs, parades and festivals that happen in the five boroughs. (For more events, check out the other chapters in the Arts & Entertainment section.) Keep in mind that before you set out or plan a trip around an event, it's always wise to call and make sure the fling is still set to swing.

Spring

Whitney Biennial

For listing, see p135 **Whitney Museum of American Art**. Dates March-May.
A captivating and often provocative showcase of contemporary works by both established and emerging artists is mounted in alternate years (even-numbered ones). The 2006 edition of the show kicks off in March.

Armory Show

Piers 90 & 92, Twelfth Avenue, between 50th & 52nd Streets (1-212 645 6440/www.thearmory show.com). Subway: C, E to 50th Street.
Dates 10-13 March.
The show that, in 1913, heralded the arrival of modern art in America has morphed into a huge contemporary-art mart.

St Patrick's Day Parade

Fifth Avenue, from 44th to 86th Streets (www.saintpatricksdayparade.com). **Date** 17 March.
This massive march is one of the city's longest-running annual traditions – it dates from 1762. If you feel like braving huge crowds and potentially nasty weather, you'll see thousands of green-clad merrymakers strutting to the sounds of pipe bands. Celebrations continue late into the night as the city's Irish bars teem with suds-swigging revellers.

Ringling Bros and Barnum & Bailey Circus Animal Parade

34th Street, from the Queens Midtown Tunnel to Madison Square Garden, Seventh Avenue between 31st & 33rd Streets (1-212 307 7171/www.ringling. com). **Dates** Spring.
Elephants, horses and zebras march through the tunnel and on to the streets of Manhattan in this unmissable spectacle. Stay up late for the midnight parades that open and close the circus's Manhattan run.

New York International Auto Show

Jacob K Javits Convention Center, Eleventh Avenue, between 34th & 39th Streets (1-800 282 3336/ www.autoshowny.com). Subway: A, C, E to 34th Street-Penn Station. **Dates** 14-23 Apr.
This gearheads' paradise has more than a thousand autos and futuristic concept cars on display.

Easter Parade

Fifth Avenue, from 49th to 57th Streets (1-212 484 1222). Subway: E, V to Fifth Avenue-53rd Street. **Date** 16 Apr.
Parade is a misnomer for this little festival of creative hat-making. Starting at 11am on Easter Sunday, Fifth Avenue becomes a car-free promenade of gussied-up crowds milling and showing off extravagant bonnets. Arrive early to secure a prime viewing spot near St Patrick's Cathedral, at 50th Street. After the parade, head to Tavern on The Green (Central Park West, at 67th Street) for the Mad Hatter's Easter Bonnet Contest, where you'll see even more head covers.

New York Antiquarian Book Fair

Park Avenue Armory, Park Avenue, between 66th & 67th Streets (1-212 777 5218/www.sanfordsmith. com). Subway: 6 to 68th Street-Hunter College.
Dates Late Apr.
Book dealers from around the globe showcase first editions, illuminated manuscripts and all manner of rare and antique tomes; you'll even find original screenplays and shooting scripts.

Tribeca Film Festival

Various Tribeca locations (1-212 941 2400/ www.tribecafilmfestival.org). Subway: A, C, 1, 2, 3 to Chambers Street. **Dates** Late Apr.
Organised by neighbourhood resident Robert De Niro, this festival is packed with hundreds of screenings of independent and international films; it's attended by more than 300,000 film fans.

Cherry Blossom Festival

For listing, see p154 **Brooklyn Botanic Garden**.
Dates Late Apr, early May.
Nature's springtime blooms adorn the garden's 200-plus cherry trees at this annual festival. Performances, demonstrations and workshops are all part of the fun.

Global Marijuana March

March starts Broadway, at Houston Street, and proceeds to Battery Park (1-212 677 7180). **Date** First weekend in May.
In addition to being a good place to meet and greet local stoners, this annual march (which takes

And they're off! 35,000 **Marathon** runners cross the Verrazano-Narrows Bridge. *See p265.*

place during the first weekend in May in cities around the world) seeks to raise awareness about marijuana-related issues.

Bike New York: The Great Five Boro Bike Tour

Battery Park to Staten Island (1-212 932 2453/ www.bikenewyork.org). Subway: A, C, J, M, Z, 1, 2, 3 to Chambers Street; R, W to City Hall; 4, 5, 6 to Brooklyn Bridge-City Hall. Then bike to Battery Park. **Date** 7 May.

Thousands of cyclists take over the city for a 42-mile (68km) Tour de New York. (Pedestrians and motorists should plan on extra getting-around time.) Advance registration is required. Event organisers suggest the trains listed above, as some subway exits below Chambers Street may be closed to bike-toting cyclists for safety reasons, and bikes are not allowed at the South Ferry (1 train), Whitehall Street (R, W) and Bowling Green (4, 5) stations.

Bryant Park Free Summer Season

Bryant Park, Sixth Avenue, at 42nd Street (1-212 768 4242/www.bryantpark.org). Subway: B, D, F, V to 42nd Street-Bryant Park; 7 to Fifth Avenue. **Dates** May-Aug.

One of the highlights of the park's free-entertainment season is the ever-popular Monday-night alfresco movie series, but there's plenty of fun in the daylight hours as well. You can catch Broadway-musical numbers as part of the Broadway in Bryant Park series; *Good Morning America* mini-concerts featuring big-name acts; and a variety of readings, classes and public-art projects.

Red Hook Waterfront Arts Festival

Various locations in Red Hook, Brooklyn (1-718 596 2507/www.bwac.org). Travel: A, C, F to Jay Street-Borough Hall, then B61 bus to Van Brunt Street; F, G to Smith-9th Streets, then B77 bus to Van Brunt Street. **Date** Late May, early June.

This rapidly evolving neighbourhood cultural bash includes dance and music performances, along with the Brooklyn Waterfront Artists' Pier Show.

Fleet Week

For listing, see p121 **Intrepid Sea-Air-Space Museum**. **Dates** Last week in May.

New York's streets swell with good-looking sailors during this week-long event honouring the armed forces. Head to the *Intrepid* to catch tugs-of-war, eating contests and more.

Lower East Side Festival of the Arts

Theater for the New City, 155 First Avenue, between 9th & 10th Streets (1-212 254 1109/www.theater forthenewcity.net). Subway: L to First Avenue; 6 to Astor Place. **Dates** 26-28 May.

This celebration of artistic diversity features performances by dozens of theatrical troupes, poetry readings, films and family-friendly programming.

Washington Square Outdoor Art Exhibit

Various streets surrounding Washington Square Park (1-212 982 6255). Subway: A, B, C, D, E, F, V to W 4th Street; R, W to 8th Street-NYU. **Dates** 27-29 May; 3, 4 June; 2-4, 9, 10 Sept.

Exhibitors here show off photography, sculpture, paintings and one-of-a-kind crafts. It's a great way for browsers and buyers to spend an afternoon.

Summer

Met in the Parks

Various locations (1-212 362 6000/www.met opera.org). **Dates** June.

The Metropolitan Opera stages free opera performances in Central Park and other NYC parks. Grab a blanket, pack a picnic (no alcohol or glass bottles) and show up in the afternoon to nab a good spot.

Central Park SummerStage

Rumsey Playfield, Central Park, entrance on Fifth Avenue, at 72nd Street (1-212 360 2777/www. summerstage.org). Subway: 6 to 68th Street-Hunter College. **Dates** June-Aug.

Arts & Entertainment

Central Park Summer Stage, when culture comes out to play.

Rockers, symphonies, authors and dance companies take over the stage at this superpopular, mostly free annual series. Show up early or plan to listen from a spot outside the gates (not such a bad option, if you bring a blanket – and some snacks!). Admission is charged for benefit shows and special events.

Shakespeare in Central Park at the Delacorte Theater

For listing, see p349. **Dates** June-Aug.
One of Manhattan's best summertime events gets bold-face stars to pull on their tights and take a whack at the Bard.

SOFA New York

Seventh Regiment Armory, 643 Park Avenue, at 67th Street (1-800 563 7632/www.sofa expo.com). Subway: 6 to 68th Street-Hunter College. **Dates** 1-4 June.
Browse this giant show of Sculptural Objects and Functional Art, and you might find that perfect conversation piece for your home.

Museum Mile Festival

Fifth Avenue, from 82nd to 105th Streets (1-212 606 2296/www.museummilefestival.org). **Date** Second Tuesday in June.
For one day each year, nine of the city's major museums open their doors free of charge to the public. You can also catch live music, street performers and other arty happenings along Fifth Avenue.

National Puerto Rican Day Parade

Fifth Avenue, from 44th to 86th Streets (1-718 401 0404). **Date** Second Sunday in June.

Salsa music blares, and scantily clad revellers dance along the route and ride colourful floats at this free-wheeling party celebrating the city's largest Hispanic community.

Broadway Bares

Roseland Ballroom, 239 W 52nd Street, between Broadway & Eighth Avenue (1-212 840 0770/ www.broadwaycares.org). Subway: 1 to 50th Street. **Dates** Mid June.
The new annual fund-raiser for Broadway Cares/ Equity Fights AIDS is your chance to see some of the Great White Way's hottest bodies sans costumes. Broadway Cares also hosts an annual auction of star-autographed teddy bears ('Broadway Bears') in February, and a show tune-filled Easter Bonnet Competition in April, as well as several other fun theatre-themed events throughout the year.

JVC Jazz Festival

Various locations (1-212 501 1390/www.festival productions.net). **Dates** Mid June.
A direct descendant of the Newport Jazz Festival, this jazz bash is an NYC institution. The fest not only fills Carnegie and Avery Fisher Halls with big draws, but also sponsors gigs in Harlem and downtown clubs.

Mermaid Parade

Coney Island, Brooklyn (1-718 372 5159/ www.coneyisland.com). Subway: D, F, N, Q to Coney Island-Stillwell Avenue. **Date** 24 June.
Decked-out mermaids and mermen of all shapes, sizes and ages share the parade route with elaborate, kitschy floats, come rain or shine. It's the wackiest

summer-solstice event you'll likely ever witness. Check the website for details, as the parade location varies from year to year.

Gay & Lesbian Pride March
From Fifth Avenue, at 52nd Street to Christopher Street (1-212 807 7433/ www.hopinc.org). **Date** 25 June.
Downtown Manhattan becomes a sea of rainbow flags as gays and lesbians from the city and beyond parade down Fifth Avenue in commemoration of the 1969 Stonewall riots. After the march, there's a massive street fair and a dance on the West Side piers.

Summer Restaurant Week
Various locations (www.nycvisit.com). **Dates** Late June, early July.
Twice a year, for two weeks at a stretch, some of the city's finest restaurants dish out three-course prix-fixe lunches for $20.06; some places also offer dinner for $30.06. (The lunch price reflects the year.) For the full list of participating restaurants, visit the website. You are advised to make reservations well in advance.

Midsummer Night Swing
Lincoln Center Plaza, Columbus Avenue, between 64th & 65th Streets (1-212 875 5766/www. lincolncenter.org). Subway: 1 to 66th Street-Lincoln Center. **Dates** Late June-mid July.
Lincoln Center's plaza is transformed into a giant dancefloor as bands play salsa, Cajun, swing and other music. Each night is devoted to a different dance style; parties are preceded by lessons.

Celebrate Brooklyn! Performing Arts Festival
Prospect Park Bandshell, Prospect Park West, at 9th Street, Park Slope, Brooklyn (1-718 855 7882/ www.celebratebrooklyn.org). Subway: F to Seventh Avenue. **Dates** Late June-late Aug.
Outdoor events include music, dance, film and spoken-word performances. Huge crowds flock to the park's bandshell to hear major artists such as They Might Be Giants and Los Lobos. A $3 donation is requested, and admission is charged for a few benefit shows.

Nathan's Famous July 4 Hot Dog Eating Contest
Outside Nathan's Famous, corner of Surf & Stillwell Avenues, Coney Island, Brooklyn (www.nathans famous.com). Subway: D, F, N, Q to Coney Island-Stillwell Avenue. **Date** 4 July.
Competitive eaters gather from all over the world to pig out at the granddaddy of pig-out contests, which has been happening annually in Coney Island for more than a decade.

Macy's Fireworks Display
East River, exact location varies (1-212 494 4495). **Date** 4 July at approximately 9pm.
This world-famous annual fireworks display is the city's star attraction on Independence Day. The pyrotechnics are launched from barges on the East River, so look for outdoor vantage points along the lower FDR Drive (closed to traffic), the Brooklyn and Long Island City waterfronts, or on Roosevelt Island. Keep in mind, however, that spectators are packed like sardines at the prime public spots.

New York Philharmonic Concerts in the Parks
Various locations (1-212 875 5709/www.newyork philharmonic.org). **Dates** July-Aug.
The New York Philharmonic has presented a varied classical-music programme in many of New York's larger parks for more than 40 years.

Seaside Summer & Martin Luther King Jr Concert Series
Various locations (1-718 469 1912/www.brooklyn concerts.com). **Dates** July-Aug.
Grab a lawn chair and listen to free pop, funk, soul and gospel at these outdoor concerts in Brooklyn.

PS 1 Warm Up
For listing, see p162. **Dates** July-Sept 3-9pm Sat.
For years, this weekly Saturday-afternoon bash in the museum's courtyard has drawn fashionable types from all over the city to dance, drink beer and relax in a beach-like environment. Local and international DJs and bands provide the soundtrack for your summer amusement.

Mostly Mozart
Lincoln Center, Columbus Avenue, between 64th & 65th Streets (1-212 875 5766/www.lincoln center.org). Subway: 1 to 66th Street-Lincoln Center. **Dates** Late July-Aug.
For more than 35 years, this four-week-long festival has been mounting a packed schedule of works by Mozart and his contemporaries.

Lincoln Center Out of Doors Festival
For listing, see p263. **Dates** Aug.
Free dance, music, theatre, opera and more make up this ambitious and family-friendly festival of classic and contemporary works.

New York International Fringe Festival
Various locations (1-212 279 4488/www.fringe nyc.org). **Dates** Aug.
Wacky, weird and sometimes great, downtown's Fringe Festival shoehorns hundreds of performances into 16 theatre-crammed days.

Central Park Zoo Chillout Weekend
Central Park, entrance on Fifth Avenue, at 65th Street (1-212 439 6500/www.wcs.org). Subway: N, R, W to Fifth Avenue-59th Street; 4, 5, 6 to 59th Street. **Dates** Early Aug.
If you're roaming the city's streets during the dog days of August, this two-day party offers the perfect chilly treat. The weekend freeze-fest features penguin and polar-bear talent shows, games, zookeeper challenges and other frosty fun.

Arts & Entertainment

Harlem Week

*Various Harlem locations (1-212 862 8477/www.
harlemdiscover.com). Subway: B, C, 2, 3 to 135th
Street.* **Dates** Aug.
Get into the groove at this massive street fair, which
serves up live music, art and food along 135th Street.
Concerts, film, dance, fashion and sports events are
on tap all week.

Howl!

*Various East Village locations (1-212 505 2225/
www.howlfestival.com).* **Dates** Last week in August.
Taking its name from the seminal poem by long-
time neighbourhood resident Allen Ginsberg, this
all-things-East Village fest is a grab bag of art
events, films, performance art, readings and much
more. A good chance to dip into local life.

Autumn

West Indian-American
Day Carnival

*Eastern Parkway, from Utica Avenue to Grand Army
Plaza, Brooklyn (1-718 467 1797/www.wiadca.org).
Subway: 2, 3 to Grand Army Plaza; 3, 4 to Crown
Heights-Utica Avenue.* **Date** 4 Sept.

The streets come alive with the jubilant clangour of
steel-drum bands and the steady throb of calypso
and soca music. Mas bands – elaborately costumed
marchers – dance along the parade route, thousands
move to the beat on sidewalks, and vendors sell
Caribbean crafts, clothing, souvenirs and food.

Broadway on Broadway

*43rd Street, at Broadway (1-212 768 1560/
www.broadwayonbroadway.com). Subway: N, Q,
R, W, 42nd Street S, 1, 2, 3, 7 to 42nd Street-Times
Square.* **Date** Early-mid Sept.
Broadway's biggest stars convene in the middle of
Times Square to belt out show-stopping numbers.
The season's new productions mount sneak pre-
views, and it's all free.

Atlantic Antic

*Atlantic Avenue, from Fourth Avenue to
Hicks Street, Brooklyn (1-718 875 8993/www.
atlanticave.org). Subway: B, Q, 2, 3, 4, 5 to
Atlantic Avenue; D, M, N, R to Pacific Street.*
Dates Mid Sept.
Entertainment, ethnic foods, kids' activities and the
World Cheesecake-Eating Contest fill the avenue at
this monumental Brooklyn festival.

Don't miss River festivals

River to River Festival

*Various venues along the West Side
& southern waterfronts of Manhattan
(www.rivertorivernyc.org).* **Dates** June-Sept.
Lower Manhattan organisations present more
than 500 free programmes in some of the
city's coolest waterfront locations. Musical
performers last year ranged from Arlo Guthrie
to Yo La Tengo. **The Hudson River Festival**
(1-212 528 2733, www.hudsonriverfestival.
com) augments the watery diversions with
visual-arts shows, walking tours, theatre,
dance and family events. And additional
concert programming is produced in
conjunction with the Seaport Music
Festival (www.seaportmusicfestival.com).

CMJ Music Marathon & FilmFest

Various locations (1-917 606 1908/www.cmj.com).
Dates Mid Sept.
The annual *College Music Journal* schmooze-fest
draws thousands of young fans and music-industry
types to one of the best showcases for new rock,
indie-rock, hip-hop and electronica acts. The
FilmFest, which runs in tandem with the music
blow-out, includes a wide range of feature and short
films, many music-related.

Feast of San Gennaro

*Mulberry Street, from Canal to Houston Streets (1-
212 768 9320/www.sangennaro.org). Subway: B, D,
F, V to Broadway-Lafayette Street; J, M, N, Q, R, W,
Z, 6 to Canal Street.* **Dates** Mid Sept.
This massive street fair stretches along the main
drag of what's left of Little Italy. Come on opening
and closing days to see the marching band of old-
timers, or after dark, when sparkling lights arch over
Mulberry Street and the smells of frying *zeppole* and
sausages hang in the sultry air.

New York Film Festival

*Alice Tully Hall, Avery Fisher Hall and Walter
Reade Theater at Lincoln Center, Broadway, at
65th Street (1-212 875 5050/www.filmlinc.com).
Subway: 1 to 66th Street-Lincoln Center.* **Dates**
Early to mid Oct.
This uptown institution, founded in 1962, is still a
worthy cinematic showcase, packed with premières,
features and short flicks from around the globe, plus
a stellar list of celebrities for the red-carpet events.

Open House New York

Various locations (1-917 583 2398/www.ohny.org).
Dates Early to mid Oct.
Get an insider's view – literally – of the city that even
most locals haven't seen. More than 100 sites of
architectural interest normally off-limits to visitors
throw open their doors and welcome the curious during a weekend of urban exploration. Lectures and
educational programmes are also on offer all week.

Next Wave Festival

For listing, see p328 **Brooklyn Academy of
Music.** **Dates** Oct-Dec.
The best of the best in the city's avant-garde music,
dance, theatre and opera scenes are performed at
this lengthy annual affair.

d.u.m.b.o. art under the bridge

*Various locations in Dumbo, Brooklyn (1-718 694
0831/www.dumboartscenter.org). Subway: A, C to
High Street; F to York Street.* **Dates** Mid Oct.
Dumbo (Down Under the Manhattan Bridge
Overpass) has become a Brooklyn art destination,
and this weekend of art appreciation, featuring concerts, forums, a short-film series and in-studio visits, is a popular event.

Village Halloween Parade

*Sixth Avenue, from Spring to 22nd Streets
(www.halloween-nyc.com).* **Date** 31 Oct at 8pm.

The sidewalks at this iconic Village shindig are
always packed beyond belief. Our advice for the best
vantage point: strap on a costume and watch from
inside the parade (line-up starts at 6.30pm on Sixth
Avenue, at Spring Street).

New York City Marathon

*Staten Island side of the Verrazano-Narrows Bridge,
to Tavern on the Green, in Central Park (1-212 423
2249/www.nycmarathon.org).* **Date** Early Nov.
The sight of 35,000 marathoners hotfooting it
through all five boroughs over a 26.2-mile (42km)
course is an impressive one. Scope out a spot somewhere in the middle (the starting and finish lines are
mobbed) to get a good view of the herd. **Photo** *p261.*

Macy's Thanksgiving Day Parade & Eve Balloon Blowup

*Central Park West, at 77th Street to Macy's,
Broadway, at 34th Street (1-212 494 4495/www.
macysparade.com).* **Date** 23 Nov at 9am.
The stars of this nationally televised parade are the
gigantic, inflated balloons, the elaborate floats and
good ol' Santa Claus. New Yorkers brave the cold
night air to watch the rubbery colossi take shape at
the inflation area on the night before Thanksgiving
(from 77th to 81st Streets, between Central Park
West and Columbus Avenue). **Photo** *p266.*

Winter

The Nutcracker

*New York State Theater, Lincoln Center, Columbus
Avenue, at 63rd Street (1-212 870 5570/www.
nycballet.com). Subway: 1 to 66th Street-Lincoln
Center.* **Dates** 24 Nov-first week in Jan.
Performed by the New York City Ballet, George
Balanchine's fantasy world of fairies, princes and toy
soldiers is a family-friendly holiday diversion.

Radio City Christmas Spectacular

For listing, see p320 **Radio City Music Hall.**
Dates Nov-early Jan.
The high-kicking Rockettes and an onstage nativi-
ty scene with live animals are the attractions at this
(pricey) annual homage to the Yuletide season.

Christmas Tree-Lighting Ceremony

*Rockefeller Center, Fifth Avenue, between 49th
& 50th Streets (1-212 332 6868/www.rockefeller
center.com). Subway: B, D, F, V to 47-50th Streets-
Rockefeller Center.* **Date** Late Nov/early Dec.
The crowds can be overwhelming here, even if you
stake out a place early. Those who brace them will-
witness celebrity appearances and pop-star performances). But there's plenty of time during the
holiday season to marvel at the giant evergreen.

The National Chorale Messiah Sing-In

*Avery Fisher Hall, Lincoln Center, Columbus Avenue,
at 65th Street (1-212 333 5333/www.lincolncenter.
org/www.nationalchorale.org). Subway: 1 to 66th
Street-Lincoln Center.* **Dates** Mid Dec.

Arts & Entertainment

Hallelujah! Chase those holiday blues away by joining with the National Chorale and hundreds of your fellow audience members in a rehearsal and performance of Handel's *Messiah*. No experience is necessary, and you can buy the score on site, though advance perusal would help novices to the work.

New Year's Eve Ball Drop

Times Square (1-212 768 1560/www.times squarebid.org). Subway: N, Q, R, W, 42nd Street S, 1, 2, 3, 7 to 42nd Street-Times Square. **Date** 31 Dec.
Meet up with half a million others and watch the giant illuminated ball descend amid a blizzard of confetti and cheering. Expect freezing temperatures, densely packed crowds, absolutely no bathrooms – and very tight security.

Macy's Thanksgiving Day Parade. *See p265.*

New Year's Eve Fireworks

Naumburg Bandshell, middle of Central Park, at 72nd Street (www.centralparknyc.org). Subway: B, C to 72nd Street; 6 to 68th Street-Hunter College. **Date** 31 Dec.
The fireworks explode at midnight, and you can participate in a variety of evening festivities, including dancing and a costume contest. The best views are from Tavern on the Green (at 67th Street), Central Park West (at 72nd Street) and Fifth Avenue (at 90th Street).

New Year's Eve Midnight Run

Naumburg Bandshell, middle of Central Park, at 72nd Street (1-212 423 2249/www.nyrrc.org). Subway: B, C to 72nd Street; 6 to 68th Street-Hunter College. **Date** 31 Dec.
Start the new year with a four-mile jog through the park. There's also a masquerade parade, fireworks, prizes and a booze-free toast at the halfway mark.

New Year's Day Marathon Poetry Reading

For listing, see p278 **The Poetry Project.**
Date 1 Jan.
Big-name bohemians (Patti Smith, Richard Hell, Jim Carroll) step up to the mic during this free, all-day spoken-word spectacle.

Winter Antiques Show

Seventh Regiment Armory, 643 Park Avenue, between 66th & 67th Streets (1-718 292 7392/www.winterantiquesshow.com). Subway: 6 to 68th Street-Hunter College.
Dates Mid to late Jan.
One of the world's most prestigious antiques shows brings together more than 70 American and international dealers.

Winter Restaurant Week

For listing, see p263 **Summer Restaurant Week.**
Dates Late Jan, early Feb.
Another opportunity to sample gourmet food at soup-kitchen prices. (Well, almost.)

Chinese New Year

Around Mott Street, Chinatown (1-212 966 0100). Subway: J, M, N, Q, R, W, Z, 6 to Canal Street.
Dates Early Feb.
Gung hay fat choy!, as the greeting goes. Chinatown bustles with energy during the two weeks of the Lunar New Year. Festivities include a staged fireworks display, a dragon parade (which snakes in and out of several restaurants), various performances and delicious food.

Art Show

Seventh Regiment Armory, 643 Park Avenue, between 66th & 67th Streets (1-212 940 8590/www.artdealers.org). Subway: 6 to 68th Street-Hunter College. **Dates** Mid to late Feb.
Whether you're a serious collector or just a casual art fan, this vast fair is a great chance to peruse some of the world's most impressive for-sale pieces dating from the 17th century to the present.

Art Galleries

Contemporary, modern, abstract, avant-garde: seek art here and you shall find.

Greene Naftali Gallery. *See p270.*

New York is America's fertile artland, with hundreds of established galleries flourishing like never before and new spaces constantly popping up in Manhattan, Brooklyn and Queens. The epicentre of the contemporary art surge lies in the West Chelsea and Meatpacking districts, where you might open a frosted glass door to a museum-quality show of a big-name artist – and then, just down the street, visit an offbeat exhibit accessible only by a rickety freight elevator. The art scene in Chelsea has grown to such a size that a comprehensive crawl is a full-day endeavour, including pit stops at local chic restaurants and designer stores.

A foray towards the Upper East Side is sure to turn out some art gems. Prestigious galleries along 57th Street offer a pageant of blue-chip shows, and on a stroll down Museum Mile you'll discover plenty of works by the Old Masters. Soho, although no longer the hotspot it was in the '80s, still lays claim to an impressive collection of non-profit spaces. Similarly, new venues in the Lower East Side and Harlem won't disappoint. In the last several years, Williamsburg, Brooklyn, has become a wellspring for new art and is well worth the trip across the East River to the neighbourhood's 40-odd galleries. Long Island City in Queens is another big attraction for art lovers, with PS 1 Contemporary Art Center (*see p166*) and notable exhibition spaces blooming all around.

Even Dumbo in Brooklyn has a burgeoning art scene along its waterfront. Thanks to the migration of artists and gallerists throughout the city, areas that were once off the beaten track are now fresh and vital art destinations.

But before you take off be sure to consult the most up-to-date listings found in *Time Out New York* magazine and the Friday and Sunday editions of the *New York Times*. The monthly *Gallery Guide* (www.galleryguide.org) is useful for uncritical (but extensive) listings; it is free in many venues or costs around $3 at newsstands.

Take heed during holiday time. Most spaces are closed for major US holidays (*see p383* **Holidays**). From May or June through to early September, many are open only on weekdays, and they often close for the entire month of August. Summer hours are listed for galleries that have set their calendar, but it's always wise to call first before you hit the pavement.

Lower East Side

Once a land of pushcarts and pickles, the Lower East Side is experiencing a renaissance. For an overview of the scene (which includes artist-run spaces too numerous to mention), take the ELS-LES walking tour (www.elsles.org).
Subway: *F to East Broadway or Delancey Street; F, V to Lower East Side-Second Avenue; J, M, Z to Delancey-Essex Streets.*

Don't throw away that old garden fence. **Barbara Gladstone** wants it...

ELS-LES (Every Last Sunday on the Lower East Side) Open Studios

Various studios and galleries in the Lower East Side (www.lowereastsideny.com/artwalkparticipant.htm). **Open** 1-7pm last Sun of the month. **Admission** free, though a donation is suggested.

A great way to get a taste of the Lower East Side's rapidly evolving art scene. On the last Sunday of every month, a number of artist- and artisan-run studios in the area open their doors to the public (download a map from the website to find the venues). Participants vary, but ABC No Rio (*see p278* **Our unorganicized reading**), Metalstone Gallery (175 Stanton Street, at Clinton Street, 1-212 253 8308) and Zito Studio Gallery (122 Ludlow Street, between Delancey and Rivington Streets, 1-646 602 2338) are likely to be among the art spaces opening their doors to interested members of the public.

Maccarone Inc

45 Canal Street, between Ludlow & Orchard Streets (1-212 431 4977). **Open** noon-6pm Wed-Sun.

Run by former Luhring Augustine director Michele Maccarone, this gallery spread over four floors, which was once a hardware store, focuses on emerging European and local talent.

Participant Inc

95 Rivington Street, between Ludlow & Orchard Streets (1-212 254 4334/www.participantinc.org). **Open** noon-7pm Wed-Sun.

Overseen by its savvy curator Lia Gangitano, Participant Inc is a glass-fronted gallery and a Lower East Side hotspot. Expect entertaining, intelligent exhibitions that cross-breed visual and performing arts with literature and new media.

Rivington Arms

102 Rivington Street, between Essex & Ludlow Streets (1-646 654 3213/www.rivingtonarms.com). **Open** *Sept-Jul* 11am-6pm Wed-Fri; noon-6pm Sat, Sun.

This intimate storefront space, run by Melissa Bent and Mirabelle Marden (painter Brice Marden's daughter), has attracted both a fashionable crowd of followers and enviable critical kudos.

Soho

The main concentration of Manhattan galleries may have shifted to the western blocks of Chelsea, but a few notables still reside here, and a number of the city's most important non-profit venues continue to make the area a vital stop on the art map.
Subway: *A, C, E, J, M, N, Q, R, W, Z, 1, 6 to Canal Street; B, D, F, V to Broadway-Lafayette Street; N, R, W to Prince Street; 6 to Spring Street.*

Deitch Projects

18 Wooster Street, between Canal & Grand Streets (1-212 343 7300). **Open** noon-6pm Tue-Sat.

Jeffrey Deitch is an art-world impresario whose gallery features live spectacles as well as large-scale – and sometimes overly ambitious – efforts by artists who work in virtually all media. (By comparison, Deitch's original Grand Street site seems small and sedate, but it's the one of his three Soho spaces that we most confidently recommend.) Solo shows here, by the likes of Yoko Ono, aim to be both complex and accessible.

Leo Koenig Inc

545 W 23rd Street, between Tenth & Eleventh Avenues (1-212 334 9255/www.leokoenig.com). **Open** 10am-6pm Tue-Sat.

Leo Koenig's father is Kasper Koenig, the internationally known curator and museum director, but Leo has been making a name for himself too by showcasing cutting-edge American and German talents – Meg Cranston, Torben Giehler and Lisa Ruyter are among the artists he's exhibited.

Peter Blum

99 Wooster Street, between Prince & Spring Streets (1-212 343 0441/www.peterblumgallery.com). **Open** 10am-6pm Tue-Fri; 11am-6pm Sat.

This elegant space is manned by a dealer with an impeccable eye and wide tastes. Past exhibitions have run the gamut from drawings by art stars Robert Ryman and Alex Katz to terracotta funerary figures from West Africa and colourful quilts by African-American folk artist Rosie Lee Tompkins.

Arts & Entertainment

... but you could try throwing some paint around.

Ronald Feldman Fine Arts

31 Mercer Street, between Canal & Grand Streets (1-212 226 3232/www.feldmangallery.com). **Open** *Sept-Jun* by appointment only Mon; 10am-6pm Tue-Sat. *Jul, Aug* 10am-6pm Mon-Thur; 10am-3pm Fri.
This Soho pioneer has brought us landmark shows of such legendary avant-gardists as Eleanor Antin, Leon Golub and Hannah Wilke. Feldman also regularly takes chances on newer talents like British photographer Keith Cottingham – all to good effect.

Chelsea

Chelsea has the city's highest concentration of galleries; just be advised that it can be hard to see even half the neighbourhood in one day. The subway takes you only as far as Eighth Avenue, so you'll have to walk at least one long block westward to get to the galleries. You can also take the M23 crosstown bus.
Subway: *A, C, E to 14th Street; C, E to 23rd Street; L to Eighth Avenue.*

Alexander and Bonin

132 Tenth Avenue, between 18th & 19th Streets (1-212 367 7474/www.alexanderandbonin.com). **Open** *Sept-Jun* 10am-6pm Tue-Sat. *Jul* 10am-6pm Tue-Fri. *Aug* by appointment only.
This long, cool drink of an exhibition space features contemporary painting, sculpture and photography by artists such as Willie Doherty, Mona Hatoum, Rita McBride, Doris Salcedo and Paul Thek.

Andrea Rosen Gallery

525 W 24th Street, between Tenth & Eleventh Avenues (1-212 627 6000/www.andrearosen gallery.com). **Open** *Sept-Jun* 10am-6pm Tue-Sat. *Jul, Aug* 10am-6pm Mon-Fri.
During the past 15 years, Andrea Rosen has established several major careers: the late Felix Gonzalez-Torres got his start here (the gallery handles the artist's estate), as did Wolfgang Tillmans, Andrea Zittel and John Currin (who left for Gagosian in 2003). Recent additions to the roster, such as the much touted young sculptor David Altmejd, promise more of the same high quality to come.

Andrew Kreps Gallery

516A W 20th Street, between Tenth & Eleventh Avenues (1-212 741 8849/www.andrewkreps.com). **Open** *Sept-Jun* 10am-6pm Tue-Sat. *Jul, Aug* 10am-6pm Mon-Fri.
The radicals in Andrew Kreps's adventurous stable of artists include Ricci Albenda, Roe Ethridge, Robert Melee and Ruth Root.

Anton Kern Gallery

532 W 20th Street, between Tenth & Eleventh Avenues (1-212 367 9663/www.antonkern gallery.com). **Open** *Sept-Jul* 10am-6pm Tue-Sat. *Aug* by appointment only.
The son of artist Georg Baselitz, Kern presents young American and European artists whose installations have provided the New York art scene with some of its most visionary shows. The likes of Kai Althoff, Sarah Jones, Michael Joo, Jim Lambie and David Shrigley all show here.

Barbara Gladstone

515 W 24th Street, between Tenth & Eleventh Avenues (1-212 206 9300). **Open** *Sept-mid Jun* 10am-6pm Tue-Sat. *Mid Jun-Labor Day* 10am-6pm Mon-Fri.
Gladstone is strictly blue-chip, with an emphasis on the conceptualist, the philosophical and the daring. Matthew Barney, Anish Kapoor and Rosemary Trockel put on exhibits here. **Photos** *p268, p269.*

Bellwether

134 Tenth Avenue, between 18th & 19th Streets (1-212 929 5959/www.bellwethergallery.com). **Open** *Sept-Jul* 11am-6pm Tue-Sat.
The hot-pink luminous neon sign in the window heralds the arrival of this former Brooklyn stalwart over the river at its new street-level digs in Chelsea. Setting trends since 1999, Bellwether represents such promising talents as Ellen Altfest, Sarah Bedford and Adam Cvijanovic.

Daniel Reich Gallery

537A W 23rd Street, between Tenth & Eleventh Avenues (1-212 924 4949/www.danielreich gallery.com). **Open** 11am-6pm Tue-Sat. Call for summer hours.

Young gallerist Daniel Reich showed out of his tiny apartment before settling into this current ground-floor space that – despite its more white-cube setting – continues to host a fresh generation of free-spirited artists, like Christian Holstad, Hernan Bas, Delia Gonzalez and Gavin Russom.

David Zwirner

525 W 19th Street, between Tenth & Eleventh Avenues (1-212 727 2070/www.davidzwirner.com). **Open** *Sept-Jun* 10am-6pm Tue-Sat. *Jul, Aug* 10am-6pm Mon-Fri.

This German expatriate has a head-turning roster of international contemporary artists on his books that includes Marcel Dzama, Toba Khedoori, Chris Ofili, Neo Rauch and Diana Thater. (*See also p274* **Zwirner & Wirth.**)

Friedrich Petzel Gallery

535 W 22nd Street, between Tenth & Eleventh Avenues (1-212 680 9467/www.petzel.com). **Open** *Sept-Jun* 10am-6pm Tue-Sat. *Jul, Aug* 10am-6pm Mon-Fri.

The Friedrich Petzel Gallery represents some of the brightest young stars on the international scene, so you can count on intriguing shows. Sculptor Keith Edmier, photographer Dana Hoey, painter and film-maker Sarah Morris, and installation artists Jorge Pardo and Philippe Parenno all show here.

Gagosian Gallery

555 W 24th Street, between Tenth & Eleventh Avenues (1-212 741 1111/www.gagosian.com). **Open** *Sept-May* 10am-6pm Tue-Sat. *Jun-Aug* 10am-6pm Mon-Fri.

Larry Gagosian's mammoth (20,000sq ft) contribution to 24th Street's top-level galleries was launched in 1999 with an exhilarating show of Richard Serra sculptures. There's been no slackening since, with follow-up exhibitions featuring works by Douglas Gordon, Ellen Gallagher, Damien Hirst, Ed Ruscha, Julian Schnabel and Andy Warhol.

Gorney Bravin + Lee

534 W 26th Street, between Tenth & Eleventh Avenues (1-212 352 8372/www.gblgallery.com). **Open** *Sept-Jun* 10am-6pm Tue-Sat. *Jul* 10am-6pm Tue-Fri. *Aug* by appointment only.

Gorney Bravin + Lee is a refreshingly friendly gallery that is especially strong in the fields of photography and sculpture. It has an attention-grabbing stable of contemporary artists, including Sarah Charlesworth, Justine Kurland, Catherine Opie and Alexis Rockman.

Greene Naftali Gallery

8th Floor, 526 W 26th Street, between Tenth & Eleventh Avenues (1-212 463 7770/www.greene naftaligallery.com). **Open** *Sept-Jun* 10am-6pm Tue-Sat. *Jul, Aug* 10am-6pm Mon-Fri.

Although this gallery is worth a visit just for its wonderful light and spectacular bird's-eye view, the keen vision of gallerist Carol Greene outdoes even the the eighth-floor view. Mavericks such as sculp-

tor Rachel Harrison, painter Jacqueline Humphries and video artist Lucy Gunning draw rave reviews from critics and collectors alike. **Photo** *p267.*

John Connelly Presents

Suite 1003, 526 W 26th Street, between Tenth & Eleventh Avenues (1-212 337 9563). **Open** *Sept-Jun* 11am-6pm Tue-Sat. *Jul, Aug* 11am-6pm Mon-Fri.

Connelly, long-time director of Andrea Rosen Gallery, recently struck out on his own and quickly earned a reputation as one of the most exciting young dealers around. Expect provocative, rambunctious works by emerging young artists, with an emphasis on installation.

Lehmann Maupin

540 W 26th Street, between Tenth & Eleventh Avenues (1-212 255 2923/www.lehmann maupin.com). **Open** *Sept-Jun* 10am-6pm Tue-Sat. *Jul-Labor Day* 10am-6pm Tue-Fri. *Aug* by appointment only.

This gallery left its Rem Koolhaas-designed loft in Soho but kept Koolhaas on board when it came to designing its new Chelsea digs in a former garage. Epic exhibitions feature hip international artists, including Teresita Fernandez, Do-Ho Suh, Kutlug Ataman and Tracey Emin.

Luhring Augustine Gallery

531 W 24th Street, between Tenth & Eleventh Avenues (1-212 206 9100/www.luhring augustine.com). **Open** *Sept-May* 10am-6pm Tue-Sat. *Jun-Aug* 10am-5.30pm Mon-Fri.

Designed by Richard Gluckman, the area's architect of choice, the Luhring Augustine Gallery features work from an impressive index of contemporary artists, such as British sculptor Rachel Whiteread, Swiss video star Pipilotti Rist, Japanese photographic artist Yasumasa Morimura, and Americans Janine Antoni, Larry Clark, Jenny Gage, Paul McCarthy and Christopher Wool.

Mary Boone Gallery

541 W 24th Street, between Tenth & Eleventh Avenues (1-212 752 2929/www.maryboone gallery.com). **Open** *Sept-Jun* 10am-6pm Tue-Sat. *Jul, Aug* by appointment only.

Mary Boone made her name in the '80s representing Julian Schnabel, Jean-Michel Basquiat and Francesco Clemente at her Soho gallery (*see p273*). She later moved to Midtown and, in 2000, added this sweeping space in Chelsea, showing established artists like David Salle, Barbara Kruger and Eric Fischl alongside the work of young up-and-comers like Kevin Zucker and Hilary Harkness.

Matthew Marks Gallery

522 W 22nd Street, between Tenth & Eleventh Avenues (1-212 243 0200/www.matthewmarks.com). **Open** *Sept-Jun* 11am-6pm Tue-Sat. *Jul, Aug* 11am-6pm Mon-Fri.

The Matthew Marks Gallery was a driving force behind Chelsea's transformation into one of the city's top art destinations, and with three outposts

Painted love

With Times Square dressed in corporate splendour and Harlem gentrifying fast, Coney Island is one of the last classic destinations in New York to retain its old-time grit. Between the Cyclone and the Parachute Jump, the hucksters and the suckers, the area's dilapidated streets and dim arcades offer plenty of faded character, but they haven't seen much fresh colour lately.

Enter the Dreamland Artist Club. Founded in 2004 by graffiti legend Steve Powers and Creative Time, a non-profit producer of public art projects, the 'club' is a loose amalgam of street and gallery artists who have made handpainted signs for mom-and-pop amusement stands that couldn't otherwise afford to have them. In 2004 the Dreamland Artist Club resulted in contributions from 25 artists, advertising everything from ice-cream and bumper cars to the Dime Toss and the Spider. Most of the signs are still in place. In the summer of 2005, Creative Time curator Alexa Coyne negotiated the placement of 17 new signs for the amusement park, including a 130ft-long Coney Island-themed mural by Os Gemeos, the Brazilian twins who painted the wall opposite the new Coney Island-Stillwell Avenue subway entrance. But there's no need to fear that Coney Island might lose

its traditional grit. 'This isn't a gentrification or renewal project,' says Powers, who got the idea three years ago when he discovered that the bulk of Coney Island's traditional signage had disappeared or been replaced by the kind that is designed on a computer. 'We're not planting trees, just putting out information. If the signs make the place more crazy, that's the artists doing their job.'

Most of the businesses involved are along Jones Walk or Bowery Street; maps are available at the Dreamland Artist Clubhouse on Surf Avenue. The artists chose their own sites and were free to paint whatever they liked, as long as they included the business name. One of the most elaborate signs is a plasma-cut number over the Balloon Dart Game, which includes sculpted cut-outs of the Man in the Moon and the Cyclone. 'I tend to overdo it,' says Swoon, the formally trained 22-year-old street artist who created it.

Creative Time's Coyne thinks the art has already produced a halo effect. 'I've noticed business owners fixing things up,' she says. 'The signs have been a motivating factor.' As for Powers, his goal now is the same as it was when he worked only in the street: 'To make the world a different place,' he says. 'Not necessarily a better one.'

A flying visit to **Paula Cooper Gallery** (also pictured right).

to its name, and it remains one of the neighbourhood's powerhouses. Matthew Marks showcases such international talent as Lucien Freud, Nan Goldin, Andreas Gursky, Ellsworth Kelly, Brice Marden and Ugo Rondinone.
Other locations: 521 W 21st Street, between Tenth & Eleventh Avenues (1-212 243 0200); 523 W 24th Street, between Tenth & Eleventh Avenues (1-212 243 0200).

Metro Pictures

519 W 24th Street, between Tenth & Eleventh Avenues (1-212 206 7100/www.metropictures gallery.com). **Open** *Sept-mid Jun* 10am-6pm Tue-Sat. *Mid Jun-Labor Day* 10am-6pm Mon-Fri.
The gallery is best known for representing art-world superstar Cindy Sherman, along with such big contemporary names as Mike Kelley, Robert Longo and the late German artist Martin Kippenberger.

PaceWildenstein Gallery

534 W 25th Street, between Tenth & Eleventh Avenues (1-212 929 7000/www.pacewildenstein. com). **Open** *Sept-May* 10am-6pm Tue-Sat. *Jun-Aug* 10am-6pm Mon-Thur; 10am-4pm Fri.
In a space designed by the artist Robert Irwin, this welcoming Chelsea branch of the famous 57th Street gallery houses grand-scale shows by major contemporary talents such as Chuck Close, Alex Katz, Sol LeWitt, Robert Rauschenberg, Elizabeth Murray and Kiki Smith.

Paula Cooper Gallery

534 W 21st Street, between Tenth & Eleventh Avenues (1-212 255 1105). **Open** 10am-6pm Tue-Sat. *Jun-Aug* 9.30am-5pm Mon-Fri.
First in Soho and early to Chelsea, Paula Cooper has built up an impressive art temple for worshippers of the contemporary. (She has also opened a second space, across the street.) The gallery is best known for minimalist and conceptualist work, including

that by photographers Zoe Leonard and Andres Serrano and sculptors such as Carl Andre, Donald Judd, Sherrie Levine and Tony Smith. You'll also see younger artists who are just starting to make a name for themselves in the art world, like Kelley Walker and John Tremblay. **Photos** *p272, p273.*
Other locations: 521 W 21st Street, between Tenth & Eleventh Avenues (1-212 255 5247).

Postmasters Gallery

459 W 19th Street, between Ninth & Tenth Avenues (1-212 727 3323/www.postmastersart.com). **Open** *Sept-Jul* 11am-6pm Tue-Sat.
Postmasters Gallery, run by the savvy duo of Magdalena Sawon and Tamas Banovich, has an emphasis on technologically inflected art (most of which leans towards the conceptualist) in the form of sculpture, painting, new media and installations from the likes of Diana Cooper, Christian Schumann and Wolfgang Staehle.

Robert Miller Gallery

524 W 26th Street, between Tenth & Eleventh Avenues (1-212 366 4774/www.robertmiller gallery.com). **Open** *Sept-Jun* 10am-6pm Tue-Sat. Call for summer hours.
This former 57th Street stalwart often shows works by well-established artists you might expect to see displayed at a museum rather than in a gallery. Exhibitors include the likes of the painters Lee Krasner, Joan Mitchell and Alice Neel, and the photographers Bruce Weber and Diane Arbus.

Sonnabend

536 W 22nd Street, between Tenth & Eleventh Avenues (1-212 627 1018). **Open** *Sept-Jul* 10am-6pm Tue-Sat. *Aug* by appointment only.
Sonnabend is a well-established stand-by in a museum-like space that shows new work by Ashley Bickerton, Gilbert & George, Candida Höfer, Jeff Koons, Haim Steinbach and Matthew Weinstein.

57th Street

The home of Carnegie Hall, Tiffany & Co, Bergdorf Goodman and a number of art galleries, the area surrounding 57th Street is a beehive of commercial activity that's lively, cultivated, chic – and expensive.
Subway: *E, V to Fifth Avenue-53rd Street; F to 57th Street; N, R, W to Fifth Avenue-59th Street.*

Greenberg Van Doren Gallery

7th Floor, 730 Fifth Avenue, at 57th Street (1-212 445 0444/www.gvdgallery.com). **Open** *Sept-May 10am-6pm Tue-Sat. Jun-Aug 10am-5pm Mon-Fri.*
This elegant gallery represents established artists Jennifer Bartlett and Richard Diebenkorn, as well as younger talent like painters Benjamin Edwards and Cameron Martin, video artist Alix Pearlstein, and photographers Tim Davis and Jessica Craig-Martin.

Mary Boone Gallery

4th Floor, 745 Fifth Avenue, between 57th & 58th Streets (1-212 752 2929/www.maryboone gallery.com). **Open** *Sept-Jun 10am-6pm Tue-Sat.*
Here, one-time Soho celeb Boone continues to produce hit shows featuring young artists, but her most prized venue is her newer gallery in Chelsea (*see p270*). The star attractions at both locations are established players such as Ross Bleckner, Peter Halley and hip provocateur Damian Loeb.

Marian Goodman Gallery

4th Floor, 24 W 57th Street, between Fifth & Sixth Avenues (1-212 977 7160/www.mariangoodman. com). **Open** *Sept-Jun 10am-6pm Mon-Sat. Jul, Aug 10am-6pm Mon-Fri.*
This well-known space offers a host of renowned names. Look for artists John Baldessari, Christian Boltanski, Maurizio Cattelan, Gabriel Orozco, Gerhard Richter, Thomas Struth and Jeff Wall.

PaceWildenstein Gallery

2nd Floor, 32 E 57th Street, between Madison & Park Avenues (1-212 421 3292/www.pace wildenstein.com). **Open** *Sept-May 9.30am-6pm Tue-Sat. Jun-Aug 9.30am-6pm Mon-Fri.*
To view shows by a few of the 20th century's most significant artists, head to this institution on 57th Street. Here you'll find pieces by such notables as Chuck Close, Agnes Martin, Pablo Picasso, Ad Reinhardt, Mark Rothko, Lucas Samaras, Elizabeth Murray and Kiki Smith. The Pace Prints division at this location exhibits works on paper by everyone from Old Masters to notable contemporaries. Not content with that, the gallery also deals in fine ethnic and world art.

Projectile Gallery

3rd Floor, 37 W 57th Street, between Fifth & Sixth Avenues (1 212 688 4673). **Open** *Sept-Jun noon-6pm Tue-Sat.* Call for summer hours.
This gallery has been the darling of European critics and curators since it opened in 1998, and its recent move from Harlem to midtown has only increased its following. Expect work by acclaimed young artists including Julie Mehretu, Peter Rostovsky and Stephen Vitiello.

Upper East Side

Many galleries on the Upper East Side sell masterpieces to billionaires. Still, anyone can look for free, and some pieces are treasures that will vanish from public view for years, if sold.
Subway: *6 to 68th Street-Hunter College or 77th Street.*

C&M Arts

45 E 78th Street, at Madison Avenue (1-212 861 0020/www.c-m-arts.com). **Open** *Sept-May 10am-5.30pm Tue-Sat. Jun-Aug 10am-5.30pm Mon-Fri.*

If you'd like to view or study the works of historic figures like Louise Bourgeois, Joseph Cornell, Franz Kline, Mark Rothko or Cy Twombly, then check out this major player in the secondary art market.

Gagosian Gallery

980 Madison Avenue, at 76th Street (1-212 744 2313/www.gagosian.com). Open Sept-May 10am-6pm Tue-Sat. Jun-Aug 10am-6pm Mon-Fri.

Long a force to be reckoned with in the world of contemporary art, Larry Gagosian commands pristine temples uptown and in Chelsea (*see p270*). Regularly featured artists include Francesco Clemente and Richard Serra, as well as younger stars like Cecily Brown and Damien Hirst.

Knoedler & Co

19 E 70th Street, between Fifth & Madison Avenues (1-212 794 0550/www.knoedlergallery.com). Open Sept-May 9.30am-5.30pm Tue-Fri. Jun-Aug 9.30am-5pm Mon-Fri.

Opened in 1846, the oldest gallery in New York represents museum-quality post-war and contemporary artists such as Lee Bontecou and John Walker.

Mitchell-Innes & Nash

5th Floor, 1018 Madison Avenue, between 78th & 79th Streets (1-212 744 7400/www.miandn.com). Open Sept-Jun 10am-5pm Tue-Sat. Jul 10am-5pm Mon-Fri. Call for Aug hours.

This 11-year-old gallery is run by two former specialists from Sotheby's who have an ambitious exhibiting programme that ranges from modern masters like Willem de Kooning to contemporary up-and-comers like Kojo Griffin.

Zwirner & Wirth

32 E 69th Street, between Madison & Park Avenues (1-212 517 8677/www.zwirnerandwirth.com). Open Sept-Jun 10am-6pm Tue-Sat. Jul-Labor Day 10am-6pm Mon-Fri.

Z&W, in a recently renovated townhouse space, exhibits modern and contemporary masters like Dan Flavin, Martin Kippenberger and Bruce Nauman. (*See also p270* **David Zwirner**.)

Harlem

Triple Candie

461 W 126th Street, between Morningside & Amsterdam Avenues (1-212 865 0783/www. triplecandie.org). Subway: A, B, C, D, 1 to 125th Street. Open noon-5pm Thur-Sun.

This multicultural arts centre brings exhibitions and educational programmes to Harlem's west side.

Brooklyn

Presently, there are about 60 galleries in Brooklyn, and that number is growing. Most are open on Sundays and Mondays, when the majority of Manhattan galleries are closed. Artists who live and work in Brooklyn have

created a thriving art scene, with Williamsburg as its uncontested hub. (For a printable map of the area's show spaces, visit www.williamsburg galleryassociation.com.)

Pierogi

177 North 9th Street, between Bedford & Driggs Avenues, Williamsburg, Brooklyn (1-718 599 2144/ www.pierogi2000.com). Subway: L to Bedford Avenue. Open Sept-Jul noon-6pm Mon, Thur-Sun and by appointment.

Pierogi, one of Williamsburg's established galleries, presents the Flat Files, a series of drawers containing works on paper by some 800 artists. Don't pass up the chance to don those special white gloves and handle the archived artwork yourself.

Plus Ultra Gallery

235 South 1st Street, at Roebling Street, Williamsburg, Brooklyn (1-718 387 3844/www.plusultragallery. com). Subway: J, M, Z to Marcy Avenue; L to Bedford Avenue. Open Sept-Jul noon-6pm Mon, Fri-Sun.

Artist Joshua Stern and art entrepreneur Ed Winkleman run the newly expanded Plus Ultra, lending shows by Leslie Brack, Joe Fig and Andy Yoder an ambience of serious fun.

Roebling Hall

390 Wythe Avenue, at South 4th Street, Williamsburg, Brooklyn (1-718 599 5352/www. brooklynart.com). Subway: J, M, Z to Marcy Avenue; L to Bedford Avenue. Open noon-6pm Mon, Fri-Sun.

Directors Joel Beck and Christian Viveros-Fauné cook up interesting and provocative shows featuring emerging local and international talent.

Non-profit spaces

apexart

291 Church Street, between Walker & White Streets (1-212 431 5270/www.apexart.org). Subway: J, M, N, Q, R, W, Z, 6 to Canal Street; 1 to Franklin Street. Open Sept-Jul 11am-6pm Tue-Sat.

apexart's inspiration comes from the independent critics, curators and artists selected for apexart's curatorial programme. The work rarely follows prevailing fashions; more often, it anticipates them.

Art in General

79 Walker Street, between Broadway & Lafayette Street (1-212 219 0473/www.artingeneral.org). Subway: J, M, N, Q, R, W, Z, 6 to Canal Street. Open Sept-Jun noon-6pm Tue-Sat.

Now celebrating its 24th year, this Chinatown oddball has a vigorous resident-artist programme that introduces newcomers – from New York, Europe, and Cuba and elsewhere in Latin America – in a homey, almost familial atmosphere.

The Drawing Center

35 Wooster Street, between Broome & Grand Streets (1-212 219 2166/www.drawingcenter.org). Subway: A, C, E, J, M, N, Q, R, W, Z, 6 to Canal Street. Open Sept-Jul 10am-6pm Tue-Fri; 11am-6pm Sat.

This 29-year-old Soho standout, a stronghold of works on paper, assembles critically acclaimed programmes that feature not only soon-to-be art stars but also museum-calibre legends such as James Ensor, Ellsworth Kelly and even Rembrandt.

Grey Art Gallery at New York University

100 Washington Square East, between Washington & Waverly Places (1-212 998 6780/www.nyu.edu/greyart). Subway: A, B, C, D, E, F, V to W 4th Street; N, R, W to 8th Street-NYU. **Open** *Mid Sept-mid Jul* 11am-6pm Tue, Thur, Fri; 11am-8pm Wed; 11am-5pm Sat. **Admission** suggested donation $3.
NYU's museum-laboratory has a multimedia collection of nearly 6,000 works covering the entire range of visual art. The emphasis is on the late 19th and the 20th centuries.

Momenta Art

72 Berry Street, between North 9th & 10th Streets, Williamsburg, Brooklyn (1-718 218 8058/www.momentaart.org). Subway: L to Bedford Avenue. **Open** *Sept-Jun* noon-6pm Mon, Fri-Sun.
Momenta is housed in a tiny Brooklyn space, yet it conveys the importance of a serious Chelsea gallery. You'll find solo and group exhibitions from a cross-section of emerging, mainly conceptualist, artists.

SculptureCenter

44-19 Purves Street, at Jackson Avenue, Long Island City, Queens (1-718 361 1750/www.sculpture-center.org). Subway: E, V to 23rd Street-Ely Avenue; G to Long Island City-Court Square; 7 to 45th Road-Court House Square. **Open** 11am-6pm Mon, Thur-Sun.
One of the best places to see work by blossoming and mid-career artists, this gallery is known for its very broad definition of sculpture. The impressive steel-and-brick digs, designed by architect Maya Lin, opened in late 2002.

Smack Mellon Gallery

56 Water Street, between Dock & Main Streets, Dumbo, Brooklyn (1-718 834 8761/www.smackmellon.org). Subway: A, C to High Street; F to York Street. **Open** noon-6pm Wed-Sun.
Avant-garde group shows fill this multidisciplinary gallery's draughty but accommodating quarters. Originally a foundry, the 6,000sq ft structure dates from before the Civil War. Call before visiting; a move to 92 Plymouth Street at Washington Street, one block away, is planned for late 2005.

Photography

New York is photo country, no doubt about it. For a comprehensive overview of local shows, look for the bimonthly directory *Photograph* ($5).

Edwynn Houk Gallery

4th Floor, 745 Fifth Avenue, between 57th & 58th Streets (1-212 750 7070/www.houkgallery.com). Subway: N, R, W to Fifth Avenue-59th Street. **Open** *Sept-Jul* 11am-6pm Tue-Sat. Call for summer hours.

The Edwynn Houk Gallery is a respected specialist in vintage and contemporary photography. Among the artists exhibited are Brassaï, Lynn Davis, Dorothea Lange, Annie Leibovitz, Man Ray and Alfred Stieglitz, each commanding, as you'd expect for talent of this calibre, the very top dollar.

International Center of Photography

1133 Sixth Avenue, at 43rd Street (1-212 857 0000/www.icp.org). Subway: B, D, F, V to 42nd Street-Bryant Park; 7 to Fifth Avenue. **Open** 10am-6pm Tue-Thur, Sat, Sun; 10am-8pm Fri. **Admission** $10; $7 seniors and students; free under-12s. Voluntary donation 5-8pm Fri.
In 2001, ICP's galleries, once split between midtown and uptown locations, were consolidated in a redesigned building that also accommodates a school and a library (a major archive of photography magazines and thousands of biographical and photographical files). Begun in the 1960s as the International Fund for Concerned Photography, ICP houses work by legendary photojournalists Werner Bischof, Robert Capa, David Seymour and Dan Weiner, who were tragically killed on assignment. True to their tradition, news and documentary photography remains an important part of the centre's programme, which also includes contemporary photos and video (in 2003, the first-ever ICP Photo Triennial further solidified ICP's position in the contemporary photographic scene). Two floors of exhibition space often showcase retrospectives devoted to a single artist; more recent shows have focused on the work of Larry Clark, Ralph Eugene Meatyard and Garry Winogrand.

Klotz/Sirmon Gallery

Suite 701, 511 W 25th Street, between Tenth & Eleventh Avenues (1-212 741 4764/www.klotzsirmon.com). Subway: C, E to 23rd Street. **Open** *Sept-Jun* by appointment only Tue, Wed; noon-6pm Thur-Sat. *Jul, Aug* noon-6pm Wed-Fri.
In addition to its stock of high-quality vintage and contemporary works, this gallery also functions as the NYC agent for the *New York Times'* extensive photographic archives, which comprises some five million prints. If you're in New York in December, don't miss the gallery's annual holiday sale. Curators and collectors rub elbows with just plain folks – and they're all looking for bargains.

Pace/MacGill

9th Floor, 32 E 57th Street, between Madison & Park Avenues (1-212 759 7999). Subway: N, R, W to Lexington Avenue-59th Street; 4, 5, 6 to 59th Street. **Open** *Sept-late Jun* 9.30am-5.30pm Tue-Fri; 10am-6pm Sat. *Late Jun-Aug* 9.30am-5.30pm Mon-Thur; 9.30am-4pm Fri.
Pace/MacGill is a well-established gallery that frequently shows work by such well-known names as Walker Evans, Robert Frank, Irving Penn and Alfred Stieglitz, in addition to ground-breaking contemporaries like Guy Bourdin, Chuck Close, Philip-Lorca DiCorcia and Kiki Smith.

Books & Poetry

Live readings and spoken-word slams are a *def* sentence.

If you're one of those people who walked out of the film version of *The Hours* and carped that the book was better, you're in luck. For book purists, New York still offers many literary pleasures that involve more than a solitary evening snuggled up with a novel. At author readings even the most reserved writers read their work with inflections and explanations that add surprising nuances to their books.

Of course, New York authors have also aimed to go beyond the simple reading-from-the-podium approach. The Moth series, for instance, is a storytelling event, with writers like Jonathan Ames improvising tales – with no notes allowed – in front of an audience (and a panel of judges). Other events, like the author2author series at Housing Works bookstore, pair up literary luminaries who use their books as a launching pad for compelling dialogues.

Whatever type of event you're drawn to, readings are like the rock shows of the book world, a place where you can see your favourite writers perform in the flesh. Some events sell out (if you like David Foster Wallace, buy tickets in advance). Others are small, cosy affairs, with authors striking up conversations with the audience. To find out who's reading when and where, call or visit each venue's website, or check out the weekly listings in *Time Out New York* magazine.

Author appearances

Asian-American Writers' Workshop

10th floor, 16 W 32nd Street, between Fifth Avenue & Broadway (1-212 494 0061/www.aaww.org). Subway: B, D, F, N, Q, R, V, W to 34th Street-Herald Square. **Admission** suggested donation $5. **No credit cards**.

Acclaimed writers of Asian heritage – including Jhumpa Lahiri and Susan Choi – together with up-and-comers lecture on the publishing biz or read from their work at this respected organisation.

Barbès

376 9th Street, at Sixth Avenue, Park Slope, Brooklyn (1-718 965 9177/www.barbesbrooklyn.com). Subway: F to Seventh Avenue; M, R to Fourth Avenue-9th Street. **Admission** free-$8. **No credit cards**.

Too many cafés host a few readings and suddenly declare themselves 'community centres'. However, Barbès, a bar and performance space owned by two French musicians, is one of the few places around that really earns itself the appellation.

Barnes & Noble

33 E 17th Street, between Broadway & Park Avenue South (1-212 253 0810/www.barnesandnoble.com). Subway: L, N, Q, R, W, 4, 5, 6 to 14th Street-Union Square. **Admission** free.

Nearly every author tour touches down at a Barnes & Noble. This Union Square location offers an especially varied schedule. Recent names include Joyce Carol Oates, Ian McEwan and Michael Cunningham.

Bluestockings

172 Allen Street, between Rivington & Stanton Streets (1-212 777 6028/www.bluestockings.com). Subway: F, V to Lower East Side-Second Avenue. **Admission** suggested donation free-$10. **Credit** AmEx, MC, V.

This self-proclaimed progressive bookstore and café hosts frequent readings and discussions, often on feminist and lesbian themes.

Books of Wonder

18 W 18th Street, between Fifth & Sixth Avenues (1-212 989 3270/www.booksofwonder.net). Subway: F, V to 14th Street; L to Sixth Avenue. **Admission** free.

Given the many successful authors trying their hands at children's books, you're just as likely to see Michael Chabon as Maurice Sendak reading here.

Coliseum Books

See p250 for listing. **Admission** free.

The new and improved Coliseum continues to draw some big guns: recent readings have included Karen Jay Fowler and David Sedaris.

Galapagos Art & Performance Space

See p316 for listing. **Admission** free-$5. **No credit cards**.

Books and beer – really, what could be better? This unconventional Brooklyn bar hosts regular readings and literary variety shows.

Half King

505 W 23rd Street, between Tenth & Eleventh Avenues (1-212 462 4300/www.thehalfking.com). Subway: C, E to 23rd Street. **Show** 7pm Mon. **Admission** free.

Co-owned by Sebastian Junger, the author of *The Perfect Storm*, the Half King features Monday night readings, with recent authors including Thomas Kelly and Siddhartha Deb.

Happy Ending Series

Happy Ending, 302 Broome Street, between Eldridge & Forsyth Streets (1-212 334 9676). Subway: F, V to Delancey Street; J, M, Z to Delancey-Essex Streets. **Admission** free.

Taking the mic at **Bowery Poetry Club**. *See p278.*

Hosted by Amanda Stern, these reading events (with musical interludes) take place in a massage-parlour-turned-watering-hole. The bar setting lends the series a laid-back, convivial vibe. Readers range from up-and-comers like Aimee Bender to near-canonical authors like Paul Muldoon.

Housing Works Used Book Cafe

See p252 for listing. **Admission** free, book donations encouraged.

The emerging and the illustrious mingle at the microphone (and in the audience) at this Soho bookstore and café, which has one of the best reading series in the city. What's more, the profits go to provide shelter and support services to homeless people living with HIV and AIDS.

Hue-Man Bookstore

2319 Frederick Douglass Boulevard (Eighth Avenue), between 124th & 125th Streets (1-212 665 7400/ www.huemanbookstore.com). Subway: A, B, C, D to 125th Street. **Admission** free.

This spacious Harlem bookstore features frequent readings as well as in-store appearances by authors (Bill Clinton, whose office is nearby, held a signing of his memoir here), with an emphasis on African-American writers and topics.

Humanities & Social Sciences Library

455 Fifth Avenue, at 42nd Street (1-212 930 0830/www.nypl.org). Subway: B, D, F, V to 42nd Street-Bryant Park; 7 to Fifth Avenue. **Open** 11am-7.30pm Tue, Wed; 10am-6pm Thur-Sat. **Admission** free. **Admission** $10. **No credit cards**.

The Celeste Bartos Forum at this branch of the New York Public Library presents excellent live interviews with such influential literary figures as JM Coetzee, as well as literary lectures and readings.

KGB

2nd floor, 85 E 4th Street, between Second & Third Avenues (1-212 505 3360/www.kgbbar.com). Subway: F, V to Lower East Side-Second Avenue; 6 to Astor Place. **Admission** free.

This dark and formerly smoky East Village hangout with an old-school Communist theme runs several top-notch weekly series, featuring NYC writers, poets, fantasy authors and more.

McNally Robinson Bookstore

50 Prince Street, between Lafayette & Mulberry (1-212 274 1160/www.mcnallyrobinson.com). Subway: N, R to Prince Street; 6 to Spring Street. **Admission** free.

McNally Robinson is an excellent new independent bookstore. To cement its reputation, it's bringing a wide range of non-fiction writers and novelists to read in its comfortable café space.

National Arts Club

15 Gramercy Park South, between Park Avenue South & Irving Place (1-212 475 3424/www. nationalartsclub.org). Subway: 6 to 23rd Street. **Admission** free, except for benefits.

A posh Gramercy Park address and grand Victorian interiors make this a suitably dramatic setting for gazing upon your literary idol. Lectures and readings are open to the public as space permits; check the website for upcoming events. And leave that hoodie at home – business attire is required.

New School University

66 W 12th Street, between Fifth & Sixth Avenues (1-212 229 5353/tickets 1-212 229 5488/www.new school.edu). Subway: F, V to 14th Street; L to Sixth Avenue. **Admission** free-$15; students free. **Credit** AmEx, MC, V.

Grace Paley, Rita Dove and Anne Carson are a few of the notable writers to participate in the New School University's wide-ranging readings and literary forums. It's also worth looking out for political discussions and poetry nights.

92nd Street Y

1395 Lexington Avenue, at 92nd Street (1-212 415 5500/www.92y.org). Subway: 6 to 96th Street. **Admission** $16-$35. **Credit** AmEx, MC, V.

Canonical novelists, journalists and poets preside over some grand intellectual feasts here, with talks by critic James Wood, as well as readings by writers like James Salter and Alice Munro. A notable recent double bill paired up Jonathan Safran Foer and William T Vollman.

192 Books

192 Tenth Avenue, at 21st Street (1-212 255 4022). Subway: C, E to 23rd Street. **Admission** free.

This independent bookstore offers a wide variety of books, focusing on literary titles and art history. Its reading series is phenomenal, bringing in quality authors, such as novelists Harry Mathews and Gary Indiana, and poet John Ashbery.

Poetry Project

St Mark's Church in-the-Bowery, 131 E 10th Street, at Second Avenue (1-212 674 0910/www.poetry project.com). Subway: L to First Avenue; 6 to Astor Place. **Admission** $8; $7 seniors and students. **No credit cards**.

The Project, housed in a beautiful old church, has hosted an amazing roster of poets since its inception way back in 1966, including creative luminaries such as Allen Ginsberg, Patti Smith, Eileen Myles and Adrienne Rich. It also offers workshops, lectures, book parties and an open poetry reading on the first Monday of each month.

Sunny's Bar

253 Conover Street, between Beard & Reed Streets, Red Hook, Brooklyn (1-718 625 8211). Travel: F, G to Smith-9th Streets, then take the B77 bus to Conover Street. **Admission** $3 donation. **No credit cards**.

If you're feeling adventurous, make the trip out to this old waterfront joint to hear a varied line-up of local literati such as the elegant writer of non-fiction Phillip Lopate and the wittily intimate poet, Vijay Seshadri. Scheduling varies, so be sure to call ahead.

Spoken word

Most spoken-word events begin with a featured poet or two before moving on to an open mic. If you'd like to participate, show up a little early and ask for the sign-up sheet. Remember to adhere to poetry-slam etiquette: feel free to express your approval out loud, but keep criticism to yourself (silence speaks louder than words). For an up-to-date schedule of events throughout the city, check out the Ultimate NYC Poetry Calendar (www.poetz.com/calendar).

Bowery Poetry Club

308 Bowery, between Bleecker & Houston Streets (1-212 614 0505/www.bowerypoetry.com). Subway: B, D, F, V to Broadway-Lafayette Street; 6 to Bleecker Street. **Admission** free-$15. **No credit cards**.

Celebrating the grand oral traditions and cyberific future of poetry, the funky BPC features spoken-word events nightly, with readings and performance in the afternoon. The Urbana National Slam team leads an open mic on Thursdays. **Photo** *p277*.

Cornelia Street Café

29 Cornelia Street, between Bleecker & W 4th Streets (1-212 989 9319/www.corneliastreetcafe.com). Subway: A, B, C, D, E, F, V to W 4th Street. **Admission** free-$6, one-drink minimum. **Credit** AmEx, MC, V.

This charming West Village restaurant is home to several long-running series of spoken-word events, along with live music and theatre. At press time, the café's basement performance space was devoting nights to Arab-, Greek- and Italian-American writers. The open-mic Pink Pony series continues on Fridays (arrive before 6pm to sign up for a slot).

Moth StorySLAM

www.themoth.org.

Better at talking than at writing? The Moth, known for its big-name monthly storytelling shows, also sponsors open slams in various venues. Ten raconteurs get five minutes each to tell a favourite story (no notes allowed!) to a panel of judges.

Nuyorican Poets Cafe

236 E 3rd Street, between Avenues B & C (1-212 505 8183/ www.nuyorican.org). Subway: F, V to Lower East Side-Second Avenue. **Admission** $5-$15. **No credit cards**.

This 30-plus-year-old community East Village arts centre is known for its long history of raucous slams, jam sessions and anything-goes open mics.

Our Unorganicized Reading

ABC No Rio, 156 Rivington Street, between Clinton & Suffolk Streets (1-212 254 3697/www.abcnorio. org). Subway: F to Delancey Street; J, M, Z to Delancey-Essex Streets. **Show** 3pm Sun. **Admission** $2. **No credit cards**.

ABC No Rio's long-running Sunday-afternoon open mic promises a welcoming vibe, no time limits and 'no BS'. Just remember, brevity is still the soul of wit.

Cabaret & Comedy

Comics and crooners will keep you laughing or crying.

Suave cabaret at **Feinstein's at the Regency**. *See p281*.

Cabaret

When some people hear the word 'cabaret', they think of the Liza Minnelli movie, or of a naughty burlesque show with girls of sullied virtue; others, perhaps, assume that 'cabaret' is a kind of red wine (and 'chanteuse' a shade of green). In New York, however, the term refers to a retro style of nightclub music, with an emphasis on tried-and-true standards. While the golden age of this genre waned with the advent of rock 'n' roll, plenty of singers and fans have found fresh ways to honour the classic sound.

Performed in relatively small venues, usually with spare accompaniment, cabaret music draws from what's known as the 'Great American Songbook', a vast repertoire of tunes derived from vintage musical theatre – Cole Porter, George Gershwin, Rodgers and Hart – and supplemented with songs by contemporary composers (Randy Newman and Billy Joel are popular). You can hear some of the same material at jazz clubs, but with a different emphasis: jazz singers focus on music, whereas cabaretists emphasise storytelling and lyrical

interpretation. The top performers can make each person in the audience feel as if he or she is being personally serenaded. More than anything else, cabaret is an act of intimacy, thus making it an excellent option for a romantic evening.

Today's cabaret venues fall into two groups. Shows at Café Carlyle, Feinstein's at the Regency and the Oak Room offer old-school New York style and sophistication; you'll feel like you've stepped into one of the better Woody Allen movies. Neighbourhood clubs such as Danny's Skylight Room and the Encore are less formal and less pricey. After a rash of closings a few years back, new venues for cabaret have popped up all over town. Mid October brings the Cabaret Convention, a showcase of the genre at Town Hall (*see p322*) that attracts top-flight performers.

At its best, cabaret can summon a world of nostalgia – for a Nick-and-Nora New York, where men wore hats and women wore gloves – while maintaining its emotional relevance in the present moment. The Great American Songbook may be old-fashioned, but until people stop falling in and out of love, it will never be out of date.

Classic nightspots

Café Carlyle

*The Carlyle, 35 E 76th Street, at Madison Avenue
(1-212 744 1600/reservations 1-800 227 5737/
www.thecarlyle.com). Subway: 6 to 77th Street.*
Shows 8.45pm Mon-Thur; 8.45pm, 10.45pm Fri, Sat.
Cover Varies, usually $75-$95. **Credit** AmEx, DC,
Disc, MC, V.
This elegant boîte in the Carlyle hotel, with its airy
murals by Marcel Vertes, is the epitome of New York
chic, attracting such top-level singers as Eartha Kitt,
Barbara Cook and Ute Lemper. Woody Allen sometimes sits in as clarinetist with Eddie Davis and his
New Orleans Jazz Band on Monday nights (call
ahead to confirm). Don't dress casually – embrace
the high life. To drink in some atmosphere without
spending quite so much, try Bemelmans Bar across
the hall, which always features an excellent pianist
(5.30pm-12.30am Mon-Sat; $20-$25 cover).

Feinstein's at the Regency

*Regency Hotel, 540 Park Avenue, at 61st Street
(1-212 339 4095/www.feinsteinsattheregency.com).
Subway: N, R, W to Lexington Avenue-59th Street;
4, 5, 6 to 59th Street.* **Shows** 8.30pm Tue-Thur;
8.30pm, 11pm Fri, Sat. **Cover** $60, $30-$40 food-and-
drink minimum. **Credit** AmEx, DC, Disc, MC, V.
Cabaret's crown prince, Michael Feinstein, draws A-
list talent to this swank room in the Regency. It's
mega-pricey, but you get what you pay for. Recent
performers have included some of the top names in
the business: Chita Rivera, Patti LuPone and Brian
Stokes Mitchell, to name a few. **Photo** *p279.*

Oak Room

*Algonquin Hotel, 59 W 44th Street, between Fifth &
Sixth Avenues (1-212 840 6800/reservations 1-212
419 9331/www.algonquinhotel.com). Subway: B, D,
F, V to 42nd Street-Bryant Park; 7 to Fifth Avenue.*
Shows 9pm Tue-Thur; 9pm, 11.30pm Fri, Sat.
Cover $50, $20 drink minimum; $50 dinner
compulsory at first Friday and Saturday shows.
Credit AmEx, DC, Disc, MC, V.
This resonant, banquette-lined room is the place to
enjoy such cabaret luminaries as Karen Akers and
Andrea Marcovicci, plus rising young stars of the
jazz world (including the great Paula West). And
yes, all you Dorothy Parker fans out there in cabaret
land, it's *that* Algonquin.

Standards

Danny's Skylight Room

*Grand Sea Palace, 346 W 46th Street, between
Eighth & Ninth Avenues (1-212 265 8130/1-212
265 8133/www.dannysgsp.com). Subway: A, C, E to
42nd Street-Port Authority.* **Shows** Times vary.
Piano bar 8-11pm daily. **Cover** $10-$25, $12-$15
food-and-drink minimum. No cover for piano bar.
Credit AmEx, DC, Disc, MC, V.
A pastel-hued nook within the Grand Sea Palace on
Restaurant Row, Danny's features up-and-comers

as well as a few of the more mature cabaret and jazz
stand-bys, such as the owlish John Wallowitch and
the ageless Blossom Dearie.

Don't Tell Mama

*343 W 46th Street, between Eighth & Ninth Avenues
(1-212 757 0788/www.donttellmama.com). Subway:
A, C, E to 42nd Street-Port Authority.* **Shows** Times
vary, 2-3 shows per night. *Piano bar* 9pm-4am daily.
Cover free-$20, two-drink minimum. **Credit** AmEx, DC,
Disc, MC, V.
Showbiz pros and piano-bar buffs adore this dank
but homey Theater District stalwart, where acts
range from the strictly amateur to potential stars of
tomorrow. The nightly line-up may include pop, jazz
or Broadway singers, as well as female imperson-
ators, magicians, comedians or musical revues.

Duplex

*61 Christopher Street, at Seventh Avenue South
(1-212 255 5438/www.theduplex.com). Subway:
1 to Christopher Street-Sheridan Square.* **Shows**
7pm, 9pm daily. *Piano bar* 9pm-4am daily. **Cover**
$5-$25, two-drink minimum. **Credit** AmEx, MC, V.
The Duplex may not have classic glamour, but it's
the city's oldest cabaret. Going strong for 50-plus
years, the place is known for campy, good-natured
fun, and has become a home away from home for
local favourites Lisa Asher and Brandon Cutrell.

Encore

*266 W 47th Street, between Broadway & Eighth
Avenue (1-212 221 3960/www.theencorenyc.com).
Subway: C, E, 1 to 50th Street.* **Shows** Times vary.
Cover $10-$20, two drink minimum. **Credit** MC, V.
The city's newest venue, located at the heart of the
Theater District, has quickly become a hub of the
cabaret community. The intimate downstairs room
boasts tasty finger food as well as a solid line-up of
New York nightclub talent, including Julie Reyburn
and the quirky duo known as Gashole.

Hideaway Room at Helen's

*169 Eighth Avenue, between 18th & 19th Streets
(1-212 206 0609). Subway: A, C, E to 14th Street;
1 to 18th Street.* **Shows** Times vary, 2-3 shows per
night. *Piano bar* 6-10pm daily. *Open mic* 10pm-4am
daily. **Cover** $15-$25, $15 food-and-drink minimum.
No cover for piano bar. **Credit** AmEx, MC, V.
This fresh, friendly boîte has risen, phoenix-like, on
the site of the late Judi's Chelsea. In addition to the
eclectic range of performers – from the legendary
Julie Wilson to a panoply of drag queens (this is
Chelsea, after all) – the venue boasts a bustling piano
bar and affordable food.

Alternative venues

Joe's Pub

See p317 for listing. **Shows** Times vary, 2 shows per
night. **Cover** $10-$30.
This plush club and restaurant in the Public Theater
is both hip and elegant, and boasts an exraodinarily

varied mix of performers (usually booked for just a single night). Among the rock, jazz and world-music acts, you'll also occasionally find a Broadway performer reaching into the world of cabaret.

Comedy

New York City and its comedy scene have a lot in common: besides having a propensity for filth, both are full of insults and feature a freaky cast of characters in desperate need of attention. Whether you prefer a standard joke told through a microphone or avant-garde antics, you'll find what your funny bone craves in the city's many clubs, bars and theatres dedicated to an endless parade of punchlines. Hit Carolines on Broadway and Gotham Comedy Club to hear late-night talk-show circuit comics (and keep your fingers crossed for surprise visits from the likes of Jerry Seinfeld and Lewis Black). Step into the Upright Citizens Brigade Theater for top-notch improvised and sketch shows by the city's riskier young comedians. Trek to Ars Nova in Hell's Kitchen for written material of a more professional (and typically musical) bent.

Ars Nova
511 W 54th Street, between Tenth & Eleventh Avenues (1-212 977 1700/www.arsnovanyc.com). Subway: C, E to 50th Street. **Shows** Times vary. **Cover** free-$20. **Average drink** $5. **Credit** AmEx, Disc, MC, V (online tickets only).
This jewel box of a theatre puts on a heady, well-selected (if somewhat erratic) repertoire of comedy, cabaret and music shows, in an environment that's focused more on the performance on stage than the cash register behind the bar. The weekly *Thursdays At Ten* showcases a rotating selection of the current comedy acts at the venue.

Carolines on Broadway
1626 Broadway, between 49th & 50th Streets (1-212 757 4100/www.carolines.com). Subway: N, R, W to 49th Street; 1, 9 to 50th Street. **Shows** 7pm, 9.30pm Mon, Tue; 7.30pm, 9.30pm Wed; 8pm, 10pm Thur, Sun; 8pm, 10.30pm, 12.30am Fri, Sat. **Cover** $10-$40, two-drink minimum. **Credit** AmEx, MC, V.
You can occasionally catch old-school comics like Paul Mooney or Robert Schimmel at this stalwart of a stand-up club, but you'll also find current stars such as *Saturday Night Live*'s Finesse Mitchell. Be warned: the bigger the star, the more you pay.

Chicago City Limits
Ground floor of the New York Improv, 318 W 53rd Street, between Eighth & Ninth Avenues (1-212 888 5233). Subway: C, E to 50th Street. **Shows** 8pm Wed-Fri; 8pm, 10pm Sat. **Cover** $15 plus two-drink minimum. **Credit** AmEx, Disc, MC, V.
The CCL, which moved from Chicago in 1979, presents topical sketches, songs and audience-inspired

improv. Explore a different medium on the first Sunday of every month, when the club hosts a short comedy film festival; for details, see www.first sundays.com. CCL's sketch- and improv-comedy revues play at the New York Improv's second stage.

Comedy Cellar
117 MacDougal Street, between Bleecker & W 3rd Streets (1-212 254 3480/www.comedycellar.com). Subway: A, B, C, D, E, F, V to W 4th Street. **Shows** 9pm, 11pm Mon-Thur, Sun; 9pm, 10.45pm, 12.30am Fri; 7.30pm, 9.15pm, 11pm, 12.45am Sat. **Cover** $10-$15, two-item minimum. **Credit** AmEx, MC, V.
This club is a good bet since *SNL* and *Tough Crowd* star Colin Quinn is almost always around, with some of his big-name friends (including Kevin Brennan, Lynne Koplitz and Godfrey) in tow.

Comedy Village
82 W 3rd Street, between Sullivan & Thompson Streets (1-212 477 0130/www.comedyvillage.com). Subway: A, B, C, D, E, F, V to W 4th Street. **Shows** 9.30pm Mon-Thur, Sun; 8pm, 10pm, 12.15am Fri, Sat. **Cover** $8 plus two-drink minimum Mon-Thur, Sun; $15 plus two-drink minimum Fri, Sat. **Credit** AmEx, MC, V.
The Boston Comedy Club has headed off to that big Sox stadium in the sky. In its place, PJ Landers opened this new venue, in which many of the same comics are due to be reincarnated.

Dangerfield's
1118 First Avenue, between 61st & 62nd Streets (1-212 593 1650/www.dangerfields.com). Subway: N, R, W to Lexington Avenue-59th Street; 4, 5, 6 to 59th Street. **Shows** 8.45pm Mon-Thur, Sun; 8.30pm, 10.30pm Fri; 8pm, 10.30pm, 12.30am Sat. **Cover** $13-$20. **Credit** AmEx, MC, V.
Opened by the late Rodney Dangerfield way back in 1969, this old-school lounge pre-dates not only its competitors, but also many of its performers. The club offers good food and cheap parking – and no drink minimum, which alone makes a visit here worthwhile… even if it gets no respect.

Gotham Comedy Club
34 W 22nd Street, between Fifth & Sixth Avenues (1-212 367 9000/www.gothamcomedyclub.com). Subway: F, N, R, V, W to 23rd Street. **Shows** 8.30pm Mon-Thur, Sun; 8.30pm, 10.30pm Fri; 8.30pm, 10.30pm, 12.30am Sat. **Cover** $10-$16, two-drink minimum. **Credit** AmEx, DC, MC, V.
Like most stand-up clubs, the charge-laden bill's arrival will make it difficult to remember how hard you just laughed. Unlike most other stand-up clubs, Gotham's line-ups – which have included Jim David, Marc Maron and Greg Giraldo – are usually worth it.

Laugh Factory
303 W 42nd Street, at Eighth Avenue (1-212 586 7829/www.laughfactory.com). Subway: A, C, E to 42nd Street-Port Authority. **Shows** 8pm Tue, Sun; 8.30pm Wed, Thur; 8.30pm, 10.30pm, 12.30am Fri, Sat. **Cover** $15-$30, two-drink minimum. **Credit** AmEx, DC, Disc, MC, V.

New York Improv.

This Times Square stand-up club is a spin-off of the long-running LA counterpart by the same name and is where you'll see slick West Coast talent such as Kathy Griffin and Dean Edwards.

Laugh Lounge nyc
151 Essex Street, between Rivington & Stanton Streets (1-212 614 2500/www.laughloungenyc.com). Subway: F to Delancey Street; J, M, Z to Delancey-Essex Streets. **Shows** 8.30pm Tue-Thur; 8.30pm, 10.30pm Fri, Sat. **Cover** $8-$15, two-drink minimum. **Credit** AmEx, Disc, MC, V.
Although their off-peak nights occasionally offer line-ups as edgy as their Lower East Side location would imply, for the most part one can expect standard club-circuit fare from this relatively new venue.

Magnet Theater
254 W 29th Street, between Seventh & Eighth Avenues (1-212 244 8824/www.magnettheater.com). Subway: A, C, E to 34th Street-Penn Station; 1 to 28th Street. **Shows** times vary Mon-Thur. **Cover** $5. **No credit cards.**
Modern-day improvisation guru Armando Diaz is behind this new Chelsea comedy spot, near the Upright Citizens Brigade Theatre (UCBT), in the neighbourhood we're calling 'the Improv District'.

New York Improv
318 W 53rd Street, between Eighth & Ninth Avenues (1-212 757 2323/www.newyorkimprov.com). Subway: C, E to 50th Street. **Shows** 9pm Mon-Thur, Sun; 9pm, 11.30pm Fri; 9pm, 11pm, 12.45am Sat. **Cover** $10-$15. **Credit** AmEx, DC, Disc, MC, V.
Originally opened in 1963, the legendary Improv's stage was graced by greats like Richard Pryor, Robin Williams and George Carlin. This recent reincarnation trots out today's rising stars, many of whom are already working the TV circuit. **Photo** *above*.

Rififi
Cinema Classics, 332 E 11th Street, between First & Second Avenues (1-212 677 5368). Subway: L to First Avenue. **Shows** times vary daily. **Cover** Free-$5. **No credit cards.**
In the back room of this movie house you'll find relief from celluloid as the performance space features almost exclusively comedy. The three weekly recurring shows – *Welcome to Our Week, Giant Tuesday Night of Amazing Inventions and Also There is a Game* and *Invite Them Up* – also happen to be three of the best shows in the city.

Stand-Up New York
236 W 78th Street, at Broadway (1-212 595 0850/ www.standupny.com). Subway: 1 to 79th Street. **Shows** 8.30pm Mon, 6pm, 9pm Tue, Wed; 6pm, 9pm, 11.30pm Thur; 8pm, 10pm, 12.30am Fri, Sat; 7pm, 9.15pm Sun. **Cover** $5-$15, two-drink minimum. **Credit** AmEx, MC, V.
You're not exactly spoiled for comedic choice on the Upper West Side: this is the only club out there. Stand-Up New York features a mix of circuit regulars (Laurie Kilmartin, Jim Gaffigan and Dean Obeidallah), along with fresh new talents.

Upright Citizens Brigade Theatre
307 W 26th Street, between Eighth & Ninth Avenues (1-212 366 9176/www.ucbtheatre.com). Subway: C, E to 23rd Street. **Shows** Times vary. **Cover** $5-$8. **No credit cards.**
The UCBT presents some of the most adventurous comedy in NYC and, even better, it's always at budget prices. You'll often see performers from *Conan, Saturday Night Live* and *The Daily Show* displaying the sketch and improv talents that put them there in the first place. (Sunday is the typical night for celebrity drop-ins.) If you're feeling funny, take a class!

Arts & Entertainment

Children

Gotham is not just for grown-ups.

In NYC, daily thrills number in the hundreds, from hearing subterranean trumpet players blast over the squeal of the subway to seeing how the blazing lights of Times Square turn night-time into fantastically garish day. No surprise, then, that the city generates excitement in young visitors, including really cool tweens and teens. Remember, it takes years for even a home-grown New York City kid to get blasé about this place. But be forewarned: all this stimulation can overload the circuits of smaller children. So take in the sights but, in between the Empire State Building and the Statue of Liberty, put away the map and have a wander. You never know what you'll see – a street performer in head-to-toe glitter, eight dogs with their walker in tow or maybe you'll spy the Olsen twins sipping coffee.

Of course, you'll want to take in some of New York's more tried-and-tested offerings, too. We've listed spots that cater to the city's little cognoscenti, as well as some traditional fare that has entertained generations of NYC children. To keep up with the child-friendly events happening during your stay, pick up a copy of *Time Out New York Kids*.

Where to stay

Most hotels, especially the big chains, will move a crib or an extra bed into your room to accommodate your tot. Ask if this service is available when you book, and check on the size of the room; sometimes, the hipper the hotel, the smaller the rooms, since most of the trendy places assume their guests will be out on the town all night. A few especially child-friendly places are listed below. For more on hotels, *see p44* **Where to Stay**.

Beacon Hotel

2130 Broadway, between 74th & 75th Streets (1-212 787 1100/1-800 572 4969/www.beaconhotel.com). For review, see p71.

Holiday Inn Midtown

440 W 57th Street, between Ninth & Tenth Avenues (1-212-581-8100/1-800 465 4329/www.hi57.com). For review, see p72 **Chain gang**.

Inn on 23rd

131 W 23rd Street, between Sixth & Seventh Avenues (1-212 463 0330/www.innon23rd.com). For review, see p46.

Roger Smith

501 Lexington Avenue, between 47th & 48th Streets (1-212 755 1400/1-800 445 0277/www. rogersmith.com). For review, see p61.

Babysitting

Baby Sitters' Guild

1-212 682 0227/www.babysittersguild.com. **Bookings** 9am-9pm daily. **No credit cards.** Long- or short-term multilingual sitters cost $20 and up per hour (four-hour minimum), plus cab fare. Babysitters are available around the clock.

Pinch Sitters

1-212 260 6005. **Bookings** 8am-5pm Mon-Fri. **No credit cards.** Charges are $16 per hour (four-hour minimum), plus cab fare after 9pm ($10 maximum).

Classic kids' New York

Astroland Amusement Park

1000 Surf Avenue, at West 10th Street, Coney Island, Brooklyn (1-718 372 0275/www.astro land.com). Subway: D, F, Q to Coney Island-Stillwell Avenue. **Open** *Mid Apr-mid Jun* noon-6pm Sat, Sun, weather permitting (plus weekdays during public-school spring break). *Mid Jun-Labor Day* noon-midnight daily. *Early Sept-early Oct* opens at noon Sat, Sun; closing time depends on weather. **Admission** $2-$5 per ride; Mon-Thur and Fri mornings $21.99 per six-hour session. **Credit** MC, V. This well-aged Coney Island amusement park has an appealing grunginess that makes it a welcome alternative to slick, mouse-themed parks. Kids over 54in (137cm) tall can ride the world-famous Cyclone roller coaster; young ones will prefer the Tilt-a-Whirl or the carousel. Coney Island is being bought by developers and may become America's newest 'family destination' – a cleaned-up clone of itself.

Dinosaurs at the Museum of Natural History

For listing, see p141 **American Museum of Natural History**.
Children of all ages request repeat visits to this old-fashioned, exhibit-based museum – especially to see the dinosaur skeletons, the enormous blue whale and, in the colder months, the free-flying butterflies. During the holiday season, look for the Christmas tree decorated with origami ornaments (they include dinosaur shapes, of course). Paper-folders are on hand to help visitors make their own.

The Nutcracker

see p264 for listing.
Generations of New York kids have counted on the New York City Ballet to provide this Balanchine holiday treat. The pretty two-act production features an onstage snowstorm, a flying sleigh, a one-ton Christmas tree and child dancers.

Storytelling at the Hans Christian Andersen Statue

Central Park, entrance on Fifth Avenue, at 72nd Street (www.centralparknyc.org). Subway: 6 to 68th Street-Hunter College. Dates Jun-Sept 11am-noon Sat. Admission free.
Children five and older have gathered for decades at the foot of this climbable statue to hear master storytellers from all over the country tell folk and fairy tales to rapt groups.

Temple of Dendur at the Met

For listing, see p135 Metropolitan Museum of Art.
The Met can be overwhelming unless you make a beeline for one or two galleries. The impressive Temple of Dendur, a real multi-roomed, ancient temple with carvings and reliefs (and graffiti), was brought here from Egypt stone by stone, and it's a perennial hit. Also check out the mummies in the Egyptian Room and the medieval arms and armour collection. Pick up a few of the Met's printed *Family Guides* (free at the museum's information desks and available for online download), which give kids the inside scoop on what they're seeing. Note that the Met now opens on most Monday holidays – and provides special children's programming – when many other museums are closed.

Winnie the Pooh & Friends

Donnell Library Center, 20 W 53rd Street, between Fifth & Sixth Avenues (1-212 621 0618). Subway: E, V to Fifth Ave-53rd Street. Open noon-6pm Mon, Wed, Fri; 10am-6pm Tue, noon-8pm Thur; noon-5pm Sat; 1-5pm Sun. Call for summer hours. Admission free.
The toys that belonged to Christopher Robin Milne are still ensconced in a glass case in this library's Central Children's Room, despite a 1998 diplomatic crisis in which the UK demanded their return.

Arts festivals

Some of the city's free annual arts festivals incorporate interesting kids' programming. Of particular note is the **Lincoln Center Out of Doors Festival** (*see p263*), which offers pared-down performances for children.

Circuses

Each spring, **Ringling Bros and Barnum & Bailey's** three-ring circus (*see p260*) comes to Madison Square Garden, and so do animal-rights picketers. You can't beat the world-famous circus for spectacle, but the one-ring alternatives listed below are more fun.

Big Apple Circus

Damrosch Park, Lincoln Center, 62nd Street, between Columbus & Amsterdam Avenues (1-212 268 2500/www.bigapplecircus.org). Subway: 1 to 66th Street-Lincoln Center. Dates Oct-Jan. Call or visit website for schedule and prices. Credit AmEx, Disc, MC, V.
New York's travelling circus was founded 28 years ago as an intimate answer to the Ringling Bros extravaganza. The clowns in this non-profit show are among the most creative in the country. The circus performs a special late-night show on New Year's Eve, at the end of which the entire audience joins the performers in the ring for a champagne (or apple juice) countdown.

UniverSoul Circus

1-800 316 7439/www.universoulcircus.com. Dates Early Apr-late May. Call or visit website for venue, schedule and prices. Credit AmEx, DC, Disc, MC, V.
This one-ring 'circus of colour' has the requisite clowns and animals with a twist: instead of familiar circus music, you get hip hop, R&B, salsa – and a morality-tale finale. The group usually appears in Brooklyn's Prospect Park in the spring.

Film

New York International Children's Film Festival

Various venues (1-212 349 0330/www.gkids.com). Dates Feb-Mar. Call or visit website for schedule and prices. Credit AmEx, MC, V.
This three-week fest is a hot ticket. An exciting mix of shorts and full-length features is presented to everyone from tots through teens. Many of the films are by international indie filmmakers – and not just those who make kids' flicks. Children determine the festival's winners, which are then screened at an awards ceremony.

Tribeca Film Festival

Various Tribeca venues (www.tribecafilmfestival.org). Dates 25 Apr-7 May 2006. Visit the website for schedule and prices. Credit AmEx, MC, V.
Robert De Niro's affair includes two weeks of screenings for kids, both commercial premières and shorts programmes, plus an outdoor street festival.

Museums & exhibitions

Museums usually offer weekend and school-break workshops as well as interactive exhibitions. Even the very young love exploring the **American Museum of Natural History**; its **Rose Center for Earth and Space** (*see p142*) features exhibits and a multimedia space show within the largest suspended glass cube in the US. Children of all ages will be fascinated by the amazing scale

Arts & Entertainment

model *Panorama of the City of New York* at the **Queens Museum of Art** (*see p165*) and by the toy collection at the **Museum of the City of New York** (*see p135*), which includes teddy bears, games, dolls and doll's houses. At the **American Museum of the Moving Image** (*see p163*), kids mess with *Jurassic Park* sound effects and play with moving-image technology. The **Intrepid Sea-Air-Space Museum** (*see p120*) houses interactive battle-related exhibits on an aircraft carrier. Many art museums offer family tours and workshops that may include sketching in the galleries, notably the **Brooklyn Museum** (*see p154*), the **Metropolitan Museum of Art** (*see p135*) and the **Whitney Museum of American Art** (*see p135*). The **Museum of Modern Art**, too (*see p124*), is now catering to families in its expanded midtown home; MoMA family programmes are free and include admission to the museum – which saves you a bundle.

Brooklyn Children's Museum

145 Brooklyn Avenue, at St Marks Avenue, Crown Heights, Brooklyn (1-718 735 4400/www.bchild mus.org). Subway: A to Nostrand Avenue; C to Kingston-Throop Avenue; 3 to Kingston Avenue. **Open** *Sept-Jun* 1-6pm Wed-Fri; 11am-6pm Sat, Sun. *Jul, Aug* 1-6pm Tue-Fri; 11am-6pm Sat, Sun. Call or visit website for holiday hours. **Admission** $4; free under-1s. **Credit** AmEx, Disc, MC, V.
Founded in 1899, BCM is the world's first museum designed for kids. It has more than 27,000 artefacts in its Collection Central gallery, including prehistoric fossils and present-day toys from around the world. Hands-on exhibits and live small animals rule the Animal Outpost, and the People Tube, a huge sewer pipe, connects four exhibit floors. On weekends, a free shuttle bus makes a circuit from the Grand Army Plaza subway station to the Brooklyn Museum and this museum. BCM is undergoing a major expansion into a new home – the world's first green museum building, scheduled to open in 2007 – so check the website before setting out.

Children's Museum of the Arts

182 Lafayette Street, between Broome & Grand Streets (1-212 941 9198/www.cmany.org). Subway: 6 to Spring Street. **Open** noon-5pm Wed, Fri-Sun; noon-6pm Thur. **Admission** $8. Voluntary donation 4-6pm Thur. **Credit** AmEx, MC, V ($35 minimum).
Kids under seven love this low-key museum and its floor-to-ceiling blackboards, art computers and vast store of art supplies.

Children's Museum of Manhattan

212 W 83rd Street, between Amsterdam Avenue & Broadway (1-212 721 1234/www.cmom.org). Subway: 1 to 86th Street. **Open** 10am-5pm Wed-Sun. Call for summer and holiday hours. **Admission** $8; $5 seniors; free under-1s. **Credit** AmEx, MC, V.
This children's museum promotes several types of literacy through interactive exhibitions. In the

Inventor Center, computer-savvy kids can take any idea they dream up – a flying bike, a talking robot – and design it onscreen using digital imaging.

New York Hall of Science

see p165 for listing.
Known for the 1964 World's Fair pavilion in which it is housed and the rockets from the US space programme that flank it, this museum has always been worth a trek for its discovery-based exhibits. Since its massive expansion in 2005, it's become a must for curious kids. The new building houses permanent hands-on exhibits that deal with 21st-century concepts such as networks, the science of sports and, in a massive preschool-science area, the urban world. From March through December, the 30,000sq ft outdoor Science Playground teaches children the principles of balance, gravity and energy. Other standouts include the first interactive exhibit devoted to maths (designed by Charles and Ray Eames).

Sony Wonder Technology Lab

Sony Plaza, 56th Street, between Fifth & Madison Avenues (1-212 833 8100/www.sonywonder techlab.com). Subway: E, V to Fifth Avenue-53rd Street; N, R, W to Fifth Avenue-59th Street. **Open** 10am-5pm Tue-Sat; noon-5pm Sun; reservations recommended. **Admission** free.
Recently refurbished and expanded, this digital wonderland lets visitors use state-of-the-art communication technology to play at designing video games, assisting in surgery, editing a TV show and operating robots. A new exhibit even lets visitors rock out in a band. Children eight and older get the most out of this place.

Outdoor places

Battery Park City Parks

Battery Park City, Hudson River, between Chambers Street & Battery Place (1-212 267 9700/www.bpc parks.org). Subway: A, C, 1, 2, 3 to Chambers Street; 1 to Rector Street. **Open** 6am-1am daily. **Admission** free.
Besides watching the boats along the Hudson, kids can enjoy one of New York's best playgrounds, an open field for ball games, Frisbee and lazing, and a park house that has balls, board games and other toys for the borrowing. Kids' events are held May to October (visit the website for a schedule). Don't miss the picnic garden near the Chambers Street entrance, where kids love to interpret (and climb on) sculptor Tom Otterness's *Real World* installation.

Riverbank State Park

Hudson River, at 145th Street (1-212 694 3600). Subway: 1 to 145th Street. **Open** 6am-11pm daily. *Ice-skating* Nov-Jan; call for hours. **Admission** free. *Rink* $1; *skate rental* $4.
Besides the skating rink and other athletic facilities, the main draw at this unusual 28-acre park is the Totally Kid Carousel (open June through August), designed by children.

Boning up on dinos at the **Museum of Natural History**. *See p284.*

Central Park

Most New Yorkers don't have their own garden – instead, they have public parks. The most popular is **Central Park**, with places and programmes just for kids. (Visit www.central parknyc.org for a calendar.) Don't miss the beautiful antique carousel (April to November 10am to 6pm daily; December to April 10am to 4.30pm Saturday and Sunday; $1.25 a ride). The Heckscher Playground (one of 20) will soon boast an up-to-date adventure area.

Central Park Zoo
see p133 for listing.
The stars of this refurbished wildlife centre are the polar bears and penguins, which live in glass habitats so you can watch their underwater antics.

Conservatory Water
Central Park, entrance on Fifth Avenue, at 72nd Street. Subway: 6 to 68th Street-Hunter College. **Open** *Jul, Aug* 11am-7pm Mon-Fri, Sun; 2-7pm Sat, weather permitting. **Admission** free.
Stuart Little Pond, named after EB White's storybook mouse, is a mecca for model-yacht racers. When the boat master is around, rent a remote-controlled vessel ($10 per hour).

Henry Luce Nature Observatory
see p133 for listing.
Inside the Gothic Belvedere Castle, telescopes, microscopes and hands-on exhibits teach kids about the plants and animals living in the park. With ID, you can borrow a Discovery Kit: binoculars, a birdwatching guide and other cool tools.
North Meadow Recreation Center
Central Park, Midpark, at 97th Street (1-212 348 4867/www.centralparknyc.org). Subway: B, C, 6 to 96th Street. **Open** Check website for hours. **Admission** free.

Park visitors with photo ID can check out the Field Day Kit, which includes a Frisbee, hula hoop, jump rope, kickball, and Wiffle ball and bat.

Victorian Gardens
Central Park, Wollman Rink (1-212 982 2229/ www.victoriangardensnyc. com). Subway: N, R, W to Fifth Avenue-59th Street. **Open** *Mid May-early Sept* 11am-7pm Mon-Fri; 10am-8pm Sat, Sun. **Admission** $6 (includes 2 rides), children under 3ft (1m) tall free with adult; additional rides $1 each or $20 for 24; pay one price (for unlimited rides) $18. **No credit cards**.
Central Park's first Disneyesque feature is this nostalgia-themed amusement park geared to young children. The mini teacup carousel and Rio Grande train are bound to be hits with little kids.

Wollman Rink
see p339 for listing.
Skating in Central Park amid snowy trees, with grand apartment buildings towering in the distance, is a New York tradition. This popular (read: crowded) rink offers lessons and skate rentals, plus a snack bar where you can warm up with hot chocolate.

Gardens

Brooklyn Botanic Garden
see p154 for listing.
In the 13,000sq ft Discovery Garden, children can play botanist, make toys out of natural materials, weave a wall, and generally get their hands dirty.

New York Botanical Garden
see p168 for listing.
The Everett Children's Adventure Garden is a whimsical museum of the natural world. In the Family Garden (open from early spring through to late October) kids can run under a giant caterpillar topiary, poke around in a touch-tank, and plant or harvest vegetables.

Arts & Entertainment

Here's to the babies who brunch

On weekends, New Yorkers do brunch. And that includes very young New Yorkers, who no longer have to whine and fidget as their parents dawdle over that third cup of coffee. Instead of just tossing a handful of crayons on the table, many restaurants now offer creative distractions for the juice-box set. Movies, live music and separate playrooms leave grown-ups free to luxuriate in a couple of almost-like-the-old-days hours. Here's where to join the locals – with tots in tow – in this popular culinary ritual.

Big City Bar and Grill

1600 Third Avenue, at 90th Street (1-212 369 0808). Subway: 4, 5, 6 to 86th Street. **Open** noon-4pm Sat, Sun. **Credit** MC, V.
This huge, noisy all-American joint offers PlayDine, an in-house play area supervised by child-care professionals, during its brunch service. (PlayDine is available during lunch and dinner, too.) For a charge of $10 per child (less for additional children), kids play out of earshot while parents indulge in a leisurely meal of fancy frittatas, eggs Benedict or apple pancakes. A quick-order kids' menu lets the wee ones scarf down some French toast before heading to the playroom.

Bubby's

1 Main Street, between Plymouth & Water Streets, Dumbo, Brooklyn (1-718 222 0666/www.bubbys.com). Subway: A, C to High Street; F to York Avenue. **Open** 10am-4pm Sat, Sun. **Credit** MC, V.
Want to skip the subway for once? From the South Street Seaport, take a fun five-minute New York Water Taxi ride across the river to the Fulton Ferry Landing. At the Brooklyn outpost of this famously family-friendly Tribeca restaurant, a well-stocked play area (plus crayons and balloons at the table) keeps little hands occupied while adults chow down on spicy huevos rancheros and the like. Bonus: across the street, there's a scenic waterfront playground. Don't forget to grab cones at the Brooklyn Ice Cream Factory nearby. Pictured right.
Other locations: 120 Hudson Street, at North Moore Street (1-212 219 0666).

Church Lounge

Tribeca Grand Hotel, 2 Sixth Avenue, between Church & White Streets (1-212 519 6677/www.tribecagrand.com). Subway: A, C, E to Canal Street. **Open** 10am-3pm Sun. **Credit** AmEx, MC, V.

Performing arts

Adventures of Maya the Bee

45 Bleecker Theater, 45 Bleecker Street, at Lafayette Street (1-212 253 9983/www.45bleecker.com/maya.html). Subway: B, D, F, V to Broadway-Lafayette Street; 6 to Bleecker Street. **Shows** *Oct-Jun* 11am Sat. **Tickets** $15. **Credit** AmEx, MC, V.
The star of the Culture Project's long-running jazz puppet play is the sweetest little bee that kids are likely to meet. But some of the creatures Maya encounters are not so nice – this is the insect world, after all. Recommended for five to nines.

Carnegie Hall Family Concerts

see p328 for listing. **Tickets** $8.
Even kids who profess to hate classical music are usually impressed by a visit to Carnegie Hall. The Family Concert series features first-rate classical, world-music and jazz performers, along with pre-concert workshops and storytelling. Concerts run from autumn through spring and are recommended for aged five to 12.

Family Matters

For listing, see p354 **Dance Theater Workshop**. **Tickets** $20; children $10.

Curated by a pair of choreographer parents and geared for children aged three and up (some shows are for pre-teens and teens), Family Matters is a quirky variety show blending art, dance, music and theatre. Call or check the website for a schedule.

Jazz for Young People

For listing, see p323.
These participatory concerts, held at Jazz at Lincoln Center's sparkling new digs and modelled on the New York Philharmonic Young People's Concerts, are led by the trumpeter and all-round jazz great Wynton Marsalis.

Kids'n Comedy

Gotham Comedy Club, 34 W 22nd Street, between Fifth & Sixth Avenues (1-212 877 6115/www.kidsncomedy.com). Subway: F, N, R, V, W to 23rd Street. **Shows** Call or visit website for schedule; reservations required. **Tickets** $15 plus one-drink minimum. **Credit** AmEx, MC, V.
Kids'n Comedy has developed a stable of funny kids, aged nine to 17, who deliver their own stand-up material, much of it mined from the homework-sucks vein (and some of it clearly culled from Daddy's last cocktail party).

For $25, adults can linger over the fabulous all-you-can-eat smörgåsbord and snort down Bloody Marys from the handsome bar, while kids gobble their $10 brunch and then watch seasonal movies. Toddlers can snack for free on whatever looks tasty, be it sushi, mac and cheese, or a Mickey Mouse-shaped waffle. It's child-friendly but quite upscale.

Iridium Jazz Club

1650 Broadway, at 51st Street (1-212 582 2121). B, D, E to Seventh Avenue; N, R, W to 49th Street; 1 to 50th Street. **Open** 11am-3pm Sun. **Credit** AmEx, MC, V.
Many folks remember Bob Dorough as the host of TV's *Schoolhouse Rock*. But Dorough, now 81, was a disciple of Charlie Parker and contributed to a '60s Miles Davis album. So the ponytailed hepcat puts a little bit of everything on the menu – including 'Conjunction Junction' – when he and his trio play the weekly jazz brunch at Iridium. Guests, some of them kids, often join him onstage, and the all-you-can-eat buffet ($22) is a treat. Older kids should have a great time here.

La Belle Epoque

827 Broadway, between 12th and 13th Streets (1-212 254 6436/www.belleepoquenyc.com). Subway: L, N, Q, R, W, 4, 5, 6 to 14th Street-Union Square. **Open** noon-3pm one Sat a month. Call for exact date. **Credit** MC, V.
At this New Orleans-style club and restaurant, the monthly baby brunch keeps little ones busy with blocks, Pack 'n' Plays, Exersaucers and doll strollers. Adults can enjoy tasty made-to-order omelettes.

Little Orchestra Society

Various venues (1-212 971 9500/www.little orchestra.org). **Tickets** $12-$50. **Credit** MC, V.
Since 1947, this orchestra has presented classical concerts for kids, including the popular interactive *Peter and the Wolf* for pre-schoolers and December's spectacular *Amahl and the Night Visitors*, complete with real live sheep.

New Victory Theater

see p349 for listing. **Tickets** $10-$50.
As New York's only full-scale young people's theatre, the New Victory presents international theatre and dance companies at junior prices. Shows often sell out well in advance, so reserve seats early.

New York Theatre Ballet

Florence Gould Hall, 55 E 59th Street, between Madison & Park Avenues (1-212 355 6160/www. nytb.org). Subway: N, R, W to Lexington Avenue-59th Street; 4, 5, 6 to 59th Street. **Tickets** $30; $25 under-12s. Tickets also available through Ticketmaster. **Credit** AmEx, MC, V.
Enjoy one-hour adaptations of classic ballets such as *The Nutcracker*. The interactive *Carnival of the Animals* teaches the audience basic dance moves, and *Alice in Wonderland* is a vaudeville-style romp.

Swedish Cottage Marionette Theater

Central Park West, at 81st Street (1-212 988 9093). Subway: B, C to 81st Street-Museum of Natural History. **Shows** *Oct-Jun* 10.30am, noon Tue-Fri; 1pm Sat. *Jul, Aug* 10.30am, noon Mon-Fri. **Tickets** $6; $5 children. **No credit cards.**
Reservations are essential at this intimate theatre, located in an old Swedish schoolhouse run by the City Parks Foundation.

Theatreworks/NYC

Lucille Lortel Theatre, 121 Christopher Street, between Bleecker & Hudson Streets (1-212 627 7373/www.theatreworksusa.org). Subway: 1 to Christopher Street. **Shows** Nov, Dec, March, Apr, Jul, Aug. **Tickets** $35. **Credit** AmEx, MC, V.
Over a period of 45 years, the travelling company Theatreworks/USA has developed a reputation for producing dependable, if somewhat bland, mostly musical adaptations of kid-lit classics. The company finally formed a New York arm in 2005. Based at the legendary Lortel Theatre, once home to Lucille Lortel, the 'Queen of Off-Broadway', it promises to uphold the Theatreworks tradition, but with better production values.

Arts & Entertainment

Urban Word NYC

Various venues (www.urbanwordnyc.org).
A DJ hosts poetry slams and open mics for 'the next generation'. Teens bring their own (uncensored) poems and freestyle rhymes or give props to other kids performing theirs.

Sports & activities

For bicycling, horseback riding and ice-skating, *see pp334-340* **Sport & Fitness**.

Downtown Boathouse

Pier 40, at Houston Street (1-646 613 0375/ www.downtownboathouse.org). Subway: 1 to Houston Street. **Open** *15 May-15 Oct* 9am-6pm daily.
From May to October, weather permitting, this volunteer-run organisation offers free kayaking (no appointment necessary) on weekends. They also offer free Wednesday-evening classes and three-hour guided kayak trips on weekend mornings. All trips are offered on a first-come, first-served basis, and you must be able to swim.
Other locations: Pier 96, at 56 Street; Riverside Park South Pier, at 72nd Street.

Chelsea Piers

Piers 59-62, W 17th through 23rd Streets, at Eleventh Avenue (1-212 336 6666/www.chelsea piers.com). Subway: C, E to 23rd Street.
A roller rink, gymnasium, pool, toddler gym and extreme-skating park help kids burn energy. You'll also find ice-skating rinks, batting cages and rock-climbing walls in this vast complex. Day passes are available. The Flip 'n' Flick programme (occasional Saturdays, 7-11pm) allows parents to get a night off while the kids enjoy athletic activities and a movie. *See also p337.*

Sydney's Playground

66 White Street, between Broadway & Church Street (1-212 431 9125/www.sydneys playground.com). Subway: J, M, N, Q, R, W, Z, 6 to Canal Street. **Open** *Sept-May* 10am-6pm daily; *Memorial Day-Labor Day* 10am-6pm Mon-Fri. **Admission** $8.50.
Credit AmEx, Disc, MC, V.
This huge, architecturally striking indoor play space has been designed to resemble a streetscape, complete with a multilevel 'climbing city', a 'roadway' for ride-on toys and a café.

Trapeze School New York

see p340 for listing.
Kids over six can fly through the air with the greatest of ease. (You can also just stop along the esplanade and watch.) Children under 12 must be accompanied by an adult.

Willy Bee's Family Lounge

302 Metropolitan Avenue, between Driggs Avenue & Roebling Street, Williamsburg, Brooklyn (1-718 599 3499/www.willybees.com).

Subway: L to Bedford Avenue. **Open** 9am-7pm Mon-Thur; 9am-8pm Fri; 10am-8pm Sat; 10am-6pm Sun. **Credit** MC, V.
NYC's hippest neighbourhood, just across the river from the Lower East Side, has started turning into baby central as its artsy residents couple and pro-create. Visit for a blast of alternakid culture and a pit stop at Willy Bee's café and play space, a favourite hangout for local parents. You can sip wine while the children check out the toys, draw on the blackboard or mess around in the backyard.

Tours

ARTime

1-718 797 1573. **Open** *Oct-Jun* 11am-12.30pm first Sat of the month. **Admission** $25 per parent-child pair, $5 each additional child. **No credit cards**.
Since 1994, art historians with education backgrounds have led contemporary-art tours of Chelsea galleries for kids aged five to ten.

Confino Family Apartment Tour

For listing, see p103 **Lower East Side Tenement Museum**.
A weekly interactive tour teaches children aged five to 14 about immigrant life in the early 20th century. Kids participate in games, try on period costumes and handle knick-knacks from that era.

Zoos

Bronx Zoo

Bronx River Parkway, at Fordham Road (1-718 367 1010/www.bronxzoo.org). Subway: 2, 5 to West Farms Square-East Tremont Avenue. **Open** *Apr-Oct* 10am-5pm Mon-Fri; 10am-5.30pm Sat, Sun, holidays. *Nov-Mar* 10am-4.30pm daily. **Admission** *Apr-Oct* $12; $9 seniors & children; free under-2s. *Nov-Mar* $8; $6 seniors & children; free under-2s. Voluntary donation Wed. (Some rides and exhibitions are extra.) **Credit** AmEx, DC, Disc, MC, V.
Inside the Bronx Zoo is the Bronx Children's Zoo, with lots of domesticated critters to pet, plus exhibits that show the world from an animal's point of view. Beyond the Children's Zoo, camel rides (April through October) and sea-lion feedings (11am and 3pm) are other can't-miss attractions for visitors with kids. Take a spin on the new Bug Carousel, where kids straddle gigantic insects. *See also p169.*

New York Aquarium

610 Surf Avenue, at West 8th Street, Coney Island, Brooklyn (1-718 265 3474/www.nyaquarium.com). Subway: D to Coney Island-Stillwell Avenue; F, Q to W 8th Street-NY Aquarium. **Open** Visit website for hours. **Admission** $11; $7 seniors and 2-12s; free under-2s. **Credit** AmEx, Disc, MC, V.
Like the rest of Coney Island, this aquarium is just a little shabby, but kids enjoy seeing the famous beluga-whale family, the scary sharks and the entertaining sea-lion show – and then taking a stroll along the Coney Island boardwalk.

Clubs

Get into the groove.

New York is high on the list of cities that helped incubate the concept of innovative clubbing. Starting with 1960's freak-out dens like the Electric Circus, continuing with musically pioneering spots such as the Loft and the Paradise Garage, and advancing the art-nightlife connection via the Mudd Club, Jackie 60 et al – the city's after-dark denizens had long pushed the notion that clubs could be more than a place to get blotto, traipse around on the dancefloor and go home with a new friend. Even more recently, in hotspots such as Twilo and Vinyl, there was always the feeling that going to clubs really meant something – forgetting about the outside world and travelling a road towards an ecstatic, almost religious sort of experience.

In the last decade or so, that type of clubbing seems to have vanished in NYC. In the '90s, most niteries existed merely to separate a sucker from their dough – and there are more

than enough of those around to fill the bevy of upscale, bottle-service spots that have opened in the last several years. (In our book, $250 and upwards for a jug of mediocre hooch is a rip – table privileges or not.) Granted, the NYC after-dark arena has always been about money to some extent. Studio 54 proprietor Steve Rubell, for instance, famously tried to evade the tax revenuers by stuffing trash bags full of cash into the ceiling of the club's basement. But even a mercenary like Rubell knows that Studio 54 was primarily a *scene,* and for all his faults – for one, he also helped to popularise the velvet rope – he expended untold energy in creating and maintaining that scene.

Still, there is an army of New Yorkers yearning for a nightlife utopia where forward-thinking frolicking is the rule, and where sub-Paris Hilton types and their striped-shirt attendants aren't the ones calling the shots. In the last few years, a number of new venues

Spirit. *See p294.*

Spirit. *See p294.*

Arts & Entertainment

have popped up – **Sullivan Room**, **Cielo** and **Love** among them – that have cool music and a great vibe as their mandate, and that strive to make nightlife the innocently tribal activity it can be. Add clubs like them to old favourites such as **Club Shelter**, **Subtonic Lounge**, the **Giant Step** parties and the **Motherfucker** soirées, and you have the makings of a nightlife that would be the envy of most burgs. The problem is in keeping up with the ever-shifting landscape. The following listings are a good place to start but also check up-to-date party-listing websites such as Rhythmism (www.rhythmism.com), subscribe to email newsletters like Beyond Events (send a mail to nyc_electronic_events_calendar-subscribe@yahoogroups.com to get on the list) or – best yet – pick up a copy of *Time Out New York*.

Note that few clubs take credit cards and those that do may require a minimum spend.

Clubs

Cielo

18 Little W 12th Street, between Ninth Avenue & Washington Street (1-212 645 5700/www.cieloclub.com). Subway: A, C, E to 14th Street; L to Eighth Avenue. **Open** 10pm-4am daily. **Cover** $5-$20. **Average drink** $10.

You'd never guess from the red carpet and the Euro dude manning the door that the attitude inside this boîte is zero, at least on weeknights. It's a wonderful little joint – the urban-ski-lodge decor looks terrific, the sunken dancefloor is a nice touch, and the place boasts one of the city's clearest sound systems. (Weekends are a slightly different matter, though, with all of the tables reserved for those willing to drop a wad for a bottle of hooch.) The club features top-shelf house from world-class DJs, with everyone from Masters at Work's Louie Vega to drum 'n' bass superstar Roni Size having plied their trade here; every Monday Cielo is treated to DJ deity François K's dub-heavy Deep Space session. The club has won a bevy of 'best club' awards in its three years of existence – and deserves them. **Photo** *p294.*

Club Shelter

20 W 39th Street, between Fifth & Sixth Avenues (1-212 719 4479/www.clubshelter.com). Subway: B, D, F, V to 42nd Street-Bryant Park; 7 to Fifth Avenue. **Open** 11pm-noon Sat. **Cover** $15-$20. **Average drink** $6.

There's only one thing you need to know about Club Shelter: it's the home of the world-famous Shelter party. DJ Timmy 'the Maestro' Regisford is the ringmaster of this long-running Saturday night affair, spinning soulful house and classics to an enthusiastic (and sexually and racially mixed) crowd that doesn't leave until long after the sun rises on Sunday. During warm weather, the roof deck offers a view of the surrounding skyscrapers, but the real magic happens indoors, under the disco ball.

Copacabana

560 W 34th Street, at Eleventh Avenue (1-212 239 2672/www.copacabanany.com). Subway: A, C, E to 34th Street-Penn Station. **Open** 6pm-3am Tue, Thur; 10pm-5am Fri, Sat. **Cover** $5-$30. **Average drink** $9.

Miami meets Las Vegas in the Copa's pink-palm-tree-lined lobby. Women throw curves in skintight pants and peekaboo blouses; gentlemen bump it up a notch with suits and ties. Some 3,000 Latinos – and those who love them – pack the Copa's 48,000sq ft to dance the night away. Upstairs, live bands play salsa and merengue as synchronised showgirls shake the large dancefloor; for house music, make your way downstairs.

Crobar

530 W 28th Street, between Tenth & Eleventh Avenues (1-212 629 9000/www.crobar.com). Subway: C, E to 23rd Street. **Open** 10pm-7am Thur-Sat. **Cover** $20-$30. **Average drink** $9.

The splendiferous Crobar is as close to a full-on superclub as NYC has to offer: it can squeeze 2,750 revellers into its amazing main room and pair of smaller party dens, it has a great sound system, and it flashes the many varieties of disco lights that modern science has produced. As with most huge ventures, though, the beats tend to lean towards the lowest-common-denominator end of the dance-music spectrum. Regardless, the club has to be commended for taking an occasional chance, organising visits from the likes of twisted-beat merchant Superchumbo and the thum-house pioneers of Miami's Murk. This is a must-see on the city's after-dark circuit.

Lightship Frying Pan

Pier 63, Twelfth Avenue, at 23rd Street (1-212 989 6363/www.fryingpan.com). Subway: C, E to 23rd Street. **Open** Dates and times vary. **Cover** $5-$10. **Average drink** $6.

A one-time floating lighthouse salvaged from the briny deep, this lightship has found new life as one of the city's more eccentric spots to toss a party. The stationary vessel is basically a lovable floating scrap heap, with ferric oxide as the design element of choice. It's hard to believe that the Frying Pan is legal for revelry. Apparently, the city has trouble believing it as well: the boat and its adjacent pier have been shut down numerous times by the city elders. When she's open for business, though, the Pan is a blast – there's something about being on the water that brings out the drunken sailor in every clubber. The best night is Friday when DJs Nickodemus and Mariano – none other than the dub-funky Turntables on the Hudson crew (*see p296*) – man the decks.

Lotus

409 W 14th Street, between Ninth Avenue & Washington Street (1-212 243 4420/www.lotusnewyork.com). Subway: A, C, E to 14th Street; L to Eighth Avenue. **Open** 10pm-4am daily. **Cover** $20. **Average drink** $8.

Lotus was one of the first upscale clubs to invade the once-scuzzy Meatpacking District, and so it immediately attracted legions of celebs, models and gawkers. Happily, the venue's trendy patina has faded, and now Lotus can be fully appreciated as a well-furnished restaurant, lounge and dance club where DJs spin a mainstream mix of sounds to an affluent bridge-and-tunnel crowd. Friday nights are still the best, when the GBH crew takes over to lend the club a sheen of downtown hipsterism. Getting past the doorman hasn't got any easier, so make sure you dress to impress.

Love
40 W 8th Street, at MacDougal Street (1-212 477 5683/www.musicislove.net). Subway: A, B, C, D, E, F, V to W 4th Street; R, W to 8th Street-NYU (W weekdays only). **Open** 10pm-4am Wed-Sat; 5pm-1am Sun. **Cover** $10-$15. **Average drink** $6.
Love, the latest addition to the city's clubbing landscape, is an anomaly; its focus is squarely on the music (mostly of the deep-house variety) and on building a scene. It's hardly a revolutionary concept, but in today's nightlife world of going for the quick buck, it helps Love to stand out. The main room is a sparely furnished bare box, but the DJ line-up is pretty impressive – names on the level of Kenny 'Dope' Gonzales, Body & Soul's Joe Claussell and Metro Area have all graced the decks here – and the sound system is one of New York's finest.

Marquee
289 Tenth Avenue, between 26th & 27th Streets (1-646 473 0202). Subway: C, E to 23rd Street. **Open** 10pm-4am Tue-Sat. **Cover** $20. **Average drink** $9.

The centrepiece of Marquee, which is located in a former garage, is a spectacular double-sided staircase that leads to the mezzanine, where a glass wall overlooks the action below. Although not quite as searingly red-hot as it was when it opened in '03, the 600-person space remains very popular – in other words, you're likely to have trouble getting past the velvet rope. The deejayed music tends towards radio-friendly, none-too-thought-provoking hip hop, pop and rock.

Pyramid
101 Avenue A, between 6th & 7th Streets (1-212 228 4888). Subway: F, V to Lower East Side-Second Avenue; L to First Avenue; 6 to Astor Place. **Open** 10pm-4am daily. **Cover** free-$15. **Average drink** $7.
In a clubbing era long gone, the Pyramid was a cornerstone of forward-thinking queer club culture. In what could be considered a sign of the times, the venue's sole remaining gay soirée is Friday night's non-progressive '80s dance-fest, 1984. Otherwise, the charmingly decrepit space features the long-running drum 'n' bass bash Konkrete Jungle, as well as a rotating roster of goth and new-wave affairs.

Roxy
515 W 18th Street, between Tenth & Eleventh Avenues (1-212 645 5156/www.roxynyc.com). Subway: A, C, E to 14th Street; L to Eighth Avenue. **Open** 8pm-2am (roller-skating only) Wed; 11pm-4am Fri; 11pm-6am Sat. **Cover** $15-$30. **Average drink** $8.
Roxy began its life as a humongous roller-skating rink (the immense main room can squeeze 2,200 revellers on to its dancefloor), but in the early '80s,

Club rules

Clubbing in NYC can be a little intimidating. Keep this simple advice in mind to avoid the most common pitfalls.

Avoid run-ins with the law
Know that you may be searched – so leave weapons at home (duh). Also, the city's nightlife crackdown has made clubs very paranoid about drug use. Be smart.

Dress the part
If you're going to a trendy spot, look sharp – those dirty Cons and XXL-size tees ain't gonna cut it. But if you're heading to a grunge pit, leave the Armani at home.

Guys, don't travel in packs
In order to maintain a gender balance, straight-oriented venues often refuse entry to large groups of men. But if you're heading to a gay-leaning spot, the more, the merrier!

Make nice at the door
Screaming 'I'm on the list!' (even if you are) won't get you anywhere with seen-it-all doormen. However, a smile and a bit of patience might. And don't forget ID!

Phone ahead
Parties can change line-up or location at a moment's notice. Before you leave, call the club, visit its website or check a current issue of *Time Out New York*.

Pick your night wisely
If possible, hit the clubs any night except Friday or Saturday; going out on weekdays ensures you'll be hanging with the cool kids.

Play it safe
The subway is a lot safer than it used to be, but if you're out late, we recommend that you take a cab or a car service home (*see p369*).

Cielo. See p292.

it became a great cross-cultural hangout, with B-boys poppin' and lockin' as downtown arty types looked on. Nowadays, it's known for Saturday night's massive boy bash, with thousands of hedonists (including a smattering of women and straight men) dancing on house beats all night long. Fridays showcase mixed sounds that range from hip hop to events featuring superstar DJs like Paul van Dyke. On Wednesdays, Roxy stays true to its roots with a roller-skating jam.

Sapphire

249 Eldridge Street, between Houston & Stanton Streets (1-212 777 5153/www.sapphirenyc. com). Subway: F, V to Lower East Side-Second Avenue. **Open** 7pm-4am daily. **Cover** $5. **Average drink** $5.

Itty-bitty Sapphire was one of the first Lower East Side bars to feature DJs, and its management had the foresight to secure a cabaret licence before the city authorities clamped down. Mondays through Wednesdays, the music falls somewhere along the

techno-house-disco continuum, and local heroes E-man and Melvin Moore are joined by the occasional slumming-it big name. Thursdays through Saturdays, hip hop and funk rule, with beloved veteran DJ Jazzy Nice often running things. A word of warning though: weekends can be quite brutally crowded, so dress to sweat.

Spirit

530 W 27th Street, between Tenth & Eleventh Avenues (1-212 268 9477/www.spiritnewyork.com). Subway: C, E to 23rd Street. **Open** 10pm-5am Fri, Sat. **Cover** free-$30. **Average drink** $8.

The sister club to one of Dublin's top niteries (www.spiritdublin.com) has had to battle the ghosts of the address's former tenant, the much-missed Twilo. Going further back in time, the spot was home to the original Sound Factory. So far, it's been a tough battle. When Spirit first opened in 2004, it tried using Twilo-style forward-thinking house and techno; crowds were sparse. Next, the club tried an utterly mainstream approach, to much the same

Sullivan Room

*218 Sullivan Street, between Bleecker & W 3rd
Streets (1-212 252 2151/www.sullivanroom.com).
Subway: A, B, C, D, E, F, V to W 4th Street.*
Open 10pm-4am Mon, Tue, Thur-Sat. **Cover**
$5-$15. **Credit** AmEx, Disc, MC, V.
Where's the party? It's right here in this unmarked
subterranean space, which hosts some of the best
deep-house, tech-house and breaks bashes the city
has to offer. It's an utterly unpretentious club, with
little of the glitz that bigger clubs feature – but hell,
all you really need are some thumpin' beats and a
place to move your feet, right?

Table 50

*643 Broadway, at Bleecker Street (1-212 253
2560/www.table50.com). Subway: B, D, F, V
to Broadway-Lafayette Street; 6 to Bleecker
Street.* **Open** 10pm-4am daily. **Cover** free-$10.
Average drink $10.
If you disregard the sometimes-sniffy door policy,
Table 50 is a fine place to while away your evening.
The fully licensed club (meaning you can actually
dance) has a speakeasy vibe to it, with its hard-to-
find door, dark lighting and exposed brick making
it a good choice for a bit of clandestine canoodling.
The music – ranging from Mark Ronson's none-too-
deep party mix to full-bore house music – can be a
bit obvious, but at least the sound system is decent.

Webster Hall

*125 E 11th Street, between Third & Fourth
Avenues (1-212 353 1600/www.webster-hall.com).
Subway: L, N, Q, R, W, 4, 5, 6 to 14th Street-Union
Square.* **Open** 10pm-5am Thur-Sat. **Cover** free-$30.
Average drink $6.
Should you crave the sight of big hair, muscle shirts
and gold chains, Webster Hall offers all that and,
well, not much more. The grand four-level space,
built in the 1800s as a dance hall, is nice enough, and
the DJs aren't bad (choose from disco, hip hop, soul,
Latin, progressive house or pop hits), but it's hard
to forget who you're sharing the dancefloor with.
Wet T-shirt and striptease contests ratchet up the
get-me-out-of-here ambience.

Lounges & DJ bars

APT

*419 W 13th Street, between Ninth Avenue &
Washington Street (1-212 414 4245/www.apt
website.com). Subway: A, C, E to 14th Street; L to
Eighth Avenue.* **Open** 7pm-4am daily. **Cover** varies.
Average drink $9.
Labelled 'snootissimo' when it opened, this bi-level
boîte is now the city's prime place for hearing cool
underground beats. Everyone from techno deity Carl
Craig to Zulu Nation founder Afrika Bambaataa has
played the platters here, in either the sleek basement
bar or the cosy, well-appointed street-level room.
The resident spinners – no slouches themselves –
include lounge-kitsch slinger Ursula 1000, the elec-
trofunky Negroclash crew, soulful-house guru Neil

effect. Things have gotten somewhat better more
recently, though, with the Made Event crew occasionally taking over the space to feature DJs of the
international calibre of prog-tech titan Danny
Tenaglia, from Tyrant, and Lee Burridge taking
control of the Technics. **Photo** *p291.*

Subtonic Lounge at Tonic

*107 Norfolk Street, between Delancey & Rivington
Streets (1-212 358 7501/www.tonicnyc.com).
Subway: F to Delancey Street; J, M, Z to Delancey-
Essex Streets.* **Open** 7.30pm-2am Thur-Sat. **Cover**
free-$12. **Average drink** $6.
Subtonic Lounge, the unadorned basement of the
Lower East Side's avant-bohemian Tonic performance space, features the Friday night Bunker bash,
where DJs spin a myriad underground beats ranging from challenging IDM to straight-up techno. The
sound system might not be all that, but the party
throwers and the patrons (who rest on banquettes
inside giant, ancient wine casks) make up for it with
sheer exuberance. For **Tonic**, *see p322.*

Arts & Entertainment

Aline and deep-disco master DJ Spun. APT becomes sardine-packed on weekends and on headliner guest nights, but at least you're squeezed in with one of the best-looking crowds in town.

Slipper Room

167 Orchard Street, at Stanton Street (1-212 253 7246/www.slipperroom.com). Subway: F, V to Lower East Side-Second Avenue. **Open** 8pm-4am Tue-Sat. **Average drink** $8.

New York City has a healthy neo-burlesque scene, and the petite Slipper Room is, if not at that scene's nexus, pretty darn near it. Many of the Victorian-looking venue's happenings, notably Friday's Hot Box hoedown, feature plenty of bump-and-grind action, with DJs spinning the appropriate beats; the occasional live band completes the picture.

Studios

Tribeca Grand Hotel, 2 Sixth Avenue, between Walker & White Streets (1-212 519 6677/www. tribecagrand.com). Subway: A, C, E to Canal Street; 1, 9 to Franklin Street. **Open** 9pm-2am daily. **Average drink** $10.

When the Tribeca Grand first started showcasing DJs and live music in its downstairs, club-like sanctum, it unexpectedly became one of the city's top spots for underground beats – thanks mostly to its totally of-the-moment electroclash and nu-rock. Things have calmed down a lot since then, but the place still rocks at the Saturday night Fixed affair, where groundbreaking DJs and live acts – folks like Glasgow's Optimo and crazed bleep-funk duo Mu – sometimes hold court. Always call before visiting as the room is also used for functions.

Triple Crown

108 Bedford Avenue, at North 11th Street, Williamsburg, Brooklyn (1-718 388 8883/ www.triplecrownpage.com). Subway: L to Bedford Avenue. **Open** 6pm-4am daily. **Average drink** $8.

Since its fall '04 opening, the sleek Williamsburg lounge Triple Crown has managed to rise to the top of the city's hip-hop venues. Granted, the competition for that status isn't exactly fierce, but when you regularly score spinners on the level of Rob Swift from the X-Ecutioners, A Tribe Called Quest's Ali Shaheed Muhammad and old-school legend Schooly D, you're obviously doing something right.

Roving & seasonal parties

New York has a number of peripatetic and season-specific shindigs. Nights, locations and prices vary, so telephone, email or hit the websites for the latest updates.

Cooper-Hewitt Summer Sessions: Design + DJs + Dancing

For listing, see p135 **Cooper-Hewitt, National Design Museum. Open** *Jul, Aug* 6-9pm Fri. **Cover** $10 (includes museum admission). **Average drink** $8.

In the warmer months, the city's premier design museum hosts after-work revelry, but these aren't garden parties in the traditional sense. DJs ranging from local funksters to international superstars work the crowd with all manner of underground beats. Still, the vibe is a lot more genteel than the similar PS 1 Warm Up party (*see below*).

Giant Step

www.giantstep.net.

Giant Step parties have been among the best of the nu-soul scene since the early '90s – back before there was a nu-soul scene. Sadly, the gang doesn't throw nearly as many fêtes as it once did, now preferring to concentrate on live shows and record promotions. But on the rare occasion that Giant Step does decide to pack a dancefloor, don't miss it: the music is always great, and the multiculti crowd is gorgeous.

Motherfucker

www.motherfuckernyc.com.

This peripatetic, polysexual trash fest, helmed by veteran NYC scenesters Justine D, Michael T, Georgie Seville and Johnny T, is generally considered the best bash going in town right now. Held on the eves of major holidays at an array of the city's biggest clubs, it features Justine, Michael and guests spinning an anarchic mix of sleazed-out electro, new wave and disco, plus an utterly deviant menagerie of club freaks that you're likely to come across nowadays. In many ways, it's a throwback to the glory days of NYC's once-decadent clubbing scene.

PS 1 Warm Up

PS 1 Contemporary Art Center, 22-25 Jackson Avenue, at 45th Road, Jackson Heights, Queens (1-718 784 2084/www.ps1.org). Subway: E, V to 23rd Street-Ely Avenue; G to 21st Street-Jackson Avenue; 7 to 45th Road-Court House Square. **Open** *Jul-Sept* 2-9pm Sat. **Cover** $8 (includes museum admission). **Average drink** $5.

Back in '97, who could have guessed that the courtyard of the Museum of Modern Art-affiliated PS 1 Contemporary Art Center would play host to some of the most anticipated clubbing events in the city? Since the Warm Up series kicked off, summer Saturdays truly haven't been the same. Thousands of dance-music fanatics pack the space, swigging beer, dancing and generally making a mockery of the soirée's arty setting. The sounds range from spiritually inclined soul to full-bore techno, spun by local stars and international DJ deities.

Turntables on the Hudson

1-212 560 5593/www.turntablesonthehudson.com.

This ultrafunky affair has a permanent Friday home at the Lightship Frying Pan (*see p292*), but it pops up all over the place on other nights of the week. DJs Nickodemus, Mariano and their guests do the dub-funky, world-beat thing, and live percussionists add to the flavour. If you like to shake it, this is as good as it gets: wherever the Turntables party happens, the dancefloor is packed all night long.

Buzzworthy

Sleepy Face & DJ Boo, DJs & party promoters

The NYC nightlife power couple Sleepyface & DJ Boo (*pictured right*) is proof that persistence pays off. The DJ-promoters – known to their families and friends as married pair Mike and Begonia Gwertzman – have been part of the city's house-music mosaic for years, but it wasn't until they brought their Basic NYC bashes to Sullivan Room in February 2004 that they finally started getting the recognition they deserve. 'Crowds here definitely need some alternatives,' Begonia says. To that end, the couple has been inviting the sort of spinners who are too underground for the megaclubs but way too talented to be relegated to a dingy lounge with a crappy sound system: DJ Garth from San Francisco's Wicked Crew, James Curd of the Greenskeepers and Chicago's DJ Diz have been some recent coups.

Tim Sweeney, DJ & radio host

'I'm a lucky guy,' Tim Sweeney (*pictured below*) admits. At 25, he's the DJ-host of WNYU's beloved *Beats in Space* show, is livin' large as the soundtrack supervisor at Rockstar Games, holds down a residency at the ever-popular APT and spins at fringe shindigs all over town. (He's also scored internships with both the precedent-setting audio collagist Steinski and DFA Records,

where he holds a paying production-duties position.) As heard in the freewheeling *Beats in Space*, which has made him one of NYC's most in-demand DJs, Sweeney has a way with a bizarro mix. 'I don't know what to call what I do,' he says. But he sure can manage to toss sounds ranging from old-school hip hop to warped techno into the mix and make it work.

Nappy G, percussionist

'For some young people, the club scene replaced spirituality,' explains rhythm master Gordon Clay, aka Nappy G. 'Going to church was about getting together and singing, a bunch of people just vibing.' The son of African Methodist Episcopalian preachers, Clay spent many Sundays of his youth playing drums in their Kentucky church. Now, Sunday mornings might find him pounding alongside a DJ at a wild NYC dance party. He's still uniting people through drumming, but the setting is far removed from the chapel. The versatile musician, DJ, producer and MC has become the secret weapon of the Turntables on the Hudson crew; when Clay takes to his drum set to improvise with the global grooves of DJs Nickodemus and Mariano, the energy of the crowd rises exponentially. His uncanny ability to find the direct link between rhythms and movement comes from years playing for African dance classes in Manhattan and Haitian voodoo ceremonies in Brooklyn.

Film & TV

Let Hollywood play make-believe; New York City is the real deal.

From the original 1933 *King Kong* bounding up the Empire State Building to 2005's supersized remake, New York City has been – and always will be – a cherished site within our cultural consciousness. Even the briefest stay in Gotham can make you feel like you've walked on to the set of your favourite TV programme or movie: from a stroll past Trump Tower ('You're fired!') to a heart-to-heart in Central Park (virtually any film by Woody Allen).

Film

Simply put, New York is unparalleled for its daily range of offerings for the movie lover. Splashy multiplexes carry the latest Hollywood releases, but New York's real cinematic treasures are its dozens of revival, independent and foreign-film houses. And film festivals and retrospectives are all over town, year-round. For current listings, check daily newspapers or pick up an issue of *Time Out New York*.

Art & revival houses

Angelika Film Center
18 W Houston Street, at Mercer Street (1-212 995 2000/www.angelikafilmcenter.com). Subway: B, D, F, V to Broadway-Lafayette Street; N, R, W to Prince Street; 6 to Bleecker Street. **Tickets** $10.50; $7 seniors and under-12s. **Credit** AmEx, MC, V.
The six-screen Angelika emphasises independent fare, both American and foreign. The complex is a zoo on weekends, so come extra early or visit the website to buy advance tickets.

BAM Rose Cinemas
For listing, see p328 **Brooklyn Academy of Music. Tickets** $10; $7 students (Mon-Thur only); $6 seniors and children. **Credit** AmEx, MC, V.
Brooklyn's premier art-film venue does double duty as a repertory house for well-programmed classics and a first-run multiplex for independent films.

Cinema Village
22 E 12th Street, between Fifth Avenue & University Place (1-212 924 3363/www.cinemavillage.com). Subway: L, N, Q, R, W, 4, 5, 6 to 14th Street-Union Square. **Tickets** $10; $7.50 students; $5.50 seniors and under-13s. **Credit** MC, V.
The three-screen Cinema Village specialises in American indie flicks and foreign movies. Check out the appealing subway turnstile that admits ticket-holders to the lobby.

Film Forum
209 W Houston Street, between Sixth Avenue & Varick Street (1-212 727 8110/www.filmforum.com). Subway: 1 to Houston Street. **Tickets** $10; $5 seniors and under-12s (senior discount before 5pm Mon-Fri). **Credit** Cash only at box office; AmEx, MC, V on website.
Though the seats and sight lines leave something to be desired, this three-screen art theatre presents great documentaries, new and repertory films, and a cute crowd of budding NYU auteurs and film geeks in horn-rimmed glasses.

IFC Center
323 Sixth Avenue, at 3rd Street (1-212 924 7771/www.ifccenter.com). Subway: A, B, C, D, E, F, V to W 4th Street. **Tickets** $10.75; $7 seniors and under-12s. **Credit** AmEx, MC, V.
The long-darkened Waverly has risen again as a modernised three-screen art house, showing the latest indie hits, choice midnight cult items and the occasional foreign classic. A high-toned café provides sweets, lattes and substantials; you may find yourself rubbing elbows with the talent on screen, since many come to introduce their work on opening night.

The ImaginAsian
239 E 59th Street, between Second & Third Avenues (1-212 371 6682/www.theimaginasian.com). Subway: N, R, W to Lexington Avenue-59th Street; 4, 5, 6 to 59th Street. **Tickets** $10; $8 seniors and under-12s. **Credit** MC, V.
Since its 2004 rechristening, this 300-seat movie palace, once named after DW Griffith, has faithfully devoted itself to all things Asian or Asian-American. Typical fare includes jolting J-horror freakouts, cutting-edge Korean dramas and the latest dance moves bustin' outta Bollywood.

Landmark's Sunshine Cinema
143 E Houston Street, between First & Second Avenues (1-212 330 8182/1-212 777 3456). Subway: F, V to Lower East Side-Second Avenue. **Tickets** $10.25; $6.75 over-63s. **Credit** AmEx, Disc, MC, V.
A beautifully restored 1898 Yiddish theatre has become one of New York's snazziest art houses, presenting some of the finest new independent cinema in stadium-seated, air-conditioned luxury.

Leonard Nimoy Thalia
Symphony Space, 2537 Broadway, at 95th Street, entrance on 95th Street (1-212 864 5400). Subway: 1, 2, 3 to 96th Street. **Tickets** $10; $8 seniors and students. **Credit** AmEx, MC, V.
The famed Thalia art house – featured in *Annie Hall* – was recently rebuilt. It's much more comfortable

now, and it continues to offer retrospectives of foreign classics, but with more cutting-edge stuff sometimes thrown into the mix.

Paris Theatre
4 W 58th Street, between Fifth & Sixth Avenues (1-212 688 3800/1-212 777 3456). Subway: F to 57th Street; N, R, W to Fifth Avenue-59th Street. **Tickets** $10; $6 seniors and children. **Credit** Cash only at box office; AmEx, MC, V on website.
Near the Plaza Hotel, this posh cinema is *de rigueur* for cinéastes who love foreign-language films.

Quad Cinema
34 W 13th Street, between Fifth & Sixth Avenues (1-212 255 8800/www.quadcinema.com). Subway: F, V to 14th Street; L to Sixth Avenue. **Tickets** $9.50; $6.50 seniors and 5-12s. **Credit** Cash only at box office; AmEx, MC, V on website.
Four small screens (in downtown's first multiplex) show a broad selection of foreign and American independent films, as well as documentaries, many dealing with politics and sexuality. Children under five are not admitted.

Two Boots Pioneer Theater
155 E 3rd Street, between Avenues A & B (1-212 591 0434/www.twoboots.com). Subway: F, V to Lower East Side-Second Avenue. **Tickets** $9; $6.50 seniors, students and children. **Credit** AmEx, Disc, MC, V.
Phil Hartman, founder of the Two Boots pizza chain, also runs this East Village alternative film centre, which shows an assortment of newish indies, revivals and themed festivals.

Museums & societies

American Museum of the Moving Image
For listing, see p165.
Moving Image, the first American museum devoted solely to the art of motion pictures, puts on an impressive schedule of more than 700 films a year, many of which are organised into some of the most creatively curated series in the city.

Anthology Film Archives
32 Second Avenue, at 2nd Street (1-212 505 5181/www.anthologyfilmarchives.org). Subway: F, V to Lower East Side-Second Avenue. **Tickets** $8; $5 seniors and students. **No credit cards**.
Housed in a crumbling landmark building, Anthology is a fiercely independent cinema showcasing foreign and experimental film and video. Upon opening in 1970, its first offering was a typewritten manifesto.

Brooklyn Museum
For listing, see p155.
The eclectic roster at Brooklyn's stately palace of fine arts concentrates on offbeat foreign films and smart documentaries.

Film Society of Lincoln Center
Walter Reade Theater, Lincoln Center, 165 W 65th Street, between Broadway & Amsterdam Avenue, plaza level above Alice Tully Hall (1-212 875 5601/www.filmlinc.com). Subway: 1, 9 to 66th Street-Lincoln Center. **Tickets** $10; $7 students; $5 seniors (before 6pm Mon-Fri). **Credit** Cash only at box office; MC, V on website.
The FSLC was founded in 1969 to support filmmakers and promote contemporary film and video. It operates the Walter Reade Theater, a state-of-the-art venue in Lincoln Center with the city's most comfortable cinema seats and best sight lines. Programmes are usually thematicwith an international perspective. In autumn, the Society hosts the New York Film Festival (*see p265*).

IMAX Theater
For listing, see p143 **American Museum of Natural History**.
The IMAX screen is an eye-popping four storeys high; child-friendly movies explore the myriad wonders of the natural world.

Metropolitan Museum of Art
For listing, see p136.
The Met offers a programme of documentaries on art – many relating to current museum exhibitions – that are screened in the Uris Center Auditorium (near the 81st Street entrance).

Museum of Modern Art
For listing, see p125.
The city's toniest destination for superb programming of art films and experimental work, drawing from a vast vault that's second to none.

Museum of Television & Radio
For listing, see p125.
The museum's collection includes thousands of TV programmes that can be viewed at private consoles.

Foreign-language films

Many of the institutions listed also above screen films in languages other than English.

Asia Society and Museum
For l isting, see p135.
See works from China, India and other Asian countries, as well as Asian-American productions.

French Institute Alliance Française
For listing, see p330 **Florence Gould Hall**.
FIAF shows French and Francophone movies.

Goethe-Institut New York
For listing, see p136.
Screens German films in various locations around the city, as well as in its own opulent auditorium.

Japan Society
For listing, see p128.
The society organises a carefully chosen schedule of current and classic Japanese fare.

Film festivals

Each spring, MoMA and the Film Society of Lincoln Center sponsor the highly regarded **New Directors/New Films** series, presenting works by on-the-cusp filmmakers from around the world. The FSLC, together with Lincoln Center's *Film Comment* magazine, also puts on the popular *Film Comment* **Selects** series, which allows the magazine's editors to showcase their favourite movies that have yet to be distributed in the US. Plus, every September and October since 1963, the FSLC has hosted the prestigious **New York Film Festival**. (For more information on any of these three festivals, visit www.filmlinc.com.) The **New York Independent Film and Video Festival** (1-212 777 7100, www.nyfilmvideo.com) lures cinéastes twice yearly, in April and November. Every April, Robert De Niro rolls out his relatively new but increasingly well-regarded **Tribeca Film Festival** (*see p260*). The popular **New York Lesbian & Gay Film Festival** screens in early June (1-212 571 2170, www.newfestival.org). January brings the annual **New York Jewish Film Festival** (1-212 875 5600) to Lincoln Center's Walter Reade Theater.

TV

Studio tapings

The Daily Show with Jon Stewart

513 W 54th Street, between Tenth & Eleventh Avenues (1-212 586 2477/www.comedycentral.com/ dailyshow). Subway: C, E to 50th Street. **Tapings** 5.30pm Mon-Thur.
Reserve tickets at least three months ahead by phone, or call at 11.30am on the Friday before you'd like to attend and see if there's a cancellation. You must be at least 18 and have a photo ID.

Last Call with Carson Daly

30 Rockefeller Plaza, Sixth Avenue, between 49th & 50th Streets (1-888 452 8499/www.1iota.com). Subway: B, D, F, V to 47th-50th Streets-Rockefeller Center. **Tapings** Call or visit website for schedule.
A couple of weeks in advance, make a reservation online or by phone. For stand-by tickets, get in line at NBC's 49th Street entrance no later than 11am on weekdays. After that, leftover tickets might be available in the lobby's NBC Experience store. Daly fans take note: unlike at *Total Request Live*, you must be at least 16 to attend this show.

Late Night with Conan O'Brien

30 Rockefeller Plaza, Sixth Avenue, between 49th & 50th Streets (1-212 664 3056/www.nbc.com/conan). Subway: B, D, F, V to 47th-50th Streets-Rockefeller Center. **Tapings** 5.30pm Tue-Fri.

Call at least three months in advance for tickets (four-ticket limit). A small number of same-day stand-by tickets are distributed at 9am (49th Street entrance); one ticket per person. You must be at least 16 and have a photo ID.

Late Show with David Letterman

1697 Broadway, between 53rd & 54th Streets (1-212 975 1003/www.lateshowaudience.com). Subway: B, D, E to Seventh Avenue. **Tapings** 5.30pm Mon-Wed; 5.30pm, 8pm Thur.
Seats can be hard to come by. Try requesting tickets for a specific date by filling out a form on the show's website. You may also be able to get a stand-by ticket by calling 1-212 247 6497 at 11am on the day of taping. You must be 18 and have a photo ID.

Saturday Night Live

30 Rockefeller Plaza, Sixth Avenue, between 49th & 50th Streets (1-212 664 3056/www.nbc.com/snl). Subway: B, D, F, V to 47th-50th Streets-Rockefeller Center. **Tapings** Dress rehearsal at 8pm; live show at 11.30pm.
Tickets are notoriously difficult to snag, so don't get your hopes up. The season is assigned by lottery every autumn. Send an email to snltickets@nbc.com anytime during August, or try the stand-by ticket lottery on the day of the show. Line up by 7am under the NBC Studio marquee (50th Street, between Fifth & Sixth Avenues). You must be at least 16.

Tours

These tours sell out, so reserve in advance.

Kramer's Reality Tour

The Producers Club, 358 W 44th Street, between Eighth & Ninth Avenues (1-800 572 6377/www.kenny kramer.com). Subway: A, C, E to 42nd Street-Port Authority. **Tours** 11.45am Sat, Sun (holiday weekends only); reservations required. **Tickets** $40. **Credit** AmEx, Disc, MC, V.
Kenny Kramer (yes, the guy who inspired that *Seinfeld* character) takes you to many of the show's locations on his tour bus.

Sex and the City Tour

Meet at Pulitzer Fountain near the Plaza Hotel, Fifth Avenue, between 58th & 59th Streets (1-212 209 3370/www.sceneontv.com). Subway: N, R, W to Fifth Avenue-59th Street. **Tours** 11am Mon-Fri; 10am, 11am, 3pm Sat; 10am, 3pm Sun. **Tickets** $35. **Credit** MC, V.
The show has long since wrapped, but it lives on in syndication and, apparently, on this tour, which takes you to more than 35 sites.

The Sopranos Tour

Meet at the giant button sculpture, Seventh Avenue, at 39th Street (1-212 209 3370/www.sceneontv.com). Subway: N, Q, R, W, 42nd Street S, 1, 2, 3, 9, 7 to 42nd Street-Times Square. **Tours** 2pm Sat, Sun. **Tickets** $40. **Credit** MC, V.
A bus takes you to New Jersey to check out Tony's haunts, from the Bada Bing! to Pizzaland.

Gay & Lesbian

New York offers everything you need to be out and about.

Belly up to the bar at **Girls Room**. *See p306.*

It might be easier to have a guide to the *non-*queer city sites. OK, slight exaggeration. But seriously, this city has got to be one of the gayest on Earth. It's truly a place where LGBT people are more often safe than in danger, more often embraced than loathed, and more often out (we hope!) than in. It's a city with not just a couple of 'gay scenes', but an unfathomable slew. You'll find niches for all homos – from wild-child queer rockers and drag-queen-lovin' rainbow wearers to bald-dyke activists and settled-down parents who haven't been to a gay bar in years. There's a community for everyone, every day of the week, in all five boroughs, whether at a bar, theatre, park, political office, restaurant or bookstore.

New York is a homo haven for many historical and social reasons. For starters, it was the home of the 1969 Stonewall riots in the West Village, which jump-started the American gay-rights movement. Plus, the city has no shortage of queer role models, including politicians, artists, performers, writers and activists. Even the laws here foster a healthy queer existence, criminalising anti-gay violence, forbidding

discrimination in the workplace and affording same-sex couples comprehensive domestic-partnership rights; the city has even pledged to respect the legal documents of gay spouses married in places where such a union is legal.

As an out-of-towner trying to find the queer world that's right for you, the **Lesbian, Gay, Bisexual & Transgender Community Center** (*see p302*) is a great first stop. The information desk attendant will be happy to supply you with an informative visitors' packet, as well as a schedule listing the gatherings of more than 300 groups that use the facility, from the Lesbian Sex Mafia to the New York Association for Gender Rights Advocacy (NYAGRA). And then there's the annual **Gay Pride Week** in June, when LGBT folks flock here from around the world to revel in queer fun by attending a swirl of parties and performances, and by joining a half-million or so spectators and participants at the Pride March (*see p263*). Other summer events include the popular **NewFest** gay film festival, held in mid June, and two July theatre festivals, the Fresh Fruit Festival and HOT!

The Annual NYC Celebration of Queer Culture. But rest assured that you'll find gay drama in this town pretty much anytime, anyplace.

Books & media

Gay bookstores, it seems, are dropping like drawers in a backroom. Blame the internet. Blame Barnes & Noble. Blame Here!TV. Still, these two reliable shops remain great places to browse or buy.

Bluestockings

172 Allen Street, between Rivington & Stanton Streets (1-212 777 6028/www.bluestockings.com). Subway: F, V to Lower East Side-Second Avenue. **Open** 1-10pm Mon-Fri; 10am-10pm Sat, Sun. **Credit** AmEx, MC, V.

This former feminist bookseller, founded in 1999, now bills itself more broadly as a radical bookstore, fair-trade café and activist resource centre. Still, it continues to stock a load of LGBT writings and erotica, and it hosts regular events such as queer political forums and monthly women's open-mic nights.

Oscar Wilde Bookshop

15 Christopher Street, between Sixth & Seventh Avenues (1-212 255 8097/www.oscar wildebooks.com). Subway: 1 to Christopher Street-Sheridan Square. **Open** 11am-7pm daily. **Credit** AmEx, Disc, MC, V.

Purportedly the world's first gay bookstore (it opened in 1967) is small but loaded with atmosphere. Come for the history, the friendly and knowledgeable staffers, the picturesque neighbourhood, and the store's collection of new and used books. Keep an eye out for first-edition classics.

Publications

Time Out New York's Gay & Lesbian section offers a lively weekly guide to city happenings. Both of New York's weekly gay entertainment magazines – *HX* and *Next* – include extensive boycentric information on bars, clubs, restaurants, events, group meetings and sex parties. The monthly *Go NYC*, 'a cultural road map for the city girl', gives the low-down on the lesbian scene. The newspaper *Gay City News* provides feisty political coverage with an activist slant; its arch-rival, the *New York Blade*, focuses on queer politics and news. All are free and widely available in street boxes or at gay and lesbian bars and bookstores. *MetroSource* ($4.95) is a bimonthly glossy with a guppie slant and tons of listings.

Television & radio

What a difference a year makes! In 2004, there were no exclusively gay TV stations; by mid 2005, there were three, all available in NYC.

Q Television, Logo and the on-demand Here!TV, all offering a cornucopia of feature films, talk shows and documentaries, are available round the clock via the local Time Warner Cable provider. And then there's the fabulous Manhattan Neighborhood Network (MNN), Manhattan's public-access station, allowing New Yorkers of all stripes to have their very own programmes. There are plenty of queer ones in the mix, with the *Gay USA* news programme and the long-running *Dyke TV* among the standouts (though programming varies by cable company, so you may not be able to watch these shows on a hotel TV.) *HX* and *Next* provide the most current gay-TV listings. On the radio, NYC's community-activist station, WBAI-FM 99.5, features the progressive gay talk show *Out-FM* on Mondays at 11am. And online, Sirius satellite radio offers the show *OutQ 24/7*, with programming from such New York personalities as Michelangelo Signorile, Frank DeCaro and Larry Flick.

Centres & helplines

Gay & Lesbian Switchboard of New York Project

1-212 989 0999/www.glnh.org. **Open** 4pm-midnight Mon-Fri; noon-5pm Sat.

This phone service offers excellent peer counselling, legal referrals, details on gay and lesbian organisations, and information on bars, hotels and restaurants. Outside New York (but within the US), callers can use the toll-free Gay & Lesbian National Hotline (1-888 843 4564).

Gay Men's Health Crisis

119 W 24th Street, between Sixth & Seventh Avenues (1-212 367 1000/AIDS advice hotline 1-212 807 6655/www.gmhc.org). Subway: F, V, 1 to 23rd Street. **Open** *Hotline* 10am-9pm Mon-Fri; noon-3pm Sat; recorded information in English and Spanish at other times. *Office* 10am-6pm Mon-Fri.

GMHC was the world's first organisation dedicated to helping people with AIDS. Its threefold mission is to push for better public policies; to educate the public to prevent the further spread of HIV; and to provide services and counselling to people living with HIV. Support groups usually meet in the evening.

Lesbian, Gay, Bisexual & Transgender Community Center

208 W 13th Street, between Seventh & Eighth Avenues (1-212 620 7310/www.gaycenter.org). Subway: A, C, E, 1, 2, 3 to 14th Street; L to Eighth Avenue. **Open** 9am-11pm daily.

Activist organisations ACT UP and GLAAD got their starts here. It provides info for gay tourists; political, cultural, spiritual and emotional support; and meeting space to 300-odd groups. The National Museum & Archive of Lesbian & Gay History and the Pat Parker/Vito Russo Library are housed here.

Buzzworthy

JD Samson and Lilly of the Valley
with Brooke Webster.

Cattyshack *See p308*

Soon after the sad closing of the Lower East Side's Meow Mix, proprietor Brooke Webster has made good on her promise to the dyke community to keep the feline spirit alive – in a brand new space and a whole new borough, that is. Meow Mix fans new and old have been packed to the rafters at the industrial-chic space on Fourth Avenue in Park Slope, within stumbling distance of the R train. The massive, low-lit club, is blessed with a breezy roof deck and a great line-up of DJs like JD Samson of Le Tigre and Lilly of the Valley.

Lesbian Herstory Archives

484 14th Street, between Eighth Avenue & Prospect Park West, Park Slope, Brooklyn (1-718 768 3953/www.lesbianherstoryarchives.org). Subway: F to 15th Street-Prospect Park. **Open** 7-9pm Wed; other times vary. Call or visit website for more information.

Located in Brooklyn's Park Slope neighbourhood, the Herstory Archives contain more than 20,000 books (cultural theory, fiction, poetry, plays), 1,600 periodicals and assorted memorabilia. The cosy space also hosts occasional film screenings, readings and social gatherings, plus an annual open house held in late June.

Michael Callen-Audre Lorde Community Health Center

356 W 18th Street, between Eighth & Ninth Avenues (1-212 271 7200/www.callen-lorde.org). Subway: A, C, E to 14th Street; L to Eighth Avenue; 1 to 18th Street. **Open** 8.30am-8pm Mon, Tue; 12.30-8pm Wed; 9am-4.30pm Thur, Fri.

This is the country's largest health centre serving primarily the gay, lesbian, bisexual and transgender community. It offers comprehensive medical care, HIV treatment, STD screening and treatment, mental-health services, peer counselling as well as free adolescent services (including a youth hotline on 1-212 271 7212).

NYC Gay & Lesbian Anti-Violence Project

Suite 200, 240 W 35th Street, between Seventh & Eighth Avenues (24-hour bilingual hotline 1-212 714 1141/1-212 714 1184/www.avp.org). Subway: A, C, E, 1, 2, 3 to 34th Street-Penn Station. **Open** 10am-8pm Mon-Thur; 10am-6pm Fri.

The Project works with local police to provide support to victims of anti-queer crimes, plus has volunteers who offer advice on how to seek help from police. Long- and short-term counselling are available.

Queer perspective

Sure, every neighbourhood has gay residents – but only a select few can be properly deemed 'gaybourhoods'. The big daddy of them all is still Chelsea, where hot, upwardly mobile men strut and cruise along the runway-like Eighth Avenue between 16th and 23rd Streets. The strip is positively bulging with muscled queens, as well as sleek boutiques, gyms, lounges and

Lounging and loafing are on the menu...

eateries. The 'hood is also headquarters for *HX*, and you'll find copies of the nightlife guide in street boxes on practically every corner. The queerness spreads north from here into Hell's Kitchen, also known as Clinton – or 'Chelsea north' in jest – which has been recently claimed as the next gay-man frontier. Positioned conveniently near Manhattan's Theater District, this is where you'll find a growing number of gay-owned eateries, bars and boutiques.

If these 'hoods, in all their clonish glory, leave you a bit bored, head downtown, where more diverse gaybourhoods await. An edgier, junkie-punkie youthful crowd thrives in the East Village, home to a vast network of bars and clubs that cater to skinny boys, quirky drag queens and pierced dykes, as well as a generous dose of wannabes. Crosstown, on Christopher Street in the **West Village**, you'll find the historic heart of gay New York. It's home to the legendary **Stonewall** (*see p307*), friendly piano bars, stores full of pink-triangle key chains and a healthy number of gay and lesbian bars. The recently remodelled Christopher Street Pier still draws gaggles of African-American and Latino gay youths.

Beyond Manhattan's borders, Brooklyn's tree-lined **Park Slope** is a long-time enclave for lesbians – especially settled-down types with kids and real careers, as the affordable-rent days that started the whole dyke settlement are long gone. During the first weekend in June, the Slope hosts the annual **Brooklyn Pride March**, a scaled-down version of Manhattan's parade. Brooklyn's hipster Williamsburg neighbourhood is also home to a growing queer population, this one closely resembling the tattooed masses of the East Village.

Other boroughs have less pronounced gay scenes, but in Queens, Jackson Heights is home to several LGBT bars and clubs and a large South American queer population. Chueca (69-04 Woodside Avenue, at 69th Street, 1-718 424 1171) is a hopping spot for salsa-dancing lesbian couples. And the **Queens Pride March**, held in Jackson Heights in mid June, is a less corporate and more ethnically diverse version of the main Pride event in Manhattan.

Men of all ages, shapes and sizes frequent fetish bars and clubs, like the Eagle (*see p307*) in Chelsea, as well as numerous private sex and fetish parties (see *HX* for listings). Gay Male S/M Activists (www.gmsma.org) holds frequent parties and workshops about kinky play. Libidinous lesbians should head to one of the friendly, dyke-owned Toys in Babeland (*see p257*) boutiques, which hold occasional workshops on topics from female ejaculation to anal pleasure, or to the wild women's sex party Submit (1-718 789 4053), where a den of slings, shower rooms and handcuffs awaits you monthly. Similarly, the monthly SPAM: Sex Party and More, is a Brooklyn-based underwear soirée that welcomes dykes, fags, trannies, bis – anyone except for straight folks, basically.

Where to stay

Chelsea Mews Guest House

344 W 15th Street, between Eighth & Ninth Avenues (1-212 255 9174). Subway: A, C, E to 14th Street; L to Eighth Avenue. **Rates** $100–$250 single/double. **No credit cards.**
Built in 1840, this guest house caters to gay men. Rooms are comfortable and well furnished and, in most cases, have semi-private bathrooms. Laundry service and bicycles are complimentary. The creepily named Anne Frank Suite has two twin beds and a private bathroom.

... or you could just have an ogle, at the **Eagle**. *See p307.*

Chelsea Pines Inn

317 W 14th Street, between Eighth & Ninth Avenues (1-212 929 1023/1-888 546 2700/www.chelseapines inn.com). Subway: A, C, E to 14th Street; L to Eighth Avenue. **Rates** $139-$219; continental breakfast included. **Credit** AmEx, DC, Disc, MC, V.

On the border of Chelsea and the West Village, Chelsea Pines welcomes gay guests, male and female. The 25 rooms are clean and comfortable; most have private bathrooms, and all include a radio, TV and refrigerator.

Colonial House Inn

318 W 22nd Street, between Eighth & Ninth Avenues (1-212 243 9669/1-800 689 3779/www.colonial houseinn.com). Subway: C, E to 23rd Street. **Rates** $85-$130 single/double with shared bath; $135-$150 single/double with private bath (higher on weekends); continental breakfast included. **Credit** MC, V.

This beautifully renovated 1850s townhouse sits on a quiet street in Chelsea. Run by and primarily for gay men, Colonial House is a great place to stay, even if some of the less expensive rooms are a bit snug. Bonuses: a fireplace in three of the deluxe rooms and a rooftop deck for all (nude sunbathing allowed!).

East Village B&B

244 E 7th Street, between Avenues C & D (1-212 260 1865). Subway: F, V to Lower East Side-Second Avenue. **Rates** $100 single; $120 double; $300 apartment; breakfast included. **No credit cards**.

This lesbian-owned gem is tucked into a turn-of-the-20th-century apartment building on a quiet East Village block. The recently remodelled space has gleaming wood floors and exposed brick, plus an eclectic art collection. The bedrooms are done up in bold colours, one of the bathrooms has a small tub, and the living room has a TV and CD player.

Incentra Village House

32 Eighth Avenue, between Jane & W 12th Streets (1-212 206 0007). Subway: A, C, E to 14th Street; L to Eighth Avenue. **Rates** $119-$169 single/double; $149–$199 suite. **Credit** AmEx, MC, V.

Two cute 1841 townhouses in the West Village make up this recently renovated guest house run by gay men. The spacious rooms have private bathrooms and kitchenettes; some have working fireplaces. A 1939 Steinway baby-grand piano is in the parlour.

Ivy Terrace

230 E 58th Street, between Second & Third Avenues (1-516 662 6862/www.ivyterrace.com). Subway: N, R, W to Lexington Avenue-59th Street; 4, 5, 6 to 59th Street. **Rates** $180-$250 single/double; $1,200-$1,500 weekly; breakfast included. **Credit** AmEx, MC, V.

This lovely lesbian-run B&B sits on the same block as boy haunts OW Bar and the Townhouse. The three cosy rooms feature wood floors and lacy bedspreads on old-fashioned sleigh beds. Owner Vinessa Milando (who runs the inn with partner and lesbian-party promoter Sue Martino) provides breakfast each morning. You're also free to create your own meals: each room is equipped with a gas stove and a full-size fridge.

Bars

Most gay bars in New York offer drink specials, happy hours and colourful theme nights; some have hot-body contests, live performances and slutty themes (dyke bars, of course, usually have pool tables). This past year has brought a bi-level dyke bar to Brooklyn, courtesy of the former Meow Mix owner, and a boys' sports bar, of all things, to Chelsea. If you wind up at a place that doesn't feel like your scene, don't fret – there are plenty of others just a few twirls away.

Lower East Side & East Village

Boysroom

9 Avenue A, between 1st & 2nd Streets (1-212 358 1440/www.tripwithus.com). Subway: F, V to Lower East Side-Second Avenue. **Open** 9pm-4am daily. **Cover** $5-$10. **Average drink** $7. **No credit cards**.

It's a dark, two-level lounge from downtown creature of the night Misstress Formika – DJ, drag queen and hostess with the mostest. Pile in for the young crowds, amateur go-go contests and porn, which is piped in on mounted TV screens. There's a different theme every night, including the popular Go-Go Idol Saturdays and Boyslife Sundays.

The Cock
29 Second Avenue, at 2nd Street (no phone).
Subway: F, V to Lower East Side-Second Avenue.
Open 9pm-4am daily. **Cover** $5-$10. **Average drink** $7. **No credit cards.**
Formerly known as the Hole, this wonderfully dark and sleazy spot has been taken over by the Cock (only in New York, folks). a legendary nasty fest that used to be just up the block. Nightly soirées feature lots of cruising, cocktail-guzzling and heavy petting among the rail-thin, messy-haired young boys.

Girls Room
210 Rivington Street, between Pitt & Ridge Streets (1-212 995 8684/www.girlsroomnyc.com). Subway: F to Delancey Street; J, M, Z to Delancey-Essex Streets. **Open** 7pm-4am Tue-Sat. **Cover** free-$3. **Average drink** $6. **No credit cards.**
Filling in the Lower East Side lesbian gap that was created when Meow Mix closed last year, this dyke bar offers theme nights five nights a week, from '80s karaoke on Wednesdays and the popular Sex for the City Girl soirée on Saturdays. Visit the website for a schedule of special events. **Photo** *p301.*

Nowhere
322 E 14th Street, at First Avenue (1-212 477 4744). Subway: L to First Avenue. **Open** 3pm-4am daily. **Average drink** $5. **No credit cards.**
A friendly, spacious watering hole – from the same folks who run the nearby Phoenix (447 E 13th Street, between First Avenue & Avenue A, 1-212 477 9979) – Nowhere attracts attitude-free crowds filled with everyone from dykes to bears, thanks to a fun line-up of theme nights.

Slide/Marquee
356 Bowery, between Great Jones & E 4th Streets (1-212 420 8885). Subway: B, D, F, V to Broadway-Lafayette Street; 6 to Bleecker Street. **Open** 5pm-4am daily. **Average drink** $5. **No credit cards.**
Located in a space that housed one of Manhattan's first openly gay bars in the 1800s, the Slide – with its infamous, party-hearty promoter Daniel Nardicio – came on the scene in 2003 to restore some pre-Mayor Giuliani sleaze to the East Village. Prepare thyself for dirty drag queens, naked go-go boys and underwear parties, and wacky shows of all kinds in its upstairs Marquee theatre.

Starlight Bar & Lounge
167 Avenue A, between 10th & 11th Streets (1-212 475 2172/www.starlightbarlounge.com). Subway: L to First Avenue. **Open** 6pm-3am Mon-Thur, Sun; 6pm-4am Fri, Sat. **Average drink** $6. **Credit** AmEx.

This reliable lounge gets mobbed on weekends, but its calmer weeknight schedule brings a wonderful rotation of performances, including comedy on Wednesdays and readings and DJs at other times. Sunday nights, the popular lesbian party Starlette is still kicking, bringing in a mix of glamour gals, tomboys and college students.

West Village

Chi Chiz
135 Christopher Street, at Hudson Street (1-212 462 0027). Subway: 1 to Christopher Street-Sheridan Square. **Open** 10pm-4am daily. **Average drink** $5. **No credit cards.**
This hotspot for men of colour, just steps from the Christopher Street Pier, is a cruisy kind of place. Swarms form at Monday night's karaoke, and both Tuesday's She-Chiz Ladies' Night and the Thursday-evening pool tournaments are equally popular.

Cubbyhole
281 W 12th Street, at 4th Street (1-212 243 9041). Subway: A, C, E to 14th Street; L to Eighth Avenue. **Open** 4pm-2am Mon-Wed; 4pm-4am Thur, Fri; 2pm-4am Sat, Sun. **Average drink** $6. **No credit cards.**
This friendly lesbian spot is always chock-full of girls tying one on, with the standard set of Melissa Etheridge or kd lang blaring in the background. Chinese paper lanterns, tissue-paper fish and old holiday decorations emphasise the welcoming home-made charm – as do the many dyke-friendly gay boys and straight folks who are often found bellying up to the bar.

Henrietta Hudson
438 Hudson Street, at Morton Street (1-212 924 3347/www.henriettahudson.com). Subway: 1 to Christopher Street-Sheridan Square. **Open** 4pm-4am Mon-Fri; 1pm-4am Sat, Sun. **Average drink** $6. **No credit cards.**
A long-time, beloved lesbian bar, Henrietta Hudson used to be more of a grubby pub than glammy lounge. But following a glossy renovation, it's definitely more the latter now. It's still attracting young hottie girls from all over the New York area, especially the nearby burbs. Every night's a new DJ party, with Mamacita Sundays and Transcend Tuesdays among the diverse and well-attended line-up. **Photo** *p307.*

The Monster
80 Grove Street, at Sheridan Square (1-212 924 3558). Subway: 1 to Christopher Street-Sheridan Square. **Open** 4pm-4am Mon-Fri; 2pm-4am Sat, Sun. **Average drink** $5. **No credit cards.**
Upstairs, locals gather to sing show tunes in the piano lounge. (And, honey, you haven't lived till you've witnessed a bunch of tipsy queers belting out the best of Broadway.) The downstairs disco caters to a young outer-borough crowd just itchin' for a bit of fun.

From shabby to fabby – the revamped **Henrietta Hudson**, as popular as ever. *See p306*.

The Stonewall

53 Christopher Street, between Seventh Avenue South & Waverly Place (1-212 463 0950). Subway: 1 to Christopher Street-Sheridan Square. **Open** 4pm-4am daily. **Average drink** $6. **No credit cards**.
This is the gay landmark, next door to the actual location of the 1969 gay rebellion against police harassment. For years, the joint was a snore, but lately, it's gotten an infusion of sexy shenanigans, such as go-go boys, strip contests and nights reserved for Latino boys.

Chelsea

Barracuda

275 W 22nd Street, between Seventh & Eighth Avenues (1-212 645 8613). Subway: C, E to 23rd Street. **Open** 4pm-4am daily. **Average drink** $6. **No credit cards**.
This long-time staple is friendlier and more comfortable than the neighbourhood competition. It's got a traditional, low-lit bar up front and a frequently redecorated lounge in the back. Drag-queen celebrities perform throughout the week, and there's never a cover charge as far as we know.

The Eagle

554 W 28th Street, between Tenth & Eleventh Avenues (1-646 473 1866/www.eaglenyc.com). Subway: C, E to 23rd Street. **Open** 10pm-4am Mon-Sat; 5pm-4am Sun. **Average drink** $5. **No credit cards**.
The Meatpacking District was once home to outpost of kink the Lure. Now the action has moved to this classic Levi's-and-leather fetish bar. Look out for beer blasts, foot-worship fêtes, leather soirées and simple nights of pool playing and cruising. **Photo** *p304*.

Gym

167 Eighth Avenue, at 18th Street (1-212 337 2439/www.gymsportsbar.com). Subway: A, C, E to 14th Street; L to Eighth Avenue. **Open** 4pm-4am daily. **Average drink** $7. **No credit cards**.
One of the newest games in town, this one is all about games – of the actual sporting variety, that is. Catch theme parties that revolve around gay sports leagues, plus pool tables, video games and pro events shown on big-screen TVs. Talk about butch.

XES Lounge

157 W 24th Street, between Sixth & Seventh Avenues (1-212 604 0212/www.xesnyc.com). Subway: F, V, 1 to 23rd Street. **Open** 4pm-4am daily. **Average drink** $7. **Credit** AmEx, MC, V.
This sleek and relatively new spot has exposed brick walls, metal coffee tables, Eames chairs and a patio, with Japanese maples, Philippe Starck furniture and a much appreciated smoking-allowed policy. Catch theme parties and drag shows on weekends.

xl

357 W 16th Street, between Eighth & Ninth Avenues (1-646 336 5574/www.xlnewyork.com). Subway: A, C, E to 14th Street; L to Eighth Avenue. **Open** 4pm-4am daily. **Average drink** $8. **No credit cards**.
This sleek trilevel bar is a study in style: witness the giant aquarium in the unisex bathroom. Fashion divas, muscle men, fag hags and a few drag queens run amok under one roof. Sunday and Monday nights feature free shows starring top-notch Broadway and cabaret performers.

A (queer) place in the sun

When you want to go further than your MetroCard can take you, check out our primer on queer summer enclaves. After all, you'd hate to be a fish out of water – or a beer-drinkin' lesbian stuck in the Fire Island Pines.

Cherry Grove, Fire Island, NY

www.cherrygrove.com
Travel time Just under 2 hours by car and ferry or Long Island Rail Road and ferry.
Who goes there Oft-naked boys from Long Island, the East Village and beyond, plus ethnically diverse dykes with two things in common: tiny budgets and a big thirst for alcohol.
Main activities Drinking, beachgoing, drinking, eating in, drinking.
Key events Drag queens raise money for abandoned pets at the annual Cherry Grove PAWS Benefit at the Ice Palace in late June. The Invasion, another drag blow-out, is 4 July. (See website for info on both events.)

East Hampton, NY

www.hamptons.com
Travel time 2 hours 30 mins by car, Long Island Rail Road or Hampton Jitney.
Who goes there Wealthy power dykes who are into golf; rich uptown fags.
Main activities Fund-raiser-hopping, seeing and being seen.
Key events Don white linen shorts and frolic on the lush grounds of a private estate to raise money for the gay lobbyist group Empire State Pride Agenda (www.prideagenda.org), which holds its Annual Hamptons Tea Dance benefit in early July. July's also the time for the Dancing on the Beach fund-raiser for the city's LGBT Community Center (www.gaycenter.org).

The Pines, Fire Island, NY

www.fipines.com
Travel time Just under 2 hours by car and ferry or Long Island Rail Road and ferry.

Midtown

OW Bar

221 E 58th Street, at Second Avenue (1-212 355 3395). Subway: N, R, W to Lexington Avenue-59th Street; 4, 5, 6 to 59th Street. **Open** 4pm-4am Mon-Sat; 2pm-4am Sun. **Average drink** $6. **Credit** AmEx, Disc, MC, V.
Oscar Wilde's initials adorn this East Side watering hole. In addition to the tony lounge area, jam-packed digital jukebox and lovely patio, there are frequent drag and cabaret performances.

Posh

405 W 51st Street, between Ninth & Tenth Avenues (1-212 957 2222). Subway: C, E to 50th Street. **Open** 4pm-4am daily. **Average drink** $6. **Credit** AmEx, MC, V.
OK, so it's not exactly the poshest place in town, but the small, homey lounge is sweet, and delish drinks and speciality evenings keep the regulars coming.

Therapy

348 W 52nd Street, between Eighth & Ninth Avenues (1-212 397 1700). Subway: C, E to 50th Street. **Open** 5pm-2am Mon-Wed, Sun; 5pm-4am Thur-Sat. **Average drink** $7. **Credit** AmEx, MC, V.
Therapy is the main event in Hell's Kitchen, and with good reasons: the minimalist yet dramatic two-level design; performances by bona fide Broadway stars; a clever cocktail menu that includes the Oral Fixation and the Freudian Sip; and the beautiful crowd of boys. You'll even find good grub here, and a fireplace to cosy up to on chilly nights.

Uptown

Candle Bar

309 Amsterdam Avenue, at 74th Street (1-212 874 9155). Subway: 1, 2, 3 to 72nd Street. **Open** 2pm-4am daily. **Average drink** $5. **No credit cards**.
This Upper West Side mainstay is a small and cruisy neighbourhood kind of place, but recent ownership has rekindled the joint's spark after years of slowing down. Catch nightly drink specials for $2.50, from ice-cold Bud to potent Margaritas.

Eight of Clubs

230 W 75th Street, between Broadway & West End Avenue (1-212 580 7389). Subway: 1, 2, 3 to 72nd Street. **Open** 7pm-4am daily. **Average drink** $5. **No credit cards**.
This tiny watering hole offers a pool table, video games and a backyard patio that hosts a variety of happenings when the weather is warm. It's not trendy, hot or particularly popular, but it possesses a down-to-earth, old-school charm that's hard to find these days.

Brooklyn

fishack

249 Fourth Avenue, between Carroll & President Streets, Park Slope (1-718 230 5740). Subway: M, R to Union Street. **Open** 2pm-4am Mon-Fri; noon-4am Sat, Sun. **Average drink** $7. **No credit cards**.
This brand-new, bilevel space is all industrial-chic, spare-design charm. It's a full-time lesbian joint,

Who goes there Chelsea boys and other well-heeled, well-sculpted men who prefer harder stuff to sipping.
Main activities Beach cruising, toasting at grandiose dinner parties, partying at the Pavilion club.
Key events The Fire Island Dance Festival, a fund-raiser for Dancers Responding to AIDS, is in mid July (www.dradance.org); the annual Pines Party fund-raiser for Gay Men's Health Crisis (www.gmhc.org) is in early August; Empire State Pride Agenda (www.prideagenda.org) throws a benefit, Rites of Summer – a magnet for party-circuit boys – in mid August.

Cape May, NJ
www.capemay.com
Travel time 2 hours 30 mins by car or NJ Transit bus (1-973 762 5100).
Who goes there Monogamous boy couples (and plenty of hetero pairs) seeking pricey Victorian B&Bs and refined cuisine.

Main activities Beach romping, bird-watching, dining out.
Key events In early August, check out the Queen Maysea Coronation ceremony, a local favourite. Talk about camp!

New Hope, PA
www.newhopepa.com
Travel time About 2 hours by car or Trans-Bridge bus (1-610 868 6001).
Who goes there Middle-American lesbians and gay men (and plenty of straight people, too) who drink Bud with lunch, prefer the country to the beach and go to bed early.
Main activities Bicycling, tchotchke shopping.
Key events The Performing Arts Festival, featuring theatre, music and art exhibitions all over town, runs from mid July through late August. For berry-picking and pie-eating – especially if you have kids – hit the annual Blueberry Festival in mid July. (See the website, above, for info on both events.)

courtesy of former Meow Mix cat Brooke Webster, and its theme nights, excellent DJs and breezy roof deck have been bringing in the crowds, from Brooklyn, downtown Manhattan and beyond.

Excelsior
390 Fifth Avenue, between 6th & 7th Streets, Park Slope (1-718 832 1599). Subway: M, R to Union Street. **Open** 6pm-4am Mon-Fri; 2pm-4am Sat, Sun. **Average drink** $7. **No credit cards.**
Refined Excelsior, bathed in red, black and chrome, has a spacious deck out back, a beautiful garden, an eclectic jukebox and an excellent selection of beers on tap. The boys are cute, local and friendly.

Ginger's Bar
363 Fifth Avenue, between 5th & 6th Streets, Park Slope (1-718 788 0924). Subway: M, R to Union Street. **Open** 5pm-4am Mon-Fri; 2pm-4am Sat, Sun. **Average drink** $6. **No credit cards.**
The front room of Ginger's, with its dark-wood bar, looks out on to a bustling street scene. The back, which has an always busy pool table, evokes a rec-room feel. Come summertime, the outdoor patio feels like a friend's yard. This congenial local hang (and Excelsior neighbour) is full of all sorts of dykes, many with their dogs – or favourite gay boys – in tow.

Metropolitan
559 Lorimer Street, at Metropolitan Avenue, Williamsburg (1-718 599 4444). Subway: G to Metropolitan Avenue, L to Lorimer Street. **Open** 3pm-4am daily. **Average drink** $5. **No credit cards.**

The hipster enclave of Williamsburg has its fair share of queers, and this is its sole gay stand-by. Stop in to refresh with icy brew while you're tooling around the neighbourhood; you'll find a mellow crowd (with lots of beards – of the facial-hair variety), video games, an outdoor patio and drinks specials galore.

Clubs

A number of New York clubs have gay parties or gay nights. For more clubs, plus additional information about some of those listed below, *see p291* **Clubs.**

Dance clubs & parties

Crobar
530 W 28th Street, between Tenth & Eleventh Avenues (1-212 629 9000/www.crobar.com). Subway: C, E to 23rd Street. **Open** 10pm-4am Mon, Thur-Sun. **Cover** $25. **Average drink** $9. **Credit** AmEx, DC, Disc, MC, V.
This incarnation of Crobar – which also has outposts in Miami and Chicago – is a massive, flashy spot with a roster of wild offerings. Among the queerest are Thursdays and Saturdays, plus the roving circuit party Alegria, which blows through every couple of months or so.

Lovergirl
Club Shelter, 20 W 39th Street, between Fifth & Sixth Avenues (1-212 252 3397). Subway: B, D, F, V

Arts & Entertainment

Better Burger NYC (*see p311*): the finest beef, the finest buns.

to 42nd Street-Bryant Park; 7 to Fifth Avenue. **Open** 10pm-5am Sat. **Cover** $10-$12. **Average drink** $6. **No credit cards**.

Lovergirl, a popular women's party, takes advantage of Club Shelter's dynamite sound system and state-of-the-art lighting. The multiracial crowd, which doesn't start flowing in until after midnight, enthusiastically shakes it to hip-hop, R&B, funk, reggae and Latin music, while ultrasexy go-go gals sport the latest in fashionable G-strings.

Motherfucker
www.motherfuckernyc.com.
If rock 'n' roll is your style, you'll want to check out Motherfucker, the wildly popular polysexual dance party that takes place about seven times a year, rarely at the same venue. (*See also p296*.)

Roxy
515 W 18th Street, between Tenth & Eleventh Avenues (1-212 645 5156). Subway: A, C, E to 14th Street; L to Eighth Avenue. **Open** 11pm-4am Sat. **Cover** $15-$25. **Average drink** $8. **Credit** MC, V.
Promoter John Blair still packs this megaclub with a tasty range of muscle-bound boys who jump all night to house and techno spun by some of the biggest names on the DJ circuit. A classic-rock lounge is kindly provided upstairs, for old-schoolers who prefer beers to bumps.

Saint at Large
1-212 674 8541/www.saintatlarge.com.
The now mythical Saint was one of the first venues where New York's gay men could enjoy dancefloor freedom. The club closed, but the clientele keeps the memory alive with a huge and très important annual circuit party: the fetishy Black Party, with mind-blowing themes that revolve around kink and sex

shows. The White Party, its angelic answer, was on hold in 2005, but check the website for updates on its buzzed-about reappearance.

Shescape
Serena, 222 W 23rd Street, between Sixth & Seventh Avenues (www.shescape.com). Subway: F, V to 23rd Street. **Open** 8pm-4am Sat, Sun. **Cover** $5. **Average drink** $7. **No credit cards**.
The Shescape crew has been offering some of the hottest lesbian bashes around since the 1970s. And while the best time to join the party is for one of their infamous special events – on Thanksgiving Eve, Pride weekend and New Year's Eve, among other times – you can now get your weekly Shescape fix at this Sunday night lounge, with low lighting, drink specials and music from DJ Francesca Magliano.

Splash
50 W 17th Street, between Fifth & Sixth Avenues (1-212 691 0073/www.splashbar.com). Subway: F, V to 14th Street; L to Sixth Avenue. **Open** 4pm-4am Mon-Thur, Sun; 4pm-5am Fri, Sat. **Cover** $5-$20. **Average drink** $7. **No credit cards**.
This Chelsea institution offers a large dance space as well as the famous onstage showers, where hunky go-go boys get wet and wild. And the supermuscular bartenders seem bigger than ever. Nationally known DJs rock the house, local drag celebs give good face, and in-house VJs flash eclectic snippets of classic musicals and videos.

Restaurants & cafés

Few New York restaurateurs would bat an eyelash at a same-sex couple enjoying an intimate dinner. But if you're concerned about being in the minority where you dine, then check out the following gayest eateries in town, where it's the straight folks who get the second glances.

Better Burger NYC
178 Eighth Avenue, at 19th Street (1-212 989 6688). Subway: C, E to 23rd Street; 1 to 18th Street. **Open** 11am-midnight Mon-Thur, Sun; 11am-1am Fri, Sat. **Average burger** $6. **Credit** AmEx, MC, V.
Gayest burger joint ever! It's also the healthiest. But don't worry, the menu – which includes lean patties of beef, turkey, ostrich, soy or veal – is as delicious as the hunky clientele. And although it is a fast-food joint, it's a classy one, listing organic beers and wines to go with your burger, air-baked fries and home-made ketchup. **Photo** *p310*.

Big Cup
228 Eighth Avenue, between 21st & 22nd Streets (1-212 206 0059). Subway: C, E to 23rd Street. **Open** 7am-12.30am Mon-Fri; 8am-1am Sat, Sun. **Average sandwich** $7. **No credit cards.**
Big Cup is as unmistakably Chelsea Boy as a pair of shiny, steroid-pumped pecs. The coffee is fine, as are the snacks – brownies and Rice Krispies Treats, plus sandwiches and soups. Not much attention is paid to those, though, because Big Cup is one of New York's classic gay meet markets.

Cafeteria
119 Seventh Avenue, at 17th Street (1-212 414 1717). Subway: 1 to 18th Street. **Open** 24hrs daily. **Average main course** $16. **Credit** AmEx, DC, MC, V.
This is the fresh-faced version of Foodbar (*see below*), where throngs of neighbourhood boys gather for updated comfort food (savoury meat loaf, mounds of mac and cheese), lean cuisine (salads, granola with fruit topping) and a list of juicy cocktails. It's open round the clock (need a post-club pick-me-up?) and even has a dark lounge of its own, down in the sexy basement.

Counter
105 First Avenue, between 6th & 7th Streets (1-212 982 5870). Subway: F, V to Lower East Side-Second Avenue. **Open** 5pm-midnight Mon-Fri; 11am-1am Sat, Sun. **Average main course** $15. **Credit** AmEx, MC, V.
This hip, lesbian-owned East Village spot takes vegetarian cuisine to a whole new level, adding a wine bar with a dozen organic offerings. Pair a glass or two with one of the lip-smackin' vegan tapas, or try bigger eats, such as portobello au poivre or curried plantain dumplings drizzled in coconut sauce. Brunch is served on weekends.

Elmo
156 Seventh Avenue, between 19th & 20th Streets (1-212 337 8000). Subway: 1 to 18th Street. **Open** 11am-midnight Mon-Thur; 11am-2am Fri, Sat; 10am-midnight Sun. **Average main course** $14. **Credit** AmEx, Disc, MC, V.

This spacious, brightly decorated eaterie has good, reasonably priced food and a bar that offers a view of the dining room, which is jammed with guys in clingy tank tops – regardless of the weather. And then there's the fun basement lounge, which hosts frequent readings, comedy and drag shows, plus the occasional chic-lesbian soirée.

Foodbar
149 Eighth Avenue, between 17th & 18th Streets (1-212 243 2020). Subway: 1 to 18th Street. **Open** 11am-midnight daily. **Average main course** $15. **Credit** AmEx, Disc, MC, V.
Foodbar's globally influenced American menu will get your mouth watering, if the customers haven't already. Balsamic-glazed roasted chicken, a Moroccan salad and steak au poivre and big-brunch omelettes are each entirely satisfying. Servers are efficient and coquettish – a combination we happen to treasure. It's a classic Chelsea hang.

44 & X Hell's Kitchen
622 Tenth Avenue, at 44th Street (1-212 977 1170). Subway: A, C, E to 42nd Street-Port Authority. **Open** 5.30pm-midnight Mon-Wed; 5.30pm-12.30am Thur, Fri; 11.30am-12.30am Sat, Sun. **Average main course** $20. **Credit** AmEx, MC, V.
Fabulous queens pack out the sleek dining space that was one of the first bright spots on quickly gentrifying Tenth Avenue. It's situated alongside the Theater District and the Manhattan Plaza high-rises, home to thousands of artistes. Oh, and the food's great, too – classics like creamy mac and cheese and American specialities like filet mignon, grilled fish and braised short ribs. It's the perfect post-theatre or pre-club pit stop.

Lips
2 Bank Street, at Greenwich Avenue (1-212 675 7710). Subway: 1, 2, 3 to 14th Street. **Open** 5.30pm-midnight Mon-Thur; 5.30pm-1am Fri, Sat; 11.30am-4pm, 5.30-11pm Sun. **Average main course** $18. **Credit** AmEx, DC, MC, V.
This festive restaurant certainly does generate an enjoyable jovial atmosphere: the drag-queen waitstaff serves tasty meals and performs for very enthusiastic patrons. Midweek events tend to be a lot gayer than the weekends, when scores of shrieking straight chicks descend on the place for their bachelorette parties. The Sunday brunch ($14.95 including copious alcohol) is quite a show.

Rubyfruit Bar & Grill
531 Hudson Street, between Charles & Washington Streets (1-212 929 3343). Subway: 1 to Christopher Street-Sheridan Square. **Open** 2pm-4am Mon-Thur; 3pm-4am Fri, Sat; 11.30am-2am Sun. **Average main course** $20. **Credit** AmEx, DC, Disc, MC, V.
The food is good, but it's not the main selling point at this dedicated lesbian restaurant and bar. An eclectic mix of music and congenial customers make for a great place for fun-loving, old-school dykes.

Arts & Entertainment

Music

At the forefront of classical and popular scenes, New York doesn't miss a beat.

Popular

Two very different New York music scenes have emerged in recent years: one involves the overhyped, trendy rock and pop acts that fill the pages of *Rolling Stone* and *NME* and is largely unknown to actual New Yorkers, while the other only comes into focus once you get to town and realise just how deep the city's music roots run. Case in point: the Bravery were touted as one of 2005's bands to watch by nearly every major music publication in the US and UK. Mention the NYC-based group's name to a music fan who lives here and you're likely to get a blank stare (unless you happen to be at a Lower East Side hipster haven, such as Pianos).

The one never-ending plotline to the city's music scene is renewal. We're not just talking about retro-rock bands bleeding the '80s dry for wan inspiration; it's the constant influx of hungry, talented youths who come to town looking to make a name for themselves that keeps things fresh. While melting-plot clichés get tossed around like lettuce – and the mix of youth and experience, not to mention local and global styles, is in evidence everywhere you look – what's special about this city is that assimilating doesn't mean giving up your roots. Musicians who come here are equally proud to be New Yorkers and to retain their roots, which is why everything from Latin pop to heavy metal can sound quintessentially New York.

That Lower East Side see-and-be-seen scene, centred on Ludlow Street, remains as colourful and bustling as ever. But if you don't count yourself among the rock 'n' roll set, you'll still find plenty to listen to – world-class jazz, hip hop, soul, folk and pretty much every international flavour and fusion, from legends and rising stars, across the five boroughs.

To help you navigate the scene, we've organised the city's most active and notable venues by genre. Note to the anal: these categories are loose. Many spots can throb with a techno beat one night and rock out the next, or skip from hip hop to Brazilian music in a single evening. A relaxed attitude helps, as does a willingness to hang around and do some people-watching: if a listing says your favourite band is going on at 11pm, you might wait till midnight or later.

A valid photo ID proving that you're 21 or over is essential, not only to drink but, often, just to get in (a passport or a driver's licence are best). NYC bouncers have heard it all, and they're notoriously impervious to excuses.

Tickets are usually available from clubs in advance and at the door. A few small and medium-size venues also sell advance tickets through local record stores. For larger events, it's wise to buy through Ticketmaster (*see p382*) on the web, over the phone or at one of the outlets located throughout the city. Tickets for some events are available through Ticket Web (www.ticketweb.com). You can also purchase them online from websites of specific venues (URLs are included in venue listings where available). For more ticket details, *see p328*. And remember to call ahead for info and show times, which may change without notice.

Arenas

Continental Airlines Arena
For listing, see p334 **Meadowlands Sports Complex**.
North Jersey's answer to Madison Square Garden recently played host to the likes of Eminem, U2, Britney Spears and Van Halen. Oldies showcases and radio-sponsored pop and hip-hop extravaganzas also happen here.

Madison Square Garden
For listing, see p334.
Madison Square Garden, one of the world's most famous arenas, is where the biggest acts – Prince, Madonna, Bob Dylan – come out to play. Whether you can see them well depends a lot on your seat, or your binoculars.

Nassau Veterans Memorial Coliseum
For listing, see p334.
Long Island's arena hosts mainstream acts like Rush, Incubus and Sarah McLachlan, punctuated by occasional teen-pop sock hops (*American Idol* Live, Hilary Duff) and garish Bollywood showcases.

Rock, pop & soul

Ace of Clubs
9 Great Jones Street, at Lafayette Street (1-212 677 6924/www.aceofclubsnyc.com). Subway: B, D, F, V to Broadway-Lafayette Street; 6 to Bleecker Street.
Cover $5-$12; doors open at 7pm. **No credit cards**.

All this cosy shoebox of a space had needed the past few years was a booker with some taste. Ask and ye shall receive, as early as 2005 it morphed from the old Under Acme into Ace of Clubs and started bringing in a diverse mix of mostly local rock (the Giraffes), blues (Corey Harris) and progressive jazz (the Jazz Passengers' Bill Ware and his Urban Vibes project). The location is about as central as they come, and if you need a bite, the restaurant Acme is on street level to satisfy your soul-food jones.

Apollo Theater
253 W 125th Street, between Adam Clayton Powell Jr Boulevard (Seventh Avenue) & Frederick Douglass Boulevard (Eighth Avenue) (1-212 531 5305/www. apollotheater.com). Subway: A, B, C, D, 1 to 125th Street. **Box office** 10am-6pm Mon, Tue, Thur, Fri; 10am-8.30pm Wed; noon-6pm Sat. **Tickets** $20-$100. **Credit** AmEx, DC, Disc, MC, V.

Visitors might think they know Harlem's venerable Apollo from TV's *Showtime at the Apollo*, but as the saying goes, the small screen adds about 10lb. Inside, the elegant yet lived-in theatre – still the city's home of R&B and soul music – is actually quite cosy. Known for launching the careers of Ella Fitzgerald, Michael Jackson and D'Angelo, to name just a few, the Apollo continues to bring in veteran talent such as Joan Armatrading and Ben E King while offering wannabe stars a legendary stage to show off their own shine.

Arlene's Grocery
95 Stanton Street, between Ludlow & Orchard Streets (1-212 995 1652/www.arlene-grocery.com). Subway: F to Delancey Street; J, M, Z to Delancey-Essex Streets. **Cover** $7; doors open 6pm-4am daily. **Credit** AmEx, MC, V.

A mid-level rung on the local-band ladder, Arlene's can pack as many as six rock acts a night, often adding afternoon shows on Saturdays. Monday night's live-band karaoke is an institution, even if the band that started it all has moved on. A lively spot in the liveliest of neighbourhoods.

BAMcafé at Brooklyn Academy of Music
For listing, see p328 **Brooklyn Academy of Music**.

Among the cornucopia of live-entertainment programmes found at BAM is the BAMcafé above the lobby, which comes to life on weekend nights with country, spoken word, hip hop, world music and more, by performers such as Son de Madre and Manze. The Next**Next** series, which began in 2002, focuses on performers in their 20s.

BB King Blues Club & Grill
237 W 42nd Street, between Seventh & Eighth Avenues (1-212 997 4144/www.bbkingblues.com). Subway: A, C, E to 42nd Street-Port Authority; N, Q, R, W, 42nd Street S, 1, 2, 3, 7 to 42nd Street-Times Square. **Box office** 10.30am-midnight daily. **Tickets** $12-$150. **Credit** AmEx, DC, Disc, MC, V.

Its location and appearance would seem geared to tourists, but BB's joint in Times Square plays host to perhaps the widest variety of music in town: cover bands and soul tributes fill the gaps between big-name bookings such as Aretha Franklin, the Neville Brothers and Judy Collins. Lately, the club has also proved a viable space for extreme metal bands (Napalm Death, Obituary, Hate Eternal) and neo-soul and hip-hop acts (such as Angie Stone, Method Man, Ghostface and assorted other Wu-Tangers). For many shows, the best seats are at the dinner tables up front, but menu prices are steep. The Harlem Gospel Choir buffet brunch, on Sundays, raises the roof, while live classic-rock, jazz and blues groups play for free most nights at Lucille's Bar & Grill, the cosy restaurant named after King's cherished guitar.

Beacon Theatre
2124 Broadway, at 74th Street (1-212 496 7070). Subway: 1, 2, 3 to 72nd Street. **Box office** 11am-7pm Mon-Fri; noon-6pm Sat. **Tickets** $15-$175. **No credit cards.**

This spacious Upper West Side theatre hosts a variety of popular acts, from Hot Tuna and Meat Loaf to Nick Cave and Sigur Ros – and once a year, the Allman Brothers take over the place for a lengthy residency. While the theatre's sound and vastness can be daunting to performer and audience alike, the stately, gilded interior and uptown location make you feel like you're having a real night out on the town.

Bowery Ballroom
6 Delancey Street, between Bowery & Chrystie Street (1-212 533 2111/www.boweryballroom.com). Subway: J, M, Z to Bowery; 6 to Spring Street. **Box office** at the Mercury Lounge, see p319. **Tickets** $13-$40. **Credit** AmEx, MC, V (bar only).

Cadillac *and* Honda – both represent the Bowery Ballroom's status on the NYC music scene. Probably the best venue in town for seeing indie bands either on the way up or holding their own, the Bowery nonetheless brings in a diverse range of artists from in town and around the world, as well as offering a clear view and loud, bright sound from just about any spot. Excellent bookings have included Rachid Taha, Teenage Fanclub, Smog and Keren Ann, while Neko Case played two spectacular shows for Valentine's Day in 2005. Not into an opening band? The spacious downstairs lounge is a great place to relax and socialise between (or during) sets.

Bowery Poetry Club
308 Bowery, at Bleecker Street (1-212 614 0505/ www.bowerypoetry.com). Subway: B, D, F, V to Broadway-Lafayette Street; 6 to Bleecker Street. **Cover** $3-$10; check website for schedule. **Credit** AmEx, MC, V (bar only).

The name of this colourful joint on the Bowery reveals its roots in the poetry-slam scene, but it's also the truest current iteration of the East Village's legendary creative-arts scene: all kinds of jazz, folk, hip hop and improv theatre can be found here routinely; if you have a taste for the bizarre and don't offend easily,

Buzzworthy

Clap Your Hands Say Yeah

Clap Your Hands Say Yeah is a baby band, with nary a release to its credit and only a pile of T-shirts to hawk after its shows. Already, however, this local quintet has its sound outlined with a precision unmatched by many veterans. The group has stockpiled a mass of oft-trampled influences, including what amounts to a 12-course meal of in-vogue '80s acts. The Reagan-era creepiness that often surfaces when contemporary acts dabble in such sounds is curtailed by Clap Your Hands' apparent affinity for the Clean and other indie slouchers, to say nothing of the harmonica strapped in front of singer Alec Ounsworth's mouth. (Republicans play keyboards, but it takes a socialist to pull off the consecrated harmonica holder.)

keep your eyes peeled for anything from the Jollyship to the Whiz-Bang musical-puppet crew. The BPC offers a range of sandwiches and hot and cold drinks, and it was a round-the-clock counterculture HQ during the Republican convention in 2004.

Cake Shop

152 Ludlow Street, between Rivington and Stanton Streets (1-212 253 0036/www.cake-shop.com). Subway: F, V to Lower East Side-Second Avenue. **Cover** $6-$8; doors open at 8pm. **No credit cards**. This narrow but clean-and-new basement space gets points for much more than its keen indie-rock bookings, such as up-and-comers Tomorrow's Friend, the !!!-offshoot Free Blood and manic noise act Aa. For one thing, it's located in the heart of the Lower East Side, between Pianos and the Living Room on Ludlow Street. What's more, it has pastries and coffee for sale upstairs. Better still (for late-night music junkies, at least) is the brightly lit back room on street level, which sells used vinyl and CDs, as well as a smattering of new releases, DVDs and other record-store ephemera. The sort of small-but-spirited spot we always thought we'd find in NYC.

CBGB

315 Bowery, at Bleecker Street (1-212 982 4052/ www.cbgb.com). Subway: B, D, F, V to Broadway-Lafayette Street; 6 to Bleecker Street. **Cover** $3-$12; check website for schedule. **No credit cards**.
The big-name bookings were so far in the past that when people learned this tarnished mecca of punk rock was fighting for its life (and lease), it seemed a little surreal. But, apparently, a fight for survival is exactly what was needed to bring the old punks back (and, often, out of retirement), with benefit shows featuring the Circle Jerks, Dead Boys and Anti-Nowhere League. You can feel the history throughout the grubby joint (especially stuck on the walls), and you can certainly smell it, too: brace yourself before a trip to the notorious bathroom. **Photo** *p316.*

CB's Lounge/CB's 313 Gallery

313 Bowery, at Bleecker Street (1-212 677 0455/ www.cbgb.com). Subway: B, D, F, V to Broadway-Lafayette Street; 6 to Bleecker Street. **Cover** $5-$10; shows start around 7pm. **Credit** AmEx, MC, V (bar only, $20 minimum).

CBGB (*see p315*): the notorious bathroom is nearly as legendary...

CBGB's smaller next-door neighbours (the Lounge is downstairs from the Gallery) are more cultivated – and, to be sure, happening – as far as current music. CB's 313 Gallery displays art (not band stickers) on its walls and up-and-coming singer-songwriters on its stage. The lower level has the feeling of a suburban rec room and showed its range with a (recently concluded) weekly jazz free-for-all.

Continental
25 Third Avenue, at St Marks Place (1-212 529 6924/www.continentalnyc.com). Subway: N, R, W to 8th Street-NYU; 6 to Astor Place. **Cover** free-$10; doors open at 4pm. **No credit cards**.
Like CBGB, the Continental's rep as a prime street-punk spot has grown in inverse proportion to its band calendar. Proof was provided recently by the club itself, when it issued a pair of live CDs with the stars of yesteryear. Today's sound-alike thrashers are nameless but competent and loud (and the volume here can be punishing), and the Continental is surely the best rock club in the city for drinking: a titillating sign above the bar reads 'FIVE SHOTS OF ANY-THING – $10'. Punk forefather Cheetah Chrome and Boston's the Real Kids still pop in for gigs now and then, but the real draw is Monday's Original Punk/Metal Karaoke Band, which will help you live out your rock 'n' roll dreams. All-ages gigs on weekend afternoons are a long-standing tradition.

Delancey
168 Delancey Street, at Clinton Street (1-212 254 9920/www.thedelancey.com). Subway: F to Delancey Street; J, M, Z to Delancey-Essex Streets. **Cover** $6-$10; doors open at 8pm. **No credit cards**.
Spitting distance from the Williamsburg Bridge (even if you're a lousy spitter) is the Delancey, which has quickly become one of Manhattan's hotter spots

on account of its frequent bookings of hyped indie bands (Clap Your Hands Say Yeah, Youth Group) and DJs – and the lovely second-floor outdoor patio (where you'd want to spit from, if you were so rude), which is always mobbed with beautiful young hipsters in the summer, doesn't hurt. **Photo** *p320*.

Don Hill's
511 Greenwich Street, at Spring Street (1-212 219 2850/www.donhills.com). Subway: C, E to Spring Street; 1 to Canal Street. **Cover** free-$10; doors open at 7.30pm. **Credit** AmEx, DC, Disc, MC, V.
This unassuming, boxy space isn't much for new live bands these days. But Saturday night's Britpoppy Tiswas party often features strong locals, and Wednesday's glam-punk bonanza Röck Cändy is always a solid bet – especially if you like cheap beer.

Galapagos
70 North 6th Street, between Kent & Wythe Avenues, Williamsburg, Brooklyn (1-718 782 5188/www. galapagosartspace.com). Subway: L to Bedford Avenue. **Cover** free-$7; show times vary. **No credit cards**.
This roomy Williamsburg art and performance space, famed for the dark pool at its entrance (and the setting for one of the scenes in *Coffee and Cigarettes*), focuses on Brooklyn artists, but its mix of music, performance art, readings and film screenings doesn't discriminate. Burlesque and vaudeville nights are weekly staples, while a recent series staged by SculptureCenter brought in Alan Licht, Aki Onda and Currituck Co, among others.

Hammerstein Ballroom
Manhattan Center, 311 W 34th Street, between Eighth & Ninth Avenues (1-212 279 7740/www. mcstudios.com). Subway: A, C, E to 34th Street-Penn Station. **Box office** noon-5pm Mon-Sat. **Tickets** $10-$50. **Credit** AmEx, MC, V.

... as the punk icons who played its stage.

Patrons can be treated like cattle and the drinks remain the most outlandish in town – upwards of ten bucks for a cheap cocktail in a plastic cup! – but there's no denying the status of this cavernous space. Unless you're on the floor (there is no general admission here), the stage might seem a distant illusion. But the once-poor sound quality has been rectified, to the point where New Order's recent NYC return could be considered a triumph, and the environment itself – dramatic, vaulted balconies hanging over a raucous floor – captures that big-show excitement. For local artists such as Interpol and the Strokes, dates here are proof they've made it big.

The Hook

18 Commerce Street, between Dwight & Richards Streets, Red Hook, Brooklyn (1-718 797 3007/www. thehookmusic.com). Subway: F, G to Carroll Street. **Open** *Show days* 8.30pm-4am. **Cover** $8-$15. **No credit cards**.
How do you survive as a nightclub in a remote spot? Do like the Hook and bring in a steady stream of must-see bands, from noisy touring outfits (Khanate, Ill Ease) to locals with followings (Animal Collective, Kid Congo Powers). The spacious club has a long bar, a wide-open floor, an easy-going vibe and a huge area out back for smokers. Even though the Red Hook area has been on the rise, the Hook itself – on a lonely block of warehouses – is still a destination venue, as opposed to one component of a night out. Bring a car service number to get home.

Irving Plaza

17 Irving Place, at 15th Street (1-212 777 6800/ www.irvingplaza.com). Subway: L, N, Q, R, W, 4, 5, 6 to 14th Street-Union Square. **Box office** noon-6.30pm Mon-Fri; 1-4pm Sat. **Tickets** $10-$60. **Credit** AmEx.

Despite recent competition, no mid-size room compares with mid-size Irving Plaza's diverse calendar. Indie legends (Slint, Mission of Burma), pillars of American music (Robert Cray, John Fogerty) and rising stars of rock (Chevelle, Static-X) and hip-hop (Madlib, Blackalicious) cram the Plaza's schedule. And from the parlour-lit lounge downstairs to the shadowy corners of the balconies, this pleasantly worn old ballroom practically whispers of New York's rock past.

Joe's Pub

The Public Theater, 425 Lafayette Street, between Astor Place & E 4th Street (1-212 539 8770/ www.joespub.com). Subway: N, R, W to 8th Street-NYU; 6 to Astor Place. **Box office** 1 6pm Mon, Sun; 1-7pm Tue Sat. **Tickets** $12-$30. **Credit** AmEx, MC, V.
One of the city's premier live-music spots for sit-down audiences, Joe's Pub brings in impeccable talent – mainly eclectic, adult-oriented fare. While some well-established names such as John Wesley Harding, Sir Richard Bishop, Malian blues nomads Tinariwen and even Vanessa Carlton have played here recently, Joe's also provides a stage for up-and-coming local singers (Essie Jain, Heather Greene). Late-night hip-hop parties combine a trendy vibe with quality beats, while the Mingus Orchestra – a city institution – recently took over Thursday nights. A small but solid menu and deep bar selection seal the deal.

Knitting Factory

74 Leonard Street, between Broadway & Church Street (1-212 219 3132/www.knittingfactory.com). Subway: A, C, E to Canal Street; 1 to Franklin Street. **Box office** 4-11pm Mon-Sat; 2-11pm Sun. **Tickets** $5-$20. **Credit** AmEx, MC, V.

Taking music outside the auditorium...

This three-floor circus was once known as NYC's downtown home of avant-garde jazz, but a couple of ownership changes later and jazz is scarce (other than the occasional Bad Plus gig). What you will find is a woolly (if inconsistent) mix of mainly indie acts (the Fall, Lilys, Richard Davies), metal (Otep, Pelican, Soilent Green) and locals (Jah Division, the Flesh), with a smattering of decent hip hop and college-campus-calibre filler. The smaller Tap Bar and claustrophobic Old Office, both under the main room (both with separate admissions), often have good DJs tucked in among the busy flow of bands.

Lakeside Lounge

162 Avenue B, between 10th & 11th Streets (1-212 529 8463/www.lakesidelounge.com). Subway: L to First Avenue; N, Q, R, W, 4, 5, 6 to 14th Street-Union Square. **Cover** free; shows start at 9.30 or 10pm. **Credit** AmEx, MC, V (bar only).
Because this cosy East Village joint is co-owned by guitarist and producer Eric Ambel (who plays in Steve Earle's band), the roadhouse and roots acts that come through tend to be at least fun. Local country-tinged talents (Tandy, Chris Harford, Jack Grace) appear often, and the bar, the jukebox and the photo booth are all attractions of their own.

Lit Lounge

93 Second Avenue, between 5th & 6th Streets (1-212 777 7987/www.litloungenyc.com). Subway: F, V to Lower East Side-Second Avenue; 6 to Astor Place. **Cover** free-$5; shows start at 9pm. **Credit** AmEx, MC, V (bar only, $20 minimum).
This likeable, if airflow-challenged, dungeon offers a stream of earnest, noisy young indie bands, but its

calendar is peppered with enough top-notch talent to keep it on the radar. You might find local avant-folk stars such as PG Six and Samara Lubelski on the tiny stage one night and gritty hard rockers Made Out of Babies the next. Occasionally, a truly memorable night will go down, such as when art-guitar god Glenn Branca joined in with Tono-Bungay. The location makes it easy to swing in and right back out if you're hitting the town.

Living Room

154 Ludlow Street, between Rivington & Stanton Streets (1-212 533 7235/www.livingroomny.com). Subway: F to Lower East Side-Second Avenue; J, M, Z to Delancey-Essex Streets. **Open** 6pm-4am Mon, Tue; 2pm-4am Wed-Sat; 6pm-2am Sun. **Cover** free; one-drink minimum. **No credit cards**.
Many local clubs try to lay claim to being the place where Norah Jones got her start, but the Living Room is really it (she even donated a piano as a way of saying thanks). Still, that was in the venue's old (and drab) location; since moving to the Lower East Side's version of Main Street, the stream of singer-songwriters that fill the schedule here has taken on a bit more gleam, and the warmly lit environs seem to be always bustling. Skilful guitarist Jim Campilongo appears regularly, as do local stalwarts such as Tony Scherr, Chris Lee and Matty Charles.

Makor

35 W 67th Street, between Central Park West & Columbus Avenue (1-212 601 1000/www.makor.org). Subway: 1 to 66th Street-Lincoln Center. **Box office** 9am-9pm Mon-Thur; 9am-5pm Fri; 7-10pm Sat; 9am-10pm Sun. **Tickets** $9-$30. **Credit** AmEx, MC, V.

Arts & Entertainment

... BAM's annual **Outside Art Festival**. *See p328*.

Behind this unassuming Upper West Side spot's doors – and down the stairs, then around the corner – lies this Jewish cultural centre's stage. Make the trek, however, and you'll find an oddly vast range of globalist sounds, from Gypsy singer Sanda Weigl to the Dimestore Danceband and hip-hop duo Airborn Audio. The location and layout makes Makor (related to the 92nd Street Y) less than ideal for simply hanging out, but surprises await.

Maxwell's

1039 Washington Street, at 11th Street, Hoboken, NJ (1-201 798 0406/www.maxwellsnj.com). Travel: PATH train to Hoboken, then take a cab, the Red Apple bus or NJ Transit 126 bus to 12th Street. **Box office** Visit website for hours. **Tickets** $7-$20. **Credit** AmEx, Disc, MC, V.

The trip out to Maxwell's can be a hassle, but the 15-minute walk – not unpleasant if the weather's on your side – from the PATH train can make you feel like you're in small-town America in a way that Brooklyn can't. The restaurant in front is big and friendly, and for dessert, you can feast on indie-rock fare from popular artists like Stars and Quintron, or any number of new local acts. Hometown heroes Yo La Tengo stage their more-or-less annual Hanukkah shows at this area institution.

Mercury Lounge

217 E Houston Street, between Essex & Ludlow Streets (1-212 260 4700/www.mercuryloungenyc.com). Subway: F, V to Lower East Side-Second Avenue. **Box office** noon-7pm Mon-Sat. **Cover** $8-$15; shows require advance tickets. **Shows** daily, times vary. **Credit** AmEx, DC, Disc, MC, V (bar only).

The unassuming, boxy Mercury Lounge is both an old stand-by and pretty much the No.1 indie-rock club in town, with solid sound and sight lines (and a cramped bar in the front room). With four-band bills almost every night, you can catch plenty of locals (the Occasion, Bishop Allen and Blues Explosion offshoot 20 Miles) and touring bands (Junior Senior, the Go-Betweens, Sam Prekop) in the course of just one week. Note that some of the Lower East Side spot's bigger shows sell out in advance, mainly through online sales.

New Jersey Performing Arts Center

1 Center Street, at the waterfront, Newark, NJ (1-888 466 5722/www.njpac.org). Travel: PATH train to Newark, then take the Loop shuttle bus to NJPAC. **Box office** noon-6pm Mon-Sat; 10am-3pm Sun. **Tickets** $12-$100. **Credit** AmEx, Disc, MC, V.

Within sight of Manhattan (and quite easy to get to, as well), NJPAC offers up legends of disco (Donna Summer) and Broadway stars in cabaret performances (Brian Stokes Mitchell), as well as crowd-pleasing swing and soul music. The summer is chock-full of outdoor entertainment geared to families, too.

92nd Street Y

www.ymcanyc.org.
Best known for the series Jazz in July (now directed by pianist Bill Charlap) and Lyrics & Lyricists, the uptown Y's schedule extends to gospel, mainstream jazz and singer-songwriters. The small, handsome theatre provides a fine setting for the sophisticated fare that plays here.

Riffing at the **Delancey**. *See p316.*

Northsix

66 North 6th Street, between Kent & Wythe Avenues, Williamsburg, Brooklyn (1-718 599 5103/ www.northsix.com). Subway: L to Bedford Avenue. **Box office** 4-11pm daily (advance online purchase recommended). **Tickets** $6-$18. **Credit** AmEx, Disc, MC, V (advance purchases only).
One of Williamsburg's top music spots, Northsix does a great job of pleasing trendy locals and music fans who might otherwise steer clear of the area. Easily accessible via the L, this warehouse-like space has hosted indie stars Lightning Bolt and Mary Timony, as well as one of the DKT/MC5 reunion shows. It's also one of the few clubs where you can still hear live hip hop (mainly of the underground variety, such as from the Definitive Jux label).

Nublu

62 Avenue C, between 4th & 5th Streets (1-212 979 9925/www.nublu.net). Subway: F, V to Lower East Side-Second Avenue. **Cover** $5-$10; doors open at 8pm. **No credit cards**.
Inversely proportional to its size – not to mention the seemingly out-of-the-way location deep in Alphabet City – has been Nublu's prominence on the local globalist club scene. A pressure cooker of creativity, Nublu gave rise to the Brazilian Girls, who started jamming at one late-night session and haven't stopped yet, as well as starting NYC's romance with the Northern Brazilian style *forró*. Even on weeknights, events usually start no earlier than 10pm and can run into the wee hours – but if you show up early (and find the unmarked door), the bar is well stocked with wine selections, among other beverages, and the staff is as warm as the music.

Pianos

158 Ludlow Street, between Rivington & Stanton Streets (1-212 505 3733). Subway: F to Delancey Street; J, M, Z to Delancey-Essex Streets. **Box office** 5pm-4am daily. **Cover** free-$12; shows start around 8pm. **Credit** AmEx, DC, MC, V.
On a Saturday night, Pianos can seem like either the centre of New York or the ninth circle of hell, depending on your tastes. But there's no denying that this style-conscious bar-cum-club brings in a weird, wild mix; one night you'll get trendy local bands (the Harlem Shakes, Unisex Salon) and the next you might get Prince Paul! The sound is often lousy and the room uncomfortably mobbed, but like it or not, there are always good reasons to go back. Darn it. Also a good bet is the emerging talent booked in the charming and free upstairs lounge.

Radio City Music Hall

1260 Sixth Avenue, at 50th Street (1-212 247 4777/ www.radiocity.com). Subway: B, D, F, V to 47-50th Streets-Rockefeller Center. **Box office** 10am-8pm Mon-Sat; 11am-8pm Sun. **Tickets** $25-$125. **Credit** AmEx, MC, V.
Few rooms scream 'New York City!' more than this gilded hall, which has recently drawn Wilco, Alanis Morissette and Carole King as headliners. Of course, the greatest challenge for any performer is not to get upstaged by the awe-inspiring art deco surroundings.

Roseland

239 W 52nd Street, between Broadway & Eighth Avenue (1-212 247 0200/www.roselandballroom. com). Subway: B, D, E to Seventh Avenue; C to 50th Street. **Box office** at Irving Plaza, *see p317.* **Tickets** $17-$75. **No credit cards**.
Roseland has always gotten the automatic bad rap that plagues most big venues, but really, other than the occasional queue to get in, there are few complaints. Good sound is always a struggle in a room this size, but Sleater-Kinney made a noisy set work recently. As at any large club, you'll find any artist who can fill the room performing here, from Aimee Mann or the Indigo Girls to Ghostface or Youssou N'Dour.

Rothko

116 Suffolk Street, between Delancey & Rivington
Streets (www.rothkonyc.com). Subway: F to Delancey
Street; J, M, Z to Delancey-Essex Streets. **Cover**
free-$8; shows start around 8pm. **No credit cards**.
The cloying vibe of trendiness that plagues a place
like Pianos is relatively absent at Rothko, just a few
blocks away. This Lower East Side shoebox has a
more refined definition of hip, drawing DJing and
electronic stars such as Diplo, Mu and Plaid in addition to rockers (Pilot to Gunner, Dance Disaster
Movement, the Ponys). The monthly hip-hop karaoke
is among the best such events you'll find in town.

Sidewalk

94 Avenue A, at 6th Street (1-212 473 7373).
Subway: F, V to Lower East Side-Second Avenue;
6 to Astor Place. **Cover** free; two-drink minimum;
shows start around 7.30pm. **Credit** AmEx, MC, V
(bar only).
Despite its cramped and awkward layout, the
Sidewalk café is the undisputed focal point of the
city's anti-folk scene – though that category means
just about anything from piano pop to wry folk.
Nellie McKay, Regina Spektor and the Moldy Peaches
all got started here; Monday's Antihootenanny with
anti-folk capo Lach is an institution.

Sin-é

150 Attorney Street, between Houston & Stanton
Streets (1-212 388 0077/www.sin-e.com). Subway:
F to Delancey Street; J, M, Z to Delancey-Essex
Streets. **Open** 7.30pm-1am daily. **Cover** $7-$15.
No credit cards.
Immortalised by a Jeff Buckley live recording (made
at an earlier incarnation), this unassuming little
Lower East Side space mainly schedules local indie
bands, many more earnest than good. But there are
more than enough great bands here, from garage
semi-legends Cheater Slicks and Boston's Big Bear
to Lubricated Goat and TV on the Radio's Kyp
Malone flying solo. One nice aspect is that, while
close enough to stroll over to Ludlow Street, down
here things are quite peaceful and untrafficked.

S.O.B.'s

204 Varick Street, at Houston Street (1-212 243
4940/www.sobs.com). Subway: 1 to Houston Street.
Box office 11am-6pm Mon-Sat. **Tickets** $10-$25.
Credit AmEx, DC, Disc, MC, V (food and bar only).
The titular sounds of Brazil are just some of many
global genres that keep this Tribeca spot hopping.
Hip hop, soul, reggae and Latin beats figure into
the mix, with MIA, Seu Jorge, Leela James and
Yellowman each appearing of late. Careful at the
bar – drinks are outrageously priced. But the sharp-
looking clientele doesn't seem to mind.

Southpaw

125 Fifth Avenue, between Sterling & St Johns
Places, Park Slope, Brooklyn (1-718 230 0236/www.
spsounds.com). Subway: B, Q, 2, 3, 4, 5 to Atlantic
Avenue; D, M, N, R to Pacific Street. **Open** Show
times vary. **Tickets** $7-$20. **No credit cards**.

Another cool space that's far enough out of
Manhattan to ensure you'll never come just to
chill out, but only to see someone specific. Which is
hardly a problem, since the calendar welcomes
prime roots outfits (Jon Langford's Waco Brothers,
Magnolia Electroc Co), the occasional psych-rock
explosion (Acid Mothers Temple) and plenty of
garage rock (Reigning Sound, the Dirtbombs,
Teengenerate). Like its Park Slope neighbourhood,
Southpaw tends to draw cool, mellow audiences, and
with all this elbow room, getting to the (huge!) bar
is hardly an issue.

Theater at Madison Square Garden

Seventh Avenue, between 31st & 33rd Streets
(1-212 465 6741/www.thegarden.com). Subway:
A, C, E, 1, 2, 3 to 34th Street-Penn Station.
Box office noon-6pm Mon-Sat. **Tickets** vary.
Credit AmEx, DC, Disc, MC, V.

Buzzworthy

The ACME Ensemble

The ACME Ensemble spans a range from
hard-core modernism to more pop-oriented
contemporary idioms. Young, smart and
hip, this group of Juilliard students and
grads has dazzled downtown crowds at
Tenri Cultural Center (43 W 13th Street)
and the Cornelia Street Café (*see p323*).
Founder and cellist Clarice Jensen keeps
the flexible ensemble – which includes
violin, viola, flute, clarinet, piano and
percussion, along with a conductor and
other instruments as needed – focused on
established 20th-century masterpieces, as
well as new music by young composers.

This smaller space within the Garden has better sound than the arena. The Theater has hosted world-music celebrations, as well as mainstream hip hop, and the last Gospelfest featured Aretha Franklin.

Tonic

107 Norfolk Street, between Delancey & Rivington Streets (1-212 358 7503/www.tonicnyc.com). Subway: F to Delancey Street; J, M, Z to Delancey-Essex Streets. **Cover** $5-$40; doors open at 7.30pm. **No credit cards.**

Overcoming great odds just to remain open early in 2005, Tonic survived mainly because of the great love that artists and audiences feel for the small former kosher winery. A string of big-name benefits – Yo La Tengo, sure, but also Yoko Ono – helped stave off eviction, and Tonic hurtles on as the home of New York's avant-garde, creative and experimental music scenes. On any night you might find challenging experimenters (Tim Barnes, Okkyung Lee or members of Sonic Youth), folk legends (Simon Finn, Michael Hurley) or local rock talent (Tomorrow's Friend, the Double). Downtown icon John Zorn and artists from his Tzadik label perform frequently. In Subtonic (*see p295*), the basement lounge, guests can loll around on banquettes built into giant former wine casks on weekends, as DJs spin hip and edgy sounds, new and old. **Photo** *p324.*

Town Hall

123 W 43rd Street, between Sixth & Seventh Avenues (1-212 997 1003/www.the-townhall-nyc.org). Subway: B, D, F, V to 42nd Street-Bryant Park; N, Q, R, W, 42nd Street S, 1, 2, 3, 7 to 42nd Street-Times Square. **Box office** noon-6pm Mon-Sat. **Tickets** $15-$85. **Credit** AmEx, MC, V ($1 surcharge).

The superb acoustics at this 'people's auditorium' make mellower sounds right at home, and there's no doubting the gravitas of the surroundings. Antony and the Johnsons, Eels and Oliver Mtukudzi have each put on stellar shows here of late, and the Broadway by the Year series brings in the best standards and stars from the nearby Great White Way.

Trash

256 Grand Street, between Driggs Avenue & Roebling Street, Williamsburg, Brooklyn (1-718 599 1000/www.thetrashbar.com). Subway: L to Bedford Avenue. **Cover** $6-$8; doors open at 8pm. **No credit cards.**

Formerly Luxx, one of Brooklyn's central locations for Electroclash (remember that? Neither do we!), this slightly grubby club tore down the glitzy wallpaper and returned to booking fun rock – including Heroin Sheiks, Wide Right and the Hunches – in its blisteringly loud, red-lit back room. Two bars and a front room with a pool table make Trash a happening place to, you know, get trashed.

Webster Hall

125 E 11th Street, between Third & Fourth Avenues (1-212 353 1600/www.websterhall.com). Subway: L to Third Avenue; N, Q, R, W, 4, 5, 6 to 14th Street-Union Square. **Open** Visit website for hours. **Tickets** free-$30. **Credit** AmEx, DC, MC, V.

Even if the bookings come in at a relative trickle, the addition of Webster Hall to the local scene provides a great-sounding alternative for bands (not to mention fans) who might have had their fill of comparably sized Irving Plaza. The folks who run Bowery Ballroom and Mercury Lounge provide the bookings here, which is why the schedule features bands that have grown out of those rooms (Broadcast, Spoon, the Raveonettes). A rare appearance from British electronica duo Autechre might not have been possible in any other room in town, given Webster's size and killer sound system.

Jazz & experimental

Barbès

376 9th Street, at Sixth Avenue, Park Slope, Brooklyn (1-718 965 9177/www.barbesbrooklyn.com). Subway: F to Seventh Avenue. **Tickets** free-$8. **Credit** Disc, MC, V (bar only).

Show up early if you want to get into Park Slope's global-bohemian club (and you do), since it's tiny. This boîte, run by musically inclined French expats, brings in jazz of the traditional swing and more daring stripes, plus world-music-derived hybrids (Las Rubias del Norte) and uncategorisable acts (the literate One Ring Zero).

Birdland

315 W 44th Street, between Eighth & Ninth Avenues (1-212 581 3080/www.birdlandjazz.com). Subway: A, C, E to 42nd Street-Port Authority. **Box office** Reservations required; call club. **Tickets** $20-$50, $10 food-and-drink minimum. **Credit** AmEx, DC, Disc, MC, V.

The name means jazz but, perhaps in deference to its Theater District digs, Birdland is also a prime destination for cabaret. The jazz names that pass through are unimpeachable (Kurt Elling, Jim Hall, Paquito D'Rivera) and the cabaret stars glowing (Christine Andreas, Christine Ebersole). Residencies are among the better ones in town (the Chico O'Farrill Afro-Cuban Jazz Orchestra owns Sundays and David Ostwald's Louis Armstrong Centennial Band hits on Tuesdays; Mondays find cabaret's waggish Jim Caruso and his Cast Party).

Blue Note

131 W 3rd Street, between MacDougal Street & Sixth Avenue (1-212 475 8592/www.bluenote.net). Subway: A, B, C, D, E, F, V to W 4th Street. **Box office** Call or visit website for reservations. **Tickets** $10-$65, $5 food-and-drink minimum. **Credit** AmEx, DC, MC, V.

Found on a bustling, slightly seedy block is the Blue Note, which prides itself on being 'the jazz capital of the world'. Bona fide musical titans (Cecil Taylor, Abbey Lincoln) rub up against hot young talents (Matthew Shipp, Jason Lindner) on the calendar, while the tables in the club get patrons rubbing up against each other. The Late Night Groove series and the Sunday brunches are the best bargain bets.

Talent loves the **55 Bar**, and the 55 Bar loves it right back.

Carnegie Hall

For listing, see p328.
As the saying indicates, Carnegie Hall means the big time. In recent years Zankel Hall – a state-of-the-art 599-seat subterranean theatre – has greatly augmented Carnegie's pop, jazz and world-music offerings. Between them both, the complex has welcomed Wayne Shorter, Keith Jarrett and Dave Brubeck of late, among many other high-wattage names.

Cornelia Street Café

29 Cornelia Street, between Bleecker & W 4th Streets (1-212 989 9319/corneliastreetcafe.com). Subway: A, B, C, D, E, F, V to W 4th Street. **Cover** $8-$12, $6 drink minimum; doors open at 9pm. **Credit** AmEx, DC, MC, V.
Upstairs is a cosy little Greenwich Village eatery. Walk downstairs and you'll find an even cosier music space that hosts adventurous jazz, poetry, world music and folk. Regular mini-festivals spotlight blues, songwriters and new concert-theatre works.

55 Bar

55 Christopher Street, between Seventh Avenue South & Waverly Place (1-212 929 9883/www.55 bar.com). Subway: 1 to Christopher Street-Sheridan Square. **Cover** free-$15; doors open 5.30pm Fri, Sat; 9.30pm Sun. **No credit cards**.
Though tiny (oh, call it intimate), this Prohibition-era dive is now one of New York's most artist-friendly rooms, thanks to its knowledgeable, appreciative audience. You can catch emerging talent almost every night at the free-of-charge early shows, while late sets regularly feature established artists, including Chris Potter and Mike Stern. **Photo** *above*.

Iridium Jazz Club

1650 Broadway, at 51st Street (1-212 582 2121/ www.iridiumjazzclub.com). Subway: 1 to 50th Street. **Box office** Reservations recommended; call venue. **Tickets** $25-$35, $10 food-and-drink minimum. **Credit** AmEx, DC, Disc, MC, V.
One of the nicer places to dine while being hit with top-shelf jazz – both from household names and cats who are more for insiders – is Iridium, located smack in the middle of Broadway's bright lights. Recent guests include Art Ensemble of Chicago, Mose Allison, and Archie Shepp and Roswell Rudd. Monday nights belong to wise-cracking guitar hero Les Paul, while Tuesdays mean the Mingus Big Band.

Jazz at Lincoln Center

Broadway, at 60th Street (1-212 258 9595/www. jazzatlincolncenter.org). Subway: A, B, C, D, 1 to 59th Street-Columbus Circle. **Box office** Call for reservations. **Tickets** $10-$30 plus minimums; shows at 7.30pm, 9.30pm. **Credit** AmEx, MC, V.
Seductively lit, decorated with elegant photography and blessed with clear sight lines and a gorgeous view of 59th Street and Central Park South, Dizzy's Club Coca-Cola: Jazz at Lincoln Center might be a Hollywood cinematographer's ideal vision of what a Manhattan jazz club ought to be. The swanky, intimate club – a regular hang for some of the most outstanding players in the business – is a class act in all but its clunky, commercialised name.

Jazz Gallery

290 Hudson Street, between Dominick & Spring Streets (1-212 242 1063/www.jazzgallery.org). Subway: C, E to Spring Street. **Box office**

Reservations strongly recommended; call club. **Tickets** $12-$15; shows at 9pm, 10.30pm. **No credit cards.**
The fact that there's no bar here should be a tip-off: the Jazz Gallery is a place to witness true works of art, from the sometimes-obscure but always interesting jazzers who play the club (Henry Threadgill, Steve Coleman) to the photos and artefacts displayed on the walls. The tiny room's acoustics are sublime.

Jazz Standard

116 E 27th Street, between Park Avenue South & Lexington Avenue (1-212 576 2232/www. jazzstandard.com). Subway: 6 to 28th Street. **Box office** Call for reservations. **Tickets** $15-$30. **Credit** AmEx, DC, Disc, MC, V.
The room's airy, multi-tiered floor plan makes for splendid sight lines to match the sterling sound quality, and in keeping with the rib-sticking chow offered upstairs (at restaurateur Danny Meyer's Blue Smoke barbecue joint), the jazz is often of the groovy, hard-swinging variety, with musicians such as pianist Vijay Iyer and tenorist David Murray. Pianist Fred Hersch's annual series of duets is a delight.

Lenox Lounge

288 Malcolm X Boulevard (Lenox Avenue), between 124th & 125th Streets (1-212 427 0253/www.lenox lounge.com). Subway: 2, 3 to 125th Street. **Cover** $5-$20 plus two-drink minimum. **Credit** Disc, MC, V.
This classy art deco lounge in Harlem once hosted Billie Holiday and has been drawing stars since the late '30s. Saxist Patience Higgins's Sugar Hill Jazz Quartet jams into the wee hours on Monday nights. *See also p222.*

Merkin Concert Hall

For listing, see p329.
Just north of Lincoln Center is this home for classical and jazz composers. Merkin's polished digs also provide an intimate setting for chamber music and jazz, folk, cabaret and experimental performers. The New York Guitar Festival mounts elaborate multi-artist tribute concerts that feature the cream of the six-string crop; other series include the New York Festival of Song, WNYC's New Sounds Live and Broadway Close Up.

Smoke

2751 Broadway, between 105th & 106th Streets (1-212 864 6662/www.smokejazz.com). Subway: 1 to 103rd Street. **Shows** 9pm, 11pm, 12.30am Mon-Sat; 6pm Sun. **Cover** free, $10 drink minimum Mon-Thur, Sun; $15-$25 Fri, Sat. **Credit** Disc, MC, V.
Not unlike a swanky living room, Smoke is a classy little joint that acts as a haven for local jazz legends and any touring artists looking to play an intimate space. Early in the week, evenings are themed: on Sunday, it's Latin jazz; Tuesday, organ jazz. On weekends, internationally renowned jazzers (Hilton Ruiz, Tom Harrell, Eddie Henderson) hit the stage, relishing the opportunity to play informal gigs uptown.

The Stone

Avenue C, at 2nd Street (no phone/www.thestonenyc. com). Subway: F, V to Lower East Side-Second Avenue. **Cover** $10; doors open at 8pm; closed Mondays. **No credit cards.**
Don't call sax star John Zorn's new non-profit venture a 'club'. You'll find no food or drinks here, and no nonsense, either – the Stone is an art space dedicated to

Tonic. *See p322.*

'the experimental and the avant-garde'. If you're down for some rigorously adventurous sounds – Jim O'Rourke, Tony Conrad, Okkyung Lee and the ever-shifting constellation of sterling players that live here and pass through – Zorn has made it easy: no advance ticket sales; all ages are admitted (and kids 19 and under get discounts); and the bookings are left to a different artist-cum-curator each month.

Sweet Rhythm
88 Seventh Avenue South, between Bleecker & Grove Streets (1-212 255 3626/www.sweetrhythmny.com). Subway: 1 to Christopher Street-Sheridan Square. **Shows** 8pm, 10pm Mon-Thur, Sun; 8pm, 10pm, midnight Fri, Sat. **Cover** $10-$25, $10 minimum per person per set. **Credit** AmEx, DC, MC, V.
In the same location as the legendary Sweet Basil you'll now find Sweet Rhythm – more of a destination to see a particular artist than a hangout (due to the uninviting seating scheme). While a variety of jazz sounds dominates (swing, standards, bop) and big names such as Sonny Fortune and Rashied Ali still drop in occasionally (not to mention Jane Ira Bloom and Carl Allen), blues and world music are also on hand. Tuesday nights are devoted to vocalists.

Swing 46
349 W 46th Street, between Eighth & Ninth Avenues (1-212 262 9554/www.swing46.com). Subway: A, C, E to 42nd Street-Port Authority. **Cover** $5-$12; shows start at 9.30pm. **Credit** AmEx, DC, MC, V.
Swing isn't a trend at this supper club – whether peppy or sappy, these cats mean it. Bands (with names like the Flying Neutrinos and the Flipped Fedoras) that jump, jive and wail await you, so be sure to wear your dancin' shoes. Dance lessons are available too.

Tonic
For listing, see p322.

Village Vanguard
178 Seventh Avenue South, at Perry Street (1-212 255 4037/www.villagevanguard.com). Subway: A, C, E, 1, 2, 3 to 14th Street; L to Eighth Avenue. **Shows** 9pm, 11pm Mon-Thur, Sun; 9pm, 11pm, 12.30am Fri, Sat. **Tickets** $20, $10 drink minimum; call or visit website for reservations. **Credit** AmEx, MC, V (online purchases only).
Seventy years old and going strong, the Village Vanguard is one of New York's real jazz meccas. History surrounds you here: Coltrane, Miles Davis and Bill Evans have all grooved in this hallowed hall, and the walls are lined with photos and artefacts. The big names, old and new, continue to fill the Vanguard's line-up, and the 16-piece Vanguard Jazz Orchestra has been the Monday night regular for almost 40 years. Reservations are strongly recommended, and the Vanguard takes only cash or travellers' cheques at the door.

Zebulon
258 Wythe Avenue, between Metropolitan Avenue & North Third Street, Williamsburg, Brooklyn

Buzzworthy

Jeremy Pelt
This rising star in mainstream jazz seems destined to make his mark as a strong trumpeter and gifted composer. He paid his dues the old-fashioned way, as a standout soloist in high-profile groups such as the Mingus Big Band and pianist Eric Reed's New York 7. Pelt now has a few solid albums under his belt, but live is the best place to get swept up in his formidable skills and clarion intensity. No wonder he's fast becoming the contemporary bop scene's man about town.

(1-718 218 6934/www.zebuloncafeconcert.com). Subway: L to Bedford Avenue. **Cover** free; doors open at 4pm. **Credit** AmEx.
For years they've been talking about Williamsburg as NYC's leading hipster enclave. But how hip could it have been without a killer jazz spot like Zebulon? Emphasising the young firebrands (such as Gold Sparkle Band and Tyshawn Sorey) over the establishment, Zebulon also welcomes the daring wing of the local rock scene (such as TV on the Radio's Kyp Malone). While the café opens in the afternoon, don't expect live music to start till closer to 10pm.

Blues, country & folk

BB King Blues Club & Grill
For listing, see p314.

Paddy Reilly's Music Bar
519 Second Avenue, at 29th Street (1-212 686 1210/www.paddyreillys.com). Subway: 6 to 28th Street. **Shows** 9.30pm Mon-Thur; 10.30pm Fri, Sat; 4-8pm Sun. **Cover** $5-$7. **Credit** AmEx, Disc, MC, V.
Patrons flock to this Gramercy institution for the silky Guinness, the house's only draft; but they stay for the lively Irish folk and rock acts that bring the room to life. Popular pub-rockers the Prodigals are regulars on Fridays, and the rest of the weekend features Irish-rock and traditional jam sessions.

Rodeo Bar & Grill
375 Third Avenue, at 27th Street (1-212 683 6500/www.rodeobar.com). Subway: 6 to 28th Street. **Cover** free; shows start at 10pm. **Credit** AmEx, DC, Disc, MC, V (bar only).
The unpretentious crowd and roadhouse atmosphere – not to mention the lack of a cover charge – make the Rodeo the city's best roots club, with a steady stream of rockabilly, country and related sounds. Rockabilly filly Rosie Flores is a regular, and bluegrass scion Chris Scruggs recently visited from Nashville to play his '50s-style rock.

Latin, reggae & world

Copacabana

560 W 34th Street, between Tenth & Eleventh Avenues (1-212 239 2672/www.copacabanany.com). Subway: A, C, E to 34th Street-Penn Station. **Cover** $10-$40, $30 at tables; doors open 6pm Tue; 10pm Fri, Sat. **Credit** AmEx, Disc, MC, V.

The city's most iconic destination for Latin music has now become a fully fledged party palace. It's still a prime stop for salsa, cumbia and merengue, but in addition to booking world-renowned stars (Ruben Blades, El Gran Combo, and Tito Nieves with Conjunto Clasico), the Copa now has an alternative nook called the House Room, where dancers can spin to disco, house and Latin freestyle.

Satalla

37 W 26th Street, between Broadway & Sixth Avenue (1-212 576 1155/www.satalla.com). Subway: N, R, W to 28th Street. **Cover** $10-$25; shows start at 8pm or 10pm. **Credit** AmEx, Disc, MC, V.

Satalla is a lounge dedicated to the globalist flavour of New York, which means that you'll find more hybrids than pure indigenous styles. Blues, Celtic bands, African drummers, Greek singing troupes and zydeco each fit the bill here, even if played by NYC-based artists. The decor is a tad psychedelic, but the couches are so comfy that it's easy to settle into the trip.

S.O.B.'s

For listing, see p321.

Zinc Bar

90 W Houston Street, between La Guardia Place & Thompson Street (1-212 477 8337/www.zincbar. com). Subway: A, B, C, D, E, F, V to W 4th Street. **Open** 6pm-3.30am daily. **Cover** $5. **Credit** AmEx, DC, Disc, MC, V (bar only).

Located where Greenwich Village meets Soho, Zinc Bar is the place to hoot and holler with die-hard night owls. The after-hours atmosphere is enhanced by the cool mix of African, flamenco, jazz and samba bands.

Summer venues

Castle Clinton

Battery Park, Battery Place, at State Street (1-212 835 2789). Subway: R, W to Rector Street; 1 to South Ferry; 4, 5 to Bowling Green. **Tickets** free.

One of the nicer views in all of Manhattan is found at its bottom tip, in the heart of Battery Park. This historic fort welcomes a handful of established stars whenever the weather is warm, with special events often found on 4 and 14 July. Lyle Lovett, Calexico, Yo La Tengo and Mavis Staples have all performed for free in the evening air, but note: those free tickets do have to be picked up in person on the day of a show, and they always go fast.

Central Park SummerStage

For listing, see p262.

Now in its 20th year, the City Parks Foundation fills summers in the park with just about every sound under the sun. Emmylou Harris and Elvis Costello seem to drop in every season, but 2005 included everyone from Dinosaur Jr and Death Cab for Cutie to Cassandra Wilson and Brad Mehldau as well. Many of the shows remain free, with a handful of high-priced benefits covering for them.

Giants Stadium

For listing, see p334 **Meadowlands Sports Complex**.

At New Jersey's Giants Stadium, you can catch Hot97's annual Summer Jam, one of the biggest hip-hop shows in the country, as well as other biggies like the Rolling Stones and Bruce Springsteen.

Lincoln Center Plaza

For listing, see p329 **Lincoln Center**.

Lincoln Center's multi-tiered floor plan allows for several outdoor stages in one sprawling facility, but the most popular venues are the North Plaza, which houses the well-loved Midsummer Night Swing dance concerts (*see p263*), and the Damrosch Park Bandshell, which rolls out the red carpet for the likes of sax icon Sonny Rollins. When the weather's hot, a wide variety of music from around the world creates a rich global feast.

Prospect Park Bandshell

For listing, see p263 **Celebrate Brooklyn! Performing Arts Festival**.

Prospect Park Bandshell is to Brooklynites what Central Park SummerStage is to Manhattan residents: the place to hear great music in the great outdoors. Adventurous programming for the summer's Celebrate Brooklyn! Festival runs the global gamut, from exotic (Africa Day) to less so (Canada Day). Of course, everything from blues titans (Bettye LaVette and Charlie Musselwhite) and Latin sounds (Eddie Palmieri, Milly Quezada) to classic movie-and-music pairings round out the calendar.

Tommy Hilfiger at Jones Beach Theatre

Jones Beach, Long Island (1-516 221 1000/www. tommyhilfigerjonesbeach.com). Travel: LIRR from Penn Station, Seventh Avenue at 32nd Street, to Freeport, then take the Jones Beach bus. **Box office** 10am-9pm Monday show days; 10am-6pm Tue-Sat; noon-6pm Sun; open till 9pm show days. **Tickets** $30-$135. **Credit** AmEx, MC, V.

It's a long haul, especially if you don't have your own wheels, and the sound is generally indifferent. Still, you can't beat the open-air setting at this beachside amphitheatre. From July to September, the biggest tours stop here, including package shows like Ozzfest and Projekt Revolution, as well as veterans such as Tom Petty, the reunited Pixies and Judas Priest, and soul stars both current (Erykah Badu) and classic (Anita Baker).

Arts & Entertainment

Classical

If the word that best characterised the past season in New York's classical-music community was 'flux', perhaps the word that best describes the season ahead is 'anticipation'. **Carnegie Hall** welcomes its new general director, Clive Gillinson, who inherits a venue arguably at the height of its power. The **Metropolitan Opera** moves into what will surely be one of the most fascinating – and potentially contentious – periods of its storied history, as general manager Joseph Volpe breaks in his successor, Peter Gelb, a former record-company executive controversial for his populist moves. Meanwhile, New York City goes from strength to strength, offering ever more fascinating fare and innovative ways to engage living composers and broader audiences alike. Columbia University's **Miller Theatre**, already known for contemporary and early music, has begun to absorb mainstream repertoire in original ways; moving in the opposite direction, **Merkin Concert Hall** offers an increasingly expansive menu every season.

Tickets

You can buy tickets directly from most venues, whether by phone, online or at the box office. However, a surcharge is generally added to tickets not bought in person. For more ticket information, *see p382.*

CarnegieCharge
1-212 247 7800/www.carnegiehall.org.
Box office By phone 8am-8pm daily. **Fee** $5.50 surcharge per ticket. **Credit** AmEx, DC, Disc, MC, V.

Centercharge
1-212 721 6500. **Box office** By phone 10am-8pm Mon-Sat; noon-8pm Sun. **Fee** $5.50 surcharge per ticket. **Credit** AmEx, Disc, MC, V.
Centercharge sells tickets for events at Alice Tully Hall, Avery Fisher Hall and the Juilliard School, as well as for the Lincoln Center Out of Doors Festival.

Metropolitan Opera
1-212 362 6000/www.metoperafamily.org/metopera/home.aspx. **Box office** By phone 10am-8pm Mon-Sat; noon-6pm Sun. **Fee** $5.50 surcharge per ticket. **Credit** AmEx, Disc, MC, V.
The Met sells tickets for performances held in its opera house, including those of the resident American Ballet Theatre.

Backstage passes

Curious music lovers can go behind the scenes at several of the city's major concert venues. Backstage at the Met (1-212 769 7020,

www.metoperafamily.org/education/calendar/backstage.aspx) shows you around the famous house during the opera season, which runs from September to May; Lincoln Center Tours (1-212 875 5350) escorts you inside Avery Fisher and Alice Tully Halls, as well as the New York State Theater; Carnegie Hall (1-212 247 7800) guides you through what is perhaps the world's most famous concert hall. For a $15 fee, you may also sit in on rehearsals of the New York Philharmonic (1-212 875 5656), usually held on the Thursday before a concert.

Concert halls

Brooklyn Academy of Music
30 Lafayette Avenue, between Ashland Place & St Felix Street, Fort Greene, Brooklyn (1-718 636 4100/www.bam.org). Subway: B, Q, 2, 3, 4, 5 to Atlantic Avenue; C to Lafayette Avenue; D, M, N, R to Pacific Street; G to Fulton Street. **Box office** noon-6pm Mon-Sat; noon-4pm Sun show days. **Admission** varies. **Credit** AmEx, MC, V.
America's oldest academy for the performing arts continues to present some of the freshest and most adventurous programming in the city. Every autumn and winter, the Next Wave Festival provides an overview of avant-garde music, dance and theatre, while spring brings lauded European opera productions to town. The BAM Harvey Theater, located nearby, offers a smaller, more atmospheric setting for new creations by composers such as Tan Dun and Meredith Monk, as well as innovative stagings of baroque opera. Meanwhile, the resident Brooklyn Philharmonic Orchestra has reached new heights of excellence under the direction of soon-to-depart conductor Robert Spano. *Photos p318-9.*

Carnegie Hall
154 W 57th Street, at Seventh Avenue (1-212 247 7800/www.carnegiehall.org). Subway: N, Q, R, W to 57th Street. **Box office** 11am-6pm Mon-Sat; noon-6pm Sun. **Admission** varies. **Credit** AmEx, DC, Disc, MC, V.
The stars – both soloists and orchestras – in the classical-music firmament continue to shine most brightly in the venerable Isaac Stern Auditorium, inside this renowned concert hall. Still, it's the spunky upstart Zankel Hall that has generated the most buzz; the below-street-level space offers an eclectic mix of classical, contemporary, jazz, pop and world music. Next door, Weill Recital Hall hosts intimate concerts and chamber-music programmes.

Florence Gould Hall
French Institute Alliance Française, 55 E 59th Street, between Madison & Park Avenues (1-212 355 6160/www.fiaf.org). Subway: N, R, W to Fifth Avenue-59th Street; 4, 5, 6 to 59th Street. **Box office** 11am-7pm Tue-Fri; 11am-3pm Sat. **Admission** $10-$35. **Credit** AmEx, MC, V.
Programming in this small, comfortable hall has a decidedly French tone, in both artists and repertoire.

Lincoln Center, a cathedral to performing arts.

Merkin Concert Hall

Kaufman Center, 129 W 67th Street, between
Broadway & Amsterdam Avenue (1-212 501 3330/
www.kaufman-center.org). Subway: 1 to 66th Street-
Lincoln Center. **Box office** noon-7pm Mon-Thur,
Sun; noon-4pm Fri. **Admission** $10-$25. **Credit**
AmEx, MC, V (advance purchases only).

Tucked away on a side street in the shadow
of Lincoln Center, this unimposing gem of a
concert hall offers a robust mix of early music and
avant-garde programming, as well as an increasing
amount of jazz, folk and some more eclectic
fare. Here, the New York Festival of Song has
finally found a comfortable home, while regular
performances sponsored by WNYC-FM afford
opportunities for casual interaction with composers
and performers.

New Jersey Performing Arts Center

For listing, see p319.

It takes only 15 or 20 minutes to reach Newark's
sumptuous performing-arts complex from midtown,
and the rewards are well worth the trip. Tickets for
big-name acts that may be sold out at Manhattan
venues can often be found here, and performances
may be slightly different from those in concurrent
Gotham gigs.

92nd Street Y

www.ymcanyc.org.

The YMCA has always stood for solidly traditional
orchestral, solo and chamber masterpieces. But it
also fosters the careers of young musicians and
explores European and Jewish-American music traditions, with innovative, far-reaching results.

Lincoln Center

Built in the 1960s, this massive complex is the
nexus of Manhattan's performing-arts scene.
Lincoln Center hosts lectures and symposia in
the Rose Building, in addition to events in the
main halls: Alice Tully Hall, Avery Fisher
Hall, Metropolitan Opera House, New York
State Theater, and the Vivian Beaumont and
Mitzi E Newhouse Theaters. Also here are
the Juilliard School (*see p333*) and the Fiorello
H La Guardia High School of Music and Art
and Performing Arts (108 Amsterdam
Avenue, between 64th & 65th Streets, www.
laguardiahs.org), which frequently hosts
professional performances.

Big stars like Valery Gergiev, Sir Colin Davis
and the Emerson Quartet are Lincoln Center's
meat and potatoes, but lately the great divide
between the flagship Great Performers season
and the relatively audacious, multidisciplinary
Lincoln Center Out of Doors Festival (*see*
p263) has begun to narrow, thanks to fresher
programming. Even the Mostly Mozart festival
(*see p263*), a long-time summer staple, has
begun drawing a younger, hipper crowd with
its progressive bookings and innovative artistic
juxtapositions.

Lincoln Center

Columbus Avenue, at 65th Street (1-212 546 2656/
www.lincolncenter.org). Subway: 1 to 66th Street-
Lincoln Center.

This is the main entry point for Lincoln Center, but the venues that follow are spread out across the square of blocks from 62nd to 66th Streets, between Amsterdam and Columbus Avenues.

Alice Tully Hall
1-212 875 5050. **Box office** 11am-6pm Mon-Sat; noon-6pm Sun. **Admission** free-$75. **Credit** AmEx, Disc, MC, V.
Home to the Chamber Music Society of Lincoln Center (1-212 875 5788, www.chambermusicsociety.org), Alice Tully Hall somehow makes its 1,096 seats feel cosy. It has no centre aisle, and the seating offers decent legroom. Its Art of the Song series is among Lincoln Center's most inviting offerings.

Avery Fisher Hall
1-212 875 5030. **Box office** 10am- 6pm Mon-Sat; noon-6pm Sun. **Admission** $20-$114. **Credit** AmEx, Disc, MC, V.
This handsome, comfortable 2,700-seat hall is the headquarters of the New York Philharmonic (1-212 875 5656, www.nyphilharmonic.org), the country's oldest symphony orchestra (founded in 1842) and one of its finest. The sound, which ranges from good to atrocious depending on who you ask, stands to be improved. Inexpensive, early evening 'rush hour' concerts and open rehearsals are presented on a regular basis. The Great Performers series features top international soloists and ensembles. **Photo** *p332.*

Metropolitan Opera House
1-212 362 6000/www.metopera.org. **Box office** 10am-8pm Mon-Sat; noon-6pm Sun. **Admission** $12-$295. **Credit** AmEx, Disc, MC, V.
The Met is the grandest of the Lincoln Center buildings, so it's a spectacular place to see and hear opera. It hosts the Metropolitan Opera from September to May, and major visiting companies during the summer. Opera's biggest stars (think Domingo, Fleming and Voigt) appear here regularly, and artistic director James Levine has turned the orchestra into a true symphonic force. Audiences are knowledgeable and fiercely partisan, with subscriptions remaining in families for generations. Still, the Met has become more inclusive; digital English-language subtitles, which appear on screens affixed to railings in front of each seat, are convenient for the novice and unobtrusive to their more seasoned neighbour. Tickets are expensive, and unless you can afford good seats, the view won't be great; standing-room-only tickets start at $15, and you'll have to queue on Saturday morning to buy them. At least you'll be able to see the eye-popping, gasp-inducing sets (by directors such as Zeffirelli) that remain the gold standard here. **Photo** *p331.*

New York State Theater
1-212 870 5570. **Box office** 10am-7.30pm Mon; 10am-8.30pm Tue-Sat; 11.30am-7.30pm Sun. **Admission** $25-$110. **Credit** AmEx, DC, Disc, MC, V.
NYST houses the New York City Ballet (www.nycballet.com) as well as the New York City Opera (www.nycopera.com). The opera company has tried

to overcome its second-best reputation by being both ambitious and defiantly populist. Rising young American singers often take their first bows at City Opera (many of them eventually make the trek across the plaza to the Met), where casts and productions tend to be younger and sexier than those of its more patrician counterpart. Known for its fierce commitment to the unconventional – from modern American works and musical-theatre productions to intriguing Handel stagings and forgotten *bel canto* gems – City Opera is considerably cooler than its neighbour and about half the price. But truly splashy grand spectacle remains the province of the Met.

Walter Reade Theater
1-212 875 5600/www.filmlinc.com. **Box office** noon-6pm Mon-Fri; 30mins before shows Sat, Sun. **Admission** $10; $7 students; $6 members; $5 6-12s. **No credit cards.** For tickets by phone, call 1-212 496 3809.
The Walter Reade Theater's acoustics are less than fabulous; still, the Chamber Music Society uses the space regularly, and the Great Performers series offers Sunday morning events fuelled by pastries and hot beverages sold in the lobby.

Opera

The Metropolitan Opera and the New York City Opera may be the leaders of the pack, but they're hardly the only game in town. Feisty upstarts and long-standing grass-roots companies ensure that Manhattan's operaphiles are among the best served in the world. Call the organisations or visit their websites for ticket prices, schedules and venue details. The music schools (*see p333*) also have opera programmes.

Amato Opera Theater
319 Bowery, at 2nd Street (1-212 228 8200/ www.amato.org). Subway: B, D, F, V to Broadway-Lafayette Street; 6 to Bleecker Street. **Admission** $30; $25 seniors, students and children. **Credit** AmEx, Disc, MC, V.
New York's beloved mom-and-pop opera shop offers charming, fully staged productions in a theatre only 20ft wide – it's almost like watching opera in your living room. Casting can be inconsistent, but many well-known singers have performed here.

American Opera Projects
South Oxford Space, 138 South Oxford Street, between Atlantic Avenue & Hanson Place, Fort Greene, Brooklyn (1-718 398 4024/www.operaprojects.org). Subway: B, Q, 2, 3, 4, 5 to Atlantic Avenue; C to Lafayette Avenue; D, M, N, R to Pacific Street; G to Fulton Street. **Admission** varies. **No credit cards.**
American Opera Projects is not so much an opera company as a living, breathing workshop that allows you the opportunity to follow a new work from gestation to completion.

Dicapo Opera Theatre

*184 E 76th Street, between Lexington & Third
Avenues (1-212 288 9438/www.dicapo.com).
Subway: 6 to 77th Street.* **Admission** *$47.50.*
Credit MC, V.

This top-notch chamber-opera troupe benefits
from City Opera-quality singers performing in a
delightfully intimate setting in the basement of St
Jean Baptiste Church.

New York Gilbert & Sullivan Players

For listing, see p332 **Symphony Space**.

Is Victorian camp your vice? This troupe presents a
rotating schedule of the Big Three (*HMS Pinafore,
The Mikado* and *The Pirates of Penzance*), plus lesser-known G&S works.

Other venues

Bargemusic

*Fulton Ferry Landing, between Old Fulton &
Water Streets, Dumbo, Brooklyn (1-718 624
2083/www.bargemusic.org). Subway: A, C to
High Street; F to York Street.* **Admission** *$25-$40.*
Credit MC, V.

This former coffee-bean barge presents four
chamber concerts a week – and a great view of
the Manhattan skyline. It's a magical experience,
but wrap up warm in winter. When the weather
warms, you can enjoy a drink on the upper deck during the concert's intermission.

Frick Collection

For listing, see p135.

Concerts in the Frick Collection's elegantly
appointed concert hall are a rare treat, generally featuring lesser-known but nonetheless world-class
performers. After holding the line for free concerts
far longer than expected, the Frick finally imposed
a $20 ticket charge in 2005; ironically, however,
this might actually make it easier to get tickets,
which were routinely snatched up by members
before the public even had a chance. Concerts
are also broadcast live in the Garden Court, where
tickets are not required.

Kaye Playhouse

*Hunter College, 68th Street, between Park
& Lexington Avenues (1-212 772 4448/
www.kayeplayhouse.hunter.cuny.edu). Subway:
6 to 68th Street-Hunter College.* **Box office**
noon-6pm Mon-Sat. **Admission** *$10-$70.*
Credit AmEx, MC, V.

Named after its benefactors – comedian Danny
Kaye and his wife Sylvia – this refurbished theatre
offers an eclectic programme of professional music
and dance performances.

The **Metropolitan Opera**'s
La Bohème. See p330.

Lorin Maazel conducting the **New York Philharmonic**. *See p330*, Avery Fisher Hall.

Kitchen

For listing, see p354.
A meeting place for the avant-garde in music, dance and theatre for more than 30 years, the Kitchen has played a less prominent role in the local scene during recent seasons. Still, edgy art can be found here, and prices range from free to $25.

Kosciuszko Foundation

15 E 65th Street, at Fifth Avenue (1-212 734 2130/ www.thekf.org). Subway: F to Lexington Avenue-63rd Street; 6 to 68th Street-Hunter College.
Admission $15-$30. **Credit** MC, V.
This East Side townhouse hosts a chamber music series with a mission: each programme usually features at least one work by a Polish composer. You're less likely to choke on Chopin than to hear something novel by Paderewski or Szymanowski.

Metropolitan Museum of Art

For listing, see p135.
When it comes to established virtuosos and revered chamber ensembles, the Metropolitan Museum's programming is consistently rich and full (and ticket prices are correspondingly high). The museum has also established a youthful resident ensemble, Metropolitan Museum Artists in Concert. Seasonally inspired early-music concerts are held uptown in the stunning Fuentidueña Chapel at the Cloisters (*see p149*).

Miller Theatre at Columbia University

Broadway, at 116th Street (1-212 854 7799/ www.millertheatre.com). Subway: 1 to 116th Street-Columbia University. **Box office** noon-6pm Mon-Fri. Show days open 2 hours before performance. **Admission** $20; $12 students.
Credit AmEx, MC, V.
Columbia's Miller Theatre has single-handedly made contemporary classical music sexy in New York City. The credit belongs to executive director George Steel, who proved that presenting challenging fare by composers such as Babbitt, Ferneyhough

and Scelsi in a casual, unaffected setting could attract a young audience – and hang on to it. Miller's early-music offerings, many of which are conducted by Steel, are also exemplary.

New York Public Library for the Performing Arts

For listing, see p141.
The library's Bruno Walter Auditorium regularly hosts free recitals, solo performances and lectures.

Symphony Space

2537 Broadway, at 95th Street (1-212 864 5400/ www.symphonyspace.org). Subway: 1, 2, 3 to 96th Street. **Box office** noon-6pm Tue-Sat.
Admission varies ($2 surcharge per order).
Credit AmEx, MC, V.
Despite its name, Symphony Space provides programming that is anything but symphony-centric: recent seasons have featured saxophone quartets, Indian classical music and politically astute performances of Purcell's *Dido and Aeneas*. The annual Wall to Wall marathons serve up a full day of music – free of charge – focusing on a particular composer, from Bach to Sondheim.

Tishman Auditorium

New School University, 66 W 12th Street, at Sixth Avenue (1-212 243 9937/Box office 1-212 229 5488). Subway: F, V to 14th Street; L to Sixth Avenue. **Admission** free-$15. **No credit cards**.
The New School's modestly priced Schneider Concerts chamber series features up-and-coming musicians. Established artists also play here – for a fraction of the prices charged elsewhere.

Churches

From sacred to secular, a thrilling variety of music is performed in New York's churches. Superb acoustics, out-of-this-world choirs and serene surroundings make these houses of worship particularly attractive venues. Bonus: some concerts are free or very cheap.

Arts & Entertainment

Cathedral Church of St John the Divine

1047 Amsterdam Avenue, at 112th Street (1-212 316 7540/www.stjohndivine.org). Subway: B, C, 1, to 110th Street-Cathedral Parkway. **Box office** 2-6pm Mon-Fri; 10am-6pm Sat, Sun. **Admission** varies. **Credit** AmEx, Disc, MC, V.

The stunning neo-Gothic, 3,000-seat sanctuary provides a heavenly atmosphere for the church choir and visiting ensembles, though acoustics are murky.

Christ and St Stephen's Church

120 W 69th Street, between Columbus Avenue & Broadway (1-212 787 2755/www.csschurch.org). Subway: 1, 2, 3 to 72nd Street. **Admission** varies. **No credit cards.**

This small, pleasant West Side church offers one of the most diverse concert rosters in the city, including an annual presentation of Bach's choral *Christmas Oratorio*.

Church of St Ignatius Loyola

980 Park Avenue, at 84th Street (1-212 288 2520/ www.saintignatiusloyola.org). Subway: 4, 5, 6 to 86th Street. **Admission** $10-$40. **Credit** AmEx, Disc, MC, V.

The Sacred Music in a Sacred Space series is a high point of Upper East Side music culture. Lincoln Center also holds concerts here, capitalizing on the church's fine acoustics and prime location.

Church of the Ascension

12 W 11th Street, between Fifth & Sixth Avenues (1-212 358 1469/www.voicesofascension.org). Subway: N, R, W to 8th Street-NYU. **Admission** $10-$50. **Credit** MC, V (advance purchases only).

There's a first-rate professional choir, the Voices of Ascension, at this little Village church. You can catch the choir at Lincoln Center on occasion, but home turf is the best place to hear it.

Corpus Christi Church

529 W 121st Street, between Amsterdam Avenue & Broadway (1-212 666 9266/www.mb1800.org). Subway: 1 to 116th Street-Columbia University. **Admission** varies. **Credit** MC, V.

Fans of early music can get their fix from Music Before 1800, a series that regularly imports the world's leading antiquarian artists and ensembles.

St Bartholomew's Church

109 E 50th Street, between Park & Lexington Avenues (1-212 378 0248/www.stbarts.org). Subway: E, V to Lexington Avenue-53rd Street; 6 to 51st Street. **Admission** varies. **Credit** AmEx, MC, V.

This magnificent church hosts the Summer Festival of Sacred Music, one of the city's most ambitious choral-music series, and fills the rest of the year with performances by resident ensembles and guests.

St Thomas Church Fifth Avenue

1 W 53rd Street, at Fifth Avenue (1-212 757 7013/ www.saintthomaschurch.org). Subway: E, V to Fifth Avenue-53rd Street. **Admission** $15-$70. **Credit** AmEx, MC, V.

The country's only fully accredited choir school for boys keeps the great Anglican choral tradition alive and well in New York. St Thomas's annual performance of Handel's *Messiah* is a must-hear that's well worth the rather steep ticket price.

Trinity Church/St Paul's Chapel

Trinity Church, Broadway, at Wall Street; St Paul's Chapel, Broadway, at Fulton Street (1-212 602 0747/www.trinitywallstreet.org). Subway: R, W to Rector Street; 4, 5 to Wall Street. **Admission** Concerts at One series $2 donation. **No credit cards.**

Historic Trinity, located in the heart of the Financial District, plays host to the inexpensive Concerts at One series. Performances are held at 1pm on Mondays at St Paul's Chapel, and Thursdays at Trinity Church.

Schools

The Juilliard School and the Manhattan School of Music are renowned for their talented students, faculty and artists-in-residence, all of whom regularly perform for free or at low cost. Lately, Mannes College of Music has made great strides to rise to the same level. Noteworthy music and innovative programming can also be found at several other colleges and schools in the city.

Juilliard School

60 Lincoln Center Plaza, Broadway, at 65th Street (1-212 769 7406/www.juilliard.edu). Subway: 1 to 66th Street-Lincoln Center. **Admission** usually free.

New York City's premier conservatory stages weekly concerts by student soloists, orchestras and chamber ensembles, as well as elaborate opera productions that often can rival many professional presentations.

Manhattan School of Music

120 Claremont Avenue, at 122nd Street (1-212 749 2802, ext 4428/www.msmnyc.edu). Subway: 1 to 125th Street. **Admission** usually free.

The Manhattan School of Music offers masterclasses, recitals and off-site concerts by its students, faculty and visiting pros. The American String Quartet, in residence since 1984, gives concerts regularly, while the Augustine Guitar Series includes recitals by top soloists.

Mannes College of Music

150 W 85th Street, between Columbus & Amsterdam Avenues (1-212 580 0210/www.mannes.edu). Subway: B, C, 1 to 86th Street. **Admission** usually free.

In addition to student concerts and faculty recitals, Mannes also mounts ambitious, historically themed concert series; the summer is given over to festivals and workshops for instrumentalists. Most of these events provide affordable performances by some of the world's leading musicians.

Sports & Fitness

Sweat it out on the bench or on the field.

The Yankee half of New York enjoys a game at **Yankee Stadium**. *See p335.*

In this city, a game is much more than just a spectator sport. Two pro football teams, three pro hockey teams, three pro basketball teams, and two major-league and two minor-league baseball teams call the area home. And if raucous cheering doesn't get your blood pumping fast enough, then you can kayak in the Hudson, go ice-skating at Rockefeller Center, swing a golf club at Chelsea Piers, ride a horse in Central Park, or pedal a bike along well-maintained park trails in any of the five boroughs – and even over the George Washington Bridge to New Jersey. Or intone your 'om' at one of the city's many yoga centres.

Spectator sports

Major venues

All advance tickets for events at these venues are sold through Ticketmaster (*see p382*).

Madison Square Garden
Seventh Avenue, between 31st & 33rd Streets (1-212 465 6741/www.thegarden.com). Subway:

A, C, E, 1, 2, 3 to 34th Street-Penn Station. **Open** *Box office* 9am-6pm Mon-Fri; 10am-6pm Sat; noon-1 hour after event begins Sun. **Tickets** $25-$350. **Credit** AmEx, DC, Disc, MC, V.

Meadowlands Sports Complex
East Rutherford, NJ (1-201 935 3900/www.meadow lands.com). Travel: NJ Transit Meadowlands Sports Complex bus from Port Authority Bus Terminal (1-212 564 8484), Eighth Avenue at 42nd Street; one way $3.50. **Open** *Box office* 11am-6pm Mon-Sat; 2 hours prior to event Sun. **Tickets** from $25. **No credit cards** for Giants and Jets games and Meadowlands Racetrack. All other events: AmEx, DC, Disc, MC, V.
Continental Airlines Arena, Giants Stadium and the Meadowlands Racetrack are part of this massive multi-venue complex across the river, and all are serviced by the same bus.

Nassau Veterans Memorial Coliseum
1255 Hempstead Turnpike, Uniondale, Long Island (1-516 794 9303/www.nassaucoliseum.com). Travel: From Penn Station, Seventh Avenue at 32nd Street, take LIRR (www.lirr.org) to Hempstead, then take the N70, N71 or N72 bus to the Coliseum. **Tickets** from $25. **Credit** AmEx, Disc, MC, V.

Baseball

Talk of the national pastime dominates the papers, airwaves and water coolers through the summer and into early autumn. New York is home to two teams – the Yankees and the Mets – and each one (along with its fan base) has a distinct personality. The American League's Yankees are the team with the rich history (Babe Ruth, Mickey Mantle), the long list of championships and a payroll that would bankrupt a small country. The National League's Mets are the relatively new kids on the block: they came along in 1961 to fill the gap created when the working-class favourite Brooklyn Dodgers moved to Los Angeles in 1958. The club's scruffy underdog personality keeps many fans rooting for them (fruitlessly, on the whole) year after year. Minor-league excitement returned in 2001, when the Staten Island Yankees and the Brooklyn Cyclones (the Mets' minor-league team) opened new ballparks in wonderful cityscape settings.

Brooklyn Cyclones
KeySpan Park, 1904 Surf Avenue, between West 17th & 19th Streets, Coney Island, Brooklyn (1-718 449 8497/www.brooklyncyclones.com). Subway: D, F, Q to Coney Island-Stillwell Avenue. **Open** *Box office 10am-4pm Mon-Sat.* **Tickets** $5-$12. **Credit** AmEx, Disc, MC, V.

New York Mets
Shea Stadium, 123-01 Roosevelt Avenue, at 126th Street, Flushing, Queens (1-718 507 8499/www. mets.com). Subway: 7 to Willets Point-Shea Stadium. **Open** *Box office 9am-5.30pm Mon-Fri; 9am-2pm Sat, Sun.* **Tickets** $5-$53. **Credit** AmEx, Disc, MC, V.

New York Yankees
Yankee Stadium, River Avenue, at 161st Street, Bronx (1-718 293 6000/www.yankees.com). Subway: B, D, 4 to 161st Street-Yankee Stadium. **Open** *Box office 9am-5pm Mon-Sat; 10am-4pm Sun; and during games.* **Tickets** $8-$95. **Credit** AmEx, Disc, MC, V. **Photo** *p334.*

Staten Island Yankees
Richmond County Bank Ballpark, 75 Richmond Terrace, at Bay Street, Staten Island (1-718 720 9200/www.siyanks.com). Travel: Staten Island Ferry to St George Terminal. **Open** *Box office 9am-6pm Mon-Fri; 10am-6pm Sat; and during games.* **Tickets** $9, $10. **Credit** AmEx, Disc, MC, V.

Basketball

Both of the area's NBA teams – the New York Knicks and the New Jersey Nets – are in what could tactfully be described as a 'rebuilding phase'. After a few years near the top of the Eastern Conference, the Nets are hoping to make the finals again by pairing younger players with star guard Jason Kidd. The Knicks, the true New York home team, have stumbled, but recent trades may help. Watching either squad in its home arena can be an exciting way to spend a night, and tickets are easier to come by these days. The Knicks play at Madison Square Garden; many seats are filled with basketball diehards (like Spike Lee), while Nets games (at the Continental Airlines Arena in New Jersey) are more family-friendly. The ladies of the WNBA's New York Liberty hold court at MSG in the summer.

New Jersey Nets
Continental Airlines Arena (for listing, see p334 **Meadowlands Sports Complex***). 1-800 765 6387/www.njnets.com.* **Tickets** $15-$150.

New York Knicks
Madison Square Garden (for listing, see p334). www.nyknicks.com. **Tickets** $34-$115.

New York Liberty
Madison Square Garden (for listing, see p334). www.nyliberty.com. **Tickets** $10-$65.

Boxing

Church Street Boxing Gym
25 Park Place, between Broadway & Church Street (1-212 571 1333/www.nyboxinggym.com). Subway: 2, 3 to Park Place; 4, 5, 6 to Brooklyn Bridge-City Hall. **Open** *Call or visit website for schedule.* **Tickets** $20-$30. **No credit cards**.
Church Street is a workout gym and amateur-boxing venue in an atmospheric cellar. Evander Holyfield, Mike Tyson and other heavy hitters have trained here before Garden matches. About ten times a year, on Fridays, the gym hosts white-collar bouts.

Gleason's Gym

83 Front Street, between Main & Washington Streets, Dumbo, Brooklyn (1-718 797 2872/ www.gleasonsgym.net). Subway: F to York Street.
Open Call or visit website for schedule.
Tickets $15. **Credit** DC, Disc, MC, V.
Although it occupies an undistinguished second-floor warehouse space in a now-groovy neighbourhood, Gleason's is the professional boxer's address in New York. The 'sweet scientists' who have trained at the city's most storied gym include Muhammad Ali and Jake (*Raging Bull*) La Motta. Monthly white-collar fights draw doctors, lawyers and stockbrokers – in and out of the ring.

Madison Square Garden

for listing, see p334. **Tickets** $30-$305.
Once the country's premier boxing venue, the Garden still hosts some pro fights and the city's annual Golden Gloves amateur championships.

Dog show

Westminster Kennel Club Dog Show

Madison Square Garden (for listing, see p334). www.westminsterkennelclub.org. **Tickets** $40-$95.
Dates February.
America's most prestigious dog show prances into Madison Square Garden each February. One of the oldest sporting events in the country, it's your chance to see some of the most beautiful, well-trained pooches on the planet compete for the coveted Best in Show – and Snausages.

Football

Every Sunday from September to January, New Yorkers get religious… about football. New York, uniquely, lays claim to two NFL teams, and the Giants and the Jets have followings that are equally rabid – so rabid that every home game for both squads is officially sold out. But the teams sometimes release a few seats (generally, those that weren't claimed by the visiting team) on the day of the game. Call for availability on the Friday before kick-off. You can also try your luck on eBay or with a scalper (risky; tickets may be counterfeit). Fans of the fast-paced, high-scoring arena-football league should head out to Nassau Coliseum to see the New York Dragons, who play from February through to May.

New York Dragons

Nassau Veterans Memorial Coliseum (for listing, see p334). 1-866 235 8499/www.newyorkdragons.com. **Tickets** $15-$110.

New York Giants

Giants Stadium (for listing, see p334 **Meadowlands Sports Complex***). 1-201 935 8222/www.giants.com.* **Tickets** $65-$85.

New York Jets

Giants Stadium (for listing, see p334 **Meadowlands Sports Complex***). 1-516 560 8100/www.newyorkjets.com.* **Tickets** $60-$80.

Hockey

The National Hockey League's 2005 season went belly-up and, at press time, there was no telling what would happen in 2006. Check newspapers to see if play is on. The formerly powerful New York Rangers have repeatedly failed to make the play-offs for an uncomfortable number of seasons. The upstart New Jersey Devils have captured three Stanley Cups in the last ten years and always play an exciting, hard-nosed brand of hockey. The New York Islanders skate at the suburban Nassau Coliseum on Long Island. Tickets for all three teams are on sale throughout the season, which runs from October to April.

New Jersey Devils

Continental Airlines Arena (for listing, see p334 **Meadowlands Sports Complex***). www.newjerseydevils.com.* **Tickets** $20-$90.

New York Islanders

Nassau Veterans Memorial Coliseum (for listing, see p334). www.newyorkislanders.com. **Tickets** $25-$175.

New York Rangers

Madison Square Garden (for listing, see p334). www.newyorkrangers.com. **Tickets** $23-$630.

Horse racing

There are three major racetracks near Manhattan: thoroughbreds run at Aqueduct, Belmont and the Meadowlands. If you don't want to trek all the way to Long Island or New Jersey, then catch the action (and the seedy atmosphere) at any off-track betting (OTB) parlour (check the *Yellow Pages* for locations).

Aqueduct Racetrack

110-00 Rockaway Boulevard, at 110th Street, Jamaica, Queens (1-718 641 4700/www. nyra.com/aqueduct). Subway: A to Aqueduct Racetrack. **Races** *Thoroughbred* Oct-May Wed-Sun. **Admission** *Clubhouse* $2; *grandstand* $1. Free 2 Jan-7 Mar. **No credit cards.**

The Wood Memorial, a test run for promising three-year-olds, is held each spring. Betting is, of course, legal at all New York tracks.

Belmont Park

2150 Hempstead Turnpike, Elmont, Long Island (1-516 488 6000/www.nyra.com/belmont). Travel: From Penn Station, Seventh Avenue at 32nd Street, take LIRR (www.lirr.org) to Belmont Park. **Races** *Thoroughbred* May-Jul, Sept, Oct Wed-Sun. **Admission** *Clubhouse* $5; *grandstand* $2. **No credit cards.**

This big beauty of an oval is home to the third and longest leg of horse racing's Triple Crown, the mile-and-a-half Belmont Stakes (10 June, in 2006).

Meadowlands Racetrack

For listing, see p334 **Meadowlands Sports Complex***. 1-201 843 2446/www.thebigm.com.* **Races** *Thoroughbred* Oct, Nov; *harness* Nov-Aug; check website for schedule. **Admission** *Clubhouse* $3; *grandstand* $1. **No credit cards.**

The Meadowlands offers both harness (trotting) and thoroughbred racing. Top harness racers compete for more than $1 million in the prestigious Hambletonian, held the first Saturday in August.

Soccer

The Brits call it football; many Americans call it boring. Still, in a city that's home to such a large immigrant population, footy commands a huge number of fans. You'll find pick-up games in many city parks, and the pro MetroStars play across the river at Giants Stadium, which also occasionally hosts top European teams (such as Manchester United) for exhibition games in front of tens of thousands of crazed hooligans. Check www.meadowlands.com for the schedule.

MetroStars

Giants Stadium (for listing, see p334 **Meadowlands Sports Complex***). 1-888 463 8768/www.metrostars.com.* **Tickets** $18-$38.

Tennis

US Open

USTA National Tennis Center, Flushing Meadows-Corona Park, Queens (1-866 673 6849/www.usopen. org). Subway: 7 to Willets Point-Shea Stadium. **Tickets** $22-$120. **Credit** AmEx, MC, V.

Tickets go on sale late in the spring for this grand-slam thriller, which the USTA says is the highest-attended annual sporting event in the world. Check the website for match schedules.

Active sports

A visit to New York means a lot of watching – watching plays, watching concerts, watching that weird cowboy guy who plays guitar in his underwear in Times Square. But if you get a hankering to do something yourself, the city won't let you down.

All-in-one sports centre

Chelsea Piers

Piers 59-62, W 17th through 23rd Streets, at Eleventh Avenue (1-212 336 6666/www. chelseapiers.com). Subway: C, E to 23rd Street.

This massive sports complex, which occupies a six-block stretch of riverfront real estate, offers just about every popular recreational activity in a bright, clean, well-maintained facility. Would-be Tigers can practise their swings at the Golf Club (Pier 59, 1-212 336 6400); bowlers can set up their pins at the AMF Lanes (between Piers 59 and 60, 1-212 835 2695). Ice-skaters spin and glide at the Sky Rink (Pier 61, 1-212 336 6100). Rather skate on wheels? Hit the Roller Rink and Skate Park (Pier 62, 1-212 336 6200). The Field House (Pier 62, 1-212 336 6500) has a toddler adventure centre, a rock-climbing wall, a gymnastics training centre, batting cages, basketball courts, indoor playing fields and more. Just looking for a spinning class or yoga session? At the Sports Center (Pier 60, 1-212 336 6000) gym, you'll find classes in everything from triathlon training to hip-hop dance. Hours and fees vary; call or consult the website for more information.

Bicycling

Hundreds of miles of paths make it easy for the recreational biker to get pretty much anywhere in New York. Construction continues on the paths that run alongside the East and Hudson Rivers, and it will soon be possible for riders to completely circumnavigate the island of Manhattan. Visitors can either take a DIY trip using rental bikes and path maps or go on organised rides. A word of caution: cycling in the city is serious business. Riders must stay alert and abide by traffic laws, especially because drivers and pedestrians often don't. If you keep your ears and eyes open – and wear a helmet – you'll enjoy an adrenaline-pumping ride. Or forget the traffic and just take a spin through one of the city's many parks, including Central and Prospect Parks.

Bike-path maps
Department of City Planning Bookstore

22 Reade Street, between Broadway & Elk Street (1-212 720 3667). Subway: J, M, Z to Chambers Street; R, W to City Hall; 4, 5, 6 to Brooklyn Bridge-City Hall. **Open** 10am-4pm Mon-Fri.

The city's Bicycle Master Plan includes nearly 1,000 miles of cycling lanes. Free annual updates are available at this shop or at www.nyc.gov.

Transportation Alternatives *Suite 1207, 115 W 30th Street, between Sixth & Seventh Avenues (1-212 629 8080/www.transalt.org). Subway: B, D, F, N, Q, R, V, W to 34th Street-Herald Square; 1, 2, 3 to 34th Street-Penn Station.* **Open** *9.30am-6pm Mon-Fri.*
TA is a non-profit citizens' group that lobbies for more bike-friendly streets. You can pop into the office to get free maps or download them from the website.

Bike rentals

Gotham Bike Shop *112 West Broadway, between Duane & Reade Streets (1-212 732 2453/www. gothambikes.com). Subway: A, C, 1, 2, 3 to Chambers Street.* **Open** *10am-6.30pm Mon-Wed, Fri, Sat; 10am-7.30pm Thur; 10.30am-5pm Sun.* **Fees** *$10 per hour; $30 for 24hrs (includes helmet).* **Credit** AmEx, MC, V.
Rent a sturdy set of wheels from this shop and ride the short distance to the Hudson River esplanade.

Loeb Boathouse *Central Park, entrance on Fifth Avenue, at 72nd Street (1-212 517 2233/www. centralparknyc.org). Subway: 6 to 68th Street-Hunter College.* **Open** *10am-6pm daily, weather permitting.* **Fees** *$6-$21 per hour (includes helmet).* **Credit** AmEx, MC, V (credit card and ID required for rental).
If you want to cruise through Central Park, this place has more than 100 bikes available.

Metro Bicycles *1311 Lexington Avenue, at 88th Street (1-212 427 4450/www.metrobicycles.com). Subway 4, 5, 6 to 86th Street.* **Open** *9.30am-6.30pm daily.* **Fees** *$7 per hour; $35 per day.* **Credit** AmEx, Disc, MC, V.
Trek and Fisher bikes are available by the day; check Metro's website or call for additional locations in Manhattan.

Organised bike rides

Bike the Big Apple *(1-201 837 1133/ www.bikethebigapple.com).*
Tag along with a tour company that combines biking with sightseeing. Trips include a Lower East Side and Brooklyn ride that makes stops at chocolate and beer factories.

Fast & Fabulous *(1-212 567 7160/ www.fastnfab.org).*
This 'queer and queer-friendly' riding group leads tours throughout the year, usually meeting in Central Park and heading out of the city.

Five Borough Bicycle Club *(1-212 932 2300 ext 115/www.5bbc.org).*
This local club always offers a full slate of leisurely rides around the city, as well as jaunts that head farther afield for more experienced riders. Best of all, most trips are free.

Time's Up! *(1-212 802 8222/www.times-up.org).*
An alternative-transportation advocacy group, Time's Up! sponsors rides year-round, including Critical Mass, in which hundreds of cyclists and skaters meet at Union Square Park (7pm on the last Friday of every month) and go tearing through the city, often ending up in Greenwich Village.

Bowling

Bowlmor Lanes

110 University Place, between 12th & 13th Streets (1-212 255 8188/www.bowlmor.com). Subway: L, N, Q, R, W, 4, 5, 6 to 14th Street-Union Square. **Open** 11am-3am Mon; 11am-2am Tue-Thur; 11am-4am Fri, Sat; 11am-1am Sun. **Fees** per person per game $6.45 weekdays before 5pm; $7.95 weekdays after 5pm, and weekends and holidays; $5 shoe rental. Under 21 not admitted after 5pm Tue-Sun. **Credit** AmEx, MC, V.
Renovation turned a seedy but historic Greenwich Village alley (Richard Nixon bowled here!) into a hip downtown nightclub. Monday evening's Night Strike features glow-in-the-dark pins and a techno-spinning DJ in addition to unlimited bowling from 10pm to 3am ($20 per scenester includes shoes).

Gyms

Many gyms offer single-day memberships. If you can schedule a workout during off-peak hours (instead of just before or after the workday), you likely won't have to compete for time on the machines. Call for class details.

Crunch

623 Broadway, between Bleecker & Houston Streets (1-212 420 0507/1-888 227 8624/www.crunch.com). Subway: B, D, F, V to Broadway-Lafayette Street; 6 to Bleecker Street. **Open** 6am-10pm Mon-Fri; 9am-7pm Sat, Sun. **Fees** Day pass $24. **Credit** AmEx, DC, Disc, MC, V.
For a downtown feel without the attitude, Crunch wins hands down. Most of the ten New York locations feature NetPulse cardio equipment, which lets you surf the web or watch a personal TV while you exercise. Visit Crunch's website for other locations.

New York Sports Club

151 E 86th Street, between Lexington & Third Avenues (1-800 301 1231/www.nysc.com). Subway: 4, 5, 6 to 86th Street. **Open** 5.30am-11pm Mon-Thur; 5.30am-10pm Fri; 8am-9pm Sat, Sun. **Fees** Day pass $25. **Credit** AmEx, MC, V.
A day membership at New York Sports Club includes aerobics classes and access to the weight room, cardio machines, steam room and sauna. The 62nd and 86th Street branches feature squash courts. Visit the website for other gym locations.

Horseback riding

Claremont Riding Academy

175 W 89th Street, between Columbus & Amsterdam Avenues (1-212 724 5100). Subway: 1 to 86th Street. **Open** 6.30am-8pm Mon-Fri; 8am-5pm Sat, Sun. **Fees** Rental $50 per hour; lessons $60 per half hour or 3 lessons for $165. **Credit** MC, V.
Beginners use an indoor arena while experienced riders can take a leisurely canter along six miles of trails in Central Park. Be prepared to prove your

English-saddle-mounted mettle: Claremont subjects all riders to an interview to determine their level of experience.

Kensington Stables

51 Caton Place, at East 8th Street, Kensington, Brooklyn (1-718 972 4588/www.kensington stables.com). Subway: F to Fort Hamilton Parkway. **Open** 10am-sunset. **Fees** *Guided trail ride* $25 per hour; *private lessons* $45 per hour. **Credit** AmEx, Disc, MC, V.

The paddock is small, but miles of lovely trails wind through Prospect Park (*see p153*), particularly in the Ravine, which was designed to be seen from horseback.

Ice-skating

Lasker Rink

Central Park, midpark between 106th & 108th Streets (1-212 534 7639/www.centralparknyc.org). Subway: B, C to 110th Street. **Open** *Nov-Mar* 10am-3.45pm Mon, Wed, Thur; 10am-10pm Tue, Fri; 12.30-10pm Sat; 12.30-4.30pm Sun. **Fees** $4.50; $2.25 children. *Skate rental* $4.75. **Credit** MC, V.

This neighbourhood rink has two skate areas: one for high-school hockey teams and the other for the average joe.

Rockefeller Center Ice Rink

1 Rockefeller Plaza, from 49th to 50th Streets, between Fifth & Sixth Avenues (1-212 332 7654/www.therinkatrockcenter.com). Subway: B, D, F, V to 47-50th Streets-Rockefeller Center. **Open** Oct-Apr; call or visit website for hours. **Fees** $9-$17; $7-$12 under-12s. *Skate rental* $7-$8. **Credit** AmEx, Disc, MC, V.

Easily among the city's most recognisable tourist attractions, Rockefeller Center's rink, under the giant statue of Prometheus, is perfect for atmosphere – but bad for elbow room. The rink opens with an energetic ice show in mid October but attracts the most visitors when the towering Christmas tree is lit.

Wollman Rink

Central Park, midpark at 62nd Street (1-212 439 6900/www.wollmanskatingrink.com). Subway: N, R, W to Fifth Avenue-59th Street. **Open** *Late Oct-Mar* 10am-2.30pm Mon, Tue; 10am-9pm Wed, Thur, Sun; 10am-11pm Fri, Sat. **Fees** *Mon-Thur* $8.50; $4.25 children; *Fri-Sun* $11; $4.50 children. *Skate rental* $4.75. **No credit cards**.

Less crowded – especially after the holidays – than Rock Center, the rink offers a lovely setting beneath the trees of Central Park.

In-line skating

In-line skating is very popular in New York: the choking traffic makes it practical, and the landscape makes it pleasurable (a beautiful paved loop circumnavigates Central Park; bike paths run along the Hudson River). Join a group skate, or go it alone. The gear shop Blades,

Board and Skate (120 W 72nd Street, between Columbus & Amsterdam Avenues, 1-212 787 3911) rents by the day ($20).

Empire Skate Club of New York

PO Box 20070, London Terrace Station, New York, NY 10011 (1-212 774 1774/www.empireskate.org). This club organises in-line and roller-skating events throughout the city, including island-hopping tours and night-time rides such as the Thursday Evening Roll: skaters meet May through October at Columbus Circle (Broadway, at 59th Street, southwest corner of Central Park) at 6.45pm.

Kayaking

Kayaking is a great way to explore New York Harbor and the Hudson River. Given the tricky currents, the tidal shifts and the hairy river traffic, it's best to go on an organised excursion.

Downtown Boathouse

Pier 26, between Hubert & North Moore Streets (1-646 613 0375/www.downtownboathouse.org). Subway: 1 to Franklin Street. **Open** 15 May-15 Oct. **Fee** free.

From May to October, weather permitting, this volunteer-run organisation offers free kayaking (no appointment necessary) in front of the boathouses at both locations. They also offer free Wednesday-evening classes and three-hour guided kayak trips on weekend mornings. All trips are offered on a first-come, first-served basis; you must be able to swim. **Other locations**: Pier 66A, Twelfth Avenue, at 26th Street.

Manhattan Kayak Company

Pier 63 Maritime, Twelfth Avenue, at 23rd Street (1-212 924 1788/www.manhattankayak.com). Subway: C, E to 23rd Street. **Open** Call or visit website for schedule and prices. **Credit** AmEx, Disc, MC, V.

Run by veteran kayaker Eric Stiller, who once paddled halfway around Australia, Manhattan Kayak offers beginner to advanced classes and tours. Adventures include the Sushi Tour ($100 per person), in which the group paddles to Edgewater, New Jersey, to dine at a sushi restaurant.

Running

The path ringing the Central Park reservoir is probably the most popular jogging trail in the entire city, but dozens of parks and paths are waiting to be explored. Just tie on a cushy pair of sneakers and go where your feet lead you.

New York Road Runners

9 E 89th Street, between Fifth & Madison Avenues (1-212 860 4455/www.nyrrc.org). Subway: 4, 5, 6 to 86th Street. **Open** 10am-8pm Mon-Fri; 10am-5pm Sat; 10am-3pm Sun. **Fees** Call or visit website. **Credit** AmEx, MC, V.

Arts & Entertainment

Laughing Lotus.

Hardly a weekend passes without some sort of run or race sponsored by the NYRR, which is responsible for the New York City Marathon. Most races take place in Central Park and are open to the public. The club also offers classes and clinics.

NYC Hash House Harriers
1-212 427 4692/www.hashnyc.com.
Fees $15 covers food and beer after the run.
This energetic, slightly wacky group has been running in the Big Apple for more than 20 years and always welcomes newcomers. A 'hash' is part training run, part scavenger hunt, part keg party. The participants follow a three- to five-mile trail that a member (called 'the hare') marks with chalk or other visual clues. After the exercise, the group retires to a local watering hole for drinks and grub.

Swimming

The Harlem, Vanderbilt and West Side YMCAs (www.ymcanyc.org) have decent-size pools (and day passes), as do some private gyms. Many hotel pools provide day-pass access as well. The city of New York maintains several Olympic-size (and plenty of smaller) facilities. Its outdoor pools are free of charge and open from late June to Labor Day: Hamilton Fish (Pitt Street, between Houston & Stanton Streets, 1-212 387 7687); Asser Levy Pool (23rd Street, between First Avenue & FDR Drive, 1-212 447 2020); Tony Dapolito Recreation Center (Clarkson Street, at Seventh Avenue South, 1-212 242 5228). Recreation Center 54 (348 54th Street, between First & Second Avenues, 1-212 754 5411) has an indoor pool. For more information, call New York Parks & Recreation (1-212 639 9675, www.nycgovparks.org).

Tennis

From April through November, the city maintains excellent municipal courts throughout the five boroughs. Single-play (one-hour) tickets cost $7. For a list of city courts, visit www.nycgovparks.org.

Trapeze

Trapeze School New York
Hudson River Park, between Canal & Vestry Streets (1-917 797 1872/www.trapezeschool.com). Subway: 1 to Canal Street. **Open** May-Nov, weather permitting. **Fees** 2-hour class $47-$65, plus $22 one-time application fee. **Credit** AmEx, Disc, MC, V.
Sarah Jessica Parker did it on an episode of *Sex and the City* a couple years ago, so it must be cool. Set in a large, cage-like construction on the bank of the Hudson River (a tent for year-round operation is in the works at Pier 40), the school will teach those ages six and up to fly through the air with the greatest of ease. You can also watch while a loved one has a fling.

Yoga

Laughing Lotus Yoga Center
3rd Floor, 59 W 19th Street, between Fifth & Sixth Avenues (1-212 414 2903/www.laughinglotus.com). Subway: F, V, N, R, W to 23rd Street. **Open** Call or check website for schedule. **Fees** Single class $10-$15. **Credit** AmEx, Disc, MC, V.
Roomy new Chelsea digs accommodate a kind of yogic community centre that has weekly holistic workshops, classes and an in-house tarot reader and astrologist. Among the regular offerings: midnight yoga, reflexology and absolute-beginner classes.

Levitate Yoga
780 Eighth Avenue, between 47th & 48th Streets (1-212 974 2288/www.levitateyoga.com). Subway: C, E, to 50th Street. **Open** Call or check website for schedule. **Fees** Single class $18; students $12. **Credit** AmEx, MC, V.
This modern-looking studio caters to beginners, tourists from area hotels, and casts and crews performing at nearby theatres. In the warm months, special classes are held on the 2,000sq ft rooftop terrace.

Om Yoga Center
6th Floor, 826 Broadway, between 12th & 13th Streets (1-212 254 9642/www.omyoga.com). Subway: L, N, Q, R, W, 4, 5, 6 to 14th Street-Union Square. **Open** Call or check website for schedule. **Fees** Single class $16. **Credit** AmEx, Disc, MC, V.
Cyndi Lee's famed yoga spot offers all-level, flowing-style *vinyasa* yoga classes with a focus on alignment.

Theatre & Dance

With so many venues, no doubt you'll be stage-struck.

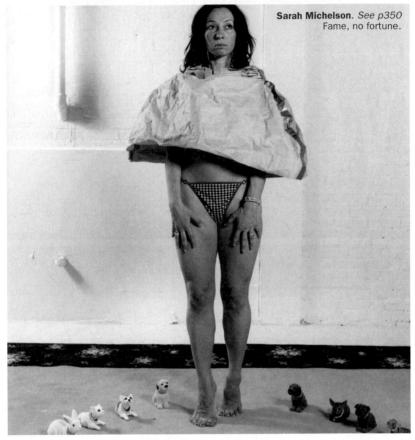

Sarah Michelson. *See p350*
Fame, no fortune.

Theatre

Perhaps you've heard the theatre referred to as the 'fabulous invalid'. The joke underscores the conundrum in the industry today: it's always thriving, yet always ailing. Although New York is still the theatre capital of the world, with hundreds of shows opening year-round – and Broadway at the top of the food chain – the economic logistics of sustaining a show are ever more daunting. Broadway flops routinely lose millions; artistic Off Broadway successes sometimes shut after a two-month run for lack of a big producer. And goodness knows how many brilliant works go unnoticed in the cash-poor precincts of Off-Off Broadway. Despite all that, New York theatre survives. And if diversity is any indication, some might even say it flourishes. There are perennial family-friendly draws like *The Lion King* and *Chitty Chitty Bang Bang*, delirious musical comedies like *The Producers* and *Hairspray* and top-

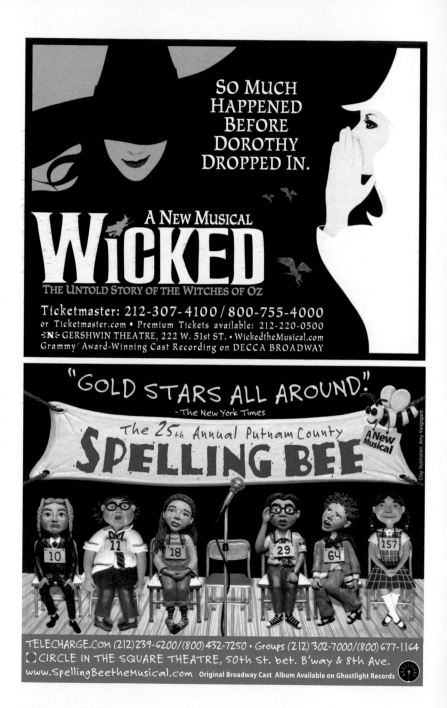

drawer drama such as John Patrick Shanley's *Doubt*. But you can also catch terrific examples of pop-driven musicals, such as the ABBA-inspired *Mamma Mia!* and Tony Award winner *Avenue Q*, an irreverent show best described as *Rent* meets *Sesame Street*.

From Midtown's landmark palaces and slightly more intimate venues to Downtown's offbeat Off Broadway and Off-Off Broadway spaces, there's a place – and a show – that will suit every taste.

BUYING TICKETS

If you have a major credit card, then buying Broadway tickets is as easy as picking up a phone. Nearly all Broadway and Off Broadway shows are served by one of the city's 24-hour ticketing agencies, which are listed in the shows' print advertisements or in the capsule reviews that run each week in *Time Out New York*. The venues' information lines can also refer you to ticket agents sometimes by merely transferring your call (for additional ticketing info, *see p382*). Theatre box offices usually charge a small fee for phone orders.

Some of the cheapest tickets on Broadway are 'rush' tickets (purchased the day of a show at the theatre's box office), which cost an average of $25 – but not all theatres offer these, and some reserve them for students. A few theatres distribute rush tickets through a lottery, usually held two hours before the performance. If a show is sold out, it's worth waiting for stand-by tickets just before curtain time. Tickets are slightly cheaper for matinées (typically on Wednesdays, Saturdays and Sundays) and previews, and for students or groups of 20 or more. For discount seats, your best bet is TKTS (*see p382*), where you can get tickets on the day of the performance for as much as 75 per cent off the face value. Arrive early to beat – or at least get a jump on – the long lines. TKTS also sells matinée tickets the day before a show. (Beware of scam artists trying to sell tickets to those waiting in line: their tickets are often fake.) You should consider purchasing a set of vouchers from the Theatre Development Fund if you're interested in seeing more than one Off-Off Broadway show or dance event.

Theatre Development Fund

1501 Broadway, between 43rd & 44th Streets (1-212 221 0013/www.tdf.org). Subway: N, Q, R, W, 42nd Street S, 1, 2, 3, 7 to 42nd Street-Times Square. **Open** 10am-6pm Mon-Fri. **No credit cards.**
For $28 TDF offers a book of four vouchers that can be purchased only at its office by visitors who bring their passport or out-of-state driver's license, or by students and residents on the TDF mailing list. Each voucher is good for one admission to an Off-Off

Broadway theatre, dance or music event at venues such as the Atlantic Theater Company, the Joyce, the Kitchen, Performance Space 122 and many more. TDF's NYC/Onstage service (1-212 768 1818) provides information by phone on all events in town.

Broadway

Technically speaking, 'Broadway' is the Theater District that surrounds Times Square on either side of Broadway (the avenue), mainly between 41st and 53rd Streets. This is where you'll find the grand theatres that were built largely between 1900 and 1930. Officially, 38 are designated as being part of Broadway – full-price tickets at one of them can cost more than $100. The big shows are hard to ignore; high-profile revivals and new blockbusters announce themselves from giant billboards and drench the airwaves with radio advertisements. Still, there's more to Broadway than splashy musicals and flashy pop spectacles. In recent years, provocative dramas like *Take Me Out* and madcap comedies such as *Urinetown* have had remarkable success, as have revivals of American classics such as Lorraine Hansberry's *A Raisin in the Sun* and Eugene O'Neill's *Long Day's Journey into Night*.

The Roundabout Theatre Company (American Airlines Theatre, 227 W 42nd Street, between Seventh & Eighth Avenues, 1-212 719 1300; Studio 54, 254 W 54th Street, between Broadway & Eighth Avenue) is critically acclaimed for putting on classics that feature all-star casts; it was also the force behind the brilliant revival of *Assassins* by Stephen Sondheim and John Weidman in 2004. You can subscribe to the Roundabout's full season or buy single tickets, if they're available.

Broadway (Theater District)

Subway: *C, E, 1 to 50th Street; N, Q, R, W, 42nd Street S, 2, 3, 7 to 42nd Street-Times Square.*

Long-running shows

Straight (non-musical) plays can provide some of Broadway's most stirring experiences, but they're less likely than musicals to enjoy long runs. If you aren't in search of song, check *Time Out New York* for current listings and reviews of new or revived dramatic plays.

Avenue Q

Golden Theater, 252 W 45th Street, between Broadway & Eighth Avenue (1-212 239 6200/ www.avenueq.com). Subway: A, C, E to 42nd Street-Port Authority. **Box office** 10am-8pm Mon-Sat; noon-7pm Sun. **Tickets** $21-$96. **Shows** 8pm Tue-Fri; 2, 8 pm Sat; 2, 7pm Sun. *Length* 2hrs 15 mins. One intermission. **Credit** AmEx, DC, Disc, MC, V.

HOTCHA.

CHICAGO
THE MUSICAL

WINNER! SIX 1997 TONY AWARDS!

TELECHARGE.COM 212-239-6200 • CHICAGOTHEMUSICAL.COM
AMBASSADOR THEATRE • 219 WEST 49TH STREET
GRAMMY® AWARD-WINNING CAST RECORDING ON RCA VICTOR

Mixing puppets and live actors with irreverent jokes and snappy songs, this clever, good-hearted musical comedy was a surprise hit. It garnered several 2004 Tonys, including Best Musical. **Photo** *p347*.

Chicago

Ambassador Theatre, 219 W 49th Street, between Broadway & Eight Avenues (1-212 239 6200). Subway: N, R, W to 49th Street; 1 to 50th Street. **Tickets** $48-$100. **Shows** 7pm Tue; 2, 8pm Wed; 8pm Sat; 2, 8pm Thur, Fri; 6.30pm Sun. *Length* 2hrs 30 mins. One intermission. **Credit** AmEx, MC, V.

This snappy 1975 John Kander-Fredd Ebb-Bob Fosse show tells the dark saga of chorus girl Roxie Hart, who murders her lover, avoids prison and – with the help of a huckster lawyer – becomes a musical star. Director Walter Bobbie and choreographer Ann Reinking's minimalist strip-club aesthetic panders to some abstract lust, but the story is wicked fun and the brassy score infectious.

Hairspray

Neil Simon Theatre, 250 W 52nd Street, between Broadway & Eighth Avenue (1-212 307 4100/ www.hairsprayonbroadway.com). Subway: C, E, 1 to 50th Street. **Box office** 10am-8pm Mon-Sat; noon-6pm Sun. **Tickets** $60-$100. **Shows** 7pm Tue; 2, 8pm Wed; 8pm Thur, Fri; 2, 8pm Sat; 3pm Sun. *Length* 2hrs 35 mins. One intermission. **Credit** AmEx, DC, Disc, MC, V.

John Waters's classic kitsch film has become an eye-popping song-and-dance extravaganza that's bigger, brighter, more satirical and much funnier than the original.

Monty Python's Spamalot

Shubert Theatre, 225 W 44th Street, between Broadway & Eighth Avenue (1-212 239 6200). **Tickets** $36.25-$101.25. **Shows** 7pm Tue; 2pm, 8pm Wed, Sat; 8pm Thur, Fri; 3pm Sun. *Length* 2hrs 15mins. One intermission. **Credit** AmEx, MC, V.

Monty Python founder Eric Idle is behind this 'lovingly ripped-off' musical adaptation of *Monty Python and the Holy Grail*. Veteran director Mike Nichols stages the mélange of greatest-hits laughs and Broadway-spoofing novelty. Winner of the 2005 Tony Award for Best Musical.

The Producers

St James Theatre, 246 W 44th Street, between Seventh & Eighth Avenues (1-212 239 6200/ www.producersonbroadway.com). Subway: N, Q, R, W, 42nd Street S, 1, 2, 3, 7 to 42nd Street-Times Square. **Box office** 10am-8pm Mon-Sat; noon-6pm Sun. **Tickets** $66-$99. **Shows** 7pm Tue; 2, 8pm Wed; 8pm Thur, Fri; 2, 8pm Sat; 3pm Sun. *Length* 2hrs 45 mins. One intermission. **Credit** AmEx, DC, Disc, MC, V.

Mel Brooks's ode to tastelessness mixes Broadway razzamatazz with Borscht Belt humour. Original stars Nathan Lane and Matthew Broderick left the cast, but the show still delivers plenty of laughs.

Wicked

Gershwin Theatre, 222 W 51st Street, between Broadway & Eighth Avenue (1-212 307 4100). Subway: C, E, 1, to 50th Street. **Box office** 10am-8pm Mon-Sat; noon-6pm Sun. **Tickets** $40-$100. **Shows** 7pm Tue; 2, 8pm Wed; 8pm Thur, Fri; 2, 8pm Sat; 3pm Sun. *Length* 2hrs 45 mins. One intermission. **Credit** AmEx, DC, Disc, MC, V.

Based on novelist Megan Maguire's 1995 riff on *The Wizard of Oz* mythology, *Wicked* provides a witty prequel to the classic children's book and movie. At press time, Joe Mantello's sumptuous production starred Megan Hilty and Shoshana Bean as young versions of Glinda the Good Witch and the Wicked Witch of the West.

Off Broadway

As the cost of mounting a show on Broadway continues to soar, many serious playwrights are opening their shows in the more adventurous (and less financially demanding) Off Broadway houses. Off Broadway theatres have between 200 and 500 seats, and tickets usually run from $20 to $70. Below are some of our favourite long-running shows, followed by a few of the best theatres and repertory companies.

Long-running shows

Altar Boyz

Dodger Stages, 340 W 50th Street, between Eighth & Ninth Avenues (1-212 239 6200). Subway: C, E, 1 to 50th Street. **Box office** 1-6pm Mon, Sun; 1-7.30pm Tue-Sat. **Tickets** $66-$69. **Shows** 8pm Mon, Tue, Thur, Fri; 2pm, 8pm Sat; 3pm, 7pm Sun. *Length* 1hr 30mins. No intermission. **Credit** AmEx, MC, V.

The Altar Boyz sing about Jesus in the unlikely idiom of boy-band pop, complete with five-part harmony, synchronised steps and prefab streetwise posturing. Mad props where mad props are due: the show's young stars really work their crosses off.

Blue Man Group

Astor Place Theater, 434 Lafayette Street, between Astor Place & E 4th Street (1-212 254 4370/www. blueman.com). Subway: N, R, W to 8th Street-NYU; 6 to Astor Place. **Box office** noon-7.45pm daily. **Tickets** $55-$65. **Shows** 8pm Tue-Thur; 7, 10pm Fri; 4, 7, 10pm Sat; 2, 5, 8pm Sun. *Length* 2hrs. No intermission. **Credit** AmEx, DC, Disc, MC, V.

Three men with extraterrestrial imaginations (and head-to-toe blue body paint) carry this long-time favourite – a show that's as smart as it is ridiculous.

Stomp

Orpheum Theater, 126 Second Avenue, between St Marks Place & E 7th Street (1-212 477 2477). Subway: N, R, W to 8th Street-NYU; 6 to Astor Place. **Box office** 1-7pm Tue-Fri. **Tickets** $35-$60. **Shows** 8pm Tue-Fri; 7, 10.30pm Sat; 3, 7pm Sun. *Length* 1hr 30 mins. No intermission. **Credit** AmEx, MC, V.

Arts & Entertainment

This show is billed as a 'percussion sensation' because there's no other way to describe it. Using garbage-can lids, buckets, brooms, sticks and just about anything they can get their hands on, these aerobicised dancer-musicians make a lovely racket.

Repertory companies & venues

Atlantic Theater Company
336 W 20th Street, between Eighth & Ninth Avenues (Telecharge 1-212 239 6200/www. atlantictheater.org). Subway: C, E to 23rd Street. **Box office** 6-8pm Tue-Fri; noon-2pm, 6-8pm Sat; 1-3pm Sun. **Credit** AmEx, Disc, MC, V.
Created in 1985 as an offshoot of acting workshops taught by playwright David Mamet and film star William H Macy, this dynamic theatre has presented nearly 100 plays, including Mamet's *Romance* and Woody Allen's *A Secondhand Memory*.

Brooklyn Academy of Music
For listing, see p328.
Brooklyn's grand old opera house – along with the Harvey Theater, two blocks away on Fulton Street – stages the famous multidisciplinary Next Wave Festival every October through December (*see p265*). The 2005 festival included avant-garde composer Philip Glass's *Orion* and the British director Edward Hall's all-male rendition of Shakespeare's *Winter's Tale*.

Classic Stage Company
136 E 13th Street, between Third & Fourth Avenues (Ticket Central 1-212 677 4210/www. classicstage.org). Subway: L, N, Q, R, W, 4, 5, 6 to 14th Street-Union Square. **Box office** noon-5pm Mon-Fri. **Credit** AmEx, MC, V.
From Greek tragedies to medieval mystery plays, the Classic Stage Company (under the tutelage of artistic director Brian Kulick) makes the old new again with open rehearsals, staged readings and full-on productions.

Dodger Stages
340 W 50th Street, between Eighth & Ninth Avenues (1-646 871 1730/www.dodgerstages.com). Subway: C, E, 1 to 50th Street. **Box office** 1-6pm Mon, Sun; 1-7.30pm Tue-Sat. **Credit** AmEx, MC, V.
Formerly a movie multiplex, this new centre boasts a shiny, space-age interior and five gorgeous, fully renovated theatres presenting everything from the underwater puppet spectacle *Symphonie Fantastique* to world premières of new musicals, like *Altar Boyz*. Dodger Theatrical, an organisation that produces Broadway shows, is behind this $20 million undertaking, which is one of the biggest in recent theatre history.

59E59
59 E 59th Street, between Madison & Park Avenues (1-212 279 4200/www.59e59.org). Subway: N, R, W to Lexington Avenue-59th Street; 4, 5, 6 to 59th Street. **Box office** noon-7pm daily. **Credit** AmEx, MC, V.

Intermission buzz at **Avenue Q**. *See p343.*

This chic new East Side venue, which comprises an Off Broadway space and two smaller theatres, made a splash in its first year with the Brits Off Broadway festival. The Off Broadway company Primary Stages now makes its home at 59E59.

Irish Repertory Theatre
132 W 22nd Street, between Sixth & Seventh Avenues (1-212 727 2737/www.irishrepertory theatre.com). Subway: F, V, 1 to 23rd Street. **Box office** 10am-6pm Mon-Fri; 11am-6pm Sat, Sun. **Credit** AmEx, MC, V.
This Chelsea company puts on compelling shows by Irish playwrights. Past productions include Frank McCourt's *The Irish and How They Got That Way* and Enda Walsh's *Bedbound*.

Lincoln Center
For listing, see p329.
The majestic Lincoln Center complex includes two amphitheatre-style drama venues: the 1,138-seat Vivian Beaumont Theater (the Broadway house) and the 338-seat Mitzi E Newhouse Theater (Off Broadway). Expect polished, often star-studded productions of classic plays (such as *Henry IV* featuring Kevin Kline and Ethan Hawke) and new musicals (Adam Guettel's *The Light in the Piazza*). The Lincoln's founding policy ensures that ticket prices are kept reasonable, averaging $32.

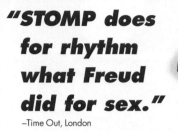

Manhattan Theatre Club

*City Center, 131 W 55th Street, between Sixth &
Seventh Avenues (1-212 581 1212/Telecharge 1-212
239 6200/www.mtc-nyc.org). Subway: B, D, E to
Seventh Avenue.* **Box office** 11am-5pm Mon, Sun;
noon-7pm Tue-Sat. **Credit** AmEx, DC, Disc, MC, V.
Manhattan Theatre Club has a history of sending
young playwrights to Broadway, as seen with such
successes as David Auburn's *Proof* and John
Patrick Shanley's *Doubt*. The club's two theatres
are located in the basement of City Center. The 275-
seat Stage I Theater features four plays a year; the
Stage II Theater offers works-in-progress, workshops and staged readings, as well as full-length
productions. MTC also has a Broadway home in the
renovated Biltmore Theatre (261 W 47th Street,
between Broadway & Eighth Avenue; tickets from
Telecharge, 1-212 239 6200).

New Victory Theater

*209 W 42nd Street, between Seventh & Eighth
Avenues (1-646 223 3020/Telecharge 1-212 239
6200/www.newvictory.org). Subway: N, Q, R, W,
42nd Street S, 1, 2, 3, 7 to 42nd Street-Times
Square.* **Box office** 11am-5pm Mon, Sun;
noon-7pm Tue-Sat. **Credit** AmEx, MC, V.
The New Victory is a perfect symbol for the transformation of Times Square. Built in 1900 by Oscar
Hammerstein II, Manhattan's oldest theatre became
a strip club and adult cinema in the '70s and '80s.
Renovated by the city in 1995, the building now
features a full season of family-friendly plays.

New York Theatre Workshop

*79 E 4th Street, between Bowery & Second Avenue
(1-212 460 5475/www.nytw.org). Subway: F, V to
Lower East Side-Second Avenue; 6 to Astor Place.*
Box office 1-6pm Tue-Sun. **Credit** AmEx, MC, V.
Founded in 1979, the New York Theatre Workshop
works with emerging directors eager to take on chal-
lenging pieces. Besides plays by the likes of Caryl
Churchill (*Far Away, A Number*) and Tony Kushner
(*Homebody/Kabul*), this company also premièred
Rent, Jonathan Larson's Pulitzer Prize-winning
musical, which still packs 'em in on Broadway.

Playwrights Horizons

*416 W 42nd Street, between Ninth & Tenth Avenues
(Ticket Central 1-212 279 4200/www.playwrights
horizons.org). Subway: A, C, E to 42nd Street-
Port Authority.* **Box office** noon-8pm daily.
Credit AmEx, MC, V.
More than 300 important contemporary plays have
premièred here, including dramas such as *Driving
Miss Daisy* and *The Heidi Chronicles*. Recent sea-
sons have included works by Craig Lucas (*Small
Tragedy*) and Lynn Nottage (*Fabulation*).

Public Theater

*425 Lafayette Street, between Astor Place & E 4th
Street (1-212 539 8500/Telecharge 1-212 239
6200/www.publictheater.org). Subway: N, R, W to
8th Street-NYU; 6 to Astor Place.* **Box office** 1-6pm
Mon, Sun; 1-7.30pm Tue-Sat. **Credit** AmEx, MC, V.
Founded by the late Joseph Papp and dedicated
to the work of new American playwrights and
performers, this Astor Place landmark is also
known for its Shakespeare productions (*see p349*
Shakespeare in the Park). The building houses five stages and the cabaret space Joe's Pub (*see
p317*). The Public recently recruited Oskar Eustis
(formerly of the Trinity Repertory Company in
Providence, Rhode Island) to serve as the new
artistic director.

Second Stage Theatre

*307 W 43rd Street, at Eighth Avenue (1-212 246
4422/www.secondstagetheatre.com). Subway: A, C, E
to 42nd Street-Port Authority.* **Box office** noon-6pm
Tue-Sun. **Credit** AmEx, MC, V.
Now located in a beautiful Rem Koolhaas-designed
space near Times Square, Second Stage produces
the works of new American playwrights, including
the New York premières of Mary Zimmerman's
Metamorphoses and Lisa Loomer's *Living Out*.

Shakespeare in the Park at the Delacorte Theater

*Park entrance on Central Park West, at 81st
Street, then follow the signs (1-212 539 8750/
www.publictheater.org). Subway: B, C to 81st
Street-Museum of Natural History.*
The Delacorte Theater in Central Park is the fair-
weather sister of the Public Theater (*see above*).
When not producing Shakespeare in the East
Village, the Public offers the best of the Bard outdoors during the New York Shakespeare Festival
(Jun-Sept). Tickets are free (two per person); they're
distributed at both theatres at 1pm on the day of
performance. Normally, 9am is a good time to begin
waiting, though the line can start as early as 6am
when big-name stars are on the bill.

Vineyard Theatre

*108 E 15th Street, at Union Square East (1 212 353
0303/box office 1-212 353 0303/www.vineyard
theatre. org). Subway: L, N, Q, R, W, 4, 5, 6 to
14th Street-Union Square.* **Box office** 10am-6pm
Mon-Fri. **Credit** AmEx, MC, V.
This theatre near Union Square produces excellent
new plays and musicals including Pulitzer Prize
winner Paula Vogel's *The Long Christmas Ride
Home* and the Tony Award-winning Broadway hit
Avenue Q (*see p343*).

Off-Off Broadway

Technically, 'Off-Off Broadway' denotes a show
that is presented at a theatre with fewer than
100 seats and created by artists who aren't
necessarily card-carrying union pros. It's where
some of the most daring writers and performers
create their edgiest work. The New York
International Fringe Festival (1-212 279 4488,
www.fringenyc.org), held every August, is a
great way to catch the wacky side of theatre.
The cheekily named National Theater of the

United States of America (www.ntusa.org), Radiohole (www.radiohole.com) and the International WOW Company (www.inter mationalwow.org) are troupes that consistently offer inspired envelope-pushing work. But Off-Off Broadway – where tickets run $10 to $25 – is not restricted to experimental or solo shows. You can also see classical works and more traditional plays staged by companies such as the Mint Theater (3rd Floor, 311 W 43rd Street, between Eighth & Ninth Avenues, 1-212 315 0231, www.minttheater.org) and at venues like HERE and Performance Space 122.
Repertory companies & venues

The Brick

575 Metropolitan Avenue, between Lorimer Street & Union Avenue, Williamsburg, Brooklyn (1-718 907 3457/www.bricktheater.com). Subway: G to Metropolitan Avenue; L to Lorimer Street. **Box office** opens 15 minutes prior to curtain. **No credit cards.**

This chic, brick-lined venue in Williamsburg presents a variety of experimental work. Last summer, it made a joyful noise with the campy, outrageous Moral Values Festival.

HERE

145 Sixth Avenue, at Broome Street (1-212 647 0202/Smarttix 1-212 868 4444/www.here.org). Subway: C, E to Spring Street. **Box office** 4-10pm daily. **Credit** AmEx, MC, V.
Containing three intimate performance spaces, an art gallery and a chic café, this lovely Tribeca arts complex, dedicated to non-profit arts enterprise, has hosted a number of exciting companies. It was the launching pad for such well-known shows as Eve Ensler's *Vagina Monologues*.

Flea Theater

41 White Street, between Broadway & Church Street (1-212 226 2407/www.theflea.org). Subway: A, C, E, J, M, N, Q, R, W, Z, 1, 6 to Canal Street. **Box office** noon-6pm Mon-Sat. **Credit** AmEx, MC, V.

Fame, no fortune

Look over the reviews and articles that have been written about choreographer Sarah Michelson and one word keeps cropping up: 'ambitious'. It's an apt description of her much-praised work, which is not so much dance as a series of living art installations. In fact, 'ambitious' is one of the few words Michelson (pictured p341) will herself use to describe her choreography. 'I try to do lots of different things,' she says, noting that the launching pad for her ideas is usually the performance space itself – what can be done with its visual organisation – and the movement takes off from there. Add to that a whopping dose of experimentation with costuming, set design, video, lighting and even what goes on in the lighting booth. In her *Shadowmann* of three years ago, Michelson dispensed with the mundane notion that a performance should be seen in one sitting. It was presented in two parts, on separate evenings, in separate venues – the Kitchen and PS 122 – each of which was visually transformed. At the Kitchen, the audience sat on the stage and faced the doors; at the start of the performance the lights went up instead of down and the doors were flung open to reveal dancers entering from the street. All of this could come off as gimmickry if not for the emotional effect of the whole. Michelson's movement, with its idiosyncratic gestures and oft-repeated phrases, moves the viewer – even if the

meaning is less than clear. (And don't bother asking her what the meaning is: 'I wouldn't say anything,' she says.) Indeed, Michelson is reticent about using any words to describe her work, but some that definitely rub her the wrong way include 'quirky' and 'fun'. With its mix of gesture and movement that sometimes appears more free-form than set, Michelson's work has a 'humanistic' quality, she says. But the choreographer is as meticulous as any ballet master. 'It's very exacting work,' she says. 'We're killing ourselves out there.'

But what's really killing the choreographer these days is the classic artist's conundrum: how to eke out a living in New York. Last year, Michelson had to postpone the première of her well-received *Daylight* by several months after cracking a bone in her foot. The money lost from the cancelled performance, along with her medical bills (she has no insurance), had her unable to pay the rent on her studio apartment and hiding from her landlord. This, from a choreographer who once set a piece for Mikhail Baryshnikov's White Oak Dance Project. (She had Mischa in a skirt and Velcro handcuffs, dancing on bubble wrap.) The situation is such that Michelson says 2006 will be her last year as a choreographer and performer; filmmaking, she thinks, might be a more viable way to make a living creatively. If this threat of retirement is real, that makes it all the more urgent to get to her potential swan song at BAM this autumn.

Arts & Entertainment

Participants in **Dance New Amsterdam**'s summer workshops. *See p354.*

Founded in fashionable Tribeca in 1997, Jim Simpson's cosy, well-appointed venue has presented both avant-garde experimentation (the work of Mac Wellman) and politically provocative satires (mostly by AR Gurney).

Performance Space 122

150 First Avenue, at 9th Street (1-212 477 5288/ www.ps122.org). Subway: L to First Avenue; 6 to Astor Place. **Box office** 11am-6pm daily. **Credit** AmEx, MC, V.

One of New York's most interesting venues, this non-profit arts centre presents experimental dance, performance art, music, film and video. Eric Bogosian, Whoopi Goldberg, John Leguizamo and others have developed projects here; of more street-level interest is the monthly bloggers' night. Australian trend-setter Vallejo Gantner recently took over as artistic director of this downtown institution, promising to make its programming more international in flavour. The dance programming is also worthy of note; *see p354.*

Dance

Home to the world's foremost dance companies and untold numbers of independent, cutting-edge choreographers, New York is a testament to the endless ways that the human body can get its move on. The city is the base for the companies of such modern dance luminaries as Martha Graham, Alvin Ailey, Merce Cunningham and Trisha Brown. For the classically minded, the New York City Ballet offers both innovative new works by resident choreographer Christopher Wheeldon and the unparalleled repertory of George Balanchine, whose choreography transformed ballet in the 20th century. New York is a virtually required stop for national and international company tours, and partly for this reason its audiences tend to be knowledgeable and enthusiastic.

In a city where, in the 1960s, the Judson Dance Theater spawned the 'postmodern' movement that changed the face of modern dance, experimentation is still alive; a host of more intimate spaces showcase exceptional artists, such as Stephen Petronio, John Jasperse, Donna Uchizono and Sarah Michelson, and there are many incubators for new talent. The World Music Institute presents a variety of ethnic dance at Symphony Space and City Center, and the Japan Society is a goldmine for discovering both avant-garde voices and the purity of traditional dance.

Some choreographers take you out of the theatre altogether with 'site-specific' works, such as those by Noemie Lafrance, who has staged performances in a clock tower and a parking garage. The renowned Japanese-born duo Eiko & Koma has offered numerous free outdoor performances, in parks, plazas and gardens throughout the city.

There are two major dance seasons – March to June, and October to December. The spring season is particularly busy: start with Paul Taylor's consistently brilliant company in March, then grab your seats for the spring programmes of the American Ballet Theatre and NYCB. That's not to say that dance is dead from July to September; indeed, summer is a great time to catch smaller modern-dance troupes and outdoor performances at the open-air Central Park SummerStage (*see p354*), the Lincoln Center Out of Doors Festival (*see p263*) and the River to River Festival (*see p87*) in lower Manhattan.

If you too yearn to unleash your creative bodily expression, there are dozens of dance schools (some affiliated with major companies) that offer classes in everything from ballet to contact improv to Afro-Caribbean and Haitian dance. Information about classes and workshops is listed in *Time Out New York*. You can call ahead for a schedule, but walk-ins are welcome at most spaces.

Traditional venues

Brooklyn Academy of Music
For listing, see p328.
BAM, which showcases superb local and out-of-town companies, is one of New York's most prominent cultural institutions. The Howard Gilman Opera House, with its Federal-style columns and carved marble, is a stunning dance venue. The Mark Morris Dance Group generally performs here in the spring. The 1904 Harvey Theater (651 Fulton Street, between Ashland & Rockwell Places, Fort Greene, Brooklyn), formerly the Majestic, has hosted choreographers John Jasperse and Ralph Lemon; the annual DanceAfrica festival, in its 29th year in 2006,

is the venue's longest-running performance series. Each autumn, BAM's Next Wave Festival highlights established and experimental dance groups; this year, look for Sarah Michelson in October.

City Center
131 W 55th Street, between Sixth & Seventh Avenues (1-212 581 7907/www.nycitycenter.org). Subway: B, D, E to Seventh Avenue; F, N, Q, R, W to 57th Street. **Tickets** $15-$110. **Credit** AmEx, MC, V ($4.75 per-ticket surcharge).
Before the creation of Lincoln Center changed the cultural geography of New York, this was the home of the American Ballet Theatre, the Joffrey Ballet and the New York City Ballet. The City Center's lavish decor is golden – as are the companies that pass through here. You can count on superb performances by the ABT in the fall, the Alvin Ailey American Dance Theater in December, the Paul Taylor Dance Company in the spring and others throughout the year.

Joyce Theater
175 Eighth Avenue, at 19th Street (1-212 242 0800/www.joyce.org). Subway: A, C, E to 14th Street; 1 to 18th Street; L to Eighth Avenue. **Tickets** $28-$45. **Credit** AmEx, DC, Disc, MC, V.
This intimate space, formerly a cinema, is one of the finest theatres in town. Of the 472 seats at the Joyce, there's not a single bad one. Companies and choreographers who present work here, including the Ballet Hispanico, David Parsons and Doug Varone, tend to be more traditional than experimental. This year look for DanceBrazil in February and Pilobolus Dance Theatre in July. During the summer, when many theatres are dark, the Joyce continues its programming. At Joyce Soho, emerging companies present work nearly every weekend.
Other locations: Joyce Soho, 155 Mercer Street, between Houston & Prince Streets (1-212 334 7479).

Metropolitan Opera House
For listing, see p328.
A range of international companies, from the Paris Opera Ballet to the Kirov Ballet, perform at the Met. In spring, this majestic space is home to the American Ballet Theatre, which presents full-length traditional story ballets, as well as contemporary classics by Frederick Ashton and Antony Tudor. The acoustics are wonderful, but the theatre is immense: get as close to the stage as you can afford.

New York State Theater
Lincoln Center, 64th Street, at Columbus Avenue (1-212 870 5570/www.nycballet.com). Subway: 1 to 66th Street-Lincoln Center. **Tickets** $20-$99. **Credit** AmEx, DC, Disc, MC, V.
The neoclassical New York City Ballet headlines at this opulent theatre, which Philip Johnson designed to resemble a jewel box. NYCB has two seasons: winter begins just before Thanksgiving and features more than a month of performances of George Balanchine's magical *The Nutcracker*; the

Times Square South

For those who prefer their haute couture served with a dollop of drama, the burgeoning Garment District theatre scene may be just the ticket. The unquestionable diva of the litter is the brand-spanking new **37 ARTS** theatre complex (450 West 37th Street, between Ninth & Tenth Avenues). Anchoring what some are now dubbing 'Times Square South', this six-storey modernist concrete structure is actually home to two distinct entertainment entities: the Baryshnikov Arts Center (BAC) and the West 37th Arts Group. The brainchild of the internationally renowned dance star Mikhail Baryshnikov, the non-profit BAC is a three-floor production and rehearsal facility dedicated to developing young artists and new interdisciplinary dance, theatre and music pieces. New works receive occasional public unveilings in the company's informal 100-seat studio theatre.

'The focus is on developing the artist rather than mounting main-stage shows, and to that end Baryshnikov is very involved artistically because it's his baby – he's there every step and every day,' says BAC's general manager Christina L Sterner.

West 37th Arts Group, on the other hand, plans to fill its three slick Off-Broadway theatres with for-profit productions of new plays and revivals. The company already struck gold when in 2005 it leased out its largest space for the star-studded (Ethan Hawke, Parker Posey, Bobby Cannavale) sold-out run of David Rabe's *Hurlyburly*.

Nearby, the **Zipper Theater** (336 West 37th Street; pictured) is perhaps more typical of the rough-hewn zeitgeist of the Garment District arts scene. Open for business shortly after 9/11, the owners worked with a tight budget to renovate an old zipper factory – carving out plenty of room for the production of edgy new American plays. 'When we moved in it was wall-to-wall shelving with zippers,' said general manager Emily Elsener. 'And we used most of what was here as material for construction so the theatre has a very industrial feel. But it's very comfortable – our audience sits in mini-van automobile seats complete with cup-holders, and everyone is encouraged to take drinks direct from our beautiful bar right into the theatre.'

Around the corner is the **Theatre Building** (312 West 36th Street), home to three more theatre companies: the Barrow Group, the Abingdon Theatre, and the Workshop Theater. All told, the companies offer six spaces dedicated to the production of new American work and New York premières. Their block party neighbour – the Dionysus Theatre's **Complex** at 270 West 36th Street – is another small two-theatre space aimed at the production of new general-interest and gay-positive plays. So, what are you waiting for? Go south!

Arts & Entertainment

season continues through February with repertory performances. The nine-week spring season usually begins in April. The best seats are in the first ring, where the music comes through loud and clear and – even better – you can enjoy the dazzling patterns of the dancers. The works are by Balanchine (the 89ft-by-58ft stage was built to his specifications); Jerome Robbins; Peter Martins, the company's ballet master in chief; and resident choreographer Christopher Wheeldon, whose work has injected the troupe with new life. Weekly cast lists are available online or at the theatre.

Alternative venues

Aaron Davis Hall
City College, Convent Avenue, at 135th Street (1-212 650 7100/www.aarondavishall.org). Subway: 1 to 137th Street-City College. **Tickets** *$15-$35.* **Credit** AmEx, MC, V.
Performances here celebrate African-American life and culture. Companies that have graced the modern, spacious theatre include the Bill T Jones/Arnie Zane Dance Company and the Alvin Ailey junior company, Ailey II.

Brooklyn Arts Exchange
421 Fifth Avenue, at 8th Street, Park Slope, Brooklyn (1-718 832 0018/www.bax.org). Subway: F, M, R to Fourth Avenue-9th Street. **Tickets** *$8-$15.* **Credit** Disc, MC, V.
Brooklyn Arts Exchange, a multi-arts non-profit organisation, presents a variety of dance concerts by emerging choreographers. There are also performances just for children.

Central Park SummerStage
For listing, see p262.
This outdoor dance series runs during the heat of summer. Temperatures can get steamy, but at least you're outside. Count on seeing traditional and contemporary dance; arrive early to secure a spot close to the stage.

Dance New Amsterdam (DNA)
280 Broadway at Chambers Street (1-212 625 8369/www.dnadance.org). Subway R, W to City Hall. **Tickets** *$10-$25.* **Credit** MC, V.
A home for downtown dance for more than 20 years, Dance Space has moved further downtown into much splashier digs and changed its name for the occasion. Now known as Dance New Amsterdam (an homage to Lower Manhattan's first moniker, circa 1600), the centre is putting a new emphasis on its role as a performance space and creative sanctuary; it's long had a rep as a great place to take classes. DNA's new 135-seat theatre will offer about 50 performances a year. **Photos** *p351.*

Dance Theater Workshop
Bessie Schönberg Theater, 219 W 19th Street, between Seventh & Eighth Avenues (1-212 924 0077/www.dtw.org). Subway: 1 to 18th Street. **Tickets** *$12-$25.* **Credit** AmEx, MC, V.

DTW, led by Cathy Edwards, hosts work by contemporary choreographers, both local and foreign. This space features a 194-seat theatre, two dance studios and an artists' media lab.

Danspace Project
St Mark's Church in-the-Bowery, 131 E 10th Street, at Second Avenue (1-212 674 8194/www.danspaceproject.org). Subway: L to Third Avenue; 6 to Astor Place. **Tickets** *$12-$20.* **No credit cards**.
This gorgeous, high-ceilinged sanctuary for downtown dance is at its most sublime when the music is live. The choreographers who take on the four-sided performance space tend towards pure movement, rather than technological experimentation.

Galapagos Art & Performance Space
For listing, see p316.
This casual Brooklyn club, which plays host to all sorts of creative types, often showcases movement-based performances, among them a burlesque evening on Mondays.

The Kitchen
512 W 19th Street, between Tenth & Eleventh Avenues (1-212 255 5793/www.thekitchen.org). Subway: A, C, E to 14th Street; L to Eighth Avenue. **Tickets** *$5-$10.* **Credit** AmEx, MC, V.
Although best known as an avant-garde theatre space, the Kitchen also offers experimental dance by inventive, often provocative artists. Choreographers Sarah Michelson and Dean Moss have worked here.

Merce Cunningham Studio
11th Floor, 55 Bethune Street, between Washington & West Streets (1-212 691 9751/www.merce.org). Subway: A, C, E to 14th Street; L to Eighth Avenue. **Tickets** *$10-$30.* **No credit cards.**
Located in the Westbeth complex on the edge of the West Village, the Cunningham Studio is rented to independent choreographers. As a result, performance quality varies, but some shows are wonderful. The stage and seating area are in a large dance studio; be prepared to take off your shoes. Arrive early, too, or you may have to sit on the floor.

Movement Research
Judson Church, 55 Washington Square South, at Thompson Street (1-212 539 2611/www.movement research.org). Subway: A, B, C, D, E, F, V to W 4th Street. **Tickets** *free.*
Construction at Judson will keep this free weekly series, devoted to experimentation and emerging artists, on the move itself. Check the website or telephone for updates.

Performance Space 122
For listing, see p351.
An appealing range of up-and-coming choreographers present unconventional new works at what was once an abandoned public school. Artists such as Ron Brown and Doug Varone started out here.

Trips Out of Town

Day Trips

Beat a speedy retreat to nearby sites.

The attractions of New York City far outshine those of its hinterland: there are no must-see destinations to combine with a NY visit. But sometimes New Yorkers need a break from the frenetic pace of the city – and so might you. Whether you prefer to hike, swim in the ocean or loose your mind on a roller coaster, you'll find plenty of options within just a few hours (or less) from the concrete jungle. Many getaway spots are accessible by public transport; save yourself the high car-rental rates (and hellish traffic in and out of town) by hopping on a bus, train or ferry.

GENERAL INFORMATION

NYC & Company, the New York visitors and convention bureau (see p386 **Websites**), has many brochures on out-of-town excursions. Look for special packages if you're planning to spend a few days away. The *New York Times*'s Sunday travel section carries advertised deals for transport and accommodation. *Time Out New York*'s annual Summer Getaways issue will also point you in the right direction.

TRANSPORT

We've included information on how to reach all listed destinations from New York City. Metro-North and the Long Island Rail Road, or LIRR (see p369), are the two main commuter-rail systems. Both offer theme tours in the summer. Call the Port Authority Bus Terminal (see p367) for information on all bus transport from the city. For a more scenic route, travel by water: NY Waterway (see p83) offers service to areas outside Manhattan. For more information on airports, buses, car rental and trains, see pp366-70.

Art attack

Dia:Beacon

Take a model example of early 20th-century industrial architecture. Combine it with some of the most ambitious and uncompromising art of the past 50 years. What do you get? One of the finest, most luxuriant aesthetic experiences on the planet. Indeed, for the 24 artists whose work is on view, and for the visiting public, Dia:Beacon – Dia Art Foundation's magnificent new outpost in the Hudson Valley – is nothing short of a blessing.

Despite its cavernous Chelsea galleries, Dia has never had adequate space to put its hugely scaled collection on permanent display. Its founders, Heiner Friedrich and his wife, Philippa de Menil, an heir to the Schlumberger oil fortune, acquired much of their holdings in the 1960s and '70s. They had a taste for the minimal, the conceptual and the monumental, and supported artists with radical ideas about what art was, what it could do and where it should happen. Together with others of their generation, the Dia circle (Robert Smithson, Michael Heizer, Walter De Maria, Donald Judd and Dan Flavin) made it difficult to consider a work of art apart from its context – be it visual, philosophical or historical – ever again. Thanks to the institution's current director Michael Govan, curator Lynne Cooke and board chairman Leonard Riggio (founder and chairman of Barnes & Noble, Inc), that context is now the biggest contemporary-art museum in the world.

An 80-minute train ride from Grand Central, Dia:Beacon sits on a 31-acre tract overlooking the Hudson River. The 300,000 square-foot complex of three brick buildings was erected in 1929 as a factory for Nabisco. No less than 34,000 square feet of north-facing skylights provide almost all of the illumination within. Nowhere does that light serve the art here better than in the immense gallery where 72 of the 102 canvases that make up Andy Warhol's rarely exhibited *Shadows* (1978-9) hang end to end like a mesmerizing series of solar flares.

What really sets the Dia:Beacon experience apart, however, is its confounding intimacy. The design of the galleries and gardens by California light-and-space artist Robert Irwin, in collaboration with the Manhattan architectural collective OpenOffice, seems close to genius. Not only does it make this enormous museum feel like a private house, it allows Cooke to draw correspondences between artworks into an elegant narrative of connoisseurship.

Dia:Beacon

Reggio Galleries, 3 Beekman Street, Beacon, NY (1-845 440 0100/www.diabeacon.org). **Open** *14 Apr-17 Oct* 11am-6pm Thur-Mon. *21 Oct-10 Apr* 11am-4pm Mon, Fri-Sun. **Admission** $10; $7 students and seniors; free under-12s. **Credit** AmEx, MC, V.
Getting there: Metro-North trains service the Beacon station, and discount rail-and-admission packages are available (www.mta.info).

Dia:Beacon: where it's hip to be square. *See p356.*

Shore thing

Sandy Hook

There's one thing you should know about Sandy Hook: there's a nude beach at its north end (it's called Gunnison Beach, and it's located at parking lot G in case you're curious). Sure, the swinger set there compels boaters with binoculars to anchor close to shore, and it's also home to a cruisy gay scene – but there's much more to this 1,665-acre natural wonderland than sunbathers in the buff. Along with seven miles of dune-backed ocean beach, the Gateway National Recreation Area is home to the nation's oldest lighthouse (the only one remaining from colonial times), as well as extensive fortifications from the days when Sandy Hook formed the outer line of defence for New York Harbor. Natural areas like the Maritime Holly Forest attract an astounding variety of birds. In fact, large stretches of beach are closed in summer to allow the endangered piping plover a quiet place to mate. The park really does offer a bit of everything – including surfers, catching waves within sight of the Manhattan skyline.

With all that the expansive Hook has to offer, it's a bit like having an island getaway at NYC's doorstep. There's even a cool way to get there:

rather than take to the roads and their hair-tearing traffic only to find at the end of the drive that the parking lots are full, hop the ferry boat from Manhattan, and turn an excursion to the beach into a scenic mini-cruise. Once you dock at Fort Hancock after the one-hour crossing, it's a short walk to most of the beaches; and if you've still got energy for more, shuttle buses will transport you to any one of the other six strands along the peninsula.

As you'd expect, typical waterside snacks like hot dogs are available at concession stands, which can be found at each of the beach areas. But for more ambitious grub, like Caesar salad with grilled tuna, head to the Seagull's Nest (1-732 872 0025), the park's one very basic restaurant; it's located at Area D, about 3 miles south of the ferry dock. Blanket picnics in the sand are permitted, so a great tip is to bring along goodies for dining alfresco. There are tables and grills for barbecues at Guardian Park at the south end of Fort Hancock.

If baking and eating in the sun all day doesn't appeal to you, there are plenty of historic sites worth exploring other than the lighthouse. The Fort Hancock Museum is located in one of the elegant century-old officer's houses that form an arc facing Sandy Hook Bay, and the abandoned forts make for an interesting day of sightseeing.

Trips Out of Town

Sandy Hook Gateway National Recreation Area

1-732 872 5970.

Getting there: Take the ferry. Board on Saturdays and Sundays (17 June through Labor Day) from the New York Waterway Dock at W 38th Street (Pier 78) at 9am and from the World Financial Center Dock at 9.20am and 11.20am. Call 1-800 533 3779 for reservations, which are suggested. The return boat leaves at 4.30pm. **Fares** $30; $16 under-12s; free under-3s. **Travel time** 55 minutes

Take a hike

Though the city's parks are great places for hanging out, if you are hankering for a *real* fresh-air escape, you need to be more than a few blocks away from Times Square. These three nearby day hikes will satisfy your desire for nature. When heading out, be sure to take bottled water and energy-inducing snacks.

Breakneck Ridge

The trek at Breakneck Ridge is a favourite of many local hikers for its accessibility, variety of trails and awe-inspiring views of the Hudson Valley. The trailhead is roughly a two-mile walk along the highway from the Cold Spring stop on Metro-North's Hudson line (on weekends the trains stops closer to the trail at the Breakneck Ridge stop). You'll find the start of the trail on the river's eastern bank, atop a tunnel that was drilled out for Route 9D; it's marked with small white paint splotches (called blazes in hiking parlance) on nearby trees. Be advised: Breakneck got its name for a reason. The initial trail ascends 500 feet in a mile and a half and gains another 500 feet by a series of dips and rises over the next few miles. The hike is not recommended if you're not in good shape. If you do choose this path, there are plenty of dramatic overlooks where you can rest, refuel with water and a snack, and stretch out on a rock. After the difficult initial climb, Breakneck Ridge offers options for all levels of hikers. Several crossings in the first few miles provide alternative routes down. Maps of all the paths, which are clearly marked with differently coloured blazes along the way, are available from the New York-New Jersey Trail Conference. Depending on your trail choices, you can spend from two hours to a full day hiking Breakneck. For trail information and to obtain a map (strongly advised!), contact the New York-New Jersey Trail Conference: 1-201 512 9348, www.nynjtc.org.

Getting there: Take the Metro-North Hudson train from Grand Central to the Cold Spring stop. You can get closer to the start of the trail by catching the line's early train to the Breakneck Ridge stop, Saturday and Sunday only 7.51am and 8.51am.

Return trains at 4.44pm and 6.55pm. **Fares** $20 round trip, off-peak. Contact the MTA for schedules. www.mta.nyc.info.

Harriman State Park

Just across the Hudson and south-west of the sprawling campus of West Point is Harriman State Park. You can access its more than 200 miles of trails and 31 lakes – many of which you can swim in – from stops on the Metro-North Port Jervis line. Of the trail options, our favourite is the Triangle Trail, an eight-mile jaunt beginning just past the parking lot at Tuxedo station – about an hour from Penn Station. Triangle leads up steadily more than 1,000 feet towards the summit of Parker Cabin Mountain before turning south to offer views of lakes Skenonto and Sebago. From there, it heads down steadily, steeply at times, and ends, after a little more than five miles total, at a path marked with red dashes on white. It's a long distance to cover, but the terrain is varied and peaceful. Also, there are intersecting short cuts you can take back to the trailhead. On a hot day, however, the best detour is a dip in one of the lakes and a nap in the sun.

Getting there: Take the Metro-North Port Jervis train, Penn Station to Tuxedo line (with a train switch in Secaucus, NJ). **Fares** $20 round trip,

Sandy Hook.

off-peak. Contact the MTA for schedules at www. mta.nyc.info. For park information and maps of all the trails in Harriman State Park, contact the New York-New Jersey Trail Conference: www.nynjtc.org, 1-201 512 9348; or Harriman State Park: 1-845 786 2701, www.nysparks.state.ny.us.

Otis Pike Wilderness

If you're looking for ocean views and a less aggressive hike, Fire Island's Otis Pike Wilderness Area is the trek for you. Though it's an hour and a half on the LIRR from Grand Central to Patchogue, followed by a half-hour ferry to the Watch Hill Visitor Center, Otis Pike's pristine beaches and wildlife are worth the journey. The stretch of preserved wilderness from Watch Hill to Smith Point is home to deer, rabbits, foxes and numerous types of seabirds, including the piping plover, which nests during the summer. Be sure you stay out of the plovers' nesting grounds, which are marked with signs, and don't feed any wildlife you see along the way.

Fire Island is completely flat, apart from a few sand dunes, though trolling the beaches and sandy paths can be slow going. After traversing the boardwalk leading from the Watch Hill Center, hike along Burma Road, a path that runs across the entire island, and in seven miles you'll arrive at the Wilderness Visitor Center at Smith Point. For a more scenic 14-mile loop, you can hike out along Burma Road and take a different route back along the shoreline – just make sure to stay on the most-travelled paths to minimise your effect on the fragile ecosystem.

Getting there: LIRR Montauk Line, Penn Station to Patchogue. **Fares** $19 round trip: call 1-718 217 5477. The Davis Park Ferry from Patchogue to Watch Hill is $14 round trip; call 1-631 475 1665 for schedules (May-Oct). For Otis Pike information, contact Fire Island National Seashore: 1-631 289 4810, www.nps.gov/fiis.

A bit of New England in New York

City Island

Out here, you've got your clam diggers and you've got your mussel suckers. Clam diggers are those folks who were born on City Island – the 1.5-by-1-mile spit of land that lies off the north-east coast of the Bronx on Long Island Sound. Mussel suckers are everybody else.

Given the modern state of medicine and transport, the number of clam diggers is dwindling. But the small-town feeling on City Island – like a tiny New England fishing village

in New York City – survives. This is despite the legions of off-islanders who cross the bridge from Pelham Bay Park each weekend to inhale fried clams at one of the restaurants lining City Island Avenue before dashing back to the city. Buffered from the rest of New York by the expanse of Pelham Bay Park, this community of 4,500 feels preserved in amber. There's even a City Island accent: a unique blend of Bronx squonk and New England bray.

The **City Island Nautical Museum** (190 Fordham Street, between Minnieford & King Avenues, 1-718 885 0008, open 1-5pm Sun only), housed in a quaint former schoolhouse, is stocked with model ships, Revolutionary War artefacts and tributes to such local heroes as Ruby Price Dill, the island's first kindergarten teacher. It also has a room devoted to the island's past as a centre of maritime activity. In its heyday, around World War II, City Island was home to no fewer than 17 shipyards. Seven America's Cup-winning yachts were built on the island (and, residents inevitably add, the Cup was lost in 1983 – the very year they stopped building the boats here).

There are still several yacht clubs in operation on these shores and a few sailmakers in the phone book, but City Islanders are more likely to head into Manhattan for work nowadays. Few commercial fishermen are left, though you'd hardly guess it walking into the **Boat Livery** (663 City Island Avenue, at Sutherland Street, 1-718 885 1843) – a bait-and-tackle shop and bar that's changed so little over the past decades that the 'updated' boat-rental prices painted next to the door still read '$2 per day'. The bar, which is dripping with fishing paraphernalia and old Christmas lights, is locally known as the Worm Hole; it serves beer in plastic cups that you can take out to the dock and drink while you watch the rented boats as they return to shore at sunset.

In summer, City Island is also worth an evening trip. With crab shanties on every corner and boats in the background, the small maritime community exudes a striking Nantucket charm. On Belden Point are **Johnny's Reef** (1-718 885 2086, 2 City Island Avenue) and **Tony's Pier Restaurant** (1-718 885 1424, 1 City Island Avenue); both have outdoor seating areas, and Johnny's Reef has telescopes too. Grab a couple of beers and a basket of fried clams, sit at one of the picnic benches and watch the boats sail by. On Wednesday evenings from mid May through mid September the island offers yacht races: the Eastchester Bay Wednesday Series.

Getting there: Take the 6 train to Pelham Bay Park and transfer to the Bx29 bus, which takes you to City Island.

Theme-park larks

Six Flags Great Adventure

If you like adrenaline-pumping rides and deep-fried junk food, with a lot of shirt-soaking water rides thrown in for good measure, have we got a theme park for you – **Six Flags Great Adventure**. Last summer, Great Adventure heralded the opening of the 'fastest and tallest roller coaster on Earth', Kingda Ka. Not for the faint of heart, this monster hurls riders 456 feet into the sky at speeds up to 128 miles per hour. (Psst! We hear that the best way to experience this thrilling ride is to eat a few burgers right before you go on and sit in the very front car.)

Whatever rides you choose, it's best to start slowly. You'll need to build courage (and stomach) for the more turbulent attractions to come. A good place to begin is on the huge Ferris wheel, which affords a bird's-eye view of all the main attractions. Swinging from a basket 150 feet in the air, you can scope out the goods on offer: 12 roller coasters lie in wait for you, not to mention the various spin and puke rides, like Spinmeister and Taz Twister. Follow up the ferris wheel with a jaunt on Skull Mountain, an in-the-dark roller coaster (think Disney World's Space Mountain, only smaller). Runaway Train is another coaster with training wheels. Or if you're feeling wimpy, just take a spin on the carousel.

Food is central to Great Adventure, so you should indulge in a corn dog and some cheese fries during a break from the rides. Post-digestion, it's time for the biggies. On the less scary side, there's Rolling Thunder, a wooden coaster that reminds New Yorkers of Coney Island's Cyclone; it's fun but bumpy. Next up, try the Great American Scream Machine, which has more loops than a Slinky. Medusa, a 61mph 'floorless' coaster (the seats are designed so that you're strapped in, but your feet dangle in the air) that plunges from a full 13 storeys in the sky is a hoot. There's also the Chiller, a terrifying-looking coaster that goes both forward and back. Or you can opt for a hot funnel cake, a sweet way to refuel after a full eight hours of adrenaline surge and burn.

Six Flags Great Adventure

Route 537, Jackson, NJ (1-732 928 1821).
Getting there: NJ Transit buses service Great Adventure daily. Buses leave Port Authority at 9.30am, returning at 8.30pm (sharp!). Call 1-800 772 2222. A round-trip ticket ($50) includes park admission.

A mood for food

Culinary Institute of America

If you're the type of person who rips the recipes out of glossy food magazines and prowls fancy kitchen-supply stores on Sunday afternoons, but you hardly ever so much as crack an egg,

Idyllic **City Island**. *See p359.*

you might need a stint at the Culinary Institute of America. Of course, no one's suggesting that you actually change your ways by enrolling in a cooking school. But if you're a food lover, a great place to spend a day is on the CIA campus in Hyde Park, where just one afternoon can fulfill all sorts of epicurean fantasies.

Sprawled over 150 hilly and beautiful acres that overlook the Hudson River, this is the country's oldest culinary college, and also a monument to the romance of the cooking life. The academy once housed a seminary, and as a result the lush campus retains a wonderful sense of calm and serenity.

Although the 2,500 full-time students here pay up to $20,000 a year for the privilege, you can get in on the action for just $5 – not much more than an issue of *Saveur*. The price buys you a tour through Roth Hall, which contains the majority of the campus's 38 kitchens and three of its four restaurants. On Mondays (10am and 4pm), Wednesdays and Thursdays (4pm), enthusiastic student guides take you past the fragrant kitchens, where aspiring chefs work on buttery sauces, vegetable sautées, roast meats and chocolate sculptures. Roth Hall was clearly designed with the voyeur in mind: windows to the instructional kitchens face the hallways, allowing you to enjoy an experience far more vivid than *Emeril Live*.

And if this isn't enough, diehard foodies can enrol in a Saturday class. You can choose from a wide range of topics listed on the CIA web site.

These six-hour classes will set you back about $165 – but just think of all the money you'll save when you start cooking at home.

When you call to sign up for a tour, it would be a good idea to book a table at one of the school's four public restaurants: St Andrews Café (serving up grilled meats and fish; vegetarian entrées), Caterina de Medici (perfect for Italian food), American Bounty (for an upscale American menu) or the Escoffier Restaurant (elegant classical French cuisine). The food alone makes a meal here almost worth the trip – with the walking tour as an added bonus. The school also has a no reservation-required place: the Apple Pie Bakery – perfect for a yummy sweet treat. If you are visiting between January and March, or September and early December, inquire about the CIA Dining Series – a selection of lectures and tastings that are sure to inspire.

The restaurants stay open for dinner, but by the time the evening rolls around, you'll be ready to board the train back home to get a head start filling out that CIA application form you picked up on your tour.

Culinary Institute of America

433 Albany Post Road, Hyde Park, NY (1-914 452 9600/www.ciachef.edu).
Getting there: Take a Metro-North train from Grand Central to Poughkeepsie ($26 round trip, off-peak). A cab ride from Poughkeepsie station to the CIA costs $7. (There's almost always a cab or two waiting at the station's taxi stand.).

Rock the Hudson

Take a ferry up the Hudson River to these opulent historic mansions

Kykuit

Neatly perched atop a hill in Westchester County, Kykuit (pictured), the Rockefeller family's stately manor, and its elaborately landscaped grounds resemble a miniature Versailles. The estate had been off-limits to the public for almost 80 years, but today a network of ferries and trains travelling from Manhattan rendezvous with buses that carry passengers to Kykuit; tours are held in conjunction with historic Philipsburg Manor in nearby Sleepy Hollow. It may be true that a Kykuit visit isn't the cheapest way to spend a day, but the chance to inspect one of the region's most remarkable interiors and get a glimpse into the lives of an incredibly influential American family really is priceless.

The ferry docks at a pier at Sleepy Hollow and the transition from ferry to bus generally goes smoothly, but some passengers may find themselves standing during the short ride to Philipsburg. Once there, visitors have about an hour in which to explore the compound, which has been restored to resemble a working 18th-century farm, complete with animals and all.

The portals to Kykuit, the Rockefeller family's primary dwelling until the 1980s, first opened to the public in 1992. The two-hour tour of the house and galleries snakes through eight of the boxy Italianate mansion's 40 rooms. Art on display includes stunning Ming vases, sculptures by Rodin and Giacometti and a dozen or so Picasso tapestries. At midpoint the tour spills into the Beaux Arts garden abutting the house; from the back terrace, verdant hills unfurl towards the Hudson like an Asher B Durand landscape. After descending into a basement-chamber-turned-art-gallery, tour groups head to the coach house – a shrine of sorts for about 30 vintage carriages and automobiles, which have been accumulated by the family over the years. Motorised vehicles on display include a Ford Model S Roadster from 1907, a 1924 Model T and Nelson Rockefeller's spectacular bulletproof black limousine.

Metro-North offers a less costly round-trip package to Sleepy Hollow and Kykuit – allowing visits to Philipsburg, Washington

Irving's old home of Sunnyside and railroad baron Jay Gould's Gothic Revival Lyndhurst castle – but the view from a train rarely compares with the ferry's stunning view of the scenery that lines the Hudson River. Once the boat glides beneath the George Washington Bridge, the apartment complexes start to disappear from the Palisades. And on the return trip, the hazy apparition on the horizon sharpens into yet another (at least partially) Rockefeller production: Manhattan's forest of skyscrapers.

Kykuit

Pocantico Hills, Tarrytown, NY 10591 (1-914 631 9491/www.hudsonvalley.org). **Open** *Late Apr-early Nov* 9am-3pm Mon, Wed-Sun. **Admission** $22; $18 seniors, children; not recommended for children under 10. **Credit** MC, V. **Getting there**: NY Waterway runs ferries including admission and buses to Philipsburg Manor and the Kykuit house and galleries tour. (May-Nov Sat, Sun, 1-800 533 3779, www.nywaterways.com). If you prefer to travel by land, you can take the train: Metro-North offers a round trip and admission package.

Other destinations

Several other magnificent historic homes (and their sprawling estates) dot the hills overlooking the Hudson River. The Historic Hudson Valley (1-914 631 8200, www. hudsonvalley.org) maintains many of these sites, which are open to the public throughout much of the year.

Lyndhurst Castle

635 South Broadway, Tarrytown, NY 10591 (1-914 631 4481/www.lyndhurst.org). **Open** *Mid Apr-Nov* 10am-4.15pm Mon holidays, Tue-Sun. *Dec-mid Apr* 10am-3.30pm Mon holidays, Sat, Sun. **Admission** $10; $9 seniors; $4 12-17s; free under-12s. *Grounds only* $4. **No credit cards**.

Several notable figures have called this Gothic Revival mansion, Lyndhurst Castle, home, including former New York City Mayor William Paulding and robber baron Jay Gould. The interior is sumptuously decorated and lovingly maintained.

Getting there: NY Waterway runs ferries including admission and bus to Lyndhurst Castle (May-Nov Sat, Sun, 1-800 533 3779,

www.nywaterways.com). Ferry departs at 10.30am at Pier 78 (at 38th Street). **Fares** $49; $25 children. If you prefer to travel by land, you can take the train: from Grand Central, the estate is a scenic 40-minute trip by Metro-North (Hudson line) to Tarrytown and a five-minute taxi ride from the train station.

Sunnyside

West Sunnyside Lane, off Route 9, Tarrytown, NY 10591 (1-914 591 8763/1-914 631 8200/www.hudsonvalley.org). **Open** *Mar* 10am-3pm Sat, Sun. *Apr-Oct* 10am-4pm Mon, Wed-Sun. *Nov, Dec* 10am-3pm Mon, Wed-Sun. **Admission** $10; $9 seniors; $6 5-17s; free under-5s. **No credit cards**.

Author Washington Irving renovated and expanded his 18th-century Dutch Colonial cottage in Tarrytown, adding a stepped-gable entrance and a Spanish-style tower.

Getting there: NY Waterway runs ferries including admission and buses to Sleepy Hollow's Sunnyside and Philipsburg Manor (May-Nov Sat, Sun, 1-800 533 3779, www.nywaterways.com). Ferry departs at 10.30am at Pier 78 (at 38th Street). **Fares** $46; $25 children. If you prefer travel by land, you can take the train: Metro-North (*see p369*).

AVOID THIS

GET THESE

TimeOut presents

Get It. Get Out.

The Other Side

An interactive CD/DVD guide to the bleeding edge of the world's great cities. Each Dual Disc features
a mix album curated by a native audio pioneer and a
DVD guide to the best bars, clubs, hotels, restaurants, art, illicit spots, shops and more.

In Record Stores October 25th

Dig Deeper: www.timeout.com/otherside

Directory

Directory

Getting to & from NYC

Airlines

Air Canada 1-800 361
5373/www.aircanada.ca.
American Airlines 1-800 433
7300/www.aa.com.
British Airways 1-800 247
9297/www.britishairways.com.
Delta Air Lines 1-800 221
1212/www.delta.com.
JetBlue Airways 1-800 538
2583/www.jetblue.com.
Northwest/KLM 1-800 374
7747/www.nwa.com.
United Airlines 1-800 241
6522/www.united.com.
US Airways 1-800 428
4322/www.usairways.com.
Virgin Atlantic 1-800 862
8621/www.virgin atlantic.com.

To & from the airport

For a list of transport services
between New York City and its
major airports, call 1-800 247
7433. Public transport is the
cheapest method, but it can
be both frustrating and
time-consuming. None of the
airports is particularly close
or convenient. Private bus or
van services are usually the
best bargains. Medallion (city-
licensed) yellow cabs, which
can be flagged on the street
or picked up at designated
locations at airports, are more
expensive but take you all the
way to your destination for a
fixed, zoned price, with any
tolls on top. (Not so in reverse.)
You may also reserve a car
service in advance to pick you
up or drop you off (see p369
Taxis & car services).
Although it is illegal, many
car-service drivers and
unlicensed 'gypsy cabs' solicit
riders around the baggage-
claim areas. Avoid them.

Bus services

New York Airport Service

1-212 875 8200/www.nyairport
service.com. Call or visit website
for schedule.
Buses operate frequently between
Manhattan and both JFK (one way
$15/round trip $27) and La Guardia
($12/$21), from early morning to late
at night, with stops near Grand
Central Terminal (Park Avenue,
between 41st and 42nd Streets), near
Penn Station (33rd Street, at Seventh
Avenue), inside the Port Authority
Bus Terminal (see p367 **By bus**) and
outside a number of midtown hotels
(for an extra charge). Buses also
operate from JFK to La Guardia
(one way $13).

Olympia Trails

1-212 964 6233/1-877 894 9155/
www.olympiabus.com. Call or visit
website for schedule.
Olympia operates between Newark
Airport and Manhattan, stopping
outside Penn Station (34th Street at
Eighth Avenue) and Grand Central
(41st between Park and Lexington),
and inside Port Authority. The fare
is $12 one way (round trip $19);
buses leave every 15 to 20 mins,
day and night.

SuperShuttle

1-212 209 7000/www.supershuttle.
com. 24hrs daily.
Blue SuperShuttle vans offer door-to-
door service between NYC and the
three major airports. Allow extra
time when catching a flight, as vans
will be picking up other passengers.
The fare varies from $13 to $22,
depending on pickup location and
destination. Always call to confirm.

Airports

Three major airports service
the New York City area, plus
the smaller MacArthur airport
on Long Island, served by
domestic flights only.

John F Kennedy International Airport

1-718 244 4444/www.panynj.gov.

At $2, the bus and subway link from
JFK is dirt cheap but it can take up
to two hours to get to Manhattan.
At the airport, look for the yellow
shuttle bus to the Howard Beach
station (free), then take the A train
to Manhattan. Thankfully JFK's
AirTrain now offers faster service
between all eight airport terminals
and the A, E, J and Z subway lines,
as well as the Long Island Rail Road,
for $5. Visit www.airtrainjfk.com for
more information. Private bus and
van services are a good compromise
between value and convenience (see
above **Bus services**). A medallion
yellow cab from JFK to Manhattan
will charge a flat $45 fare, plus toll
(varies by route, but usually $4) and
tip (if service is fine, give at least $5).
Although metered (not a flat fee), the
fare to JFK from Manhattan will be
about the same cost. Check out
www.nyc.gov/taxi for the latest cab
rates.

La Guardia Airport

1-718 533 300/www.panynj.gov.
Seasoned New Yorkers take the
M60 bus ($2), which runs between
the airport and 106th Street at
Broadway. The ride takes 40 minutes
to an hour (depending on traffic) and
runs from 4.30am to 1.30am daily.
The route crosses Manhattan at
125th Street in Harlem. Get off at
Lexington Avenue for the 4, 5 and
6 trains; at Malcolm X Boulevard
(Lenox Avenue) for the 2 and 3; or at
St Nicholas Avenue for the A, B, C
and D trains. You can also disembark
on Broadway at 116th or 110th Street
for the 1 and 9 trains. Less time-
consuming options: private bus
services cost around $14; taxis and
car services charge about $25, plus
toll and tip.

MacArthur Airport

1-631 467 3210/
www.macarthurairport.com.
Some flights into this airport in Islip,
Long Island, may be cheaper than
flights into those above. Getting to
Manhattan, of course, 50 miles
away, will take longer and be more
expensive, unless you take the LIRR.
Fares are generally $13 and a shuttle
from the airport to the train station
is $5. For car service Colonial
Transportation (1-631-589 3500) will
take up to four people to Manhattan
for $143, including tolls and tip.

Newark Liberty International Airport

1-973 961 6000/www.newark airport.com.

Although it's in next-door New Jersey, Newark has good mass transit access to NYC. The best bet is a 40-minute, $11.55 trip by the New Jersey Transit to or from Penn Station. The airport's monorail, AirTrain Newark (www.airtrain newark.com), is now linked to the NJ Transit and Amtrak train systems. For inexpensive buses, see bus services below. A car service will run about $40 and a taxi around $45, plus toll and tip.

By bus

Buses are an inexpensive means of getting to and from New York City, though the ride takes longer and is sometimes uncomfortable. Buses are particularly useful if you want to leave in a hurry; many don't require reservations. Most out-of-town buses come and go from the Port Authority Bus Terminal.

Bus stations

George Washington Bridge Bus Station

4211 Broadway, between 178th & 179th Streets (1-800 221 9903/ www.panynj.gov). Subway: A, 1 to 181st Street.
A few bus lines that serve New Jersey and Rockland County, New York, use this station.

Port Authority Bus Terminal

625 Eighth Avenue, between 40th & 42nd Streets (1-212 564 8484/www. panynj.gov). Subway: A, C, E to 42nd St-Port Authority.
This somewhat unlovely terminus is the hub for many transportation companies offering commuter and long-distance bus services to and from New York City. If you have an early departure, bring your own breakfast, as the concessions don't open until around 7am. As with any tranport terminal, watch our for petty criminals, especially late at night.

Long-distance lines

Greyhound Trailways

1-800 229 9424/www.greyhound. com. 24hrs daily. **Credit** AmEx, DC, Disc, MC, V.

Greyhound offers long-distance bus travel to destinations across North America.

New Jersey Transit

1-973 762 5100/1-800 772 2222/ www.njtransit.com. Call or visit website for schedules. **Credit** MC, V.
NJT provides bus service to nearly everywhere in the Garden State and some destinations in New York State; most buses run around the clock.

Peter Pan

1-800 343 9999/www.peterpanbus. com. 24hrs daily. **Credit** MC, V.
Peter Pan runs extensive service to cities across the Northeast; its tickets are also valid on Greyhound.

By car

If you drive to the city, you may encounter delays at bridge and tunnel crossings (check www.nyc.gov and www.panynj.gov before driving in). Tune your car radio to WINS (1010 on the AM dial) for up-to-the-minute traffic reports. Delays can run anywhere from 15 minutes to two hours – plenty of time to get your money out for the toll ($4 is average). It makes sense, of course, to time your arrival and departure against the commuter flow.

For driving in the city, *see p370.*

Parking

We recommend that if you drive to NYC, you should head for a garage, park your car, and leave it there. Parking on the street is problematic and car theft not unheard of. Garages are plentiful but expensive. If you want to park for less than $15 a day, try a garage outside Manhattan and take public transport into the city. Listed below are Manhattan's better deals. For other options, see the Yellow Pages.

Central Kinney System

www.centralparking.com. **Open** 24hrs daily, most locations. **Credit** AmEx, MC, V.
One of the city's largest parking companies, Kinney is accessible and

reliable, though not the cheapest in town. Rates vary, so call for prices.

GMC Park Plaza

1-212 888 7400. **Open** 24hrs daily, most locations. **Credit** AmEx, MC, V.
GMC has more than 70 locations in the city. At $23 overnight, including tax, the one at 407 E 61st Street, between First and York Avenues (1-212 838 4158) is the least expensive.

Icon Parking

1-877 727 5464/www.iconparking. com. **Open** 24hrs daily, most locations. **Credit** AmEx, MC, V.
Choose from more than 160 locations via the website to guarantee a spot and price ahead of time.

Mayor Parking

Pier 40, West Street, at W Houston Street (1-800 494 7007). **Open** 24hrs daily. **Rates** $16 for 12 hours. **Credit** AmEx, MC, V.
Mayor Parking, another of the city's large chains, offers indoor and outdoor parking. Call for information and other locations.

By train

America's national rail service is run by Amtrak. Nationwide routes are slow, infrequent and unreliable (if characteral), but there are some good fast services linking the eastern seaboard cities. For commuter rail services, *see p369.*

Train stations

Grand Central Terminal

From 42nd to 44th Streets, between Vanderbilt & Lexington Avenues. Subway: 42nd St S, 4, 5, 6, 7 to 42nd St-Grand Central.
Grand Central is home to Metro North, which runs trains to more than 100 stations throughout New York State and Connecticut. Schedules are available at the terminal. As well as one of New York's loveliest buildings, it's a big retail centre with some excellent eating and drinking venues, including the famous Oyster Bar.

Penn Station

31st to 33rd Streets, between Seventh & Eighth Avenues. Subway: A, C, E, 1, 2, 3 to 34th St-Penn Station.
Amtrak, Long Island Rail Road and New Jersey Transit trains depart from this terminal, which has printed schedules available.

Directory

Getting Around

Orientation

Manhattan is divided into three major sections: downtown, which includes all neighborhoods south of 14th Street; midtown, roughly the area between 14th and 59th Streets; and uptown, north of 59th Street.

Generally, avenues run north-south along the length of Manhattan. They are parallel to one another and are logically numbered, with a few exceptions, such as Broadway, Columbus and Lexington Avenues. Manhattan's centre is Fifth Avenue, so all buildings located east of it will have 'East' addresses, with numbers getting higher towards the East River, and those west of it will have 'West' numbers that get higher towards the Hudson River. Streets are also parallel to one another, but they run east to west, or crosstown, and are numbered, from 1st Street up to 220th Street.

The neighbourhoods of lower Manhattan – including the Financial District, Tribeca, Chinatown and Greenwich Village – were settled prior to urban planning and can be confusing to walk through. Their charming lack of logic makes frequent reference to a map essential.

Public transport

Changes to subway and bus schedules can occur at the last minute, so pay attention to the posters on subway station walls and any announcements you may hear in trains and on subway platforms.

Metropolitan Transportation Authority (MTA)
Travel info 1-718 330 1234/updates 1-718 243 7777/www.mta.info.

The MTA runs the subway and bus lines, as well as a number of alternative commuter services to points outside Manhattan. You can get news of service interruptions and download the most current MTA maps from the website.

City buses

MTA buses are fine… if you're not in a hurry, or just using them for sightseeing. They are white and blue and display a digital destination sign on the front, along with a route number preceded by a letter (M for Manhattan). The $2 fare is payable with a **MetroCard** (*see below*) or exact change (coins only; no pennies). MTA's express buses usually head to the outer boroughs for a $5 fare.

MetroCards allow automatic transfers from bus to bus and between buses and subways. If you pay cash, and you're travelling uptown or downtown and want to go crosstown (or vice versa), ask the driver for a transfer when you get on – you'll be given a ticket for use on the second leg of your journey, valid for two hours. Maps are posted on most buses and at all subway stations; they're also available from NYC & Company (*see p383* **Tourist information**). The Manhattan bus map is reprinted in this guide (*see p413*). All buses are equipped with wheelchair lifts. Contact the MTA for further information.

Subways

The subway is the fastest way to get around town during the day, and it's far cleaner and safer than it was 20 years ago. The city's system is one of the world's largest and cheapest – $2 will get you from the depths of Brooklyn to the furthest reaches of the Bronx and anywhere in between (though

the subway doesn't service Staten Island). Trains run around the clock, but with sparse service and fewer riders at night, it's advisable (and usually quicker) to take a cab after 10pm.

Ongoing improvements have resulted in several changes. This guide provides the most current subway map at press time (*see p416*); you can also ask MTA workers in service booths for a free copy.

To ensure safety, don't stand near the edge of the platform. Late at nights and early in the morning, board the train from the designated off-peak waiting area, usually near the middle of the platform; this area is more secure than the ends of the platforms or the outermost cars, which are often less populated at night. Standard urban advice: hold your bag with the opening facing you, keep your wallet in a front pocket and don't wear flashy jewellery. Remember that petty crime increases during the holidays.

METROCARDS
To enter the subway system, you need a MetroCard (it also works on buses), which you can buy from a booth inside the station entrance or from one of the brightly coloured MetroCard vending machines, which accept cash, debit cards and credit cards (AmEx, Disc, MC, V) and can usually give change when available. Free transfers between buses and subways are available only with a **MetroCard**.

There are two types of cards: pay-per-use and unlimited-ride. Any number of passengers can use a pay-per-use card, which is sold in denominations from $4 (two trips) to $80. A $20 card offers

12 trips for the price of 10. If you're planning to use the subway or buses often, the unlimited-ride MetroCard is great value. These cards are offered in three amounts: a one-day Fun Pass ($7, available at station vending machines but not at booths), a seven-day pass ($24) and a 30-day pass ($76). These are good for unlimited rides, but you can't share a card with your travel companions, since you can only swipe it once every 18 minutes at a given subway station or on a bus.

SUBWAY LINES
Trains are identified by letters or numbers and are colour-coded according to the line on which they run. Stations are most often named after the street on which they're located. Entrances are marked with a green globe (open 24 hours) or a red globe (limited hours). Many stations have separate entrances for the uptown and downtown platforms – look before you pay.

Local trains stop at every station on the line; express trains make major-station stops only.

Train
The following commuter services ply NY's hinterland.

Long Island Rail Road
1-718 217 5477/www.lirr.org.
LIRR provides rail service from Penn Station, Brooklyn and Queens.

Metro-North
1-212 532 4900/1-800 638 7646/www.mnr.org.
Commuter trains service towns north of Manhattan and leave from Grand Central Terminal.

New Jersey Transit
1-973 762 5100/1-800 772 2222/ www.njtransit.com.
Service from Penn Station reaches most of New Jersey, some points in New York State and Philadelphia.

PATH Trains
1 800 234 7284/www.pathrail.com.

PATH (Port Authority Trans-Hudson) trains run from six stations in Manhattan to various places across the Hudson River in New Jersey, including Hoboken, Jersey City and Newark. The system is fully automated, and entry costs $1.50. You need change or crisp bills for the ticket machines, and trains run 24 hours a day. Manhattan PATH stations are marked on the subway map (*see p416*).

Taxis & car services

Taxicabs
Yellow cabs are hardly ever in short supply – except, of course, at rush hour and in nasty weather. Use only yellow medallion (licensed) cabs; avoid unregulated gypsy cabs. If the centre light on top of the taxi is lit, that means the cab is available and should stop if you flag it down. Jump in and then tell the driver where you're going. (New Yorkers generally give cross streets rather than addresses.)

Taxis carry up to four people for the same price: $2.50 plus 40¢ per fifth of a mile, with an extra 50¢ charge from 8pm to 6am and a $1 surcharge during rush hour (weekdays from 4 to 8pm). The average fare for a three-mile ride is $9-$11, depending on the time of day and on traffic (the meter adds another 20¢ per minute while the car is idling). Cabbies rarely allow more than four passengers in a cab (it's illegal, unless the fifth person is a child under seven), though it may be worth asking.

Not all drivers know their way around the city, so it helps if you know where you're going – and speak up. By law, taxis cannot refuse to take you anywhere inside the five boroughs or to New York airports, so don't be duped by a reluctant cabbie. They may still refuse; to avoid an argument, get out and try another cab. If you have a

problem, take down the medallion and driver's numbers, posted on the partition. Always ask for a receipt – there's a meter number on it. To complain or to trace lost property, call the Taxi & Limousine Commission (1-212 227 0700, 8am-4pm Mon-Fri) or visit www.nyc.gov/taxi. Tip 15-20%, as you would at a restaurant.

Late at night, cabs stick to fast-flowing routes. Try the avenues and key streets (Canal, Houston, 14th, 23rd, 34th, 42nd, 57th, 72nd and 86th). Bridge and tunnel exits are good for a steady flow of taxis returning from airports, and cabbies will usually head for nightclubs and big hotels. Otherwise, try the following:

Chinatown
Chatham Square, where Mott Street meets the Bowery, is an unofficial taxi stand. You can also try hailing a cab exiting the Manhattan Bridge at Bowery and Canal Street.

Lincoln Center
The crowd heads towards Columbus Circle for a cab; those in the know go west to Amsterdam Avenue.

Lower East Side
Katz's Deli (Houston Street at Ludlow Street) is a cabbies' hangout; also try Delancey Street, where cabs come in over the Williamsburg Bridge.

Midtown
Penn Station, Grand Central Terminal and the Port Authority Bus Terminal attract cabs all night.

Soho
If you're on the west side, try Sixth Avenue; east side, the intersection of Houston Street and Broadway.

Times Square
This busy area has 30 taxi stands – look for the yellow globes on poles.

Tribeca
Cabs head up Hudson Street. The Tribeca Grand (2 Sixth Avenue, between Walker and White Streets) is another good bet.

Car services
Car services are also regulated by the Taxi & Limousine

Directory

Commission (*see p368*). Unlike cabs, they aren't yellow and drivers can make only pre-arranged pickups. If you see a black Lincoln Town Car, it most likely belongs to a car service. Don't try to hail one, and be wary of those that offer you a ride; they may not be licensed or insured, and you could get ripped off.

The following companies will pick you up anywhere in the city, at any time of day or night, for a set fare.

Carmel
1-212 666 6666.

Dial 7
1-212 777 7777.

Tri-State Limousine
1-212 777 7171/1-212 410 7600.

Driving

Manhattan drivers (especially cabbies) are fearless; so taking to the streets is not for the faint of heart. It's best to try to restrict your driving to evening hours, when traffic is lighter and there's more street parking available. Even then, keep your eyes on the road and stay alert.

Car rental

Car rental is much cheaper in the city's outskirts and in New Jersey and Connecticut than in Manhattan; reserve ahead for weekends. Another way to save money is to rent from an independent agency, such as **Aamcar**. Log on to www.carrentalexpress.com for more independent companies.

Companies located outside New York State do not include LDW (loss/damage waiver) insurance in their rate, which means you will need to pay for any damage to the car unless you are covered under another policy or by your credit card. Rental companies in New York State are required by law to insure their own cars, though

the renter pays for the first $100 in damage to the rental vehicle. Personal liability insurance is advised wherever you rent (unless your travel insurance or home policy covers it). UK residents may find rental car insurance more cheaply on www.insurance4carhire.com.

You will need a credit card (or a large cash deposit) to rent a car, and you usually have to be at least 25 years old. All car-rental companies listed below add sales tax (8.625 per cent). If you know you want to rent a car before you travel, ask your travel agent or airline to check for special deals and discounts, or look online.

Aamcar
315 W 96th Street, between West End Avenue & Riverside Drive (1-800 722 6923/1-212 222 8500/ www.aamcar.com). Subway: 1, 2, 3, 9 to 96th Street. **Open** 7.30am-7.30pm Mon-Fri; 9am-midnight Sat; 9am-5pm Sun. **Credit** AmEx, DC, Disc, MC, V.
Compact rates from $49.95 per day, unlimited mileage; $39.95 with 100 free miles.

Alamo *US: 1-800 462 5266/www. alamo.com. UK: 0870 400 562/ www.alamo.co.uk.*
Avis *US: 1-800 230 4898/www.avis. com. UK: 0870 606 0100/www. avis.co.uk.*
Budget *US: 1-800 527 0700/ www.budget.com. UK: 0870 153 170/ www.budget.co.uk.*
Dollar *US: 1-800 800 3665/ www.dollar.com. UK: 0800 085 578/ www.dollar.co.uk.*
Enterprise *US: 1-800 261 7331/ www.enterprise.com. UK: 0870 350 3000/www.enterprise.com/uk.*
Hertz *US: 1-800 654 3131/ www.hertz.com. UK: 0870 844 8844/ www.hertz.co.uk.*
National *US: 1-800 227 7368. UK: 0116 217 3884. Both: www.nationalcar.com.*
Thrifty *US: 1-800 847 4389/www. thrifty.com. UK: 01494 51600/www.thrifty.co.uk.*

Street parking

Make sure you read parking and meter signs and never park within 15 feet (five metres) of a fire hydrant (to avoid a $115 ticket and/or

having your car towed). Parking is off-limits on most streets for at least a few hours every day. The Department of Transportation (dial 311) provides information on daily changes to parking regulations. If precautions fail, call 1-718 935 0096 for towing and impoundment information.

Emergency towing

Citywide Towing
514 W 39th Street, between Tenth & Eleventh Avenues (1-212 244 4420). **Open** 24hrs daily; repairs 9am-5pm daily. **Credit** MC, V.
All types of repairs are carried out on domestic and foreign vehicles.

24-hour gas stations

Exxon
24 Second Avenue, at 1st St (1-212 979 7000). **Credit** AmEx, MC, V. Repairs.

Hess
502 W 45th Street, at Tenth Ave (1-212 245 6594). **Credit** AmEx, DC, Disc, MC, V. No repairs.

Cycling

Aside from the immensely pleasurable bicycling in Central Park, and along the wide bike paths around the perimeter of Manhattan – which is now virtually circumnavigated by paths – biking in the busy city streets is no picnic and is not recommended for urban beginners. Still, zipping through bumper-to-bumper traffic holds a certain allure – especially for those with good cycling skills, a helmet and a motorists-be-damned attitude. For bike rentals and citywide bike paths, *see p337*.

Walking

One of the best ways to take in NYC is on foot. Most of the streets are laid out in a grid pattern and are relatively easy to navigate. Our full set of street maps (*pp402-412*) makes it even easier.

Resources A-Z

Age restrictions

In NYC, you must be 18 to buy tobacco products and 21 to buy or to be served alcohol. Some bars and clubs admit patrons between 18 and 21, but you'll be ejected if you're caught drinking alcohol. Always carry picture ID as even those well over 21 can be asked to show proof of age and identity.

Business

Consumer information

Better Business Bureau

1-212 533 6200/ www.newyork.bbb.org.
The BBB offers advice on consumer-related complaints (shopping, services, etc). Each phone enquiry costs $5 (plus New York City tax) and must be charged to a credit card; the online service is free.

New York City Department of Consumer Affairs

42 Broadway, between Beaver Street & Exchange Place (311 local, 1-212 639 9675 out of state/www.nyc.gov/consumer. Subway: 4, 5 to Bowling Green.
Open 9am-5pm Mon-Fri.
File complaints on consumer-related matters here.

New York City 311 Call Center

311.
This non-emergency three-digit number was established in 2004 as a means for residents to get answers and register complaints about city issues ranging from parking regulations and small claims court to real estate auctions and consumer tips.

International couriers

DHL Worldwide Express

Call to find the office nearest you or to arrange a pickup at your door (1-800 225 5345/www.dhl.com). **Credit** AmEx, DC, Disc, MC, V.
DHL will send a courier to pick up packages at any NYC address, or you can deliver packages in person to one of its offices or drop-off points. Cash is not accepted.

FedEx

Call to find the office nearest you or to arrange a pickup at your door (1-800 247 4747/www.fedex.com). **Credit** AmEx, DC, Disc, MC, V.
Packages headed overseas should be dropped off by 6pm for International Priority delivery (depending on destination), and by 9pm for packages to most destinations in the US (some locations have a later cut-off time; call to check).

UPS

Various locations throughout the city; free pickup at your door (1-800 742 5877/www.ups.com). Hours vary by office; call for locations and times. **Credit** AmEx, MC, V.
Like DHL and FedEx, UPS will send a courier to pick up parcels at any address in the five boroughs. The city's 30 retail locations (formerly Mail Boxes Etc) also offer mailbox rental, mail forwarding, packaging, phone-message service, copying and faxing. UPS provides domestic and international service.

Messenger services

A to Z Couriers

106 Ridge Street, between Rivington & Stanton Streets (1-212 253 6500/www.atozcouriers.com). Subway: F to Delancey Street; J, M, Z to Delancey-Essex Streets. **Open** 8am-8pm Mon-Fri. **Credit** AmEx, MC, V.
These cheerful couriers will deliver in the city (also national and international).

Breakaway

335 W 35th Street, between Eighth & Ninth Avenues (1-212 947 4455/www.breakawaycourier.com). Subway: A, C, E to 34th Street-Penn Station. **Open** 7am-9pm Mon-Fri; 9am-5pm Sat; noon-5pm Sun. **Credit** AmEx, MC, V.
Breakaway is a recommended local delivery service that promises to pick up and deliver within 90 minutes.

Jefron

55 Walker Street, between Church Street & West Broadway (1-212 431 6610/www.jefron.com). Subway: 1, 2, 3 to Chambers Street. **Open** 4am-8pm Mon-Fri. **No credit cards.**
Jefron specialises in transporting import and export documents.

Photocopying & printing

Dependable Printing

44 E 21st Street, at Park Avenue South (1-212 533 7560). Subway: N, R, W to 23rd Street. **Open** 8.30am-7pm Mon-Fri; 10am-4pm Sat. **Credit** AmEx, MC, V.
Dependable provides offset, laser and colour printing; fax; large-format photocopies; binding and more.
Other locations: 71 W 23rd Street, between Fifth & Sixth Avenues (1-646 336 6999).

Servco

1150 Sixth Avenue, between 44th & 45th Streets (1-212 575 0991).

Travel advice

For current information on travel to a specific country— including the latest news on health issues, safety and security, local laws and customs – contact your home country's government department of foreign affairs. Most have websites with useful advice for would-be travelers.

Australia
www.dfat.gov.au/travel

Ireland
www.irlgov.ie/iveagh

United Kingdom
www.fco.gov.uk/travel

Canada
www.voyage.gc.ca

New Zealand
www.mft.govt.nz/travel

USA
www.state.gov/travel

Subway: B, D, F, V to 47th-50th Streets-Rockefeller Center; 7 to Fifth Avenue. **Open** 8.30am-8pm Mon-Fri. **No credit cards.**
Photocopying, offset printing, blueprints and binding services are available.

Translation & language services

All Language Services

77 W 55th Street, between Fifth & Sixth Avenues (1-212 986 1688/fax 1-212 265 1662). Subway: 42nd Street S, 4, 5, 6, 7 to 42nd Street-Grand Central. **Open** 24hrs daily. **Credit** AmEx, MC, V.
ALS will type or translate documents in any of 59 languages and provide interpreters.

Consulates

Check the phone book for a complete list of consulates and embassies. *See also p371.* **Travel advice.**

Australia
1-212 351 6500.

Canada
1-212 596 1628.

Great Britain
1-212 745 0200.

Ireland
1-212 319 2555.

New Zealand
1-212 832 4038.

Customs

US Customs allows foreigners to bring in $100 worth of gifts (the limit is $800 for returning Americans) without paying duty. One carton of 200 cigarettes (or 50 cigars) and one litre of liquor (spirits) are allowed. Plants, meat and fresh produce of any kind cannot be brought into the country – not even a sandwich. You will have to fill out a form if you carry more than $10,000 in currency. You will be handed a white form on your inbound flight to fill in, confirming you have not exceeded any of these allowances.

If it is essential for you to bring prescription drugs into the US, make sure the container is clearly marked, and bring your doctor's statement or a prescription. Marijuana, cocaine and most opiate derivatives, along with a number of other drugs and chemicals, are not permitted: possession of them is punishable by a stiff fine and/or imprisonment. Check with the **US Customs Service** (www.customs.gov) before you arrive if you have any questions about what you can bring.

New York might be one of the world's great shopping destinations, but bear in mind that UK customs still allows returning visitors to bring only £145 worth of 'gifts, souvenirs and other goods' into the country duty-free, along with the usual duty-free goods.

Disabled access

Under New York City law, all facilities constructed after 1987 must provide complete access for the disabled – restrooms, entrances and exits included. In 1990, the Americans with Disabilities Act made the same requirement federal law. In the wake of this legislation, many older buildings have added disabled-access features. There has been widespread (though imperfect) compliance with the law, but it's always a good idea to call ahead and check.

New York can be challenging for a disabled visitor. One useful resource is *Access for All*, a guide to New York's cultural institutions published by Hospital Audiences Inc (1-212 575 7660, www.hospaud.org). The online guide tells how accessible each location really is and includes information on the height of telephones and water fountains; hearing and visual aids; and passenger-loading zones and alternative

entrances. HAI's service for the visually impaired provides recordings of commentaries of theatre performances.

All Broadway theatres are equipped with devices for the hearing-impaired; call **Sound Associates** (1-212 582 7678, 1-888 772 7686) for more information. There are a number of other stage-related resources for the disabled. **Telecharge** (1-212 239 6200) reserves tickets for wheelchair seating in Broadway and Off Broadway venues while Theatre Development Fund's **Theater Access Project** (1-212 221 1103, www.tdf.org) arranges sign-language interpretation and captioning in American Sign Language for Broadway and Off Broadway shows. **Hands On** (1-212 740 3087, www.hands on.org) does the same.

Lighthouse International

111 E 59th Street, between Park & Lexington Avenues (1-212 821 9200/www.lighthouse.org). Subway: N, R, W to Lexington Avenue-59th Street; 4, 5, 6 to 59th Street. **Open** 10am-6pm Mon-Fri; 10am-5pm Sat.
In addition to running a store that sells handy items for the vision-impaired, this organisation provides helpful information for blind residents of and visitors to New York City.

Mayor's Office for People with Disabilities

2nd Floor, 100 Gold Street, between Frankfort & Spruce Streets, second floor (1-212 788 2830). Subway: J, M, Z to Chambers Street; 4, 5, 6 to Brooklyn Bridge-City Hall. **Open** 9am-5pm Mon-Fri.
This city office provides a broad range of services for the disabled.

New York Society for the Deaf

315 Hudson Street, between Vandam & Spring Streets (1-212 366 0066/ www.nysd.org). Subway: C, E, to Spring Street; 1 to Houston Street. **Open** 9am-5pm Mon-Thur; 9am-4.30pm Fri.
The deaf and hearing-impaired come here for information and services.

Society for Accessible Travel & Hospitality

Suite 610, 347 Fifth Avenue, between 33rd & 34th Streets (1-212 447 7284/www.sath.org). Subway: B, D, F, N, Q, R, V, W to 34th Street-Herald Square.

This non-profit group was founded in 1976 to educate the public about travel facilities for people with disabilities and to promote travel for the disabled worldwide. Membership is $45 a year ($30 for seniors and students) and includes access to an information service and a quarterly travel magazine. No drop-ins; membership by mail only.

Electricity

The US uses 110-120V, 60-cycle alternating current rather than the 220-240V, 50-cycle AC used in Europe and elsewhere. The transformers that power or recharge many newer electronic devices such as laptop computers are designed to handle either current and may need nothing more than an adaptor for the wall outlet. However, most electrical appliances, including hairdryers, will require a power converter as well. Adaptors and converters of various sorts can be purchased at airport shops, at several pharmacies and department stores, and at Radio Shack branches around the city (consult the phone book for store locations), and they can sometimes be borrowed at better hotels.

Emergencies

Ambulance

In an emergency only, dial **911** for an ambulance or call the operator (dial 0). To complain about slow emergency service or poor treatment, call the Fire Department Complaint Hotline (1-718 999 2646).

Fire

In an emergency only, dial **911**.

Police

In an emergency only, dial **911**. For the location of the nearest police precinct or general information about police services, call 1-646 610 5000.

Gay & lesbian

For gay/lesbian resources, *see pp301-311* **Gay & Lesbian**.

Health & medical facilities

The public health-care system is virtually non-existent in the United States, and private health care is prohibitively expensive. If possible, make sure you have comprehensive medical insurance when you travel to New York.

Clinics

Walk-in clinics offer treatment for minor ailments. Most require immediate payment, though some will send their bill directly to your insurance company if you're a US resident. You will have to file a claim to recover the cost of prescription medication.

D•O•C•S

55 E 34th Street, between Madison & Park Avenues (1-212 252 6000). Subway: 6 to 33rd Street. **Open** *Walk-in* 8am-8pm Mon-Thur; 8am-7pm Fri; 9am-3pm Sat; 9am-2pm Sun. *Extended hours* by appointment. **Base fee** $80 and up. **Credit** AmEx, Disc, MC, V.

These excellent primary-care facilities, affiliated with Beth Israel Medical Center, offer by-appointment and walk-in services. If you need X-rays or lab tests, go as early as possible – no later than 6pm – Monday through Friday.

Other locations: 202 W 23rd Street, at Seventh Avenue (1-212 352 2600).

Dentists

NYU College of Dentistry

345 E 24th Street, between First & Second Avenues (1-212 998 9872/after-hours emergency care 1-212 998 9828). Subway: 6 to 23rd Street. **Open** 8.30am-7pm Mon-Thur; 8.30am-3pm Fri. **Base fee** $90. **Credit** Disc, MC, V.

If you need your teeth fixed on a budget, the final-year students here are slow but proficient, and an experienced dentist is always on hand to supervise. Go before 2pm to ensure a same-day visit.

Emergency rooms

You will be billed for emergency treatment. Call your travel-insurance company's emergency number before seeking treatment to find out which hospitals accept your insurance. Emergency rooms are always open at:

Cabrini Medical Center

227 E 19th Street, between Second & Third Avenues (1-212 995 6000). Subway: L to Third Avenue; N, Q, R, W, 4, 5, 6 to 14th Street-Union Square.

Mount Sinai Hospital

Madison Avenue, at 100th Street (1-212 241 7171). Subway: 6 to 103rd Street.

New York – Presbyterian Hospital/Weill Cornell Medical Center

525 E 68th Street, at York Avenue (1-212 746 5454). Subway: 6 to 68th Street.

St Luke's – Roosevelt Hospital

1000 Tenth Avenue, at 59th Street (1-212 523 6800). Subway: A, B, C, D, 1 to 59th Street-Columbus Circle.

St Vincent's Hospital

153 W 11th Street, at Seventh Avenue (1-212 604 7998). Subway: F, V, 1, 2, 3 to 14th Street; L to Sixth Avenue.

Gay & lesbian health

See p302 **Centers & helplines**.

House calls

NYHotel Urgent Medical Services

Suite 1D, 952 Fifth Avenue, between 76th & 77th Streets (1-212 737 1212/www.travelmd.com). Subway: 6 to 77th Street. **Open** 24hrs daily; appointments required. **Fees** Weekday hotel-visit fee $165 and up; weekday office-visit fee $55-$165 (higher for nights and weekends). **Credit** AmEx, MC, V.

Dr Ronald Primas and his partners provide specialist medical attention right in your Manhattan hotel room or private residence, from a simple prescription to urgent medical care.

Directory

Pharmacies

Be aware that pharmacies will not refill foreign prescriptions and may not sell the same over-the-counter products.

Duane Reade

224 W 57th Street, at Broadway (1-212 541 9708/www.duane reade.com). Subway: N, Q, R, W to 57th Street. **Open** 24hrs daily. **Credit** AmEx, MC, V.
This chain operates all over the city, and some stores are open 24 hours. Check the website for additional branches.
Other 24-hour locations: 24 E 14th Street, at University Place (1-212 989 3632); 155 E 34th Street, at Third Avenue (1-212 683 3042); 1279 Third Avenue, at 74th Street (1-212 744 2668); 2465 Broadway, at 91st Street (1-212 799 3172).

Rite Aid

303 W 50th Street, at Eighth Avenue (1-212 247 8736/www.riteaid.com). Subway: C, E to 50th Street. **Open** 24hrs daily. **Credit** AmEx, Disc, MC, V.
Selected Rite Aid stores have 24-hour pharmacies. Call 1-800 748 3243 or check the website for a listing of all branches.
Other 24-hour locations: 408 Grand Street, at Clinton Street (1-212 529 7115); 301 W 50th Street, at Eighth Avenue (1-212 247 8384); 146 E 86th Street, between Lexington & Third Avenues (1-212 876 0600); 2833 Broadway, at 110th Street (1-212 663 3135).

STDs, HIV & AIDS

Chelsea Clinic

303 Ninth Avenue, at 28th Street (1-212 239 1718/1-212 239 0843). Subway: C, E to 23rd Street. **Open** 8.30am-4.30pm Mon-Fri; 9am-2pm Sat.
Hours of walk-in clinics may change, so call ahead before visiting. Arrive early, because testing is offered on a first-come, first-served basis. (Check the phone book or see www.nyc.gov for other free clinics.)

Women's health

Liberty Women's Health Care of Queens

37-01 Main Street, at 37th Avenue, Flushing, Queens (1-718 888 0018/ www.libertywomenshealth.com). Subway: 7 to Flushing-Main Street. **Open** By appointment only. **Credit** MC, V.

Size charts

Women's clothing

UK	Europe	US
4	32	2
6	34	4
8	36	6
10	38	8
12	40	10
14	42	12
16	44	14

Women's shoes

UK	Europe	US
3	36	5
4	37	6
5	38	7
6	39	8
7	40	9
8	41	10
9	42	11

Men's suits

UK	Europe	US
34	44	34
36	46	36
38	48	38
40	50	40
42	52	42
44	54	44
46	56	46

Men's shoes

UK	Europe	US
6	39	7
71/2	40	71/2
8	41	8
8	42	81/2
9	43	91/2
10	44	101/2
11	45	11

This facility provides surgical and non-surgical abortions until the 24th week of pregnancy. Unlike many other clinics, Liberty uses abdominal ultrasound before, during and after the abortion to ensure safety.

Parkmed Eastern Women's Center

5th Floor, 44 E 30th Street, between Madison Avenue & Park Avenue South (1-212 686 6066/www.eastern womenscenter.com). Subway: 6 to 28th Street. **Open** By appointment only. **Credit** AmEx, Disc, MC, V.
Urine pregnancy tests are free. Counselling, contraception services and non-surgical abortions are also available.

Planned Parenthood of New York City

Margaret Sanger Center, 26 Bleecker Street, at Mott Street (1-212 965 7000/1-800 230 7526/www.ppnyc.org). Subway: B, D, F, V to Broadway-Lafayette Street; N, R, W to Prince Street; 6 to Bleecker Street. **Open** 8am-4.30pm Mon, Tue; 8am-6.30pm Wed-Fri; 7.30am-4.30pm Sat. **Credit** AmEx, MC, V.
This is the best-known, most reasonably priced network of family-planning clinics in the US. Counselling and treatment are available for a full range of needs, including abortion, contraception, HIV testing and treatment of STDs. Call for more information on other services or to make an appointment at any of the centres.

Walk-in clients are welcome for emergency contraception and free pregnancy tests.
Other location: 44 Court Street, between Joralemon & Remsen Streets, Brooklyn Heights, Brooklyn (appointments 1 212 965 7000).

Helplines

Alcohol & drug abuse

Alcoholics Anonymous

1-212 647 1680. **Open** 9am-10pm daily.

Cocaine Anonymous

24-hour recorded information 1-212 262 2463.

Drug Abuse Information Line

1-800 522 5353. **Open** 8am-10pm daily.
This hotline refers callers to recovery programmes around the state as well as to similar programmes in the rest of the US.

Pills Anonymous

24-hour recorded information 1-212 874 0700.
This helpline offers recorded information on drug-recovery programmes for users of marijuana, cocaine, alcohol and other addictive substances, as well as referrals to Narcotics Anonymous meetings. You

can also leave a message so that a counsellor can call you back.

Child abuse

Childhelp USA's National Child Abuse Hotline

1-800 422 4453. **Open** 24hrs daily. Counsellors provide general crisis consultation and can help in an emergency. Callers include abused children, runaways and parents having problems with children.

Gay & lesbian

See p302 **Centers & helplines**.

Health

Visit the Centers for Disease Control and Prevention (CDC) website (www.cdc.gov) for up-to-date national health information, or call one of the toll-free hotlines below.

National STD & AIDS Hotline

1-800 342 2437. **Open** 24hrs daily.

Travelers' Health

1-877 394 8747 or visit CDC website. **Open** 24hrs daily. Provides alerts on disease outbreaks and other information via a recording.

Psychological services

Samaritans

1-212 673 3000. **Open** 24hrs daily. People who may be thinking of committing suicide or suffering from depression, grief, sexual anxiety or alcoholism can call this volunteer organisation for advice and a listening ear.

Rape & sex crimes

Safe Horizon Crisis Hotline

1-212 577 7777/www.safe horizon.org. **Open** 24hrs daily. SH offers telephone and in-person counselling for any victim of domestic violence, rape or other crime, as well as practical help with court procedures, compensation and legal aid.

Special Victims Liaison Unit of the New York Police Department

Rape hotline 1-212 267 7273. **Open** 24hrs daily. Reports of sex crimes are fielded by a female detective from the Special Victims Liaison Unit. She will inform the appropriate precinct, send an ambulance if requested, and provide counselling and medical referrals. Other issues handled: violence against gays and lesbians, child victimisation, and referrals for the families and friends of crime victims.

St Luke's – Roosevelt Hospital Crime Victims Treatment Center

1-212 523 4728. **Open** 9am-5pm Mon-Fri. The Rape Crisis Center provides a trained volunteer who will accompany you through all aspects of reporting a rape and getting emergency treatment.

Holidays

See p383 **Holidays**.

Insurance

If you are not an American, it's advisable to take out comprehensive insurance before arriving here; insurance for foreigners is almost impossible to arrange in the US. Make sure you have adequate health coverage; medical costs are high. For a list of New York urgent-care facilities, *see p373* **Emergency rooms**.

Internet

Internet access

Cyber Café

250 W 49th Street, between Broadway & Eighth Avenue (1-212 333 4109). Subway: C, E, 1, 9 to 50th Street; N, R, W to 49th Street. **Open** 8am-11pm Mon-Fri; 11am-11pm Sat, Sun. **Cost** $6.40 per half hour; 50¢ per printed page. **Credit** AmEx, MC, V. This is a standard internet-access café that also happens to serve great coffee and snacks.

FedEx Kinko's

1-800 463 3339/www.kinkos.com.

Outposts of this ubiquitous and very efficient computer and copy centre can be found throughout the city.

New York Public Library

www.nypl.org The branch libraries throughout the five boroughs are great places to email and surf the web for free. However, the scarcity of computer stations may make for a long wait, and user time is limited. The Science, Industry and Business Library, 188 Madison Avenue, at 34th Street, has more than 40 workstations that you can use for up to an hour per day.

Wi-Fi

NYCWireless

www.nycwireless.net. This group has established 113 nodes in the city for free wireless access. (For example, most parks below 59th Street are covered.) Visit the website for more information.

Starbucks

www.starbucks.com. **Credit** AmEx, MC, V. Many branches offer wireless access through T-Mobile (10¢ per minute).

Legal assistance

If you're arrested for a minor violation (disorderly conduct, harassment, loitering, rowdy partying, etc) and you are very polite to the officer during the arrest (and carry proper ID), then you'll probably get fingerprinted and photographed at the station and be given a desk-appearance ticket with a date to show up at criminal court. Then, you'll most likely get to go home.

Arguing with a police officer or engaging in more serious criminal activity (possession of a weapon, drunken driving, illegal gambling or prostitution, for example) might get you 'processed', which means a 24- to 30-hour journey through the system. If the courts are backed up (and they usually are), you'll be held temporarily at a precinct pen. You can make a phone call after you've been

Directory

fingerprinted. When you get through central booking, you'll arrive at 100 Centre Street for arraignment. A judge will decide whether you should be released on bail and will set a court date. If you can't post bail, then you'll be held at Rikers Island. The bottom line: try not to get arrested, and if you are, don't act foolishly.

Legal Aid Society
1-212 577 3300/www.legal-aid.org. **Open** 9am-5pm Mon-Fri.
Legal Aid gives general information and referrals on legal matters.

Sandback, Birnbaum & Michelen Criminal Law
1-800 640 2000. **Open** 24hrs daily.
You might want to carry these numbers with you, in case you find the cops reading you your rights in the middle of the night. If no one at this firm can help you, then you'll be directed to lawyers who can.

Libraries

See p375 **New York Public Library**.

Locksmiths

The emergency locksmiths listed below are open 24 hours. Both require ID and proof of car ownership or residency (driving licence, car registration, utility bill).

Champion Locksmiths
30 locations in Manhattan (1-212 362 7000). **Cost** $15 service charge; $39 minimum to replace the lock they have to break. **Credit** AmEx, Disc, MC, V.

Elite Locksmiths
470 Third Avenue, between 32nd & 33rd Streets (1-212 685 1472). Subway: 6 to 33rd Street. **Cost** $55 during the day; $85 at night. **No credit cards**.

Lost property

For property lost in the street, contact the police. For lost credit cards or travellers' cheques, *see pp378-9*.

Buses & subways
New York City Metropolitan Transit Authority, 34th Street-Penn Station, *near the A-train platform (1-212 712 4500).* **Open** 8am-noon Mon-Wed, Fri; 11am-6.30pm Thur.
Call if you've left something on a subway train or a bus.

Grand Central Terminal
1-212 340 2555. **Open** 7am-6pm Mon-Fri; 8.45am-5pm Sat.
Call if you've left something on a Metro-North train.

JFK Airport
1-718 244 4444, or contact your airline.

La Guardia Airport
1-718 533 3400, or contact your airline.

Newark Liberty International Airport
1-973 961 6230, or contact your airline.

Penn Station
1-212 630 7389. **Open** 7.30am-4pm Mon-Fri.
Call for items left on Amtrak, New Jersey Transit or the Long Island Rail Road.

Taxis
1-212 692 8294/www.nyc.gov/taxi. Call for items left in a cab.

Media

Daily newspapers

Daily News
The *News* has drifted politically from the Neanderthal right to a more moderate but tough-minded stance under the ownership of real-estate mogul Mort Zuckerman.

New York Post
Founded in 1801 by Alexander Hamilton, the *Post* is the nation's oldest continuously published daily newspaper. It has swerved sharply to the right under current owner Rupert Murdoch. The *Post* includes more gossip than any other local paper, and its headlines are often sassy and sensational.

The New York Times
As Olympian as ever after more than 150 years, the *Times* remains the city's, and the nation's, paper of record. It has the broadest and deepest coverage of world and national events and, as the masthead proclaims, it delivers 'All the News That's Fit to Print'. The mammoth *Sunday Times* can weigh a full 5lb and typically contains hundreds of pages, including a well-regarded magazine

as well as book-review, travel, real-estate and other sections.

Other dailies
The *Amsterdam News*, one of the nation's oldest black newspapers, offers a trenchant African-American viewpoint. New York also supports three Spanish-language dailies: *El Diario, Hoy* and *Noticias del Mundo*. *Newsday* is a Long Island-based daily with a tabloid format but a sober tone (it also has a city edition). *USA Today* keeps weary travellers abreast of national news. You may even find your own local paper at a Universal News shop (check the phone book for locations).

Weekly newspapers

Downtown journalism is a battlefield, pitting the *New York Press* against the *Village Voice*. The *Press* consists largely of opinion columns; it's full of youthful energy and irreverence as well as cynicism and self-absorption. The *Voice* is sometimes passionate and ironic but just as often strident and predictable. Both papers are free. In contrast, the *New York Observer* focuses on the doings of the upper echelons of business, finance, media and politics. *Our Town, Chelsea Clinton News*, the *West Sider* and *Manhattan Spirit* are on the sidelines; these free sister publications feature neighbourhood news and local political gossip, and they can be found in street-corner dispensers around town. In a class all its own is the hilarious, satirical national weekly the *Onion*.

Magazines

New York
This magazine is part newsweekly, part lifestyle reporting and part listings.

The New Yorker
Since the 1920s, the *New Yorker* has been known for its fine wit, elegant prose and sophisticated cartoons. Today, it's a forum for serious long-form journalism. It usually makes for a lively, intelligent read, in both paper form and on the well-made website.

Time Out New York

Of course, the best place to discover what's going on in town is *Time Out New York*. Based on the tried-and-trusted format of its London parent, TONY is an indispensable guide to the life of the city (if we do say so ourselves). Its hot 100 restaurants are an essential read.

Other magazines

Since its launch in 1996, the bimonthly *Black Book Magazine* has covered New York high fashion and culture with intelligent bravado. *Gotham*, a monthly from the publisher of the glossy gab-rags *Hamptons* and *Aspen Peak*, unveiled its larger-than-life celeb-filled pages in 2001. And for two decades now, *Paper* has reported monthly on the city's trend-conscious, offering plenty of insider buzz on bars, clubs, downtown boutiques – and the people you'll find in them.

Radio

Nearly 100 stations serve the New York area. On the AM dial, you can find talk radio and phone-in shows that attract everyone from priests to sports nuts. Flip to FM for free jazz, the latest Franz Ferdinand single or any other auditory craving. Radio highlights are printed weekly in *Time Out New York*, and daily in the *Daily News*.

College radio

College radio is innovative and free of commercials. However, smaller transmitters mean that reception is often compromised by Manhattan's high-rise topography.

WNYU-FM 89.1 and **WKCR-FM 89.9** are, respectively, the stations of New York University and Columbia; programming spans the musical spectrum. **WFUV-FM 90.7**, Fordham University's station, plays mostly folk and Irish music but also airs a variety of shows, including *Beale Street Caravan*, the most widely distributed blues programme in the world.

Dance & pop

American commercial radio is rigidly formatted, which makes most pop stations extremely tedious and repetitive during the day. Tune in on evenings and weekends for more interesting programming. **WQHT-FM 97.1**, 'Hot 97,' is a commercial hip-hop station with all-day rap and R&B. **WKTU-FM**

103.5 is the premier dance-music station. **WWPR-FM 105.1**, 'Power 105,' plays top hiphop, and a few old-school hits. **WBLS-FM 107.5** showcases classic and new funk, soul and R&B.

Jazz

WBGO-FM 88.3 is strictly jazz. Dee Dee Bridgewater's weekly *JazzSet* programme features many legendary artists. **WKCR-FM 89.9**, the student-run radio station of Columbia University, is where you'll hear legendary jazz DJ Phil Schaap.

Rock

WSOU-FM 89.5, the station of Seton Hall University, a Catholic college, focuses primarily on hard rock and heavy metal. **WAXQ-FM 104.3** offers classic rock. **WXRK-FM 92.3**'s alternative music format attracts morning listeners with Howard Stern's 6-10am weekday sleaze-fest.

Other music

WQEW-AM 1560, 'Radio Disney,' has kids' programming. **WNYC-FM 93.9** and **WQXR-FM 96.3** serve up a range of classical music; **WNYC** tends towards the progressive end of the classical spectrum. **WCAA-FM 105.9** and **WZAA-FM 92.7** spin Spanish and Latin.

News & talk

WABC-AM 770, **WCBS-AM 880**, **WINS-AM 1010** and **WBBR-AM 1130** (see also below Sports) offer news throughout the day, plus traffic and weather reports. WABC hosts a morning show featuring the street-accented demagoguery of Guardian Angels founder Curtis Sliwa along with civil-rights attorney Ron Kuby (weekdays 5-10am). Right-winger Rush Limbaugh also airs his views here (noon-3pm).

WNYC-AM 820/FM 93.9, a commercial-free, public radio station, provides news and current-affairs commentary. **WBAI-FM 99.5** is a left-leaning community radio station. **WLIB-AM 1190** is the flagship station of Air America, a liberal answer to right-wing talk radio.

Sports

WFAN-AM 660 airs Giants, Nets, Mets and Devils games. Talk-radio fixture Don Imus offers his opinion on… everything (5.30-10am Mon-Fri). **WCBS-AM 880** covers the Yankees, New York's pride and joy. **WEPN-AM 1050** is devoted to news and sports talk and is the home of the Jets, Knicks and Rangers. **WBBR-AM 1130** broadcasts Islanders games. **WADO-AM**

1280 provides Spanish-language coverage of many sports events.

Television

A visit to New York often includes some TV time, which can cause culture shock, particularly for British and European visitors.

Time Out New York offers a rundown of TV highlights. For full schedules, save the *Sunday New York Times* TV section or buy a daily paper.

Networks

Six major networks broadcast nationwide. All offer ratings-driven variations on a theme.

CBS (Channel 2 in NYC) has the top investigative show, *60 Minutes*, on Sundays at 7pm; overall, programming is geared to a middle-aged demographic, but CBS also screens reality shows like *Survivor*. **NBC** (4) is the home of *Law & Order*, the long-running sketch-comedy series *Saturday Night Live* (11.30pm, Sat), and popular primetime shows including *The Apprentice*, *Fear Factor*, *ER*, *Scrubs* and *Will & Grace*. **Fox-WNYW** (5) is popular with younger audiences for shows like *The Simpsons* and *The OC*. **ABC** (7) is the king of daytime soaps and family-friendly sitcoms. Recently, ABC has scored huge hits with *Desperate Housewives* and *Lost*.

WXTV and **WNJU** are Spanish-language channels that offer game shows and racy Mexican dramas. They're also your best non-cable bets for soccer.

Public TV

Public TV is on channels 13, 21 and 25. Documentaries, arts shows and science series alternate with *Masterpiece Theatre* and reruns of British shows like *Inspector Morse*. Channel 21 broadcasts BBC World News daily at 6am and at 7 and 11pm.

Cable

For channel numbers for Time Warner Cable or for other cable systems, such as Cablevision or RCN, check a local newspaper's TV listings.

Nickelodeon presents shows suitable for kids and adults nostalgic for shows like *The Brady Bunch* and *Happy Days*. **NY1** focuses on local news. The **History Channel**, **Sci Fi** and the **Weather Channel** are self-explanatory. **Discovery Channel** and **The Learning Channel** feature educational nature and science programmes.

Directory

VH1, MTV's mature sibling, airs the popular *Behind the Music* series, which delves into the lives of artists such as LL Cool J, TLC, Vanilla Ice and the Partridge Family. **MTV** increasingly offers fewer music videos and more of its original programming (*The Osbournes*, *Punk'd* and *The Real World*). **FUSE**, a new music-video channel, aims for early MTV style.

FSN (Fox Sports Network), **MSG** (Madison Square Garden), **ESPN** and **ESPN2** are all-sports stations.

Bravo shows arts programming, such as *Inside the Actors Studio*, art-house films and *Queer Eye for the Straight Guy*.

Comedy Central is all comedy, airing *South Park* and *The Daily Show* with Jon Stewart.

Cinemax, the **Disney Channel**, HBO, the **Movie Channel** and **Showtime** are premium channels often available in hotels. They show uninterrupted feature films, exclusive specials and acclaimed original series such as *The Sopranos* and *Six Feet Under*.

Money

Over the past few years, much of American currency has undergone a subtle facelift – partly to deter increasingly adept counterfeiters. However, 'old' money still remains in circulation. All denominations except for the $1 bill have recently been updated by the US Treasury. One dollar ($) equals 100 cents (¢). Coins include copper pennies (1¢) and silver-coloured nickels (5¢), dimes (10¢) and quarters (25¢). Half-dollar coins (50¢) and the gold-coloured dollar coins are less commonly seen, except as change from vending machines.

All paper money is the same size, so make sure you fork over the right bill. It comes in denominations of $1, $2, $5, $10, $20, $50 and $100 (and higher, but you'll never see those bills). The $2 bills are quite rare and make a smart souvenir. Small shops will seldom break a $50 or $100 bill, and cab drivers aren't required to change bills larger than $20, so it's best to carry smaller denominations.

ATMs

The city is full of automated teller machines (ATMs), located in bank branches, delis and many small shops. Most accept American Express, MasterCard, Visa and major bank cards, if they have been registered with a personal identification number (PIN). Commonly, there's a usage fee of $1.50 to $2, though the superior exchange rate often makes ATMs worth the extra charge. Holders of accounts at out-of-country banks can also use ATMs but the fees can be high. Though you don't always pay the local charge, some UK banks charge up to £4 per transaction plus a variable payment to cover themselves against exchange rate fluctuations. Yes, it sounds as dodgy to us as it does to you.

US bank account holders who have lost their PIN or whose card is damaged can usually get cash from branches of their bank with proper ID.

Most ATM cards now double as charge cards, if they bear the Maestro or Cirrus logo. You can get cashback on this at supermarkets, UK customers included – theoretically, and for a percentage charge – though in practice it seems to only work at certain outlets.

Banks & currency exchange

Banks are generally open from 9am to 3pm Monday through Friday, though some stay open longer and on Saturdays. You need a photo ID, such as a passport, to cash travellers' cheques. Many banks will not exchange foreign currency, and the bureaux de change, limited to tourist-trap areas, close between 6 and 7pm. It's best to arrive with a few dollars in cash and to pay

mostly with credit cards or travellers' cheques (accepted in most restaurants and larger stores – but ask first, and be prepared to show ID). In emergencies, most large hotels offer 24-hour exchange facilities; the catch is that they charge high commissions and don't give good rates.

Chase Bank
1-888 935 9935/www.chase.com. Chase's website gives information on foreign currency exchange, banking locations and credit cards. For foreign currency delivered in a hurry, call the number listed above.

Commerce Bank
1-888 751 9000/www.commerce online.com. All of Commerce's 17 Manhattan locations are open seven days a week.

People's Foreign Exchange
3rd Floor, 575 Fifth Avenue, at 47th Street (1-212 883 0550). Subway: E, V to Fifth Avenue-53rd Street; 7 to Fifth Avenue. **Open** 9am-6pm Mon-Fri; 10am-3pm Sat, Sun.
People's provides foreign exchange on bank notes and travellers' cheques of any denomination for a $2 fee.

Travelex
29 Broadway, at Morris Street (1-212 363 6206). Subway: 4, 5 to Bowling Green. **Open** 9am-5pm Mon-Fri.
A complete range of foreign-exchange services is offered.
Other location: 510 Madison Avenue at 53rd Street (1-212 753 0117).

Credit cards

Bring plastic if you have it, or be prepared for a logistical nightmare. Credit cards are essential for renting cars and booking hotels, and handy for buying tickets over the phone and the internet. The five major cards accepted in the US are American Express, Diners Club, Discover, MasterCard and Visa. If cards are lost or stolen, contact:

American Express
1-800 528 2122.

Diners Club
1-800 234 6377.

Discover
1-800 347 2683.

MasterCard/Maestro
1-800 826 2181.

Visa/Cirrus
1-800 336 8472.

Travellers' cheques

Like credit cards, travellers' cheques are also routinely accepted at banks, stores and restaurants throughout the city. Bring your driver's licence or passport for identification. If cheques are lost or stolen, contact:

American Express
1-800 221 7282.

Thomas Cook
1-800 223 7373.

Visa
1-800 336 8472.

Wire services

If you run out of cash, don't expect the folks at your consulate to lend you money. In case of an emergency, you can have money wired to you from your home.

MoneyGram
1-800 926 400/www. moneygram.com.

Western Union
1-800 325 6000/www. westernunion.com.

Postal services

Stamps are available at all US post offices and from drugstore vending machines and at most newstands. It costs 37¢ to send a 1oz (28g) letter within the US. Each additional ounce costs 23¢. Postcards mailed within the US cost 23¢; for international postcards, it's 70¢. Airmailed letters to anywhere overseas cost 80¢ for the first ounce and 75¢ for each additional ounce.

For faster Express Mail, you must fill out a form, either at a post office or by arranging a

pickup. Twenty-four-hour delivery to major US cities is guaranteed. International delivery takes two to three days, with no guarantee. Call 1-800 275 8777 for more information.

General Post Office
421 Eighth Avenue, between 31st & 33rd Streets (24-hour information 1-800 275 8777/www.usps.com). Subway: A, C, E to 34th Street-Penn Station. **Open** 24hrs daily. **Credit** MC, V.
This is the city's main post office; call for the branch nearest you. Queues are long, but stamps are available from vending machines. Branches are usually open 9am-5pm Mon-Fri; hours vary Sat.

General Delivery
390 Ninth Avenue, between 31st & 33rd Streets (1-212 330 3099). Subway: A, C, E to 34th Street-Penn Station. **Open** 10am-1pm Mon-Sat.
US residents without local addresses can receive their mail here; it should be addressed to the recipient, General Delivery, 390 Ninth Avenue, New York, NY 10001. You will need to show a passport or ID card when picking up letters.

Poste Restante
Window 29, 421 Eighth Avenue between 31st & 33rd Streets (1-212 330 2912). Subway: A, C, E to 34th Street-Penn Station. **Open** 8am-6pm Mon-Sat.
Foreign visitors can receive mail here; mail should be addressed to the recipient, General Post Office, Poste Restante, 421 Eighth Avenue, attn: Window 29, New York, NY 10001. Be sure to bring ID.

Religion

Here are just a few of New York's many places of worship. Check the phone book for more listings.

Baptist

Abyssinian Baptist Church
See p145 for listing.

Buddhist

New York Buddhist Church
331-332 Riverside Drive, between 105th & 106th Streets (1-212 678

0305/www.newyorkbuddhistchurch. org). Subway: 1 to 103rd Street.

Catholic

St Patrick's Cathedral
See p121 for listing.

Episcopal

Cathedral Church of St John the Divine
See p142 for listing.

Jewish

UJA–Federation of New York Resource Line
1-212 753 2288/www.young leadership.org. **Open** 9am-5pm Mon-Thur; 9am-4pm Fri.
This hotline provides referrals to other organisations, groups, temples, philanthropic activities and synagogues, as well as advice on kosher food in the city.

Methodist

Church of St Paul & St Andrew, United Methodist
263 W 86th Street, between Broadway & West End Avenue (1-212 362 3179/www.spsanyc.org). Subway: 1 to 86th Street.

Muslim

Islamic Cultural Center of New York
1711 Third Avenue, between 96th & 97th Streets (1-212 722 5234). Subway: 6 to 96th Street.

Presbyterian

Madison Avenue Presbyterian Church
921 Madison Avenue, at 73rd Street (1-212 288 8920/www.mapc.com). Subway: 6 to 72nd Street.

Restrooms

See p381 **Toilet talk.**

Safety

New York's crime rate, particularly for violent crime, has waned during the past

Directory

decade. Most crime occurs late at night in low-income neighbourhoods. Don't arrive thinking your safety is at risk wherever you go; it is unlikely that you will ever be bothered.

Still, a bit of common sense won't hurt. Don't flaunt your money and valuables, and try not to look obviously lost. Avoid deserted and poorly lit streets; walk facing oncoming traffic so no one can drive up alongside you undetected, and close to or on the street; muggers prefer to hang back in doorways and shadows. If you are threatened, hand over your valuables at once (your attacker will likely be as anxious to get it over with as you), then dial 911 as soon as you can (it's a free call).

Be extra alert to pickpockets and street hustlers – especially in crowded tourist areas like Times Square – and be wary of diversionary jostles.

Smoking

New Yorkers live under some of the strictest anti-smoking laws on the planet. The 1995 NYC Smoke-Free Air Act makes it illegal to smoke in virtually all indoor public places, including the subway and cinemas. Recent legislation went even further, banning smoking in nearly all restaurants and bars; for a list of exceptions, *see p216* **Butting in**. Be sure to ask before you light up.

Students

Student life in NYC is unlike it is anywhere else in the world. An endless extracurricular education exists right outside the dorm room – the city is both teacher and playground. For further guidance, check the *Time Out New York Student Guide*, available in August for free on campuses, and $2.95 at Hudson News outlets (consult the phone book for locations).

Student identification

Foreign students should get an **International Student Identity Card** (ISIC) as proof of student status and to secure discounts. These can be bought from your local student-travel agent (ask at your student union or see STA Travel below). If you buy the card in New York, then you will also get basic accident insurance – a bargain.

Student travel

Most agents offer discount fares for those under 26. Specialists in student deals include:

STA Travel
205 E 42nd Street, between Second & Third Avenues (1-212 822 2700/for other locations 1-800 777 0112/www.statravel.com). Subway: 42nd Street S, 4, 5, 6, 7 to 42nd Street-Grand Central. **Open** 10am-6pm Mon-Sat.

Tax & tipping

In restaurants, it is customary to tip at least 15 per cent, and since NYC tax is 8.625 per cent, a quick method for calculating the tip is to double the tax. In many restaurants, when you are with a group of six or more, the tip will be included in the bill. For tipping on taxi fares, *see p369*.

Telephones

New York, like most of the world's busy cities, is overrun with telephones, cellular phones, pagers and faxes. (Check with your network operator to be sure that service will be available here.) This increasing dependence on a dial tofne accounts for the city's abundance of area codes. As a rule, you must dial 1 + the area code before a number, even if the place you are calling is in the same area code. The area codes for

Manhattan are 212 and 646; Brooklyn, Queens, Staten Island and the Bronx are 718 and 347; 917 is reserved mostly for mobile phones and pagers. Long Island area codes are 516 and 631; codes for New Jersey are 201, 551, 848, 862, 609, 732, 856, 908 and 973. Numbers preceded by 800, 877 and 888 are free of charge when dialled from anywhere in the US.

General information

The Yellow Pages and the White Pages phone books contain a wealth of useful information in the front, including theatre-seating diagrams and maps; the blue pages in the centre of the White Pages directory list all government numbers and addresses. Hotels will have copies; otherwise, try libraries or Verizon (the local phone company) payment centres.

Collect calls & credit card calls
Collect calls are also known as reverse-charge calls. Dial 0 followed by the number, or dial AT&T's 1-800 225 5288, MCI's 1-800 265 5328 or Sprint's 1-800 663 3463.

Directory assistance
Dial 411 or 1 + area code + 555 1212. Doing so may be free, depending on the payphone you are using; carrier fees may apply. Long-distance directory assistance may also incur long-distance charges. For a directory of toll-free numbers, dial 1-800 555 1212.

Emergency
Dial 911. All calls are free (including those from pay- and mobile phones).

International calls
Dial 011 + country code (Australia 61; New Zealand 64; UK 44), then the number.

Operator assistance
Dial 0.

Pagers & mobiles

Most US mobile phones will work in NY but since the US doesn't have a standard national network, visitors should check with their provider that their phone will work here, and whether they need to unlock a roaming option. Visitors from other countries will need a tri-band handset and a roaming agreement, and may find charges so high that rental, or, depending on the length of their stay, purchase of a US phone (or SIM card) will make better economic sense.

If you carry a mobile phone, make sure you turn it off on trains and buses and at restaurants, plays, movies, concerts and museums. New Yorkers are quick to show their annoyance at an ill-timed ring. Some establishments

even post signs designating 'cellular-free zones'.

InTouch USA
1-800 872 7626. **Open** 8am-5.30pm Mon-Fri. **Credit** AmEx, DC, Disc, MC, V.
InTouch, the city's largest mobile-phone rental company, leases equipment by the day, week or month.

Public payphones & phonecards

Public payphones are easy to find. Some of them even work (non-Verizon phones tend to be poorly maintained). Phones take any combination of silver coins: local calls usually cost 25¢ for three minutes; a few

payphones require 50¢ but allow unlimited time on the call. If you're not used to US phones, then note that the ringing tone is long; the 'engaged' tone, or busy signal, is short and higher pitched.

To call long-distance or to make an international call from a payphone, you need to go through one of the long-distance companies. Most payphones in New York automatically use AT&T, but phones in and around transportation hubs usually contract other long-distance carriers, and charges can be outrageous. MCI and Sprint are respected brand names (*see p380* **Collect calls &**

Toilet talk
When nature calls, here's where to answer.

Visitors to New York are always on the go. But in between all that go, go, go, sometimes you've really got to go. Contrary to what your nose may sometimes lead you to believe, the streets and alleys are no place to find relief. The real challenge lies in finding a legal public place to take care of your business. Although they don't exactly have an open-door policy, the numerous McDonald's restaurants, Starbucks coffee shops and Barnes & Noble bookstores contain (usually clean) restrooms.

If the door to the loo is locked, you may have to ask a cashier for the key. Don't announce that you're not a paying customer and you should be all right. The same applies to most other fast-food chains (Au Bon Pain, Wendy's, etc), major stores (Barneys, Macy's, Toys 'R' Us) and hotels and bars that don't have a host stationed at the door. Here are a few other options that can offer sweet relief in the city (though you may have to hold your breath and forgo soap and towel).

Downtown

Battery Park
Castle Clinton. Subway: 1 to South Ferry; 4, 5 to Bowling Green.

Tompkins Square Park
Ave A at 9th St. Subway: L to First Ave; 6 to Astor Pl.

Washington Square Park
Thompson St at Washington Sq South. Subway: A, B, C, D, E, F, V to W 4th St.

Midtown

Bryant Park
42nd St between Fifth and Sixth Aves. Subway: B, D, F, V to 42nd St-Bryant Park; 7 to Fifth Ave.

Grand Central Terminal
42nd St at Park Ave, Lower Concourse. Subway: 42nd St S, 4, 5, 6, 7 to 42nd St-Grand Central.

Penn Station
Seventh Ave between 31st and 33rd Sts. Subway: A, C, E, 1, 2, 3 to 34th St-Penn Station.

Uptown

Avery Fisher Hall at Lincoln Center
Broadway at 65th St. Subway: 1, 9 to 66th St-Lincoln Ctr.

Charles A Dana Discovery Center
Central Park, north side of Harlem Meer, 110th St at Malcolm X Blvd (Lenox Ave). Subway: 2, 3 to 110th St-Central Park North.

Delacorte Theater
Central Park, midpark at 81st St. Subway: B, C to 81st St-Museum of Natural History.

Directory

credit-card calls). Make the call by either dialling 0 for an operator or dialling direct, which is cheaper. To find out how much a call will cost, dial the number, and a computerised voice will tell you how much money to deposit. You can pay for calls with your credit card.

The best way to make long-distance calls is with a phonecard, available from any post-office branch or from chain stores like Duane Reade or Rite Aid (*see p374* **Pharmacies**). Delis and newspaper kiosks sell phonecards, including the New York Exclusive, which has favourable international rates. Instructions are on the card.

Telephone answering service

Messages Plus Inc

1317 Third Avenue, between 75th & 76th Streets (1-212 879 4144). Subway: 6 to 77th Street. **Open** 24hrs daily. **Credit** AmEx, DC, Disc, MC, V.
Messages Plus provides an answering service with specialised (medical, bilingual, etc) receptionists, if required, and plenty of ways to deliver your messages. It also offers telemarketing, voicemail and interactive website services.

Tickets

It's always show time somewhere in New York. And depending on what you're after – music, sports, theatre – scoring tickets can be a real hassle. Smaller venues often have their own box offices. Large arenas like Madison Square Garden have ticket agencies – and many devoted spectators. You may have to try more than one tactic to get into a popular show.

Box-office tickets

Fandango

1-800 326 3264/www.fandango.com. 24hrs daily. **Surcharge** $1.50 per ticket. **Credit** AmEx, Disc, MC, V.

Passport update

People of all ages (children included) who enter the US on the Visa Waiver Progam (VWP; *see p384*) are now required to carry their own machine-readable passport, or MRP. MRPs are recognisable by the double row of characters along the foot of the data page. All burgundy EU and EU-lookalike passports issued in the UK since 1991 (that is, all that are still valid) should be machine readable. Some of those issued outside the country may not be, however; in this case, holders should apply for a replacement even if the passport has not expired. Check at your local passport-issuing post office if in any doubt at all.

The US's requirement for passports to contain a 'biometric' chip applies only to those issued from 26 October 2006. By then, all new and replacement UK passports should be compliant, following a gradual phase-in. The biometric chip contains a facial scan and biographical data.

Though it is being considered for 2008 (when ID cards may be introduced), there is no current requirement for UK passports to contain fingerprint or iris data. The application process remains as it was, except for new guidelines that ensure that the photograph you submit can be used to generate the facial scan in the chip.

Further information for UK citizens is available from www.passport.gov.uk/0870 521 0410. Nationals of other countries should check well in advance of their journey whether their current passport meets the requirements for the time of their trip, at http://travel.state.gov/visa and with the issuing authorities of their home country.

Fandango is one of the newer services to offer advance credit-card purchase of movie tickets online or over the phone. Tickets can be picked up at an automated kiosk in the theatre lobby (not available in all theatres).

Moviefone

1-212 777 FILM/www.moviefone. com. 24hrs daily. **Surcharge** $1.50 ($1 if purchased online) per ticket. **Credit** AmEx, Disc, MC, V.
Purchase advance film tickets by credit card over the phone or online; pick them up at an automated kiosk in the theatre lobby. This service is not available for every theatre.

Telecharge

1-212 239 6200/www.telecharge. com. 24hrs daily. **Average surcharge** $6 per ticket. **Credit** AmEx, DC, Disc, MC, V.
Broadway and Off Broadway shows are on offer here.

Ticket Central

416 W 42nd Street, between Ninth & Tenth Avenues (1-212 279 4200/

www.ticketcentral.org). Subway: N, Q, R, W, 42nd Street S, 1, 2, 3, 7 to 42nd Street-Times Square. **Box office & phone orders** noon-8pm daily. **Surcharge** varies with ticket price. **Credit** AmEx, MC, V.
Off and Off-Off Broadway tickets are available at the office or by phone.

Ticketmaster

1-212 307 4100/www.ticket master.com. **Surcharge** $3-$10 per ticket. **Credit** AmEx, DC, Disc, MC, V.
This reliable service sells tickets to rock concerts, Broadway shows, sports events and more. You can buy tickets by phone, online or at outlets throughout the city – Tower Records, J&R Music and Computer World, and Filene's Basement, to name a few.

TKTS

Duffy Square, 47th Street, at Broadway (1-212 221 0013/www.tdf. org). Subway: N, Q, R, W, 42nd Street S, 1, 2, 3, 7 to 42nd Street-Times Square. **Open** 3-8pm Mon-Sat; 11am-7pm Sun. Matinée tickets

10am-2pm Wed, Sat; 11am-2pm Sun.
Surcharge $3 per ticket. **No credit cards**.
TKTS has become a New York tradition. Broadway and Off Broadway tickets are sold at discounts of 25, 35 and 50% for same-day performances; tickets to other highbrow events are also offered. The queue can be long, but it's often worth the wait.

Holidays

The majority of banks and government offices are closed on the major US holidays, but you will usually find a smattering of restaurants and shops have stayed open, along with some museums. If you are in New York during or around a holiday, be sure to call the venues you'd like to visit to enquire about special hours.

New Year's Day
January 1

Martin Luther King Day
Third Monday in January

Presidents' Day
Third Monday in February

Memorial Day
Last Monday in May

Independence Day
July 4

Labor Day
First Monday in September

Columbus Day
Second Monday in October

Veterans Day
November 11

Thanksgiving Day
Fourth Thursday in November

Christmas Day
December 25

Other locations: 199 Water Street; booth is at the corner of Front and John Streets.

Scalpers & standby tickets

When a show sells out, there's always the illegal scalper option, though the risk that you might end up with a forged ticket does exist. Before you part with any cash, make sure the ticket has the correct details, and be warned: the police have been cracking down on such trade.

Some venues also offer standby tickets right before show time, while others give reduced rates for tickets purchased on the same day as the performance.

Ticket brokers

Ticket brokers function like scalpers but are legal because they operate from out of state. They can almost guarantee tickets, however costly, for sold-out events and tend to deal only in better seats. They also tend to be less seedy and more regularly patronised than their UK equivalents. For brokers, look under Ticket Sales in the Yellow Pages.

Apex Tours
1-800 248 9849/www.tixx.com.
Open 9am-5pm Mon-Fri. **Credit** AmEx, Disc, MC, V.

Prestige Entertainment
1-800 243 8849/www.prestige entertainment.com. **Open** 8am-6pm Mon-Fri; 8am-5pm Sat; 11am-3pm Sun. **Credit** AmEx, MC, V.

TicketCity
1-800 765 3688/www.ticketcity.com.
Open 8.30am-8pm Mon-Fri; 10am-6pm Sat; 11am-4pm Sun. **Credit** AmEx, Disc, MC, V.

Time & date

New York is on Eastern Standard Time, which extends from the Atlantic coast to the eastern shore of Lake Michigan and south to the Gulf of Mexico. This is five hours behind Greenwich Mean Time. Clocks are set forward one hour in early April for Daylight Savings Time and back one hour at the end of October. Going from east to west, Eastern Time is one hour ahead of Central Time, two hours ahead of Mountain Time and three hours ahead of Pacific Time. In the US, the date is written as month, day and year; so 2/8/05 is 8 February 2005. Forms that foreigners may need to fill in, however, are often the other way round, including immigration cards.

Toilets

See p381 **Toilet talk**.

Tourist information

Hotels are usually full of maps, brochures and free tourist magazines that include paid listings (so the recommendations cannot be viewed as objective). Many local magazines, including *Time Out New York*, offer opinionated, reliable information and updates on events and exhibitions.

NYC & Company
810 Seventh Avenue, between 52nd & 53rd Streets (1-800 NYC VISIT/ www.nycvisit.com). Subway: B, D, E to Seventh Avenue. **Open** 8.30am-6pm Mon-Fri; 9am-5pm Sat, Sun. The city's official visitors' and information centre doles out maps, leaflets, coupons and advice.
Other locations: 33-34 Carnaby Street, London W1V 1CA, UK (020 7437 8300).

Times Square Visitors Center
1560 Broadway, between 46th & 47th Streets (1-212 869 1890). Subway: N, Q, R, W, 42nd Street S, 1, 2, 3, 7 to 42nd Street-Times Square. **Open** 8am-8pm daily. This centre offers discount coupons for Broadway tickets, internet access, MetroCards, and other useful goods and services, predominantly for Theatreland.

Directory

Visas & immigration

Visas

Some 27 countries participate in the **Visa Waiver Program** (VWP). Citizens of Andorra, Australia, Austria, Belgium, Brunei, Denmark, Finland, France, Germany, Iceland, Ireland, Italy, Japan, Liechtenstein, Luxembourg, Monaco, the Netherlands, New Zealand, Norway, Portugal, San Marino, Singapore, Slovenia, Spain, Sweden, Switzerland and the UK do not need a visa for stays in the US shorter than 90 days (business or pleasure) as long as they have a machine-readable passport valid for the full 90-day period and a return ticket. *See also p382* **Passport alert**.

If you do not qualify for entry under the VWP, that is if you are not from one of the eligible countries or are visiting for any purpose other than pleasure or business, you will need a visa. Media workers and students note: this includes you. If you are in the slightest doubt, check ahead. You can obtain application forms from your nearest US embassy or consulate or its website. Enquire several months ahead of travel how long the application process is currently taking.

Canadians travelling to the US need visas only in special circumstances.

Whether or not you have a visa, it is not advisable to travel on a passport with six months or less to run.

If you lose your passport inside the US, contact your consulate (*see p372*).

Immigration

Your airline will give all visitors an immigration form to be presented to an official when you land. Fill it in clearly and be prepared to give an address at which you are staying (a hotel is fine).

Upon arrival, you may have to wait an hour or, if you're unlucky, considerably longer, in Immigration, where owing to tightened security you can expect slow-moving queues. You may be expected to explain your visit; be polite and prepared. Note that all visitors to the US are now photographed and fingerprinted on arrival on every trip. You will usually be granted an entry permit.

US Embassy Visa Information

In the US, 1-202 663 1225/in the UK, 09055 444 546, 60p per minute/http://travel.state.gov/visa.

When to go

There is no bad time to visit New York, and visitor numbers are fairly steady year-round. The weather can be unpleasantly hot in summer and charmingly, then tediously, snowy in winter, but there are compensations at each season. *See below* **Climate**.

Working in NY

Non-nationals cannot work in the US without the appropriate visa; these are hard to get and generally require you to prove that your job could not be done by a US citizen. Contact your local embassy for further information. Some student visas allow part-time work after the first academic year.

UK students who want to spend a summer vacation working in the States should contact the British Universities North America Club (BUNAC) for help in arranging a temporary job and the requisite visa (16 Bowling Green Lane, London, EC1R 0QH; 020 7251 3472, www.bunac.org/uk).

Climate

New York is fairly predictable: winters are windy and frigid (with a sun that sits low in the southern sky, so you might want to plan your walks northward, from downtown to uptown, to avoid the glare); summers are hot and humid, with occasional brief showers. Spring is typically blustery and changeable, and fall/autumn is generally dry, cool and gorgeous. Below is a snapshot of the city's weather averages. Just remember that no matter what it's like outside, there's always something to do indoors.

	Temperature		Rain/snow	Full sun
	Hi °F/°C	Low °F/°C	days	days
Jan	38/3	25/-4	11	8
Feb	40/5	27/-3	10	8
Mar	50/10	35/2	11	9
Apr	61/16	44/7	11	8
May	72/22	54/12	11	8
Jun	80/27	63/17	10	8
Jul	85/30	68/20	11	8
Aug	84/29	67/20	10	9
Sept	76/25	60/16	8	11
Oct	65/18	50/10	8	12
Nov	54/12	41/5	9	9
Dec	43/6	31/-1	10	9

Source: National Weather Service

Directory

Further Reference

Books

See also p18.

Edward F Bergman *The Spiritual Traveler: New York City* A guide to sacred and peaceful spaces in the city.
Eleanor Berman *Away for the Weekend: New York* Trips within a 200-mile radius of New York City. *New York Neighborhoods* Foodie guide focussing on ethnic enclaves.
William Corbett *New York Literary Lights* A compendium of information about NYC's literary past.
Dave Frattini *The Underground Guide to New York City Subways*
Gerri Gallagher and Jill Fairchild *Where to Wear* A staple for shopaholics.
Suzanne Gerber *Vegetarian New York City.*
Alfred Gingold and Helen Rogan *Cool Parent's Guide to All of New York .*
Hagstrom *New York City 5 Borough Pocket Atlas* You won't get lost when you carry this thorough street map.
Colleen Kane (ed) *Sexy New York City* Discover erotica in the Naked City.
Chuck Katz *Manhattan on Film 2*
Lyn Skreczko and Virginia Bell *The Manhattan Health Pages*
Earl Steinbicker (ed.) *Daytrips New York*
Linda Tarrant-Reid *Discovering Black New York* Museums, landmarks, more.
Time Out *New York Eating & Drinking 2005* The annual comprehensive critics' guide to thousands of places to eat and drink in the five boroughs.

Architecture

Richard Berenholtz *New York, New York* Mini panoramic images of the city through the seasons.
Stanley Greenberg *Invisible New York* Photographic account of hidden architectural triumphs.
Landmarks Preservation Commission *New York City Landmarks Preservation Guide*
Karl Sabbagh *Skyscraper* How the tall ones are built.
Robert AM Stern et al. *New York 1930* A massive coffee-table slab with stunning pictures.
Norval White & Elliot Willensky *AIA Guide to New York City* A comprehensive directory of important buildings.
Gerard R Wolfe New York: *A Guide to the Metropolis* Historical and architectural walking tours.

Culture & recollections

Irving Lewis Allen *The City in Slang* How NY has spawned new words and phrases.
Candace Bushnell *Sex & the City; Trading Up* Smart women, superficial New York.
George Chauncey *Gay New York* The evolution of gay culture from 1890 to 1940.
Martha Cooper and Henry Chalfant *Subway Art*
Josh Alan Friedman *Tales of Times Square* Sleaze and decay in the old Times Square.
Nelson George *Hip Hop America* The history of hip-hop, from Grandmaster Flash to Puff Daddy.
Robert Hendrickson *New Yawk Tawk* Dictionary of NYC slang.
Jane Jacobs *The Death and Life of Great American Cities*
AJ Liebling *Back Where I Came From* Personal recollections from the *New Yorker* columnist.
Gillian McCain and Legs McNeil *Please Kill Me* Oral history of the '70s punk scene.

Frank O'Hara *The Collected Poems of Frank O'Hara* The great NYC poet found inspiration in his hometown.
Andrés Torres *Between Melting Pot and Mosaic* African-American and Puerto Rican life in the city .
Heather Holland Wheaton *Eight Million Stories in a New York Minute*
EB White *Here Is New York* A clear-eyed love letter to Gotham.

Fiction

Kurt Andersen *Turn of the Century Millennial* Manhattan seen through the eyes of media players.
Paul Auster *The New York Trilogy: City of Glass, Ghosts, and the Locked Room* A search for the madness behind the method of Manhattan's grid.
Kevin Baker *Dreamland* A poetic novel about Coney Island's glory days.
James A Baldwin *Another Country* Racism under the bohemian veneer of the 1960s.
Michael Chabon *The Amazing Adventures of Kavalier and Clay* Pulitzer Prize-winning account of Jewish comic-book artists in the 1940s.
Bret Easton Ellis *Glamorama* A satirical view of dazzling New York City nightlife.
Jack Finney *Time and Again* An illustrator travels back to 19th-century NY.
Larry Kramer *Faggots* Devastating satire of gay NY.
Phillip Lopate (ed) *Writing New York* An excellent anthology of short stories, essays and poems.
Tim McLoughlin (ed) *Brooklyn Noir* An anthology of crime tales set in Brooklyn.
Time Out *Book of New York Short Stories* Naturally, we like these original short stories by 23 US and British authors.

Toni Morrison *Jazz* 1920s Harlem.
David Schickler *Kissing in Manhattan* Explores the lives of quirky tenants in a Manhattan block.
Hubert Selby Jr *Last Exit to Brooklyn* Dockland degradation, circa 1950s.
Edith Wharton *Old New York* Four novellas of 19th-century New York.
Colson Whitehead *The Colossus of New York: A City in 13 Parts* A lyrical tribute to city life.
Tom Wolfe *The Bonfire of the Vanities* Rich/poor, black/white. An unmatched slice of 1980s New York.

History

See p18 **Further reading**.

Films

Annie Hall (1977) Woody Allen co-stars with Diane Keaton in this appealingly neurotic valentine to living and loving in Manhattan.
Breakfast at Tiffany's (1961) Blake Edwards gave Audrey Hepburn her signature role as the cash-poor socialite Holly Golightly.
Dog Day Afternoon (1975) Al Pacino makes for a great antihero as a Brooklyn bank robber in Sidney Lumet's uproarious classic.
Do the Right Thing (1989) The hottest day of the summer leads to racial strife in Bedford-Stuyvesant in Spike Lee's incisive drama.
The French Connection (1971) As detective Jimmy 'Popeye' Doyle, Gene Hackman ignores all traffic lights to chase down drug traffickers in William Friedkin's thriller.
The Godfather (1972) and **The Godfather: Part II** (1974) Francis Ford Coppola's brilliant commentary about capitalism in America is told through the violent saga of Italian gangsters.

Mean Streets (1973) Robert De Niro and Harvey Keitel shine as small-time Little Italy hoods in Martin Scorsese's breakthrough film.
Midnight Cowboy (1969) Street creatures 'Ratso' Rizzo and Joe Buck face an unforgiving Times Square in John Schlesinger's dark classic.
Spider-Man (2002) The comic-book web-slinger from Forest Hills comes to life in Sam Raimi's pitch-perfect crowd pleaser.
Taxi Driver (1976) Robert De Niro is a crazed cabbie who sees all of New York as a den of iniquity in Martin Scorsese's bold drama.

Music

Beastie Boys 'No Sleep Till Brooklyn' These now middle-aged hip-hoppers began showing their love for their fave borough two decades ago.
Leonard Cohen 'Chelsea Hotel #2' Of all the songs inspired by the Chelsea, this bleak vision of doomed love is on a level of its own.
Billy Joel 'New York State of Mind' This heartfelt ballad exemplifies the city's effect on the souls of its visitors and residents.
Charles Mingus 'Mingus Ah Um' Mingus brought the gospel to jazz and created a NY masterpiece.
Public Enemy 'It Takes a Nation of Millions to Hold Us Back' A ferociously political tour de force from the Long Island hip-hop group whose own Chuck D once called rap 'the CNN for black America'.
Ramones 'Ramones' Four Queens roughnecks, a few buzzsaw chords, and clipped musings on turning tricks and sniffing glue – it transformed rock and roll.
Frank Sinatra 'Theme song from New York, New York' Trite and true, Frank's bombastic love letter melts those little-town blues.

Bruce Springsteen 'My City of Ruins' The Boss praises the city's resilience post-September 11 with this track from 'The Rising'.
The Strokes 'Is This It' The effortlessly hip debut of this hometown band garnered praise and worldwide attention.
The Velvet Underground 'The Velvet Underground & Nico' Lou Reed and company's first album is still the gold standard of downtown cool.

Websites

www.timeoutny.com The Time Out New York website covers all the city has to offer. When planning your trip, check out the New York City Guide section for a variety of itineraries that you can use in conjunction with this guide.
eatdrink.timeoutny.com Subscribe to the TONY Eating & Drinking online guide and instantly search thousands of reviews written by our critics.
www.nycvisit.com The site of NYC&Company, the local convention and visitors' bureau.
www.mta.info Subway and bus service changes are always posted here.
www.nyc.gov City Hall's official New York City website has lots of links.
www.nytimes.com 'All the News That's Fit to Print' from the *New York Times*.
www.clubplanet.com Follow the city's nocturnal scene and buy advance tickets to big events.
www.livebroadway.com 'The Official Website of Broadway' is the source for theaters, tickets and tours.
www.hipguide.com A short 'n' sweet site for those looking for what's considered hip.
www.forgotten-ny.com Remember old New York here.
www.manhattanusersguide. com An insiders' guide to what's going on around town.

Index

Advertisers' Index

Please refer to relevant page for contact details

Place of interest and/or entertainment	▮
Hospital or college	▮
Railway station	▮
Parks	▮
River	▮
Freeway	▬478▬
Main road	
Main road tunnel	
Pedestrian road	▬
Airport	✈
Church	✚
Subway station	Ⓜ
Area name	SOHO
Hotels	❶
Restaurants	❶
Bars	❶

Maps

Street Index

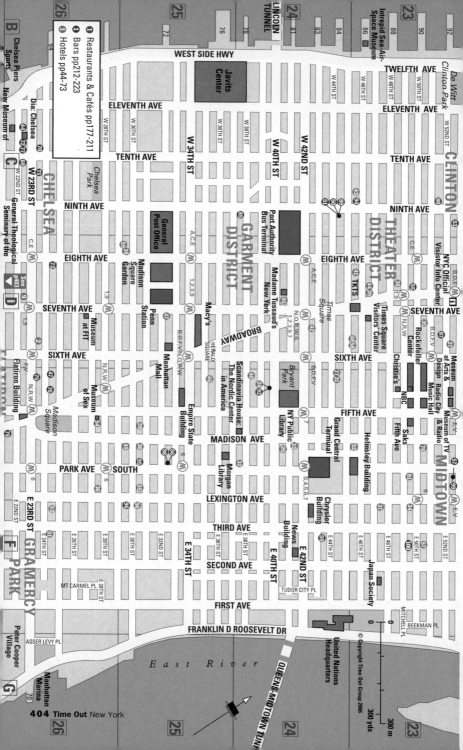

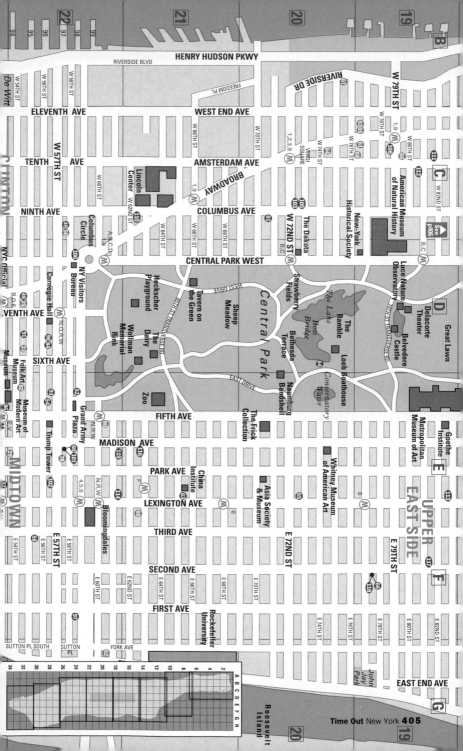

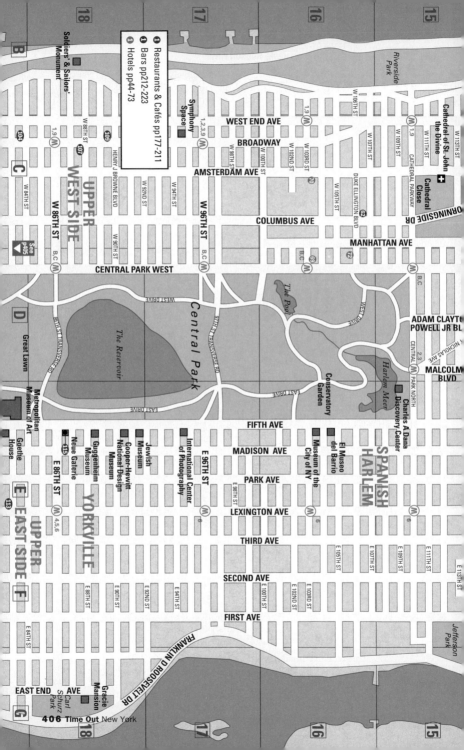

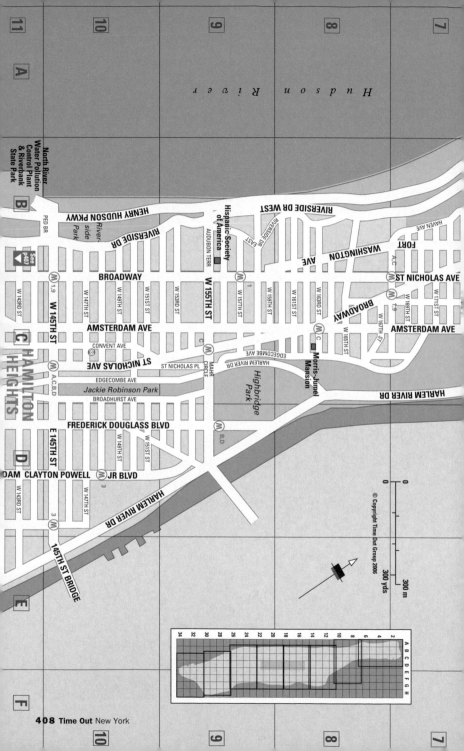

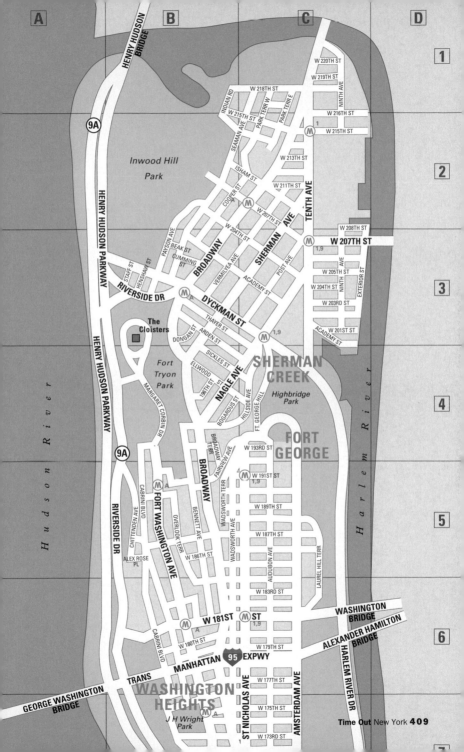

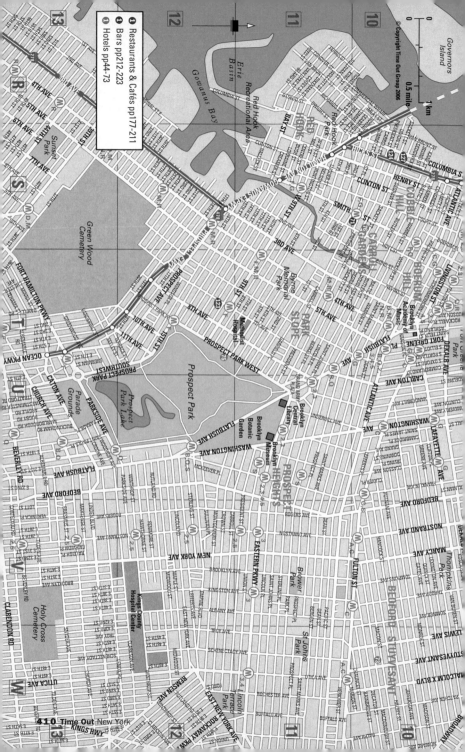

Hudson River

Upper Bay

BROOKLYN-BATTERY TUNNEL

BATTERY PARK CITY

WEST SIDE HWY

WHITEHALL ST

TRIBECA

HUDSON ST

HUDSON ST

CHURCH ST

WEST BROADWAY

WEST BROADWAY

FRANKLIN D ROOSEVELT DR

BROADWAY

VARICK ST

CENTRE ST

AVENUE OF THE AMERICAS

GREENWICH VILLAGE

PARK ROW

CHINATOWN

FIFTH AVE

SOHO

BROADWAY

LAFAYETTE

THE BOWERY

PARK AVE SOUTH

BROOKLYN BRIDGE

PEARL ST

EAST BROADWAY

LOWER EAST SIDE

THIRD AVE

GRAMERCY PARK

SECOND AVE

FURMAN ST

CADMAN PLZ

EAST VILLAGE

FRANKLIN D ROOSEVELT DR

NASSAU ST

Industrial Park

Wallabout Bay

Brooklyn Navy Yard

East River

See pp402–403

See p412

KENT AVE

BEDFORD AVE

GREENPOINT

GREENPOINT AVE

McGUINNESS BLVD

FLUSHING AVE

BEDFORD AVE

DRIGGS AVE

BERRY ST

NASSAU AVE

McCarren Park

McGolrick Park

NORMAN AVE

KINGSLAND AVE

Newtown Creek

MARCY AVE

RODNEY ST

WILLIAMSBURG

UNION AVE

GRAND STREET EXT

HUMBOLDT ST

COOPER Park

495

LEWIS AV

BUSHWICK

BROADWAY

BUSHWICK AVE

MYRTLE AVE

VANDERVOORT AVE

METROPOLITAN AVE

GRAND ST

FLUSHING AVE

Calvary Cemetery

LAUREL HILL

GREENPOINT AVE

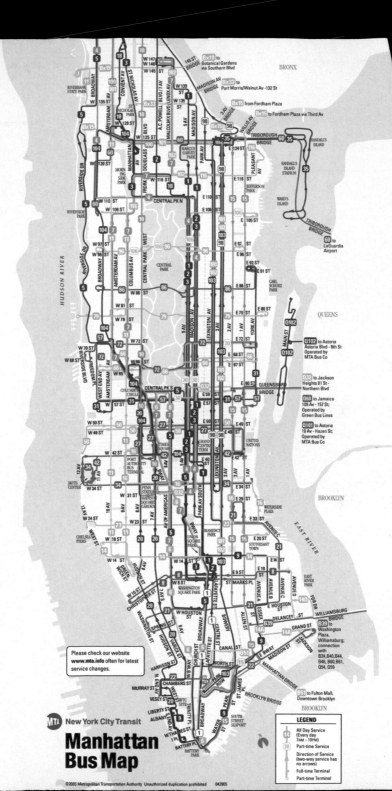

Manhattan Bus Map

MTA New York City Transit

©2005 Metropolitan Transportation Authority   Unauthorized duplication prohibited   042905